T0180898

Lecture Notes in Computer Science　　10729

Commenced Publication in 1973
Founding and Former Series Editors:
Gerhard Goos, Juris Hartmanis, and Jan van Leeuwen

More information about this series at http://www.springer.com/series/7408

Antonio Cerone · Marco Roveri (Eds.)

Software Engineering and Formal Methods

SEFM 2017 Collocated Workshops:
DataMod, FAACS, MSE, CoSim-CPS, and FOCLASA
Trento, Italy, September 4–5, 2017
Revised Selected Papers

 Springer

Editors
Antonio Cerone (iD)
Nazarbayev University
Astana
Kazakhstan

Marco Roveri (iD)
Fondazione Bruno Kessler
Povo
Italy

ISSN 0302-9743 ISSN 1611-3349 (electronic)
Lecture Notes in Computer Science
ISBN 978-3-319-74780-4 ISBN 978-3-319-74781-1 (eBook)
https://doi.org/10.1007/978-3-319-74781-1

Library of Congress Control Number: 2018930886

LNCS Sublibrary: SL2 – Programming and Software Engineering

Printed on acid-free paper

This Springer imprint is published by Springer Nature
The registered company is Springer International Publishing AG
The registered company address is: Gewerbestrasse 11, 6330 Cham, Switzerland

Preface

This volume contains the technical papers presented at the five workshops collocated with the 15th International Conference on Software Engineering and Formal Methods (SEFM 2017). The workshops took place at the Fondazione Bruno Kessler, Trento, Italy, during September 4–5, 2017.

The SEFM 2017 conference brought together leading researchers and practitioners from academia, industry, and government, to advance the state of the art in formal methods, to facilitate their uptake in the software industry, and to encourage their integration within practical software engineering methods and tools. The satellite workshops provided a highly interactive and collaborative environment to discuss emerging areas of software engineering, software technologies, model-driven engineering, and formal methods.

The five workshops whose papers are included in this volume are:

- **DataMod 2017** – 6th International Symposium From Data to Models and Back September 4–5, 2017. Organized by: Vashti Galpin (University of Edinburgh, UK), Paolo Milazzo (Università di Pisa, Italy), and André Teixeira (Delft University of Technology, The Netherlands).
- **FAACS 2017** – First Workshop on Formal Approaches for Advanced Computing Systems, September 4, 2017. Organized by: Paolo Arcaini (Charles University, Czech Republic), Marina Mongiello (Politecnico di Bari, Italy), Elvinia Riccobene (Università degli Studi di Milano, Italy), and Patrizia Scandurra (University of Bergamo, Italy).
- **MSE 2017** – First Workshop on Microservices: Science and Engineering, September 4, 2017. Organized by: Marcello M. Bersani (Politecnico of Milan, Italy), Antonio Bucchiarone (FBK, Italy), Nicola Dragoni (Technical University of Denmark and Örebro University, Sweden), Luca Ferrucci (ISTI-CNR, Pisa, Italy), Manuel Mazzara (Innopolis University, Russia), and Fabrizio Montesi (University of Southern Denmark).
- **CoSim-CPS 2017** – First Workshop on Formal Co-Simulation of Cyber-Physical Systems, September 5, 2017. Organized by: Cinzia Bernardeschi (University of Pisa, Italy), Peter Gorm Larsen (Aarhus University, Denmark), and Paolo Masci (Universidade do Minho, Portugal).
- **FOCLASA 2017** – 15th International Workshop on Foundations of Coordination Languages and Self-Adaptive Systems, September 5, 2017. Organized by: Carlos Canal (University of Malaga, Spain) and Gwen Salaün (University of Grenoble Alpes, France).

We would like to thank each organizer of the five workshops at SEFM 2017 for the interesting topics and resulting talks, as well as the respective Program Commitee members and external reviewers who carried out thorough and careful reviews, created the program of each workshop, and made the compilation of this high-quality volume possible. We also thank the paper contributors and attendees of all workshops. We would like to extend our thanks to all keynote speakers for their excellent presentations. A special thanks goes to Annalisa Armani and to all the other members of the Ufficio Eventi of FBK, who largely contributed to the success of the SEFM 2017 conference and workshops. We also thank the developers and maintainers of the EasyChair conference management system, which was of great help in handling paper submission, reviewing, discussion, for all workshops, and in the preparation of this volume. Finally, we would like to thank the organizers of SEFM 2017, Alessandro Cimatti and Marjan Sirjani, for useful insights and discussions, as well as the Fondazione Bruno Kessler that hosted the workshops and the conference.

November 2017   Antonio Cerone
                                                            Marco Roveri

Contents

MSE 2017

CoSim-CPS 2017

FOCLASA 2017

DataMod 2017

DATAMOD 2017 Organizers' Message

The 6th International Symposium From Data to Models and Back (DataMod 2017) was held in Trento, Italy, during September 4–5, 2017. The symposium aims at bringing together practitioners and researchers from academia, industry, government and non-government organizations to present research results and exchange experiences, ideas, and solutions for modeling and analyzing complex systems and using knowledge management strategies, technology, and systems in various domain areas such as ecology, biology, medicine, climate, governance, education, and social software engineering. After a careful review process, the Program Committee accepted nine papers for presentation at the symposium. The program of DataMod 2017 was also enriched by the keynote speeches of Bruno Lepri titled "Understanding and Rewiring Cities Using Big Data," Siobhán Clarke titled "Exploring Change Planning in Open, Complex Systems," and Simone Tini titled "Applications of Weak Behavioral Metrics in Probabilistic Systems." Additionally, Paolo Milazzo gave a tutorial titled "On DataMod Approaches to Systems Analysis."

Several people contributed to the success of DataMod 2017. We are grateful to the whole Steering Committee, and in particular to Paolo Milazzo for his assistance in the organization of the event. We would like to thank the organizers of SEFM 2017, and in particular the workshops chairs, Antonio Cerone and Marco Roveri. We would also like to thank the Program Committee and the additional reviewers for their work in reviewing the papers. The process of reviewing and selecting papers was significantly simplified through using EasyChair. We thank all attendees of the symposium and hope that this event enabled a good exchange of ideas and generate new collaborations among attendees. The organization of DataMod 2017 was supported by the research project "Metodologie informatiche avanzate per l'analisi di dati biomedici (Advanced computational methodologies for the analysis of biomedical data)" funded by the University of Pisa (PRA_2017_44).

November 2017

Vashti Galpin
André Herdeiro Teixeira

Organization

DataMod 2017 - Steering Committee

Antonio Cerone   Nazarbayev University, Kazakhstan
Jane Hillston   University of Edinburgh, UK
Marijn Janssen   Delft University of Technology, The Netherlands
Stan Matwin   University of Ottawa, Canada
Paolo Milazzo   University of Pisa, Italy
Anna Monreale   University of Pisa, Italy

DataMod 2017 - Program Committee

Ezio Bartocci   TU Wien, Austria
Bettina Berendt   KU Leuven, Belgium
Luca Bortolussi   University of Trieste, Italy
Giulio Caravagna   University of Edinburgh, UK
Antonio Cerone   Nazarbayev University, Kazakhstan
Chiara Damiani   University of Milano-Bicocca, Italy
Cheng Feng   Imperial College London, UK
Giuditta Franco   University of Verona, Italy
Ilenia Fronza   Free University of Bolzano/Bozen, Italy
Rosalba Giugno   University of Verona, Italy
Vashti Galpin (Co-chair)   University of Edinburgh, UK
Yiwei Gong   Wuhan University, China
Rocio Gonzalez-Diaz   University of Seville, Spain
Tias Guns   Vrije Universiteit Brussel, Belgium
Joris Hulstijn   Delft University of Technology, The Netherlands
Mouna Kacimi   Free University of Bozen-Bolzano, Italy
Donato Malerba   University of Bari, Italy
Emanuela Merelli   University of Camerino, Italy
Anna Monreale   University of Pisa, Italy
Charles Morisset   Newcastle University, UK
Patrick Mukala   Enidhoven University of Technology, The Netherlands
Laura Nenzi   IMT, Lucca, Italy
Nicola Paoletti   Stony Brook University, USA
Anna Philippou   University of Cyprus, Cyprus
Carla Piazza   University of Udine, Italy
Silvio Ranise   Fondazione Bruno Kessler, Trento, Italy
Giulio Rossetti   ISTI-CNR and University of Pisa, Italy

Matteo Rucco	United Technologies Research Center, Trento, Italy
Marc Sterling	Nazarbayev University, Kazakhstan
André Teixeira (Co-chair)	Delft University of Technology, The Netherlands
Luca Tesei	University of Camerino, Italy
Roberto Trasarti	ISTI-CNR, Pisa, Italy
Luca Viganò	King's College London, UK
Nicola Zannone	Eindhoven University of Technology, The Netherlands
Roberto Zunino	University of Trento, Italy

DataMod 2017 - Additional Reviewers

Peter Carmichael	Newcastle University, UK
Laura Genga	Eindhoven University of Technology, The Netherlands
Simone Righi	University of Bologna, Italy

Understanding and Rewiring Cities Using Big Data
(Keynote Talk)

Bruno Lepri

Fondazione Bruno Kessler, Italy

In the last decades, cities have been largely acknowledged as complex and emergent systems as opposed to top-down planned entities. Thus, a new city science is emerging that aims at an empirical analysis of urbanization processes. However, it is evident the lack of understanding of the dynamics that regulate people interactions, their relationship with urban characteristics, and their influence on social and economic outcomes of cities. Nowadays, massive streams of human behavioural data and urban data combined with increased analytical capabilities are creating unprecedented possibilities for understanding global patterns of human behaviour and for helping researchers to better understand relevant problems for cities and also for whole societies. For example, analysing the digital traces people leave every day (e.g., mobile phones and social media data, credit card transactions, etc.) researchers were able, among the other things, to estimate the socio-economic status of territories, to monitor the vitality of urban areas and to predict neighbourhoods' crime levels. In my keynote talk, I describe some recent works where my group and other collaborators have leveraged data from public (e.g., national census, household surveys, cadastral data) and from commercial entities (e.g., Foursquare, mobile phone data, credit card transactions, Google Street View images, etc.) in order (i) to infer how vital and liveable a city is, (ii) to find the urban conditions (e.g., mixed land use, mobility, safety perception, etc.) that magnify and influence urban life, (iii) to study their relationship with societal outcomes such as poverty, criminality, innovation, segregation, etc., and (iv) to envision data-driven guidelines for helping policy makers to respond to the demands of citizens. Our results open the door for a new research framework to study and to understand cities, and societies, by means of computational tools (i.e. machine learning approaches) and novel sources of data able to describe human life with an unprecedented breath, scale and depth. Finally, I also describe and discuss several potential policy applications of our results.

Exploring Change Planning in Open Complex Systems (Keynote Talk)

Siobhán Clarke

Trinity College Dublin, Ireland

Modern, complex systems are likely to execute in open environments (e.g., applications running over the Internet of Things), where changes are frequent and have the potential to cause significant negative consequences for the application. A better understanding of the data in the environment will enable applications to better plan for change and remain resilient in the face of loss of data sources through, for example, mobility or battery loss. This talk explored our recent work on models for change planning in such open, complex systems. The approaches include static, multi-layer system and change modelling, through to multi-agent systems that learn and adapt to changes in the environment, and finally collaborative models for emergent behaviour detection, and for resource sharing.

We studied large-scale, multi-layer systems in the context of a crisis management case study that had organisational, behavioural and services layers, and asked questions such as what happens when a problem occurs in one layer, and that problem is likely to manifest itself across multiple layers of the system? What data model is needed to support decision-making as to the best thing to do when a fault occurs? We devised a model whereby we could do flexible, extensible look-up for adaptation processing when an error is triggered. Remaining challenges for the research community include how to find the root cause of a problem to generate the correct trigger, and automating an adaptation process when the environment is inherently unstable. More of our work that contributes to addressing some of these challenges includes automated detection of emergent behaviour in multi-agent systems, which may indicate anomalies that require correction. This distributed algorithm enables constituent agents in complex adaptive system to collaboratively detect emergent events, relying on the feedback that occurs naturally from the system level to the component level when emergent behaviour or properties appears, facilitating detection using only data local to each agent.

Our focus on open, unstable environments also lead us to consider multi-agent systems with learning techniques, in particular exploring challenges with community-based residential energy sharing. We used reinforcement learning for decision-making on energy usage while catering for both changing individual household needs and the dynamics of renewable energy availability and corresponding energy availability for the community. Data of interest included both knowledge relating to the availability of energy (particularly renewable), and information about the householders' needs. Of course, an interesting challenge in providing such automated decision-making as to the use of energy in residential homes is ensuring that there is a happy balance when addressing the needs of all residents. Different households may have different goals and policies for energy use that may conflict, and some may not be willing to collaborate. In this talk, I also introduced our work on enabling cooperative, neighbourly behaviour in open systems, where we use social reasoning techniques to build a social dependency model that enables agents to adjust their behaviour when sharing constrained resources, and balance both personal and society benefits. Agents share only minimal personal data for building the social dependency model. The talk also illustrated how this model was applied to ad hoc ride-sharing, where results showed more efficient use of vehicles, thereby reducing carbon emissions.

Applications of Weak Behavioral Metrics in Probabilistic Systems
(Keynote Talk)

Simone Tini

Department of Science and High Technology,
University of Insubria, Via Valleggio 11, Como, Italy

Probabilistic process algebras, such as probabilistic CCS and CSP, are languages that are employed to describe probabilistic concurrent communicating systems. The most general semantic model employed to describe the behaviour of these systems is that of *nondeterministic probabilistic labelled transition systems*, or PTSs for short, which combine labelled transition systems and discrete time Markov chains, thus allowing us to model, at the same time, the reactive system behaviour, nondeterministic choices and probabilistic choices. In order to compare the behaviour of systems in the PTS model, behavioural *metric semantics* have been proposed as notions of *behavioural distance* that characterize how far the behaviour of two systems is apart.

The notion of *weak bisimulation metric* proposed by Desharnais, Jagadeesan, Gupta and Panangaden is a metric semantics which allows us to abstract from non-observable, or internal, transition steps. The asymmetric variant, called *weak simulation quasi-metric*, has been proposed by Lanotte, Merro and Tini to reason on protocols where the systems under consideration are not approximately equivalent. In this talk we discuss how this notion can be used to evaluate the performances of gossip protocols.

In order to specify and verify systems in a compositional manner, it is necessary that the behavioural semantics is compatible with all operators of the language that describe these systems. In the probabilistic setting, the intuitive idea is that two systems that are close according to the considered notion of distance should be approximately inter-substitutable: Whenever a system s in a language context $C[s]$ is replaced by a close system s', the obtained context $C[s']$ should be close to $C[s]$. In other words, there should be some relation between the behavioural distance between s and s' and the behavioural distance between $C[s]$ and $C[s']$ so that any limited change in the behaviour of a sub-component s implies a smooth and limited change in the behaviour of the composed system $C[s]$. *Uniform continuity* proposed by Gebler, Larsen and Tini guarantees the compatibility of the metric semantics with language operators. Lanotte, Merro and Tini investigated the compositionality of both weak bisimilarity metric and weak similarity quasimetric semantics with respect to a variety of standard process algebra operators. In this talk we discuss how these compositionality results can be successfully used to conduct compositional reasoning to estimate the performances of group key update protocols in a multicast setting.

Temporal Analytics for Software Usage Models

Oana Andrei$^{(\boxtimes)}$ and Muffy Calder

School of Computing Science, University of Glasgow, Glasgow G12 8RZ, UK
oana.andrei@glasgow.ac.uk

Abstract. We address the problem of analysing how users *actually* interact with software. Users are heterogeneous: they adopt different usage patterns and each individual user may move between different patterns, from one interaction session to another, or even during an interaction session. For analysis, we require new techniques to model and analyse temporal data sets of logged interactions with the purpose of discovering, interpreting, and communicating meaningful patterns of usage. We define new probabilistic models whose parameters are inferred from logged time series data of user-software interactions. We formulate hypotheses about software usage together with the developers, encode them in probabilistic temporal logic, and analyse the models according to the probabilistic properties. We illustrate by application to logged data from a deployed mobile application software used by thousands of users.

1 Introduction

Software users are heterogeneous: they adopt different usage patterns for the same software, furthermore, each individual user may move between different patterns, from one interaction session to another, or even during a session. This may be for a variety of contextual reasons, for example, time of day, time since last session, length of session, purpose of engagement, environment (e.g. on a train or at a desk) or device (PC, tablet, wearable). To analyse these differing and dynamic usage patterns, we require new techniques to model and analyse temporal data sets of logged interactions with the purpose of discovering, evaluating, and communicating meaningful patterns of usage. We define new probabilistic models of software usage that are generated from logged data using statistical methods. Analysis is performed by model checking probabilistic temporal logic properties.

Our approach consists of:

- two new parametrised, admixture discrete-time Markov models that include latent (unobserved) and observed states and depend on a finite number K of usage patterns,
- segmented logged time series data encapsulating different usage time intervals, e.g. interactions over first day, first week, first month, second month,
- use of maximum-likelihood parameter estimation techniques for inferring model parameters,

© Springer International Publishing AG 2018
A. Cerone and M. Roveri (Eds.): SEFM 2017 Workshops, LNCS 10729, pp. 9–24, 2018.
https://doi.org/10.1007/978-3-319-74781-1_1

– an encoding of the inferred usage models in the PRISM model checker [1] and use of temporal logics PCTL and PCTL* for analysis.

It is important to note we are not inferring the underlying software structure, which is determined by the designed functionality of the software. We are investigating the differing generating processes of software *usage* over a dynamic, heterogeneous population of a users. The logged data are user-initiated events: we refer to the time series data as *user traces*, where each user trace consists of all the logged sessions for that user/device. We identify basic common traits of usage emerging within such a population of users and classify users as *admixtures* of basic traits. In statistical modelling, in a mixture model each user trace is mapped to one single behavioural trait, whereas in admixture models each user trace has a distribution over all behavioural traits. To the best of our knowledge, inferring admixture temporal structures has not been described in prior work outside our group. Figure 1 summarises our approach. This work builds on two previous studies: an initial analysis of AppTracker using PAM models [2], and earlier, in [3], analysis of individual user models for a mobile game application. Major differences here include formal definitions of PAM, new GPAM model, generic properties, and use of parameter K as exploratory tool.

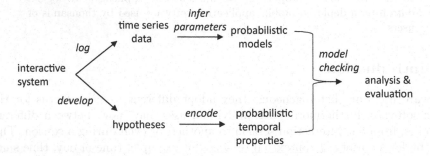

Fig. 1. Role of inference and probabilistic model checking in defining and analysing software usage models.

The main contributions of the paper are:

– two new latent state Markov models: population admixture model (PAM) and generalised population admixture model (GPAM),
– flattened form of the GPAM model as discrete time Markov chain and encoding in the probabilistic model checker PRISM,
– generic and GPAM-specific temporal logic properties,
– an example based on a deployed user-intensive mobile application software (mobile app) used by tens of thousands of users, working in close collaboration with the app developers.

In the next section we give background definitions. The new latent variable Markov models, PAM and GPAM, are introduced in Sect. 3. In Sect. 4 we define classes of probabilistic temporal properties for analysing PAMs and GPAMs. In Sect. 5 we give an overview of our example interactive software and evaluate its usage by PAM and GPAM analysis. We reflect on our approach in Sect. 6 and conclusions are in Sect. 7.

2 Technical Background

2.1 Markov Models

We assume familiarity with Markov models, probabilistic logics PCTL and PCTL* with rewards, and model checking [1,4,5]; basic definitions are below.

Let $\mathcal{A}$ be a finite set of atomic propositions. A **discrete-time Markov chain (DTMC)**, also called a first-order Markov chain model, is a tuple $(S, \bar{s}, \mathbf{P}, \mathcal{L})$ where: S is the set of states; $\bar{s} \in S$ is the initial state, $\mathbf{P} : S \times S \to [0, 1]$ is the transition probability function (or matrix) such that for all states $s \in S$ we have $\sum_{s' \in S} \mathbf{P}(s, s') = 1$; $\mathcal{L} : S \to 2^{\mathcal{A}}$ is a labelling function associating to each state s in S a set of valid atomic propositions from the set $\mathcal{A}$. A *path* (or execution) of a DTMC is a non-empty sequence $s_0 s_1 s_2 \dots$ where $s_i \in S$ and $\mathbf{P}(s_i, s_{i+1}) > 0$ for all $i \geq 0$. For DTMC $\mathcal{D}$ the set of paths starting from state s is $Path^{\mathcal{D}}(s)$. A transition is also called a *time-step*.

We will distinguish between latent (unobserved or hidden), and observed states. The standard latent variable Markov model is the hidden Markov model, which does not include transitions between observed states. Formally, a **first-order hidden Markov model (HMM)** is a tuple $(\mathcal{X}, \mathcal{Y}, \pi, A, B)$ where: $\mathcal{X}$ is the set of hidden (or latent) states $\mathcal{X} = \{1, \dots, K\}$; $\mathcal{Y}$ is the set of observed states generated by hidden states; $\pi : \mathcal{X} \to [0, 1]$ is an initial distribution, where $\sum_{x \in \mathcal{X}} \pi(x) = 1$; $A : \mathcal{X} \times \mathcal{X} \to [0, 1]$ is the transition probability matrix, such that for all $x \in \mathcal{X}$ we have $\sum_{x' \in \mathcal{X}} A(x, x') = 1$; $B : \mathcal{X} \times \mathcal{Y} \to [0, 1]$ is the observation probability matrix, such that for all $x \in \mathcal{X}$ we have $\sum_{y \in \mathcal{Y}} B(x, y) = 1$.

A less common, but more useful model than HMM for us, is the auto-regressive hidden Markov model, which also permits transitions between observed states. Formally, a **first-order auto-regressive hidden Markov model (AR-HMM)** is a tuple $(\mathcal{X}, \mathcal{Y}, \pi, A, B)$ where: $\mathcal{X}, \mathcal{Y}, \pi, A$ are as defined for HMM; $B : \mathcal{X} \times \mathcal{Y} \times \mathcal{Y} \to [0, 1]$ is the observation probability matrix, such that for all $x \in \mathcal{X}$ and $y \in \mathcal{Y}$ we have $\sum_{y' \in \mathcal{Y}} B(x, y, y') = 1$.

2.2 Probabilistic Logics and Model Checking

Probabilistic Computation Tree Logic (PCTL) and its extension *PCTL** allow one to express a probability measure of the satisfaction of a temporal property by a DTMC. Their syntax is the following:

$$
\begin{array}{rl}
\textit{State formulae} & \Phi ::= \textit{true} \mid a \mid \neg \Phi \mid \Phi \wedge \Phi \mid \mathsf{P}_{\bowtie p}[\Psi] \mid \mathsf{S}_{\bowtie p}[\Phi] \\
\textit{PCTL Path formulae} & \Psi ::= \mathsf{X}\,\Phi \mid \Phi \mathsf{U}^{\leq N}\,\Phi \\
\textit{PCTL* Path formulae} & \Psi ::= \Phi \mid \Psi \wedge \Psi \mid \neg \Psi \mid \mathsf{X}\,\Psi \mid \Psi \mathsf{U}^{\leq N}\,\Psi
\end{array}
$$

where a ranges over a set of atomic propositions $\mathcal{A}$, $\bowtie \in \{\le, <, \ge, >\}$, $p \in [0, 1]$, and $N \in \mathbb{N} \cup \{\infty\}$.

This is a minimal set of operators, the propositional operators *false*, disjunction and implication can be derived. Two common derived path operators are: the *eventually* operator F where $\mathsf{F}^{\le n} \Phi \equiv true \ \mathsf{U}^{\le n} \Phi$ and the *always* operator G where $\mathsf{G} \Psi \equiv \neg(\mathsf{F} \neg \Psi)$. If $N = \infty$ then the superscript N is omitted. In PRISM $\mathsf{P}_{=?}[\Psi]$ computes the probability for Ψ to hold in a given state (initial state by default). $\mathsf{S}_{=?}[\Phi]$ computes the steady-state (long-run) probability of being in a state which satisfies a Boolean-valued state formula Φ. PRISM supports a *reward*-based extension of PCTL called *rPCTL* that assigns non-negative real values to states and/or transitions. $\mathsf{R}_{rwd=?}\left[\mathsf{C}^{\le N}\right]$ computes the reward named *rwd* accumulated along *all* paths within N time-steps, $\mathsf{R}_{rwd=?}[\mathsf{F} \ \phi]$ computes the reward named *rwd* accumulated along *all* paths until ϕ is satisfied. Filters check for properties that hold from sets of states satisfying given propositions. Here we use **state** as the filter operator: e.g., **filter**(**state**, ϕ, *condition*) where ϕ is a state formula and *condition* a Boolean proposition uniquely identifying a state in the DTMC.

3   Probabilistic Models for Software Usage

Our experience indicates that useful usage models do *not* depend only on static attributes such as the location, gender, age of users, but on *dynamic* attributes such as *patterns* of use, that may change over time. Users are heterogeneous and each individual user may move between different patterns, from one interactive session to another, or even during an interaction session. We need new models of dynamic usage patterns and new ways to analyse those models. To encapsulate the patterns of dynamic and heterogeneous users, we define models that are:

- *probabilistic*: statistical models of the different generating processes of heterogeneous, dynamic users,
- *Markovian*: behaviour is determined by current state, not process history,
- *admixture*[1]: usage patterns (or, more generally, behavioural traits) are complex and drawn from a probability distribution, i.e. individuals move between different patterns during an observed trace.

First-order Markov models have been shown to provide a good modelling approach for human navigation on the Web [6–10] (where the states correspond to visited webpages) as well as within mobile applications [3, 11] (where the states correspond to device screen events). We model the usage pattern as a hidden/latent state and the user-initiated events as observed states. Each hidden state defines a first-order discrete time Markov chain (DTMC) over observed states, which we call *activity pattern*.

Let $\mathcal{P}$ be a population of M user traces, with each user trace $\alpha^1, \ldots, \alpha^M$ a finite sequence over a set $\mathcal{A}$ of n events (labels of logged user interactions). Some

---

[1] Admixture models derive from genetic analysis of populations where individuals have mixed ancestry: each individual inherits a fraction of his/her genome from ancestors.

events are distinguished by the unique labels startS and stopS to denote the beginning and end (resp.) of a user *session* within a trace. Each user trace is a concatenation of sessions. It is important to note that each user trace contains a variable number of sessions, and each session is a variable length sequence of events. We now define two different usage models for a given population of user traces.

Definition 1 (Population admixture model). *For a given positive integer K, a population admixture model (PAM) for the user trace population $\mathcal{P}$ is a tuple $(\mathcal{X}, \mathcal{Y}, B, \mathcal{L}, \Theta)$ where:*

- $\mathcal{X}$ *is the set of latent states,* $\mathcal{X} = \{1, \ldots, K\}$,
- $\mathcal{Y}$ *is the set of observed states,* $\mathcal{Y} = \{0, \ldots, n-1\}$,
- B *is the observation probability matrix with $B : \mathcal{X} \times \mathcal{Y} \times \mathcal{Y} \to [0,1]$ such that for all $x \in \mathcal{X}$ and $y \in \mathcal{Y}$ we have $\sum_{y' \in \mathcal{Y}} B(x, y, y') = 1$,*
- $\mathcal{L} : \mathcal{Y} \to \mathcal{A}$ *is the labelling function,*
- $\Theta = \{\theta_1, \ldots, \theta_M\}$ *is the set of distributions over all latent states for each user trace in the population, such that for all m, $1 \leq m \leq M$, $\theta_m : \mathcal{X} \to [0,1]$ with $\sum_{x \in \mathcal{X}} \theta_m(x) = 1$.*

Definition 2 (Generalised population admixture model). *For a given positive integer K, a generalised population admixture model (GPAM) for the user trace population $\mathcal{P}$ is a tuple $(\mathcal{X}, \mathcal{Y}, \pi, A, B, \mathcal{L})$ where $(\mathcal{X}, \mathcal{Y}, \pi, A, B)$ is an AR-HMM and $\mathcal{L} : \mathcal{Y} \to \mathcal{A}$ is the labelling function.*

Definition 3 (Activity patterns). *For any PAM $(\mathcal{X}, \mathcal{Y}, B, \mathcal{L}, \Theta)$ or GPAM $(\mathcal{X}, \mathcal{Y}, \pi, A, B, \mathcal{L})$, and any latent state $x \in \mathcal{X}$, the tuple $(\mathcal{Y}, \mathcal{L}^{-1}(startS), B(x), \mathcal{L})$ is a discrete-time Markov chain we call* activity pattern.

Hidden Markov models express relationships only between latent states, but not between observed states, so they are not suitable for our purpose of analysing user-software interaction. PAM models are admixtures of first-order Markov chains (DTMCs) that express relationships between observed states, with Θ defining distributions over the latent states. PAM models are well-suited for user-intensive software, in particular because we can study the values for Θ across all users or subpopulations thereof. In the PAM models, it is not possible to relate changes to latent states to changes in the observed states. If this is important, then AR-HMMs (GPAM) are more suitable because they express explicit relationships between both observed and latent states.

Each of the models PAM and GPAM (pictorial representation in Fig. 2) offers a different perspective on usage behaviours, and consequently affords different analysis. Both are based on K mixture components (or latent states), with each component a DTMC (an activity pattern). Each component DTMC has the same set of states, but the transition probabilities are different, as indicated by the thickness of transitions. The number of mixture components/activity patterns, K, is an exploratory tool: we do not try to find the "correct" or optimal value

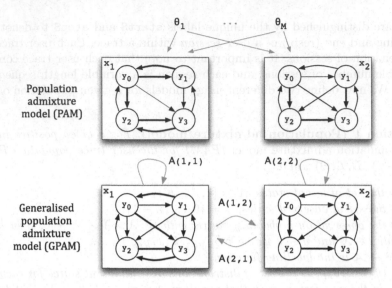

Fig. 2. Pictorial representation of PAM and GPAM for two latent states (or activity patterns as DTMCs in each box) x_1 and x_2, $K = 2$, four observed states $y_0 - y_3$, M user traces, $1 \leq m \leq M$

for K, instead we explore the variety of activity patterns that are meaningful to software evaluation (e.g. we might develop distinct versions for three or four different activity patterns).

3.1 Learning Model Parameters

The size of the latent state set $\mathcal{X}$ (the number K of the activity patterns), the set of n observed states (user-initiated events) $\mathcal{Y}$, and the labelling function $\mathcal{L}$ are pre-determined for both PAM and GPAM. It remains to define the observation matrix B and distributions Θ for PAM, and the transition matrix A, observation matrix B, and initial distribution π for GPAM. We *learn* these parameters from sets of user traces using statistical methods for maximum likelihoods.

We segment the user traces according to intervals over days, weeks, or months, based on timestamps associated with each logged event (the time stamps are then discarded). Intervals have the form $[d_1, d_2]$, which includes the user traces from the d_1^{th}-th up to the d_2^{th} day of usage.

Given a set $\mathcal{P}$ of user traces, we compute $n \times n$ transition-occurrence matrices for each trace α such that α_{ij} at position (i, j) is the number of times the subsequence α_i, α_j occurs in α. This is the input data for parameter inference.

For PAM we employ the local non-linear optimisation Expectation–Maximisation (EM) algorithm [12] for finding maximum likelihood parameters of observing each trace, restarting the algorithm whenever the log-likelihood has multiple-local maxima. EM converges provably to a local optimum of the criterion, in this case the likelihood function. For GPAM (AR-HMM) we employ the Baum–Welch algorithm [13], which uses also the EM algorithm. We use EM, as opposed to say Markov chains Monte Carlo methods, because it is fast and computationally efficient for our kind of data.

3.2 Encoding Models in the PRISM Modelling Language

For both PAM and GPAM we analyse each activity pattern as a DTMC in PRISM. In addition, for GPAM we *flatten* the whole AR-HMM model, which has two types of states and three types of transitions (between latent states, between observed states, from latent states to observed states) into a DTMC (and subsequently analyse it in PRISM) as follows. We pair each observed state with a hidden state. The transition probability between two any such pairs of states (y, x) and (y', x') is the probability of moving from hidden state x to hidden state x' times the probability of moving between the observed states y to y' while in the current hidden state x', i.e., $\mathbf{P}((y, x), (y', x')) = A(x, x') \cdot B(x', y, y')$. The initial state $(\mathcal{L}^{-1}(\mathsf{startS}), 0)$ is a dummy that encodes the global initial distribution. This flattening operation shares similarities with the composition between an HMM and a deterministic finite state machine (see [14]), however we are composing an HMM with a DTMC.

Definition 4. *Given a GPAM* $(\mathcal{X}, \mathcal{Y}, \pi, A, B, \mathcal{L})$*, we flatten it into the DTMC* $(S, (\bar{y}, 0), \mathbf{P}, \mathcal{L})$ *where:*

- $S = \mathcal{Y} \times (\{0\} \cup \mathcal{X})$*, where* $\mathcal{X} = \{1, \dots, K\}$*,*
- $\bar{y} = \mathcal{L}^{-1}(\mathsf{startS})$ *is the initial observed state with the label* startS*,*
- $\mathbf{P}((y, x), (y', x')) = A(x, x') \cdot B(x', y, y')$*, for* $x > 0$*,*
- $\mathbf{P}((\bar{y}, 0), (y, x)) = \begin{cases} \pi(x) \ if \ y = \bar{y} \ and \ x' > 0 \\ 0 \qquad otherwise \end{cases}$
- $\mathcal{L}(y, x) = \mathcal{L}(y) \times \{x\}$*.*

For clarification, DTMCs are used at two levels of abstraction: to represent individual activity patterns and to represent the more complex GPAM Markov models in which the activity patterns are embedded, as a flattened GPAM.

4 Temporal Properties for Analysing Usage Models

We present *generic* rPCTL properties for analysing: (1) individual activity patterns of both PAM and (flattened)[2] GPAM models, and (2) *GPAM-specific* rPCTL and PCTL* properties that involve moving *between* activity patterns. It is important to note we cannot check properties from the latter set on PAM models because PAMs include a distribution over activity patterns and not transition probabilities between activity patterns, as in GPAMs.

---

[2] All results are for flattened GPAMs.

4.1 Generic Properties for Individual Patterns in PAM and GPAM

We consider the following classes of state formulae:

$$Observed\ state\ formulae\ \varphi ::= \mathbf{true} \mid \ell \mid y = j \mid \neg\varphi \mid \varphi \wedge \varphi$$
$$Hidden\ state\ formulae\ \gamma ::= \mathbf{true} \mid x = i \mid \neg\gamma \mid \gamma \wedge \gamma$$
$$Non\text{-}probabilistic\ state\ formulae\ \phi ::= \varphi \mid \gamma \mid \neg\phi \mid \phi \wedge \phi$$

where ℓ ranges over the set of observed state labels $\mathcal{A}$, j over the set of observed states identifiers $\{0,\ldots,n-1\}$ and i over the set of hidden state identifiers $\{0,1,\ldots,K\}$ (with 0 denoting a dummy hidden state for the PRISM encoding). We define the following reward structures for all values of $j \in \{0,\ldots,n-1\}$ and $i \in \{1,\ldots,K\}$: rLabelj and rLabeljAPi for computing the expected number of visits to an observed state j and to a state (i,j) respectively, and rSteps and rStepsAPi for computing the number of all time steps in the model and the number of all time steps in activity pattern i respectively. Note that rLabeljAPi and rStepsAPi are defined exclusively for GPAM models. The PRISM definitions of these rewards are as follows:

```
rewards "rLabelj" (y=j): 1; endrewards
rewards "rLabeljAPi" (y=j) & (x=i) : 1; endrewards
rewards "rSteps" [] true : 1; endrewards
rewards "rStepsAPi" [] (x=i) : 1; endrewards
```

Table 1 lists three classes of generic properties: VisitProb, VisitCount, and StepCount, where the reward name $rewardV$ can be either of rLabelj and rLabeljAPi, while $rewardS$ can be either of rSteps and rStepsAPi. We adopt the following interpretation of the model checking results for activity patterns in the same model (either PAM or GPAM), and the same value of N, when comparing the states. We say that a pair of observed state j and activity pattern i scores a better (resp. worse) result that (j',i') if: VisitProb returns a higher (resp. lower) value, VisitCount a higher (resp. lower) value, StepCount a positive lower (resp. higher) value for the pair (j,i) than for (j',i').

Table 1. Classes of rPCTL properties applicable in PAM and GPAM model.

Prop.	Description	rPCTL formula
VisitProb	Probability that starting from state satisfying ϕ_0, ϕ_1 holds until reaching a state in which ϕ_2 holds, within N time-steps	$\mathbf{filter}(\mathbf{state}, \mathsf{P}_{=?}[\phi_1 \mathsf{U}^{\leq N}\phi_2], \phi_0)$
VisitCount	Starting from state satisfying ϕ_0, expected reward cumulated over N time-steps	$\mathbf{filter}(\mathbf{state}, \mathsf{R}_{rewardV=?}[\mathsf{C}^{\leq N}], \phi_0)$
StepCount	Starting from state satisfying ϕ_0, expected number of steps cumulated before reaching a state satisfying ϕ_1	$\mathbf{filter}(\mathbf{state}, \mathsf{R}_{rewardS=?}[\mathsf{F}\,\phi_1], \phi_0)$

Table 2 illustrates some instances of the property classes in Table 1. VP1 and VP2 are simple reachability properties for a particular state in either an activity pattern (AP) or a GPAM respectively. VP3 computes the reachability probability for a state j in pattern i while always being in pattern i in an GPAM. SC1 and SC2 compute the expected number of steps needed to reach a particular state in either an AP or a GPAM, while SC3 computes only the steps takes in the pattern i to reach a state in an GPAM. VC1 computes the expected number of visits to a state j in an AP, while VC2 computes only the number of visits to state j while the pattern i in a GPAM.

Table 2. Instances of VisitProb, VisitCount, and StepCount applicable to activity pattern (AP) i in PAM or GPAM, parametrised by observed state j and pattern i.

Prop.	DTMC	rPCTL formula
VP1	AP/PAM	filter(state, $P_{=?}[\text{true U}^{\leq N}(y = j)]$, startS)
VP2	GPAM	filter(state, $P_{=?}[\text{true U}^{\leq N}(x = i \wedge y = j)]$, (startS $\wedge\, x = 0$))
VP3	GPAM	filter(state, $P_{=?}[(x = i)\ \text{U}^{\leq N}(x = i \wedge y = j)]$, (startS $\wedge\, x = i$))
SC1	AP/PAM	filter(state, $R_{\text{rSteps}=?}[F\,(y = j)]$, startS)
SC2	GPAM	filter(state, $R_{\text{rSteps}=?}[F(x = i \wedge y = j)]$, (startS $\wedge\, x = 0$))
SC3	GPAM	filter(state, $R_{\text{rStepsAPi}=?}[F(x = i \wedge y = j)]$, (startS $\wedge\, x = i$))
VC1	AP/PAM	filter(state, $R_{\text{rStatej}=?}[C^{\leq N}]$, startS)
VC2	GPAM	filter(state, $R_{\text{rStatejAPi}=?}[C^{\leq N}]$, (startS $\wedge\, x = i$))

4.2 GPAM-Specific Properties

For GPAM, it is possible to consider properties that involve multiple activity patterns. A few such rPCTL/PCTL* properties are listed in Fig. 3.

> **PG1 :** filter(state, $P_{=?}[(\neg\textsf{UseStop})\ \text{U}\ (x = i_1 \wedge y = j_1)]$, $(x = i_0 \wedge y = j_0)$)
>
> **PG2 :** filter(state, $R_{\text{rSteps}=?}[F\,(y = j_1)]$, $(x = i_0 \wedge y = j_0)$)
>
> **PG3 :** filter(state, $R_{\text{rSteps}=?}[F\,(x = i_1 \wedge y = j_1)]$, $(x = i_0 \wedge y = j_0)$)
>
> **PG4 :** filter(state, $R_{\text{rStepsAPi}=?}[F\,(x = i_1 \wedge y = j_1)]$, $(x = i_0 \wedge y = j_0)$)
>
> **PG5 :** $P_{\geq 1}[F\,(x = i \wedge y = j)] \wedge P_{\geq 1}[G\,((x = i \wedge y = j) \Rightarrow P_{>p}[(x = i)\ \text{U stopS}])]$
>
> **PG6 :** $P_{\geq 1}[F\,\phi_1] \wedge P_{\geq 1}[F\,\phi_2] \wedge P_{\geq 1}[F\,((\neg\phi_1 \wedge \neg\phi_2)\ \text{U}\ P_{\geq 1}[(\phi_1 \wedge \neg\phi_2)\ \text{U}\ P_{\geq p}[X\,\phi_2]])]$
>
> **PG7 :** $S_{=?}[x = i]$

Fig. 3. rPCTL* properties where i, i_0, i_1 range over hidden states, j, j_1, j_2 over observed states, $p \in [0, 1]$.

Property PG1 is an instance of VisitProb (reasoning over reachability within the same user session), while PG2 – PG4 are instances of StepCount. PG5 helps us identify most likely states and patterns that lead to the end of the session (this is useful for user engagement analysis across different time intervals). PG6 checks for correlations between two properties (that might involve states and activity patterns): if eventually one property holds (for a period of time), then immediately afterwards, the second property holds. PG7 computes the long-run probability of the population of user traces of being in each of the activity patterns and it gives us more insight into the popularity of the patterns.

5   Example Software Usage Analysis: AppTracker

AppTracker [15] is a personal productivity iOS mobile application that runs in the background, monitoring the opening and closing of (other) apps. It displays a series of charts and statistics, offering insight to users into the time spent on their device, the most used apps, how these stats fluctuate over time, etc. The main menu screen offers four main options (Fig. 4(a)). The first menu item, *Overall Usage*, contains summaries of all the data recorded since AppTracker was installed and opens the views `OverallUsage` and `Stats` (Fig. 4(b)). The second menu item, *Last 7 Days*, opens the view `StackedBars` and displays a chart indicating activity recorded over the last 7 days. The third menu item, *Select by Period*, opens the view `PeriodSelector` and shows statistics for a selected period of time. For example, this could be which apps were used most since last Saturday, or how time spent on Facebook varied each day last month, or hourly device usage for a particular day (Fig. 4(c)). The final menu option, *Settings*, allows a user to start and stop the tracker, or to reset their recorded data. We are interested in the 16 user-initiated events that switch between views, as illustrated by the state diagram in Fig. 5. These events determine the atomic propositions used in our models. The state labels denoting the start and the end of a session are `UseStart` and `UseStop` respectively. The log data is stored in a MySQL database by the SGLog framework. Raw data is extracted from the database and processed using JavaScript to obtain user traces in JSON format has the following format: information about the user's device, start and end data of AppTracker usage, and list of sessions. For example, the start of a user trace may look like the following:

```
[{"deviceid":"_","firstSeen":"2013-08-20 09:10:59","lastSeen":"2014-03-24
09:57:32","sessions":[[{"timestamp":"2013-08-20 09:11:01","data":
"UseStart"},{"timestamp":"2013-08-20 09:11:02","data":"T&C"},{"timestamp":
"2013-08-20 09:11:23", "data":"Main"},{"timestamp":"2013-08-20 09:11:46",
"data":"OverallUsage"},...]}]
```

AppTracker was first released in 2013 and downloaded over 35,000 times; our data sets are taken from a sample of 489 users traces during 2013 and 2014. For learning parameters, the EM algorithm was restarted 200 times with 100 maximum number of iterations for each restart. As example performance, we implemented the algorithm for GPAM parameters in Java and ran it on a 2.8 GHz Intel Xeon (single thread, one core); for the first week of logged usage data, the

(a) Main menu   (b) Overall stats   (c) Daily device usage

Fig. 4. Screenshots from AppTracker.

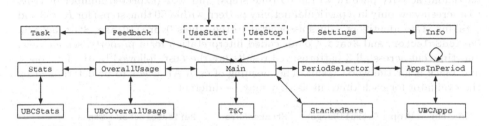

Fig. 5. AppTracker state diagram. `UseStart` labels the initial state; all (15) outgoing and incoming arrows are omitted for `UseStart` and `UseStop`.

algorithm takes 1.7 min for $K = 2$, 2.5 min for $K = 3$, and 3.7 min for $K = 4$. Note that complexity of the inference depends on the n and value of K, not on the size of the data sets.

Analysis of individual patterns. This helps us identify distinct characteristics of each pattern and give patterns names that are meaningful. In [2] we considered five properties for PAM: the ones listed in Table 2 and two instances of the VisitProb and StepCount (where the starting state corresponds to a screen view different from `UseStart`). Here, as an example of properties for GPAM, we give results for VP2 and VC2 in Table 3 for $K = 3$. For the first month of usage, AP1 has the best results for `Stats` and almost the worst for the other states, AP2 has the best results for `OverallUsage`, poor results for `StackedBars` and `PeriodSelector`, and worst for `Stats`, while AP3 has the best results for `StackedBars` and `PeriodSelector`, however `OverallUsage` scores better, and `Stats` has also good results. Therefore for the first month, we conclude that AP1 identifies activity around `Stats` only, AP2 is a Glancing pattern (based around the screen view `OverallUsage`), and AP3 is an Overall Viewing pattern (based around high level exploration of the app). For the second month of usage we see different results. AP1 is more likely a Glancing pattern, AP2 an Overall Viewing pattern, and AP3 an In-depth Viewing pattern (based around in-depth visualisations of usage statistics for specific periods of interest). For the third month, AP1 is an In-depth Viewing pattern, AP2 is an Overall Viewing pattern, and AP3 is a Glancing pattern.

We draw two main conclusions: (1) during the first month there is an exceptional activity around `Stats` screen view compared to the later months (we will see additional information revealed by the analysis of PG5); (2) during the second month and the third month of usage we can identify a distinctive Glancing pattern characterised by frequent visits to `OverallUsage` and, surprisingly, to `StackedBars`, though that is almost 5 times less frequent. These interpretations, based of the results listed in Table 3, gives only a glimpse of the characteristics of the patterns. More information is obtained by analysing the other properties and correlating the results.

Table 3. GPAM results for properties VP2 (probability to reach screen view in a particular activity pattern within 50 time steps) and VC2 (expected number of visits to a screen view only in a particular activity pattern within 50 time steps) for $K = 3$ and j taking state identifiers values associated to the labels `OverallUsage`, `StackedBars`, `PeriodSelector`, and `Stats`. Colour-coded interpretation for a property, screen view, and time cut across all 3 patterns: red results are the best, followed by the blue ones, and black is for the worst result. The meaning of each AP needs to be determined by the evaluator for each time cut as they may be different.

Time cut	Prop.	OverallUsage			StackedBars			PeriodSelector			Stats		
		AP1	AP2	AP3	AP1	AP2	AP3	AP1	AP2	AP3	AP1	AP2	AP3
1st month	VP2	0.24	0.99	0.85	0.19	0.30	0.75	0.28	0.24	0.54	0.75	0.01	0.68
	VC2	0.52	6.23	1.98	0.21	0.36	1.44	0.37	0.49	0.79	1.66	0.01	1.17
2nd month	VP2	0.73	0.98	0.23	0.00	0.76	0.66	0.04	0.14	0.64	0.21	0.23	0.79
	VC2	2.47	5.52	0.26	0.00	1.55	1.19	0.05	0.15	1.79	0.25	0.33	1.99
3rd month	VP2	0.39	0.40	0.97	0.60	0.21	0.69	0.46	0.48	0.29	0.67	0.20	0.33
	VC2	0.55	1.38	5.63	1.06	0.31	1.26	0.72	1.07	0.67	1.36	0.55	0.48

Analysis specific to GPAM. We analysed 18 GPAM models ($K \in \{2, 3, 4\}$; 6 time cuts) using the properties of Table 2 and PG1–PG7 instantiated for various combinations of states and activity pattern identifiers. The results confirmed that AppTracker has three major activity patterns: Overall Viewing, In-depth Viewing, Glancing, moreover the patterns do not correlate with the top-level menu structure (we observe this when we consider larger values for K). In addition, the GPAM-specific properties PG1–PG4 bring new information compared to the PAM analysis such as: (a) finer insight into each pattern characteristics in relation to the other patterns and (b) a stronger case for a distinct activity pattern, Glancing, for short interactions around the `OverallUsage` screen view, especially for time intervals excluding the first few days of usage.

Due to space constraints, we give details for only one property, PG5, which concerns user disengagement. This property computes the probability that *always from a screen view j in a pattern i, eventually, without changing the pattern, the session ends*. Analysing this property allows us to identify most likely screen views and patterns that diminish user engagement (i.e. lead to end of the session). Table 4 lists the results for PG5, two cases, $K = 2$ and $K = 3$. For the first month of usage (and this also holds for all time intervals starting from first day of usage), the views Stats, UBCOverall and UBCApps are the most likely to disengage users in Glancing and Overall Viewing patterns where the probabilities p to do so are the highest over all states (see in bold), while in the In-depth Viewing pattern PG5 either does not hold, or it holds for close to zero values of p. While for the views UBCOverall and UBCApps this effect was expected because of their lowest level in the hierarchical menu, we were intrigued by the results for Stats. We discussed these results with the designers of AppTracker and found out that Stats does not show much information up until the first 30 days of usage; therefore they subsequently suggested changing the monthly Stats view to show something engaging (e.g. default illustrations of monthly stats and/or quick tutorial) up until the first 30 days of usage so that users do not get put off and end the session. During the second month of usage, for $K = 2$ the probabilities p are similar for both patterns. For $K = 3$, during the first month of usage Stats is most likely across all screen views to disengage users, whereas during the second month we see other screen views such as OverallUsage and StackedBars as likely as Stats to disengage users.

Table 4. GPAM results for property PG5, for $K = 2$ and $K = 3$, and first and second months of usage. The two values in each cell are the probability bound p for the first month and the second month of usage respectively such that PG5 holds; if no value for p is given, the property does not hold for any value of p.

State label	$K = 2$		$K = 3$		
	Overall	In-depth	Overall	In-depth	Glancing
OverallUsage	0.39/0.63	−/0.69	0.55/0.17	−/0.08	0.33/0.87
StackedBars	0.46/0.63	−/0.76	0.55/0.66	−/0.01	0.37/−
PeriodSelector	0.26/0.43	−/0.62	0.37/0.05	−/0.09	0.14/0.51
AppsInPeriod	0.15/0.14	0.07/0.56	0.28/0.03	0.06/0.01	0.12/0.32
Stats	**0.71**/0.59	−/0.68	**0.68**/0.22	0.01/0.13	**0.62**/0.86
UBCOverall	**0.81**/0.56	−/−	0.38/−	0.02/0.02	0.08/0.77
UBCApps	**0.84**/0.14	0.01/−	**0.61**/0.02	−/0.05	0.47/−

6   Discussion

Which models, which temporal properties. PAM and GPAM analyses with generic properties and models generated from different usage intervals provide insight into the main characteristics of the patterns. We suggest this is a good starting point for any study of usage patterns. This is followed by GPAM-specific analysis, which allows us to reason about changing patterns within a temporal property. This analysis may be focused around interesting characteristics revealed during the initial, generic analysis (e.g. the unusual activity around Stats view). A feature of PAM is the user trace distribution: this informs us about which user traces are "interesting" to investigate further. Here we gave only PAM and GPAM results, ideally we would also pick certain individual user traces (e.g. those engaged for a long/short time period), define sub-populations (according to ranges of θ), and analyse the relevant models.

Temporal aspects. Our approach has two temporal aspects: data logging intervals and path formulae in the generated model, they should not be confused as they are at different scales.

Effect of parameter inference. Models depend on the data and inferred parameters, so property checking will give different results for different models (and different runs of the inference algorithm), but we expect to see similar ratios between sets of learnt parameters.

Longitudinal and other types of analysis. Our example indicates results may be sensitive to the chosen time interval for logged data. Common sense indicates this is to be expected, for example differences between the first day of use and use after several weeks. However, there may be software-specific temporal sensitivities: our example indicated an unanticipated sensitivity in the first month of use. We note there are other categorisations: device type, timezone, length of user trace in number of sessions, frequency of sessions, and average length of sessions, to name a few. The plethora of possible categorisations and parametrised properties can be overwhelming and even more so the consideration of how to present the analysis results (e.g. as tables, as plots). Systematic approaches to categorisation and interpretation of results are needed.

Related work. User behaviours are considered in [10] where models are based on static user attributes rather than on inferred behaviours, assuming within-class use to be homogeneous, whereas we demonstrate within-class variation. Zang et al. [16] extended probabilistic model checking to HMMs, this is not applicable as we are interested in properties involving both latent and observed states; moreover, we do not analyse properties directly on AR-HMMs, but on their flattened version as DTMCs. The two hidden Markov models we use, PAM and GPAM, are examples of dynamic Bayesian networks (DBNs) [5,17]. DBNs can be analysed using Bayesian statistical model checking [18], however our models are easily encoded and analysed using probabilistic model checking. Extensive works on inferring parameters for first-order HMM models (as DBNs) from user traces for runtime verification purposes can be found in [14,19], however we are looking at a different class of HMM, namely admixture models, for identifying and analysing usage models within a population of user traces.

7 Conclusions and Future Work

We have defined new models of software usage based on two new admixture, latent variable Markov models: PAM and GPAM. Both models are admixtures of activity patterns (DTMCs) and are generated from logged data sets of interactions of actual deployments, over different time intervals. Temporal logic property analysis is by model checking. We defined two sets of (parametrised) temporal logic properties: generic ones for analysis of individual activity patterns and GPAM-specific for properties that combine patterns. The generic properties provide insight into the main characteristics of the patterns, and we suggest this is a good starting point for any study of usage patterns. This is followed by GPAM-specific analysis, which may be focused around interesting or unusual results from the generic analysis. Application to logged data from a real-life interactive software system indicates that out approach is tractable and useful; future work includes guidance on how and when to investigate each of the models, and a systematic approach to interpretation of results.

Acknowledgement. This research is supported by EPSRC Programme Grant *A Population Approach to Ubicomp System Design* (EP/J007617/1).

References

1. Kwiatkowska, M.Z., Norman, G., Parker, D.: PRISM 4.0: verification of probabilistic real-time systems. In: Gopalakrishnan, G., Qadeer, S. (eds.) CAV 2011. LNCS, vol. 6806, pp. 585–591. Springer, Heidelberg (2011). https://doi.org/10.1007/978-3-642-22110-1_47
2. Andrei, O., Calder, M., Chalmers, M., Morrison, A., Rost, M.: Probabilistic formal analysis of app usage to inform redesign. In: Ábrahám, E., Huisman, M. (eds.) IFM 2016. LNCS, vol. 9681, pp. 115–129. Springer, Cham (2016). https://doi.org/10.1007/978-3-319-33693-0_8
3. Andrei, O., Calder, M., Higgs, M., Girolami, M.: Probabilistic model checking of DTMC models of user activity patterns. In: Norman, G., Sanders, W. (eds.) QEST 2014. LNCS, vol. 8657, pp. 138–153. Springer, Cham (2014). https://doi.org/10.1007/978-3-319-10696-0_11
4. Baier, C., Katoen, J.P.: Principles of Model Checking. The MIT Press, Cambridge (2008)
5. Murphy, K.P.: Machine Learning: A Probabilistic Perspective. The MIT Press, Cambridge (2012)
6. Borges, J., Levene, M.: Data mining of user navigation patterns. In: Masand, B., Spiliopoulou, M. (eds.) WebKDD 1999. LNCS (LNAI), vol. 1836, pp. 92–112. Springer, Heidelberg (2000). https://doi.org/10.1007/3-540-44934-5_6
7. Chierichetti, F., Kumar, R., Raghavan, P., Sarlós, T.: Are web users really Markovian? In: Mille, A., Gandon, F.L., Misselis, J., Rabinovich, M., Staab, S. (eds.) Proceedings of the 21st World Wide Web Conference 2012 (WWW 2012), pp. 609–618. ACM (2012)
8. Singer, P., Helic, D., Taraghi, B., Strohmaier, M.: Detecting memory and structure in human navigation patterns using Markov chain models of varying order. PLoS One **9**(7), 1–21 (2014)

9. Singer, P., Helic, D., Hotho, A., Strohmaier, M.: HypTrails: a Bayesian approach for comparing hypotheses about human trails on the web. In: Gangemi, A., Leonardi, S., Panconesi, A. (eds.) Proceedings of the 24th International Conference on World Wide Web (WWW 2015), pp. 1003–1013. ACM (2015)

10. Ghezzi, C., Pezzè, M., Sama, M., Tamburrelli, G.: Mining behavior models from user-intensive web applications. In: Proceedings of the 36th International Conference on Software Engineering (ICSE 2014), pp. 277–287. ACM (2014)

11. Kostakos, V., Ferreira, D., Gonçalves, J., Hosio, S.: Modelling smartphone usage: a Markov state transition model. In: Lukowicz, P., Krüger, A., Bulling, A., Lim, Y., Patel, S.N. (eds.) Proceedings of the 2016 ACM International Joint Conference on Pervasive and Ubiquitous Computing (UbiComp 2016), pp. 486–497 (2016)

12. Dempster, A.P., Laird, N.M., Rubin, D.B.: Maximum likelihood from incomplete data via the EM algorithm. J. Roy. Stat. Soc.: Ser. B (Methodol.) **39**(1), 1–38 (1977)

13. Welch, L.: Hidden Markov models and the Baum-Welch algorithm. IEEE Inf. Theory Soc. Newslett. **53**(4), 10–13 (2003)

14. Bartocci, E., Grosu, R., Karmarkar, A., Smolka, S.A., Stoller, S.D., Zadok, E., Seyster, J.: Adaptive runtime verification. In: Qadeer, S., Tasiran, S. (eds.) RV 2012. LNCS, vol. 7687, pp. 168–182. Springer, Heidelberg (2013). https://doi.org/10.1007/978-3-642-35632-2_18

15. Bell, M., Chalmers, M., Fontaine, L., Higgs, M., Morrison, A., Rooksby, J., Rost, M., Sherwood, S.: Experiences in logging everyday app use. In: ACM Proceedings of Digital Economy 2013 (2013)

16. Zhang, L., Hermanns, H., Jansen, D.N.: Logic and model checking for hidden Markov models. In: Wang, F. (ed.) FORTE 2005. LNCS, vol. 3731, pp. 98–112. Springer, Heidelberg (2005). https://doi.org/10.1007/11562436_9

17. Sucar, L.E.: Probabilistic Graphical Models: Principles and Applications. ACVPR. Springer, London (2015). https://doi.org/10.1007/978-1-4471-6699-3

18. Langmead, C.J.: Generalized queries and Bayesian statistical model checking in dynamic Bayesian networks: application to personalized medicine. In: Proceedings of CSB 2009 (2009)

19. Stoller, S.D., Bartocci, E., Seyster, J., Grosu, R., Havelund, K., Smolka, S.A., Zadok, E.: Runtime verification with state estimation. In: Khurshid, S., Sen, K. (eds.) RV 2011. LNCS, vol. 7186, pp. 193–207. Springer, Heidelberg (2012). https://doi.org/10.1007/978-3-642-29860-8_15

Sequential Pattern Mining for ICT Risk Assessment and Prevention

Michele D'Andreagiovanni, Fabrizio Baiardi, Jacopo Lipilini,
Salvatore Ruggieri[✉], and Federico Tonelli

Dipartimento di Informatica, Università di Pisa,
Largo B. Pontecorvo 3, 56127 Pisa, Italy
ruggieri@di.unipi.it

Abstract. Security risk assessment and prevention in ICT systems rely on the analysis of data on the joint behavior of the system and its (malicious) users. The Haruspex tool models intelligent, goal-oriented agents that reach their goals through attack sequences. Data is synthetically generated through a Monte Carlo method that runs multiple simulations of the attacks against the system. In this paper, we present a sequential pattern mining analysis of the database of attack sequences. The intended objective is twofold: (1) to exploit the extracted patterns for the design of attack counter-measures, and (2) for gaining a better understanding of the "degree of freedom" available for the attackers of a system. We formally motivate the need for using maximal sequential patterns, instead of frequent or closed sequential patterns, and report on the results on a specific case study.

Keywords: Security risk assessment · Attack sequences
Sequential pattern mining · Maximum coverage problem

1 Introduction

Approaches for security risk assessment and prevention in ICT systems rely on the analysis of data on the joint behavior of the system and its (malicious) users. Such data is typically collected over time after the deployment of a system. This results in two main drawbacks. First, the approach cannot assess and manage risk at design time, but only with *a-posteriori* sub-optimal remedies. This prevents a principled *by-design* approach in risk analysis and management [8]. Second, the data available for the analysis is both scarce and biased because one has to wait for *real* attacks to take place and extreme events such as low frequency - high impact attacks are not included.

The Haruspex tool [2] aims at predicting the behavior of a system under attacks even before its deployment. It models intelligent, goal-oriented agents that reach their goals through attack sequences. Data is synthetically generated through a Monte Carlo method that runs multiple simulations of the attacks against the system. Simulations rely on formal models of the target system and

© Springer International Publishing AG 2018
A. Cerone and M. Roveri (Eds.): SEFM 2017 Workshops, LNCS 10729, pp. 25–39, 2018.
https://doi.org/10.1007/978-3-319-74781-1_2

of the threat agents and they return a large sample of attack sequences. The analysis of such data can reveal paths of successful attacks in an ICT network, and suggest possible patches that block them at design-time.

This paper intends to improve simple statistical summaries of attack sequences. We exploit knowledge discovery approaches to extract informative patterns from the data in the form of sequential patterns. The intended objective is twofold: (1) to exploit the extracted patterns for the design of attack counter-measures, and (2) for gaining a better understanding of the "degree of freedom" available for the attackers of a system. Objective (1) can be achieved by using data mining models for making predictions on the next attack of a threat agent that is following a matched pattern [4,9,11], hence enforcing dynamic counter-measures. We instead take a different approach that selects from the set of extracted patterns a set that covers as much as possible the successful attack sequences of the threat agent. Such a set represents a global description of the strategies of the agent. By reasoning on such characterization, we claim that an analyst can derive useful information for the design of static counter-measures, which are especially useful at system design time. Such a description, possibly at alternative abstraction levels, is also useful to understand the "degree of freedom" of an attacker that targets the ICT system, namely objective (2).

The paper is organized as follows. Section 2 introduces the Haruspex tool. Section 3 describes a case study including a sample ICT system and modeling of threat agents. Classes of sequential patterns and measures of interest for the field of ICT risk assessment are then introduced in Sect. 4. Next, in Sect. 5, we introduce a notion of covering for sets of sequential patterns and formally prove that maximal sequential patterns is the most appropriate class for computing covers. Section 6 discusses the covers found for attack sequences of our case study. Finally, we discuss related work and summarize the contribution of the paper.

2   ICT Risk Assessment: The Haruspex Approach

This section describes the tools of the Haruspex suite [1] that simulate the attacker behaviors to produce synthetic attack sequences. In the following, we denote by *user* the team that interacts with such tools to assess and manage the security risks of an ICT system. Such a *target system* can be already existing or only in its design phase. The suite builds the models of the target system and of the threat agents, or *attackers*, to simulate the agent attacks in the scenario of interest. The accuracy of the simulation depends on the accuracy of the tools that build the model of the system and those of the agents. Table 1 defines the abbreviations we use in the following.

The *builder* and the *descriptor* are the Haruspex tools that model, respectively, the system infrastructure and the agents. Then, the *engine* uses these models to apply the Monte Carlo method and to run a number of simulations of the agent attacks.

Table 1. List of abbreviations.

S	The target system
n	A node of S
ag	A threat agent (attacker)
at	An elementary attack
v	A vulnerability
$v(at)$	The vulnerabilities enabling at
$pre(at)$	The rights to execute at
$res(at)$	The resources to execute at
$post(at)$	The rights granted if at succeeds
$succ(at)$	The success probability of at
$time(at)$	The execution time of at
$\lambda(ag)$	The look-ahead of ag

2.1 Modeling an Infrastructure

The *builder* is the first tool the user applies to build a model of the target
system S that decomposes S into a network of nodes and the resulting nodes
into components, i.e. hardware/software modules. Each component is affected
by zero or more *vulnerabilities* that enable some *attacks* [13,15,16]. Haruspex
covers social engineering attacks by modeling users of S as further components
with the proper vulnerabilities. If any vulnerability in $v(at)$ is effective, at is
enabled and succeeds with a probability $succ(at)$, otherwise it fails. For each
vulnerability v that affects a node n, the *builder* computes $pre(at)$ and $post(at)$
for each attack v enables. These properties drive the sequence that an agent will
compose. The *builder* computes $pre(at)$ and $post(at)$ by matching predefined
patterns against the description of v in some *de facto* standard databases, e.g.
the Common Vulnerability Enumeration [1,15]. The *builder* considers any attack
sequence of ag, even those that involve distinct nodes of S. To let the *builder*
model sequences that involve distinct nodes, the user has to describe to the
builder the logical topology of nodes in S and the components of S that controls
it, e.g. firewalls.

2.2 Modeling Agents

The *descriptor* builds an agent model starting from four properties the user
defines for each agent:

1. the initial rights;
2. the goal(s);
3. the selection strategy;
4. the value of $\lambda(ag)$ of the look-ahead.

A goal is the set of rights that ag get after reaching the target node n_f, and it results in an *impact*, i.e. a loss for the owner of S [3]. An agent ag can attempt an elementary attack at. The attack is successful if the agent owns the rights defined in $pre(at)$, either as initial rights or as rights granted after previous successful attacks. ag sequentially executes elementary attacks. The attack sequence is *successful* if it reaches n_f.

Each ag is paired with a selection strategy that ranks the next attack sequences ag may execute according to its goals, its current set of rights and its preferences. $\lambda(ag)$ defines the look-ahead of ag, i.e., the largest number of attacks in the sequences ag ranks to select the one to execute. The strategy always selects one of the sequences leading to a goal, if it exists. Otherwise, the strategy ranks sequences according to attack attributes only. In this case, ag may select a sequence with useless attacks, i.e. their granted rights are useless to reach a goal. In the current version of the suite, the user can pair ag with one of the following strategies:

1. *maxProb:* returns the sequence with the best success probability,
2. *maxIncr:* returns the sequence granting the largest set of rights,
3. *maxEff:* returns the sequence with the best ratio between success probability and execution time of attacks,
4. *maxAtt:* returns the sequence granting the rights that enable the execution of the largest number of attacks,
5. *SmartSubnetFirst:* returns any attack that ag may execute and that increases these rights. It prefers attacks that enable ag to enter another subnetwork.

If $\lambda(ag) = 0$, then ag can only adopt the *SmartSubnetFirst* strategy, This strategy prefers the attacks that enable ag to enter a distinct subnetwork and it is *Smart* because it prefers the attacks that ag can execute.

Haruspex models both the time to implement the attack and the one to collect information to select the attack. Larger values of $\lambda(ag)$ result in a more accurate selection that may avoid useless attacks, on the other hand, the time ag spends to acquire information on the target system increases with $\lambda(ag)$.

2.3   Simulation Engine

The *engine* uses the infrastructure model and those of the agents to apply the Monte Carlo method. It executes an experiment with several independent runs that simulate, for a maximum time period, the attacks of a set of agents and the discovery of potential vulnerabilities. To guarantee run independence, the *engine* re-initializes the state of S and of any agent before starting a new run. An experiment ends either after executing the specified number of runs or when a predefined statistic reaches the required confidence level. Each experiment returns a database of attack sequences collected in the runs.

In each time step, the *engine* considers any idle agent that still has to reach a goal. For each agent ag, the *engine* considers the current set of rights of ag and computes the sequences with, at most, $\lambda(ag)$ attacks that ag can select.

Then the *engine* applies the selection strategy of *ag* and it simulates *at*, the first attack of the sequence the strategy returns. If *at* succeeds and *ag* has reached a goal, the *engine* updates the corresponding impact.

3   Case Study

In this section, we describe a case study that will be the subject of sequential pattern mining analysis later on. Figure 1 shows the topology of the target system network. It consists of 36 nodes (hosts) plus routers and switches (they are not part of the model). The node $n_e = 0$ is the entry node, i.e., all attack sequences start from it, and the node 34 is the goal node, i.e., $n_f = 34$. An attack sequence is then considered successful if it reaches n_f.

The system vulnerabilities result in 2,859 elementary attacks, belonging to 192 attack types. An elementary attack *at* is specific of a vulnerability at a node, i.e. the same attack that targets different nodes give raises to distinct elementary attacks. Attack types group elementary attacks according to the CVE [1,15] vulnerability they exploit.

Example 1. An example of elementary attack is one that grants administrative privileges on the software HP Data Protector at node 1. The attack has type:

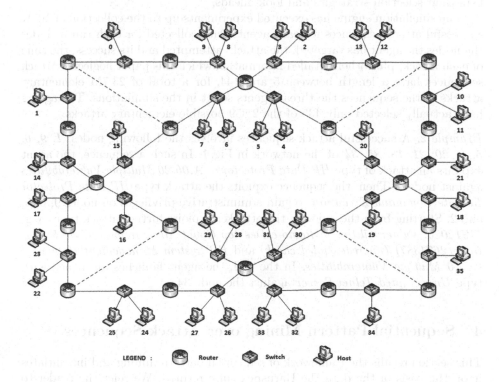

Fig. 1. Topology of the case study system.

Table 2. Threat agents in the case study.

ag	Strategy	$\lambda(ag)$
A0	*SmartSubnetFirst*	0
A1	*maxIncr*	1
A2	*maxIncr*	2
A3	*maxProb*	1
A4	*maxProb*	2
A5	*maxAtt*	2

HP Data Protector Remote Command Execution. An attack of the same type but at another node is a different elementary attack.

As another example, if an attacker wants to remotely execute arbitrary code may exploit an attack of type *MS12020: Vulnerabilities in Remote Desktop Could Allow Remote Code Execution (2671387) (uncredentialed check).*

As a third example, the *Unencrypted Telnet Server* type models an attack to steal sensitive information through Telnet protocol.

The risk assessment in the case study considers 6 threat agents A0-A5. Table 2 lists their selection strategies and look-aheads.

The simulation engine has executed experiments up to the collection of 100K successful attack sequences for each agent. Data collected for each run includes the nodes the agent has targeted, the attacks attempted and its success, the time of each attack, plus other detailed information which this paper neglects. Attack sequences have a length between 5 and 144, for a total of 23.7M elementary attacks in the sequences the threat agents select in the simulations. The agents have actually selected only 435 of the 2,859 possible elementary attacks.

Example 2. A successful attack sequences involves the following nodes: *1, 9, 6, 5, 2, 20, 21, 18, 35, 34* of the network in Fig. 1. In such a sequence, the agent exploits an attack of type *HP Data Protector < A.06.20 Multiple Vulnerabilities* against node 1. Then, the sequence exploits the attack type *HP Data Protector Remote Command Execution* to gain administrative privileges on nodes 9, 6, 5, and 2. Starting from these nodes, the attacker exploits further attack types, e.g. *MS12020: Vulnerabilities in Remote Desktop Could Allow Remote Code Execution (2671387) (uncredentialed check)* and *HP System Management Homepage < 7.0 Multiple Vulnerabilities.* In the end, the agent launches an attack with type *Unencrypted Telnet Server* against the node 34.

4   Sequential Pattern Mining over Attack Sequences

This section recalls the framework of sequential pattern mining and instantiates it on the basis of the data the Haruspex suite returns. We refer the reader to

[6,12,14] for surveys on sequential pattern mining theory and applications. A large suite of algorithms for extracting classes of sequential patterns is implemented in Java [5].

4.1 Sequence Databases

Let $I = \{i_1, \ldots, i_m\}$ be a fixed set of *items*, where $m > 0$. Items can be symbols or, simply, natural numbers. An *itemset* A is a set of items, i.e., $A \subseteq I$. A *sequence* $S = \langle A_1, \ldots, A_l \rangle$ is an ordered list of non-empty itemsets. We write $l(S) = l$ to denote the length $l \geq 0$ of S. A sequence $S_1 = \langle A_1, \ldots, A_l \rangle$ is a *sub-sequence* of $S_2 = \langle B_1, \ldots, B_k \rangle$ if there exists $1 \leq \pi_1 < \ldots < \pi_l \leq k$ such that $A_1 \subseteq B_{\pi_1}, \ldots, A_l \subseteq B_{\pi_l}$. In such a case, we write $S_1 \sqsubseteq S_2$. Also, we say that S_2 *contains* S_1. We write $S_1 \sqsubset S_2$ when $S_1 \sqsubseteq S_2$ and $S_1 \neq S_2$, and say that S_2 *strictly contains* S_2. A *sequence database* $\mathcal{D} = \{S_1, S_2, \ldots, S_n\}$ is a multiset of sequences. $|\mathcal{D}|$ is the size of $\mathcal{D}$.

With reference to the case study, attack sequences can be modeled by considering items at different granularities. We will consider two scenarios (several others are possible).

Definition 1. *In scenario S1, items are elementary attacks at. Since each agent executes one attack at a time, itemsets $A \subseteq I$ are singletons of elementary attacks, i.e., $|A| = 1$. Moreover, in this scenario, we include in a sequence $S = \langle at_1, \ldots, at_l \rangle$ only successful elementary attacks at_i's.*

Example 3. Reconsider Example 2. The attack sequence in scenario S1 would be modeled as $\langle at_1, at_9, at_6, at_5, at_2, at_{20}, at_{21}, at_{18}, at_{35}, at_{34} \rangle$, where at_j is some elementary attack attempted at node n_j. E.g., at_9 is the HP Data Protector Remote Command Execution at node n_9.

Definition 2. *In scenario S2, items are eithers nodes n or attack types t. Again, since agents execute the attacks sequentially, itemsets either consists of node and type ($\{n, t\}$), or of node only ($\{n\}$), or of type only ($\{t\}$). Also in this scenario, we include in a sequence $S = \langle \{n_1, t_1\}, \ldots, \{n_l, t_l\} \rangle$ only information from successful attacks.*

Example 4. Reconsider Example 2 again. The attack sequence in scenario S2 would be modeled as $\langle \{n_1, t_1\}, \{n_1, t_9\}, \{n_1, t_6\}, \{n_1, t_5\}, \{n_1, t_2\}, \{n_1, t_{20}\}, \{n_1, t_{21}\}, \{n_1, t_{18}\}, \{n_1, t_{35}\}, \{n_1, t_{34}\} \rangle$, where t_j is the attack type attempted at node n_j. E.g., t_9 is the *HP Data Protector Remote Command Execution* attack type.

4.2 Sequential Patterns and Measures of Interest

Sequences can be adopted as abstractions (patterns) of subsets of $\mathcal{D}$. We denote such abstractions as sequential patterns to differentiate them from sequences in $\mathcal{D}$. Formally, a *sequential pattern* SP is a sequence. The *cover* of a sequential pattern SP is the set of sequences in $\mathcal{D}$ that contain SP. In symbols, $cover_{\mathcal{D}}(SP) = \{S \in \mathcal{D} \mid SP \sqsubseteq S\}$. The goal of *sequential pattern mining* is to extract from a sequence database a set of interesting sequential patterns. An objective measure of interest is support. The *absolute support* (or, simply, support) of SP is the size of its cover: $supp_{\mathcal{D}}(SP) = |cover_{\mathcal{D}}(SP)|$. The *relative support* of SP is the fraction of its cover over $\mathcal{D}$: $relsupp_{\mathcal{D}}(SP) = |cover_{\mathcal{D}}(SP)|/|\mathcal{D}|$. We omit the subscripts $\mathcal{D}$ when clear from the context.

Example 5. An example sequential pattern in scenario S1 is the following: $SP = \langle at_9, at_2, at_{21} \rangle$. It covers all sequences that perform at some point attack at_9 (which is, say, at node n_9), and after zero or more steps attack at_2 (at node n_2), and after zero or more steps attack at_{21} (at node n_{21}). The sample sequence of Example 3 is in the cover of SP.

Besides support, other measures of interest can be devised to rank sequential patterns. The following may be specifically defined to the problem of risk assessment:

- *Length $l(SP)$*, the longer a pattern is the more information it provides on a (successful) strategy of a threat agent.
- *Score $score(SP) = supp(SP) \cdot 2^{l(SP)-1}$*, defined as a combination of support and length, where length is exponentially weighed.
- *Success distance $success(SP)$*. For a sequence S, the success distance is defined as the number of itemsets in S between the last one matching SP and the last in S. The success distance $success(SP)$ is the mean success distance over the sequences in the cover of SP. Intuitively, the smaller the success distance, the higher is the risk that an ongoing sequence matching the pattern will become successful (the agent reach its goal).
- *Right distance $right(SP)$*. For a sequence S, the right distance is defined as the number of new rights in S acquired between the last itemset matching SP and the last itemset in S. The right distance $right(SP)$ is the mean right distance over the sequences in the cover of SP. This is a refinement of success distance that considers the number of missing rights before the success instead of the number of steps before the agent is successful.

Example 6. The sequence of Example 3 contributes to the success distance of SP in Example 5 with a value of 3, because it attempts 3 more attacks after the last match with SP, namely after at_{21}.

4.3 Frequent, Closed, and Maximal Sequential Patterns

While a measure of interest can prompt useful patterns from an initial collection, the number of all possible sequential patterns is exponentially large (in the number of items and pattern length). It is then important to concentrate on specific collections of sequential patterns. The frequent pattern mining literature has proposed several collections and efficient algorithms to extract them from sequence databases.

Consider a fixed minimum support threshold $minsup > 0$. A sequential pattern SP is *frequent* if $supp(SP) \geq minsup$. We denote by $\mathcal{FP}$ the set of frequent sequential patterns. Since two frequent sequential patterns may actually denote the same set of sequences, i.e., they have a same cover, restricting to patterns with distinct covers is a lossless strategy to reduce the number of extracted patterns and to avoid duplicate analyses. SP is *closed* if it is frequent and not strictly contained in a sequential pattern SP' with the same support, i.e., $supp(SP) \geq minsup \wedge \nexists SP'. (SP \sqsubset SP' \wedge supp(SP') = supp(SP))$. We denote by $\mathcal{CP}$ the set of closed sequential patterns. Closed sequential patterns are the longest sequential patterns in the class of equivalence of patterns with a same cover. A further condensed representation consists of restricting to the longest frequent sequential patterns only. SP is *maximal* if it is frequent and not strictly contained in another frequent sequential pattern SP' i.e., $supp(SP) \geq minsup \wedge \nexists SP'. (SP \sqsubset SP' \wedge supp(SP') \geq minsup)$. We denote by $\mathcal{MP}$ the set of closed sequential patterns. Maximal sequential patterns are closed, but the converse does not necessarily holds. In summary, $\mathcal{FP} \supseteq \mathcal{CP} \supseteq \mathcal{MP}$. For non-trivial sequence databases, the inclusion is strict.

Next lemma is referred to as the *anti-monotonicity* property of *cover* (or, equivalently, of *supp*). It is a trivial consequence of transitivity of relation $\sqsubseteq$.

Lemma 1. *If* $SP_1 \sqsubseteq SP_2$ *then* $cover(SP_1) \supseteq cover(SP_2)$.

5   The Covering Problem

5.1   Motivation

Sequential patterns provide a useful abstraction for understanding the strategies an agent adopts to reach its goal. Ranking patterns using one of the measures of interest from Sect. 4.2 prompts sub-sequences that occur with high frequency among the successful ones (using support as measure) that are characterized in higher detail (using length), or that are close to success (using success/right distance). In particular, the last ranking appears extremely useful in the design of *dynamic counter-measures*, such as blocking an agent that is following a pattern of successful attack before it reaches the goal. In this paper, however, we concentrate on a different approach, which tries and overcome the main limitation of (sequential) patterns, namely the *local view* each of them provides. A *global understanding* of the behavior of agents is missing. It is not obvious how to grasp a set of strategies that characterize the behavior of a threat agent[1]. Such a set provides a better understanding of how exposed is the target system to the attack strategies of the agent. Furthermore, it also supports what-if analyses and the selection of *static counter-measures*, such as network redesign and software patches. For instance, the integration of the Haruspex suite and sequential pattern mining in iteration generate sequence databases, characterize agent strategies, design counter-measures, and then repeat the process on the revised system.

---

[1] A further problem is to extract a set of strategies that, in addition, are also specific to a threat agent because they are not (often) used by the other agents. In this sense, they define a *signature* of the threat agent.

5.2   The Covering Problem

Let us extend the *cover* notation to sets of sequential patterns.

Definition 3. *For a set C, we define: $cover_D(C) = \cup_{SP \in C} cover_D(SP)$.*

We say that C *covers* the sequence database D if every sequence in D is covered by some pattern in C. The problem of finding a set C such that $cover_D(C) = D$ is an instance of the well-known set cover problem [7]. Typically, however, one aims at finding a set C of a maximum size k (called *budget*). In our case study, for instance, domain experts may have to examine the set C. Hence, it needs to be sufficiently small for human inspection. A cover of size k may not exist, hence one aims at finding a set C of size at most k which maximizes $|cover_D(C)|$ – the number of covered sequences from D. This is an instance of the maximum coverage problem [7]. As a final generalization, we assume that sequential patterns in C are constrained to belong to a pre-determined set P, e.g., frequent, closed or maximal sequential patterns.

Definition 4. *Let P be a set of sequential patterns, and $k \geq 1$. We define the k-cover of P: $\mathbf{Cov}(k, P) = argmax_{C \subseteq P \wedge |C| \leq k} |cover(C)|$.*

More than one subset $C \subseteq P$ can maximize the objective function. Thus, we write $C \in \mathbf{Cov}(k, P)$ to denote any such subset.

Computing the k-cover is an NP-hard problem in general. A greedy algorithm chooses sequential patterns from P according to one rule: at each stage, choose the one whose cover contains the largest number of sequences uncovered by the already chosen elements. Such a greedy algorithm achieves an approximation ratio of ≈ 0.632 w.r.t. the optimal cover [7].

We will now formally show that frequent FP and closed CP sequential patterns are not suitable choices for P in the computation of a cover, while maximal MP sequential patterns are. First, we introduce a notation for the minimal elements of a set of patterns w.r.t. the $\sqsubseteq$ relation.

Definition 5. $Min(P) = \{SP \in P \mid \nexists SP' \in P. \ SP' \sqsubset SP\}$.

The next key result shows that when looking for the k-cover of P, one can restrict to select only minimal elements from P.

Theorem 1. *Let $C \in \mathbf{Cov}(k, P)$. There exists $C' \in \mathbf{Cov}(k, Min(P))$ such that $cover(C) = cover(C')$ and $|C| \geq |C'|$.*

Proof. We define the set C' as follows. For every $SP \in C$ choose any $SP' \in Min(P)$ such that $SP' \sqsubseteq SP$. For a given SP, at least one such a SP' exists – it could be SP itself, if it is minimal in P. Any of such SP''s can be chosen. By construction $|C'| \leq |C| \leq k$ (in fact, a same minimal element can be chosen for two SP's in C). By Lemma 1, $cover(SP) \subseteq cover(SP')$. As a consequence:

$$cover(C) = \cup_{SP \in C} cover(SP) \subseteq \cup_{SP' \in C'} cover(SP') = cover(C').$$

Since C is a k-cover and $P \supseteq Min(P)$, then $|cover(C)|$ is maximal, which implies that the inclusion above is an equality. Finally, observe that a k-cover from

$\mathbf{Cov}(k, Min(\mathcal{P}))$ cannot cover more sequences than a k-cover of $\mathcal{P}$, by definition of maximization. Since $\mathcal{C}' \subseteq Min(\mathcal{P})$ and $|\mathcal{C}'| \leq k$ and $|cover(\mathcal{C}')|$ is maximal, we conclude $\mathcal{C}' \in \mathbf{Cov}(k, Min(\mathcal{P}))$. □

The consequence of this result is considerable. It makes no sense to try and cover a database of sequences using frequent patterns or closed patterns.

Example 7. It is readily checked that the minimal element of frequent sequential patterns $\mathcal{FP}$ is the empty sequence, namely $Min(\mathcal{FP}) = \{\langle\rangle\}$. Trivially, $\{\langle\rangle\}$ is a cover of any sequence database. By Theorem 1, $\{\langle\rangle\} \in \mathbf{Cov}(k, \mathcal{FP})$. Unfortunately, the empty sequential pattern is of no practical help in any application.

When not considering the empty sequential pattern, the result is not interesting, because sequential patterns are not needed at all when looking for a cover. As an example, a standard approach for entity selection can apply the greedy algorithm of the maximum coverage problem [7] to select items (and not sequential patterns) that have the largest residual frequency in the yet uncovered sequences.

Example 8. Consider non-empty frequent sequential patterns: $\mathcal{FP}' = \mathcal{FP} \setminus \{\langle\rangle\}$. We have that $Min(\mathcal{FP}') = \{FP \in \mathcal{FP} \mid \exists i \in I.\ FP = \langle\{i\}\rangle\}$. Then, to find a cover, we can consider only sequential patterns with one frequent item. In other words, there would be no need of extracting sequential patterns at all.

For closed sequential patterns $\mathcal{CP}$, one can reason as in the above example, and reach similar conclusions. To find a way out, one may consider $\mathbf{Cov}(k, \mathcal{P})$ for $\mathcal{P}$ being a set of frequent or closed sequential patterns with support in a range $[minsup, maxsup]$. However, which maximal threshold $maxsup$ to choose remains unclear. We propose, instead, to use maximal sequential patterns $\mathcal{MP}$, for two reasons. First, minimal elements of maximal patterns are themselves:

$$Min(\mathcal{MP}) = \mathcal{MP}.$$

The drawbacks highlighted for frequent sequential patterns are then overcome. Second, albeit a k-cover $\mathcal{C} \subseteq \mathcal{MP}$ is not a partition of $\mathcal{D}$, for any two patterns in $\mathcal{C}$ the number of sequences shared by them can be upper-bounded. This is a useful property when a business action has to be done for each sequential pattern in a cover, but sequences should not be subject to several business actions. In our case study, in particular, we aim at finding a cover consisting of sequential patterns which abstract alternative attack strategies.

Lemma 2. *Let* $SP_1, SP_2 \in \mathcal{MP}$ *with* $SP_1 \neq SP_2$. *We have:* $|cover(SP_1) \cap cover(SP_2)| < 3 \cdot minsup - 2$.

Proof. Let SP be the maximal initial sub-sequence shared by SP_1 and SP_2. Since $SP_1 \neq SP_2$, at least one between SP_1 and SP_2 is longer than SP. Since SP_1 and SP_2 are maximal, both SP_1 and SP_2 are longer than SP (otherwise, one of them would be contained in the other). Thus, let $SP_1 = SP \cdot \langle A \rangle \cdot \hat{SP}_1$ and $SP_1 = SP \cdot \langle B \rangle \cdot \hat{SP}_2$, where $\cdot$ is the sequence appending operator, and $A \neq B$.

Any $S \in cover(SP_1) \cap cover(SP_2)$ either satisfies: (1) $SP \cdot \langle A, B \rangle \cdot \hat{SP}_1 \sqsubseteq S$; or (2) $SP \cdot \langle B, A \rangle \cdot \hat{SP}_1 \sqsubseteq S$; or (3) $SP \cdot \langle A \cup B \rangle \cdot \hat{SP}_1 \sqsubseteq S$. Assume now, by absurd, that $|cover(SP_1) \cap cover(SP_2)| \geq 3 \cdot minsup - 2$. Then, the number of sequences that satisfy (1) (resp., (2) or (3)) are at least one third of $3 \cdot minsup - 2$, i.e., at least $minsup$. Therefore, SP_1 cannot be maximal. □

A better bound can be stated when the sequences are made of singleton itemsets, as in the case of scenario S1 (see Definition 1).

Lemma 3. *Assume a sequence database where itemsets are singletons. Let* SP_1, $SP_2 \in \mathcal{MP}$ *with* $SP_1 \neq SP_2$. *We have* $|cover(SP_1) \cap cover(SP_2)| < 2 \cdot minsup - 1$.

Proof. By assumption, the case (3) in the proof of Lemma 2 cannot occur. □

6   Covering Attack Sequences of the Case Study

Recall that the input dataset in our case study consists of 600 K successful attack sequences, 100K for each of the six threat agents (see Table 2). The empirical distribution of sequence lengths is reported in Fig. 2 (left). It is a mixture of two distributions. Sequences of threat agents A1 and A2 have length 12 or 13. Sequence lengths of the other agents, instead, are well approximated by Gaussian distribution with mean 32.3. Figure 2 (right) shows the empirical cumulative distribution of the rank of attacks. Let $rk(at)$ be the rank of attack at, with 1 being the rank of the most frequent attack, 2 of the second most frequent, etc. The cumulative distribution $CDF(rk(at))$ is the probability that an attack occurrence in the database belongs to one of the top $rk(at)$ most frequent attacks. It is well-fitted by a cumulative exponential distribution $1 - e^{-\lambda \cdot rk(at)}$ with $\lambda = 0.0213$. A naïve approach that tries and patches the top most frequent attacks, has to deploy 33 patches to cover half of the occurrences of attacks in the sequence database, and 108 to cover 90% of the occurrences. Such an approach is naïve because sequences include multiple attacks, hence after patching the vulnerability that enables an attack, all the sequences containing such an attack does not need further patches. Therefore, a covering approach should be considered, e.g., by applying a greedy algorithm that selects an attack on the basis of residual support (number of covered sequences among those not covered by previously selected attacks). Covering sequences using elementary attacks, however, does not result in an effective approach. In fact, the last attack of any sequence is a specific one on the target node n_f. Thus, such an attack alone will cover *all* sequences. But, since it occurs as the last attack: (1) first, it cannot enable dynamic counter-measures, because after the attack has been attempted the goal of the agent is already reached; (2) second, it gives no hint on the possible strategies of the attacker for reaching the final node.

The approach followed in this paper is instead more refined. We search for a covering using sequential patterns rather than elementary attacks. Consider the scenario S1. For each threat agent, we extract the maximal sequential patterns from the 100K attack sequence of the agent, assuming $minsup = 5K$, namely 5%

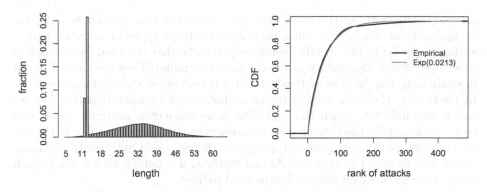

Fig. 2. Left: distribution of sequence lengths. Right: CDF of attack ranks.

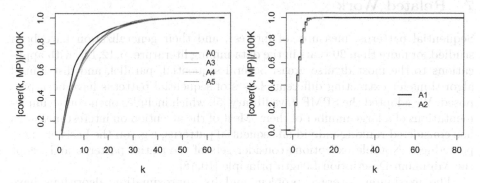

Fig. 3. Covering sequences. Left: Scenario S1. Right: Scenario S2.

relative minimum support threshold. Starting from the set of maximal sequential pattern, we compute a k-cover using the greedy algorithm. Figure 3 (left) shows the fraction of the 100K sequences that are covered by $cover(k, \mathcal{MP})$ at the variation of k for threat agents A0, A3–A5. In all cases, the top 20 sequential patterns do provide a covering of more than 85% of the attack sequences. The mean length of the top 20 sequential patterns is 3.75 for A0, 4.67 for A3, 3.6 for A4, and 3.7 for A5 (all patterns include the final node n_f). This means the k-cover provides some useful information on the strategies adopted by the threat agent. Let us consider as an example, M0. The top 7 sequential patterns in the result of the greedy algorithm cover 66% of the sequences. One specific elementary attack occurs in 4 of them, and another in the other 3 of them. Patching such two attacks will then result in an effective means for blocking 66% of the successful attack sequences. This shows that the discovery of patterns strongly reduces the number of patches to deploy without decreasing the effectiveness of the patching strategy.

Let us consider now the scenario S2. Figure 3 (right) shows the fraction of the 100K sequences that are covered by $cover(k, \mathcal{MP})$ at the variation of k for threat agents A1 and A2 and with $minsup = 15K$. The covered fraction grows rapidly with k. However, such sequential patterns cannot be used for designing countermeasures, since they include attack types or attacked nodes, without specifying the specific elementary attacks that are used (and possibly covering different elementary attacks at the same node). They are instead useful in evaluating the "degree of freedom" of a threat agent on the target system. In particular, the sequential patterns highlight the (maximal) paths that an agent may follow to reach the goal. The more sequential patterns are needed to reach a certain fraction of covered sequences, the more complex is the set of strategies/paths the agent can implement/follow – and, ultimately, the more complex is to stop the attacker. At one extreme, a topology with a single path would produce a single maximal sequential pattern.

7   Related Work

Sequential patterns, measures of interest, and their generalization have been studied for more than 20 years in the data mining literature [6,12,14], with applications to the most diverse areas. Several sequential, parallel, and distributed algorithms for extracting different classes of sequential patterns have been proposed. We adopted the SPMF Java library [5], which includes open-source implementations of a large number of them. Most of the attention on interest measures has considered ranking individual sequential patterns, e.g., on the basis of unexpectedness. Notable exceptions consider sets of sequential patterns and adopt the Minimum Description Length principle [10,18].

The maximum coverage problem and its approximation algorithms have been considered in many application contexts and variants [7]. The approach most related to ours is the computation of Coverage Patterns, a class of (non-sequential) itemsets X, such that the items in X cover a specified percentage of transactions and they overlap at most for a specified threshold [17].

Finally, the usage of data mining models in IDS has been widely adopted, e.g., using classifiers [11], association rules [9], and closed sequential patterns [4]. All of them struggle with the lack of enough data for building accurate models.

8   Conclusions

We have proposed a novel data-driven approach, based on sequential pattern mining, in ICT risk assessment and prevention that offers potentials at design-time. Starting from a sequence database generated through Monte Carlo simulations, we formally showed that maximal sequential patterns are the most appropriate classes for such a context. On a sample case study, we have shown that a maximal k-cover based on sequential patterns can provide an abstraction which is useful both for designing countermeasures and for providing to the security analyst an abstraction of the strategies of attackers on the target system.

References

1. Baiardi, F., Corò, F., Tonelli, F., Sgandurra, D.: A scenario method to automatically assess ICT risk. In: Euromicro International Conference on Parallel, Distributed, and Network-Based Processing (PDP 2014), pp. 544–551. IEEE (2014)
2. Baiardi, F., Telmon, C., Sgandurra, D.: Haruspex: simulation-driven risk analysis for complex systems. ISACA J. **3**, 46–51 (2012)
3. Baiardi, F., Tonelli, F., Bertolini, A.: CyVar: extending Var-At-Risk to ICT. In: Seehusen, F., Felderer, M., Großmann, J., Wendland, M.-F. (eds.) RISK 2015. LNCS, vol. 9488, pp. 49–62. Springer, Cham (2015). https://doi.org/10.1007/978-3-319-26416-5_4
4. Brahmi, H., Yahia, S.B.: Discovering multi-stage attacks using closed multi-dimensional sequential pattern mining. In: Decker, H., Lhotská, L., Link, S., Basl, J., Tjoa, A.M. (eds.) DEXA 2013. LNCS, vol. 8056, pp. 450–457. Springer, Heidelberg (2013). https://doi.org/10.1007/978-3-642-40173-2_38
5. Fournier-Viger, P., Gomariz, A., Gueniche, T., Soltani, A., Wu, C., Tseng, V.S.: SPMF: a Java open-source pattern mining library. J. Mach. Learn. Res. **15**, 3389–3393 (2014)
6. Fournier-Viger, P., Lin, J.C.-W., Kiran, R.U., Koh, Y.S., Thomas, R.: A survey of sequential pattern mining. Data Sci. Pattern Recogn. **1**, 54–77 (2017)
7. Hochbaum, D.S.: Approximating covering and packing problems: set cover, vertex cover, independent set, and related problems. In: Hochbaum, D.S. (ed.) Approximation Algorithms for NP-hard Problems, pp. 94–143. PWS Publishing Co. (1997)
8. Joint Task Force Transformation Initiative Interagency Working Group. SP 800–30 revision 1: Guide for conducting risk assessments. National Institute of Standards & Technology (2012)
9. Katipally, R., Gasior, W., Cui, X., Yang, L.: Multistage attack detection system for network administrators using data mining. In: Proceedings of the Cyber Security and Information Intelligence Research Workshop (CSIIRW 2010), pp. 51. ACM (2010)
10. Lam, H.T., Mörchen, F., Fradkin, D., Calders, T.: Mining compressing sequential patterns. Stat. Anal. Data Min. **7**(1), 34–52 (2014)
11. Lee, W., Stolfo, S.J., Mok, K.W.: Adaptive intrusion detection: a data mining approach. Artif. Intell. Rev. **14**(6), 533–567 (2000)
12. Mabroukeh, N.R., Ezeife, C.I.: A taxonomy of sequential pattern mining algorithms. ACM Comput. Surv. **43**(1), 3:1–3:41 (2010)
13. MITRE: Common Weakness Enumeration. https://cwe.mitre.org/
14. Mooney, C., Roddick, J.F.: Sequential pattern mining - approaches and algorithms. ACM Comput. Surv. **45**(2), 19:1–19:39 (2013)
15. NIST: National Vulnerability Database. https://nvd.nist.gov/
16. Schiffman, M.: Common Vulnerability Scoring System. https://www.first.org/cvss
17. Srinivas, P.G., Reddy, P.K., Trinath, A.V., Sripada, B., Kiran, R.U.: Mining coverage patterns from transactional databases. J. Intell. Inf. Syst. **45**(3), 423–439 (2015)
18. Tatti, N., Vreeken, J.: The long and the short of it: summarising event sequences with serial episodes. In: Proceedings of International Conference on Knowledge Discovery and Data Mining (KDD 2012), pp. 462–470. ACM (2012)

Student Performance Prediction and Optimal Course Selection: An MDP Approach

Michael Backenköhler[✉] and Verena Wolf

Computer Science Department, Saarland Informatics Campus,
Saarbrücken, Germany
michael.backenkoehler@uni-saarland.de

Abstract. Improving the performance of students is an important challenge for higher education institutions. At most European universities, duration and completion rate of degrees are highly varying and consulting services are offered to increase student achievement. Here, we propose a data analytics approach to determine optimal choices for the courses of the next term. We use machine learning techniques to predict the performance of a student in upcoming courses. These prediction form the transition probabilities of a Markov decision process (MDP) that describes the course of studies of a student. Using this model we plan to explore the effect of different strategies on student performance.

1 Introduction

Understanding and improving learning conditions of students has always been an important objective in educational institutions and different policies and interventions have been developed to improve learning processes and students' performance. Recently, educational data has been systematically analysed and used to predict students' future learning. This includes the design of models that incorporate information such as students' knowledge, talents, motivation, and attitudes. This newly emerging field, called educational data mining (EDM), focuses on the exploration and analysis of data that comes from the educational setting [7]. One goal is the prediction of students' performance and the decrease of high dropout rates at higher education institutions since high dropout rates obviously have social and economic disadvantages. In addition to dropout, also the time-to-degree and study success is an important issue on the European policy agenda and continuously monitored by higher education research institutes. Completion rates at European universities range from 39% to 85% and are highly program dependent, while the average time-to-degree is around 3.5 years for a Bachelor degree [9].

In many study programs, students can choose between different courses, the order in which they take courses, or change the degree program. In the latter case, if the newly chosen program is similar to the previous one, the accomplishments of some earlier courses can be transferred. The goal of this work is to use data of students' performance to analyse the efficiency of choices made by students concerning the courses and the program and to predict their performance

A. Cerone and M. Roveri (Eds.): SEFM 2017 Workshops, LNCS 10729, pp. 40–47, 2018.
https://doi.org/10.1007/978-3-319-74781-1_3

for different organisational strategies. For this, we preprocessed (anonymized) performance data of 3889 computer science students since 2006 which have been enrolled at Saarland University. We design a Markov decision process (MDP) that describes the performance and course selection of a student for every semester until graduation. A state of the MDP corresponds to the transcript of the student in a certain semester and the possible actions correspond to subsets of course that the student may take in the upcoming semester. The MDP will be equipped with costs/rewards that are related to the number of credit points of the course as well as the number of semesters and the expected final graduation grade. We are interested in reaching goal states where the student has successfully graduated. It is possible to consider optimization criteria such as timely graduation or best grades, however, students may only fix bounds for the number of semesters, credit points, and grade and consider other objectives such as maximize knowledge in a certain field,etc. Hence, we aim at a general MDP model that allows an analysis w.r.t. different objectives and constraints. Moreover, our goal is to analyze whether students chose their courses in a suboptimal way and check whether failure of courses or a disadvantageous order of courses could have been avoided.

A key challenge is the estimation of transition probabilities of the MDP, i.e., the probability to achieve certain grades in a certain set of courses. Grade prediction or the simpler task of estimating the probability of passing a course has been studied earlier using linear regression and matrix factorization models [1,6]. While online learning environments provide richer information for grade prediction, estimations for traditional learning environments rely on similarities between currently offered courses and courses offered in earlier semesters as well as similarities between students.

In this paper, we present preliminary results for the grade prediction based on different machine learning methods. These results were computed on the basis of the data mentioned above. In addition, we discuss our idea of an higher education studies MDP and important challenges that arise during its construction and analysis. Our findings indicate that individual study counseling can be improved by course recommendation that are based on results of the proposed MDP model.

2   Background

We propose to model the higher education studies of a student using an MDP, which necessitates the estimation of model parameters. This and the design of the MDP require careful analysis of real-world data provided by electronic administrative systems of the educational institution. Here, we use data from computer science students at Saarland University, which includes some basic metadata regarding the students, as well as information about course performance. The performance of a student in a certain course is described by an entry that includes the course title, the name of the lecturer, the awarded credit points (CP) in the European credit transfer and accumulation system (ECTS), the number of attempts, and the final grade. Some of the courses are offered regularly such as basic and core lectures. About the student, the year of birth, nationality, gender, and enrolment history is known.

There are many case-specific data-related challenges which make the analysis difficult. For example, the available records do not provide reliable information to which category a certain course belongs. Moreover, grades may be missing since student's have some freedom to choose which grades contribute to their final GPA [8]. Those that do not contribute are removed in the database, which naturally introduces an upward bias in the available data.

3   MDP for Higher Education Studies

In this section we define the Markov decision process (MDP) that models the progression of a student through the program of studies. A state of the MDP is given by the student's birth date, nationality, and transcript $T \in \mathcal{T}$ after t semesters, where t is a non-negative integer that denotes the semester relative to the student beginning the program and $\mathcal{T}$ is the set of all possible transcripts. The transcript consists of tuples (C, G), where C describes a course and $G \in \{1, 1.3, 1.7, 2, 2.3, 2.7, 3, 3.3, 3.7, 4, 5\}$ the assigned grade, where 1 is best and 5 is worst. For courses, we record the title, lecturer, amount of awarded credit points, and the category c according to the program regulations.

The available actions of the student are given by all possible subsets of the set of courses offered in the upcoming semester, constrained by the program regulations. The grades of a student, i.e. the outcome probabilities, are predicted using the methods described in Sect. 4. At the core of the model there is the reward function, that specifies how *valuable* a certain outcome is to the student. We consider two primary goals which are universal for a great majority of students:

1. Achieve a good overall grade.
2. Obtain a degree in a timely manner.

The first goal can be dealt with by a defining function $g : \mathcal{T} \to [1, 5]$ of an arbitrary (non-empty) transcript to the current overall grade according to the program's regulations. This function can now be used to compute the improvement (positive or negative) the outcome of some action imposes on the current overall grade. The second goal can be handled by consideration of the amount a certain course contributes to obtaining a degree. A program usually prescribes a certain amount of credit points that have to be achieved in certain categories along with some mandatory courses. All necessary credit points amount to a fixed number of credit points. The progress towards reaching that number gives a measure of the second goal. Let $p : \mathcal{T} \to [0, 1]$ be a function that computes the ratio of completed to missing requirements for some degree. With these two measures at our disposal we can define the reward as some combination, e.g. a linear function, of both criteria.

Following the above intuition we can now define an MDP that describes higher education studies of a student over time (HES-MDP).

Definition 1. HES-MDP. *Let $\mathcal{T}_0$ be an initial non-empty transcript of the student under consideration.* Then the Higher Education Studies MDP (HES-MDP) *is the tuple $(\mathcal{T}, \{\mathcal{A}_t | t > 0\}, P, R_c)$ where each component is defined as follows.*

- *The* state space $\mathcal{T}$ *is the set of all transcripts of grades $T \in \mathcal{T}$.*
- *The* set *of* actions, $\mathcal{A}_t$, *that are possible at time t consists of all subsets of available courses that the student can choose in semester t.*
- *The* transition probability function $P : \mathcal{T} \times \mathcal{A}_{t+1} \times \mathcal{T} \rightarrow [0,1]$ *computes for a given transcript in semester t the probability of each possible transcript after semester t if the student chooses a certain set of courses in semester t. Thus, if T_t is the transcript in semester t then, for a set A of courses, $P(T_t, A, T_{t+1})$ is the probability to achieve transcript T_{t+1} after semester t.*
- *For a fixed scaling factor $c > 0$, the* (immediate) reward function $R_c : \mathcal{T} \times \mathcal{T} \rightarrow \mathbb{R}$ *computes the reward gained during a state transition from T_t to T_{t+1} as the linear combination $R_c(T_t, T_{t+1}) = c \cdot (g(T_t) - g(T_{t+1})) + p(T_{t+1}) - p(T_t)$.*

The above MDP model can be simplified by disregarding the specific grade of a student and only recording whether the student passed the course or not. Accordingly, the grade difference term is dropped from the reward function.

Since we are considering the progression of a student through a program, not only the course performance is important. Additionally, a student may drop out of the program at any given time. There are two possible drop-out scenarios: (i) The student is forced out of the program due to poor performance. (ii) The student chooses to quit. In case of scenario (i) there are simply no applicable actions left. While (i) can be computed based on the transcript, (ii) is an event that, in principle, can occur for any student. Here, it could be sensible to train a separate model, predicting a dropout probability, which is then used to condition the grade prediction. Then the set of possible actions of a state is enriched by a transition to an absorbing state corresponding to student dropout with the probability taken from the dropout model.

3.1   Simulation

We plan to investigate the MDP by means of a standard Monte-Carlo tree search (MCTS) algorithm. In each semester a student has, in principle, the opportunity to select any subset of offered lectures. It is therefore sensible to exclude choices which are "unreasonable", which primarily bounds the size of considered subsets of courses.

Furthermore it is not known a-priori for many lectures whether they will be offered in some future semester. For example, advanced lectures or seminars may only be offered only once or irregularly. Therefore we can only assume to know which lectures are offered in the next semester. In other future semesters courses can be treated as dummies of the corresponding category. Consequently, outcome probabilities are computed by aggregation of all courses of the same category. The simulation could be done by standard algorithms such as MCTS with UCB action selection [3].

4   Performance Prediction

We now discuss the estimation of MDP transition probabilities, which amounts to the prediction of grades. The prediction of grade values can be interpreted as either a *classification* problem, or a *regression* problem in which the grade domain is extended to the real line. Here we consider the latter approach.

4.1   Prediction of Course Performance

We obtained the most reliable predictions when using aggregated performance features instead of individual performances. As features for a fixed pair of student and course, we use the current

- percentage of achieved CP w.r.t. the attempted CPs
- grade point average (GPA) weighted by credit points
- average achieved CPs per semester
- GPA weighted by the correlation of the course with other courses
- semesters of the student in the program
- age of the student
- number of attempts for the course
- overall number of CPs
- deviation of attempted CPs in a semester from the average achieved CPs

If there is no data for an aggregate value such as a mean the overall mean is imputed. As the response variable we used the grade value as given by the course data. A fundamental challenge in the prediction of grades is, that the failing grade 5 does not capture how far the student was from not failing.

All of these features are normalized to mean 0 and standard deviation 1. To perform grade predictions, we trained models separately for individual (recurring) courses. The techniques considered here are

- a simple linear regression (LR)
- Regularized linear regression (LASSO)
- Random Forests (RF)
- Gaussian Processes (GPR)
- Nearest Neighbors regression (NNR)

Except for the first two, each of the methods returns not only an estimated grade but also estimated variances, which can be used to fit a discretised normal distribution over possible grades. For LR and LASSO, variances can be obtained via bootstrapping. When simulating the MDP, we run the grade prediction in an on-the-fly fashion for the current state. For details on the above methods we refer the interested reader to the common literature [2,4].

Despite factors that take into account the semester workload of the student, the fitted models do often not realistically predict the performance, when a large set of courses is chosen. In general, the performance may be worse due to the high workload. Information on attempted versus completed courses is in general sparse since students can revoke their registration late in the semester. Thus, the data does not include lectures that have been dropped earlier in the semester. An approach to tackle this, is to estimate the expected amount of credit points per semester for a student. However, it is possible to learn models to estimate the amount of credit points a student is going to complete in a given model. For example, Fig. 1 (left) shows that students with higher GPA clearly achieve on average more credit points per semester.

For now, we make the simplifying assumption that, as long as the sum of the CPs of the chosen courses (attempted CPs) remains in a certain range, obtained grades are independent. Hence, assume that the student chooses m courses in the current semester. Then, we estimate the probability of obtaining a corresponding vector of m grades based on a multivariate normal distribution, whose vector of means contains the estimated grades (cf. Fig. 1 (right)) using one of the methods mentioned above and whose covariance matrix is a diagonal matrix with the corresponding variances. Methods like GPR directly yield such distributions while other methods such as linear regression may require bootstrapping. The grades drawn from the normal distribution have then to be discretised in order to keep the state space discrete. For example, a threshold has to be fixed which corresponds to a student failing a lecture (cf. Fig. 1 (right)). Depending on the computational effort one can also scale the "resolution" to larger ranges to reduce the state space's size.

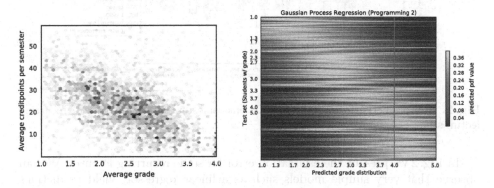

Fig. 1. (left) The average number of CPs per semester versus the overall average grade. Outliers above an average of 60CPs are excluded for clarity. The Pearson correlation coefficient is approx. -0.5217. (right) The predicted probability densities resulting from GPR for the lecture "Programming 2" in the summer semester 2013.

5 Evaluation

A prototype implementation of the feature extraction, grade prediction, and simulation was implemented in Python using standard libraries. Notably, the implementations of the machine learning methods as provided by Scikit-learn [5] were used.

5.1 Evaluating Course Performance

For a fixed semester t and a fixed course, we split the data into test and training data, i.e., all previous data $(t < t_k)$ constitutes the training data, while the data of the threshold semester $(t = t_k)$ gives the test data. We compute hyperparameters of the model using a three-fold cross validation on the training-data. Then the regressor is refitted on all the training data and grade estimation on the test data is performed. This is performed for all semesters in which the course was offered (except for the first two times to avoid a cold start).

We evaluate the predictor quality by a metric that normalizes the mean squared error (MSE) of the predictor with the MSE of the mean predictor. Consider a test set of N students with transcripts T_i and grade G_i in a fixed course ($i \in \{1, 2 \ldots, N\}$). Let $R(T_i)$ be the estimated grade in model R. Then, we define

$$E_R(\{T_1, \ldots, T_N\}) = 1 - \frac{\sum_i (G_i - R(T_i))^2}{\sum_i (G_i - \bar{G}^{\text{train}})^2}$$

where $\bar{G}^{\text{train}}$ is the average grade over the training data.

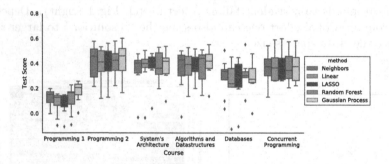

Fig. 2. The prediction error over in different semesters for a selection of recurring lectures.

In Fig. 2 we present the estimation error for some recurring lectures. We can observe that very simple models such as a linear regressor, yield predictions of similar accuracy as more involved models. The weaker results for the lecture "Programming 1" (left) are due to the fact, that for most students no information beyond their metadata is available. Here we can also observe that GPR outperforms other methods such as simple linear models. Disregarding "Programming 1" the average scores over basic lectures is highest using GPR (0.4106) while it is slightly lower using other techniques: The average values are 0.3716 (LR), 0.3947 (LASSO), 0.3950 (NNR), and 0.4033 (RF).

6 Conclusion

In this work, we sketched a Markov decision process to describe the choices of a student during her higher education studies. We identified challenges and strategies to perform simulations of that MDP based on data from earlier semesters. To this end we used machine learning methods to predict in each semester the grades the student is likely to obtain based on her previous performance. This prediction can be used to determine the transition probabilities of the MDP and simulate the progress and performance of the student until graduation.

We found that for regularly offered large courses, accurate predictions are possible, while in uncommon cases (e.g. predicting a grade for an advanced maths course if basic maths courses have not been taken before) obviously an accurate prediction is hard. As future work, we plan to improve the estimation of transition probabilities by modeling and predicting dropout (probabilities), and by investigating further the dependency between workload and obtained grades. We will analyse the MDP in detail and compare action choices which are optimal w.r.t. certain criteria against the choice that students made. Finally, we plan to provide a tool that suggests for each student and semester a set of courses optimal w.r.t. adjustable criteria.

Acknowledgments. We thank Jens Dittrich, Endre Palatinus, and Thilo Krüger for pre-processing the data and interesting discussions.

References

1. Elbadrawy, A., Polyzou, A., Ren, Z., Sweeney, M., Karypis, G., Rangwala, H.: Predicting student performance using personalized analytics. Computer **49**(4), 61–69 (2016)
2. Friedman, J., Hastie, T., Tibshirani, R.: The Elements of Statistical Learning, vol. 1. Springer series in statistics Springer, Berlin (2001). https://doi.org/10.1007/978-0-387-84858-7
3. Kocsis, L., Szepesvári, C.: Bandit based Monte-Carlo planning. In: Fürnkranz, J., Scheffer, T., Spiliopoulou, M. (eds.) ECML 2006. LNCS (LNAI), vol. 4212, pp. 282–293. Springer, Heidelberg (2006). https://doi.org/10.1007/11871842_29
4. Murphy, K.P.: Machine Learning: A Probabilistic Perspective. MIT press, Cambridge (2012)
5. Pedregosa, F., Varoquaux, G., Gramfort, A., Michel, V., Thirion, B., Grisel, O., Blondel, M., Prettenhofer, P., Weiss, R., Dubourg, V., Vanderplas, J., Passos, A., Cournapeau, D., Brucher, M., Perrot, M., Duchesnay, E.: Scikit-learn: machine learning in python. J. Mach. Learn. Res. **12**, 2825–2830 (2011)
6. Polyzou, A., Karypis, G.: Grade prediction with models specific to students and courses. Int. J. Data Sci. Anal. **2**(3–4), 159–171 (2016)
7. Romero, C., Ventura, S.: Educational data mining: a review of the state of the art. IEEE Trans. Syst. Man Cybern. Part C (Appl. Rev.) **40**(6), 601–618 (2010)
8. Bachelor Program Regulations, Saarland University (2015). http://www.ps-mint.uni-saarland.de/fileadmin/user_upload/_imported/fileadmin/Benutzerdaten/Downloads/Formulare/Informatik/StO_PO/StO_BA_Informatik_2015.pdf. Accessed June 2017
9. Vossensteyn, H., Kottmann, A., Jongbloed, B., Kaiser, F., Cremonini, L., Stensaker, B., Hovdhaugen, E., Wollscheid, S.: Dropout and completion in higher education in Europe: main report (2015)

An Algorithm for Simulating Human Selective Attention

Giovanna Broccia[1], Paolo Milazzo[1(✉)], and Peter Csaba Ölveczky[2]

[1] Department of Computer Science, University of Pisa, Pisa, Italy
{giovanna.broccia,milazzo}@di.unipi.it
[2] Department of Informatics, University of Oslo, Oslo, Norway
peterol@ifi.uio.no

Abstract. The brain mechanism of *selective attention* plays a key role in determining the success of a human's interaction with a device. If the user has to perform concurrent tasks by interacting simultaneously with more than one device, her/his attention is directed at one of the devices at a time. Attention can therefore be seen as a shared resource, and the attentional mechanisms play the role of a task scheduler. In this paper we propose an algorithm for simulating the human selective attention. Simulations can then be used to study situations in which a user has to interact simultaneously with multiple devices. This kind of study is particularly important in safety-critical contexts in which failures in the main task, such as driving a car or setting an infusion pump, may have serious consequences.

Keywords: Simulation algorithm · Human-computer interaction
Selective attention · Cognitive load

1 Introduction

A key goal of interface design is to make it easy for the user to perform the tasks at hand (e.g., driving a car or withdrawing money) by interacting with a device (such as the car driver interface or an ATM). Good interface design therefore requires understanding how the user perceives and interprets the state of the device, recognizes the enabled actions, memorizes information, and makes decisions based on such information. These cognitive processes can be modeled [5], and techniques such as simulation and model checking can be applied to analyze and predict users' behaviors.

Reasoning about users' behaviors is nontrivial even with one task, such as withdrawing money from an ATM, and becomes an even more complex problem when the user has to perform multiple tasks concurrently. In particular, it is very hard to reason analytically about how the user distributes attention to the different tasks. Analyzing attention is particularly important in order to predict the behavior of users involved in concurrent tasks.

A. Cerone and M. Roveri (Eds.): SEFM 2017 Workshops, LNCS 10729, pp. 48–55, 2018.
https://doi.org/10.1007/978-3-319-74781-1_4

Working memory is among the cognitive resources that are mostly involved in interactions with computers and other technological devices. It is a volatile memory used to store and process the information necessary for performing a task. Several models of the working memory have been proposed in the psychological literature, based on different hypotheses about the structure and functioning of such a cognitive system [2,3,6,8,10]. These models all agree on the central role of (selective) attention in the regulation of the working memory activity.

According to some psychological studies [9], the *cognitive load* of each task (i.e., the amount of cognitive resources each task requires) influences the activity of the attentional mechanisms. In particular, focusing attention on a "main" task (such as driving a car) may be impeded by a secondary "distractor" task (such as finding an interesting radio show) with a high cognitive load.

Another factor influencing attention is the fact that some tasks (e.g. driving a car or setting an infusion pump) might be more critical than others (e.g. setting the address in a satellite navigator or resizing the window of the virtual clinical folder application). If the user is involved in different concurrent tasks, one of which is safety-critical and the others non-critical but characterized by a high cognitive load, such a cognitive load of the non-critical tasks could cause the attention of the user to be moved away from the safety-critical task.

We propose an algorithm that allows us to simulate the human selective attention of users involved in multiple concurrent tasks, some of which may be safety-critical. Simulations allow us to get a quick feedback about whether a human can safely perform multiple such tasks, or about which changes should be made to the interface of a device to make interacting with it not too distracting from another (possibily critical) task. We also show that the proposed algorithm is consistent with the description of human selective attention in the psychological literature.

2   Cognitive Load and its Influence on Selective Attention

The *cognitive load* of a task is a measure of the amount of the user's cognitive resources required for completing the task. For example, solving a sudoku puzzle is a task with a high cognitive load, since the player has to repeatedly perform difficult computations. On the other hand, chatting with a friend on a social networking website has a lower cognitive load since the actions to be perfomed are easier and less frequent (one has to wait for the friend to reply).

The main cognitive resource used during the execution of a task is the *working memory (WM)* [1,12]. The WM is a form of memory with limited capacity that is responsible for the transient holding and processing of information. It is involved in accomplishing cognitive activities such as reasoning, decision making, learning and problem solving [7].

Different models have been proposed in the literature to explain how the WM works [2,3,6,8,10]. Although these models are based on different hypotheses, they all agree on two important aspects of the WM: it can store a limited amount of items (that dacay over time; i.e., are quickly forgotten) and it is responsible for both processing and storage activities. The limited capacity of the WM is thought to be the cause of the phenomenon known as the processing-storage trade-off: under heavy memory load, resources that are devoted to storage are no longer available for processing, and performance deteriorates.

There are several hypotheses regarding the nature of the items decay. One is that memory traces in WM decay within a few seconds, unless refreshed through rehearsal, and because the speed of rehearsal is limited, we can maintain only a limited amount of information [14]. The theory most successful in explaining experimental data on the interaction of maintenance and processing in WM is the "Time-Based Resource Sharing Model" [4]. This theory assumes that items in WM decay unless they are refreshed, and that refreshing them requires an attentional mechanism.

The attentional mechanism is also needed for any processing task executed concurrently with memory refreshment, especially when the processing components require retrieval from long-term memory. Both processing and maintenance of information in the WM therefore share the same resource: the attention. When there are small time intervals in which the processing task does not require attention, this time can be used to refresh memory traces. When attention is switched away from the items to be recalled, their activation suffers from a time-related decay. This effect would be particularly pronounced when the processing component involves memory retrieval from long-term memory.

The amount of forgetting therefore depends on the temporal density of attentional demands of the processing task. Such a temporal density is actually the measure of the task cognitive load considered in [4]. It is formalized as a value CL denoting the fraction of the time during which a task totally captures the user's attention, and impedes refreshing decaying memory traces. As this time increases, the pauses during which the attention can be directed at refreshing decaying items become less frequent and shorter.

A task can be seen as a sequence of basic activities, each one requiring the user's attention. Basic activities can be of different types (pressing a button, reading a text, etc.) and difficulties. When such activities are performed at a constant pace, the CL denotes the following value:

$$CL = \sum a_i n_i / T \tag{1}$$

where n_i corresponds to the number of activities of type i, a_i is a parameter that represents the difficulty of such activity (i.e., the time during which they totally capture attention), and T is the total duration of the task.

Figure 1 shows a schematic representation of a portion of a WM span task in which the goal of the interaction is to remember a sequence of letters (the ones in the white boxes) while performing some processing activities (e.g., reading aloud some digits or performing an arithmetic operation) that require successive retrievals (gray boxes marked R). The three panels in Fig. 1 illustrate variants of the same task that differ in the amount of cognitive load.

Several studies show how attentional limitations could cause trouble when performing concurrent tasks [9,11,13,15]. In particular, [9] describes the roles

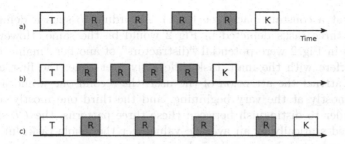

Fig. 1. Working memory tasks with different *CL* values: (b) has the highest, (c) has the lowest and (a) has a value between the other two.

of the WM, the *CL*, and the attentional mechanism in the interaction with two concurrent tasks (a "main" task and a "distractor" task). It is shown that when the *CL* of the "distractor" task increases, the interaction with the "main" task could be impeded.

3   The Simulation Algorithm

A task can be seen as a sequence of *basic tasks*: single actions that cannot be further decomposed. For example, in the task described in Sect. 2, the basic tasks are actions such as read and store a letter, solve an operation, read aloud a digit, and so on. In the task of sending an email, the basic tasks could be: typing a character, looking for a button in the interface, clicking on the button, etc.

Each basic task is charcterized by a *duration* and a *level of difficulty* (e.g., typing a character is faster and easier than selecting an entry in a dropdown menu). Two consecutive basic tasks may have some idle time between them. Such a time could be necessary for the user to switch from one basic task to the next, but also to the device to process the received input and enable the execution of the next basic task.

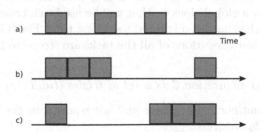

Fig. 2. Three different tasks with basic tasks denoted as gray boxes.

In [4], the time between two basic tasks is not explicitly taken into account, since the definition of the *CL* of a task assumes that the single actions are performed at a constant pace (see Eq. 1). According to such a definition, the CL of the three tasks depicted in Fig. 2 would be the same. However, if the three tasks in Fig. 2 were potential "distractors" of another "main" task, they would interfere with the main task differently over time: the first one would repeatedly attract the attention of the user, the second one would attract the attention mostly at the very beginning, and the third one mostly after some time. In order to distinguish between these three patterns, the CL should not be computed statically as an average value over the whole task duration, but should be computed dynamically as long as the task is performed. In this way, the second task in Fig. 2 would have a higher CL at the beginning and a lower CL later on, while the third task would have the opposite.

We propose an algorithm for simulating the selective attention in which the CL of the concurrent tasks is dynamically recomputed each time a basic task is completed. The CL is computed simply as the product of the difficulty and the duration of the next basic task. The CL values of the different tasks are then used in order to choose which task to execute next.

The free time between two tasks is modeled as a waiting time before the execution of a basic task (i.e., information is included in the basic task that will follow such a free time). Moreover, each task has a *criticality level* denoting to what degree it is perceived as safety-critical.

Definition 1. *A basic task is defined as a triple $\langle w, t, d \rangle \in \mathbb{R}^3$ where:*

- *w is the* waiting time *before the basic task is enabled;*
- *t is the* duration *of the basic task; and*
- *d is the* difficulty *of the basic task, with $0 < d \leq 1$.*

Definition 2. *A task is a sequence of basic tasks associated with a criticality level $C \in \mathbb{R}$ with $0 < C \leq 1$.*

We represent a task as a pair $[t_1.t_2.....t_n, C]$, with each t_i a basic task, where ε denotes an empty sequence, and where C is the task's criticality level. Consequently, the pair $[\varepsilon, C]$ represents a *completed task*.

The state of a simulation is given by a *configuration* $\mathcal{C}$, essentialy the set of active tasks, and by a global clock gc that will be used to increase the probability of choosing a task that has been ignored for a long time. For this reason, also the timestamps of the last executions of all the tasks are stored in the configuration.

Definition 3. *A configuration $\mathcal{C}$ is a set of triples (tid, T, ts) where:*

- *tid is a task identifier (of any type and not repeated in the configuration);*
- *T is a task $[t_1.t_2.....t_n, C]$;*
- *ts is a timestamp storing the last time the task with identifier tid was executed.*

We define a few auxiliary functions that are used by the simulation algorithm.

Given a task T, functions $hd(T)$ and $tl(T)$ give its first basic task and the sequence of the other basic tasks, respectively. Moreover, $criticality(T)$ gives the

---

Algorithm 1. Algorithm for simulating selective attention

1: **while not** $completed(\mathcal{C})$ **do**
2:   **if** $enabled(\mathcal{C}, gc) \neq \emptyset$ **then**
3:     **for all** $(tid, T, ts) \in enabled(\mathcal{C}, gc)$ **do**
4:       $\alpha_{tid} := c \cdot t \cdot d \cdot (1 + (gc - ts))$
5:       where $\langle w, t, d \rangle = hd(T)$ and $c = criticality(T)$
6:     **end for**
7:     choose $(\overline{tid}, \overline{T}, \overline{ts}) \in enabled(\mathcal{C}, gc)$ with probability $\dfrac{\alpha_{\overline{tid}}}{\sum_{(tid,T,ts) \in enabled(\mathcal{C},gc)} \alpha_{tid}}$

8:     $gc := gc + \overline{t}$ where $\langle \overline{w}, \overline{t}, \overline{d} \rangle = hd(\overline{T})$
9:     $\mathcal{C} := (\mathcal{C} \setminus (\overline{tid}, \overline{T}, \overline{ts})) \cup (\overline{tid}, tl(\overline{T}), gc)$
10:   **else**
11:     $gc := min\{ts + w \mid (tid, T, ts) \in \mathcal{C} \wedge \langle w, t, d \rangle = hd(T)\}$
12:   **end if**
13: **end while**

---

criticality level of T. Given a configuration $\mathcal{C}$, $enabled(\mathcal{C}, gc)$ gives the set of the tasks that are enabled at time gc. A task can be performed if the waiting time of its first basic task has passed since the execution of the previous basic task:

$$enabled(\mathcal{C}, gc) = \{(tid, T, ts) \in \mathcal{C} \mid \langle w, t, d \rangle = hd(T) \wedge gc - ts \geq w\}.$$

Furthermore, $completed(\mathcal{C})$ is true if and only if all tasks in $\mathcal{C}$ are completed:

$$completed(\mathcal{C}) = \forall(tid, T, ts) \in \mathcal{C}. \exists C \in \mathbb{R}. T = [\varepsilon, C].$$

Our simulation algorithm of selective attention is defined in Algorithm 1. The algorithm performs a main loop that essentially executes one basic task in each iteration. The basic task to be executed is the first basic task of one of the enabled tasks. For each such candidate basic task, an *attention attraction factor* α_{tid} is computed as the product of the criticality level, duration, difficulty and time since the last execution. Each of the candidate basic tasks then has a probability of being chosen that is proportional to α_{tid}. Once a basic task has been chosen, it is removed from the configuration and the global clock gc is updated. If the algorithm reaches a configuration in which no task is enabled, the main loop performs an iteration in which only the global clock gc is updated.

In order to show that the proposed simulation algorithm simulates selective attention in accordance with relevant literature, let us first consider, for the sake of simplicity, a variant of the algorithm that does not take the task times-tamp into account when computing the attention attraction factor α_{tid}. This corresponds to modifying line 4 of the algorithm to $\alpha_{tid} := c \cdot t \cdot d$.

Let us consider two concurrent tasks with the same criticality level and each consisting of k identical basic tasks:

$$T_1 = \langle w_1, t_1, d_1 \rangle . \langle w_1, t_1, d_1 \rangle . \ldots \langle w_1, t_1, d_1 \rangle$$
$$T_2 = \langle w_2, t_2, d_2 \rangle . \langle w_2, t_2, d_2 \rangle . \ldots \langle w_2, t_2, d_2 \rangle$$

In order to complete both tasks, the simulation algorithm performs exactly $2k$ steps (where a step represents the execution of a single basic task). Since the two tasks have the same criticality level, the probability of completing task T_1 at step n, with $k \leq n \leq 2k$, is

$$P(T_1, n) = \left(\frac{t_1 d_1}{t_1 d_1 + t_2 d_2} \right)^k \left(\frac{t_2 d_2}{t_1 d_1 + t_2 d_2} \right)^{(n-k)} \binom{n-1}{n-k}.$$

The expected number of steps necessary to complete task T_1 can therefore be given as $E[T_1] = \sum_{n=k}^{2k} P(T_1, n) n$, that corresponds to

$$E[T_1] = \left(\frac{t_1 d_1}{t_1 d_1 + t_2 d_2} \right)^k \sum_{n=k}^{2k} \left(\frac{t_2 d_2}{t_1 d_1 + t_2 d_2} \right)^{(n-k)} \binom{n-1}{n-k} n.$$

The formula shows that the expected number of steps for the completion of T_1 increases with the difficulty and duration of the basic tasks of T_2, namely, it increases when the CL of T_2 increases. Hence, the algorithm simulates the switching of attention in agreement with what described in [4, 9]. However, since the task timestap is not taken into account, this variant of the algorithm could lead to unrealistic starvation cases (e.g., the algorithm could repeatedly skip a task with very low criticality level and CL).

Let us now discuss what changes when the task timestamp is taken into account, namely when line 4 is exactly as in the algorithm definition. Formula $E[T_1]$ becomes more complex since the repeated probabilistic events are no longer independent. However, the structure of the formula remains the same, with a result that is still increasing with the difficulty and duration of the basic tasks of T_2 (in agreement with [4, 9]). In addition to this, the timestamps tend to favor at each step the task that has not been choosen in the previous step. As a consequence, the regular alternation of T_1 and T_2 is promoted with, as a result, a reduced variance in the distribution of the number of steps necessary to complete T_1. Hence, the use of timestamps reduces the probability of unnatural starvation among the tasks.

4   Conclusion

We have proposed a probabilistic algorithm for simulating the human selective attention, based on current knowledge of this cognitive mechanism. The algorithm takes into account the cognitive load and the criticality level of the tasks to be performed. It could be used to simulate the interaction of a user with more than one device. Simulating this kind of situation is particularly interesting when one of the devices is associated to a safety-critical task such as driving a car or using an infusion pump. By mean of simulations it could be possible to identify situations in which the non-critical tasks could represent a too high distraction for the user and could lead to failures in the safety-critical task.

The implementation of the algorithm is available at http://www.di.unipi. it/msvbio/software/AttentionSim.html. In future work, we plan to validate the algorithm against data collected by running some experiments with real users concurrently involved in more than one task.

Acknowledgements. This work has been supported by the project "Metodologie informatiche avanzate per l'analisi di dati biomedici (Advanced computational methodologies for the analysis of biomedical data)" funded by the University of Pisa (PRA_2017_44).

References

1. Atkinson, R.C., Shiffrin, R.M.: Human memory: a proposed system and its control processes. Psychol. Learn. Motiv. **2**, 89–195 (1968)
2. Baddeley, A.: The episodic buffer: a new component of working memory? Trends Cognit. Sci. **4**(11), 417–423 (2000)
3. Baddeley, A.D., Hitch, G.: Working memory. Psychol. Learn. Motiv. **8**, 47–89 (1974)
4. Barrouillet, P., Bernardin, S., Camos, V.: Time constraints and resource sharing in adults' working memory spans. J. Exp. Psychol. Gen. **133**(1), 83 (2004)
5. Cerone, A.: A cognitive framework based on rewriting logic for the analysis of interactive systems. In: De Nicola, R., Kühn, E. (eds.) SEFM 2016. LNCS, vol. 9763, pp. 287–303. Springer, Cham (2016). https://doi.org/10.1007/978-3-319-41591-8_20
6. Cowan, N.: Attention and Memory: An Integrated Framework. Oxford University Press, Oxford (1998)
7. Diamond, A.: Executive functions. Annu. Rev. Psychol. **64**, 135–168 (2013)
8. Ericsson, K.A., Kintsch, W.: Long-term working memory. Psychol. Rev. **102**(2), 211 (1995)
9. de Fockert, J.W., Rees, G., Frith, C.D., Lavie, N.: The role of working memory in visual selective attention. Science **291**(5509), 1803–1806 (2001)
10. Just, M.A., Carpenter, P.A.: A capacity theory of comprehension: individual differences in working memory. Psychol. Rev. **99**(1), 122 (1992)
11. Lavie, N., Hirst, A., De Fockert, J.W., Viding, E.: Load theory of selective attention and cognitive control. J. Exp. Psychol. Gen. **133**(3), 339 (2004)
12. Miller, G.A., Galanter, E., Pribram, K.H.: Plans and the Structure of Behavior. Adams Bannister Cox, Eugene (1986)
13. Pashler, H.: Dual-task interference in simple tasks: data and theory. Psychol. Bull. **116**(2), 220 (1994)
14. Towse, J.N., Hitch, G.J., Hutton, U.: On the interpretation of working memory span in adults. Mem. Cognit. **28**(3), 341–348 (2000)
15. Wickens, C.D.: Processing resources and attention. Mult.-task Perform. **1991**, 3–34 (1991)

Learning Decision Trees from Synthetic Data Models for Human Security Behaviour

Peter Carmichael and Charles Morisset[✉]

School of Computing, Newcastle University, Newcastle upon Tyne, UK
{p.j.carmichael,charles.morisset}@ncl.ac.uk

Abstract. In general, in order to predict the impact of human behaviour on the security of an organisation, one can either build a classifier from actual traces observed within the organisation, or build a formal model, integrating known existing behavioural elements. Whereas the former approach can be costly and time-consuming, and it can be complicated to select the best classifier, it can be equally complicated to select the right parameters for a concrete setting in the latter approach. In this paper, we propose a methodical assessment of decision trees to predict the impact of human behaviour on the security of an organisation, by learning them from different sets of traces generated by a formal probabilistic model we designed. We believe this approach can help a security practitioner understand which features to consider before observing real traces from an organisation, and understand the relationship between the complexity of the behaviour model and the accuracy of the decision tree. In particular, we highlight the impact of the norm and messenger effects, which are well-known influencers, and therefore the crucial importance to capture observations made by the agents. We demonstrate this approach with a case study around tailgating. A key result from this work shows that probabilistic behaviour and influences reduce the effectiveness of decision trees and, importantly, they impact a model differently with regards to error rate, precision and recall.

1 Introduction

Employees of organisations are known to regularly circumvent or bypass security procedures, leading to a relaxed security culture [2]. In order to identify the security culture of an organisation, a security practitioner could collect data from different sources and build a classifier model to predict the security preference of employees. For example, sources such as CCTV, interviews and physical logs (smart card data) can be used to classify employees preferences. There are three main challenges with this - (1) It is costly both in time and financially, as demonstrated by Caufield and Parkin [4]. (2) It is error prone as we rely on humans to interpret human behaviour. (3) Given the dataset, it is difficult to identify which features are relevant to build a classifier model.

To address the three challenges, we propose an assessment of classifier models known as decision trees to predict the impact behavioural elements have on

© Springer International Publishing AG 2018
A. Cerone and M. Roveri (Eds.): SEFM 2017 Workshops, LNCS 10729, pp. 56–71, 2018.
https://doi.org/10.1007/978-3-319-74781-1_5

the security culture of an organisation. Firstly, we generate synthetic data from parameterised models with behavioural elements. Secondly, we interpret the data to assess features based on the dataset. Finally, using traditional data mining techniques, we use cross validation to train and test each model independently. One of our results shows different parameters for human behaviour impact the accuracy of decision trees.

Our approach is inspired by online marketing techniques, where peoples behaviour is logged and suggestions are made based on purchases of others who have similar behaviour trends [19]. In the context of security, building a classifier model, an employee performing a security violation should be more substantial to the models rules than the same employee moving between locations. Identifying relevant features, indicates that human behaviour is required, in some form at least. Influences, such as *Social Proof* from Cialdini, or the *Messenger* effect from MINDSPACE can shift the culture of an organisation [7,9]. An employee in the right location at the right time may be influenced by the behaviours of others. If they observe the same action multiple times, or have an influential relationship with the instigator of the behaviour, then they may align their behaviour with this authoritative figure.

We analyse a tailgating case study simulating parameterised models, each model generates a trace we use to assess the accuracy of decision trees. We believe that a security practitioner can understand the relevant features and can begin to understand the relationship between the complexity of human behaviour and the accuracy of decision trees. As a security practitioner, acquiring knowledge where vulnerabilities are present, allows for insights towards defence strategies and interventions. For example, investing in turnstiles to reduce tailgating, or limiting the capabilities of employees who are flagged as a vulnerability.

The main contributions of this work are (1) Parameterised models to simulate and generate synthetic data with known behavioural elements. (2) The methodology for the assessment of decision trees constructed from a synthetic dataset.

The paper is split into the following Sections. In Sect. 2 we discuss the problem, provide an intuition for how we are approaching it and build on existing literature. In Sect. 3 we introduce our Multi Agent System (MAS) alongside a scenario focusing on tailgating. In Sect. 4 we discuss the MAS towards simulation with multiple parameters. In Sects. 5 and 6 we discuss our assessment methodology and analyse the case study. Section 7 is the conclusion and future work.

2   Problem Formulation

A security practitioner observes employee behaviour in an organisation and accumulates information about security incidents. Using this data, they wish to learn the security preference of employees. One possible solution to this is to use machine learning.

The data generated from observing employees forms a trace, where an entry in a trace describes who did what and when. It is similar to an intrusion detection system, where the logs of what happened are the entries, a collection of logs/entries forms a trace. The problem is, given a trace of interactions, can we use machine learning techniques to correctly identify the security preferences of agents? Let us consider a simple example, where an agents security preference can be *usable* or *secure*. A *usable* agent is more likely not to follow a policy, whereas a *secure* agent is. Table 1 lists four agents, the number of violations and preventions for a policy and their security preference. Given this data, the Decision Tree in Fig. 1 can be formed. It is deterministic and will resolve to a value of *usable* or *secure* dependent on the entry being evaluated. In this case, an entry is the log of violations and preventions for an agent. The resolution/decision returned is the security preference.

Table 1. A collection of entries forming a number of violations and preventions for four agents. Each agent is accompanied with a known security preference.

Agent	Violations	Preventions	Security preference
Alice	4	1	*Usable*
Bob	2	3	*Secure*
Charlie	1	0	*Usable*
Dan	2	5	*Secure*

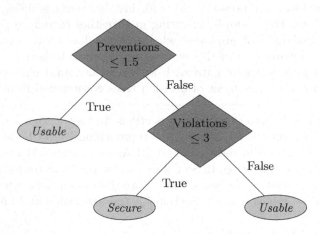

Fig. 1. Learned decision tree from the data in Table 1. A diamond is a decision point, an oval is a decision.

This is a small sample, however, an accurate tree has been learned with 100% accuracy for the training data. A decision tree offers predictive power and, given an agent with some information, we wish to predict their security preference. This is complex, as the decision tree from Fig. 1 can be easily fooled.

For example, an agent with 10 preventions and 5 violations will return as *usable*, even though they have acted securely for the most part.

Establishing which features to consider could provide meaningful results for observing the security culture of employees in an organisation. Unfortunately, the problem is of greater complexity than what we identify here, as human behaviour is complex in itself and leads us to the problem, can we use machine learning to learn from complex behaviour.

2.1 Security Culture Uncertainty

Within an organisation, a security culture exists for how individuals and groups respond to security incidents. Depending on the type of security incident and those involved, it could become a security violation or it could be prevented. We hope that individuals trained to perform tasks are security aware, but we regularly find that they circumvent organisational security policies [3].

Consider working with a company for a short period of time in order to identify the security preference of employees. We could ask them, where responses from interviews have led to popular theories such as the compliance budget [2]. Of course, respondents could lie, answer honestly but not behave consistently, or even fail to acknowledge that their behaviour is insecure.

Even if survey respondents answer honestly, it does not mean that this holds for the future. A secure employee interacting with a usable (non-secure) employee may be influenced towards usable behaviours, creating an insecure culture. Of course, this is bi-directional where secure behaviour can inform more secure behaviour.

From a security officers perspective, they only have so many tools to establish the security culture. For example, they could interview employees, then manually observe them via CCTV recordings to establish if their security preference matches their behaviour [4]. This is of course, costly and time consuming, where we would need to manually record the exact behaviour of each employee.

To add further complexity to the uncertainty of a security culture, some one who is secure may make a judgement of error causing a security incident. For example, Zhu *et al.* showed they could get more information from people simply by providing them with information up front, exploiting a concept known as reciprocity [20]. They were able to influence people to sacrifice more information than they would usually part with.

The security culture of a company can be changed, for example, via training employees [15]. This behaviour change is one that impacts how people respond to security incidents, for example a recently trained employee may have more awareness for *spear phishing* emails, and is less likely to click suspicious links.

3 Multi Agent System

Behaviour surrounding security policies is dependent on different factors. We see three main elements which impact this security culture physical locations, observations and behaviour change. In this section, we introduce a scenario and provide formal notation to express these three elements as a Multi Agent System.

Scenario: *Agents arrive at the back of a workplace reception and there are two possibilities. Firstly, if nobody is at the front of the reception, the agent must progress to the front of the reception. Secondly, if the newly arrived agent is usable, they will attempt to tailgate. A perfectly secure agent will never attempt to tailgate. If an agent is being tailgated, they can either permit or deny the action, where a permit would allow both agents in to the main building, a deny would force the tailgater to the front of the reception. A perfectly usable agent will always permit tailgating, a secure agent will deny tailgating. The scenario runs for a working week of five days.*

3.1 Location Based Agents

Some security policies rely upon physical locations. For example, tailgating relies locations connected by some entry system such as door, corridor and so on. Furthermore, employees express unique behaviours for moving between multiple locations. In recent work, it has been shown that malicious insider behaviour can be detected by using historical data from a building access control system [6]. The data allows for suitable models to be learned surrounding movement behaviour. For our work, these physical movement models provide validation techniques. Using such techniques, Hidden Markov Models can predict with up to 92% accuracy, the next movement of someone given some historical data [12].

Decisions to enforce or circumvent security policies are individual to each employee. Typically, attitudes towards policies can be impacted by personality, past experiences and a productivity trade-off, to name a few [1]. We call these attitudes a *context*, where an employees *context* informs their decision.

Formally, in a Multi Agent System, the entities are known as agents. From here on, we refer to employees or people as agents. In general, we assume the existence of a set A of agent identifiers.

Definition 1 (Location Based Agents). *Given a set of agents A, a set of locations L, and a set of contexts C, we define the set of location based agents as $LBA = A \times C \times L$.*

Definition 2 (Location Based Actions). *Given an agent a and two locations l and l', a location based action is defined as $\mathsf{m}(a, l, l')$, indicating that a moved from l to l'. A location based action does not modify the context of the agent.*

In general, there could be many different ways to capture the concrete set of location based actions in a system, for instance by going through the actual logs of a smart card system. For the sake of simplicity, we consider here a set of links $Link \subseteq L \times L$ where (l_1, l_2) indicates a physical link between the location l_1 and l_2. Intuitively speaking, any agent can move from a location to another as long as there is a link between them. We characterise this with the following rule:

$$\frac{(l, l') \in Link}{(a, c, l) \xrightarrow{\mathsf{m}(a,l,l')} (a, c, l')} \tag{1}$$

The action 1 is defined as an inference rule at the atomic level expressing that one agent moves from one location to another, provided the two locations are connected. In general, we write $(a_1, c_1, l_1) \mid \ldots (a_n, c_n, l_n)$ for a set of location based agents. Given a set of agents $LA \subseteq LBA$, we can extend the rule above as follow

$$\frac{(a, c, l) \xrightarrow{\mathsf{m}(a,l,l')} (a, c, l')}{(a, c, l) \mid LA \xrightarrow{\mathsf{m}(a,l,l')} (a, c, l') \mid LA} \tag{2}$$

The tailgating scenario is a policy breach for an organisation. Whilst it is not the case that an agent is just *usable* or just *secure*, for now, we use these polar opposites to express our model.

We introduce two actions, $\mathsf{tgp}(a_1, a_2, l, l')$ and $\mathsf{tgd}(a_1, a_2, l, l')$, indicating that a_1 and a_2 tailgated, and that a_2 denied a tailgate from a_1, respectively. Intuitively speaking, a *usable* agent is permitted as they tailgate a *usable* agent. Secondly, a *usable* agent is denied as they tailgate a *secure* agent. Formally:

$$\frac{(a_1, c_1, l) \xrightarrow{\mathsf{m}(a_1,l,l')} (a_1, c_1, l') \quad (a_2, c_2, l) \xrightarrow{\mathsf{m}(a_2,l,l')} (a_2, c_2, l') \quad c_1 = c_2 = usable}{(a_1, c_1, l), (a_2, c_2, l) \mid LA \xrightarrow{\mathsf{tgp}(a_1,a_2,l,l')} (a_1, c_1, l'), (a_2, c_2, l') \mid LA} \tag{3}$$

$$\frac{(a_2, c_2, l) \xrightarrow{\mathsf{m}(a_2,l,l')} (a_2, c_2, l') \quad c_1 = usable \quad c_2 = secure}{(a_1, c_1, l), (a_2, c_2, l) \mid LA \xrightarrow{\mathsf{tgd}(a_1,a_2,l,l')} (a_1, c_1, l), (a_2, c_2, l') \mid LA} \tag{4}$$

The rules introduced so far explain how agents with a context move between locations. They can either just move, or they can tailgate and be either permitted or denied. A permit moves them into the tailgated location, the denied leaves an agent in the same location before the action occurred.

3.2   Observing Agents

In an organisation, when an action happens, people may notice. In our example, this translates to agents observing security policies being enforced or exploited. Much like in the workplace, if someone is challenged for tailgating, people within close proximity will notice. One report recorded that users security sensitivity for other peoples security behaviour was prominent in a working environment [8]. We know that people have security awareness in the workplace, particularly when policies are regularly followed.

We began with Location Based Agents, where the interactions of agents are restricted by physical locations and the security preference of each agent. We extend this notion and introduce Observing Agents:

Definition 3 (Observing Agents). *We define $OA \subseteq A \times C \times L \times \mathbb{P}(\Theta)$ as the set of observing agents where A is the set of agents, C is the set of contexts, L is the set of Locations and $\Theta \subseteq A \times Act_\theta$. We introduce a set of observable Actions Act_θ, where any act $\in Act_\theta$ can be observed by an agent.*

Let us consider that $Act_\theta = \{permit, deny\}$, which refer to the permitting or denying of tailgating. An Observing Agent during the course of their interactions, may accumulate observations of other agents permitting or denying tailgating. As it is currently defined, an agent can only observe and store one observation for each agent. At the atomic level, an inference rule for an observation would take the form:

$$(a, c, l, \Theta_a) \xrightarrow{\text{obs}(\theta)} (a, c, l, \Theta_a' \cup \theta) \tag{5}$$

Intuitively, an agent a_1 with the action $\text{obs}(a_2, permit)$ would indicate that they have observed a_2 permitting tailgating.

For an agent observing a particular act, such as tailgating, we must consider all agents in the observable area. We provide the following definition to make use of earlier rules:

$$loc : OA \to LA$$

$$loc(a, c, l, \theta_a) = (a, c, l)$$

Therefore, the observable actions for tailgating are as follows:

$$\frac{\begin{array}{c}(a_1, c_1, l, \Theta_{a_1}) \xrightarrow{\text{obs}(permit)} (a, c, l, \Theta_{a_1} \cup permit) \\ \forall (a', c', l, \Theta_a') \in OA \Rightarrow (a', c', l, \Theta_a') \xrightarrow{\text{obs}(permit)} (a', c', l, \Theta_a' \cup permit) \\ \hline (a_1, c_1, l), (a_2, c_2, l)|loc(OA) \xrightarrow{\text{tgp}(a_1,a_2,l,l')} \\ (a_1, c_1, l'), (a_2, c_2, l')|loc(OA)\end{array}}{(a_1, c_1, l, \theta_{a_1}), (a_2, c_2, l, \theta_{a_2})|OA \xrightarrow{\text{p}(a_1,a_2,l,l',permit)} (a_1, c_1, l', \theta_{a_1}), (a_2, c_2, l', \theta_{a_2})|OA'} \tag{6}$$

$$\frac{\begin{array}{c}(a_1, c_1, l, \Theta_{a_1}) \xrightarrow{\text{obs}(deny)} (a, c, l, \Theta_{a_1} \cup deny) \\ \forall (a', c', l, \Theta_a') \in OA \Rightarrow (a', c', l, \Theta_a') \xrightarrow{\text{obs}(deny)} (a', c', l, \Theta_a' \cup deny) \\ \hline (a_1, c_1, l), (a_2, c_2, l)|loc(OA) \xrightarrow{\text{tgd}(a_1,a_2,l,l')} \\ (a_1, c_1, l), (a_2, c_2, l')|loc(OA)\end{array}}{(a_1, c_1, l, \theta_{a_1}), (a_2, c_2, l, \theta_{a_2})|OA \xrightarrow{\text{d}(a_1,a_2,l,l',deny)} (a_1, c_1, l, \theta_{a_1}), (a_2, c_2, l', \theta_{a_2})|OA'} \tag{7}$$

3.3 Behaviour Change Agents

The concept of behaviour change as a body of research contains many different models. Not all of the models are fit for our purpose. However, the COM-B model splits behaviour change into three elements; Capabilities, Opportunities and Motivation [13]. In this paper, we focus on the aspect of Motivation, which can be changed by influencing effects. Such effects as *Messenger* and *Social Norms* are of interest to us [10]. The former relates to those people/agents we perceive to be in a position of authority, the latter is all about those people around us in our immediate vicinity [7].

In our MAS, a behaviour change would be a change of context. A *secure* agent can become *usable* and vice versa. The following rule captures behaviour change for security preferences:

$$\frac{c \neq c'}{(a, c, l, \Theta_a) \xrightarrow{\text{bchange}(c')} (a, c', l, \{\})} \tag{8}$$

Whilst we don't validate the notion of behaviour change in this work, we do hope to establish meaningful results at a later point. For example, observing and interviewing users in a social experiment where a security preference is present is one possible stream to substantiate the synthetic inference rules defined.

To the best of our knowledge, for the influencing effects *Messenger* and *Social Norms* there does not exist a strategy to quantify formally these effects. Unsurprisingly, an effect is unique to each agent. As the purpose of this work is to assess the effectiveness of decision trees, we introduce the following rules which capture effects as identical for all agents:

Definition 4 (Influencing Agents). *The set $IA \subseteq A \times A$ captures Influencing Agents, where any $(a, a') \in IA$ indicates that a' can influence a and $a \neq a'$.*

The influencing agents is for the purpose of defining inference rules for the *Messenger* effect. The following rules capture this:

$$\frac{(a, c, l, \Theta_a) \xrightarrow{\text{bchange}(usable)} (a, c', l, \Theta_a)\ (\exists(a', permit) \in \Theta_a \wedge (a, a') \in IA)}{(a, c, l, \Theta_a)|IA \xrightarrow{\text{messP}(usable)} (a, c', l, \Theta_a)|IA} \tag{9}$$

$$\frac{(a, c, l, \Theta_a) \xrightarrow{\text{bchange}(secure)} (a, c', l, \Theta_a)\ (\exists(a', deny) \in \Theta_a \wedge (a, a') \in IA)}{(a, c, l, \Theta_a)|IA \xrightarrow{\text{messD}(secure)} (a, c', l, \Theta_a)|IA} \tag{10}$$

For *Social Norms*, we care about the number of agents that have been observed for a particular action. Given a set of observations, we can establish how many agents have been observed performing a particular action. The importance of this work is not the formal definitions of influences, but rather the accuracy of decisions trees when these effects are in place. As such, we don't provide the notation for the *Social Norms* effect.

4 Multi Agent System - Simulation

For clarification, we acknowledge that at times, certain rules within the system can be executed synchronously. For example, it is possible that a behaviour change rule and an observing rule can occur synchronously. For now, we consider that a behaviour change rule takes priority. In the case of two similar rules conflicting with each other, we let the simulation tool use a random number generator to address this. We hope to improve this in later work.

4.1 Model Parameters

For the simulation, we reflect behaviours and attributes that we know exist. We understand that, whilst we will not have a model that truly reflects human behaviour, we at least can parameterise concepts that we know exist from the literature. Our parameters are as follows:

- p_1: Expected Arrival Rate - Agents arrive stochastically to the workplace reception, the arrival rate follows a normal distribution, agents can arrive at any point within some bounds. For example, if a start time for work is 9AM, we might expect some agents to turn up early, just before, just after, late or precisely on time.
- p_2: Probabilistic Decision - Assumptions have been made towards individuals as being *homo economicus*, where we make decisions based on personal gain or internal heuristics for guiding behaviour which look to maximise some reward [11]. Additionally, each day, experience is slightly different and for an agent, this could be the difference between a *secure* agent acting *usable* and vice versa, which is what we capture with our probabilistic decision, the ability for agents to act against their security preference [16].
- p_3: Social Norms Influence - Social proof, where individuals assume the actions of those they have observed in order to reflect the interpreted cultural norms is apparent in many societies [14].
- p_4: Messenger Influence - *Authority*, is influencing by social/professional status, those we perceive to be in a position of power or responsibility can influence our behaviours [7,9].
- p_5: Personality - Different personalities react differently to the same influences. We implement personality traits for agents, where different personalities are subject to different influences:
    1. *Conscientiousness* - influenced by *Messenger*.
    2. *Agreeableness* - influenced by *Social Norms* and *Messenger*.
    3. *Extroversion* - influenced by *Social Norms* [18].

In a model, there is a distinct set of actions and observations recorded for agents. A trace generated from a model records agents moving between locations, tailgating being permitted or denied, agents successfully tailgating, agents failing to tailgate and agents observing tailgating being permitted or denied. This is all public information, the private information, such as the model parameters and agent contexts are not in a trace. A trace does not contain information such as if an agent can be influenced by *Messenger* or *Social Norms*. We do this to see if decision trees can determine the underlying rules for the different parameterised models.

5 Assessment Methodology

We define a model with a set of parameters such that each model contains a different set of parameters. However, the initial state of each model is identical in terms of agent context and agent location. We then run a number of simulations for each model and generate a trace for each simulation run. A model will therefore, be associated with many traces.

A trace contains the number of entries equal to the number of agents, where an entry contains all of the features for an agent and is accompanied by the final security preference of that agent. The features of agents are the number of violations, preventions, attempts at tailgating and the number of times an agent is in close proximity when tailgating between other agents occurs.

Given all of the traces for a model, we use cross validation to construct and assess the accuracy of using decision trees for each model. The cross validation consists of a training and testing phase, where the training is inclusive for the security preference of an agent and the testing phase is exclusive of the security preference.

A prediction from a decision tree is either *usable* or *secure*. If we consider secure as our target value then a *true-positive* (tp) is a correct prediction for *secure*, *true-negative* (tn) is a correct prediction for *usable*. *False-positive* (fp) is an incorrect prediction for *secure* and *false-negative* (fn) is an incorrect prediction for *usable*. From these we can calculate the error rate, precision and recall:

$$err(fp, fn, tp, tn) = \frac{fp + fn}{tp + tn + fp + fn} \tag{11}$$

$$(tp, fp) = \frac{tp}{tp + fp} \quad r(tp, fn) = \frac{tp}{tp + fn} \tag{12}$$

The cross validation creates a number of decision trees for each parameterised model. Given a set of Decision Trees D where a set of testing traces T are present. A testing trace contains a set of entries E excluding the security preference, where a function $f : D \times E \to O$ takes a decision tree, an entry and returns an outcome O where $O = \{fp_o, fn_o, tp_o, tn_o\}$.

$$g : \mathbb{N} \times \mathbb{N} \times \mathbb{N} \times \mathbb{N} \times D \times \mathbb{P}(E) \to \mathbb{N} \times \mathbb{N} \times \mathbb{N} \times \mathbb{N}$$

$$g(i,j,k,l,d,E) = \begin{cases} g((i+1),j,k,l,d,(E \setminus e)), & \exists e \in E \text{ where } f(d,e) = fp_0 \\ g(i,(j+1),k,l,d,(E \setminus e)), & \exists e \in E \text{ where } f(d,e) = fn_0 \\ g(i,j,(k+1),l,d,(E \setminus e)), & \exists e \in E \text{ where } f(d,e) = tp_0 \\ g(,j,k,(l+1),d,(E \setminus e)), & \exists e \in E \text{ where } f(d,e) = tn_0 \\ (i,j,k,l) & \text{otherwise} \end{cases}$$

$$(13)$$

Using the function g we can calculate the number of different types of outcomes a decision tree produces. We can then use the function $calc$ to assess the accuracy of a decision tree:

$$calc : D \times \mathbb{P}(P) \to [0,1]$$

$$calc(d,E) = err(g(0,0,0,0,d,E)) \tag{14}$$

Once we can calculate the error rate for one decision tree, we can then assess the accuracy of all the decision trees generated for a particular model:

$$\mu_{error}(D,E) = \frac{\sum_{d \in D} calc(d,E)}{|D|} \tag{15}$$

We do the same for the precision and recall of the decision trees, however, we do not provide the notation for this. Each model is associated with a set of decision trees. Therefore, for each model we can calculate μ_{error} to identify the accuracy of decision trees for a given set of parameters.

6 Analysis - Case Study

In this section we discuss the use of parameterised models and make remarks surrounding the results for three different cases.

The number of possible parameterised models is 2^5, we only consider 11 of these 32. The expected arrival rate is included in the majority of the parameterised models, as we do not consider too many models where all agents always arrive at the exact same time, of course this could happen, but it is very unlikely. The personality parameter is dependent upon a behaviour change parameter being present, therefore, it does not add to a model if *Social Norms* and/or the *Messenger* parameters are not included.

We used the *Julia* programming language to implement our case study and made use of the SysModels package [5,17]. We generated synthetic data on a Toshiba laptop with a 2.4 GHz i5 processor and 8 GB RAM. To generate the data for 11 models with 200 agents it took 22 min which is roughly 2 min per model. Each model is generated with 10 traces each starting from an identical initial state for each model.

For the analysis we performed four test cases and used 50, 100 and 200 agents. Table 2 is the results for the 100 agents, the results for 50 and 200 agents are in the Appendix in Tables 3 and 4 respectively.

Table 2. 100 Agents: p_1: Expected Arrival Rate; p_2: Probabilistic Decision; p_3: Norms Influence (Social Proof); p_4: Messenger Influence; p_5: Personality; $\mu(error)$: Average error rate of a model; $pr(s)$: The precision of the model towards *secure*; $r(s)$: The recall of the model for *secure*;

p_1	p_2	p_3	p_4	p_5	Model	$\mu(error)$	$\sigma(error)$	$pr(s)$	$r(s)$
					m_1	0.255	0.067	0.659	0.830
✓					m_2	0.001	0.002	1	0.997
✓	✓				m_3	0.234	0.028	0.697	0.712
✓		✓			m_4	0.073	0.019	0.963	0.953
✓			✓		m_5	0.160	0.024	0.884	0.898
✓		✓	✓		m_6	0.094	0.018	0.928	0.938
✓			✓	✓	m_7	0.114	0.016	0.904	0.910
✓	✓	✓			m_8	0.271	0.024	0.724	0.731
✓	✓		✓		m_9	0.367	0.031	0.634	0.624
✓		✓	✓	✓	m_{10}	0.027	0.012	0.975	0.969
✓	✓	✓	✓	✓	m_{11}	0.277	0.028	0.675	0.675

For each test case, we calculated the average error rate, the standard deviation, the precision and the recall of each parameterised model, where Table 2 shows the parameters for each model. We now make remarks regarding the results we have obtained.

Remark 1. *The average error rate for model m_1 is significantly more accurate with 50 than 100 or 200 agents.*

With regards to Remark 1, as the expected arrival time is not set, all agents arrive at the same time. The majority of agents don't ever permit, deny or attempt to tailgate, therefore, a decision tree will make inaccurate predictions for some agents, particularly when more than 50 agents are used.

Remark 2. *If the probabilistic parameter is set, then the average error rate significantly increases. In particular, it impacts more than both the Messenger and Social Norms parameters.*

The use of the probabilistic parameter significantly increases the average error rate of the decision trees. Due to the uncertainty of agent behaviour, i.e. *secure* agents acting *usable* and vice versa, a *secure* agent could have always behaved as *usable*. A classifier model would always conclude that they are *usable* when they are in fact *secure*. Whilst Remark 2 is not surprising, the impact of uncertain behaviour against social influences is a useful result for a security practitioner. In the real world, some people will always be *secure* or *usable*, some hover between the two and some are slightly more *secure* or slightly more *usable*, some insight towards these numbers would allow us to calculate the impact of agents towards a model.

Remark 3. *The Messenger influence has a slightly more of an impact to the error rate, precision and recall of a model than Social Norms. It is true for all four of the test cases. They both impact the error rate, precision and recall of every model.*

The influences themselves differ in how they are implemented. The *Messenger* relies on an agent observing a behaviour of another agent that they consider to be an authoritative figure. The *Social Norms* is a cumulative influence, where the number of observations of a particular action can trigger the security preference of an agent to change. For Remark 3, the interest is that they are not probabilistic behaviours, they are private behaviours.

We have defined very simple rules for our influences. We wish to know if decision trees are capable of generating rules to deal with these simple behaviour changes. Given the data for our number of agents. We can see a slight improvement when 200 agents are present. However, the decision trees still perform poorly for these basic implementations of influences.

Remark 4. *On average, the models for 200 agents are more accurate than 50 and 100 agents.*

A trend emerged for the accuracy of models as we increased the number of agents. Whilst some of the models were more accurate for 50 agents, in general Remark 4 holds, in particular for the complex models where influences and probabilistic decisions are present. This is due to an increase number of entries to train decision trees, improving its accuracy.

Overall, we can see that with some basic aspects of human behaviour such as an uncertainty of decisions between *secure* and *usable* agents, the decision trees perform poorly. Even more so that we are just considering the polar opposites for security preferences. Whilst the influencing effects implemented are relatively simple, we believe as they increase in complexity, i.e. become heterogeneous for each agent, this would reduce the accuracy of decision trees even more. On another note, and mainly due to processing limitations, it's not clear if the accuracy can be improved by generating thousands of traces to use in the cross validation analysis.

7 Conclusion

In this paper we designed a multi agent system to generate synthetic data. Secondly, we identified features from the synthetic data. Finally, using cross validation we trained and tested many different decision trees for four test cases.

The generated decision trees showed that as the complexity of human behaviour increases, the less accurate decision trees are for predicting attributes, in this case, the security preference of employees. The remarks from Sect. 6 highlight the important features of the models with regards to the parameters. For example, probabilistic decisions impact the model significantly more than influences with regards to the error rate, precision and recall. Between the influences, the *Messenger* influence had a greater impact, however, this is partially down to how a security practitioner or designer implements behaviour change.

The insights towards the impact of these different parameters allows for an understanding between the limitations of decision trees and predicting security preferences. In particular, the certainty in the accuracy of the decision trees.

The three elements of the MAS allow for the bigger problem to be broken down into manageable chunks towards validation. For example, focusing on how we observe and formalising this notion will further support the work carried out here. Interviews to evaluate how our behaviour changes, again, will improve the MAS presented in this work.

The future of this work will target the unanswered questions that we can draw from this paper. Providing validation for those three elements of the multi agent system which are the physical locations, observations and behaviour change. Calculating the impact the parameters have towards error rate, precision and recall would allow a security practitioner to identify when probabilistic agents, influences or any other behaviours are present without having prior knowledge as we did. The techniques for building classifier models will be explored, for example, by considering different algorithms for building classifier trees, or sampling a range of features to assess the importance of each feature.

Appendix A Additional Results

Table 3. 50 Agents; See Table 2 for column definitions.

Model	$\mu(error)$	$\sigma(error)$	$pr(s)$	$r(s)$
m_1	0.070	0.037	0.896	0.943
m_2	0.018	0.010	0.974	0.980
m_3	0.279	0.035	0.658	0.642
m_4	0.050	0.025	0.947	0.950
m_5	0.162	0.029	0.853	0.867
m_6	0.031	0.018	0.955	0.977
m_7	0.091	0.030	0.893	0.937
m_8	0.266	0.039	0.701	0.686
m_9	0.365	0.051	0.694	0.656
m_{10}	0.017	0.012	0.976	0.986
m_{11}	0.325	0.056	0.622	0.581

Table 4. 200 Agents; See Table 2 for column definitions.

Model	$\mu(error)$	$\sigma(error)$	$pr(s)$	$r(s)$
m_1	0.201	0.135	0.861	0.912
m_2	0.006	0.003	0.996	0.998
m_3	0.170	0.013	0.910	0.888
m_4	0.014	0.006	0.993	0.993
m_5	0.050	0.009	0.976	0.972
m_6	0.024	0.007	0.984	0.990
m_7	0.047	0.011	0.976	0.973
m_8	0.140	0.021	0.933	0.912
m_9	0.277	0.029	0.833	0.812
m_{10}	0.040	0.008	0.975	0.980
m_{11}	0.161	0.016	0.920	0.892

References

1. Bartsch, S., Sasse, M.A.: How users bypass access control and why: the impact of authorization problems on individuals and the organization (2012)
2. Beautement, A., Sasse, M.A., Wonham, M., The compliance budget: managing security behaviour in organisations. In: Proceedings of 2008 Workshop on New Security Paradigms, pp. 47–58. ACM (2009)
3. Blythe, J., Koppel, R., Smith, S.W.: Circumvention of security: good users do bad things. IEEE Secur. Priv. **11**(5), 80–83 (2013)
4. Caulfield, T., Parkin, S.: Case study: predicting the impact of a physical access control intervention. In: STAST (Socio-Technical Aspects of Security and Trust) (2016, in publication)
5. Caulfield, T., Pym, D.: Improving security policy decisions with models. IEEE Secur. Priv. **13**(5), 34–41 (2015)
6. Cheh, C., Chen, B., Temple, W.G., Sanders, W.H.: Data-driven model-based detection of malicious insiders via physical access logs. In: Bertrand, N., Bortolussi, L. (eds.) QEST 2017. LNCS, vol. 10503, pp. 275–291. Springer, Cham (2017). https://doi.org/10.1007/978-3-319-66335-7_17
7. Cialdini, R.B., Garde, N.: Influence, vol. 3. A. Michel (1987)
8. Das, S., Kim, T.H.-J., Dabbish, L.A., Hong, J.I.: The effect of social influence on security sensitivity. In: Proceedings of SOUPS, vol. 14 (2014)
9. Dolan, P., Hallsworth, M., Halpern, D., King, D., Metcalfe, R., Vlaev, I.: Influencing behaviour: the mindspace way. J. Econ. Psychol. **33**(1), 264–277 (2012)
10. Dolan, P., Hallsworth, M., Halpern, D., King, D., Vlaev, I.: Mindspace: influencing behaviour for public policy (2010)
11. Frank, R.H.: If homo economicus could choose his own utility function, would he want one with a conscience? Am. Econ. Rev. **77**, 593–604 (1987)
12. Gellert, A., Vintan, L.: Person movement prediction using hidden Markov models. Stud. Inform. Control **15**(1), 17 (2006)
13. Michie, S., van Stralen, M.M., West, R.: The behaviour change wheel: a new method for characterising and designing behaviour change interventions. Implement. Sci. **6**(1), 42 (2011)

14. Rao, H., Greve, H.R., Davis, G.F.: Fool's gold: social proof in the initiation and abandonment of coverage by wall street analysts. Adm. Sci. Q. **46**(3), 502–526 (2001)
15. Shaw, R.S., Chen, C.C., Harris, A.L., Huang, H.-J.: The impact of information richness on information security awareness training effectiveness. Comput. Educ. **52**(1), 92–100 (2009)
16. Thaler, R.H.: From homo economicus to homo sapiens. J. Econ. Perspect. **14**(1), 133–141 (2000)
17. Tristanc: SysModels Package, February 2017. https://github.com/tristanc/SysModels. Accessed 08 June 2017
18. Uebelacker, S., Quiel, S.: The social engineering personality framework. In: 2014 Workshop on Socio-Technical Aspects in Security and Trust (STAST), pp. 24–30. IEEE (2014)
19. Witten, I.H., Frank, E., Hall, M.A., Pal, C.J.: Data Mining: Practical Machine Learning Tools and Techniques. Morgan Kaufmann, Burlington (2016)
20. Zhu, F., Carpenter, S., Kulkarni, A., Kolimi, S.: Reciprocity attacks. In: Proceedings of 7th Symposium on Usable Privacy and Security, p. 9. ACM (2011)

Controlling Production Variances in Complex Business Processes

Paul Griffioen[1], Rob Christiaanse[1,2(✉)], and Joris Hulstijn[3]

[1] Delft University of Technology, Delft, Netherlands
p.r.griffioen@tudelft.nl
[2] EFCO Solutions, Amsterdam, Netherlands
r.christiaanse@efco-solutions.nl
[3] Tilburg University, Tilburg, Netherlands
j.hulstijn@uvt.nl

Abstract. Products can consist of many sub-assemblies and small disturbances in the process can lead to larger negative effects downstream. Such variances in production are a challenge from a quality control and operational risk management perspective but also it distorts the assurance processes from an auditing perspective. To control production effectively waste needs to be taken into account in normative models, but this is complicated by cumulative effects. We developed an analytical normative model based on the bill of material, that derives the rejection rates from the underlying processes without direct measurement. The model enables improved analysis and prediction. If the rejection rate is not taken into account the function of the bill of material as a reference model deteriorates and therefore output measures become more opaque and harder to verify. As a consequence it is extremely difficult or even impossible to assess efficiency and effectiveness of operations. Secondly it is impossible to judge whether net salable assets represent the correct amount and finally it is impossible to assert whether the operations do comply to company standards and applicable laws.

1 Introduction

Technological advances have enabled more and more sophisticated production processes. This leads to a vision of smart manufacturing: "fully-integrated, collaborative manufacturing systems that respond in real time to meet changing demands and conditions in the factory, in the supply network, and in customer needs" [8,17]. However, the flexibility allowed by smart manufacturing, also leads to challenges for quality control and operational risk management. Products can consist of many sub-assemblies and small disturbances in the process can lead to larger negative effects downstream. Such variances in production processes are a challenge from a control perspective. Here control can be understood in the sense of feedback and feed forward mechanisms for optimizing the production process [10], but also in the sense of management control [14] or internal control [5]. All types of control and assurance processes require reliable predictions and a reliable information systems of what actually happened to support management

© Springer International Publishing AG 2018
A. Cerone and M. Roveri (Eds.): SEFM 2017 Workshops, LNCS 10729, pp. 72–85, 2018.
https://doi.org/10.1007/978-3-319-74781-1_6

decisions about production planning, budget, resource allocation and so on, but also to ensure compliance with laws and regulations. In order to assess whether objectives are met, a *reference model* is needed, that generates a set of criteria to test evidence against [4,22]. In case of manufacturing, such a reference model is based on the way engineers have designed the product and therefore the production process. So the reference model can be depicted as known numerical ratios between different parts of an enterprise's value creation process. Hence by design input and output of resources, equipment and finished products are related by certain specific ratios, depending on the construction of an end-product. Typically, such ratios appear in the Bill of Material (BoM). In accounting theory, such ratios are used to cross-verify accuracy and completeness of reporting [19]. It needs no elaboration that similar equations are used in materials resource planning to control the production process, for planning and scheduling, and for ordering resources [11]. To manage the production process we look at the production volumes using the BoM. The BoM takes a central position in the relationship between volumes and cost. It can be used to decompose products into atomic units and conversely to accumulate quantities from basic units to composite products. Although the BoM is static, it must somehow be reflected in the production process that transforms the parts into the end product.

In this paper we develop a method to specify an analytic normative model of a production process, based on the BoM to relate the volume of end products with the total production volume. The BoM contains all the necessary information to calculate the volume ratios for different products flowing through a process without looking at the actual process details. The computations are an adaptation of Leontief's input output models. Leontief matrices were originally developed to model the input and output of different sectors on a macro economic scale [20]. These models were later extended with parameters for waste and used to indirectly measure how wasteful various parts of the economy were [1,12]. This idea of measuring indirectly is the basis for the computations in this paper, but applied to production processes. Besides the application to input output models, Leontief matrices are also useful for the netting problem in production planning. In this case the bill of material is used to relate input and output volumes of business processes [9]. The computations are similar, but now in a micro economic setting. Given the BoM and the actual volumes we extend the model to calculate the rejection rate. The rejection percentage per product or part gives a fair view of the quantity of waste. In cases the rejection rate is not taken into account, the expected waste is hard to predict because of the cumulative effect. In this circumstance the function of the BoM as a reference model deteriorates. Calculations become more opaque and harder to verify. As a consequence it is impossible to assess efficiency and effectiveness of operations, it is impossible to judge whether net salable assets represent the correct amount and finally it is impossible to assert whether the operations do comply to company standards and applicable laws.

This research makes a scientific contribution to literature about smart manufacturing [8] and use of ICT in production processes [13], but also to literature about computational auditing techniques [16]. Especially we concentrate on a specific measurement problem which has important implications in designing performance management systems.

The outline of the paper is as follows. In Sect. 2 we discuss the role of reference models and motivate why they are needed. In Sect. 3 we provide in an illustrative case: production of integrated circuits which serves as a running example to enhance comprehensibility. In Sect. 4 we start with the nature of a BoM and how the exploded BoM is used from a normative setting to calculate the component variances. In Sects. 5 and 6 we extend the BoM computations with rejection and provide in detail how a BoM can be represented and how waste can be accounted for. In Sects. 7 and 8 we discuss the results applicable in control settings and end up with some conclusions.

2   Reference Models

When data are being processed and used by people for decision making or control purposes, the reliability of the data (accuracy and completeness) becomes a necessary condition [21]. Information integrity concerns the *representational faithfulness* of the information relative to the condition or subject matter being represented [2]. Representational faithfulness involves both accuracy and completeness and therefore timeliness too, as well as the validity with respect to applicable rules and regulations [2]. Reliability and integrity are closely related to information quality in general: reliability buttresses relevance and usability of information. In other words the presented information is bound to be less relevant or usable, when it cannot be relied upon.

Designing reliable information systems is crucial for many stakeholders. For example, business controllers need detailed information to judge whether business operations are efficient and effective. Financial accountants are concerned whether the general ledger is complete and faithfully represents the financial outcomes of business transactions. Internal auditors monitor the effectiveness of the internal controls, to ensure (1) effectiveness and efficiency of operations, (2) reliability of financial reporting, and (3) compliance with applicable laws and regulations [6,7]. Thus, information systems have several functions. They may help to (i) collect and analyze evidence in order to monitor, detect and correct undesired behavior, and (ii) to facilitate the organization to be 'in control' by preventing undesired behavior. Both these functions rely on formal models of the processes and procedures. Business controllers, financial accountants and internal auditors share a common problem. To judge the outcomes of business transactions from an operational, financial or compliance point of view, requires a reference model to assess any flaws in the inter- and intra-organizational workflows. For instance, in case participants do not comply with company standards, additional control measures like rewards and punishment should be put in place [15,18]. However, production processes may lead to production variances that are difficult to control.

Reference models must therefore be able to handle the production variances to preserve predictability – representational faithfulness – and ensure usability for decision purposes. In general, production variances play a central role for material resource planning and control purposes [11]. The financial department is interested in the production variances to determine the actual losses on production and determine the net salable assets. Internal and external auditors use the variance analysis to determine the audit approach and the audit techniques to gather assertion based audit evidence in audit engagements like financial statement audits. It needs no elaboration that for production processes such analysis can become very difficult.

3   Motivating Case

An example of a production process with varying material usage is the production of Integrated Circuits (IC). To produce integrated circuits, assembly companies need to accurately deal with information flow through wafer delivery, receiving, storage, wafer receiving, packaging, testing, finishing, and shipping in order to fulfill customer demand. This means that companies need to integrate various kinds of internal and external data by means of ICT in order to improve productivity [13].

The production of an integrated circuit transforms silicon and various other materials into an integrated circuit. The first step is to produce wafers from silicon. Wafers are discs of silicon on which various layers of other materials are placed. These layers make up the logical circuits. Many identical circuits are printed and later the wafer is cut into dies. Each die is placed in a case and connected with wires to pins. The following table gives some hypothetical material usage in a finished IC. In this case 200 dies are cut from a single wafer.

Product	Material
IC	Die, Case, Wire 0.8 mg
Die	Wafer 1/200
Wafer	Silicon 10 g, Metal 0.12 g

Suppose management is faced with varying cost of materials for production runs with similar production volumes. How can such varying costs be controlled? Since total cost does not provide much information, management could look at production numbers. For example after production of 50,000 ICs and 400 wafers in two subsequent runs the following total production numbers are reported.

Product	Volume I	Volume II
IC	53800.0	53700.0
Die	125900.0	82000.0
Case	53900.0	54000.0
Wafer	1460.0	1150.0
Wire	43700.0 mg	43600.0 mg
Silicon	14700.0 g	11600.0 g
Metal	176.0 g	139.0 g

From a business control perspective these numbers are quite challenging. In the case we compare the outputs from the two subsequent production batches we expect that the used materials and components measured show some logical pattern. How do we judge the extreme upsweep in the used Die, Wafer and Silicon compared to 100 used IC's. In the next section we introduce the BoM as a means for judgement.

4   The Bill of Material

The bill of material (BoM) serves as a reference for product data and contains a list of the parts or components that are required to build a product [11]. A BoM is a multi-level document that provides build data for multiple sub-assemblies (products within products) and includes for each item: part number, approved manufacturers list (AML), mechanical characteristics and a whole range of component descriptors. In some cases the BoM may also include attached reference files, such as part specifications, CAD files and schematics. Managing a production process is equivalent to managing the BoM, in order to track product changes and maintain an accurate list of required components at a certain phase in the production process.

For this paper the most important information in a product's BoM is the parts from which it is composed and in what amount. A product can be atomic, meaning it has no parts, or it can be composed from other products. The amount is needed because the same type of part may be used more than once. If parts can be arbitrarily divided, for example in the case of liquids, the amount need not be restricted to integers.

The BoM for a given collection of products specify a numerical relation among those products. For two products it tells how much of one product is used in the composition of the other. For computational purposes the relation formed by the bills of material is written as a matrix, say matrix B with

$$B_{i,j} = \text{"The amount of product } i \text{ that is used by product } j.\text{"}$$

Each column j in this B-matrix contains the amounts from the bill of material of the j-th product. In the remainder of the paper the distinction between the individual bills and the matrix is not made and the term *bill of material* or abbreviation *bom* is used to refer to the entire collection.

The IC example of the previous section gives the following BoM matrix:

$$B = \begin{pmatrix} 0 & 0 & 0 & 0 & 0 & 0 & 0 \\ 1 & 0 & 0 & 0 & 0 & 0 & 0 \\ 1 & 0 & 0 & 0 & 0 & 0 & 0 \\ 0 & 0.005 & 0 & 0 & 0 & 0 & 0 \\ 0.800 & 0 & 0 & 0 & 0 & 0 & 0 \\ 0 & 0 & 0 & 10.000 & 0 & 0 & 0 \\ 0 & 0 & 0 & 0.120 & 0 & 0 & 0 \end{pmatrix}$$

The rows and columns are indexed by the products {IC, Die, Case, Wafer, Wire, Silicon, Metal} in that order.

A BoM can be 'exploded' to handle its recursive structure. For any vector x containing some product volume, multiplication $B \cdot x$ is the volume of all parts from which the products are directly composed. We could compute $B \cdot B \cdot x$ to obtain the volume at the next level and if we continue this indefinitely and add all results we obtain the volume of all direct and indirect parts. An elegant solution from operations research uses the mathematical fact that $I + B + B^2 + B^3 + \cdots$ equals $(I - B)^{-1}$, which is the generalization of identity $(\Sigma i : 0 \leq i : a^i) = (1 - a)^{-1}$ for the geometric series for scalars [9,20]. Define function Υ.

$$\Upsilon(B) = \sum_{0 \leq n} B^n = (I - B)^{-1}$$

Matrix $\Upsilon(B)$ is called the exploded BoM and can be used to compute total volume from output volume.

Example. With the exploded BoM the total production volume can be computed from the output volume

$$ideal = \Upsilon(B) \cdot output$$

$$= \begin{pmatrix} 1 & 0 & 0 & 0 & 0 & 0 & 0 \\ 1 & 1 & 0 & 0 & 0 & 0 & 0 \\ 1 & 0 & 1 & 0 & 0 & 0 & 0 \\ 0.005 & 0.005 & 0 & 1 & 0 & 0 & 0 \\ 0.800 & 0 & 0 & 0 & 1 & 0 & 0 \\ 0.050 & 0.050 & 0 & 10.000 & 0 & 1 & 0 \\ 0.001 & 0.001 & 0 & 0.120 & 0 & 0 & 1 \end{pmatrix} \cdot \begin{pmatrix} 50000.0 \\ 0 \\ 0 \\ 400.0 \\ 0 \\ 0 \\ 0 \end{pmatrix} = \begin{pmatrix} 50000.0 \\ 50000.0 \\ 50000.0 \\ 650.0 \\ 40000.0 \\ 6500.0 \\ 78.0 \end{pmatrix}$$

These numbers specify the ideal volume to produce 50,000 ICs and the 400 wafers. Often these are the products that end up in the end product, but as in the case for wafers it can also be an intermediate product.

Waste corresponds to the produced items that do not end up in an end product. Knowing the ideal parts we can compute it by subtracting that from the total volume. The waste in the running example is

$$waste = totvol - ideal = \begin{pmatrix} 53800.0 \\ 125900.0 \\ 53900.0 \\ 1460.0 \\ 43700.0 \\ 14700.0 \\ 176.0 \end{pmatrix} - \begin{pmatrix} 50000.0 \\ 50000.0 \\ 50000.0 \\ 650.0 \\ 40000.0 \\ 6500.0 \\ 78.0 \end{pmatrix} = \begin{pmatrix} 3800.0 \\ 75900.0 \\ 3900.0 \\ 810.0 \\ 3700.0 \\ 8200.0 \\ 98.0 \end{pmatrix}$$

Vector *totvol* is the reported total volume given in the case description.

Dividing the waste by the total volume gives waste fraction

Product	Waste I	Waste II
IC	7.1%	6.9%
Die	60.3%	39.0%
Case	7.2%	7.4%
Wafer	55.5%	43.5%
Wire	8.5%	8.3%
Silicon	55.8%	44.0%
Metal	55.7%	43.9%

The exploded BoM surely helps to analyse from a normative stance to analyse the extreme upsweep in the used Die, Wafer and Silicon compared to 100 used IC's as identified in Sect. 3. There is one problem we have to address. A BoM models an ideal world. In reality however production plans do address the possibility that components and half fabricates get rejected due to norm deviations. Consequently the above waste calculations I and II are smudged by the components and half fabricates that get rejected. The waste calculations suffer from what we coin the cumulative effect caused by this type of measurement error. So instead of modelling waste we have to model rejections. This can be done by extending the exploded BoM with a reject vector as we will see in the next section.

5   Modeling Rejection Computationally

The computation from the previous section requires the output and the production volume to be specified as vectors. Total production is denoted by *totvol*:

$totvol_i$ = "The total production volume of the i-th product."

and vector *output* is the volume of end-products:

$output_i$ = "The end-product volume of the i-th product."

Whether a product is an end product or not is a property of physical products, not of abstract products. A subset of an abstract product's instances might be used as end products, while the rest is used as part in other products. Since every produced end product must have been processed, inequality *output* $\leq$ *totvol* must always hold. For products with end products only this turns into equality.

To model waste and rejection the characteristic recursive equation of the exploded bill of material is extended with a reject vector. Equation

$$totvol = \Upsilon(B) \cdot output \tag{1}$$

from the previous section is a solution to recursive equation

$$totvol = output + B \cdot totvol \tag{2}$$

This recursive equation expresses the nesting in the products' bills of material. Instead of working with rejection, it is mathematically more convenient to work with the fraction of products that is accepted:

$\alpha_i = $ "the fraction of product i's volume that is accepted."

$= 1 - $ "the fraction of product i's volume that is rejected."

The basic equation that relates the quantities from the introduction is

$$\alpha \times totvol = output + B \cdot totvol \tag{3}$$

Everything in the remainder of this paper is derived from this equation. Before explaining it, the term $B \cdot totvol$ is examined first.

Value $B \cdot totvol$ is the key to the recursion in the equation. Earlier we saw the $B.x$ is the volume of all parts from which the products are directly composed, but now we are interested in special case $B \cdot totvol$. Since $totvol$ is the total flow $B \cdot totvol$ contains each end product's direct parts but also the parts at deeper levels of composition, but in ideal amounts. The amounts have to be corrected for rejected parts. So the interpretation of $B \cdot totvol$ is that it is the volume of all non rejected parts flowing through the process.

Continuing from the interpretation of $B \cdot totvol$ of the previous paragraph we derive that since $output$ is the ideal end-product volume that the sum of $output$ and $B \cdot totvol$ must equal the total ideal flow. Another expression for the total ideal flow is $\alpha \times totvol$. Putting both expressions together gives the equation.

The hardest problem is to calculate $totvol$ given $output$ and α. If $totvol$ and $output$ are given we can directly calculate α by rewriting the equation to

$$\alpha = (output + B \cdot totvol) / totvol$$

Calculation $output$ from $totvol$ and α is done by rewriting the equation to

$$output = \alpha \times totvol - B \cdot totvol$$

For real physical production processes this result cannot contain negative numbers. The next section deals with the solution if $output$ and α are known. First we give an example computing α.

Example. Given the bill of material from the previous example and the following volumes we can calculate α. Compute

$$\alpha = \frac{output + B \cdot totvol}{totvol}$$

$$= \frac{\begin{pmatrix} 50000.0 \\ 0 \\ 0 \\ 400.0 \\ 0 \\ 0 \\ 0 \end{pmatrix} + \begin{pmatrix} 0 & 0 & 0 & 0 & 0\ 0\ 0 \\ 1 & 0 & 0 & 0 & 0\ 0\ 0 \\ 1 & 0 & 0 & 0 & 0\ 0\ 0 \\ 0 & 0.005 & 0 & 0 & 0\ 0\ 0 \\ 0.800 & 0 & 0 & 0 & 0\ 0\ 0 \\ 0 & 0 & 0 & 10.000 & 0\ 0\ 0 \\ 0 & 0 & 0 & 0.120 & 0\ 0\ 0 \end{pmatrix} \cdot \begin{pmatrix} 53800.0 \\ 125900.0 \\ 53900.0 \\ 1460.0 \\ 43700.0 \\ 14700.0 \\ 176.0 \end{pmatrix}}{\begin{pmatrix} 53800.0 \\ 125900.0 \\ 53900.0 \\ 1460.0 \\ 43700.0 \\ 14700.0 \\ 176.0 \end{pmatrix}}$$

$$= \begin{pmatrix} 0.9294 \\ 0.4273 \\ 0.9981 \\ 0.7051 \\ 0.9849 \\ 0.9932 \\ 0.9955 \end{pmatrix}$$

Now we have the actual reject. For comparison the waste table is repeated.

Product	Waste I	Waste II	Reject I	Reject II
IC	7.06%	6.89%	7.06%	6.89%
Die	60.29%	39.02%	57.27%	34.51%
Case	7.24%	7.41%	0.19%	0.56%
Wafer	55.48%	43.48%	29.49%	29.57%
Wire	8.47%	8.26%	1.51%	1.47%
Silicon	55.78%	43.97%	0.68%	0.86%
Metal	55.68%	43.88%	0.45%	0.72%

We think it needs no elaboration that introducing the reject vector extending the exploded BoM model was very effective. Comparing the results waste versus reject it becomes clear that Cases, Wire, Silicon and Metal waste is mostly caused by cumulative effects. Hence the Reject is measured indirectly so we are still not sure whether our calculations give a good picture to judge production outputs. As we will show in the next section we can model reject directly instead of indirectly. We expect to obtain the insightful results.

6   Using Rejection as Norm

Instead of computing the rejection from the waste, we can also use rejection as norm and compute normative production volumes and waste from it. Rejection can be used as norm by reversing the usage of the equation.

The central equation is conveniently solved with the aid of adjusted bill of material B/α. Matrix B/α is defined by

$$(B/\alpha)_{i,j} = B_{i,j} \: / \: \alpha_i$$

Matrix B's i-th row is scaled by the i-th factor from α. The result is that a matrix multiplication followed by a compensation for waste is combined into a single operation. It is easy to show that

$$(B/\alpha) \cdot x = (B \cdot x) \: / \: \alpha \tag{4}$$

Product $B \cdot x$ measures the usage of the product and dividing by α compensates for waste. We now can state a non-recursive equation for $totvol$. Applying it to the result of above derivation we get:

$$totvol \: = \: output/\alpha \: + \: (B/\alpha) \cdot totvol \tag{5}$$

Exploding then gives

$$totvol = \Upsilon(B/\alpha) \: \cdot \: (output/\alpha) \tag{6}$$

Vector $output/\alpha$ is the number of end-products adjusted for waste. Now we can calculate

$$totvol = \Upsilon(B/\alpha) \: \cdot \: (output/\alpha)$$

$$= \begin{pmatrix} 1 & 0 & 0 & 0 & 0\,0\,0 \\ 2.222 & 1 & 0 & 0 & 0\,0\,0 \\ 1 & 0 & 1 & 0 & 0\,0\,0 \\ 0.016 & 0.007 & 0 & 1 & 0\,0\,0 \\ 0.800 & 0 & 0 & 0 & 1\,0\,0 \\ 0.162 & 0.073 & 0 & 10.204 & 0\,1\,0 \\ 0.002 & 0.001 & 0 & 0.120 & 0\,0\,1 \end{pmatrix} \cdot \begin{pmatrix} 52631.6 \\ 0 \\ 0 \\ 571.4 \\ 0 \\ 0 \\ 0 \end{pmatrix}$$

$$= \begin{pmatrix} 53800.0 \\ 125900.0 \\ 53900.0 \\ 1460.0 \\ 43700.0 \\ 14700.0 \\ 176.0 \end{pmatrix}$$

So to produce the 50,000 ICs and 400 wafers we expect these numbers of products to flow through the process.

From the planned production we can also compute planned waste. First we determine planned waste given the normative reject fractions used earlier. The second table is the same planned waste, except the reject of the die is lowered from 55% to 35%. This causes a cumulative effect on wafers, silicon and metal of more than 10%.

Product	Reject I	Reject II	Waste I	Waste II
IC	5.00%	5.00%	5.00%	5.00%
Die	55.00%	35.00%	57.25%	38.25%
Case	0%	0%	5.00%	5.00%
Wafer	30.00%	30.00%	53.80%	43.47%
Wire	0%	0%	5.00%	5.00%
Silicon	2.00%	2.00%	54.72%	44.60%
Metal	0%	0%	53.80%	43.47%

The results are clear. By using rejection as norm and compute normative production volumes and waste from it gives us the precise insights. The calculations show that a product's waste may vary considerably, even when its reject does not vary.

7   Application in Control Environments

The example illustrates how only a little disturbance in the rejection rate will cause considerable effects in the assembly line of integrated circuits. Therefore it is more convenient to take rejection into account in reference models and derive waste from it. This can be done by extending the exploded BoM by a so called accept vector, which is defined as the fraction of product volume that is not rejected. Given the BoM and the actual volumes we can calculate the rejection rate. The rejection percentage per product or part gives a fair view of the quantity of waste.

Being in control starts with the key question: "can we judge production volumes and compare the results". We would like to defend that in general production volumes are difficult to judge without knowing the relationship between volumes of different products as we have seen in Sect. 3. The BoM gives a controller and managers insights in the normative relationships. Sure they should be reflected in the process, but misses process efficiency and occupancy rate norms. This is what we have seen in the end of Sect. 4. Without these norms the cumulative effect will give difficult to control varying numbers. As we have demonstrated process efficiency norms can be computed from ideal BoM and overall numbers. Needless to say that these numbers should correspond to the actual process and are additionally very useful for benchmarks, cross-checking and reconsolidation controls.

The implication is that we can infer that the information based on the exploded BoM extended with the reject vector is consistent so that differences between reject percentages actually inform us about the efficiency and effectiveness of the assembly processes. Waste suffers from cumulative effects which gives us the wrong information so that it is impossible to verify the actual outcome in terms of rational expectations and costing behavior. Any procedure to assess waste without the reject vector is bound to be an illusion.

In that case also the costing behavior will be harder to predict and it will be harder to judge whether generated volumes correspond to predicted volumes, to find out whether records are represented faithfully. Indeed the hidden error would influence inventory levels and therefore affect procurement decisions. We expect that the return on investment will be negatively influenced by hidden errors caused by the cumulative effect. But there is another catch. In case the rejection rate is not taken into account, the expected waste is hard to predict. In this circumstance the function of the BoM as a reference model deteriorates. Calculations become more opaque and harder to verify. As a consequence it is impossible to assess efficiency and effectiveness of operations, it is impossible to judge whether net salable assets represent the correct amount and finally it is impossible to assert whether the operations do comply to company standards and applicable laws.

8 Conclusion

In this paper we have addressed the verification problem required by management, quality managers, and financial accountants or imposed by legal authorities. Verification of the accuracy and completeness of records, as guaranteed by a system of internal controls, requires a reference model. However, such models usually do not account for waste or losses. The issue was how to control the production variability in production processes.

A sound way to do this is to use the bill of material (BoM). The BoM takes a central position in the relation between volumes and cost. The BoM contains the information to calculate the volume ratios for different products flowing through a process. This can be quite difficult, because of the recursive nature of the calculations required for material handling, warehousing or procurement purposes. Using the BoM we do not need detailed registrations for every task executed in the processes to determine reject ratios.

In this paper we show how to define the relation between end products, waste, and components by a recursive matrix equation, that is based on the BoM. By exploding the BoM the ideal ratios can be calculated and compared with the actual outcome of the production process.

Auditors or financial controllers make use of so called audit equations, that capture the numerical ratios between the parts used in a value creation process [3]. Any waste disturbs the equations and consequently needs to be taken into account. Here we show, that in order to do predict the total volume of waste, it is enough to estimate the rejection rate, for each end-product or intermediate product. This research makes a scientific contribution to literature about smart manufacturing [8] and the use of ICT and data in production processes [13], but also contributes to the literature about computational auditing techniques [16]. In addition, it has practical value, for all those professionals who need a reference model to verify reports against, such as process controllers, as well as internal and external auditors. They need to account for waste too.

Acknowledgement. The research in this paper was supported by the SATIN research project, funded by NWO.

References

1. Baumol, W.J., Wolff, E.N.: A key role for input-output analysis in policy design. Reg. Sci. Urban Econ. **24**(1), 93–113 (1994)
2. Boritz, J.E.: Is practitioners' views on core concepts of information integrity. Int. J. Account. Inf. Syst. **6**(4), 260–279 (2005)
3. Christiaanse, R., Griffioen, P., Hulstijn, J.: Adaptive normative modelling: a case study in the public-transport domain. In: Janssen, M., Mäntymäki, M., Hidders, J., Klievink, B., Lamersdorf, W., van Loenen, B., Zuiderwijk, A. (eds.) I3E 2015. LNCS, vol. 9373, pp. 423–434. Springer, Cham (2015). https://doi.org/10.1007/978-3-319-25013-7_34
4. Christiaanse, R., Griffioen, P., Hulstijn, J.: Reliability of electronic evidence: an application for model-based auditing. In: Proceedings of 15th International Conference on Artificial Intelligence and Law, ICAIL 2015, pp. 43–52. ACM, New York (2015)
5. COSO: Internal control - integrated framework. Report, Committee of Sponsoring Organizations of the Treadway Commission (1992)
6. COSO: Enterprise risk management - integrated framework. Report, Committee of Sponsoring Organizations of the Treadway Commission (2004)
7. COSO: Guidance on monitoring internal control systems. Report, Committee of Sponsoring Organizations of the Treadway Commission, USA (2009)
8. Davis, J., Edgar, T., Porter, J., Bernaden, J., Sarli, M.: Smart manufacturing, manufacturing intelligence and demand-dynamic performance. Comput. Chem. Eng. **47**(20), 145–156 (2012)
9. Elmaghraby, S.E.: A note on the 'explosion' and 'netting' problems in the planning of materials requirements. Oper. Res. **11**(4), 530–535 (1963)
10. Engell, S.: Feedback control for optimal process operation. J. Process Control **17**, 203–219 (2007)
11. Jacobs, F.R., Weston Jr., F.C.: Enterprise resource planning (ERP)-a brief history. J. Oper. Manag. **25**, 357–363 (2007)
12. Leontief, W.: Environmental repercussions and the economic structure: an input-output approach. Rev. Econ. Stat. **52**(3), 262–271 (1970)
13. Liu, C.-M., Chen, L.S., Romanowski, R.M.: An electronic material flow control system for improving production efficiency in integrated-circuit assembly industry. Int. J. Adv. Manuf. Technol. **42**, 348–362 (2009)
14. Merchant, K.A.: Modern Management Control Systems, Text and Cases. Prentice Hall, Upper Saddle River (1998)
15. Merchant, K.A.: The control function of management. Sloan Manag. Rev. **23**(Summer), 43–55 (1982)

16. Moffitt, K.C., Vasarhelyi, M.A.: Accounting information systems in an age of big data. J. Inf. Syst. **27**(2), 1–19 (2013)
17. Rachuri, S.: Smart manufacturing systems design and analysis. Report, National Institute of Standards and Technology (NIST) (2014)
18. Simons, R.: Levers of Control: How Managers Use Innovative Control Systems to Drive Strategic Renewal. Harvard Business School Press, Boston (1995)
19. Starreveld, R.W., de Mare, H.B., Joëls, E.J.: Bestuurlijke informatieverzorging, volume deel 1: Algemene grondslagen, 2nd edn. Samson Uitgeverij, Aplhen aan den Rijn/Brussel (1988). (in Dutch)
20. Strang, G.: Linear Algebra and its Applications. Brooks Cole, Belmont (1988)
21. Strong, D.M., Lee, Y.W., Wang, R.Y.: Data quality in context. Commun. ACM **40**(5), 103–110 (1997)
22. Weigand, H., Elsas, P.: Model-based auditing using REA. Int. J. Account. Inf. Syst. **13**(3), 287–310 (2012). 2011 Research Symposium on Information Integrity & Information Systems Assurance

A Computational Model of Internet Addiction Phenomena in Social Networks

Lucia Nasti and Paolo Milazzo[✉]

Dipartimento di Informatica, Università di Pisa,
Largo Bruno Pontecorvo 3, 56127 Pisa, Italy
{lucia.nasti,milazzo}@di.unipi.it

Abstract. Addiction is a complex phenomenon, stemming from environmental, biological and psychological causes. It is defined as a natural response of the body to external stimuli, such as drugs, alcohol, but also job, love and Internet technologies, that become compulsive needs, difficult to remove. At the neurological level, the Dopamine System plays a key role in the addiction process. Mathematical models of the Dopamine System have been proposed to study addiction to nicotine, drugs and gambling. In this paper, we propose a Hybrid Automata model of the Dopamine System, based on the mathematical model proposed by Gutkin et al. Our model allows different kinds of addiction causes to be described. In particular, we consider the problem of Internet addiction and its spread through interaction on social networks. This study is undertaken by performing simulations of virtual social networks by varying the network topology and the interaction propensity of users. We show that scale-free networks favour the emergence of addiction phenomena, in particular when users having a high propensity to interaction are present.

Keywords: Computational model · Hybrid Automata · Simulation
Scale-free networks · Dopamine System · Internet addiction
Social networks

1 Introduction

Addiction is a social and complex phenomenon that has had different interpretations over the years. We can define it as a natural response of the body to some substances and external stimuli that, having a strong repercussion on the organism, become a compulsive need. This condition is difficult to remove because addiction produces a false feeling of wellness, which leads to a total loss of control and to repeat the same actions periodically. Many factors contribute to the development of addiction; it can be influenced by biological, psychological and environmental factors.

From the biological point of view, the brain has the central role: many neural circuits and, above all, the Dopamine System, are involved in the addiction process [16]. Dopamine is a neurotransmitter and has many functions in the

© Springer International Publishing AG 2018
A. Cerone and M. Roveri (Eds.): SEFM 2017 Workshops, LNCS 10729, pp. 86–100, 2018.
https://doi.org/10.1007/978-3-319-74781-1_7

body. In the brain, it has a key role in the reward system: the level of dopamine changes after a desired external stimulus is received (the achievement of a goal, the intake of a chemical substance, etc.), producing a sensation of pleasure. Such a sensation may induce the subject to look for a repetition of the stimulus. If repetition happens too frequently, the subject may enter an addiction state in which the effect of dopamine decreases (tolerance). This can cause the addict to look for stronger stimuli and to suffer in case of absence of stimuli.

Environmental aspects of addiction are the subject of recent studies [2], focusing on the impact of age, sex and social background on the spread of addiction, on which the effect of the peer group acts too. Indeed, some habits are easily shared in social aggregation because of the emulation principle for which people in a group tend to imitate each other.

In this paper, we study Internet addiction, namely the excessive Internet (and technology) use that may interfere with daily life, and the way it spreads through the interaction on social networks. In particular, we show that the scale-free topology of social networks could be a favoring factor for the spread of Internet addiction among their users.

To facilitate and improve the comprehension of this particular kind of addiction, we examined it from a computational perspective. Our hypothesis combines the last theories about the use of social networks by the users [8] and the available computational models of addiction to drugs [15] and nicotine [9] (since up to our knowledge there are no other models on Internet addiction in the literature).

We start from the mathematical model proposed by Gutkin et al. in [9] for the study of nicotine addiction. Such a model describes the main neurological processes involved in addiction phenomena and it has been validated against experimental data [6]. Moreover, the model describes the interaction between dopamine and neurological receptors that lead to persistent changes in brain structures (due to neuronal plasticity) that really occur in the case of addiction.

In our work, we simplify and, subsequently, extend the model proposed by Gutkin et al. in order to adapt it to different forms of addiction. To this purpose, we define our model in terms of Hybrid Automata [10], that allow us to better describe the different responses of the Dopamine System to stimuli of different intensities, and to better separate the description of the neural structures from the description of the external stimuli that are the cause of addiction.

In order to show that our model is a conservative modification and extension of the model in [9], we perform simulations that reproduce the results on nicotine addiction already obtained by Gutkin et al. Subsequently, we move to the problem of Internet addiction by performing simulations of networks of individuals, rather than of a single subject. This means that in each simulation experiment the model is replicated as many times as the number of individuals of the network. Moreover, stimuli for an individual are represented by messages sent to and received from other individuals in the network. Consequently, each individual has his/her own dopamine level and stimuli may cause some of the individuals to become addict.

We perform simulation experiments of three kinds of network: a 2-nodes network, a star graph and scale-free networks. The first two kinds of network are used to reason on the model parameters (in particular, on the interaction propensity factor of social network users), while the scale-free networks (that may represent the structure of a real social network) are used to show that such a topology may actually favor the spread of Internet addiction.

2   The Model of the Dopamine System

We start from the model proposed by Gutkin et al. [9], which defines the working principles of the Dopamine System in the case of constant stimuli.

Mathematical Model. The model consists of differential equations describing the dynamics of the Dopamine System, of the Action-Selection circuits and of synaptic plasticity.

We give a simplified definition of the model by describing the Action-Selection and synaptic plasticity components by means of a simpler differential equation representing, in a abstract way, the "memorization" of the received stimuli. Moreover, we replace the sigmoid functions used in the model to implement threshold-based switches, with simpler differential equations defined by cases. As a result, we obtain a model consisting of two differential equations:

- *Dopamine concentration.* We have an equation describing the dynamics of variable D representing the dopamine concentration in the prefrontal cortex:

$$\frac{dD}{dt} = \alpha \left(-D + k + \begin{cases} 1, & if \ r - M \geq \theta_p \\ 0, & if \ \theta_n \leq r - M \leq \theta_p \\ -\frac{D*M}{2}, & if \ r - M \leq \theta_n \end{cases} \right)$$

The dynamics of D is calculated by considering the following parameters:
- k is the basal production rate of dopamine;
- r is the perceived stimulus;
- M is the memory of the stimulus, whose value is given by the second differential equation;
- θ_p is the positive threshold, in the simulation is set to 80;
- θ_n is the negative threshold, in the simulation is set to -30;
- $\alpha = 0.3$ is a unique time-scaling parameter.

Apart from standard decay and basal production, the differential equation describes the dynamics of the dopamine concentration by considering three cases given by the comparison of the current stimulus r with the memory M and the two thresholds (both chosen by performing simulations). When the stimulus is largely greater than the memory, the dopamine concentration increases. When the stimulus and the memory are comparable the dopamine concentration does not increase. Finally, when the stimulus is largely smaller than the memory, the dopamine concentration decreases with a rate that depends both on D and on M.

– *Memory.* The second differential equation describes, in an abstract way, the opponent process (in psychology defined as a contrary emotional reaction to a previous stimulus) that is modeled as a "memorization" process of previous stimuli.

$$\frac{dM}{dt} = \alpha \left(-M + \begin{cases} \frac{r-M}{2}, & if \ r > M \\ 0, & otherwise \end{cases} \right)$$

Dopamine and memory take different times to reach "high" values: Memory requires some time to reach values comparable to the stimulus r, but when it reaches such a level, it contrasts the increase of dopamine concentration in the brain.

To establish if a user became addicted, we considered properly the memory level, because it represents the tolerance and so the phenomenon that better characterizes the addiction. As threshold we selected $M \geq 15$, because at that point in the performed simulations, the users showed peaks and consequently decreases in dopamine trend.

Hybrid Automata Model. Hybrid Automata [3,10] are finite state automata in which states are associated to differential equations that describe the dynamics of a set of continuous variables. Transitions of Hybrid Automaton can update the values of the variables in a discrete way. Moreover, by moving to a different state, transitions can also activate a different set of differential equations.

We propose a Hybrid Automata model to analyse the mechanisms of Dopamine System in an addiction context. It is an extension of the model by Gutkin et al. because it allows different types of stimuli to be dealt with. The stimulus is no longer a simple parameter of the differential equations, but becomes a continuous variable whose dynamics is governed by a Hybrid Automaton.

Indeed, by exploiting the modularity of Hybrid Automata, we can separate the part of the model describing the Dopamine System from the part of the model describing the dynamics of the stimuli. The two parts are described by two different automata that are composed in parallel. In order to consider a different stimulus (or a stimulus with a different dynamics) it will be enough to change the relevant automaton, without changing the automaton of the Dopamine System.

In order to validate our model and to show that it is a conservative modification and extension of the one proposed by Gutkin et al., we used it to reproduce the experiments on nicotine addiction presented in [9].

In Fig. 1 the two automata constituting our model are depicted. The biggest one is the automaton describing the Dopamine System. It essentially corresponds to the already described differential equations of the dopamine concentration D and of the memory M, in which the cases are made explicit as different states of the automaton. The initial values of D and M are 0.2 and 0, which represent, in percentage, the neural activation as in [9]. The initial state of this automaton depends on the initial value of the stimulus r.

The smaller automaton is the one describing the stimulus, i.e. the continuous variable r. In this case, the stimulus dynamics is the same considered in

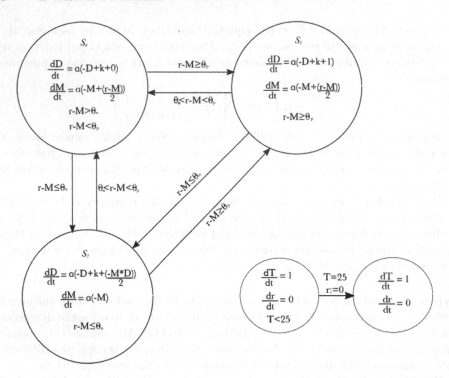

Fig. 1. Hybrid Automata of the Dopamine System and of a stimulus that remains constant for 25 days and then is interrupted.

[9]: initially set to 100, then constant for 25 days and then interrupted (by the transition that updates r into 0). The parameter, representing the constant stimulus, is experimentally obtained from the performed simulations, to reproduce the achieved results in [9]. The continuous variable T and the corresponding differential equations are used only to make it possible to define the guard on the elapsed time (25 days), considering that in [9] the nicotine administration is for 25 days on 50 examined.

Simulation. The simulation and, in particular, the resolution of the differential equations are implemented using GNU Octave [11]. In Octave, the differential equation is written in the form of a vector *xdot* that is passed to the standard ODE solver LSODE. The discrete transitions are implemented as *if-then-else* conditions inside the functions computing *xdot*. The Octave source code of the model is freely available online [1].

Graphical Results. From the performed simulations, we obtained three graphs (depicted in Fig. 2), representing respectively dopamine and memory trends, in relation to stimuli.

The dopamine trend, similar to graphs in [9], shows an initial peak resulting in withdrawal symptoms before the stimulus interruption after 25 days. Subsequently, the dopamine concentration is sustained only by the basal production rate. The performance of the memory, however, corresponds to the opponent process, that in the motivational theory has the function to quiet a previous process, which becomes weaker.

The memory ensures the pulse is absorbed and routinized, reducing its perception. It grows slower than the dopamine and shows no peaks, but its growth counteracts the constant dopamine trend, causing a spike down when the impulse is interrupted.

In order to study the possible scenarios of addiction development, in [13], we modified the automaton describing the stimulus in order to describe non-constant stimuli. In particular, we studied how the dopamine response changes to stimuli provided at regular intervals and to impulsive stimuli in which both the frequency and the intensity change dynamically

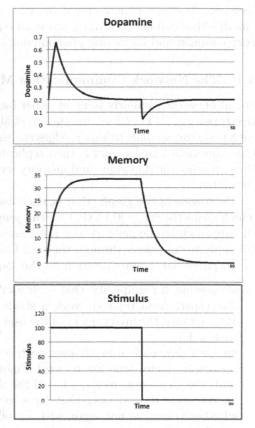

Fig. 2. Results of simulation at constant stimulus

in response to changes in the dopamine concentration (in order to simulate a subject that looks for more frequent or stronger stimuli when the feeling of satisfaction due to the high dopamine concentration disappears).

3 The Internet Addiction

In few years, the impact of Internet and technology has fundamentally changed the way we relate and communicate with each other [20]. People, especially the younger ones, tend to prefer non-verbal communication, choosing text messages to communicate with their peers [8]. Adopting a computer-mediated communication has multiple consequences, such as the loss of empathy and the increase of cortisol, resulting in increased stress and addiction [12]. Usually, users show a different attitude to this communication form, which mainly depends on their level of stress, sense of isolation and inadequacy [14]. To investigate this type of behaviour, we decided to use our model of addiction to study different kinds of scenario. Among all the kinds of Internet addiction, we choose to consider the one due to social network usage since, as reported in some recent studies, it is a very common and increasing phenomenon [18,19].

3.1   The Network Communication Model

Social networks, similarly to many other Internet related networks, have a scale-free topology [7]. Therefore, in order to study them, we consider graphs in which each node corresponds to a user, edges corresponds to social network connections. Our automata-based model is then replicated once for each node of the graph, thus allowing the dopamine and memory levels of each user to be considered and simulated.

Each node of the graph (that is, each user) is also associated to a parameter, which spans the range [0,1], that we call *propensity factor*. Such a factor, governs the approach to the network and influences the probability of such user to send (or reply to) messages through the social network.

In particular, communication on the social network is simulated as follows:

– we assume, for simplicity, that each user can send at most one message each day (apart from replies). Such a single message actually represents, in an abstract way, the involvement of the user in social network interactions during such a day;
– on each day, each user chooses with a probability proportional to his/her propensity factor whether to send a message to his/her neighbors or not. If sent, the message is received by all the neighbors;
– on the same day, all user that have received one or more messages choose whether to reply or not, again with a probability proportional to their propensity factors.

The exchange of messages causes stimuli to be received by users. In normal conditions, when in the model a user receives a message, it receives also a stimulus of intensity 100, that is comparable to the stimulus considered in the model of nicotine addiction presented in the previous section. Moreover, when the user becomes addict to such a stimulus, that is when the memory becomes greater than a threshold level of 15, it receives an additional stimulus of intensity 150 at the time of sending a message. This additional stimulus is due to a particular aspect of the Dopamine System, presented by Samson et al. in [17]: in the presence of addiction, the dopamine concentration increases also when the subject waits for a stimulus to whom he is particularly sensitive. Namely, addiction causes the dopamine level to increase as a consequence of *the expectation* of a reward. This phenomenon is often referred to as *prediction error*, as it is related with withdrawal symptoms when a stimulus is expected, but then not obtained.

3.2   The Experiments

We study our model on three forms of computer-mediated communication, represented as different graphs: (i) with only two nodes; (ii) with multiple nodes constituting a star-graph; and, (iii) with multiple nodes constituting a scale-free network. The 2-nodes graph allows us to better understand the role of the propensity factor in the dynamics of the Dopamine System. The star-graph, instead, allows us to better understand how the number of neighbors of a node influences addiction development and propagation. Finally, the scale-free networks allow us to study the role of topology and of the presence of users with high propensity factors in the spread of addiction through social networks.

We performed several simulation experiments for each graph topology and by varying the propensity factors of users. In all experiments, the simulated time corresponds to 50 days (as in the model of nicotine addiction described in the previous section and in [9]). All the experiments have been performed by implementing the model in the Python programming language. The source code of the model is available at [1].

Communication Between Two Users. The first network topology, depicted below, describes the communication between only two users, A and B.

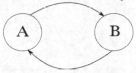

This graph is used to examine the role of the propensity factor. All the possible combinations of users have been tested, in this simple communication, to study the behaviour of the Dopamine System in different situations (summarised in Table 1). For each combination, we made 100 simulations and measured the number of times in which one or both users became addicted (i.e. $M \geq 15$).

These experiments allow us to identify three representative values for the propensity factor (low, medium and high). As regards low and high values we choose 0.2 and 0.9, respectively. Indeed, it can be seen that in the case of two users with propensity 0.2, none of the two becomes addict; in the case of two users with propensity 0.9, both of them become addict; finally, in the case of one user with propensity 0.2 and the other with 0.9, only one becomes addict. To find the medium value, we performed additional simulations (results not shown) by varying the propensity factors of both users in the range [0.3, 0.4] by steps of 0.05. We repeated these simulations 500 times for each combination of parameters and, in the end, we identified 0.35 as medium value.

The Star Graph. This network is a particular kind of tree, in which every node n is linked to the central one c. Each node interacts only with its neighbours.

So, when, for example, the node c sends a message, it is received by all peripheral nodes n; instead, when one of the peripheral nodes sends a message, it is received only by node c. To study the propagation of addiction in a graph, we start by considering how many peripheral nodes are necessary to cause addiction of the central node c.

Table 1. Each cell represents a simulation of the communication between two users, with a different combination of propensity factors. On the vertical and horizontal axis, there are the propensities of User A and User B respectively. The reported values and the color intensity, express the number of times each users became addicted.

User B

User A	0	0.1	0.2	0.3	0.4	0.5	0.6	0.7	0.8	0.9	1
0	A=0; B=0	A=0; B=0	A=0; B=0	A=0; B=0	A=0; B=0	A=0; B=0	A=0; B=0	A=0; B=0	A=0; B=0	A=0; B=0	A=0; B=0
0.1	A=0; B=0	A=0; B=0	A=0; B=0	A=0; B=0	A=0; B=0	A=0; B=0	A=0; B=0	A=0; B=0	A=0; B=66	A=0; B=97	A=0; B=99
0.2	A=0; B=0	A=0; B=0	A=0; B=0	A=0; B=0	A=0; B=83	A=0; B=100	A=0; B=100	A=0; B=100	A=0; B=100	A=0; B=100	A=0; B=100
0.3	A=0; B=0	A=0; B=0	A=0; B=0	A=0; B=0	A=0; B=95	A=1; B=100	A=2; B=100	A=6; B=100	A=6; B=100	A=5; B=100	A=8; B=100
0.4	A=0; B=0	A=0; B=0	A=90; B=0	A=96; B=3	A=95; B=96	A=93; B=100	A=91; B=100	A=96; B=100	A=91; B=100	A=94; B=100	A=93; B=100
0.5	A=0; B=0	A=0; B=0	A=100; B=0	A=100; B=5	A=100; B=94	A=100; B=100	A=100; B=100	A=100; B=100	A=100; B=100	A=100; B=100	A=100; B=100
0.6	A=0; B=0	A=0; B=0	A=100; B=0	A=100; B=6	A=100; B=96	A=100; B=100	A=100; B=100	A=100; B=100	A=100; B=100	A=100; B=100	A=100; B=100
0.7	A=0; B=0	A=0; B=0	A=100; B=0	A=100; B=2	A=100; B=95	A=100; B=100	A=100; B=100	A=100; B=100	A=100; B=100	A=100; B=100	A=100; B=100
0.8	A=0; B=0	A=51; B=0	A=100; B=0	A=100; B=2	A=100; B=99	A=100; B=100	A=100; B=100	A=100; B=100	A=100; B=100	A=100; B=100	A=100; B=100
0.9	A=0; B=0	A=88; B=0	A=100; B=0	A=100; B=5	A=100; B=96	A=100; B=100	A=100; B=100	A=100; B=100	A=100; B=100	A=100; B=100	A=100; B=100
1	A=0; B=0	A=99; B=0	A=100; B=0	A=100; B=2	A=100; B=96	A=100; B=100	A=100; B=100	A=100; B=100	A=100; B=100	A=100; B=100	A=100; B=100

None □   One ▪   Both ■

As depicted in the figure, in the simulations, we added peripheral nodes one by one (all with the same propensity factor) until c became addict, and we counted how many peripheral nodes are necessary in order to reach such a result.

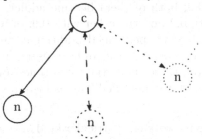

As summarised in Table 2, we used the three previously identified propensity values both for the central node c and the peripheral nodes n.

With 0.2, we add the greater number of nodes, confirming that, with this value, the interaction is really low. After studying how addiction influences the network's central node, we study how one of the peripheral nodes x whose propensity factor is 0.2 (fixed) can be influenced by the others (both c and n).

Table 2. Each cell represents the average number of nodes added in the graph to make susceptible to the addiction the central node c. On the vertical and horizontal axis, there are the different propensity factors of the central node and added nodes respectively, used during the simulations.

Nodes n

Node c	0.2	0.35	0.9
0.2	9	7	4
0.35	3	1	1
0.9	1	1	1

Few Nodes ■   More Nodes ■

This time, by changing the propensity factor of the central node c, we count how many nodes n we have to add to the graph until the target node x becomes addicted (as shown in the figure).

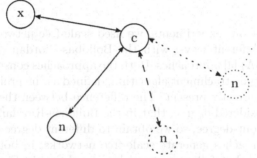

Changing the propensity factor of the added nodes n, we are able to examine different situations to notice what influences more between the central node and the added nodes. As shown in Table 3, the number of nodes to add is proportional to the propensity factor and, in particular, it is influenced by the central node, because it has a direct connection with the node x.

Scale-Free Networks. The study of the two previous networks allowed us to test the model and to delineate the significant values of the propensity factor.

Now, with the aim of understanding what happens in social networks, we start studying scale-free network topology. The characteristics of scale-free networks is the presence of few nodes with a very high degree. These high-degree nodes are called *hubs* and are responsible for many phenomena in this kind of network. In particular, one of the most relevant is the robustness to random failures: information, as well as phenomena like diseases or computer viruses, spread differently on a scale-free network depending on whether the propagation started from low-degree nodes or from the hubs. In the first case, the nodes

Table 3. Each cell represents the average number of nodes added in the graph to make susceptible to the addiction the target node x. On the vertical and horizontal axis, there are respectively the different propensity factors of the central node and added nodes, used during the simulations.

Nodes N

		0.2	0.35	0.9
Node C	0.2	44	36	17
	0.35	17	13	5
	0.9	15	7	4

Few Nodes   More Nodes

propagation is slower than the second case. This is caused by the limited role of low-degree nodes in network integrity.

Experiments. For our experiments, we used scale-free networks of 100 nodes generated in two different ways: with the Bollobás-Riordan (BR) [5] and the Barábasi-Albert (BA) [4] approaches. Both the approaches construct the network by using a preferential attachment algorithm, defined as the probability to attach a new node to one already present. The difference between the two approaches is based on the considered degree, that in the Bollobás-Riordan is distinguished into in-degree and out-degree, so we obtain to different degree distributions.

Since both approaches generate scale-free networks, in both cases we have degree distributions that follow a power law, as shown in Fig. 3; with the BR approach we usually obtain more hubs than with the BA approach. To compare the spread of addiction in the two kinds of scale-free networks, we test our model by associating different propensity factors to the users. In the first experiment, each user in the networks has a propensity factor equal to 0.2.

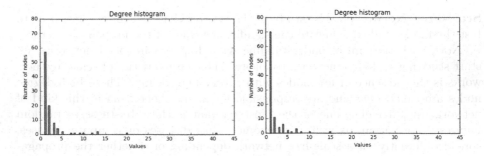

Fig. 3. Example of degree distribution of two scale-free networks generated with Bollobás-Riordan (BR), on the left, and with Barábasi-Albert (BA), on the right.

As we can notice in the Fig. 4, the propagation of the addiction is influenced by the topology of the network. Indeed, in the scale-free network generated by the BR model, there are more hubs and as a consequence we obtain more addicted nodes. To explore the difference between networks, we associated medium and high propensity factors to particular nodes. In the first case, we made more inclined to communication some random nodes to study how changes the messages sharing; in the second case we made inclined an increasing number of hubs, to compare the result with the first experiment. How shown in Fig. 5, in line with

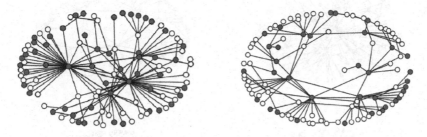

Fig. 4. On the left, there is the graph of scale-free network generated by BR; on the right, the graph of scale-free generated by BA. When all nodes have propensity equal to 0.2, 52 nodes become addicted (red color) in the first graph, 35 in the second one.

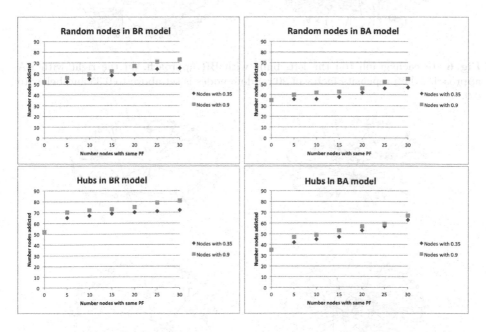

Fig. 5. The difference between the number of the addicted users in BR and BA networks, when we change the propensity factor of random nodes (on the top) among hubs (on the bottom).

the scale-free network features, we notice that in the second case we obtain in the end a greater number of addicted users.

In Fig. 6 we present different scale-free networks, generated by the two algorithms (BR and BA), in which we change the propensity factor of 20 random nodes. In Fig. 7, instead, we change the propensity factor of 20 hubs. As we expected, we obtain the greater number of addicted nodes in the BR model, and in general, if we change the propensity factor of hubs.

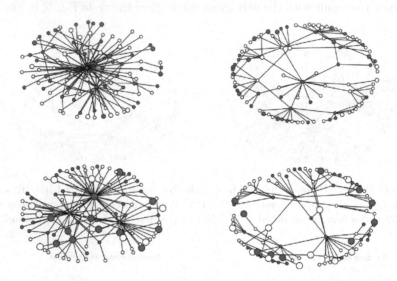

Fig. 6. In each graph (on the left, built with BR approach, on the right with BA approach), the propensity factor of 20 random nodes is set above to 0.35 and below to 0.9.

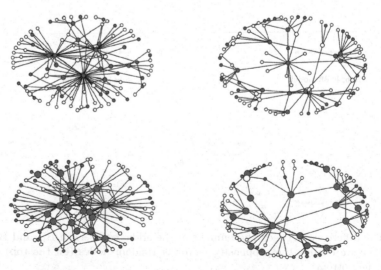

Fig. 7. In each graph (on the left, built with BR approach, on the right with BA approach), the propensity factor of 20 hubs is set above to 0.35 and below to 0.9

4   Conclusions

We proposed a computational framework for the study of addiction, taking into account both neurological and sociological characteristics. To achieve this, we decided to proceed gradually, to understand the complexity and dynamics of the phenomenon. Starting from the model proposed by Gutkin et al., we developed a simplified modular model of the Dopamine System, using the theory of Hybrid Automata. This allowed us to develop a hybrid system consisting of two components, the Dopamine System and a generator of stimuli, in order to dynamically grasp the trend of neurological activity, in relation to many environmental factors. After a general overview we decided to focus mainly on Internet addiction because it is an unexplored phenomenon, that have many sociological and psychological implications. Linked to this, we decided to study how addiction is correlated to network topologies, testing how people in a social network can influence each other.

Our model can be further developed: in the future, we plan to explore other kinds of communication, using networks with a greater number of nodes, to better investigate different stimuli (like for example non-deterministic stimuli) and to consider non-constant propensity factors.

Acknowledgement. We thank Prof. Gerald Moore (Durham University) for comments and discussions on the preliminary phases of this work. This work has been supported by the project "Metodologie informatiche avanzate per l'analisi di dati biomedici (Advanced computational methodologies for the analysis of biomedical data)" funded by the University of Pisa (PRA_2017_44).

References

1. Web page with the scripts used in this paper. http://www.di.unipi.it/msvbio/software/InternetAddiction.html
2. Alexander, B.K., Hadaway, P.F.: Opiate addiction: the case for an adaptive orientation. Psychol. Bull. **92**(2), 367 (1982)
3. Alur, R., Courcoubetis, C., Henzinger, T.A., Ho, P.-H.: Hybrid automata: an algorithmic approach to the specification and verification of hybrid systems. In: Grossman, R.L., Nerode, A., Ravn, A.P., Rischel, H. (eds.) HS 1991-1992. LNCS, vol. 736, pp. 209–229. Springer, Heidelberg (1993). https://doi.org/10.1007/3-540-57318-6_30
4. Barabási, A.-L., Albert, R.: Emergence of scaling in random networks. Science **286**(5439), 509–512 (1999)
5. Bollobás, B., Borgs, C., Chayes, J., Riordan, O.: Directed scale-free graphs. In: Proceedings of the Fourteenth Annual ACM-SIAM Symposium on Discrete Algorithms, pp. 132–139. Society for Industrial and Applied Mathematics (2003)
6. Corrigall, W.A., Franklin, K.B.J., Coen, K.M., Clarke, P.B.S.: The mesolimbic dopaminergic system is implicated in the reinforcing effects of nicotine. Psychopharmacology **107**(2), 285–289 (1992)
7. Ebel, H., Mielsch, L.I., Bornholdt, S.: Scale-free topology of e-mail networks. Phys. Rev. E **66**(3), 035103 (2002)

8. Greenfield, S.: Mind Change: How Digital Technologies are Leaving Their Mark on Our Brains. Random House, New York (2015)
9. Gutkin, B.S., Dehaene, S., Changeux, J.-P.: A neurocomputational hypothesis for nicotine addiction. Proc. Natl. Acad. Sci. U.S.A. **103**(4), 1106–1111 (2006)
10. Henzinger, T.A.: The theory of hybrid automata. In: Inan, M.K., Kurshan, R.P. (eds.) Verification of Digital and Hybrid Systems. NATO ASI Series (Series F: Computer and Systems Sciences), vol. 170, pp. 265–292. Springer, Heidelberg (2000). https://doi.org/10.1007/978-3-642-59615-5_13
11. Hauberg, S., Eaton, J.W., Bateman, D., Wehbring, R.: GNU Octave Version 3.8.1 Manual: A High-Level Interactive Language for Numerical Computations. CreateSpace Independent Publishing Platform (2014). ISBN 1441413006
12. Kuss, D.J., Griffiths, M.D.: Online social networking and addiction? A review of the psychological literature. Int. J. Environ. Res. Public Health **8**(9), 3528–3552 (2011)
13. Nasti, L.: Modelling and simulation of dopaminergic system. The case of internet addiction. Master thesis, University of Pisa, Largo Bruno Pontecorvo, 3, 56127, Pisa, Italy (2016)
14. Raskin, R., Terry, H.: A principal-components analysis of the narcissistic personality inventory and further evidence of its construct validity. J. Pers. Soc. Psychol. **54**(5), 890 (1988)
15. Redish, D.A.: Addiction as a computational process gone awry. Science **306**(5703), 1944–1947 (2004)
16. Roberts, A.J., Koob, G.F.: The neurobiology of addiction: an overview. Alcohol Res. Health **21**(2), 101 (1997)
17. Samson, R.D., Frank, M.J., Fellous, J.-M.: Computational models of reinforcement learning: the role of dopamine as a reward signal. Cogn. Neurodyn. **4**(2), 91–105 (2010)
18. Smith, K.P., Christakis, N.A.: Social networks and health. Annu. Rev. Sociol. **34**, 405–429 (2008)
19. Syvertsen, T.: "Caught in the Net": online and social media disappointment and detox. In: Media Resistance, pp. 77–97. Springer, Cham (2017). https://doi.org/10.1007/978-3-319-46499-2_5
20. Zhao, S., Grasmuck, S., Martin, J.: Identity construction on Facebook: digital empowerment in anchored relationships. Comput. Hum. Behav. **24**(5), 1816–1836 (2008)

What Belongs to Context?

A Definition, a Criterion and a Method for Deciding on What Context-Aware Systems Should Sense and Adapt to

Sélinde van Engelenburg(✉) ⓘ, Marijn Janssen ⓘ,
and Bram Klievink ⓘ

Faculty of Technology, Policy and Management,
Delft University of Technology, Delft, The Netherlands
{S. H. vanEngelenburg, M. F. W. H. A. Janssen,
A. J. Klievink}@tudelft.nl

Abstract. Context-awareness refers to the ability to sense and adapt to context. With the rise of context-aware systems, designers are struggling with what variables should be sensed from the context. According to the definitions found in the literature, whether something belongs to context, has to do with whether it is relevant. However, what it means to be relevant is left implicit in these definitions. Most work on context-aware systems is based on assumptions of the context that should be taken into account. Hence, it is unclear how to decide whether something belongs to context or should be left out. In this paper, first we analyse what is meant with context and provide a definition. In this definition we introduce the notion of a context variable, defined as an attribute of an object that is relevant. Context is then defined as the set of context variables. We establish explicit criteria for deciding whether an attribute of an object is a context variable based on the proposed definition and the designer's goal. We also provide a straightforward method to help designers to determine whether the criterion is met and a variable should be included in the context. This method is based on filling out a scheme to describe context variables.

Keywords: Context-aware systems · Context · Business-to-government
Information sharing · Context variable · Context relationship

1 Introduction

In 1994, Schillit and Theimer [1] were among the first to introduce the term 'context-aware'. Hong et al. [2] provide an extensive overview of context-aware systems. Their work shows that context-awareness involves acquiring, sensing or being aware of context as well as adapting to it or using it. In concordance with this observation, we simply define a context-aware system to be a system that senses and adapts to context.

The definitions of context in the literature suggest that what belongs to context has to do with what is relevant to something, or whether it has a certain relationship with

© Springer International Publishing AG 2018
A. Cerone and M. Roveri (Eds.): SEFM 2017 Workshops, LNCS 10729, pp. 101–116, 2018.
https://doi.org/10.1007/978-3-319-74781-1_8

something (see e.g., [3–5]). However, what it means for something to be relevant or what kind of relationship is meant, is never made explicit in these definitions. This makes it hard to establish criteria for determining what does and does not belong to the context a context-aware system should sense, when designing such a system.

Designers of context-aware systems typically do not use such criteria because they focus on a certain part of context, such as location (see e.g., [6, 7]) or do not know the relevance in advance. This introduces the risks of (1) leaving out parts of the context that could aid them in achieving their goal, (2) taking things into account that do not help them with achieving their goal or that might result into complications, and (3) different people arriving at difference outcomes.

Investigating context can require the consideration of a vast amount of variables that could be relevant, which complicates design. We experienced this in our own work on designing a context-aware architecture for business-to-government (B2G) information sharing [8]. We performed interviews to determine what context is relevant for the architecture to sense. During these interviews, we experienced various times that an interviewee or researcher got confused about what should be modelled as part of context and what not. For example, we found that the relationships between businesses (e.g., competition) is part of the context of information flows. Yet, the opportunity to build new relationships is part of the context of projects in which flows of information might be implemented. While the former is relevant to sense for the architecture, the latter is not. However, this is hard to discern without a clear criterion and systematic and structured method.

In this paper we provide a criterion based on a definition of context for determining whether something should be modelled as context, as well as a simple method for deciding whether the criterion is met. This helps designers to deal with the high complexity of investigating context by allowing them to easily decide what is and what is not relevant.

We first discuss the theoretical background in Sect. 2. In Sect. 3, we present a definition of context that is the basis for the criterion and the method. We will use the investigations of context for designing a context-aware B2G information sharing architecture as a running example throughout the paper. We will also use it to illustrate the use of our method to determine what belongs to context in Sect. 4. We believe this example is especially suitable because of its high complexity and the fact that we have data on it from the study of a real-life case. If the method works for this example, it is likely that it works in less complex cases as well.

2   Theoretical Background

The notion of context originally referred to constructing the meaning of a text, based on the surrounding text in linguistics [9]. The large volume of literature on context-aware systems contains many different definitions as well. The earlier work contains definitions by synonym (e.g., situation, environment), or by example (e.g., location) [3]. This leads to generality in the former and to incompleteness in the latter case [4]. For designers of context-aware systems, such definitions thus respectively provide too little guidance for deciding what belongs to context, or could exclude parts of context that should be included in the design of the system.

In the literature, several attempts have been made to define context for operational use without relying on synonyms or examples. Especially the work of Dey and Abowd is often used as a basis for application-specific or domain-specific definitions (see e.g., [10–14]). Dey and Abowd [3] define context as follows: *"Context is any information that can be used to characterize the situation of an entity. An entity is a person, place, or object that is considered relevant to the interaction between a user and an application, including the user and applications themselves."*

According to the definition by Dey and Abowd [3], the most important characteristics for belonging to context are (1) characterising a situation and (2) being considered relevant. However, the definition cannot be used as a basis for criteria to decide this, as their definition leaves implicit what it means to be considered relevant to an interaction and to characterise a situation. We need to know what the notions 'relevance' and 'characterising' mean to be able to decide whether something belongs to context.

Winograd [9] argues that the definition by Dey and Abowd [3] is too broad. He argues that: *"Something is context because of the way it is used in interpretation, not due to its inherent properties."* [9]. Zimmerman et al. [4], mention this issue with the definition of Dey and Abowd [3] as well. Their solution is categorising context into the fundamental categories of individuality, activity, location, time, and relations. According to them, the activity predominantly adds the relevance of context elements.

According to Winograd [9] and Zimmerman et al. [4] something is context because of its relationship to something else. This conforms with the interactional view on context described by Dourish [15]. When viewed as an interactional problem, according to Dourish [15], *"contextuality is a relational property that holds between objects or activities"*. The interactional view implies that something belongs to context, when it has relational property with something else. However, we still have no certainty about when this is exactly the case.

Context is always a context of something. According to Brézillon [5] this 'something' is a focus of an actor. He views context as knowledge and the focus helps to discriminate irrelevant external knowledge from relevant contextual knowledge. However, as Brézillon [5] himself states *"the frontier between external and contextual knowledge is porous"*. When, in his model for task accomplishment, a discrepancy is found between the model and what a user does, the user is simply asked for an explanation [5]. The new knowledge is then added to the model. This means that Brézillon [5] does not make explicit what belongs to context either. This decision is ultimately left to the user.

The notion of a contextual element is central to the definition of context by Vieira et al. [16]. A contextual element is *"any piece of data or information that can be used to characterize an entity in an application domain"* [16]. In a similar vein as in the work of Brézillon [5], contextual elements are relevant to a focus, which is determined by a task and an agent [16].

A contextual element is an attribute of a contextual entity [16]. The contextual entity is an entity that should be considered for the purpose of context manipulation [16]. Contextual elements can be identified from the attributes and relationships the entity has [16]. Vieira et al. [16] already note that the criterion to identify a property as a contextual element in their case is subjective and depends on the context requirements and a conceptual model. Therefore, the question of what belongs to context becomes a question of what should be in the conceptual model. The problem of determining what belongs to context has thus been moved instead of solved.

In the work above, there is a focus on the relevance of something as arising from an activity or actor. Similarly, other work discussing relevance focuses on determining the relevance of something at runtime and dynamically defining context for the specific task or activity at hand (see e.g., [16, 17]). It is important to make clear the distinction between such work and our work. The work presented in this paper is concerned with supporting the determining of what is relevant and what should be included in the modelled context when designing a system. We thus focus on what a context-aware system should be able to sense and what adaptations it should be able to make based on what is sensed.

Bauer et al. [18] discuss the way designers view context. In the first phase of designing a context-aware system, designers typically frame the design space to include certain things in the context based on their concept of context [18]. Designers already start with making assumptions on what belongs to context. These assumptions might be subject to changes in later phases. Often designers have difficulty to produce artefacts that can be used to test the way in which context would impact the user's interaction with the system [18]. Making choices early without testing them results in relying on assumptions.

Having a clear definition of context and a method for deciding whether something belongs to context, might help to include the appropriate variables and aid designers with testing their assumptions. This might help them with relying less on assumptions from the start.

3   A Definition of Context, a Criterion and a Method for Deciding

In the first part of this section, we will provide a definition of context. The aim of this definition is to be universal in the sense that it can be used by designers in a variety of domains with a variety of goals. In the second part of this section, we will provide a method for determining whether something belongs to context. This method is based on the definition of content and the goal of the designer.

3.1   A Definition of Context

The definitions we propose in this paper are separated into two parts. In the first part, we provide the definition of focus and of some basic notions that form the basis of our definition of the context. This is necessary to make our definition specific enough. In the second part, we provide the definition of the context. To illustrate our definitions, we use the running example introduced in the beginning of the paper of a context-aware architecture supporting B2G information sharing.

Basic Notions and the Focus of a Context

In definitions from a interactional point of view, such as that of Vieira et al. [16] context elements are viewed as attributes of entities [15]. This fits with our purposes of supporting designer's decisions of what belongs to context. Something belongs to context because an object having a certain value for an attribute has an effect on something else.

Notions such as 'object' and 'attribute', discussed below, are elementary and abstract. Providing precise definitions is therefore difficult and might lead to interesting, albeit long and out-of-scope philosophical discussions. To avoid these, we used simple and generally accepted definitions, selected on basis of their ease for determining whether something is an object or attribute, as this will be important later on to determine whether something belongs to context. Looking at objects has the advantage that there is a focus on things that can be concretely observed.

Definition 1 (object): *"something material that may be perceived by the senses"* [19].

Example 1 (object): Businesses, systems and data can be viewed as objects, as they can be perceived by the senses. The concept of justice is not an object.

In our example, we want to support B2G information sharing in which businesses are willing to participate. The attribute of sensitivity of the data that is shared is relevant, since when it has a value of 'sensitive' businesses might not be willing to participate in certain flows of information. We should thus determine whether sensitivity of data shared is relevant for our system, by looking at it as an attribute of the data that is shared and at the effect of it having a certain value.

Definition 2 (attribute): *"a quality, character, or characteristic ascribed to someone or something"* (adapted from [20]).

Example 2 (attribute): Sensitivity is an attribute of data and an attribute of a system is whether it broadcasts information.

Sensitivity of data can also be viewed as a relationship. Data can be sensitive for a certain business. In that case, sensitivity can be viewed as a relationship between information and a business, instead of as an attribute of the information. Scholars disagree on whether relationships should be viewed as attributes or properties [21]. In our case, we see no clear advantages of including relationships as part of context. Furthermore, including only attributes as part of context increases simplicity and clearness of our definitions.

The values of attributes of objects can vary. A state of the world, or a situation, is different from another when at least one value of an attribute is different. For a system to be context-aware, it should adapt to these differences when they are relevant. Furthermore, it should only consider situations that could exist in the real world, and for instance not situations that are inconsistent.

Definition 3 (situation): *A situation is a state of the world, determined by a combination of values of attributes of objects that is possible in the real world.*

Example 3 (situation): A situation in which data is sensitive, is different from one in which data is not sensitive.

A context is always a context of something, such as the willingness of businesses to participate in information sharing in our example. In linguistics, this 'something' is called a 'focal event' [22]. In Dey [23] it is the interaction between a user and an application and for Brézillon [5] and Vieira et al. [16] it is a focus.

We want our definition of context to be universal to make it useful for a variety of domains in which a context-aware system is designed. Our scope is the design of context-aware systems and this scope does apply to our definition. To achieve a universal definition, we want to define the 'something' that a context is a context of, to be as broad as possible. In our definition, this 'something' is thus an attribute of an entity. 'Entity' is meant in the broadest sense and could include concrete objects as well as for instance processes. Just as Brézillon [5] and Vieira et al. [16], we will call it a focus.

In Brézillon [5] and Vieira et al. [16], the focus of context is related to an actor. In our case, the focus is related to a designer of a B2G information sharing architecture. A designer has a goal and they want to design the system to reach that goal. Such a goal can be expressed as wanting an attribute of an entity to have a certain value or be within a certain range of values.

Definition 4 (focus): *A focus of a designer is the attribute of an entity that the designer needs to have a certain value to reach their goal.*

Example 4 (focus): A designer can have the goal to develop a context-aware architecture that supports flows of information in which businesses are willing to participate. To reach this goal the architecture should only support *flows of information* in which *businesses are willing to participate*. The focus of the designer is thus the willingness of businesses to participate (attribute) in a flow of information (entity).

The Context of a Focus

At first sight, achieving a universal definition of context seems problematic, since what belongs to a context might be different for each focus. However, context is determined by its relationship with its focus. In fact, something is only context if it has some relationship with the focus. The type of relationship is not specific to a certain focus, but the same for all foci. In this way, it can be used to formulate an universal definition of context. From this definition, what belongs to the context of a specific focus can be derived.

There is a relationship between a focus and one or more attributes of objects, if and only if the value of the focus depends in some way on the value of the attributes of the objects. The focus is only dependent on the attributes if there are values for these attributes, such that in all situations where they have these values, the focus has a certain value as well. In a sense, the context restricts the value that the focus can have in those situations.

In addition, there should be situations in which the attributes have different values. This restriction is necessary because all attributes that always have the same value would otherwise have a context relationship with every focus. Furthermore, attributes that always have the same value do not need adapting to by a context-aware system.

Definition 5 (context relationship): *A context relationship is a relationship between a focus and a set of one or more attributes of objects, where there are values for each of these attributes, such that:*

- *in each situation where they have these values, the value of the focus is the same, and*
- *for each attribute there is at least one situation in which they have a different value.*

When a set of attributes has a context relationship with a focus, we say that they restrict the focus.

Example 5 (context relationship): We assume that businesses are never willing to share their data, when the data is sensitive and there is a system in the flow of information that broadcasts it. This means that the value of the attribute willingness is limited in those situations to unwilling for at least one business. Therefore, the attributes of sensitivity and being broadcast have a context relationship with the focus of willingness. In opposition, what the authors of this paper have for dinner does not have a context relationship with willingness, because, realistically, there is nothing that they could have for dinner that would restrict the value of willingness. The speed of light in a vacuum does not have a context relationship with willingness as well, since it is always the same.

Considering Example 5, it is important to note that businesses might be either willing or unwilling to share when the information is not sensitive, not broadcast, or neither. This is possible considering the context relationship we have identified. There is only a restriction on willingness when both the data is sensitive and broadcast. Context relationships, however, in other cases might constrain the value of a focus for multiple values of their attributes of objects as well. In addition, there might be multiple sets of attributes that have a context relationship with a single focus.

Using the notion of context relationship, we can determine if an attribute of an object belongs to context. An attribute belongs to the context of a focus, if and only if it is part of a set of attributes that has a context relationship with the focus.

Definition 6 (context variable): *A context variable of a focus is an attribute of an object that is part of a set of attributes of objects that have a context relationship with the focus.*

We say that the context variable impacts the focus. Information on the value of a context variable is called context information.

Example 6 (context variable): Sensitivity of data and whether a system broadcasts the data are context variables of the focus willingness to participate in an information flow. What the authors of this paper have for dinner and the speed of light are not.

When an attribute is a context variable of a focus, this means that it is relevant to the designer. According to Definition 4, a designer achieves their goal when the focus has a certain value. To achieve the goal, they thus have to design the context-aware system, such that the focus has this value when it is used. A context variable of the focus restricts the value of that focus. Therefore, the system needs to be designed such that it can sense the context variable and adapt to it if it causes the focus to have the wrong value. This makes the context variable relevant to the design and therefore to the designer.

The definition of context is based on the other notions defined above. It is simply the set of context variables.

Definition 7 (context): *The context of a focus is the set of all its context variables that impact it.*

Example 7 (context): The context of willingness of businesses to participate in a flow of information includes the sensitivity of data and whether a system broadcasts it.

3.2   A Criterion for Deciding What Belongs to Context

To determine what belongs to context a clear and explicit criterion is needed. According to Definition 7, something belongs to the context of a focus, if it is a context variable of that focus. To determine whether an attribute belongs to context of a focus, we thus have to determine whether it is a context variable of that focus. By Definition 6, an attribute is a context variable of a focus, if it is part of a set of attributes of objects that have a context relationship with the focus. According to Definition 5, a set of attributes has a context relationship with a focus if the value of the focus is restricted by the attributes. By combining Definitions 5 and 6, we can establish a criterion to decide for an attribute whether it is a context variable of a focus.

Criterion: An attribute is a context variable of a focus, if and only if:

- *it is part of a set of attributes of objects, such that there are values for each of the attributes in the set, such that in each situation where they have these values, the value of the focus is the same, and*
- *there is at least one situation in which it has a different value.*

This criterion is precise, but also very abstract. This means that it is hard to use in practice when in the middle of collecting and analysing data. Since in the end this is the situation in which we want to support determining what belongs to context, we need a simple method to decide whether this criterion is met.

3.3   A Method for Deciding What Belongs to Context

The method for deciding what belongs to context can be used to determine for an attribute whether it belongs to the context of a focus according the criterion presented in Sect. 3.2. This criterion, is based on the definitions in Sect. 3.1. The method for deciding whether an attribute is a context variable, consist of two steps:

1. Identify the focus belonging to the goal of the designer
2. Test whether attributes meet the criterion.

Identify the Focus Belonging to the Goal of the Designer
To identify the focus, we propose that a designer performs the following steps:
(1) make explicit the problem the system should solve, (2) make explicit the goal of the

designer, (3) describe the world as it should be when the goal is reached, and (4) identify the relevant entity and attribute of the entity that is the focus.

The *first* step is aimed at identifying the problem. Solving this problem can be viewed as the goal of the designer. For the *second* step, the goal can then be expressed as what the system should be able to do at a very high level in order to solve the problem.

According to Definition 4, a focus is an attribute of an entity that a designer wants to have a certain value to reach their goal. A goal is reached when the world is in a certain state. The *third* step therefore is to exactly describe the world as it should be when the goal is reached. Such a description will include the entities, their attributes and the values that they should have when the goal is reached. The *fourth* step is identifying these from the description.

It is possible that a goal can lead to multiple foci, or that there are multiple goals. This should not be a problem. However, each of the foci will have their own context relationships and context variables.

We will demonstrate the four steps using the running example. In the example, the goal is to develop a context-aware architecture for B2G information sharing. More specifically, we focus on B2G information sharing in the container-shipping domain. For step *one*, we identify the problem we want the architecture to solve. In our case, this requires some insight into the domain of container-shipping.

In the container-shipping domain, an important task of Customs is to monitor the flow of goods [24]. When goods are shipped in containers, Customs cannot view them without opening the container. The volume of containers is so high, that it is not even remotely possible for Customs to open each and every one of them to see what is inside [25]. However, they can use information gathered by businesses to perform risk assessment and target high-risk containers for inspection [26, 27].

The information that Customs receives from businesses is often of low quality [24]. Businesses gather information that is of high quality because their own commercial operations depend on it [28]. This information could be reused by Customs according to the piggy-backing principle [28]. Customs can also be expected to contribute to the competitiveness of their country [29]. To protect competitiveness, Customs will therefore want to keep the administrative burden of businesses low. Obligating businesses to share their information, will increase their administrative burden. Therefore, whether businesses share their high-quality information with Customs, depends on whether they are willing to do so. The problem that we want to solve is that Customs requires businesses to share information with them, but that businesses are not always outright willing to do so.

For step *two*, we have to formulate our goal explicitly. What the system should do to solve this problem is to support flows of information in which businesses are willing to participate. Our goal is thus to design a context-aware architecture that support such flows of information.

For step *three*, we should describe the world as it should be when the goal is reached. The goal is reached when the context-aware system only supports flows of information in which all businesses are willing to participate.

For step *four*, we identify the entity and attribute that are the focus. The entity that is important is 'flow of information' and its attribute is the 'willingness of businesses to participate' in it. The focus is thus the attribute 'willingness of businesses to participate' of the entity 'flow of information'.

Test Whether Attributes Meet the Criterion

The second step of the method is to test whether attributes are context variables of the focus identified in the first step. In contrast with the criterion, such a test should be simple and straightforward. We can determine what the test should be, based on understanding when the criterion is met.

An attribute meets the first part of the criterion if for all situations where it has a certain value and a set of attributes of objects have a certain value, the value of the focus is the same. Of course we cannot list all possible situations to check this. In the real world, there are far too many other attributes that vary to do so. Therefore, it is also not possible to be certain that all attributes belonging to a set that have a context relationship with a focus are found.

The solution is to reduce the testing of the criterion to testing whether information collected or analysed by the designer supports the conclusion that the criterion is met. For an attribute, the information supports the conclusion that the criterion is met, if the following can be found: information on the value of the attribute and values of other attributes, and information indicating that in all situations in which these attributes have these values, the attribute of the focus is limited to a certain value. Furthermore, for each of the attributes they should establish based on the information whether there are situations in which they have a different value.

If all the information above is available, the designer should be able to fill out the scheme below. Filling out the scheme, is a test to determine whether there is support to conclude that the criterion is met. If the designer is able to fill out the scheme, then they have identified a new context variable, if they are not, then they cannot conclude this based on the information that they have. Furthermore, it is important to keep in mind that according to Definition 3, situations only include things that can happen in the real world. The designer has to fill out the scheme by filling in the information between the square brackets, of the type mentioned in the underlined text. The test consist of two parts, corresponding to the two parts of the criterion.

Test whether an attribute meets the criterion:

1. *It is possible to fill out the following scheme, such that it is supported by the information: If [attribute of object] of [object] has value [value of attribute of object], and the following is true [list of values of other attributes of objects], then [attribute in focus] of [entity in focus] has value [value of attribute in focus].*
2. *There is support to conclude that there is at least one situation in which [attribute of object] has a different value.*

We can illustrate the use of the test using the running example again. During our investigations, we found that businesses are not willing to share data if it is sensitive to them and if it will be broadcast by a system in the flow of information. We also found that data is not always sensitive. Based on this, we are able to fill out the scheme as follows:

1. It is possible to fill out the following scheme, such that it is supported by the information: If [the sensitivity] of [data shared in the flow of information] has value [sensitive to a business], and the following is true [a system in the flow of information has the value 'true' for 'whether it broadcasts the data'], then [willingness of businesses to participate] of [the flow of information] has value [not all businesses willing to participate].
2. There is support to conclude that there is at least one situation in which [sensitivity] has a different value.

   In the next section, we will provide an illustration in which attributes can be determined to be context variables or not.

4 Illustration of the Method

In this section, we will illustrate the definition and the use of the method described in Sect. 3.3. We will first show that the notions of context variables and context relationships can be used to describe the context of a context-aware tour guide. Next, we illustrate and test the method in practice with the designing of a context-aware system for B2G information sharing in the container-shipping domain.

Context-aware architectures are a type of context-aware system. Furthermore, the context that the context-aware architecture should take into account is highly complex, involving a high variety of parties with different interests and different types of information that is shared, amongst others. Due to this high complexity, what parts of context should be taken into account becomes less obvious, resulting in missing elements and even ambiguity. Our method should overcome this.

4.1 Context-Aware Tour Guide

The first type of context-aware systems that were developed in the 90's were location-aware systems, such as context-aware tour guides [30]. Such tour guides provide information based on the current location of the user [30]. A thorough investigation of what belongs to context, was usually not part of the design process of such systems. Typically, location is assumed to be relevant and is the only part of context taken into account. Nevertheless, the proposed definition of context can still be used to describe the context that should be taken into account for such systems, including location.

It would seem logical that the goal of a designer of a tour guide is to provide information on sights that is relevant to the user. The focus is thus relevance to users (attribute) of the information on sights (entity). When this is the focus, then location (attribute) of the user (object) would be the most straightforward context variable to identify. An example of a context relationship that would relate this variable to the focus is "Information on sights is restricted to not relevant to the user if the location of the sight is more than 10 m from the location of the user".

This relationship includes the location of the sights as well. Whether it is necessary for the tour guide to sense this, depends on whether the location of the sights might change or not in the domain for which the tour guide is designed. For instance, if the sights are animals that move freely in a certain area, it might be useful to sense their location. If the sight is a pyramid that has been at a certain location for millennia, then this is not necessary.

From the definition of context relationship (Definition 5) it follows that there should be at least one situation in which the value of an attribute is different, for it to be a context variable. Therefore, the location of the pyramid is not a context variable according to our definition. As context variables are meant to be sensed by the context-aware systems, this is according to what should be the case. The context relationship could then be changed to for instance "Information on the great pyramid of Giza is restricted to not relevant to the user if their location is more than 150 m from coordinates 29°58′45.03″N 31°08′03.69″E".

To develop a more advanced context-aware tour guide, a designer could take into account more than only the current location of the user. In the literature, several suggestions are provided for other parts of the context that should be taken into account, e.g., history of location of the user, location of other users [7] and interests of the user [31]. When designing a new tour guide, for each of these attributes, it could be checked whether they are context variables using the method proposed in this paper.

This example of a context-aware tour guide is simple and tour guides are a common type of context-aware system. It is therefore interesting to show how the definitions proposed in this paper can be used to describe the context for such systems. However, to test the method, it should be applied to the context of a more complex context-aware system as well, such as a context-aware architecture for B2G information sharing.

4.2   Context-Aware Architecture for B2G Information Sharing

In the running example of this paper, the focus is the willingness of businesses to participate in a flow of information. In our research, we used the proposed method for determining whether something belongs to context of this focus for a case of B2G information shipping in the container-shipping domain. The case is an international supply chain in which goods are shipped in containers. A shipping information pipeline supporting the sharing of information directly from the source was implemented and tested [27]. This pipeline supported the sharing of data between businesses as well as sharing the data with Customs.

The implementation of such a pipeline involves a lot of negotiating between different stakeholders. This, of course, is a good opportunity to get the insight into the effects of context on willingness. To collect information, secondary data were studied and three in-depth interviews were conducted with several people from the businesses and researchers involved in the project. We analysed transcripts of the interviews by determining for all statements whether they could be used to fill out the scheme in the test.

In many cases we were able to fill out the scheme presented in the previous section based on the information provided by the interviewees. For example, in the flow of information, as implemented in the project, Customs could merely view the data and not store it. We asked about this and the interviewees stated that this was because competitive sensitive data was aggregated. The supplier of this information was therefore not willing to share this type of sensitive data if Customs would have stored the data. Based on this information, we can fill out the scheme for the attribute of storing data of the object system of the government organization:

If [the attribute storing data in the flow] of [the system of the government organization] has value [true], and the following is true [information in the flow has the value true for the attribute of containing competitive sensitive data when aggregated], then [the willingness of businesses to participate] of [the flow of information] has value [not all businesses willing to participate].

We have established that whether the system of the government organization stores data is a context variable. Furthermore, we have established that the other attribute, competitive sensitivity of data when aggregated, listed in the scheme is a context variable as well.

Attributes were suggested by the interviewees that were not context variables. For instance, one of the interviewees stated that it is important to what extent the systems in the flow are able to integrate with each other. We could view ease of integration with other systems as an attribute of a system. However, based on this statement alone, we cannot conclude that ease of integration is a context variable. It is unclear whether or how the value of willingness is restricted by this attribute.

A similar example is that an interviewee mentioned that it was hard to find a suitable data model for the data pipeline. Based on the statements of the interviewee, we could not fill out the scheme because we do not know the effects on willingness and these might not exist.

Another example, already mentioned in the introduction, is that interviewees stated that benefits were that they could meet new parties and build relationships with them. This of course does not affect their willingness to be in specific flows of information, but their willingness to be in a certain project. Indeed, the precise effect on willingness could not be established and thus the scheme could not be filled out. This means that these benefits do not belong to context. What makes statements like this even harder to deal with without a clear criterion, is that having a certain relationship with another party, such as being their competitor, was established to be a context variable based on some other statements.

A limitation is that the protocols used for the interviews were already partially fed by the ideas about context presented in this paper. This means that it was already established that the effects of context on willingness needed to be investigated for designing the architecture. Something that clearly stands out during the interviews is that asking explicit questions about willingness results in exactly the information that is required to determine what context variables are. This indicates that establishing the focus already is a very important step in determining what belongs to context. Furthermore, its shows that it might be worthwhile to adapt data collection techniques to the focus at hand.

5   Conclusion

Defining context is challenging. In this paper we defined context as follows: "the context of a focus is a set of context variables that have a context relationship with the focus". A focus is an attribute of an entity that should have a certain value to obtain the goal of the designer. Context variables are attributes of objects that are relevant to the focus because they have a context relationship with the focus. They have such a relationship when, together with other context variables, they restrict the value of the focus in some situations.

Context variables are dependent on the foci. An example of a focus is the willingness of businesses to participate in a flow of information. Context variables for such a focus are sensitivity of data shared and whether data is stored in a system in the flow of information, as the values of these context variables affect businesses' willingness. For other foci, there might be other context variables.

We also provided a method for establishing for attributes whether they belong to context. This method consists of two parts. The first part is first determining what the focus is. For the second part, the designer should attempt to fill out the following scheme for each attribute based on the information on it available to them: If [attribute of object] of [object] has value [value of attribute of object], and the following is true [list of values of other attributes of objects], then [attribute in focus] of [entity in focus] has value [value of attribute in focus].

If the designer succeeds in filling out this scheme then the attribute is a context variable and belongs to context. We found this method to be useful to reduce complexity when designing a context-aware architecture for B2G information sharing in the container-shipping domain.

Further research could focus on using the method with additional ways of data collection, in different domains and by a variety of designers. Furthermore, additional research can be done on whether and how the notions defined in this paper could be used to structure information on context and translate it to requirements for the design of context-aware systems. Additionally, the definitions could be made formal using technical notation, or a taxonomy could be developed using this method.

Acknowledgements. The work in this paper is part of the project JUridical and context-aware Sharing of informaTion for ensuring compliance (JUST). This project is funded by the Netherlands Organisation for Scientific Research (NWO) as part of the ISCOM programme (Innovation in Supply Chain Compliance and Border Management) under grant number 438-13-601.

References

1. Schilit, B.N., Theimer, M.M.: Disseminating active map information to mobile hosts. IEEE Netw. **8**, 22–32 (1994)
2. Hong, J.-Y., Suh, E.-H., Kim, S.-J.: Context-aware systems: a literature review and classification. Expert Syst. Appl. **36**, 8509–8522 (2009)
3. Abowd, G.D., Dey, A.K., Brown, P.J., Davies, N., Smith, M., Steggles, P.: Towards a better understanding of context and context-awareness. In: Gellersen, H.-W. (ed.) HUC 1999. LNCS, vol. 1707, pp. 304–307. Springer, Heidelberg (1999). https://doi.org/10.1007/3-540-48157-5_29
4. Zimmermann, A., Lorenz, A., Oppermann, R.: An operational definition of context. In: Kokinov, B., Richardson, D.C., Roth-Berghofer, T.R., Vieu, L. (eds.) CONTEXT 2007. LNCS (LNAI), vol. 4635, pp. 558–571. Springer, Heidelberg (2007). https://doi.org/10.1007/978-3-540-74255-5_42

5. Brézillon, P.: Task-realization models in contextual graphs. In: Dey, A., Kokinov, B., Leake, D., Turner, R. (eds.) CONTEXT 2005. LNCS (LNAI), vol. 3554, pp. 55–68. Springer, Heidelberg (2005). https://doi.org/10.1007/11508373_5
6. Kerer, C., Dustdar, S., Jazayeri, M., Gomes, D., Szego, A., Caja, J.A.B.: Presence-aware infrastructure using web services and RFID technologies. In: Proceedings of 2nd European Workshop on Object Orientation and Web Services (2004)
7. Abowd, G.D., Atkeson, C.G., Hong, J., Long, S., Kooper, R., Pinkerton, M.: Cyberguide: a mobile context-aware tour guide. Wirel. Netw. **3**, 421–433 (1997)
8. van Engelenburg, S., Janssen, M., Klievink, B.: Design of a business-to-government information sharing architecture using business rules. In: Bianculli, D., Calinescu, R., Rumpe, B. (eds.) SEFM 2015. LNCS, vol. 9509, pp. 124–138. Springer, Heidelberg (2015). https://doi.org/10.1007/978-3-662-49224-6_11
9. Winograd, T.: Architectures for context. Hum.-Comput. Interact. **16**, 401–419 (2001)
10. Wang, Y.-K.: Context awareness and adaptation in mobile learning. In: 2nd IEEE International Workshop on Wireless and Mobile Technologies in Education, pp. 154–158 (2004)
11. Crowley, J.L., Coutaz, J., Rey, G., Reignier, P.: Perceptual components for context aware computing. In: Borriello, G., Holmquist, L.E. (eds.) UbiComp 2002. LNCS, vol. 2498, pp. 117–134. Springer, Heidelberg (2002). https://doi.org/10.1007/3-540-45809-3_9
12. Benou, P., Vassilakis, C.: The conceptual model of context for mobile commerce applications. Electron. Commer. Res. **10**, 139–165 (2010)
13. Yang, Z., Qilun, Z., Fagui, L.: An extended context model in a RFID-based context-aware service system. In: Proceedings - 2nd 2008 International Symposium on Intelligent Information Technology Application Workshop, IITA 2008 Workshop, Shanghai, pp. 693–697 (2008)
14. Khedo, K.K.: Context-aware systems for mobile and ubiquitous networks. In: International Conference on Networking, International Conference on Systems, International Conference on Mobile Communications and Learning Technologies, p. 123 (2006)
15. Dourish, P.: What we talk about when we talk about context. Pers. Ubiquitous Comput. **8**, 19–30 (2004)
16. Vieira, V., Tedesco, P., Salgado, A.C.: Designing context-sensitive systems: an integrated approach. Expert Syst. Appl. **38**, 1119–1138 (2011)
17. Brézillon, P., Pomerol, J.: Contextual knowledge sharing and cooperation in intelligent assistant systems. Le Travail Humain **62**, 223–246 (1999)
18. Bauer, J.S., Newman, M.W., Kientz, J.A.: What designers talk about when they talk about context. Hum.-Comput. Interact. **29**, 420–450 (2014)
19. Object. https://www.merriam-webster.com/dictionary/object
20. Attribute. https://www.merriam-webster.com/dictionary/attribute
21. Orilia, F., Swoyer, C.: Properties. Stanford Encyclopedia of Philosophy. Metaphysics Research Lab, Stanford University (2016)
22. Goodwin, C., Duranti, A.: Rethinking Context: An Introduction. Rethinking Context: Language as an Interactive Phenomenon, pp. 1–42. Cambridge University Press, Cambridge (1992)
23. Dey, A.K.: Understanding and using context. Pers. Ubiquitous Comput. **1**, 4–7 (2001)
24. Hesketh, D.: Weaknesses in the supply chain: who packed the box. World Cust. J. **4**, 3–20 (2010)
25. Levinson, M.: The World the Box Made. The Box: How the Shipping Container Made the World Smaller and the World Economy Bigger, pp. 1–15. Princeton University Press, Princeton (2010)

26. Tan, Y.-H., Bjørn-Andersen, N., Klein, S., Rukanova, B.: Accelerating Global Supply Chains with IT-Innovation. Springer, Heidelberg (2011). https://doi.org/10.1007/978-3-642-15669-4
27. Klievink, B., van Stijn, E., Hesketh, D., Aldewereld, H., Overbeek, S., Heijmann, F., Tan, Y.-H.: Enhancing visibility in international supply chains: the data pipeline concept. Int. J. Electron. Gov. Res. **8**, 14–33 (2012)
28. Bharosa, N., Janssen, M., van Wijk, R., de Winne, N., van der Voort, H., Hulstijn, J., Tan, Y.-H.: Tapping into existing information flows: the transformation to compliance by design in business-to-government information exchange. Gov. Inf. Q. **30**, S9–S18 (2013)
29. Customs Administration of the Netherlands: Pushing Boundaries: The Customs Administration of The Netherlands' Point on the Horizon for the Enforcement on Continuously Increasing Flows of Goods (2014)
30. Baldauf, M., Dustdar, S., Rosenberg, F.: A survey on context-aware systems. Int. J. Ad Hoc Ubiquitous Comput. **2**, 263 (2007)
31. Cheverst, K., Davies, N., Mitchell, K., Friday, A., Efstratiou, C.: Developing a context-aware electronic tourist guide. In: Proceedings of SIGCHI Conference on Human Factors Computing Systems - CHI 2000, pp. 17–24 (2000)

Finding All Minimum-Size DFA Consistent with Given Examples: SAT-Based Approach

Ilya Zakirzyanov[1,2]([✉]), Anatoly Shalyto[1], and Vladimir Ulyantsev[1]

[1] ITMO University, Saint Petersburg, Russia
{zakirzyanov,ulyantsev}@rain.ifmo.ru, shalyto@mail.ifmo.ru
[2] JetBrains Research, Saint Petersburg, Russia

Abstract. Deterministic finite automaton (DFA) is a fundamental concept in the theory of computation. The NP-hard DFA identification problem can be efficiently solved by translation to the Boolean satisfiability problem (SAT). Previously we developed a technique to reduce the problem search space by enforcing DFA states to be enumerated in breadth-first search (BFS) order. We proposed symmetry breaking predicates, which can be added to Boolean formulae representing various automata identification problems. In this paper we continue the study of SAT-based approaches. First, we propose new predicates based on depth-first search order. Second, we present three methods to identify all non-isomorphic automata of the minimum size instead of just one—the #P-complete problem which has not been solved before. Third, we revisited our implementation of the BFS-based approach and conducted new evaluation experiments. It occurs that BFS-based approach outperforms all other exact algorithms for DFA identification and can be effectively applied for finding all solutions of the problem.

Keywords: Grammatical inference · Automata identification
Symmetry breaking · Boolean satisfiability

1 Introduction

A variety of models exists in automata theory but a *deterministic finite automaton* (DFA) is the basic one and among the most important ones. DFA is a model that recognizes regular languages [1]. The essence of the DFA identification (induction, learning, synthesis) problem is to find a minimum-size DFA (a DFA with the minimum number of states) that is consistent with a given set of labeled examples—positive-labeled strings that must be accepted by the built DFA and negative-labeled strings that must be rejected. A smaller DFA is simpler and, because of well-known Occam's razor principle, is a model which better explains the observed examples. Thus the DFA learning problem is to find the regular language that most likely was used to generate a set of labeled examples. This problem is among the best-explored ones in grammatical inference [2].

© Springer International Publishing AG 2018
A. Cerone and M. Roveri (Eds.): SEFM 2017 Workshops, LNCS 10729, pp. 117–131, 2018.
https://doi.org/10.1007/978-3-319-74781-1_9

This problem was shown to be NP-hard in [3]. Nevertheless, several efficient DFA learning approaches were developed, see, e.g., [2]. DFA identification using evolutionary computation methods is one of historically the first and effective approaches, see, e.g., [4,5]. Subsequent research resulted in development of a method for evolving DFA using a multi-start random hill climber, see, e.g., [6].

Later approaches are based on heuristic algorithms. The *evidence driven state-merging* algorithm (EDSM) is the most commonly used and the only one which can handle large-sized target DFA [7]. This algorithm is greedy and works in polynomial time. Despite its efficiency in terms of solving time this approach usually finds only a local optimum but not a global one. The performance of EDSM was several times improved by using specialized search procedures, see, e.g., [8,9]. In [6] Lucas and Reynolds compared the EDSM algorithm and the evolutionary algorithm (EA) mentioned above. They found that the EDSM-based approach outperforms the EA in terms of solving time on almost all instances.

The methods mentioned above are not exact—they cannot guarantee that the found DFA is one of the minimum-sized ones. Heule and Verwer proposed so-called *translation-to-SAT* approach which can be applied to DFA identification [10]. This approach, as it can be obtained from the name, is based on the translation the original problem to well-studied *Boolean satisfiability problem* (SAT). The performance of SAT solvers has significantly improved over the last decade. This computational strength can be used in other problems by *translating* these problems into SAT instances, and subsequently running a modern SAT solver on them. This approach was shown to be very competitive for some problems, see, e.g., [11–14]. The authors have shown that translation-to-SAT is effective for solving DFA identification as well. The SAT-based method is exact as opposed to EA and EDSM algorithms, which is important because of the mentioned Occam's razor principle. The authors also proposed a combined approach, which used a few EDSM steps as a preprocessing step, and won the first prize at the *StaMInA* competition [15]. We do not consider of this step in our paper because EDSM is not an exact algorithm.

There are *symmetries* in many combinatorial problems. *Symmetry breaking predicates* can be added as constraints to SAT formula with purpose of elimination some or all symmetries and thus reduce the search space, see, e.g., [16]. When we talk about DFA the most obvious symmetries are groups of isomorphic automata. Heule and Verwer in [10] proposed simple but effective greedy *maximal clique* (max-clique) algorithm. It allows reducing the amount of isomorphic automata in each group from $n!$ to $(n - k)!$, where n is the size of the DFA and k is the size of the found clique. We proposed symmetry breaking predicates which enforce DFA states to be enumerated in the breadth-first search (BFS) order in [17]. These predicates can be added to a Boolean formula before passing it to a SAT solver. This approach allows to reduce the amount of isomorphic automata in each group from $n!$ to only one representative—the BFS-enumerated one. The results for the exact case still were not very good in our previous paper. However, the BFS-based approach is more flexible than max-clique—we demonstrated its flexibility by developing a modification of the noiseless translation-to-SAT technique for the noisy case (some examples are wrong-labeled).

In this paper we propose new symmetry breaking predicates based on depth-first search (DFS) order. This is the modification of our previous BFS-based approach. BFS-based predicates were not good enough to compete with the max-clique algorithm in DFA identification in our previous paper. Therefore we revisited our implementation of this technique. It occurs that both BFS-based and DFS-based approaches clearly outperform current state-of-the-art DFASAT from [10]. We also propose a method based on these techniques for solving the *problem of finding all automata* (find-all) with the minimum number of states which are consistent with a given set of examples. This problem has not been solved efficiently before. Moreover, none of the existing approaches for the DFA learning are applicable, even with slight modifications, to solve the find-all problem due to their nature. We use two ways of launching SAT solvers: relaunching a non-incremental solver and using an incremental solver. We also developed the heuristic backtracking method (almost similar to the one presented in the paper [18]) as a baseline for comparing it with SAT-based ones.

2   Preliminaries and Previous Work

2.1   Encoding DFA Identification into SAT

We assume the reader to be familiar with the theory of languages and automata. The purpose of the DFA identification problem is to find the minimum DFA which is consistent with two given sets of strings: a set of positive examples (S_+) and is a set of negative examples (S_-). In other words, the desired DFA must accept all strings from S_+ and reject all strings from S_-. In this paper it is assumed that DFA states are numbered from 1 to C and the start state has number 1. The example of the minimum DFA for $S_+ = \{aba, bb, bba\}$ and $S_- = \{b, ba\}$ is shown in Fig. 1a.

We briefly describe the current state-of-the-art approach for solving the considered problem. The first step of the technique proposed by Heule and Verwer in [10] is to build an *augmented prefix tree acceptor* (APTA) from the given sets S_+ and S_-. An APTA is a tree-shaped automaton based on a prefix tree for the sets S_+ and S_- but with labeled states. It is called augmented because it may contain states which are not accepting or rejecting. The APTA for S_+ and S_- mentioned above is shown in Fig. 1b.

The second step is to construct the *consistency graph* (CG) for the built APTA. The set of the CG vertices is the same as the APTA vertices set. Two vertices in the CG are adjacent if their merging in the APTA and subsequent determinization process will cause an inconsistency: a situation when an accepting state is merged with a rejecting one. The CG for APTA from Fig. 1b is shown in Fig. 1c.

The third step of the method is to divide the CG vertices set into C disjoint sets. Each set has to contain all vertices equivalent to the corresponding APTA states which will be merged into one state in the resulting DFA. If such a separation can be made, then the automaton with C states consistent with the given sets of strings exists and it can be easily built. C can be iterated from 1 and until

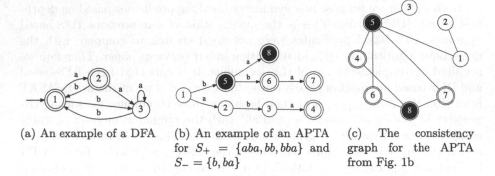

(a) An example of a DFA

(b) An example of an APTA for $S_+ = \{aba, bb, bba\}$ and $S_- = \{b, ba\}$

(c) The consistency graph for the APTA from Fig. 1b

Fig. 1. An example of an APTA and its consistency graph

such a partition is found. Thus it is guaranteed that the found C-sized DFA is the minimum DFA consistent with given behavior examples. This can be viewed as a *graph coloring* problem and we need to color CG vertices into the minimum number of colors in such a way that adjacent vertices have different colors.

The next step in the considered algorithm is to translate the graph coloring problem into SAT. Authors proposed so-called *compact encoding* where they use three kinds of Boolean variables to formulate all constraints in CNF: *color variables* $x_{v,i}$ which indicate whether the vertex v in the CG is i-colored; *parent relation variables* $y_{a,i,j}$ which indicate whether there is an a-labeled transition from the i-colored state to the j-colored state in the target DFA; *accepting color variables* z_i which indicate whether the i-colored state in the target DFA is accepting. There are four mandatory and four redundant types of clauses in the proposed compact encoding. The reader can read about them in detail in [10]. The final step of the translation-to-SAT approach is to run an external SAT solver with the built CNF formula. If the formula is satisfiable, then the target DFA can be easily constructed from the found satisfying assignment. Otherwise, the number of colors C is increased.

2.2   Symmetry Breakings Predicates

Large Clique Predicates. Heule and Verwer used symmetry breaking predicates in their algorithm [10]. In the case when the CG cannot be colored into C colors the SAT solver tries to solve the same problem $C!$ times—one time for each permutation of colors. In other words the solver considers $C!$ isomorphic automata. The authors suggested to find some large clique in the CG and to fix the colors of its vertices. It helps to reduce the number of unnecessary considerations because in any valid graph coloring all vertices in a clique obviously have different colors. Thus, assuming that the size of the found clique is k, the solver considers only $(C - k)!$ isomorphic automata. Moreover, the process of iterating over C can be started from k instead of 1.

BFS-based Predicates. We proposed the new approach to symmetry breaking in our previous research [17]. Its main idea is to enforce DFA states to be enumerated in the *breadth-first search* (BFS) order. If some order (say lexicographical) on the transition symbols is fixed then only one representative of each equivalence class with respect to the isomorphic relation is BFS-enumerated due to the uniqueness of such BFS traversal. We call a DFA *BFS-enumerated* if its enumeration corresponds to the order of states processing during the BFS traversal. In other words, if we consider a BFS tree, built for some DFA and if we arrange the children of each state from left to right according to the chosen order on the transition symbols then numbers of states should increase from left to right on the same depth (*layer-order*) and from top to bottom (*depth-order*). In [17] we used the definition based on a BFS-queue which is equivalent to the one described above but less apprehensible. An example of a BFS-enumerated DFA is shown in Fig. 2a, and its BFS tree is shown in Fig. 2b.

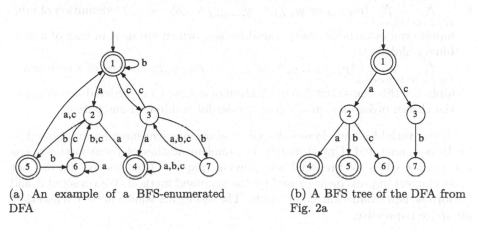

(a) An example of a BFS-enumerated DFA

(b) A BFS tree of the DFA from Fig. 2a

Fig. 2. A BFS-enumerated DFA and its BFS-tree

If such predicates are used then while a SAT solver searches for a DFA consistent with the given samples, it is restricted to only BFS-enumerated ones. To implement this we proposed three additional kinds of Boolean variables:

1. parent variables $p_{j,i}$ which are true if and only if state i is the parent of state j in the BFS tree;
2. transition variables $t_{i,j}$ which are true if and only if there is a transition from state i to state j;
3. minimum symbol variables $m_{l,i,j}$ which are true if and only if there is a l-labeled transition from state i to state j and there are no such transitions labeled with a smaller symbol (according to the choosen order on symbols). These variables are used only in the case of a non-binary alphabet.

BFS-enumeration is enforced with the following seven clauses:

1. $\bigwedge\limits_{1\leqslant i<j\leqslant C} (t_{i,j} \Leftrightarrow y_{l_1,i,j} \vee \ldots \vee y_{l_L,i,j})$—definition of transition variables using variables $y_{l,i,j}$;

2. $\bigwedge\limits_{1\leqslant i<j\leqslant C} (p_{j,i} \Leftrightarrow t_{i,j} \wedge \neg t_{i-1,j} \wedge \ldots \wedge \neg t_{1,j})$—definition of parent variables using variables $t_{i,j}$;

3. $\bigwedge\limits_{2\leqslant j\leqslant C} (p_{j,1} \vee p_{j,2} \vee \ldots \vee p_{j,j-1})$—each state except the start one holds a parent with a smaller number (depth-order);

4. $\bigwedge\limits_{1\leqslant k<i<j<C} (p_{j,i} \Rightarrow \neg p_{j+1,k})$—the ordering of children must be the same as the ordering of parents (layer-order for children of different parents);

5. $\bigwedge\limits_{1\leqslant i<j<C} (p_{j,i} \wedge p_{j+1,i} \Rightarrow y_{a,i,j})$—in case of a binary alphabet this constraint is sufficient to order two children j and $j+1$ of state i (layer-order for children of one parent);

6. $\bigwedge\limits_{1\leqslant i<j\leqslant C} \bigwedge\limits_{1\leqslant n\leqslant L} (m_{l_n,i,j} \Leftrightarrow y_{l_n,i,j} \wedge \neg y_{l_{n-1},i,j} \wedge \ldots \wedge \neg y_{l_1,i,j})$—definition of minimum symbol variables using variables $y_{l,i,j}$ which are used in case of a non-binary alphabet;

7. $\bigwedge\limits_{1\leqslant i<j<C} \bigwedge\limits_{1\leqslant k<n\leqslant L} (p_{j,i} \wedge p_{j+1,i} \wedge m_{l_n,i,j} \Rightarrow \neg m_{l_k,i,j+1})$—in case of a non-binary alphabet this constraint forces children of a state to be ordered according to the chosen order on symbols (layer-order for children of one parent).

Using variables and clauses described above one can force an automaton to be BFS-enumerated. Unfortunately the implementation of these methods was not perfect when we prepared our previous paper [17] so the results did not show the real improvement caused by the proposed method. We revisited it and performed new evaluation experiments. The results are shown in Sect. 5 and they are quite impressive.

3   DFS-Based Symmetry Breaking Predicates

In this section we propose a new way to fix automata states enumeration to avoid consideration of isomorphic automata during SAT solving. This approach is a modification of our BFS-based predicates. It enforces automata states to be enumerated in the *depth-first search* (DFS) order. We describe the method briefly, paying attention only to the differences between DFS- and BFS-based approaches. Detailed information about BFS-based predicates can be found in Sect. 2.2.

During DFS processing it is necessary to find all adjacent unvisited states for each unvisited state of the DFA. Firstly, the DFS algorithm handles the initial DFA state. Then the algorithm processes the children of this state and recursively executes for each of them. We process child states in some particular (e.g., alphabetical) order of symbols l on transitions $i \xrightarrow{l} j$. Thus again only one representative of each equivalence class with respect to the isomorphic relation will be processed. We call a DFA *DFS-enumerated* if its states are numbered in the order of handling them by DFS traversal with chosen symbol order. Although there is no traversal, we refer to it for the definition and explanation. The set of developed constraints enforces DFS. An example of a DFS-enumerated DFA is shown in Fig. 3a. A DFS tree for this DFA is shown in Fig. 3b.

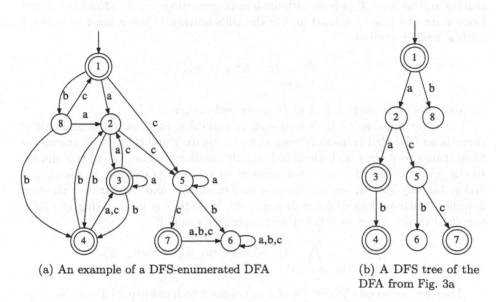

(a) An example of a DFS-enumerated DFA

(b) A DFS tree of the DFA from Fig. 3a

Fig. 3. A DFS-enumerated DFA and its DFS tree

All variables which were used for the BFS enumeration are also used for the DFS enumeration, but some the constraints must be changed. In the DFS enumeration $p_{j,i}$ variables ($p_{j,i}$ is true if and only if state i is the parent of j in the DFS tree) are defined differently. Due to the greediness of the DFS algorithm, state i is the parent of state j if it has the maximum number among states that have a transition to j:

$$\bigwedge_{1 \le i < j \le C} (p_{j,i} \Leftrightarrow t_{i,j} \wedge \neg t_{i+1,j} \wedge \ldots \wedge \neg t_{j-1,j}),$$

where $t_{i,j} \equiv 1$ if and only if there is a transition between i and j (these variables in their turn are defined by using $y_{l,i,j}$ variables).

Moreover, in the DFS enumeration instead of the children ordering constraint we use the following one. If i is the parent of state j and k is a state between i and j ($i < k < j$) then there is no transition from state k to state q, where q is bigger than j:

$$\bigwedge_{1 \le i < k < j < q < C} (p_{j,i} \Rightarrow \neg t_{k,q}).$$

Indeed, since $i < k < j$, state k has to be considered by the DFS algorithm before state j. Hence if such a transition would exist then state k must have a lower number than state j.

Now, to enforce the DFA to be DFS-enumerated we have to order children according to symbols on transitions (e.g., alphabetically). We consider two cases: alphabet Σ consists of two symbols $\{a, b\}$ and more than two symbols $\{l_1, \ldots, l_L\}$. In the case of two symbols state i can have only two transitions: to state j and to state k (where without loss of generality $j < k$). If the transition from state i to state j is used during the DFS traversal then it must be labeled with a smaller symbol:

$$\bigwedge_{1 \le i < j < k < C} (p_{j,i} \wedge t_{i,k} \Rightarrow y_{a,i,j}),$$

because otherwise state k had to be processed earlier.

In the second case we have to use $m_{l,i,j}$ variables: $m_{l,i,j}$ is true if and only if there is an l-labeled transition from state i to state j and there is no transition from state i to state j with an alphabetically smaller symbol. The idea is similar to the previous case. For state i it remains to arrange its children in the chosen order. For any two transitions from state i to state j and from state i to state k (where without loss of generality $j < k$), if state j is used during the DFS traversal then it must be labeled with a smaller symbol:

$$\bigwedge_{1 \le i < j < k \le C} \bigwedge_{1 \le m < n \le L} (p_{j,i} \wedge t_{i,k} \wedge m_{l_n,i,j} \Rightarrow \neg m_{l_m,i,k}).$$

Thus we proposed the new set of constraints which enforce a DFA to be DFS-enumerated. The predicates (for the case of three or more symbols) translated into $\mathcal{O}(C^4 + C^3 L^2)$ (where C is the number of colors and L is the alphabet size) CNF clauses which are listed in Table 1 together with BFS-based predicates, which are translated into $\mathcal{O}(C^3 + C^2 L^2)$ clauses.

Table 1. DFS-based and BFS-based symmetry breaking clauses

	Clauses	Range
Both	$t_{i,j} \Rightarrow (y_{l_1,i,j} \vee \ldots \vee y_{l_L,i,j})$	$1 \le i < j \le C$
	$y_{i,j,l} \Rightarrow t_{i,j}$	$1 \le i < j \le C;\ l \in \Sigma$
	$p_{j,i} \Rightarrow t_{i,j}$	$1 \le i < j \le C$
	$p_{j,1} \vee p_{j,2} \vee \ldots \vee p_{j,j-1}$	$2 \le j \le C$
	$m_{l,i,j} \Rightarrow y_{l,i,j}$	$1 \le i < j \le C;\ l \in \Sigma$
	$m_{l_n,i,j} \Rightarrow \neg y_{l_k,i,j}$	$1 \le i < j \le C;\ 1 \le k < n \le L$
	$(y_{l_n,i,j} \wedge \neg y_{l_{n-1},i,j} \wedge \ldots \wedge \neg y_{l_1,i,j}) \Rightarrow m_{l_n,i,j}$	$1 \le i < j \le C;\ 1 \le n \le L$
DFS	$p_{j,i} \Rightarrow \neg t_{k,j}$	$1 \le i < k < j \le C$
	$(t_{i,j} \wedge \neg t_{i+1,j} \wedge \ldots \wedge \neg t_{j-1,j}) \Rightarrow p_{j,i}$	$1 \le i < j \le C$
	$p_{j,i} \Rightarrow \neg t_{k,q}$	$1 \le i < k < j < q \le C$
	$(p_{j,i} \wedge p_{k,i} \wedge m_{l_n,i,j}) \Rightarrow \neg m_{l_m,i,k}$	$1 \le i < j < k \le C;\ 1 \le m < n \le L$
BFS	$p_{j,i} \Rightarrow \neg t_{k,j}$	$1 \le k < i < j \le C$
	$(t_{i,j} \wedge \neg t_{i-1,j} \wedge \ldots \wedge \neg t_{1,j}) \Rightarrow p_{j,i}$	$1 \le i < j \le C$
	$p_{j,i} \Rightarrow \neg p_{j+1,k}$	$1 \le k < i < j < C$
	$(p_{j,i} \wedge p_{j+1,i} \wedge m_{l_n,i,j}) \Rightarrow \neg m_{l_m,i,j+1}$	$1 \le i < j < C;\ 1 \le m < n \le L$

4   The Find-All Problem

In this section we consider the problem of finding all non-isomorphic DFA (*find-all problem*) with the minimum number of states which are consistent with a given set of strings. We propose a way to modify the SAT-based method of solving regular DFA identification problem in order to apply it to the find-all problem. We consider two ways of using SAT solvers: restarting a non-incremental solver after finding each automaton and using an incremental solver—if such a solver finds a solution, it retains its state and is ready to accept new clauses. The most common interface and technique for incremental SAT solving was proposed in [19]. We also propose the heuristic backtracking method as a baseline for comparing it with SAT-based ones.

4.1   SAT-Based Methods

The main idea of SAT-based methods of solving the find-all problem is to ban satisfying interpretations (variable values) which have already been found. It is obvious that if the proposed symmetry breaking predicates are not used then this approach finds many isomorphic automata—exactly $C!$ for each equivalence class where C is the DFA size. Since max-clique predicates fix k colors only (where k is the clique size), the algorithm of Heule and Verwer finds $(C - k)!$ isomorphic automata which is still bad. The BFS-based and DFS-based symmetry breaking predicates allow us to ban isomorphic DFA from one equality class by banning an accordingly enumerated representative. It must be noted that although the idea to discard satisfying interpretations is classic for such methods, it cannot be used in practice without effective symmetry breaking techniques. There were no known techniques to deal with factorial number of isomorphic automata earlier, and thus the considered problem could not be solved effectively. Proposed symmetry breaking predicates change the situation and bring the solution. It is easy to implement this by adding a *blocking* clause into the Boolean formula. Since we know that $y_{l,i,j}$ variables define the structure of the target DFA entirely, it is enough to forbid only values of these variables from the found interpretation:

$$\neg y_1 \vee \neg y_2 \vee \ldots \vee \neg y_{n|\Sigma|},$$

where y_k is some $y_{l,i,j}$ from the found interpretation for $1 < k < n|\Sigma|$.

There are two different ways of using SAT solvers as it was stated above. First, we can restart a non-incremental SAT solver with the new Boolean formula with the blocking clause after finding each automaton. The second approach is based on incremental SAT solvers: after each found automaton we add the blocking clause to the solver and continue its execution.

It is necessary to mention the case when some transitions of the found DFA are not covered by the APTA. It means that there are some *free* transitions which are not used during processing any given word and each such transition can end in any state, since this does not influence the consistency of the DFA with a given set of strings. But in the case of the find-all problem basically we do not wish to find all these automata distinguished only by such transitions. Thus we propose a way to force all free transitions to be self-loops—end in the same state as they start. To achieve that we add auxiliary 'used' variables: $u_{l,i}$ is true if and only if there is an l-labeled APTA edge from the i-colored state:

$$\bigwedge_{l\in\Sigma}\bigwedge_{1\le i\le C} u_{l,i} \Leftrightarrow x_{1,i} \vee \ldots \vee x_{|V_l|,i},$$

where V_l is the set of all the APTA states which have an outcoming edge labeled with l. To force unused transitions to be self-loop we add the following constraints:

$$\bigwedge_{l\in\Sigma}\bigwedge_{1\le i\le C} \neg u_{l,i} \Rightarrow y_{l,i,i}.$$

These additional constraints are translated into $\mathcal{O}(C|L|)$ clauses. See Fig. 4 for an example of an APTA for $S_+ = \{ab, b, ba, bbb\}$ and $S_- = \{abbb\}$ and its consistent DFA with an unused transition. If we add the proposed constraints, then this transition will be forced to be a loop as shown by a dashed line in Fig. 4b.

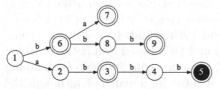
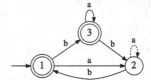

(a) An example of an APTA for $S_+ = \{ab, b, ba, bbb\}$ and $S_- = \{abbb\}$

(b) The DFA is built from the APTA from Fig. 4a with unused a-labeled transition from state 2

Fig. 4. An example of an APTA and its consistent DFA

4.2   Backtracking Algorithm

The solution based on backtracking does not use any external tools like SAT solvers. This algorithm works as follows. Initially there is an empty DFA with n states. Also there is a *frontier*—the set of edges from the APTA which are not yet represented in the DFA. Initially the frontier contains all outcoming edges of the APTA root. The recursive function Backtracking maintains the frontier in the proper state. If the frontier is not empty, then the function tries to augment the DFA with one of its edges. Each found DFA is checked to be consistent with the APTA and if the DFA complies with it then an updated frontier is found. If the frontier is empty then the DFA is checked for completeness (a DFA is complete if there are transitions from each state labeled with all alphabet symbols). If it is not complete and there are nodes which have the number of outcoming edges less than the alphabet size then we add missing edges as self-loops with function MakeComplete. Algorithm 1 illustrates the solution. The function FindNewFrontier returns the new frontier for the augmented DFA or null if the DFA is inconsistent with the APTA. This algorithm is an exact search algorithm based on the one from [18].

Data: augmented prefix tree acceptor APTA, current DFA (initially empty),
        frontier (initially contains all APTA root outcoming edges)
DFAset ← new Set<DFA>
edge ← any edge from frontier
foreach destination ∈ 1..|S| do
    source ← the state of DFA from which edge should be added
    DFA' ← DFA ∪ transition(source, destination, edge.label)
    frontier' ← FindNewFrontier(APTA, DFA', frontier)
    if frontier' ≠ *null* then
        if frontier' = ∅ then
           | DFAset.add(MakeComplete(DFA'))
        else
           | DFAset.add(Backtracking(APTA, DFA', frontier'))
        end
    end
end
return DFAset

Algorithm 1. Backtracking solution

---

5   Experiments

All experiments were performed using a machine with an AMD Opteron 6378 2.4 GHz processor running Ubuntu 14.04. All algorithms were implemented in Java, the *lingeling* SAT solver was used [20]. As far as we know all common benchmarks are too hard for solving by exact algorithms without some heuristic non-exact steps. Thus our own algorithm was used for generating problem instances. This algorithm builds a set of strings with the following parameters: size N of DFA to be generated, alphabet size A, the number S of strings to be generated. The algorithm is arranged as follows. First of all N states are generated and uniquely numerated from 1 to N. Each state is equiprobably set to be accepting or rejecting. Next on step i the algorithm picks state i, evenly chooses another state from $[i + 1; N]$ and adds a random-labeled transition from the first state to the second. After $N - 1$ such steps we have partially built an automaton where all states are reachable from the initial one (1-numbered). In the end the algorithm picks each state one by one and add all missing (in terms of automaton completeness) transitions with destination randomly chosen among all states. Finally S strings are generated by processing the automaton.

The distribution of the words' length is shifted to longer words. These strings with the accepting or rejecting labels form the instance of the DFA identification problem.

For DFA identification we used the following parameters: $N \in [10; 30]$ with step 2, $A = 2$, $S = 50N$. We compared the SAT-based approach with three types of symmetry breaking predicates: the max-clique algorithm from [10] (the current state-of-the-art) and the proposed DFS-based and BFS-based methods. Each experiment was repeated 100 times. The time limit was set to 3600 s. The results are listed in Table 2. It can be seen from the table that both DFS-based and BFS-based strategies clearly outperform the max-clique approach. BFS-based strategy in its turn notably outperforms DFS-based one when target automaton size is larger than 14. These results for the BFS-based approach were not obtained in our previous research due to weaker technical implementation.

Table 2. Median execution times of exact solving DFA identification in seconds

N	DFS	BFS	max-clique
10	20.9	20.5	23.3
12	40.4	37.6	240.3
14	82.2	62.4	TL
16	205.1	114.1	TL
18	601.7	181.9	TL
20	2501.6	293.7	TL
22	TL	453.3	TL
24	TL	625.1	TL
26	TL	925.8	TL
28	TL	1314.4	TL
30	TL	1635.5	TL

The second experiment concerned the find-all problem. A random dataset was also used here. We used the following parameters: $N \in [5; 15]$, $A = 2$, $S \in \{5N, 10N, 25N\}$. We compared the BFS-SAT-based method with the restarting strategy (REST column in the table), the BFS-SAT-based method with the incremental strategy (INC) and the backtracking method (BTR). Each experiment was repeated 100 times as well. The time limit was set to 3600 s. The results are given in Table 3. The first column in each subtable contains the number of instances which have more than one DFA in the solution (> 1). If less than 50 instances were solved then TL is shown instead of a value. It can be seen from the table that SAT-based methods work significantly faster than the backtracking one when the size of the automaton is greater than 8. It happens because the SAT-based methods with BFS-based predicates consider only one DFA for each equivalence class with respect to the isomorphic relation instead

Table 3. Median execution times in seconds of SAT-based restart method, SAT-based incremental method and backtracking method

$|N|$	$S = 5|N|$				$S = 10|N|$				$S = 25|N|$			
	>1	REST	INC	BTR	>1	REST	INC	BTR	>1	REST	INC	BTR
5	53	2.3	2.0	0.8	40	3.6	3.3	1.3	17	4.1	3.4	1.5
6	56	2.8	2.4	2.1	31	4.7	3.9	1.7	27	5.4	4.3	1.7
7	87	3.9	2.5	4.1	27	3.7	3.0	3.1	13	7.4	6.7	2.5
8	80	4.6	3.7	87.2	34	7.0	6.5	41.7	16	10.1	8.9	11.6
9	91	7.6	3.9	475.1	50	7.7	6.4	121.6	10	13.8	13.0	61.4
10	89	15.7	5.3	2756.2	47	8.6	7.0	974.7	11	18.8	16.1	276.8
11	94	19.9	7.3	TL	63	18.5	13.8	3108.0	9	24.5	21.9	1158.4
12	90	28.0	9.9	TL	49	22.3	16.7	TL	8	33.5	27.2	3289.1
13	92	185.5	18.1	TL	57	36.9	22.6	TL	12	62.0	51.4	TL
14	87	408.5	49.0	TL	71	85.1	41.8	TL	4	67.0	56.2	TL
15	95	571.1	174.1	TL	69	193.3	95.7	TL	6	29.2	26.2	TL

of $N!$. As we see, the incremental strategy in its turn clearly outperforms the restart strategy. It can be explained as incremental SAT solver saves its state but non-incremental solver does the same actions on each execution.

Our implementation of proposed predicates and algorithms is available on our laboratory github repository[1].

6   Conclusions

We have proposed DFS-based symmetry breaking predicates. They can be added to the Boolean formula before passing it to a SAT solver while solving various DFA identification problems with SAT-based algorithms. Using these predicates allows reducing the problem search space by enforcing DFA states to be enumerated in the depth-first search order.

We have revisited our implementation of the proposed symmetry breaking predicates and compared the translation-to-SAT method from [10] to the same one with proposed symmetry breaking predicates instead of original maxclique predicates. The proposed approach clearly improved the translation-to-SAT technique which was demonstrated with the experiments on randomly generated input data. The BFS-based approach has shown better results than the DFS-based one if the target DFA size is large.

Then, we have proposed a solution for the find-all DFA problem. The proposed approach can efficiently solve the problem that the previously developed methods cannot be applied for. We performed the experiments which have shown

---

[1] https://github.com/ctlab/DFA-Inductor.

that our approach with the incremental SAT solver clearly outperfoms the Backtracking algorithm.

Acknowledgements. The authors would like to thank Igor Buzhinsky, Daniil Chivilikhin, Maxim Buzdalov for useful comments. This work was financially supported by the Government of Russian Federation, Grant 074-U01.

References

1. Hopcroft, J., Motwani, R., Ullman, J.: Introduction to Automata Theory, Languages, and Computation. Addison-Wesley, Boston (2006)
2. De La Higuera, C.: A bibliographical study of grammatical inference. Pattern Recogn. **38**(9), 1332–1348 (2005)
3. Gold, E.M.: Complexity of automaton identification from given data. Inf. Control **37**(3), 302–320 (1978)
4. Dupont, P.: Regular grammatical inference from positive and negative samples by genetic search: the GIG method. In: Carrasco, R.C., Oncina, J. (eds.) ICGI 1994. LNCS, vol. 862, pp. 236–245. Springer, Heidelberg (1994). https://doi.org/10.1007/3-540-58473-0_152
5. Luke, S., Hamahashi, S., Kitano, H.: Genetic programming. In: Proceedings of the genetic and evolutionary computation conference, vol. 2, pp. 1098–1105 (1999)
6. Lucas, S.M., Reynolds, T.J.: Learning DFA: evolution versus evidence driven state merging. In: The 2003 Congress on Evolutionary Computation, 2003. CEC 2003, vol. 1, pp. 351–358. IEEE (2003)
7. Lang, K.J., Pearlmutter, B.A., Price, R.A.: Results of the Abbadingo one DFA learning competition and a new evidence-driven state merging algorithm. In: Honavar, V., Slutzki, G. (eds.) ICGI 1998. LNCS, vol. 1433, pp. 1–12. Springer, Heidelberg (1998). https://doi.org/10.1007/BFb0054059
8. Lang, K.J.: Faster algorithms for finding minimal consistent DFAs. Technical report (1999)
9. Bugalho, M., Oliveira, A.L.: Inference of regular languages using state merging algorithms with search. Pattern Recogn. **38**(9), 1457–1467 (2005)
10. Heule, M.J.H., Verwer, S.: Exact DFA identification using SAT solvers. In: Sempere, J.M., García, P. (eds.) ICGI 2010. LNCS (LNAI), vol. 6339, pp. 66–79. Springer, Heidelberg (2010). https://doi.org/10.1007/978-3-642-15488-1_7
11. Lohfert, R., Lu, J.J., Zhao, D.: Solving SQL constraints by incremental translation to SAT. In: Nguyen, N.T., Borzemski, L., Grzech, A., Ali, M. (eds.) IEA/AIE 2008. LNCS (LNAI), vol. 5027, pp. 669–676. Springer, Heidelberg (2008). https://doi.org/10.1007/978-3-540-69052-8_70
12. Galeotti, J.P., Rosner, N., Pombo, C.G.L., Frias, M.F.: TACO: efficient SAT-based bounded verification using symmetry breaking and tight bounds. IEEE Trans. Softw. Eng. **39**(9), 1283–1307 (2013)
13. Ulyantsev, V., Tsarev, F.: Extended finite-state machine induction using SAT-solver. In: Proceedings of ICMLA 2011, vol. 2, pp. 346–349. IEEE (2011)
14. Zbrzezny, A.: A new translation from ECTL* to SAT. Fundamenta Informaticae **120**(3–4), 375–395 (2012)
15. Walkinshaw, N., Lambeau, B., Damas, C., Bogdanov, K., Dupont, P.: STAMINA: a competition to encourage the development and assessment of software model inference techniques. Empirical Software Engineering **18**(4), 791–824 (2013)

16. Crawford, J., Ginsberg, M., Luks, E., Roy, A.: Symmetry-breaking predicates for search problems. KR **96**, 148–159 (1996)
17. Ulyantsev, V., Zakirzyanov, I., Shalyto, A.: BFS-based symmetry breaking predicates for DFA identification. In: Dediu, A.-H., Formenti, E., Martín-Vide, C., Truthe, B. (eds.) LATA 2015. LNCS, vol. 8977, pp. 611–622. Springer, Cham (2015). https://doi.org/10.1007/978-3-319-15579-1_48
18. Ulyantsev, V., Buzhinsky, I., Shalyto, A.: Exact finite-state machine identification from scenarios and temporal properties. Int. J. Softw. Tools Technol. Transf. 1–21 (2016)
19. Eén, N., Sörensson, N.: An extensible SAT-solver. In: Giunchiglia, E., Tacchella, A. (eds.) SAT 2003. LNCS, vol. 2919, pp. 502–518. Springer, Heidelberg (2004). https://doi.org/10.1007/978-3-540-24605-3_37
20. Biere, A.: Splatz, lingeling, plingeling, treengeling, YalSAT entering the SAT competition 2016. In: Proceedings of SAT Competition, pp. 44–45 (2016)

FAACS 2017

FAACS 2017 Organizers' Message

The First International Workshop on Formal Approaches for Advanced Computing Systems (FAACS 2017) was held in Trento, Italy, on September 4, 2017.

The way services and information are currently delivered to a multitude of end-users is changing impressively thanks to the availability of systems built on new technologies (such as IoT connectivity and smart devices) and exposing complex computational models (such as mobile, cloud, autonomic, adaptive, etc.). The development of these *advanced computing systems* requires the integration of heterogeneous methods, techniques, and solutions already individually tested in specific contexts. Moreover, owing to the employment of emerging technologies, assuring reliability, safety, and availability of such systems is a very challenging issue that requires rigorous modeling and analysis techniques. *Formal approaches* have been widely applied in the area of classic distributed systems. The challenge now is how to deal with the new problems (e.g., uncertainty, untrustworthiness, information loss, etc.) that are emerging in the development and maintenance of advanced computing systems.

The FAACS workshop was a forum for researchers and practitioners to discuss the suitability of formal methods for the specification and analysis of advanced computing systems, as well as the upcoming challenges for the formal method community in devising rigorous approaches able to deal with characteristics of the emerging technologies and computational models of this class of systems.

The workshop received six submissions, which were carefully reviewed by the three Program Committee members; four papers were accepted for presentation. There were interdisciplinary research contributions mostly related to formal approaches for monitoring cloud-enabled large-scale distributed systems, for intercepting security attacks in mobile ad hoc networks, for testing machine-learning computer programs, and for run-time verification of microservice-oriented applications. The authors of the papers presented at the workshop were invited to submit extended versions of their papers to these proceedings, taking into account feedback from the reviewers as well as discussions during the workshop and the mini-panels following each session.

We would like to thank the Program Committee and reviewers, who did an excellent job reviewing and subsequently participating in the discussion for acceptance of the papers. Furthermore, we want to thank the organizers of SEFM 2017 for their impressive responsiveness and help, and in particular the workshop chairs, Antonio Cerone and Marco Roveri.

We also extend our gratitude to EasyChair for its support in the organization process of FAACS 2017.

September 2017

Paolo Arcaini
Marina Mongiello
Elvinia Riccobene
Patrizia Scandurra

Organization

FAACS 2017 - Steering Committee

Paolo Arcaini	Charles University, Czech Republic
Marina Mongiello	Politecnico di Bari, Italy
Elvinia Riccobene	Università degli Studi di Milano, Italy
Patrizia Scandurra	University of Bergamo, Italy

FAACS 2017 - Program Committee

Yamine Ait Ameur	IRIT, France
Alessandro Bianchi	University of Bari, Italy
Chiara Braghin	University of Milan, Italy
Antonio Bucchiarone	Bruno Kessler Foundation of Trento, Italy
Georg Buchgeher	SCCH, Austria
Matteo Camilli	University of Milan, Italy
Tommaso Di Noia	Politecnico di Bari, Italy
Antonio Filieri	Imperial College London, UK
Stefan Hallerstede	Aarhus University, Denmark
Roxana Holom	RISC Software GmbH, Austria
Sungwon Kang	KAIST, Korea
Jan Kofroň	Charles University, Czech Republic
Elizabeth Leonard	Naval Research Laboratory, USA
Martina Maggio	Lund University, Sweden
Dominique Méry	LORIA, France
Raffaela Mirandola	Politecnico di Milano, Italy
Francesco Nocera	Politecnico di Bari, Italy
Hongyu Pei-Breivold	ABB Corporate Research, Sweden
Diego Pérez-Palacin	University of Zaragoza, Spain
Andreas Prinz	University of Agder, Norway
Alexander Raschke	Universität Ulm, Germany
Ella Roubtsova	Open Universiteit, The Netherlands
Guido Salvaneschi	TU Darmstadt, Germany
Neeraj Kumar Singh	INPT-ENSEEIHT/IRIT, France
Colin Snook	University of Southampton, UK
Romina Spalazzese	Malmö University, Sweden
Paola Spoletini	Kennesaw State University, USA

FAACS 2017 - Additional Reviewers

Taehyun Park	KAIST, Korea

Intercepting Blackhole Attacks in MANETs: An ASM-based Model

Alessandro Bianchi[⊠] , Sebastiano Pizzutilo ,
and Gennaro Vessio

Department of Informatics, University of Bari, Via Orabona 4, 70125 Bari, Italy
{alessandro.bianchi,sebastiano.pizzutilo,
gennaro.vessio}@uniba.it

Abstract. The inherent features of Mobile Ad-hoc NETworks (MANETs) make them vulnerable to various kinds of security attacks. In particular, in a so-called blackhole attack, one or more malicious hosts can send fake routing information towards an initiator, compromising the reliability of the network in the whole. In this paper, we propose a refinement of the NACK-based Ad-hoc On-demand Distance Vector (N-AODV) protocol, namely Blackhole-free N-AODV (BN-AODV), as a solution to intercept (cooperative) blackhole attacks in MANETs. Thanks to a formalization through an Abstract State Machine-based model, the correctness of the proposed protocol is formally proved.

Keywords: Abstract State Machines · Mobile Ad-hoc NETworks Blackhole

1 Introduction

Mobile Ad-hoc NETworks (MANETs for short) are collections of nomadic hosts which communicate in a wireless way without the need of any fixed physical infrastructure [1]. The lack of infrastructure and the continuous topology change due to movement require the definition of specific routing protocols: in most cases a communication session between two hosts is set and maintained by a number of hosts lying in the path between the two communicants. All routing protocols for MANETs, in their basic definition, assume the trustworthiness of each host. However, because of its inherent features, in the presence of malicious hosts the reliability of a MANET is vulnerable to various kinds of attacks: flooding, wormhole, blackhole, and so on [2].

In a blackhole attack the malicious host sends fake routing information towards an initiator, claiming to know the best route to reach destination [3]. Packets are so routed towards the malicious host allowing it to misuse or discard them. Sometimes, the attack involves several malicious hosts that work cooperatively. Blackholes negatively impact the performance of a MANET, making worse the inherent problem of packet loss, due to mobility, for which there is no guarantee, in general, that a destination is reachable. Unfortunately, since it takes advantage of the characteristics of the protocols' mechanism, such an attack is easy to be carried out and intercepting it is difficult.

© Springer International Publishing AG 2018
A. Cerone and M. Roveri (Eds.): SEFM 2017 Workshops, LNCS 10729, pp. 137–152, 2018.
https://doi.org/10.1007/978-3-319-74781-1_10

The literature proposes several solutions to intercept blackhole attacks, both single and cooperative ([2–4] are surveys on this topic). Nevertheless, all these solutions are described in a conventional (often informal) way, which is not rich enough to enable rigorous analysis about the capability of the protocol to intercept such attacks. Conversely, the availability of a high-level, formal environment could provide a way to analyze solutions to blackhole attacks rigorously.

To this end, the present paper proposes Blackhole-free NACK-based Ad-hoc On-demand Distance Vector (BN-AODV), a variant of the recently proposed NACK-based Ad-hoc On-demand Distance Vector (N-AODV) routing protocol [5, 6]. BN-AODV is here formally specified using Abstract State Machines (ASMs) [7], and its ability to intercept blackhole attacks is proved. In the following, several reasons for choosing the ASM formalism are presented. Firstly, it represents a general model of computation which subsumes all other classic computational models [8]. Secondly, it provides a way to describe algorithmic issues in a simple abstract pseudo-code, which can be translated into a high level programming language source code in a quite simple manner [9]. Moreover, considering methodological issues, it has been successfully applied for the design and analysis of critical and complex systems in several domains, and a specific development method came to prominence in the last years [7]. Finally, considering the implementation point of view, the capability of translating formal specifications into executable code, in order to conduct simulations of the models, is provided by tools like AsmL [10] (which is not maintained anymore), CoreASM [11] and ASMETA [12].

The rest of this paper is organized as follows. Section 2 summarizes the related literature. Section 3 overviews both ASM and N-AODV. Section 4 informally introduces BN-AODV, that is formally modeled in Sect. 5. Section 6 proves the correctness of the protocol. Section 7 concludes the paper and sketches future research.

2 Related Work

Traditionally, the literature discusses MANET protocols simulating the network behavior (e.g., [13, 14]). The simulation-based approach is very effective from the execution viewpoint, mainly for evaluating performance and comparing different solutions. However, it takes into account only a limited, predictable range of scenarios and it is not able to formally prove properties of interest. Conversely, formal methods are useful for reasoning about MANET behavior and provide more reliable results. In literature, some process calculi specifically tailored for MANETs have been proposed, for example: the ω-calculus [15], CMN (Calculus of Mobile Ad Hoc Networks) [16], and AWN (Algebra for Wireless Networks) [17]. They capture essential characteristics of nodes: from their mobility to the packet broadcasting and unicasting. However, they are not directly executable, so, conducting simulations is not possible. Moreover, process calculi are typically based on mathematical notions that developers could find unfamiliar. Various general purpose state-based models have also been used in the MANET domain, for example, finite state machines [18] and Petri nets [19, 20]. In particular, Petri nets have been employed to study several issues: modeling and verification of routing protocols [21, 22]; evaluation of their performance [23]; application to vehicular networks [24]. With respect to process calculi, state-based models provide a comfortable way for representing algorithmic issues, especially from the graphical point of view. Moreover, they are typically equipped with tools, such as CPN Tools [25], that allow one to execute the models. Nevertheless, state-based models lack of expressiveness: basically, they provide only a single level of abstraction and cannot support refinements to executable code. Moreover, according to [26], when compared to ASMs in modelling a variety of distributed systems, PNs are considered "neither intuitively clear nor formally simple". In order to overcome these limitations, our research makes use of Abstract State Machines (ASMs) [7].

The capability of ASMs to subsume other classic computational models has been stated in several works, e.g. [8, 27, 28], and an ASM sequential thesis has been proved in [29]. It states that ASMs suffice to capture the behavior of wide classes of sequential systems at any desired level of abstraction. This thesis has then been extended to parallel [30] and concurrent [31, 32] computations.

For what specifically concerns blackhole attacks, the literature includes several proposals, surveyed in [2, 3], but for the purposes of this work we only consider the solutions based on the AODV protocol and its variants. We can classify these solutions into two main categories, according to the approach they implement: topology-based and table-based. Solutions in the first category take into account the neighbourhood of the nodes in the MANET [33], or the existence of more than one route between a source and a destination [34, 35]. The second category [36–38] includes solutions in which nodes store information about all received packets in a new table. Except of [37, 38], all these proposals are useless in case of cooperative blackhole. Instead, the solution we propose is able to identify both single and cooperative attacks.

3 Background

In the following, the main concepts concerning Abstract State Machines and NACK-based Ad-hoc On-demand Distance Vector routing protocol for Mobile Ad-hoc NETworks are summarized. Detailed descriptions can be found in the related literature.

3.1 Abstract State Machines

Informally speaking, Abstract State Machines are finite sets of so-called *rules* of the form **if** *condition* **then** *updates* which transform the *abstract* states of the machine [29]. The concept of abstract state extends the usual notion of *state* occurring in finite state machines: it is an arbitrary complex structure, i.e. a domain of objects with functions and relations defined on them. On the other hand, a rule reflects the notion of *transition* occurring in traditional transition systems: *condition* is a first-order formula whose interpretation can be *true* or *false*; while *updates* is a finite set of assignments of the form $f(t_1, \ldots, t_n) := t$, whose execution consists in changing in parallel the value of the specified functions to the indicated value.

According to [7], pairs of function names together with values for their arguments are called *locations*: they abstract the notion of memory unit. The current configuration of locations together with their values determines the current state of the ASM. In each state, all conditions are checked, so that all updates in rules whose conditions evaluate to *true* are simultaneously executed, and the result is a transition of the machine from one state to another, i.e. from a configuration of values in locations to another. Moreover, for the unambiguous determination of the next state, updates must be *consistent*, i.e. no pair of updates must refer to the same location. The formalism also supports the mechanism of procedure calls; this is achieved by the definition of ASM *submachines*, i.e. parameterized rules. They support the declaration of *local* functions, so that each call of a submachine works with its own instantiation of its local functions in addition to the functions of the supermachine calling it.

Distributed ASMs (DASMs) [7] represent a generalization of basic ASMs: they capture the formalization of multiple agents acting in a distributed environment. Essentially, a DASM is intended as an arbitrary but finite number of independent agents (which are elements of a set *Agents*), each executing its own underlying ASM. In a DASM the keyword **self** is used for supporting the relation between local and global states and for denoting the specific agent which is executing a rule.

In order to properly manage the complexity of the modeled systems, the ASM formalism includes several constructs [7]. For our purposes, we consider: the *let* rule, in the form **let** $x = t$ **in** P, aimed at assigning the value of t to x, and then executing the rule P; the *forall* rule (**forall** x **with** φ **do** P), which executes P in parallel for each x satisfying φ; the *choose* rule (**choose** x **with** φ **do** P), which chooses an x satisfying φ, and then executes P; the *seq* rule (P **seq** Q) which sequentially executes P and then Q.

3.2   NACK-Based Ad-Hoc On-Demand Distance Vector Routing Protocol

The interception mechanism of blackhole attacks here proposed is derived from NACK-based Ad-hoc On-demand Distance Vector (N-AODV) [5]: it is a variant of the popular Ad-hoc On-demand Distance Vector (AODV) [39]. Its aim is to improve the network topology awareness of the network nodes through the adoption of a specific control packet named NACK (Not ACKnowledgement) [6]. N-AODV is a reactive protocol in which routes are discovered on-demand, and stored into *routing tables* within each node. The routing table associated with each node lists all the discovered (still valid) routes towards other nodes in the network and information on them. In particular, an entry of the routing table of the host i concerning a node j includes: the *address* of j; the last known *sequence number* of j; the *hop count* field expressing the distance between i and j; and the *next hop* field identifying the next node in the route to reach j. The sequence number is a monotonically increasing value maintained by each node: it helps other nodes to express the freshness of the information about it.

When an initiator wants to start a communication, it first checks if the destination is in its neighborhood (so that it is directly reachable), or a route to it is currently stored in its routing table. If so, the protocol ends and the communication simply starts. Otherwise, initiator fires the route discovery mechanism, by broadcasting route request (RREQ) packets to all its neighbors. Among the others, an RREQ packet includes: *initiator address* and *broadcast id*; *destination address*; *destination sequence number*, which expresses the latest available information about destination; and *hop count*, initially set to 0, and increased by each intermediate node. Note that the pair *initiator address* and *broadcast id* uniquely identifies the packet; in this way, duplications of RREQs that nodes have handled before can be ignored.

When an intermediate node *n* receives an RREQ, it updates the routing table entry for initiator, concerning both the sequence number of initiator and its next hop field; if an entry for initiator does not exist, it is created. Then the process is reiterated: *n* checks if the destination is a neighbor, or if it knows a route to destination with corresponding sequence number greater than or equal to the one contained into the RREQ (this means that its knowledge about the route is more recent). In both cases, *n* unicasts a route reply (RREP) packet back to initiator; an RREP contains: *initiator* and *destination address*; *destination sequence number* and *hop count*. Otherwise, *n*: updates the hop count field; rebroadcasts the RREQ to all its neighbors; and unicasts a NACK packet back to initiator. The NACK is so used to inform all nodes between *n* and initiator that, roughly speaking, *n* "does not know anything" about destination. Each NACK packet includes the addresses and the sequence numbers of *n* and initiator and their distance.

The route discovery successfully ends when a route to destination is found. While the RREP travels towards initiator, routes are set up inside the routing tables of the traversed hosts by creating an entry for destination when needed. Once initiator receives the RREP, the communication session can start. Conversely, the route discovery fails when: no RREQ reaches a node which is in the destination neighborhood; or no RREQ reaches a node whose routing table contains a route to destination; or a previously set timeout expires while initiator is waiting for RREPs. The first two cases depend on the non-reachability of destination; instead, the last case can be due to either the isolation of the destination, or too long distances, or changes in the topology during the packet transmission.

4   Blackhole-Free N-AODV

The solution here proposed for intercepting blackholes relies on N-AODV, and it adopts two additional control packets, namely *Challenge* (CHL) and *Response* (RES) packets, aimed at ensuring that no blackhole is in the discovered route. To this end, asymmetric cryptography is followed: every node *j* is associated with a public key (denoted by K_j) and a private key (denoted by K_j^{-1}). Data packets exchanged during communication sessions, as well as CHL and RES packets, that are to be routed to a node *j*, must then be encrypted with K_j, and only *j* can decrypt them by using the corresponding K_j^{-1}. Conversely, RREQ and RREP packets are not encrypted. The public keys are spread over the network by the RREQ and NACK packets. More precisely, both RREQ and NACK are enriched with a field storing the public key of the host producing the packet. In this way, each node receiving these packets knows the public key associated with the issuer; in other words: when a node *i* learns about the identity of a node *j*, then *i* also learns K_j.

The main idea behind BN-AODV is that every intermediate node lying in the discovered route to reach destination is *responsible* of the trustworthiness of the next hop of such route. To this end, if a node *n* receives an *RREP* directed to initiator from one of its neighbours *m*, then *n* must check the trustworthiness of the received *RREP*.

This is accomplished by sending a *CHL* packet to destination d, through m, encrypted with K_d, The *CHL* can simply consist of a nonce to be decremented by d. If the *CHL* safely reaches d, then d must reply with a *RES* packet, encrypted with K_n, to be unicasted towards n. If n receives back the proper *RES*, then it considers the *RREP* to be trusted and forwards the packet to the next hop in the reverse route to reach initiator. The process is then reiterated by every intermediate node in the route, until the *RREP* reaches initiator, which checks the trustworthiness of the *RREP* for the last time. If the last *RES* is received, the communication session can start. Conversely, if an intermediate node n, waiting for a *RES*, does not receive back the expected packet, it suspects the next hop m, in the route to reach d, to be a blackhole. As a consequence, n stops forwarding the *RREP*. If destination is not safely reachable and no alternative secure route is discovered until the timeout expiration, the route discovery fails.

In the case of cooperative attack, it is worth noting that one or more colluders could confirm the trustworthiness of the fake *RREP*. Nevertheless, the approach here proposed is able to intercept such an attack thanks to the last control executed by initiator. In fact, in this way, the protocol is able to judge secure or not the entire route, so intercepting not only single blackholes but also cooperative attacks. Note that, in this case, BN-AODV detects only one of the malicious nodes involved in the attack. More precisely, suppose we have a group of colluders $c_1, c_2, ..., c_n$ and a main blackhole b, lying consecutively in the route to reach destination d between a host h and d, i.e. $h, c_1, c_2, ..., c_n, b, ..., d$. The fake *RREP* generated by b then goes through the chain $c_n, ..., c_2, c_1$, before reaching h. Thanks to the protocol, h is able to stop the route discovery, however it can only suspect that c_1 is malicious, without any possibility to deduct something about the next nodes of the chain. Nevertheless, the other malicious nodes can be detected, one by one, in successive route discovery executions.

The proposed approach is quite draconian: if a node does not forward the correct *RES*, then it is suspected to be a blackhole. Unfortunately, the loss of correct *RES* packets (*CHL* packets) may be caused by node movement: in this case an honest node may be incorrectly considered a blackhole. In order to mitigate this effect, we introduce *trust levels* associated with each node. If a node n suspects one of its neighbours b to be a blackhole, then n adds b in a *trust table*. The b-th entry of the trust table of a node n expresses the trust level n has gained about b during past executions of the route discovery. Every time a node is suspected to be a blackhole, its trust level is decreased; every time it forwards the correct *RES* packet, its trust level is increased. In this way, a node is not excluded from routing activities at once, but only when its trust level reaches a lower limit. We assume a lower limit equals to $-\theta$; when a node i discovers the existence of a node j, i creates an entry concerning j in its trust table and initializes the trust level of j to 0. Every time the trust level associated with j drops to $-\theta$, i marks j as malicious. As a consequence, all packets coming in from j are always discarded by i, moreover i does not send packets to j anymore.

Finally, note that the use of cryptography is crucial to prevent blackholes from manipulating messages. In fact, without using keys, a blackhole could send fake responses. In other words, malicious nodes are forced to behave properly, otherwise their possible attacks are immediately intercepted. It is worth noting that both trust levels and tables, and cryptographic issues are not considered in the present model.

5   ASM-based Model

A MANET adopting BN-AODV can be modeled by a DASM including a set of $Hosts = \{h_1, ..., h_n\}$, where each h_1 models the behavior of a single node executing the protocol. We can think about each h_1 as univocally identified by its address. For the purposes of the present paper, each host behaves either as an honest node, or as a blackhole, or as a colluder, so three ASMs are presented, for describing the three different cases.

5.1   Honest ASM

All honest hosts behave homogeneously in accordance with the protocol, therefore we here discuss only one ASM. For space reasons, only the main issues are described below, leaving at an abstract level the less important details. Each *honest* ASM includes the following functions:

- *neighb: Hosts* → PowerSet(*Hosts*), which specifies the neighborhood of each host;
- *wishToInitiate: Hosts* → *boolean*, which indicates whether a new communication session is required;
- *initiateTo: Hosts* × *Hosts* → *boolean*, which specifies the destination of the desired communication;
- *hasToVerify: Hosts* × *Hosts* × *Hosts* → *boolean*, which establishes if the received RREP has to be verified or not;
- *trusted: Hosts* × *Hosts* → *boolean*, which acts as a flag to indicate whether an RREP packet concerning a destination has been judged to be trusted or not.

The meaning of the arguments of the functions above is quite obvious, except for *hasToVerify:* its first argument indicates the node to which the verified RREP must be forwarded; the second is the host from which the (un)verified RREP comes; the third is the destination of the current route discovery.

In order to model broadcasting and unicasting of packets, every node is associated with five queues of messages: *requests, replies, challenges, responses* and *nacks*, which include RREQ, RREP, CHL, RES and NACK packets, respectively. These queues are managed by the functions *isEmpty* and *top*, and by the rules *enqueue* and *dequeue* whose purpose is in accordance with the respective names. The access of a field f of a packet p is denoted by the form $p.f$. Note that in the protocol specification each control packet does not include information about the router forwarding it; however, in the following, we provide an additional field ($p.sender$) in each control packet for modelling reasons. Moreover, each node is associated with a *routing table* plus a *trust table* representing the information the nodes store about other nodes.

At the initial state of the computation all tables and queues are empty; the neighbourhood of each host is pre-set, depending on the initial MANET topology; all hosts are inactive, i.e. *wishToInitiate* and *initiateTo* evaluate to *false* for each node and for each pair of nodes, respectively; *hasToVerify* evaluates to *false* for each triple of nodes; *trusted* evaluates to *undef* for each pair of nodes.

The ASM pseudo-code of the i-th host is shown below, as *HostProgram*:

```
HostProgram ≡

    if ¬isEmpty(requests(self)) then {
      let RREQ = top(requests(self)), previousHop = RREQ.sender in
        UpdateRoutingTable(self, RREQ)                                    ⎤
        Router(RREQ, previousHop)                                        ⎥ HR1
        dequeue RREQ from requests(self)                                 ⎦
    }
    if wishToInitiate(self) = true then                                  ⎤
      forall dest ∈ Hosts with dest ≠ self do                           ⎥ HR2
        if initiateTo(self, dest) = true then                           ⎥
          Initiator(dest)                                                ⎦
    if ¬isEmpty(replies(self)) then                                      ⎤
      let RREP = top(replies(self)), nextHop = RREP.sender in            ⎥
        if RREP.init ≠ self then {                                       ⎥
          choose entry ∈ routingTable(self) with entry.dest = RREP.init  ⎥ HR3
          previousHop := entry.nextHop seq                               ⎥
          hasToVerify(previousHop, nextHop, RREP.dest):=true             ⎥
        }                                                                ⎦
    forall previousHop ∈ neighb(self) do                                 ⎤
      forall nextHop ∈ neighb(self) do                                   ⎥
        forall dest ∈ Hosts do                                          ⎥ HR4
          if hasToVerify(previousHop, nextHop, dest) then               ⎥
            Verify(top(replies(self)), previousHop, nextHop, dest)       ⎦
    if ¬isEmpty(challenges(self)) then {                                 ⎤
      let CHL = top(challenges(self)) in                                 ⎥
        if CHL.dest = self then {                                        ⎥
          let previousHop = CHL.sender in                                ⎥
            create_RES seq                                               ⎥
            enqueue RES into responses(previousHop)                      ⎥
            dequeue CHL from challenges(self)                            ⎥
        }                                                                ⎥ HR5
        if CHL.dest ≠ self then {                                        ⎥
          choose entry ∈ routingTable(self) with entry.dest = CHL.dest   ⎥
          nextHop := entry.nextHop seq                                   ⎥
          enqueue CHL into challenges(nextHop)                           ⎥
          dequeue CHL from challenges(self)                              ⎥
        }                                                                ⎥
    }                                                                    ⎦
    if ¬isEmpty(responses(self)) then {                                  ⎤
      let RES = top(responses(self)) in                                  ⎥
        if RES.dest ≠ self then {                                        ⎥
          choose entry ∈ routingTable(self) with entry.dest = RES.dest   ⎥ HR6
          previousHop := entry.nextHop seq                               ⎥
          enqueue RES into responses(previousHop)                        ⎥
          dequeue RES from responses(self)                               ⎥
        }                                                                ⎦
    }

    if ¬isEmpty(nacks(self)) then {                                      ⎤
      let NACK = top(nacks(self)) in                                     ⎥
        if NACK.dest ≠ self then {                                       ⎥
          choose entry ∈ routingTable(self) with entry.dest = NACK.dest  ⎥
          previousHop := entry.nextHop seq                               ⎥ HR7
          UpdateRoutingTable(self, NACK)                                 ⎥
          enqueue NACK into nacks(previousHop)                           ⎥
          dequeue NACK from nacks(self)                                  ⎥
        }                                                                ⎦
    }
```

Informally speaking, each host is inactive as long as no rule is applicable; the idleness is left when one of the events guarding the conditions of the seven rules of the machine happens. These events concern: an RREQ is received, then the rule HR1 fires, leading to the execution of the *Router* submachine; the need to start a new communication session is required, leading to the execution of the *Initiator* submachine (rule HR2); an RREP is received, so HR3 establishes the need to verify its trustworthiness; HR4 executes the *Verify* submachine when needed; a CHL is received (HR5) so the node must reply with an RES (if the CHL was directed to that node), or it must simply forward the CHL; an RES is received (HR6), so it has to be forwarded if it is not directed to that node; a NACK is received (HR7), so it has to be forwarded if it is not directed to that node.

The *create_RES* statement in HR5 has the effect to generate a new RES packet: it is not formally specified for abstracting from the specific representation of the packet. Analogous statements occur in the machines described in the following.

Note that the *Router* and the *BroadcastRREQ* submachines are analogous to the homonymous machines used for modelling the N-AODV routing protocol we proposed in [5], so, for space reasons, they are not formally modelled here: it is sufficient to state that they behave accordingly to the respective names. Analogous considerations for the *UpdateRoutingTable* and *UpdateTrustTable* submachines. Therefore, in the following we only focus on the *Initiator* and *Verify* submachines: their ASM description will then be useful for proving the correctness of the proposed protocol.

The *Verify* submachine includes two local functions:

- *verify_waiting: Hosts × Hosts → boolean*, which acts as a flag indicating whether the host is still waiting for the RES directed to it. Its initial value is *false*;
- *verify_timeout: Hosts × Hosts → ℕ*, which models the waiting time for the RES.

The ASM pseudo-code of *Verify* is shown below:

```
Verify(RREP, previousHop, nextHop, dest) ≡

  if ¬verify_waiting(self, dest) then {          ⎫
    create_CHL seq                               ⎪
    enqueue CHL into challenges(nextHop)         ⎬ VR1
    verify_waiting(self, dest) := true           ⎪
    verify_timeout(self, dest) := default_value  ⎪
  }                                              ⎭


  if verify_waiting(self, dest) then {                              ⎫
    if ¬isEmpty(responses(self)) then                              ⎪
      if ReliableRREP(self, top(responses(self))) then {           ⎪
        trusted(self, dest) := true                                ⎬ VR2
        verify_waiting(self, dest) := false                        ⎪
        dequeue top(responses(self)) from responses(self)          ⎪
      }                                                            ⎪
    verify_timeout(self, dest) := verify_timeout(self, dest) - 1   ⎪
  }                                                                ⎭
  if verify_waiting(self, dest)∧verify_timeout(self, dest)=0 then{ ⎫
    trusted(self, dest) := false                                   ⎬ VR3
    verify_waiting(self, dest) := false                            ⎪
  }                                                                ⎭
  if trusted(self, dest) then {                  ⎫
    UpdateRoutingTable(self, RREP)               ⎪
    UpdateTrustTable(self, nextHop)              ⎪
    dequeue RREP from replies(self)              ⎬ VR4
    if previousHop ≠ null then                   ⎪
      enqueue RREP into replies(previousHop)     ⎪
  }                                              ⎭
  if ¬trusted(self, dest) then {                 ⎫
    UpdateTrustTable(self, nextHop)              ⎬ VR5
    dequeue RREP from replies(self)              ⎪
  }                                              ⎭
```

ReliableRREP (**self**, top(*responses*(**self**))) is a predicate that evaluates to *true* when the received RES packet is correct, so the respective RREP can be considered reliable. It simply verifies that the content of the RES packet is exactly the expected value.

The submachine includes five rules, aimed at: creating and sending the CHL (VR1); establishing (VR2) or denying (VR3) the trustworthiness of the previously received RREP; updating both the routing table and the trust table if the RREP is trusted (VR4); updating only the trust table if the RREP is not trusted (VR5). The *verify_waiting* function avoids the node to create the same CHL more than one time. While the node is waiting, it checks the incoming RESs: if an RES directed to it is received, and its correctness is verified, then the RREP is judged to be trusted. Otherwise, the timeout is decreased: when the timeout expires, the node assumes the *RREP* to be not trusted. Finally, note that VR4 (according to [7]) uses the constant *null*, and it requires that *previousHop* is not equal to it. This is due to the case in which *Verify* is called by the *Initiator* submachine: if so, the *RREP* must not be forwarded to any other host.

Similarly to *Verify*, the *Initiator* submachine includes the following local functions:

- *initiator_waiting: Hosts × Hosts → boolean*, which acts as a flag indicating whether initiator is still waiting for (at least) an RREP directed to it. Its initial value is *false*;
- *initiator_timeout: Hosts × Hosts → ℕ*, which models the waiting time for RREPs.

The ASM pseudo-code of *Initiator* is shown below:

```
Initiator(dest) ≡

    if dest ∈ neighb(self) ∨ dest ∈ routingTable(self) then {        ⎤
        CommunicationSession(dest)                                    ⎥ IR1
        initiateTo(self, dest) := false                              ⎦
    }
    if dest ∉ neighb(self) ∧ dest ∉ routingTable(self) then {        ⎤
        create_RREQ seq                                               ⎥
        BroadcastRREQ(RREQ)                                           ⎥ IR2
        initiator_waiting(self, dest) := true                         ⎥
        initiator_timeout(self, dest) := default_value               ⎦
    }
    if initiator_waiting(self, dest) then                            ⎤
        initiator_timeout(self,dest):=initiator_timeout(self,dest)-1 seq ⎥
        if ¬isEmpty(replies(self)) then                              ⎥ IR3
            forall r∈replies(self) with r.init=self and r.dest =dest do ⎥
                if trusted(self, dest) = undef then                  ⎥
                    let nextHop = r.sender in Verify(r, null, nextHop, dest) ⎦
    if trusted(self, dest) then {                                    ⎤
        CommunicationSession(dest)                                    ⎥
        initiateTo(self, dest) := false                              ⎥ IR4
        initiator_waiting(self, dest) := false                       ⎦
    }
    if initiator_waiting(self, dest) ∧ ¬isEmpty(nacks(self)) then {  ⎤
        forall n ∈ nacks(self) with n.dest = self do {               ⎥
            UpdateRoutingTable(self, n)                               ⎥ IR5
            dequeue n from nacks(self)                                ⎥
        }                                                             ⎦
    }
    if initiator_waiting(self, dest) ∧ initiator_timeout(self, dest)=0 ⎤
    then {                                                            ⎥
        initiateTo(self, dest) := false                              ⎥ IR6
        initiator_waiting(self, dest) := false                       ⎦
    }
```

If a route to destination is already known, the communication session simply starts (IR1). Otherwise, the route discovery process is initiated (IR2). Until the timeout is greater than 0 (IR3), the incoming RREPs are checked. If (at least) an RREP directed to the host is received, the last CHL is sent. If the last RES is received, then the communication session can start (IR4). If NACKs directed to the host are received during the waiting for RREPs (IR5), the routing table is updated. The last rule (IR6) simply resets the node to inactivity.

The initiator is the last host verifying the trustworthiness of the *RREP*, so in IR3 the *Verify* submachine is called with a *null* value, instead of *previousHop* argument.

Note that an initiator could receive multiple RREPs concerning the same *dest*; in order to reduce redundancy, the protocol requires to discard them once the reliability of a route has been verified. However, for space reasons, this computation is not described.

5.2 Malicious ASMs

The literature does not provide a univocal, formal definition of blackhole (and colluder). In the following, we firstly provide a precise definition for this concept; then we present a model of malicious ASM.

Definition 1 (Forward neighbor). A *forward neighbor* f_n of a node n is the next hop of n in the route to reach the destination d, i.e. $n, f_n, ..., d$.

Thanks to the notion of forward neighbor, a blackhole is recursively defined:

Definition 2 (Blackhole). A *blackhole* is: (*i*) a main blackhole if it originates fake RREPs; or (*ii*) a colluder if its forward neighbor is a blackhole.

Therefore, differently from honest hosts, malicious hosts can behave heterogeneously in accordance with two ASMs, depending on whether the host is the main blackhole or one of its colluders.

Note that for both the blackhole and colluder nodes we assume the worst possible scenario: they behave maliciously without executing any other route discovery activity. Moreover, we assume that malicious nodes never behave honestly. Finally, we assume that the respective queues are initially empty for both malicious ASMs.

Blackhole program. The *malicious* ASM of the host behaving as main blackhole acts as a router claiming to know the best route to reach destination. This is done independently from the knowledge the blackhole has about destination. Its model is:

```
BlackholeProgram ≡

  if ¬isEmpty(requests(self)) then {
    let RREQ = top(requests(self)), previousHop = RREQ.sender in
      UpdateRoutingTable(self, RREQ)
      MaliciousRouter(RREQ, previousHop)
      dequeue RREQ from requests(self)
  }
```

where the *MaliciousRouter* submachine is simply:

```
MaliciousRouter(RREQ, previousHop) ≡

  create_RREP seq
  enqueue RREP into replies(previousHop)
```

In words: every time an RREQ reaches the blackhole, its routing table is updated and a fake RREP is sent back: it is created in accordance with the information stored in that RREQ.

Colluder program. The colluder node a priori forwards RREP packets independently from their reliability. Its model is as follows:

```
ColluderProgram ≡

  if ¬isEmpty(replies(self)) then {
    let RREP = top(replies(self)) in
      if RREP.init ≠ self then {
        choose entry ∈ routingTable(self) with entry.dest = RREP.init
        let previousHop := entry.nextHop seq
          enqueue RREP into replies(previousHop)
          dequeue RREP from replies(self)
      }
  }
```

6 Correctness

The ASMs modelling the malicious nodes are quite simple, so it is not necessary to prove their correctness. Instead, this section aims at proving that possible attacks are intercepted in every protocol execution. To this end, we assume *perfect encryption:* encrypted messages cannot be read without knowing the corresponding decryption key; this assumption leads to state that the *Verify* submachine consider reliable only the RREPs actually produced by the proper hosts. Secondly, it is worth remarking that multiple route discoveries can be executed in parallel and that each host can participate in different route discoveries playing different roles. Moreover, we only consider single communication attempts between couples of nodes: this does not compromise generality. We firstly provide the following definition:

Definition 3 (Backward neighbor). A *backward neighbor* b_n of a node n is the next hop of n in the route to reach initiator i, i.e. $i, ..., bn, n$.

The correctness of the protocol modelled by the ASMs in Sect. 5 is stated by the two following theorems: the first one assumes that the network only includes one malicious host (i.e., no colluders are considered); the second theorem generalizes the claim to networks including colluders.

Theorem 1. *The honest hosts intercept any single blackhole attack.*

Proof. Let N be the set of network nodes, and let *fRREP* be the fake RREP produced by the blackhole $b \in N$. In order to prove the claim, it must be proved that *fRREP* is discarded by the backward neighbor, $n_k \in N$, of b. Let $n_0, n_1, ..., n_{k-1}, n_k, b$ the route between the initiator n_0 and the blackhole. Formally, it must be proved that *fRREP* $\notin$ *replies* (n_{k-1}). The only rule allowing n_k to enqueue an RREP into the *replies* queue of n_{k-1} is the rule VR4 in the *Verify* submachine. More precisely, the RREP is forwarded only if *trusted*(**self**, *dest*) evaluates to *true*; in turn, the value of this location is initially set to *undef*, and it is set to *true* only inside the VR2 of the same submachine, when the proper RES is received back by n_k. Since *Verify* does not state the trustworthiness of *fRREP, trusted*(**self**, *dest*) evaluates to *false*, so the received RREP is discarded in the last line of VR4 (**dequeue** *RREP* **from** *replies*(**self**)). Thus, the protocol always intercepts single blackhole attacks.   □

Theorem 2. *The honest hosts intercept any cooperative blackhole attack.*

Proof. Let k be the number of colluders $c_i \in N$, $(1 \leq i \leq k)$ of the main blackhole b. Each c_i forwards RREP packets without checking their trustworthiness, in accordance with *ColluderProgram*. In order to prove the claim, let's consider the worst scenario, in which all nodes between the initiator n_0 and b are colluders, i.e. the route is $n_0, c_1, c_2, ..., c_k, b$. It must be proved that when *fRREP* $\in$ *replies*(n_0) the communication does not start. If *fRREP* $\in$ *replies*(n_0) then n_0 executes the IR3 rule of the *Initiator* submachine. In turn, this rule executes the verification of the RREP, and the communication session can start only if that RREP is trusted, otherwise it is discarded: since *fRREP* is not trusted by definition, it is discarded, and the communication cannot start. The case in which there is at least one honest node in the route between n_0 and b is captured by Theorem 1. Therefore, the protocol always intercepts cooperative attacks.   □

7 Conclusion

The diffusion of MANETs imposes the need to properly manage security issues. The present paper proposed the Blackhole-free NACK-based AODV (BN-AODV) routing protocol for intercepting blackhole attacks: differently from analogous proposals, we formally specified the protocol using Abstract States Machines and thanks to the formalism the capability to identify *all* nodes responsible of the attack has been proved.

Unfortunately, the formal static approach followed in this paper is not sufficient for evaluating the capability of the protocol to identify *only* malicious nodes. In fact, the draconian approach to the discovery of blackholes could label an honest node as malicious, simply because of the change of the topology, due to the hosts' movements.

The next step of the research will implement the model into the ASMETA tool [12] with a twofold purpose. On one hand, the execution of the model in a proper environment will allow us to discover possible errors and to identify improvements: for example, thanks to the implementation, the concept of time (e.g., the time nodes must wait for the proper responses) will be better treated in order to consider real time events. On the other hand, the behaviour of the protocol will be empirically investigated.

References

1. Agrawal, D., Zeng, Q.: Introduction to Wireless and Mobile Systems. Thomson Brooks/Cole, Pacific Grove (2003)
2. Kannhavong, B., Nakayama, H., Nemoto, Y., Kato, N., Jamalipour, A.: A survey of routing attacks in MANET. IEEE Wirel. Commun. **14**(5), 85–91 (2007)

3. Tseng, F.H., Chou, L.D., Chao, H.C.: A survey of black hole attacks in wireless MANET. Hum.-Centric Comput. Inf. Sci. **1**, 4 (2011)
4. Agrawal, P., Ghosh, R.K., Das, S.K.: Cooperative black and gray hole attacks in mobile ad hoc networks. In: 2nd International Conference on Ubiquitous Information Management and Communication, pp. 310–314 (2008)
5. Bianchi, A., Pizzutilo, S., Vessio, G.: Preliminary description of NACK-based ad-hoc on-demand distance vector routing protocol for MANETs. In: 9th International Conference on Software: Engineering and Applications, pp. 500–505 (2014)
6. Bianchi, A., Pizzutilo, S., Vessio, G.: CoreASM-based evaluation of the N-AODV protocol for mobile ad-hoc networks. J. Mobile Multimedia **12**, 31–51 (2016)
7. Börger, E., Stärk, R.: Abstract State Machines: A Method for High-Level System Design and Analysis. Springer, Heidelberg (2003). https://doi.org/10.1007/978-3-642-18216-7
8. Gurevich, Y.: Evolving algebras 1993: Lipari guide. In: Börger, E. (ed.) Specification and Validation Methods. Oxford University Press, pp. 9–36 (1995)
9. Börger, E.: High level system design and analysis using abstract state machines. In: Hutter, D., Stephan, W., Traverso, P., Ullmann, M. (eds.) FM-Trends 1998. LNCS, vol. 1641, pp. 1–43. Springer, Heidelberg (1999). https://doi.org/10.1007/3-540-48257-1_1
10. Gurevich, Y., Rossman, B., Schulte, W.: Semantic Essence of AsmL. Theor. Comput. Sci. **342**(3), 370–412 (2005)
11. Farahbod, R., Gervasi, V., Glässer, U.: CoreASM: An Extensible ASM Execution Engine. Fundamenta Informaticae **77**(1–2), 71–103 (2007)
12. Gargantini, A., Riccobene, E., Scandurra, P.: Model-driven language engineering: the ASMETA case study. In: 3rd International Conference on Software Engineering Advances, pp. 373–378 (2008)
13. Jayakumar, G., Gopinath, G.: Performance comparison of two on-demand routing protocols for ad-hoc networks based on random way point mobility model. Am. J. Appl. Sci. **5**(6), 659–664 (2008)
14. Goyal, P.: Simulation study of comparative performance of AODV, OLSR, FSR and LAR routing protocols in MANET in large scale scenarios. In: World Congress of Information and Communication Technologies, pp. 283–286 (2012)
15. Singh, A., Ramakrishnan, C.R., Smolka, S.A.: A process calculus for mobile ad hoc networks. In: Lea, D., Zavattaro, G. (eds.) COORDINATION 2008. LNCS, vol. 5052, pp. 296–314. Springer, Heidelberg (2008). https://doi.org/10.1007/978-3-540-68265-3_19
16. Merro, M.: An observational theory for mobile ad hoc networks. Inf. Comput. **207**(2), 194–208 (2009)
17. Fehnker, A., Glabbeek, R.V., Höfner, P., McIver, A., Portmann, M., Tan, W.L.: A process algebra for wireless mesh networks. In: 21st European Symposium on Programming, pp. 295–315 (2012)
18. Delzanno, G., Sangnier, A., Zavattaro, G.: Parameterized verification of ad hoc networks. In: Gastin, P., Laroussinie, F. (eds.) CONCUR 2010. LNCS, vol. 6269, pp. 313–327. Springer, Heidelberg (2010). https://doi.org/10.1007/978-3-642-15375-4_22
19. Bianchi, A., Pizzutilo, S.: Studying MANET through a Petri net-based model. In: 2nd International Conference of Evolving Internet, pp. 220–225 (2010)
20. Bianchi, A., Pizzutilo, S.: A Coloured nested Petri nets model for discussing MANET properties. Int. J. Multimedia Technol. **3**(2), 38–44 (2013)
21. Xiong, C., Murata, T., Tsai, J.: Modeling and simulation of routing protocol for MANET using colored petri nets. In: Conference on Application and Theory of Petri Nets: Formal Methods in Software Engineering and Defence Systems, vol. 12, pp. 145–153 (2002)

22. Xiong, C., Murata, T., Leigh, J.: An approach for verifying routing protocols in mobile ad hoc networks using Petri nets. In: 6th IEEE Symposium on Circuits and Systems, vol. 2, pp. 537–540 (2004)
23. Erbas, F., Kyamakya, K., Jobmann, K.: Modelling and performance analysis of a novel position-based reliable unicast and multicast routing method using coloured Petri nets. In: Vehicular Technology Conference, vol. 5, pp. 3099–3104 (2003)
24. Jahanian, M.H., Amin, F., Jahangir, A.H.: Analysis of TESLA protocol in vehicular ad hoc networks using timed colored Petri nets. In: 6th International Conference on the Information and Communication Systems, pp. 222–227 (2015)
25. Jensen, K., Kristensen, L.M., Wells, L.: Coloured Petri nets and CPN tools for modelling and validation of concurrent systems. Int. J. Softw. Tools Technol. Transf. 9(3–4), 213–254 (2007)
26. Börger, E.: Modeling distributed algorithms by abstract state machines compared to Petri nets. In: Butler, M., Schewe, K.-D., Mashkoor, A., Biro, M. (eds.) ABZ 2016. LNCS, vol. 9675, pp. 3–34. Springer, Cham (2016). https://doi.org/10.1007/978-3-319-33600-8_1
27. Reisig, W.: The expressive power of abstract state machines. Comput. Inform. 22, 209–219 (2003)
28. Dershowitz, N.: The generic model of computation. In: Electronic Proceedings in Theoretical Computer Science (2013)
29. Gurevich, Y.: Sequential abstract state machines capture sequential algorithms. ACM Trans. Comput. Logic 1(1), 77–111 (2000)
30. Blass, A., Gurevich, Y.: Abstract state machines capture parallel algorithms. ACM Trans. Comput. Logic 4(4), 578–651 (2003)
31. Glausch, A., Reisig, W.: An ASM-characterization of a class of distributed algorithms. In: Abrial, J.-R., Glässer, U. (eds.) Rigorous Methods for Software Construction and Analysis. LNCS, vol. 5115, pp. 50–64. Springer, Heidelberg (2009). https://doi.org/10.1007/978-3-642-11447-2_4
32. Börger, E., Schewe, K.D.: Concurrent abstract state machines. Acta Informatica 53(5), 469–492 (2016)
33. Sun, B., Guan, Y., Chen, J., Pooch, U.W.: Detecting blackhole attack in mobile ad hoc networks. In: 5th Conference on Personal Mobile Communications, pp. 490–495 (2003)
34. Al-Shurman, M., Yoo, S.M., Park, S.: Black hole attack in mobile ad hoc network. In: 42nd Annual Southeast Regional Conference, pp. 96–97 (2004)
35. Tamilselvan, L., Sankaranarayanan, V.: Prevention of blackhole attack in MANET. In: 2nd International Conference on Wireless Broadband and Ultra Wideband Communications, p. 21 (2007)
36. Raj, P.N., Swadas, P.B.: DPRAODV: a dynamic learning system against blackhole attack in AODV based MANET. Int. J. Comput. Sci. Issues 2, 54–59 (2009)
37. Ramaswamy, S., Fu, H., Sreekantaradhya, M., Dixon, J., Nygard, K.: Prevention of cooperative black hole attack in wireless ad hoc networks. In: International Conference on Wireless Networks (2003)
38. Tamilselvan, L., Sankaranarayanan, V.: Prevention of co-operative black hole attack in MANET. J. Netw. 3(5), 13–20 (2008)
39. Perkins, C.E., Belding-Royer, E., Das, S.R.: Ad hoc On-Demand Distance Vector (AODV) Routing. RFC 3561 (2003). http://tools.ietf.org/html/rfc3561

Formalizing Monitoring Processes for Large-Scale Distributed Systems Using Abstract State Machines

Andreea Buga[✉] and Sorana Tania Nemeş

Christian Doppler Laboratory for Client-Centric Cloud Computing,
Johannes Kepler University of Linz, Software Park 35, 4232 Hagenberg, Austria
{andreea.buga,t.nemes}@cdcc.faw.jku.at

Abstract. Large-Scale Distributed Systems are characterized by high complexity and heterogeneity, which might lead to unexpected failures. The role of a robust monitoring framework is to gather low-level data and assess the status of the components of the system. The framework collaborates with adapters for ensuring steady recovery plans and improving the availability of services. Monitors, as part of the system, are also affected by unavailability or random failures. In order to increase the reliability of the solution we verify the trustworthiness of the monitors and emphasize the need of redundancy. This paper introduces a formal approach for modeling and verifying a monitoring solution for Large-Scale Distributed Systems. We formalize the behavior of the monitors with the aid of Abstract State Machines and employ the ASMETA toolset for simulating and analyzing properties of the model. The tool also supports the verification process by translating a simplified version of the model to an NuSMV specification, on top of which model checking can be applied. Properties of the model are expressed with the aid of computation tree logic.

Keywords: Formal modeling · Abstract State Machines · Monitoring
Failure detection · Model validation · Computation Tree Logic

1 Introduction

Service-oriented architecture (SOA) permits orchestrating resources of various providers with the aim of delivering highly available and effective services to the end user. The development of such systems relies on techniques and algorithms specific to Large-Scale Distributed Systems (LDS). Problems encountered by any component lead to bigger failures, from which the system needs to recover.

Traditionally, monitoring refers to collecting specific data from components of the system and interpreting them in order to detect possible issues. Complemented with a robust adaptation framework, monitors ensure that the system meets its requirements and performs according to the promises expressed in terms of service-level agreement (SLA).

© Springer International Publishing AG 2018
A. Cerone and M. Roveri (Eds.): SEFM 2017 Workshops, LNCS 10729, pp. 153–167, 2018.
https://doi.org/10.1007/978-3-319-74781-1_11

Monitors are components of the LDS and are also faced with unavailability or misbehavior. False reports on problems of the nodes trigger unnecessary adaptation plans, while the impossibility to correctly detect an issue leads to lower performance of the system or even its complete failure. The goal of the monitoring service we propose is to precisely detect unavailability and crash failures of system nodes.

The current paper addresses the accuracy of the monitoring processes and adopts a formal approach for modeling their correct behavior. We impose redundancy for monitoring processes and introduce a measure for the accuracy of the monitors, referred throughout the paper as confidence degree. We specified the model for the monitoring framework with the aid of Abstract State Machines (ASM). In this sense, we engaged the methodology proposed by Arcaini et al. [4] for simulating, validating and verifying ASM models.

The remainder of the paper is organized as follows. Section 2 presents relevant work in the area. In Sect. 3 we define the architecture of the system and discuss desired behavior, which is translated into a formal specification in Sect. 4. Section 4 also contains a brief presentation of ASM specific concepts. Verification of system properties is carried out in Sect. 5. Limitations of the approach are discussed in Sect. 6, after which conclusions are drawn in Sect. 7.

2   Related Work

Lattice framework [13] proposed for the evaluation of cloud federations uses different components for executing monitoring processes. It addresses data collection, encapsulation and communication and serves as a guideline for the monitor behavior proposed by our ground model. Our work approaches the problem from the formal point of view, while Lattice discusses implementation details.

mOSAIC [21] relies on SOA and provides an Application Programming Interface (API) for communication. Every LDS component is specified in terms of resource requirements (storage, computing and communication, and budget). Brokering is done via SLA contracts at both component and application level and it is handled by the Resource Broker. S-Cube proposes also monitoring and adaptation services from the perspective of SLA violation [14]. While the focus of mOSAIC and S-Cube is on the delivery of promised SLAs, our work details the monitoring unavailability and crash failures.

ASM formal method has been used for specifying and verifying different aspects of LDS. Ma et al. introduced the notion of Abstract State Services based on ASMs and described it for a flight booking over a cloud service case study [16], while Bolis et al. proposed a formal approach for testing the conformance of web applications using ASM method [6].

In [1], Arcaini et al. propose an ASM model for analyzing Monitor-Analyze-Plan-Execute over a shared Knowledge (MAPE-K) loops of self-adapting systems that follow a decentralized architecture. Flexibility and robustness to silent node failures of the specification are validated and verified with the aid of the ASMETA toolset. The monitoring part of the MAPE-K loops was, however, not included. Arcaini et al. also addressed the specification and verification of the adaptation component for cloud systems [4].

Grid systems were also analyzed in terms of ASMs with respect to job and execution management by [5]. Differences between traditional distributed systems and grids were presented in an ASM formal description by [20]. The previously mentioned work on ASM specifications for distributed systems is representative for our understanding of distributed ASMs and their elaboration.

In our earlier work, we discussed the requirements of the monitoring solution for cloud-enabled Large-Scale Distributed Systems (CELDS) with respect to two areas of high interest for the development of smart cities [11,12]. In [11] we presented the requirements of the monitoring services for a traffic system and translated them to an ASM ground model that has been simulated. The model has been discussed in correlation with a healthcare system deployed in CELDS and his previous versions have been validated in [10,12]. The current paper extends this work and focuses on the verification of the ASM model. If the desired properties are ensured, the model can be further expanded to an actual prototype.

3 System Overview

LDS are composed of resources and services offered by various providers. One of the successful business models relying on algorithms and principles of LDS is cloud computing. While single providers cover the basic computing requirements, the increasing amount of data to be processed led to interconnecting clouds. The services are heterogeneous and their internal structure is unknown to the monitors. However, they allow the collection of a specific set of metrics, relevant for the assessment of their status. The current work has been extended on the frame of the monitoring services for CELDS, whose foundation has been presented in [17].

CELDS compose resources and services from different providers to respond to the needs of the clients. For instance, when there is a peck of requests, resources are asked from other providers. The system is a black box for the user, who is interested only in the quality of the services he requests. The execution layer, whose model and definition we take from [9], needs to be continuously monitored for flaws that might affect the availability or reliability. The role of the monitors is to detect and correctly assess faulty situations and submit this information further for system adaptation. The monitoring and adaptation components communicate intensively in order to detect and resolve problems occurring at the execution layer.

3.1 System Architecture

CELDS consist of different tiers as shown in Fig. 1. From the client-side, a large number of devices can send requests to providers. All the requests and replies are handled by a client-provider middleware formalized by [9]. Each provider,

Provider$_i$, of the system consists of a set of nodes $\{N_{i1}, N_{in}\}$, whose resources are composed and offered as services to users. Nodes can refer to a processing or a storage unit. Every node is assigned a set of monitors $\{m_1, m_i\}$ that evaluate its status. The monitoring layer communicates with the adaptation component by providing meaningful information for reconfiguration plans, which bring the system into a normal working state. The adaptation processes have been previously defined and formalized in [18,19].

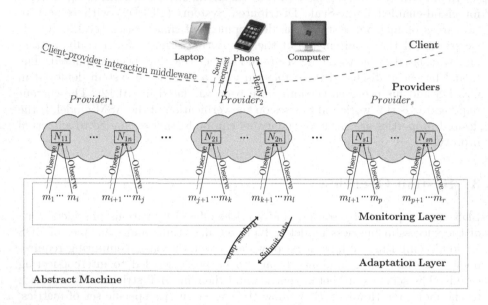

Fig. 1. Architecture of the system

3.2   Structure of the Monitoring Component

The monitoring layer continuously runs in the background of the execution layer and collects data related to each node. Monitors face also own issues. They might be unresponsive or submit random information, rather than the correct one. We introduce the notion of confidence degree based on their relative accuracy. The more imprecise evaluations a monitor does, the lower its confidence. The accuracy of a monitor is calculated as the deviation of the diagnosis it provides in comparison with the diagnosis voted by the majority of the monitors. If the confidence degree of one monitor falls below a certain threshold, it is deactivated. We assume that this process is correctly performed by the middleware and do not model this aspect.

Assessment of one monitor is not sufficiently reliable as data unavailability does not necessarily imply node failure. It can also indicate a problem of the monitor itself or of the communication link. We, then, need more monitors to contribute to the assessment. We assume that each node is observed by at least three monitors, which can collaborate and that the assignment is executed by the middleware. The minimum number of monitors represents the minimum number of participants in a voting quorum. We introduce the notion of leader of the monitors assigned to a node, which coordinates collective diagnoses whenever an issue is reported by one of the them. As shown in Fig. 2, all the monitors observe the node. $Monitor_j$ discovers a problem and reports it to the leader, which afterwards requests data from all the monitors associated to the node.

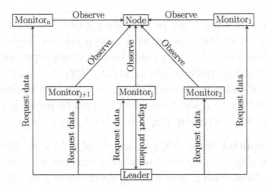

Fig. 2. View on the monitoring set assigned to a node

The leader is a different agent type, which settles a diagnosis based on the information received from all the monitors. The decision is taken based on a voting method, where each monitor inputs its own evaluation with a weight equal to its confidence degree. At the end, the diagnosis preferred by the most trustworthy majority is chosen and each of the monitor recalculates its confidence degree as follows. If the monitor inputs the same diagnosis as the one calculated by the leader, its confidence degree value does not modify. Otherwise, a penalty factor is applied. The number of similar diagnoses also contributes to the recalculation of the confidence degree. The larger the number of equivalent diagnoses to the one given by the monitor, the lower the decrease. It is, thus, considered that assessments shared by a larger number of monitors are more likely to be correct. Equation 1 shows the formula used to recalculate the confidence degree. The penalty factor is defined at initialization, depending on how critical the system is. The number of similar diagnoses represents the number of monitors who submitted the same assessment as $monitor_i$, while the number of diagnoses represents the total number of monitors who submitted their assessment.

$$conf\_degree(i) = conf\_degree(i) - \frac{|diagnoses| - |similar\_diagnoses(i)|}{|diagnoses|} \cdot *penalty\_factor,$$

$$where\ i \in Monitors(n), n \in Nodes \tag{1}$$

4   Formal Specification of the System

4.1   Background on ASM Theory

ASM is a formal method, which enhances the notion of Finite State Machine (FSM) with the possibility to express data structures for the *in* and *out* states connected by a transition. An ASM machine M is defined as a tuple $M = (\Sigma, S_0, R, R_0)$, where Σ is the signature (the set of all functions), S_0 is the set of initial states of Σ, R is the set of rule declarations, R_0 is the main rule of the machine.

A model consists of a finite set of transition rules of type: **if** *Condition* **then** *Updates*, where the *Condition* is an arbitrary predicate logic formula and the *Updates* is defined as a set of assignments to a *location* represented as a function f having a list of dynamic parameters $t_1, \ldots, t_n$: $f(t_1, \ldots, t_n) := t$. The method permits expressing synchronous parallelism, in which an update might attempt to assign distinct values to a location, thus leading to inconsistent updates. The following definition supported by Fig. 3 has been given by [7].

Definition 1. *A* control state ASM *is an ASM following the structure of the rules illustrated in Fig. 3: any control state i verifies at most one true guard, $cond_k$, triggering, thus, $rule_k$ and moving from state i to state s_k. In case no guard is fulfilled, the machine does not perform any action.*

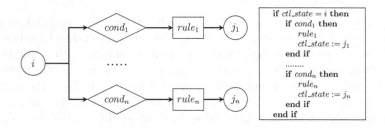

Fig. 3. Structure of a control state ASM

Rules of an ASM indicate control structures emphasizing parallelism (`par`), sequentiality (`seq`) and causality (`if...then`). With the `forall` expression, a machine can enforce concurrent execution of a rule R for every element x that satisfies a condition φ: `forall` x `with` φ `do` R. Non-determinism is expressed through the `choose` rule: `choose` x `with` φ `do` R.

Kossak and Mashkoor compared different formal models in [15] with respect to their expressiveness, easiness to use, integration in the software development process, and learning curve. ASM and Temporal Logic of Actions (TLA+) methods proved a good suitability for distributed systems. Petri Nets were not included in the study, but a comparison with the ASM method on concrete examples was carried out by Börger in [8], where Petri Nets proved to generate more complex and hard to follow specifications.

4.2 Overall Workflow of Model Specification and Analysis

Elaboration, validation and verification of the model follow a set of steps depicted
in Fig. 4. System requirements are first captured by an ASM model, which can
be easily defined with the AsmetaL language. Transformation of the monitoring
processes requirements to ASM ground models has been previously expressed
in [11,12]. The ASMETA model can be further simulated or validated by building
specific scenarios as detailed in [10]. The tool permits also automatic review of
the model for properties like conciseness or for design issues using the AsmetaMA
adviser, and the AsmetaSMV tool generates a NuSMV model, which can be
verified against desired properties.

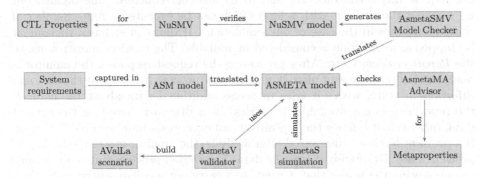

Fig. 4. Overall workflow of the modeling and verification processes

4.3 ASM Specification of the Monitoring Solution

The ASM specification of the monitoring solution closely matches the description from Sect. 3.2 and its structure is depicted in Fig. 5. The model consists of
a middleware agent, responsible for initializing the system and administration
operations (assignment of monitors, deactivation of untrustworthy components).
The model contains two main modules, one for the monitor and one for the
leader. We also used the *CTLlibrary* offered by the ASMETA toolset for verification. CELDS nodes are defined as elements of a domain and they contain a
few functions relevant for the monitoring processes. We left abstract their formal
specification and focused on the monitoring part. For the verification part, the
model has been reduced to one agent and the functions have been simplified so
that they contain primitive, finite data types.

The monitor module corresponds to the ground model depicted in Fig. 6 and
relies on the description of [10,11]. Each monitor is initialized by the middleware
agent in the *Inactive* state. As soon as it is deployed, it is assigned to a node and
moves to the *Active* state. From this state it sends a ping request (referred further
in the paper as heartbeat request) to verify if the node is available and moves
to the *Wait for response* state. There, it checks two guards. First, it verifies
if a reply arrived and if so, it processes the response. Otherwise, it checks if

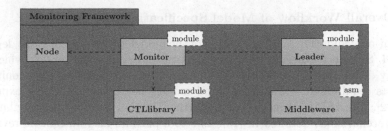

Fig. 5. Structure of the ASM monitoring specification

the request has a timeout. We had to let abstract concrete time details, but we replaced the timeout with a loop which can be executed a finite number of times (ten times in the case of our simulation). If the request has a timeout, it is stopped and the node is considered unavailable. The monitor moves, thus, to the *Report problem* state. After processing the request response, the monitor is ready to *Collect data* and after it finishes this process it moves to the *Retrieve information* state, where it tries to access additional data about the node. If the repository is not available, it carries out a diagnosis based on the current data, otherwise it queries the repository and executes a more complex analysis. If a problem has been discovered after analysis, the monitor moves to the *Report problem* state. Otherwise, it logs the data. The *Report problem* state corresponds to announcing the leader that it needs to a carry out a collaborative evaluation. After logging the data related to the current monitoring cycle, a guard verifies if its confidence degree is higher than the minimum accepted. In this case, the monitor starts a new cycle, otherwise it is deactivated by the middleware agent.

Table 1. Correlation between monitored data and node state

	Latency [ms]	CPU usage [percentage]	Memory usage [percentage]	Storage usage [percentage]	Work capacity [percentage]
Normal	<100	<40	<40	<40	>85
Critical	<100	>40	>40	>40	<85
Failed	>100	NA	NA	NA	NA

Data collected by the monitors capture a small set of parameters reflecting usage of resources and response time, which indicate possible unavailability and failure problems. We considered three possible diagnoses established by the monitors, $\{Normal, Critical, Failed\}$. Normal state corresponds to a small latency, small resource usage and high work capacity. Critical state refers to small latency, but high resource usage and small work capacity. Failure points to unavailability indicated by a high latency. The correspondence between the metrics collected by the monitor and the diagnosis it sets is depicted in Table 1. The values used for the classification are the ones expected generally for a service accessed through a high speed internet connection.

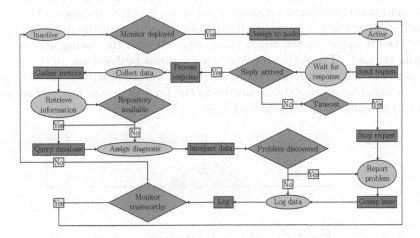

Fig. 6. Ground model of the monitor module

The rule responsible for collecting data from the node is captured in Code 1. It iterates through a set of specified metrics and for each of them checks if a value is defined and adds it to the gathered data.

```
rule r_GatherMetrics ($m in Monitor) =
  let ($count = 0) in
    while ($count < size(Metric)) do
      seq
        if (isDef(metric_value)) then
          monitor_measurements ($m) := append(monitor_measurements($m), (at
                (asSequence(Metric),iton($count)), metric_value))
        else
          monitor_measurements ($m) := append(monitor_measurements($m), (at
                (asSequence(Metric),iton($count)), 0))
        endif
        $count := $count + 1
      endseq
  endlet
```

Code 1. Monitor rule to gather metrics

If no value is defined, it simply adds zero, which is considered neutral by the specification. Data collection is done sequentially because a parallel execution tries to update the measurement list with different values at the same time. The inconsistency error was detected at simulation time with the aid of the AsmetaS tool. We leave as a future work the elaboration of transaction specific operations, which would permit submitting simultaneously multiple monitored values to the list of metrics.

The leader module focuses on collecting information from all the monitors of a node and using it for a final decision in case of reported issues. It starts from a state in which it waits for the *Evaluation requested* guard to become true. This guard is activated when a monitor reports a problem and moves the leader to the *Evaluate* state from where it requests data from all the monitors of the node. Then it moves to the assess state, where it uses the voting algorithm to evaluate the node. The voting method is a consensus problem and in comparison with previous algorithms, we require that each voter (monitor) contributes to a weight equal to its confidence degree to the final decision. The control state ASM of the leader is illustrated by Fig. 7.

Fig. 7. Ground model of the leader module

The leader coordinates evaluations executed by different monitors assigned to the node. It, thus, aims to increase the accuracy of the monitoring services. We can analyze its role on the following example. Let us assume a node is observed by three monitors, all having the confidence degree equal to 100. One of them reports that the node is unavailable, making in this way the *Evaluation requested* guard. The real issue is that the communication link between it and the node is broken. In parallel, the other two monitors receive responses from the node and continue their assessment. On the request of the leader, they submit their evaluation and vote that there is no problem with the node. The leader analyzes all three responses and decides that the node does not exhibit any actual problem (by the voting procedure). The monitoring framework prevents in this way a false positive report of a problem, that would trigger an unnecessary adaptation of the node.

The middleware agent is expressed as an ASM where all the functions and instances are initialized. It contains only one state, *Executing*, and we assume that all the actions carried out by it are reliable and correctly executed.

5   Verification of the Model

5.1   Analysis of Model Quality

The AsmetaMA model reviewer tool establishes the quality of the model by checking its compliance to a set of properties and indicating which functions, rules and control states are not necessary or not well specified. The tool relies on the translation of the model to an NuSMV specification. We list below the list of properties we checked, but we refer the reader to [3] for the complete list of properties and more details on the review procedure.

1. MP1 - No inconsistent updates are performed.
   Result: NONE (NONE indicates that no violations have been found).
2. MP2 - Every conditional rule is complete
   Result: ConditionalRule if (heartbeat_timeout(self)) is not complete.
   ConditionalRule if (isUndef(has_leader($n))) is not complete.
3. MP4 - No assignment is always trivial
   Result: Trivial update of location trigger_gossip(MONITOR_3). When the
   condition is (TRUE & !(monitor_state(monitor_3) = INACTIVE) & (moni-
   tor_state(monitor_3) = LOG_DATA)) its value is always the same of the term
   FALSE.
4. MP5 - For every domain element e there exists a location which has value e
   Result: None
5. MP7 - Every controlled location is updated and every location is read.
   Result: Functions middleware_state, has_leader, assigned_node, confidence_
   degree could be defined static.

The result of the model quality analysis was used for refining the model and
removing unnecessary functions or reviewing incomplete conditional structures.

5.2   Verification of Specification Properties

ASMETA toolset allows verifying properties of the model by using Computation
Tree Logic (CTL) operators. The framework supports the translation of the
model to an NuSMV specification that can be further checked. NuSMV supports
only finite domains and simple data structures. Hence, the AsmetaL initial model
had to be oversimplified. CTL properties were translated into AsmetaL functions,
which are part of the *CTLlibrary* described by [2].

We carried out the verification of a set of properties, which handle aspects
related to the communication between modules. We are interested in the correctness of the monitoring processes. We propose for the future work the inclusion of
the confidence degree values in the verification process. As the verification phase
is constrained to using finite sets, we defined one node to which we assigned three
monitors having one leader. We simplified functions to contain finite Integer values instead of Real ones (for confidence degree or metric values) and focused on
the correctness of the monitoring workflow. All the properties were specified in
CTL and verified on a Windows machine having Intel(R) Core(TM) i7 CPU @
2 GHz, 8 GB RAM with the aid of the AsmetaSMV Eclipse Plug-in.

Any monitor that is assigned to a node, being thus in the *Active* state,
eventually reaches the state where he logs the information collected, *Log_data*.
We ensure in this case that a monitoring cycle is eventually completed.

CTLSPEC (forall $m **in** Monitor **with** ag((monitor_state($m) = ACTIVE) implies
    ef(monitor_state($m) = LOG_DATA)))

If a monitor submits a request and does not receive a response for it, the
monitor reports the issue. We ensure in this way, that unavailability of the node
is communicated further.

CTLSPEC (forall $m **in** Monitor **with** ag((monitor_state($m) =
WAIT_FOR_RESPONSE and not(heartbeat_response_arrived($m))) implies
ax(monitor_state($m) = REPORT_PROBLEM)))

Monitors having a lower confidence degree are dismissed and move to the
inactive state. This property does not allow faulty monitors to analyze nodes of
the CELDS and aims to enforce a fail-safe behavior of the monitoring solution.

CTLSPEC (forall $m **in** Monitor **with** ag((confidence_degree($m) <
min_confidence_degree) implies ax(monitor_state($m) = INACTIVE)))

If any of the monitors reports a problem, the leader starts the evaluation
of the node. The property verifies that all reported issues are handled by the
system.

CTLSPEC (forall $m **in** Monitor **with** ag((trigger_gossip($m) = true) implies
ef(leader_state(leader_1) = EVALUATE)))

A leader that starts the evaluation must reach a conclusion and establish
an assessment. This property guarantees that the evaluation process provides a
result to the system.

CTLSPEC (forall $l **in** Leader **with** ag((leader_state($l) = EVALUATE) implies
ef(isDef(assessment($l)))))

```
> NuSMV -dynamic -coi -quiet C:\Work\Specs\ASMeta_Specs\code\Verification\SingleModelVerification.
  smv
-- specification ((AG (monitor_state(monitor_2) = ACTIVE -> EF monitor_state(monitor_2) = LOG_DATA) &
   AG (monitor_state(monitor_1) = ACTIVE -> EF monitor_state(monitor_1) = LOG_DATA)) & AG (
   monitor_state(monitor_3) = ACTIVE -> EF monitor_state(monitor_3) = LOG_DATA)) is true
-- specification ((AG ((!heartbeat_timeout(monitor_2) & (monitor_state(monitor_2) = WAIT_FOR_RESPONSE
   & heartbeat_response_arrived(monitor_2))) -> AX monitor_state(monitor_2) = COLLECT_DATA) & AG
   ((!heartbeat_timeout(monitor_1) & (heartbeat_response_arrived(monitor_1) & monitor_state(monitor_1) =
   WAIT_FOR_RESPONSE)) -> AX monitor_state(monitor_1) = COLLECT_DATA)) & AG ((!
   heartbeat_timeout(monitor_3) & (monitor_state(monitor_3) = WAIT_FOR_RESPONSE &
   heartbeat_response_arrived(monitor_3))) -> AX monitor_state(monitor_3) = COLLECT_DATA)) is true
-- specification ((AG ((monitor_state(monitor_2) = WAIT_FOR_RESPONSE & !heartbeat_response_arrived(
   monitor_2)) -> AX monitor_state(monitor_2) = REPORT_PROBLEM) & AG ((!
   heartbeat_response_arrived(monitor_1) & monitor_state(monitor_1) = WAIT_FOR_RESPONSE) -> AX
   monitor_state(monitor_1) = REPORT_PROBLEM)) & AG ((monitor_state(monitor_3) =
   WAIT_FOR_RESPONSE & !heartbeat_response_arrived(monitor_3)) -> AX monitor_state(monitor_3) =
   REPORT_PROBLEM)) is true
-- specification ((AG (confidence_degree(monitor_3) < 80 -> AX monitor_state(monitor_3) = INACTIVE) &
   AG (confidence_degree(monitor_1) < 80 -> AX monitor_state(monitor_1) = INACTIVE)) & AG (
   confidence_degree(monitor_2) < 80 -> AX monitor_state(monitor_2) = INACTIVE)) is true
-- specification ((AG (trigger_gossip(monitor_2) -> EF leader_state(leader_1) = EVALUATE) & AG (
   trigger_gossip(monitor_3) -> EF leader_state(leader_1) = EVALUATE)) & AG (trigger_gossip(monitor_1)
   -> EF leader_state(leader_1) = EVALUATE)) is true
-- specification AG (leader_state(leader_1) = EVALUATE -> EF assessment(leader_1) != undef) is true
-- specification AG (leader_state(leader_1) = IDLE_LEADER -> EF assessment(leader_1) != undef) is false
```

Code 2. AsmetaSMV Trace

A leader that is in idle state is not allowed to assign a diagnosis. This property checks that the leader does not misbehave and starts to randomly carry
out assessments. The property must be evaluated to false and the tool offers a
counterexample as well.

CTLSPEC (forall $l **in** Leader **with** ag((leader_state($l) = IDLE_LEADER)
implies ef(isDef(assessment($l)))))

The AsmetaSMV result of the property verification is captured by the snippet
from Code 2.

6   Discussions and Limitations

The current ASM specification focuses on achieving correct behavior of the monitors. It emphasizes the importance of establishing an accurate diagnosis of a component of the CELDS, given a set of partial views of the system submitted by each monitor assigned to the component. Although the ASM method permits a straightforward translation of the requirements into a formal model, our approach suffers of several limitations as follows.

In the validation stage, we had to simplify the specification by removing the non-deterministic character of the *choose* rules. The verification process implied translating the model to an NuSMV specification, which could be model checked. Hence, infinite domains had to be removed or replaced by finite sets of Integer/-Natural or enumerations. Another problem we encountered was the impossibility of assigning the value of a function as parameter for another function. Time related aspects of the solutions were also not supported by the ASM method. The ASM models can be complemented by other formal specifications focused on timing aspects like TLA+, for example.

The simplification of the model widens the gap to the high complexity of CELDS. However, the specification still captures important insights on the behavior of the monitors and helps identifying design flaws.

The research work described in this paper encompasses the steps executed to transform the requirements of the monitoring processes for CELDS to an actual formal model, which can be analyzed and verified. Once we had the ASM ground model, we could easily translate the states and rules to an AsmetaL model. The ASMETA toolset integrated with the Eclipse plug-in supported the simulation, validation and verification of the model, which were carried out gradually. However, there are still a number of open questions to be answered. For instance, the model adviser tool identifies unnecessary functions or incomplete conditional structures, but it does not assess the coverage of the model with respect to the problem domain. Validation by scenarios provides useful insights as long as the scenarios defined by the modeler are representative enough. In the verification phase, the understanding of the properties by the modeler determines the importance of model checking results. We consider that ASMETA toolset supports the designer in elaborating the specifications, assessing their quality, and eventually finding related drawbacks, but it still needs the human expertise in order to provide relevant answers.

7   Conclusions and Future Work

The paper addresses the monitoring aspect for CELDS from a formal perspective. We presented the methodology for elaborating and assessing a formal model for monitoring processes of CELDS using the ASMETA toolset. The focus of our work was on ensuring the correctness of the monitors, and hence enhancing the reliability and availability of the whole system. The work focuses on translating monitoring related processes to a formal model and verifying its properties.

Through rigorous analysis of the model we can identify design flaws, that otherwise, would propagate to the implementation phase of software development.

The model we propose is still open to future refinements, in which interpretation of data can be improved by considering aggregation of parameters into higher-level metrics. The spectrum of properties to verify can be enlarged by elaborating more the dependencies between the components and encompassing quantitative aspects of the voting process.

References

1. Arcaini, P., Riccobene, E., Scandurra, P.: Modeling and analyzing MAPE-K feedback loops for self-adaptation. In: 2015 IEEE/ACM 10th International Symposium on Software Engineering for Adaptive and Self-managing Systems, pp. 13–23, May 2015
2. Arcaini, P., Gargantini, A., Riccobene, E.: AsmetaSMV: a way to link high-level ASM models to low-level NuSMV specifications. In: Frappier, M., Glässer, U., Khurshid, S., Laleau, R., Reeves, S. (eds.) ABZ 2010. LNCS, vol. 5977, pp. 61–74. Springer, Heidelberg (2010). https://doi.org/10.1007/978-3-642-11811-1_6
3. Arcaini, P., Gargantini, A., Riccobene, E.: Automatic review of abstract state machines by meta property verification. In: Proceedings of Second NASA Formal Methods Symposium - NFM 2010, 13–15 April 2010, Washington D.C., USA, pp. 4–13 (2010)
4. Arcaini, P., Holom, R.-M., Riccobene, E.: ASM-based formal design of an adaptivity component for a cloud system. Form. Asp. Comput. **28**(4), 567–595 (2016)
5. Bianchi, A., Manelli, L., Pizzutilo, S.: An ASM-based model for grid job management. Informatica (Slovenia) **37**(3), 295–306 (2013)
6. Bolis, F., Gargantini, A., Guarnieri, M., Magri, E., Musto, L.: Model-driven testing for web applications using abstract state machines. In: Grossniklaus, M., Wimmer, M. (eds.) ICWE 2012. LNCS, vol. 7703, pp. 71–78. Springer, Heidelberg (2012). https://doi.org/10.1007/978-3-642-35623-0_7
7. Börger, E., Stark, R.F.: Abstract State Machines: A Method for High-Level System Design and Analysis. Springer-Verlag, New York Inc., Secaucus (2003). https://doi.org/10.1007/978-3-642-18216-7
8. Börger, E.: Modeling distributed algorithms by abstract state machines compared to petri nets. In: Butler, M., Schewe, K.-D., Mashkoor, A., Biro, M. (eds.) ABZ 2016. LNCS, vol. 9675, pp. 3–34. Springer, Cham (2016). https://doi.org/10.1007/978-3-319-33600-8_1
9. Bósa, K., Holom, R.-M., Vleju, M.B.: A formal model of client-cloud interaction. In: Thalheim, B., Schewe, K.D., Prinz, A., Buchberger, B. (eds.) Correct Software in Web Applications and Web Services, pp. 83–144. Springer, Cham (2015). https://doi.org/10.1007/978-3-319-17112-8_4
10. Buga, A., Nemes, S.T.: A formal approach for failure detection in large-scale distributed systems using abstract state machines. In: Benslimane, D., Damiani, E., Grosky, W.I., Hameurlain, A., Sheth, A., Wagner, R.R. (eds.) DEXA 2017. LNCS, vol. 10438, pp. 505–513. Springer, Cham (2017). https://doi.org/10.1007/978-3-319-64468-4_38
11. Buga, A., Nemes, S.T.: Towards modeling monitoring of smart traffic services in a large-scale distributed system. In: CLOSER 2017 - Proceedings of the 7th International Conference on Cloud Computing and Services Science, 24–26 April 2017, Porto, Portugal, pp. 455–462 (2017)

12. Buga, A., Nemes, S.T.: Towards modeling monitoring services for large-scale distributed systems with abstract state machines. In: Radar Track at the 22nd International Working Conference on Evaluation and Modeling Methods for Systems Analysis and Development (EMMSAD) Co-located with the 29th International Conference on Advanced Information Systems Engineering 2017 (CAiSE 2017), June 2017, Essen, Germany, vol. 1859. CEUR (2017)

13. Clayman, S., Galis, A., Mamatas, L.: Monitoring virtual networks with Lattice. In: Network Operations and Management Symposium Workshops (NOMS Wksps), pp. 239–246. IEEE/IFIP, April 2010

14. Fugini, M., Siadat, H.: SLA contract for cross-layer monitoring and adaptation. In: Rinderle-Ma, S., Sadiq, S., Leymann, F. (eds.) BPM 2009. LNBIP, vol. 43, pp. 412–423. Springer, Heidelberg (2010). https://doi.org/10.1007/978-3-642-12186-9_39

15. Kossak, F., Mashkoor, A.: How to select the suitable formal method for an industrial application: a survey. In: Butler, M., Schewe, K.-D., Mashkoor, A., Biro, M. (eds.) ABZ 2016. LNCS, vol. 9675, pp. 213–228. Springer, Cham (2016). https://doi.org/10.1007/978-3-319-33600-8_13

16. Ma, H., Schewe, K.D., Wang, Q.: An abstract model for service provision, search and composition. In: 2009 IEEE Asia-Pacific Services Computing Conference (APSCC), pp. 95–102, December 2009

17. Moreno-Díaz, R., Pichler, F., Quesada-Arencibia, A. (eds.): Computer Aided Systems Theory - EUROCAST 2015. Lecture Notes in Computer Science, vol. 9520. Springer, Cham (2015). https://doi.org/10.1007/978-3-319-27340-2

18. Nemes, S.T., Buga, A.: Towards a case-based reasoning approach to dynamic adaptation for large-scale distributed systems. In: Aha, D.W., Lieber, J. (eds.) ICCBR 2017. LNCS (LNAI), vol. 10339, pp. 257–271. Springer, Cham (2017). https://doi.org/10.1007/978-3-319-61030-6_18

19. Nemes, S.T., Buga, A.: Towards modeling adaptation services for large-scale distributed systems with abstract state machines. In: Proceedings of the Seventh International Symposium on Business Modeling and Software Design, BMSD, vol. 1, pp. 193–198. INSTICC, SciTePress (2017)

20. Németh, Z.N., Sunderam, V.: A formal framework for defining grid systems. In: 2002 14th IEEE/ACM International Symposium on Cluster, Cloud and Grid Computing, p. 202 (2002). http://dblp.uni-trier.de/rec/bibtex/conf/ccgrid/NemethS02

21. Petcu, D., Crăciun, C., Neagul, M., Panica, S., Di Martino, B., Venticinque, S., Rak, M., Aversa, R.: Architecturing a sky computing platform. In: Cezon, M., Wolfsthal, Y. (eds.) ServiceWave 2010. LNCS, vol. 6569, pp. 1–13. Springer, Heidelberg (2011). https://doi.org/10.1007/978-3-642-22760-8_1

Design-Time to Run-Time Verification
of Microservices Based Applications
(Short Paper)

Matteo Camilli[✉], Carlo Bellettini, and Lorenzo Capra

Department of Computer Science, Università degli Studi di Milano, Milan, Italy
{camilli,bellettini,capra}@di.unimi.it

Abstract. Microservice based architectures have started to gain in popularity and are often adopted in the implementation of modern cloud, IoT, and large-scale distributed applications. Software life cycles, in this context, are characterized by short iterations, where several updates and new functionalities are continuously integrated many times a day. This paradigm shift calls for new formal approaches to systematic verification and testing of applications in production infrastructures. We introduce an approach to continuous, *design- to run-time verification*, of microservice based applications. This paper describes our envisioned approach, the current stage of this ongoing work, and the challenges ahead.

Keywords: Microservices · Cloud applications · Formal verification
Formal methods @ runtime · Petri nets

1 Introduction and Background

The microservice architectural style [1] represents an upward trending approach to the development of modern cloud, IoT, or more in general large-scale distributed application. Services implement individual functional areas of the application and they may be written using different programming languages and technologies. Moreover, they are independently deployable by automated procedures. This approach has been proposed to cope with many problems associated with monolithic applications, especially as more applications are being deployed into cloud platforms [2]. Among all the issues associated with monolithic products, some notable examples are: hard maintainability; scalability issues; technology lock-in for developers; and expensive delivery of latest builds.

The microservice style is not novel or innovative: it is inspired by service-oriented computing [3] and we can find its roots in the design principles of Unix [2]. However, the shift towards microservices is a sensitive matter nowadays. In fact, several companies are switching to this paradigm by applying major refactoring activities. Netflix, Inc. [4] is a leading example: they recently moved from their previous monolithic application to a microservices architecture with

© Springer International Publishing AG 2018
A. Cerone and M. Roveri (Eds.): SEFM 2017 Workshops, LNCS 10729, pp. 168–173, 2018.
https://doi.org/10.1007/978-3-319-74781-1_12

hundreds of services working together to stream multimedia contents to millions of users every day. The whole architecture builds on Netflix CONDUCTOR engine [5], an open source framework designed by Netflix Inc. and used daily in their production environment. CONDUCTOR allows the creation of complex process flows in which individual tasks are implemented by microservices. The process flow blueprint is defined using a JSON based DSL and includes a set of *system* tasks (e.g., fork, join, conditional, etc.) executed by CONDUCTOR's engine, and *worker* tasks (e.g., file encryption) that are the functional areas of the application, running on remote machines. In this context, formal verification and testing activities can be challenging. In fact, rapidly evolving services potentially require formal models and tests to be recreated or modified. Moreover, microservices' polyglot nature potentially requires multiple testing tools because of different programming languages and runtime environments.

To deal with these open problems, we introduce an approach to formal design-to run-time verification (RV) of microservice-based process flows built on top of CONDUCTOR. In particular, we have automated the modeling phase by mechanically translating the CONDUCTOR blueprint into a formal specification given in terms of Time Basic Petri nets [6] (from now on simply TB nets). TB nets are an expressive time-extension of Petri nets (PNs) provided with a clear and rigorous semantics, and represent an effective formal specification of distributed systems with time constraints. The TB nets formalism is nicely supported by powerful off-the-shelf software tools covering both modeling and verification phases [7,8]. The RV technique is currently implemented as a prototypal JAVA library, built on top of MAHARAJA [9], a lightweight pluggable tool supporting the verification of behavioral and temporal aspects of JAVA programs.

The paper is organized as follows. In Sect. 2, we introduce our proposed approach, pointing out the current stage of this ongoing work. We report some related work in Sect. 3, finally we draw our conclusions, discussing the challenges ahead, in Sect. 4.

2 Overview of the Approach

Figure 1 shows the two main phases of our approach: (*i*) model generation and verification; and (*ii*) runtime verification. A description of the two phases follows. As a running example, used throughout the discussion, we use a taxi-hailing application, such as Uber [10]. Each microservice implements a particular functional area of the application (e.g., access control, passenger management, trip management, payment, etc.) and exposes a REST API to other microservices or the clients of the application. For example, the *passenger management* service uses the *notification* service to notify a passenger about an available driver. An API gateway exposes a public API used by mobile clients or web UIs. We assume that the process flow of the application is specified with CONDUCTOR and is deployed on a cloud platform running the CONDUCTOR's engine.

(*i*) **Model generation and offline verification** – This phase tries to deal with the rapid evolution of microservice systems by formalizing the CONDUCTOR

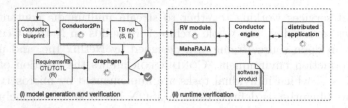

Fig. 1. High level schema of our envisioned approach.

blueprint as a TB nets model, describing both the system under development (S) and the environment (E). Every time a change is made to the process flow, the formal specification is automatically kept in sync. The translation process is fully automated by means of the CONDUCTOR2PN component. Our modeling approach abstracts from functional aspects and looks at each service as a black box. We use TB net places to represent the state of a worker task (i.e., scheduled, in progress, timed out, or failed) and transitions to represent both task primitives and events coming from the surrounding environment. We leverage TB nets' temporal functions associated with transitions to specify temporal constraints on scheduling and execution. The proposed formal semantics is complete, i.e., covers all the language constructs of CONDUCTOR.

As an example, the CONDUCTOR blueprint of the taxi-hailing application contains different worker tasks, among which: *Access control* (validating user requests); *Passenger management* (storing and processing passengers data); *Driver management* (looking for available drivers near passengers). System tasks[1] define the process flow. For instance, an *event handler* can be used to elaborate incoming user requests; a *fork* task can be used to execute in parallel the *Access control* functionality and a search for static contents in a *cache* service.

The model generation process is fully compositional, relying on the identification of translation patterns for the involved microservices (Worker tasks) and the execution flow (specified by System tasks). The final model is the composition of the TB net patterns of the microservices and execution flow constructs. It can be used to perform different verification steps, such as interactive simulation and model checking, with the aid of GRAPHGEN module. A common property to check is deadlock/livelock absence. More generally, it is possible to verify *invariant, safety, liveness* and *bounded-response time* properties corresponding to TCTL formulas [11]. For instance, we can verify whether it is possible to complete the payment and the billing processes within a certain time bound.

(*ii*) **Runtime verification** – A model (re)generated in the previous step can be also used to perform verification activities at runtime, on the production infrastructure (the CONDUCTOR engine running on a cloud platform). The objective is to run and monitor several executions in order to stress the system under scrutiny (SUS) and increase our confidence about its correctness.

---

[1] A list of all the available system tasks can be found in [5].

The RV module exploits the MAHARAJA open source tool [9]. This framework supplies the ability to map methods of interests (i.e., *action methods*) to TB net transitions. At runtime, the MAHARAJA framework performs a monitoring activity through the co-execution of the formal specification (triggered by running action methods) and the SUS. The monitor continuously evaluates the conformance of the execution timed trace, observed from the SUS, with respect to its formal specification. Since the CONDUCTOR engine is written in JAVA, the MAHARAJA framework can be directly plugged-in to monitor at runtime its own execution. As an example, different executions of the taxi-hailing application can be stimulated by issuing user requests, such as: trip computation for a given ⟨source, destination⟩ pair, by a passenger user; pick-up acceptance, by a driver user. Thus, we verify that the involved services act as expected, within the temporal constraints defined in the formal specification, by comparing the observed execution traces with feasible execution paths of the TB net model.

In addition, the RV module can be tuned to distinguish operations under the control of a tester (i.e., *controllable* action methods) from operations that can only be observed (i.e., *observable* action methods). If the running system is in a state of *quiescence* [12], a legal *controllable* action (e.g., a user request in our taxi-hailing example) is randomly chosen by applying a user-defined strategy (based on either fixed or decrementing weights [12]), to automate user interaction. In order to help assess the quality of the runtime verification activity, we allow the user to check if certain requirements (i.e., *goal states*, expressed as reachable TB net markings) are met and we gather some coverage information in terms of executed controllable/observable action methods.

Current Stage of the Work – The model generation is implemented by the CONDUCTOR2PN [13] JAVA tool. We validated our approach by translating a variety of benchmarking examples. We are currently in the process of trying it out on real-world applications. The generated model can be formally verified using the GRAPHGEN model checker [7,8,14]. The RV module, built on top of MAHARAJA [9], is a prototypal implementation and has not yet been fully validated. So far, it has been employed to monitor the execution of the taxi-hailing application running on a locally simulated environment. This has permitted us to discover a number of errors both in the blueprint and the implementation. Most conceptual errors were early discovered at the design-time, what dramatically reduced the number of bugs discovered during testing and RV.

3   Related Work

Although descriptive formalisms for distributed systems are very popular, the adoption of operational specifications offers some advantages with respect to declarative ones [15]. In fact, most operational models are visual and are usually easier to write and understand by non expert users. Automata-based formalisms support the specification of both behavioral and temporal aspects, but PN-based models are more concise and scalable [16]. Moreover, aspects like messaging and communication protocols, commonly used in service oriented and microservice-based architectures, are difficult to model using the language primitives of automata-based formalisms [17].

The automatic model generation, during the design phase, is somehow inspired by previous studies on Business Process Execution Language (BPEL) for Web Services [18]. However, these approaches cannot be directly applied in the context of microservices, where emerging new languages and frameworks, such as CONDUCTOR, are being adopted as major references for orchestration.

JOLIE [19] is an interpreter engine of microservice workflows specified by using a JAVA-like syntax orchestration language. The supplied formal specifications of its semantics (in terms of process algebra [20]) can be used for computer-aided verification. This framework does not support runtime verification on production infrastructures.

The approach presented in [21] aims at dealing with environmental dynamism in service-based applications. The proposed modeling approach allows for partial definition of services in order to perform late (i.e., at runtime) incremental composition, when the execution context is discovered. This approach does not support formal verification of requirements at design-time.

4   Conclusion and Future Work

This paper describes an ongoing research activity on the application of formal methods to continuously support the development of microservices based cloud applications. The approach gets solid foundations from well-established formal methods and connects them to microservices based process flows. In particular, we make use of TB nets formalism to support design- to run-time verification of cloud applications built on top of CONDUCTOR.

The design-time phase aims at coping with continuously evolving specifications by keeping automatically updated the formal specification. The RV phase provides a way to support integration testing activity in a formal setting by means of a single software tool, although each service is independent and potentially implemented using different programming languages and technologies.

We are going to validate the RV module with a realistic case study deployed on a cloud platform. In addition, we are interested in expanding on this work in different directions. We want to extend the RV module in order to support online model-based testing with different *scenario control* techniques [12]. Moreover, we aim at expanding the translation to stochastic PNs (supporting probabilistic model checking) to deal with the intrinsic uncertainty of the environment.

References

1. Dragoni, N., Giallorenzo, S., Lafuente, A.L., Mazzara, M., Montesi, F., Mustafin, R., Safina, L.: Microservices: yesterday, today, and tomorrow. Present and Ulterior Software Engineering, pp. 195–216. Springer, Cham (2017). https://doi.org/10.1007/978-3-319-67425-4_12

2. Microservices: a definition of this new architectural term, June 2017. https://martinfowler.com/articles/microservices.html
3. Erl, T.: Service-Oriented Architecture: Concepts, Technology, and Design. Prentice Hall PTR, Upper Saddle River (2005)
4. Netflix, Inc., June 2017. https://www.netflix.com/
5. Conductor, June 2017. https://netflix.github.io/conductor/
6. Ghezzi, C., Mandrioli, D., Morasca, S., Pezzè, M.: A unified high-level petri net formalism for time-critical systems. IEEE Trans. Softw. Eng. **17**, 160–172 (1991)
7. Camilli, M., Gargantini, A., Scandurra, P.: Specifying and verifying real-time self-adaptive systems. In: 2015 IEEE 26th International Symposium on Software Reliability Engineering (ISSRE), Nov 2015, pp. 303–313 (2015)
8. Camilli, M.: Petri nets state space analysis in the cloud. In: Proceedings of the 34th International Conference on Software Engineering, ser. ICSE 2012, pp. 1638–1640. IEEE Press, Piscataway (2012)
9. Camilli, M., Gargantini, A., Scandurra, P., Bellettini, C.: Event-based runtime verification of temporal properties using time basic petri nets. In: Barrett, C., Davies, M., Kahsai, T. (eds.) NFM 2017. LNCS, vol. 10227, pp. 115–130. Springer, Cham (2017). https://doi.org/10.1007/978-3-319-57288-8_8
10. Uber Technologies, Inc., June 2017. https://www.uber.com/
11. Alur, R., Courcoubetis, C., Dill, D.: Model-checking in dense real-time. Inf. Comput. **104**(1), 2–34 (1993)
12. Veanes, M., Campbell, C., Schulte, W., Tillmann, N.: Online testing with model programs. SIGSOFT Softw. Eng. Notes **30**(5), 273–282 (2005)
13. Conductor2Pn, June 2017. https://bitbucket.org/seresearch_unimi/conductor2pn
14. Camilli, M., Bellettini, C., Capra, L., Monga, M.: CTL model checking in the cloud using mapreduce. In: 2014 16th International Symposium on Symbolic and Numeric Algorithms for Scientific Computing, pp. 333–340, September 2014
15. Liang, H., Dong, J.S., Sun, J., Wong, W.E.: Software monitoring through formal specification animation. Innov. Syst. Softw. Eng. **5**(4), 231–241 (2009)
16. Ramchandani, C.: Analysis of asynchronous concurrent systems by timed petri nets. Technical report, Cambridge, MA, USA (1974)
17. Lee, W.J., Cha, S.D., Kwon, Y.R.: Integration and analysis of use cases using modular petri nets in requirements engineering. IEEE Trans. Softw. Eng. **24**(12), 1115–1130 (1998)
18. Hinz, S., Schmidt, K., Stahl, C.: Transforming BPEL to petri nets. In: van der Aalst, W.M.P., Benatallah, B., Casati, F., Curbera, F. (eds.) BPM 2005. LNCS, vol. 3649, pp. 220–235. Springer, Heidelberg (2005). https://doi.org/10.1007/11538394_15
19. Montesi, F., Guidi, C., Lucchi, R., Zavattaro, G.: JOLIE: a java orchestration language interpreter engine. Electron. Notes Theor. Comput. Sci. **181**, 19–33 (2007)
20. Fokkink, W.: Introduction to Process Algebra, 1st edn. Springer-Verlag, New York Inc., Secaucus (2000). https://doi.org/10.1007/978-3-662-04293-9. Ed. by W. Brauer, G. Rozenberg, and A. Salomaa
21. Bucchiarone, A., De Sanctis, M., Pistore, M.: Domain objects for dynamic and incremental service composition. In: Villari, M., Zimmermann, W., Lau, K.-K. (eds.) ESOCC 2014. LNCS, vol. 8745, pp. 62–80. Springer, Heidelberg (2014). https://doi.org/10.1007/978-3-662-44879-3_5

Generalized Oracle for Testing Machine Learning Computer Programs

Shin Nakajima[✉]

National Institute of Informatics, Tokyo, Japan
nkjm@nii.ac.jp

Abstract. Computation results of machine learning programs are not possible to be anticipated, because the results are sensitive to distribution of data in input dataset. Additionally, these computer programs sometimes adopt randomized algorithms for finding sub-optimal solutions or improving runtime efficiencies to reach solutions. The computation is probabilistic and the results vary from execution to execution even for a same input. The characteristics imply that no deterministic test oracle exists to check correctness of programs. This paper studies how a notion of oracles is elaborated so that these programs can be tested, and shows a systematic way of deriving testing properties from mathematical formulations of given machine learning problems.

1 Introduction

Software testing is a practical method for informal assurance on the quality of computer programs. It relies on *deterministic* test oracles with prescribed correct values usually given as design specifications. These oracles show the same behavior, for the same input data, returning the same checking result even for different executions of the target program.

Exact correct values of machine learning (ML) programs are not known in advance because they discern *unknown* valuable information from input dataset. Such programs are considered *non-testable* [5]. In addition, because ML problems are mostly NP-hard and intractable, ML programs may implement randomized algorithms for obtaining sub-optional solutions (e.g. [1]). This randomness makes computation results different from executions to executions. Deterministic oracles are not available for ML programs.

This paper studies a new notion of oracles for testing ML programs. Section 2 studies characteristics of ML programs from testing views, and presents a general method to use metamorphic testing (MT) [2]. Sections 3 and 4 present example cases of applying the proposed method to two machine learning problems, support vector machines (SVM) and neural networks (NN), which is followed by concluding discussions in Sect. 5.

2 Generalized Test Oracles

Deterministic test oracles for software testing rely on two key features. Given a specific test input data (X), a target program reaches a final state with a

© Springer International Publishing AG 2018
A. Cerone and M. Roveri (Eds.): SEFM 2017 Workshops, LNCS 10729, pp. 174–179, 2018.
https://doi.org/10.1007/978-3-319-74781-1_13

commutation result (Y). Firstly, those oracles determine whether the results are equal to prescribed correct values with respect to the input $(Y = C^X)$. Secondly, the oracles behave the same for different executions of the target when the input is the same. ML programs violates assumptions for deterministic oracles; (1) correct values are not known in advance, (2) returned values are varied due to randomness. We mainly consider the first aspect and then studies the second one for the case of a certain ML problem.

Pseudo oracles are using relative correct values instead of absolute correctness [5]. Such correct values are results of program executions. When two program versions (f_1 and f_2) exist, computation results of either one, say f_1, plays a role of *golden outputs*, correct values for the other (f_2). Alternatively, metamorphic testing (MT) [2] uses just one program, and considers two executions of f_1 with two different inputs (X_1 and X_2). The test inputs are related by a translation function T ($X_2 = T(X_1)$), and a certain relation R_T holds for outputs of two executions, $R_T(f_1(X_1), f_1(X_2))$. For a given translation T on the input test data, R_T is a *metamorphic relation* between the outputs. *Metamorphic testing* is a testing method that uses the relation R_T as a basis for pseudo oracles. We consider that some faults are in the program when R_T is violated, because R_T is so chosen that the two executions are expected to be the same. In simple cases, R_T is an identity ($f_1(X_1) = f_1(T(X_1))$).

The translation T and metamorphic relation (MR) M_T must respect functional requirements of the program. A systematic method to derive T and M_T from a problem description is needed so that identified pseudo oracles are effective to uncover faults with respect to the requirements.

Statistical machine learning is formulated as an optimization problem [1]. For a given machine learning task such as classifying a set of data, a problem is formulated as a mathematical function $F^C(\theta; x)$, where θ is a set of parameters to be determined. An ML problem is introducing a family of θ-indexed functions, $\{F^C(\theta; x)\}^\theta$, accompanied with *hyper-parameters* C defining a problem instance. Machine learning is searching for parameter values θ^* such that an objective function $\mathcal{E}$, referring to $F^C(\theta; x)$, to be optimal. If the optimality refers to a minimization, then $\theta^* = arg\,min\ \mathcal{E}(\theta; \{Z^n\})$, where $\{Z^n\}$ is a dataset from which some valuable information is derived. An ML program is numerically solving such a problem to obtain θ^*. They are approximate because F^C are generally non-linear and so is $\mathcal{E}$. A *learnt* model defines a function $F(\theta^*; X)$ to calculate a result for a new data X. Note that hyper-parameters are constants in the optimization process. Thus, the parameters θ are dependent on C (θ^C). Obtaining optimal C is one of the major issues, but can be conducted only after the software testing.

From software testing views, ML computer programs can be characterized as follows. (1) An ML task is declaratively specified as an optimization problem, from which metamorphic properties are derived. (2) Learning is a process of obtaining (sub-) optimal parameters, which is solved by numerical searches. It implies that *correct* parameter values are not known in advance. (3) The learnt result $F(\theta^*; X)$ with the optimal parameters is an *application program*, and its behavior is dependent on the parameter values θ^*.

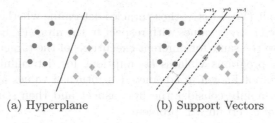

(a) Hyperplane   (b) Support Vectors

Fig. 1. Support vector machines

From these observations, the optimization program is what should be tested, but without known absolute correct results. Thus, that program is a *quasi-testable* core with relative correctness criteria. As in existing work [4,6], MT can be a basis for pseudo oracle for testing ML programs. We will study two concrete problems, because the information that is checked against the correctness criteria is dependent on ML tasks.

3   Support Vector Machines

A support vector machine (SVM) is a supervised machine learning classifier (e.g. Chapter 7 in [1]). Figure 1 (b) illustrates the concept of support vectors as opposed to a naive classifier in Fig. 1 (a). The support vectors lie on the dotted hyperplanes parallel to the resultant separating hyperplane. *Margin*, a minimum gap between the support hyperplane and separating hyperplane, is so chosen to be maximum.

SVM is a constrained optimization problem. Below, $\langle x^n, \ell^n \rangle$ are data points $(n = 1, \ldots, N)$. x^n is a D-dimensional vector and ℓ^n is its label of either -1 or $+1$. w and b are two parameters defining hyperplanes.

$$arg\min_{w,b} \frac{1}{2} \| w \|^2 \qquad \textbf{s.t. } \ell^n(w^T \cdot x^n + b) \geq 1$$

The problem is turned into a *dual* representation of a Lagrangian, $\mathcal{L}(\alpha_1, \ldots, \alpha_N)$, where α_n are Lagrange multipliers. It is actually a *soft* margin SVM and a hyperparameter C is a measure allowing noise.

$$arg\max_{\alpha_n} \sum_{n=1}^{N} \alpha_n - \frac{1}{2}\sum_{n=1}^{N}\sum_{m=1}^{N} \alpha_n\alpha_m\ell^n\ell^m(x^n \cdot x^m)$$

$$\textbf{s.t. } 0 \leq \alpha_n \leq C \; (1 \leq n \leq N), \qquad \sum_{n=1}^{N}\alpha_n\ell^n = 0$$

The resultant multipliers constitute hyperplane parameters, where S is a set of indices of the support vectors (Fig. 1(b)).

$$w = \sum_{n \in S}\alpha_n\ell^n x^n, \qquad b = \frac{1}{|S|}\sum_{m \in S}(\ell^m - \sum_{n \in S}\alpha_n\ell^n(x^n \cdot x^m))$$

Sequential minimal optimization (SMO) is a standard algorithm to solve SVM problems. SMO decomposes the optimization problem into subproblems, each referring to two data points. A problem $W(a_1, a_2)$ consists of two Lagrange multipliers with all the rest to be assumed as constants, and is analytically solvable. The algorithm continues until solutions converge.

Programs are implementing the SMO algorithm, and are our test target. We derive metamorphic properties to test them from the Lagrangian $\mathcal{L}$ and functional behavior of the SMO algorithm. For example, interchanging indices of two data points, $x^n \rightleftharpoons x^m$, does not change $\mathcal{L}$, and multipliers are interchanged as well, $\alpha_n \rightleftharpoons \alpha_m$. The MR R^T is identity for this case. Another interesting property is *Reverse Labels*, $\langle x^n, \ell^n \rangle \rightharpoonup \langle x^n, -\ell^n \rangle$ for all n. Hyperplane parameters are changed accordingly, and thus $R^T = (w^{(1)} = -w^{(2)}) \wedge (b^{(1)} = -b^{(2)})$.

A metamorphic property *Reduce Margin* in [4] was effective for testing SVM programs. The property is a special instance of *Inclusive* property [6]. Its basic idea is adding a new data point to the input dataset for enabling *corner-case* testing. Because corner cases differ for different ML tasks, *Reduce Margin* takes into account the SVM characteristics that the problem is to determine separating hyperplanes with support vectors. Namely, we put newly added data points near the existing separating hyperplanes. [4] describes details about it.

4   Neural Networks

A neural network (NN) is a general framework for machine learning tasks, regressions or classifiers (e.g. Chapter 5 in [1]). A perceptron (Fig. 2 (a)) is a basic unit. Receiving a set of input $\{x_i\}$, it emits a signal y calculated by applying an activation function σ to a weighted sum of its input; $y = \sigma(\sum_{i=1}^{d} w_i x_i)$. An NN is a two layered network of perceptrons (Fig. 2 (b)). All the input signals are fed into perceptrons in the hidden layer, and then all the signals from these perceptrons are input to perceptrons in the output layer. Let h and r be two activation functions. Given D-dimensional vector x and M perceptrons consisting of the hidden layer, signals ($k = 1, \ldots, R$) from the output layer is mathematically defined as below.

$$y_k(W; \ x) = r(\ \sum_{j=0}^{M} v_{kj} h(\sum_{i=0}^{D} w_{ji} x_i)\ )$$

where v_{kj} and w_{ji} are weights, which are compactly written as W.

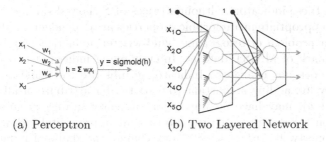

(a) Perceptron   (b) Two Layered Network

Fig. 2. Neural network

For a set of input data $\{\langle x^n, t^n \rangle\}$ $(n = 1, \ldots, N)$, NN machine learning is an optimization problem using a loss function $\mathcal{E}$. Below, y is a R-dimensional vector of the output signals.

$$\mathcal{E}(W; \{\langle x^n, t^n \rangle\}) = \frac{1}{2} \sum_{n=1}^{N} \| t^n - y(W; x^n) \|^2, \quad arg \min_{W} \mathcal{E}(W; \{\langle x^n, t^n \rangle\})$$

A naive algorithm to solve this optimization problem numerically is a steepest descent method (SD), calculating new weights until the values are converged; $\{W^{(new)} = W^{(old)} - \eta \nabla \mathcal{E}(W^{old})\}$ where η (> 0) is a hyper-parameter, called a learning rate.

A standard learning algorithm employs the back propagation (BP) for calculating $\nabla \mathcal{E}(W^{old})$ efficiently. Furthermore, NN training methods adopt several *learning tricks*. With the input normalization trick, all components x_i^n of x^n are pre-adjusted to follow a normal distribution of $Norm$ (0,1) for each i. Stochastic gradient descent (SGD) is a randomized version of the SD. These techniques complicate the algorithm, and thus make programs difficult to test.

Interpretation of parameters θ in NN learning is quite different from the SVM case. In the latter, learning parameters are Lagrange multipliers to define a hyperplane, which is a good indicator to provide relative correctness criteria. Contrarily in NN learning, parameters θ are weights in W. These are just numerical values and define no mathematical object. In addition, NN computer program executions are characterized by temporal behavior in view of convergence and/or optimality; programs may reach a stable state, but be trapped in local minimums. Therefore, such behavioral information is an important indicator, which must faithfully represent how W are changed as learning proceeds. However, a trace of loss function $\mathcal{E}$ or an accuracy for a given testing dataset, which is usually used, does not represent behavior faithfully. These pieces of information are influenced by slight changes in input training dataset.

Because the number of weights is very large in general, we cannot check the weights individually. Instead, we calculate statistical averages and deviations. Let $\alpha(e)$ be values of α at an epoch e, and $g[\alpha](e)$ be $\alpha(e+1) - \alpha(e)$. We calculate $g[\alpha](e)$ where α refers to statistical averages $(\mu(e))$ and deviations $(\sigma^2(e))$ of weights. These values constitute *indicator graph* with respect to epoch indices. We compared two graphs, one obtained from a probably correct program and another from a bug-injected one. The two show quite different behavior when viewed from these indicators, although traces of $\mathcal{E}$ showed similar curves.

Because appropriate metamorphic properties are dependent on ML problems, we studied a problem of recognizing hand-written numerical numbers, a standard benchmark of MNIST dataset. Interchanging indices of two data points, $x_n \rightleftharpoons x_m$, does not change $\mathcal{E}$. Indicator graphs are the same as well. *Additive* property [6], adding a constant to a particular attribute of all data points $(x_i^n \rightarrow x_i^n + b)$, may have no impact on indicator graphs because the input normalization takes care of the pre-adjustment appropriately. However, *Multiplicative* property [6] $(x_i^n \rightarrow a \times x_i^n)$ may change the shape of indicator graphs in that the convergence becomes slow.

Because indicator graphs represent temporal changes in statistical summaries of weight values, we call R^T to be *behavioral oracle*. It may be considered a statistical approach, but is different from *statistical oracle* [3], which employs statistical hypothesis testing to refute the correctness of probabilistic programs. NN programs employ a notion of probability specifically for efficiency reasons. Statistical oracles may be used for systems with inherent randomness.

5 Discussions and Concluding Remarks

Testing is an unknown-unknown task. We do not know whether a program has bugs or not, and thus may conduct testing in search of non-existing bugs. Nevertheless, a new way of testing is important for ML programs.

As machine learning results are sensitive to slight changes in input training dataset, changing distribution of data points in the dataset is a key issue for corner-case testing, which we call *dataset diversity*. This is similar to *Machine Teaching* [7], which is concerned with automatic generation of dataset for a given machine learning tasks. The generated dataset is biased in that ML process converges to given learning parameter values. Namely, the method is concerned with generating *well-biased* critical data points. Our future work includes studying a systematic method to obtain *dataset diversity* for corner-case testing.

References

1. Bishop, C.M.: Pattern Recognition and Machine Learning. Springer, New York (2006)
2. Chen, T.Y., Chung, S.C., Yiu, S.M.: Metamorphic testing - a new approach for generating next test cases, HKUST-CS98-01. The Hong Kong University of Science and Technology (1998)
3. Guderlei, R., Mayer, J., Schneckenburger, C., Fleischer, F.: Testing randomized software by means of statistical hypothesis tests. In: Proceedings of SOQUA 2007, pp. 46–54 (2007)
4. Nakajima, S., Bui, H.N.: Dataset coverage for testing machine learning computer programs. In: Proceedings of 23rd APSEC, pp. 297–304 (2016)
5. Weyuker, E.J.: On testing non-testable programs. Comput. J. **25**(4), 465–470 (1982)
6. Xie, X., Ho, J.W.K., Murphy, C., Kaiser, G., Xu, B., Chen, T.Y.: Testing and validating machine learning classifiers by metamorphic testing. J. Syst. Softw. **84**(4), 544–558 (2011)
7. Zhu, X.: Machine teaching: an inverse problem to machine learning and an approach toward optimal education. In: Proceedings of 29th AAAI, pp. 4083–4087 (2015)

MSE 2017

MSE 2017 Organizers' Message

MSE 2017 Organizers' Message

The Second International Workshop on Microservices: Science and Engineering (MSE 2017) was held in Trento, Italy, on September 4, 2017. The workshop brought together contributions by scientists and practitioners to shed light on the development of scientific concepts, technologies, engineering techniques, and tools for a service-based society, with a particular focus on microservices.

After a careful review process, the Program Committee accepted the following papers for presentation and publication:

- Matteo Camilli, Carlo Bellettini, Lorenzo Capra and Mattia Monga — "A Formal Framework for Specifying and Verifying Microservice-Based Process Flows"
- Florian Rademacher, Sabine Sachweh, and Albert Zündorf — "Towards a UML Profile for Domain-Driven Design of Microservice Architectures"
- Moh. Afifun Naily, Maya Retno Ayu Setyautami, Radu Muschevici, and Ade Azurat — "A Framework for Modelling Variable Microservices as Software Product Lines"
- Antonio Brogi, Andrea Canciani, Davide Neri, Luca Rinaldi and Jacopo Soldani — "Towards a Reference Dataset of Microservice-Based Applications"
- Martin Garriga — "Towards a Taxonomy of Microservices Architectures"

Several people contributed to the success of MSE 2017. We would like to thank all the workshop organizers as well as the general chair and the members of the Program Committee for their work in reviewing the contributions. The process of reviewing and selecting papers was significantly simplified through the use of EasyChair. We thank all attendees of the workshop and hope that this event facilitated a good exchange of ideas and generated new collaborations among attendees.

October 2017

Marcello M. Bersani
Antonio Bucchiarone
Nicola Dragoni
Luca Ferrucci
Manuel Mazzara
Fabrizio Montesi

Organization

MSE 2017 - Steering Committee

Marcello M. Bersani	Politecnico di Milano, Italy
Antonio Bucchiarone	Fondazione Bruno Kessler, Trento, Italy
Nicola Dragoni	Technical University of Denmark and Örebro University, Sweden
Luca Ferrucci	ISTI-CNR, Italy
Manuel Mazzara	Innopolis University, Russia
Fabrizio Montesi	University of Southern Denmark, Denmark

MSE 2017 - Program Committee

Larisa Safina	Innopolis University, Russia
Damian Andrew Tamburri	Politecnico di Milano, Italy
Matteo Camilli	University of Milan, Italy
Angelo Spognardi	Technical University of Denmark, Denmark
Silvio Ghilardi	University of Milan, Italy
Sung-Shik T. Q. Jongmans	Open University of the Netherlands, The Netherlands
Cruz-Filipe Luis	University of Southern Denmark, Denmark
Carlo Bellettini	University of Milan, Italy
Martin Garriga	Universidad Nacional del Comahue, Argentina
Madalina Erascu	West University of Timisoara, Romania
Marisol Garcia-Valls	Universidad Carlos III de Madrid, Spain
Md. Ariful Islam	Carnegie Mellon University, Pennsylvania, USA
Stéphane Demri	LSV, CNRS and ENS de Cachan, France
Soren Debois	University of Copenhagen, Denmark

MSE 2017 - Additional Reviewers

Elena Pagani	University of Milan, Italy

A Linguistic Approach for Microservices
(Keynote Talk)

Claudio Guidi

italianaSoftware s.r.l., Italy

Cloud computing and containerization technologies are going to revolutionize the nature of computational resources: from the idea of a single computable machine to that of a sea of small computational containers, which interact with each-other. But programming technologies have been always conceived to target single computational resources instead of a native distributed machine. That's why programming languages are usually focused on computation instead of communication.

In such a scenario, microservices are emerging as a leading approach for designing and developing applications in the containerized cloud. They are logic artifacts obtained by the combination of frameworks and programming languages focused on well known paradigms such as the object or the functional oriented ones. In particular, frameworks are needed for dealing with specific communication aspects like protocols and endpoint definitions. In the area of service and microservice programming these frameworks play a fundamental role because distributed systems, like the service based ones, are more focused on communication instead of computation. The main problem is that frameworks change very quickly and need continuous updates and specific management, thus they absorb a lot of time and knowledge of developers, engineers and architects. On the contrary programming languages are more stable, syntax and semantics change less frequently, but they do not permit to natively express communication concepts.

In this keynote, I propose to revolutionize service oriented programming by exploiting a new generation of native programming languages which crystallize the core aspects of communication and coordination. Such an approach will allow developers to think and program directly in services by reducing the knowledge required for managing specific frameworks. As a concrete example I will discuss the experience we had in the realization of Jolie programming language whose operational semantics is formalized by exploiting a CCS based process calculus and its syntax is very intuitive. At present Jolie is exploited in industry for implementing orchestrators and microservice based middleware processes that specifically target system integration issues.

Microservices Are Not Just Tiny Web Services
(Keynote Talk)

Luciano Baresi

DEIB - Politecnico di Milano, Italy

One may think of *microservices* as nothing but tiny, small services. This is not true, and size does not matter. There is a significant shift in the motivations and problems behind the different waves of services.

Web services were conceived as autonomous software systems that can be advertised, located, and accessed through standard-based XML messages, with the idea of pushing for modular, reusable, and standardized software entities. The problem was to slice monolithic applications into reusable chunks and support their (dynamic) composition. The many proposed standards (e.g., WSDL and BPEL) were supposed to break the barriers among proprietary systems and propose common languages and technologies to ease the integration of heterogenous, distributed components and foster the cooperation among independent parties. Web services push a share-as-much-as-possible architectural style.

While applications are not monolithic anymore, their components, often organized in layers, are still too big and, given the complexity of many software systems (e.g., Netflix), still too complex to maintain. Even small problems can preclude the operation of the whole application. This is where *microservices* enter the scene. They describe a particular way of designing software applications as suites of independently deployable services. While one may also say that it is nothing but "the SoA done right", now the focus is not on standardization and composition, but it is on isolation, and autonomy. Services are *micro* as for their contribution to the application, not because of their lines of code. They are entities that embed everything (GUI, data, and business logic) and that can be conceived, implemented, and deployed independently. Each single component (service) must be changable without impacting the operation and performance of the others. Instead of having different groups responsible for the different parts (layers) of an application, a single group controls all the aspects of a microservice. Microservices push a share-as-little-as-possible architectural style.

Microservices do not come with specific supporting technologies, but they foster a particular approach towards the realization of complex software systems. This new way of designing software systems paves the ground to a number of research directions, from more theoretical conceptualizations to concrete supporting environments and tools. After *spaghetti*-like programs and systems, someone proposed the idea of layers (*lasagne*-like), but microservices are now pushing us towards the era of *ravioli*-like software systems, and good recipes to cook them are still to come.

Microservices Are Not Just Tiny Web Services (Keynote Talk)

Luciano Baresi

DEIB - Politecnico di Milano, Italy

A Formal Framework for Specifying and Verifying Microservices Based Process Flows

Matteo Camilli[✉], Carlo Bellettini, Lorenzo Capra, and Mattia Monga

Department of Computer Science, Università degli Studi di Milano, Milan, Italy
{camilli,bellettini,capra,monga}@di.unimi.it

Abstract. The microservices architectural style is changing the way in which software is perceived, conceived and designed. Thus, there is a call for techniques and tools supporting the problem of specifying and verifying communication behavior of microservice systems. We present a formal semantics based on Petri nets for microservices based process flows specified using the CONDUCTOR orchestration language: a JSON-based domain specific language designed by Netflix, Inc. We give a formal semantics in terms of a translation from CONDUCTOR specifications into Time Basic Petri net models, *i.e.*, Petri nets supporting the definition of temporal constraints. The Petri net model can be used for computer aided verification purposes by means of well-known techniques implemented by powerful, off-the-shelf model checking tools.

Keywords: Microservices · Orchestration · Formal methods
Petri nets · Verification · Time analysis

1 Introduction

One of the most successful mantras of the so called Unix' philosophy is: "Do one thing and do it well". In fact, the Unix' offspring is characterized by a highly component-oriented architecture, with many small and specialized black-boxes (like `grep`, `sort`, or `cut`) that people use everyday to assembly—often just by using the glue provided by the shell and its piping capabilities—higher level tasks. If Service Oriented Architectures (SOA) promise to bring black-box components to distributed systems, the current call for a *microservices* attitude aims at having small and specialized pieces of functionalities. According to some of the proposers of the term microservices, a single application should be built "as a suite of small services, each running in its own process and communicating with lightweight mechanisms, often an HTTP resource API" [1,2].

In order to establish cooperation among services, *orchestration* [3] has recently seen a renewed interest [4]. An orchestration engine is in charge of enacting a script (sometimes called the *blueprint* of the high level service) defining the high level control and data flows. Thus, in order to make the composite service predictable, it is important to develop the ability of reasoning at this higher

© Springer International Publishing AG 2018
A. Cerone and M. Roveri (Eds.): SEFM 2017 Workshops, LNCS 10729, pp. 187–202, 2018.
https://doi.org/10.1007/978-3-319-74781-1_14

level. Since orchestration languages have a very simple structure and the number of components is usually small (for example, Netflix declares their "workflows" are made, on average, of six tasks, with the largest composed by 48 [5]), this seems a very good opportunity to apply formal methods, whose major weakness is often their scalability in front of real world applications complexity.

In this paper we propose to use Time Basic Petri nets [6], *i.e.*, a particular extension of Petri nets supporting the definition of temporal constraints, to analyze the properties of microservice-oriented applications orchestrated by the Netflix CONDUCTOR engine [4], an open source framework designed by Netflix Inc. and used daily in their production environment [5]. The CONDUCTOR 'Orchestrator' is driven by a workflow script, written in a JSON-based domain specific language. The Orchestrator tracks and manages workflows and it has the ability to pause, resume and restart the microservice tasks. We defined a formal semantics for the workflow language in which microservices are black-box described by Petri net modules. The formal semantics is supported by a Java tool CONDUCTOR2PN that translates CONDUCTOR specifications into a Time Basic Petri net model, which can be exploited for computer aided verification purposes by means of well-known techniques implemented by powerful, off-the-shelf model checking tools.

The paper is organized as follows: in Sect. 2 we recall some background notions on Time Basic Petri nets, in Sect. 3 we present a running example, in Sect. 4 we describe the semantics we defined, in Sect. 5 we apply the given semantics to verify some properties of the running example, in Sect. 6 we discuss some related work, and in Sect. 7 we present our conclusions and future work.

2   Background

Time Basic Petri nets—Time Basic Petri nets (TB) nets are Petri nets (PNs or P/T nets) [7], where system time constraints are introduced as linear functions associated with each transition, representing possible firing instants computed since transition's enabling. Tokens are atomically produced by firing transitions and they have timestamps with values ranging over $\mathbb{R}_{\geq 0}$. This modeling formalism represents an effective formal specification of time-dependent systems. It supports a mixed time semantics, *i.e.*, both *urgent* and *non-urgent* transitions can be used to define mandatory and optional events, respectively. TB nets are also nicely supported by powerful open source software tools considering both modeling and verification aspects [8,9]. Although other modeling formalisms such as timed-automata [10] or finite-state-machines [11] support the modeling of temporal or behavioral aspects, PNs-based approaches can be more concise and scalable [12]. Furthermore, aspects such as messaging, communication protocols, which are commonly used in distributed architectures, such as service oriented architectures and microservices, can be difficult to model with the language primitives of automata-based formalisms [12,13].

The structure of a TB net extends the P/T net one (P, T, F), where P is a finite set of places, T is a finite set of transitions such that $P \cap T = \emptyset$, and

$F \subseteq (P \times T) \cup (T \times P)$ is a set of arcs (or flows) connecting places to transitions and transitions to places. Let $v \in P \cup T$: ${}^\bullet v$, $v^\bullet$ denote the backward and forward adjacent sets of v according to F, respectively, also called pre/post-sets of v. A timestamp *binding* of $t \in T$ is a map $b_t : {}^\bullet t \rightarrow Bag(\mathbb{R}_{\geq 0})$. Moreover, each transition t is associated with a *time function* f_t which maps a binding b_t to a (possibly empty) set of $\mathbb{R}_{\geq 0}$ values, denoted by $f_t(b_t)$. f_t is formally defined as a pair of linear functions $[l_t, u_t]$, denoting parametric interval bounds.

A *marking* (or state) is a mapping $m : P \rightarrow Bag(\mathbb{R}_{\geq 0})$, where $Bag(X)$ represents the set of multisets over X. According to the *non-urgent* (or *weak*) semantics, t can fire at any instant $\tau \in f_t(b_t)$. The *urgent* (or *strong*) interpretation states that t must fire at an instant $\tau \in f_t(b_t)$, unless it is disabled by the firing of any conflicting transitions before the latest firing time of t. Given a binding b_t, a pair (b_t, τ), s.t. $\tau \in f_t(b_t)$, is said a firing instance of t. The firing instance (b_t, τ) produces a new reachable marking m' by applying the following *firing rules*:

- $\forall p \in {}^\bullet t \setminus t^\bullet \; m'(p) = m(p) - b_t(p)$
- $\forall p \in t^\bullet \setminus {}^\bullet t \; m'(p) = m(p) + \{\tau\}$
- $\forall p \in t^\bullet \cap {}^\bullet t \; m'(p) = m(p) - b_t(p) + \{\tau\}$
- for all remaining places, $m'(p) = m(p)$.

Figure 1b shows a TB net that models the lifecycle of a single microservice. We use it in the following to illustrate the background concepts. A single token with timestamp $T_0 = 0$ in place $\langle name \rangle$_schedule represents that the microservice $\langle name \rangle$ has been scheduled at time 0. In this marking, the transition $\langle name \rangle$_S2P is the only one enabled to fire by the following binding: $\{\langle name \rangle$_schedule $\rightarrow \{1 \cdot T_0\}, \langle name \rangle$_ready $\rightarrow \{1 \cdot T_A\}\}$. Possible firing time instants are obtained by evaluating the parametric bounds of $f_{\langle name \rangle$_S2P}: $[\tau_e, \tau_e + 200]$, where τ_e is the transition's enabling time (the value 0 in this case). Given a valid timestamp value $\tau \in [0, 200]$ (*e.g.*, the value 150), according to the firing rules, we get a new marking with a new token $T_0 = 150$ in place $\langle name \rangle$_inProgress (*i.e.*, the execution of the microservice starts from time 150). In this new marking, two transitions are concurrently enabled to fire: the *non-urgent* $\langle name \rangle$_P2C in the time interval $[0, \infty]$, and the *urgent* $\langle name \rangle$_P2T in the time interval $[1200, 1200]$. Thus, the service can either complete the execution or enter a timeout state. In the latter case, the system retries to execute the service a fixed number of times, depending on the number of tokens in place $\langle name \rangle$_retryCount. Whenever the task is timed out (*i.e.*, the place $\langle name \rangle$_timeout is marked) and the retryCount limit has been reached (*i.e.*, the place $\langle name \rangle$_retryCount is empty), the task enters a failure state (*i.e.*, the place $\langle name \rangle$_fail is marked by the firing of $\langle name \rangle$_P2F). The symbol ε in $f_{\langle name \rangle$_P2F} represents an infinitesimal delay used to set a precedence between the conflicting transitions $\langle name \rangle$_P2T and $\langle name \rangle$_P2F. Whenever a final state is entered (*i.e.*, either the place $\langle name \rangle$_complete or the place $\langle name \rangle$_fail is marked), the transitions $\langle name \rangle$_C2R and $\langle name \rangle$_F2R restart the service by removing all the tokens from $\langle name \rangle$_retryUsed and refilling $\langle name \rangle$_retryCount.

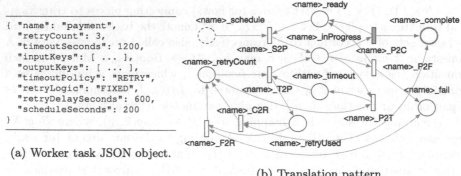

```
{ "name": "payment",
  "retryCount": 3,
  "timeoutSeconds": 1200,
  "inputKeys": [ ... ],
  "outputKeys": [ ... ],
  "timeoutPolicy": "RETRY",
  "retryLogic": "FIXED",
  "retryDelaySeconds": 600,
  "scheduleSeconds": 200
}
```

(a) Worker task JSON object.

(b) Translation pattern.

Initial marking: $\langle name \rangle\_ready\{T_A\}$, $\langle name \rangle\_retryCount\{\langle retryCount \rangle \cdot T_A\}$

Transition	Time function
$\langle name \rangle\_S2P$	$[\tau_e, \tau_e + \langle scheduleSeconds \rangle]$
$\langle name \rangle\_P2C$	$[\tau_e, \tau_e + \infty]$
$\langle name \rangle\_P2T$	$[\tau_e + \langle timeoutSeconds \rangle, \tau_e + \langle timeoutSeconds \rangle]$
$\langle name \rangle\_P2F$	$[\tau_e + \langle timeoutSeconds \rangle + \varepsilon, \tau_e + \langle timeoutSeconds \rangle + \varepsilon]$
$\langle name \rangle\_T2P$	$[\tau_e + \langle retryDelaySeconds \rangle, \tau_e + \langle retryDelaySeconds \rangle]$
$\langle name \rangle\_F2R/\_C2R$	$[\tau_e, \tau_e]$

Fig. 1. Translation pattern of a RETRY timeout-policy worker with FIXED retry-logic. *Non-urgent* transitions are depicted in gray.

Time Reachability Graph—By using consolidated analysis techniques it is possible to construct a finite symbolic state space of a TB net model, called its *Time Reachability Graph* (*TRG*) [8]. The *TRG* construction is automated by the GRAPHGEN software tool [8,9,14]. It basically relies on a *symbolic state* notion: each reachable state is a pair: $S = (M, C)$, where M (symbolic marking) maps places into elements of $Bag(TS)$ (*i.e.,* multisets of timestamps) and C (constraint) is a logical predicate formed by linear inequalities defined in terms of $TS \cup \{T_L, T_A\}$, where the symbol T_L represents the state creation instant, and the symbol T_A represents an anonymous timestamp (*i.e.,* a timestamp whose time value does not influence the evolution of the system). The constraint C contains *relative* time dependencies between timestamps. An example of initial symbolic state for the model in Fig. 1b can be $S_0 = (M_0, C_0)$, such that:

$$M_0 := \langle name \rangle\_schedule\{T_0\}, \langle name \rangle\_retryCount\{3 \cdot T_A\}$$
$$C_0 := T_0 \geq 0 \ \wedge \ T_0 \leq 10 \ \wedge \ T_L = T_0.$$

Since T_A symbols are unessential for the computation of firing times associated with enabled transitions, they do not appear in the symbolic constraint C_0.

Given the *TRG* structure, model checking algorithms can be applied to verify the correctness of the system against requirements expressed as specific *Time Computation Tree Logic* (TCTL) properties [15,16]. The model checking technique is fully automated by the GRAPHGEN software tool.

3   A Running Example: The Taxi-Hailing Application

To illustrate the use of CONDUCTOR2PN, we consider a taxi-hailing application example, such as Uber [17]. This application has a modular architecture: at the core is its business logic, which is implemented by modules that define domain objects and events. Surrounding the core are adapters (*e.g.*, database access components, messaging components, *etc.*) that interact with the external world, and web components that either expose APIs or implement a user interface (UI). Many organizations in this context are re-engineering their monolithic applications to adopt microservice architectures. The idea is to split the application into a set of smaller cohesive, independent process services interacting via messages.

A possible decomposition of the taxi-hailing system is shown in Fig. 2. This schema follows the notation introduced in [4] and shows all the services and the overall workflow. It can be automatically generated from the CONDUCTOR blueprint (by using the CONDUCTOR framework).

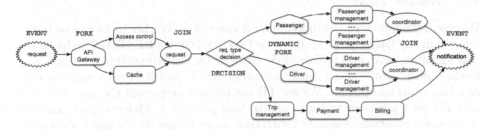

Fig. 2. High level schema of the taxi-hailing orchestration.

Each microservice (*i.e.*, a rectangular shape in Fig. 2) implements a (micro) functionality (*e.g.*, access control, trip management, payment, etc.) and is deployed independently, possibly into cloud virtual machines or Docker containers [18]. Moreover it exposes a REST API consumed by other microservices or by the application's clients. For instance, the *Passenger management* uses the *Notification* service to notify a passenger about an available driver. The *API gateway* instead, exposes a public API used by mobile clients or web UIs.

Other shapes represent control and data flow primitives (*e.g*, EVENT, FORK, JOIN, *etc.*) executed within the CONDUCTOR orchestration server to manage the execution and scalability of the entire process flow. For instance, *req. type decision* allows to choose between alternative flows depending on the request type. The *Passenger* and the *Driver* components use the dynamic fork primitive to dispatch user requests to different (possibly replicated) services, geographically located in different areas. A complete list of all available workflow primitives of CONDUCTOR is available in Table 2. They will be described more in depth in Sect. 4.2.

It is worth noting that this example is intended to represent a fictional but significant microservice system. We have designed it to highlight several features supported by our formal framework.

4   Time Basic Net Semantics for Conductor

This section introduces the semantics we defined for microservice process flows. The semantics is defined by giving the translation from the CONDUCTOR blueprint into a TB net formal model. We provide a translation for each construct of the CONDUCTOR language, *i.e.*, a JSON-based domain specific language that describes both the involved microservices (*Worker tasks*) and the execution flow (*System tasks*). The model generation process is guided by the identification of *translation patterns* of each individual component. Each pattern has *input/output* elements for joining it with other patterns. The final model is the composition (*i.e.*, the union by joining input/output elements) of different TB net patterns of the corresponding microservices and execution flow constructs. The translation process is fully automated by the CONDUCTOR2PN[1] JAVA software tool.

4.1   Worker Tasks

Worker tasks represent the individual microservices. Worker tasks can be implemented in any language and talk to the CONDUCTOR via REST API endpoints to poll for other tasks and update their status after execution. Our modeling approach abstracts away from implementation details and it views a single worker as a black-box component. We use TB net places to represent the state of a task and TB net transitions to represent the task primitives. Moreover, we make use of temporal functions associated with transitions to specify temporal constraints upon scheduling and execution.

Figure 1a represents an example of worker task metadata definition using the CONDUCTOR domain specific language. This example contains a JSON object which lists a number of fields used to tell the CONDUCTOR engine how to manage the microservice lifecycle. Accordingly, we apply the corresponding translation pattern (Fig. 1b). In this example, a timeout (*i.e.*, the `timeoutSeconds` property) has been set. Thus, if the `payment` task does not complete within 1200 ms, CONDUCTOR retries the task again (*i.e.*, the `RETRY timeoutPolicy`) up to 3 times (*i.e.*, the `retryCount` property). Upon timeout, the task is rescheduled after a fixed delay (*i.e.*, the `FIXED retryLogic`) of 600 ms (*i.e.*, `retryDelaySeconds` property). The tasks need up to 200 ms to be scheduled (*i.e.*, `scheduleSeconds` property).

Figure 1b depicts the translation pattern of the worker task listed in Fig. 1a. The pattern can be instantiated by replacing each ⟨`field`⟩ with the corresponding value read from the JSON object. Dashed line shapes represent the *input* elements. Therefore, the `payment` task is being executed whenever the `payment_schedule` place become marked. Double line shapes represent *output* elements. In this example, the `payment_complete` is the element used to join the `payment` task to other subsequent patterns.

---

[1] CONDUCTOR2PN has been released as open-source software. It is available for download at: https://bitbucket.org/seresearch_unimi/conductor2pn.

Table 1. Metadata associated with worker tasks.

Field	Description	Notes
Name	Worker task name	Unique
retryCount	#retries to attempt when a task is marked as timed out	-
timeoutSeconds	Timeout (ms) to complete a task after transiting to inProgress status	No timeouts if set to 0
timeoutPolicy	Task's timeout policy	Possible values: RETRY, ALERT_ONLY, TIME_OUT_WF
retryLogic	Mechanism for the retries	Possible values: FIXED, EXPONENTIAL_BACKOFF
scheduleSeconds	Time (ms) needed to schedule a task	User defined assumption
terminateSeconds	Time (ms) needed to end a task upon termination request	User defined assumption

Table 1 contains the complete description of metadata associated with worker tasks. Fields marked as *user defined assumption* are not part of the CONDUCTOR language, but represent additional information used by our translation process to define the user assumption on time required by specific lifecycle operations. If not defined (*e.g.,* no prior information is available, or they have negligible values), a default value is supplied. Different combinations of values assigned to timeoutPolicy and retryLogic fields determine different semantics and different corresponding translation patterns, as follows.

- The RETRY timeoutPolicy along with FIXED retryLogic is described above and the corresponding translation pattern is shown in Fig. 1b.
- The ALERT_ONLY timeoutPolicy means that the worker task just registers a counter upon timeout. The translation pattern can be easily obtained starting from Fig. 1b and by erasing the places: ⟨name⟩_retryCount, ⟨name⟩_timeout, ⟨name⟩_retryUsed, and the transitions: ⟨name⟩_T2P, ⟨name⟩_F2R, and ⟨name⟩_C2R, (along with incoming/outgoing edges). Meaning that the task does not retry the execution, but it goes into a failure state after the first timeout.
- The TIME_OUT_WF timeoutPolicy means that the entire workflow is marked as timed out and terminated upon worker's timeout. This translation pattern is shown in Fig. 3a. The dashed box represents a foreach macro substitution and it means that the inner elements are repeated for each element e (*i.e.,* for each ⟨name⟩_ready, ⟨name⟩_inProgress and ⟨name⟩_inProgress places, in this specific pattern).

– The RETRY timeoutPolicy along with EXPONENTIAL_BACKOFF retryLogic means that upon timeout, the task is rescheduled after retryDelaySeconds multiplied by the attempt number. This translation pattern is shown in Fig. 3b. Likewise the RETRY-FIXED pattern (Fig. 1b), the generated model retries to execute a timed out task a fixed number of times, but with a different timeout foreach retry attempt. The for macro substitution is used here to replicate the inner elements so that each retry attempt is constructed with the correct temporal constraint. The place ⟨name⟩_retryUsed along with transitions ⟨name⟩_C2R and ⟨name⟩_F2R are used to implement the same mechanism used in RETRY-FIXED tasks to refill the ⟨name⟩_retryCount place, once a termination state is reached.

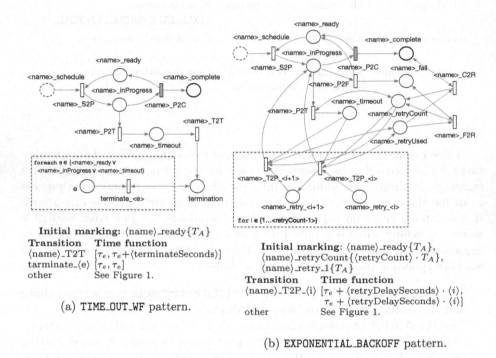

Initial marking: ⟨name⟩_ready{T_A}

Transition	Time function
⟨name⟩_T2T	[$\tau_e, \tau_e + \langle$terminateSeconds$\rangle$]
tarminate_⟨e⟩	[τ_e, τ_e]
other	See Figure 1.

(a) TIME_OUT_WF pattern.

Initial marking: ⟨name⟩_ready{T_A},
⟨name⟩_retryCount{⟨retryCount⟩ · T_A},
⟨name⟩_retry_1{T_A}

Transition	Time function
⟨name⟩_T2P_⟨i⟩	[$\tau_e + \langle$retryDelaySeconds$\rangle \cdot \langle i \rangle$, $\tau_e + \langle$retryDelaySeconds$\rangle \cdot \langle i \rangle$]
other	See Figure 1.

(b) EXPONENTIAL_BACKOFF pattern.

Fig. 3. Translations of a TIME_OUT_WF, and a RETRY EXPONENTIAL_BACKOFF worker tasks, respectively. *Non-urgent* transitions are depicted in gray.

The TB net models of the individual microservices' lifecycle represent the basic components that are joined together with the system task models.

4.2   System Tasks

The overall process flow in CONDUCTOR is a sequence of worker tasks (denoted, in the CONDUCTOR language, by the SIMPLE value associated with the type field) and system tasks (Table 2 lists all possible system task types). System tasks represent the execution flow primitives and their execution/scalability is managed by the CONDUCTOR engine. Our translation process defines a formal semantics for all system tasks, however, for the sake of space, we describe in the following the translation pattern of some representative examples used in our taxi-hailing application.

Table 2. Description of all available system tasks.

Type name	Purpose
DYNAMIC	A worker task which is dynamically derived based on the input to the task, rather than being statically defined
DECISION	Similar to the switch case statement in a programming language
FORK	Fork is used to schedule a parallel set of tasks
FORK_JOIN_DYNAMIC	Same as fork, except that the list of tasks to be forked is provided at runtime using task's input. A JOIN task must follow the dynamic fork
JOIN	Join task is used to wait for completion of multiple tasks spawned by a (dynamic) fork tasks
SUB_WORKFLOW	Sub Workflow task allows for nesting a workflow within another workflow
WAIT	A wait task is implemented as a gate that remains in inProgress state unless marked as completed or failed by an external trigger
HTTP	An HTTP task is used to make calls to another microservice over HTTP
EVENT	Publish an event (message) to either Conductor or an external system. They are useful for creating event based dependencies for workflows and tasks

Event Task—This system task publishes an event (*i.e.*, a message) to either CONDUCTOR or an external system. Messages to CONDUCTOR can create event based dependencies for workflows and tasks by using event handlers. Handlers execute specific actions (*i.e.*, either start a workflow, fail a task, or complete a task) when a matching event occurs. In our taxi-hailing application example we make use of an event handler to start the workflow upon a *request* event. Moreover, an event task (*i.e.*, *notification*) is used whenever a core functionality must notify a user. Figure 4a lists an example of an event task defined by using the CONDUCTOR language. It requires the following configuration parameters: the inputParameters is a map where keys are parameters' reference name and values are inputs parameters of the event tasks; the sink represent the recipient

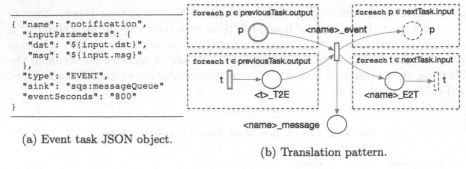

```
{ "name": "notification",
  "inputParameters": {
    "dst": "${input.dst}",
    "msg": "${input.msg}"
  },
  "type": "EVENT",
  "sink": "sqs:messageQueue"
  "eventSeconds": "800"
}
```

(a) Event task JSON object.

(b) Translation pattern.

Initial marking: ∅

Transition	Time function
⟨key⟩_decision	$[\tau_e, \tau_e + \langle \text{eventSeconds} \rangle]$

Fig. 4. Translation pattern of an EVENT system task.

of the event which can be either CONDUCTOR or an external system like Amazon Simple Queue Service (SQS) [19] used in our example; the eventSeconds defines an additional assumption on the time required by the event generation process (*i.e.*, 800 ms in our example). Figure 4b shows the corresponding translation pattern. It connects all output elements of the previous task (*i.e.*, previousTask.output) to the ⟨name⟩_event transition that produces the event (*i.e.*, a new token into the ⟨name⟩_message). The postset of this transition also includes all the input elements of the subsequent task (*i.e.*, nextTask.input). Tokens in the ⟨name⟩_message place can be consumed by the different event handlers, if any.

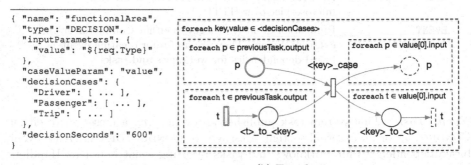

```
{ "name": "functionalArea",
  "type": "DECISION",
  "inputParameters": {
    "value": "${req.Type}"
  },
  "caseValueParam": "value",
  "decisionCases": {
    "Driver": [ ... ],
    "Passenger": [ ... ],
    "Trip": [ ... ]
  },
  "decisionSeconds": "600"
}
```

(a) Decision task JSON object.

(b) Translation pattern.

Initial marking: ∅

Transition	Time function
⟨key⟩_decision	$[\tau_e, \tau_e + \langle \text{decisionSeconds} \rangle]$

Fig. 5. Translation pattern of a DECISION system task.

Decision task—A decision task represents a `switch-case` like statement. In our taxi-hailing application, it is used to decide over alternative process flows, depending on the user type of an incoming request. An example is shown in Fig. 5a. The `caseValueParam` is the name of the parameter in task input whose value will be used as a switch; the `decisionCases` is a map where keys are possible values for `caseValueParam` and values are lists of tasks to be executed; the `decisionSeconds` defines an additional assumption on time required by the decision process. Figure 5b shows the translation pattern of a decision task. Since the `decisionCases` in Fig. 5a has three `key-value` pairs, by applying the external macro substitution we obtain three transitions: `Driver_case`, `Passenger_case`, and `Trip_case` which represent a non-deterministic choice between three different alternative execution flows. The output elements of the previous task in the process flow (*i.e.*, `previousTask.output`) represent the preset of these transitions, while the input elements of the first task in the value list (*i.e.*, `value[0].input`) represent their postset.

Dynamic Fork Join task—Dynamic fork join tasks are used in our taxi-hailing application to dispatch requests to the appropriate services, depending on the geographical location of the user. The request may be dispatched to multiple replicated services to increase the resilience. Figure 6a shows an example which defines two system tasks: the *dynamic fork* and the *join* (that must always follow the former one). The `dynamicForkTasksParam` is the name of the parameter in task input whose value contains the list of tasks to be

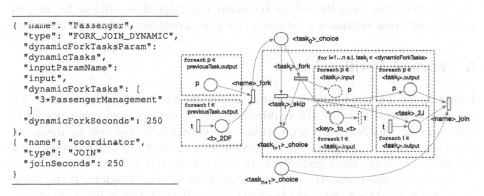

```
{ "name": "Passenger",
  "type": "FORK_JOIN_DYNAMIC",
  "dynamicForkTasksParam":
  "dynamicTasks",
  "inputParamName":
  "input",
  "dynamicForkTasks": [
    "3*PassengerManagement"
  ]
  "dynamicForkSeconds": 250
},
{ "name": "coordinator",
  "type": "JOIN"
  "joinSeconds": 250
}
```

(a) A dynamic fork followed by a join task JSON objects.

(b) Translation pattern.

	Initial marking: $\emptyset$	
Transition	**Time function**	
$\langle name \rangle$_fork	$[\tau_e, \tau_e + \langle dynamicForkSeconds \rangle]$	
$\langle name \rangle$_join	$[\tau_e, \tau_e + \langle joinSeconds \rangle]$	
$\langle task_i \rangle$_fork/_skip	$[\tau_e, \tau_e]$	

Fig. 6. Translation pattern of a `FORK_JOIN_DYNAMIC` system task. *Non-urgent* transitions are depicted in gray.

executed in parallel. The `inputParamName` is a map where keys are forked task's reference name and values are inputs parameters of forked tasks. The `dynamicForkTasks` represents an additional user defined assumption used to identify at design time the set of tasks that can be launched during the execution of the dynamic fork. The example in Fig. 6a shows that `Passenger` task can spawn any combination of worker tasks chosen from the following multiset: $\{3 \cdot \texttt{PassengerManagement}\}$, *i.e.*, the taxi-hailing application can dispatch the request to up to three `PassengerManagement` tasks to deal with the user requests. If the `dynamicForkTasks` is not defined, the default assumption is $\{1 \cdot \texttt{task}\}$ for each `task` in the worker tasks set. The `dynamicForkSeconds` and the `joinSeconds` define additional assumption on time required by the dynamic fork and join processes, respectively.

Figure 6b shows the translation pattern of a dynamic fork task followed by a join task. The initial component generated by the translation process is the `Passenger_fork` transition. The preset of this transition is composed of all the output components of the previous task. The external `for` macro substitution (on the right side), allows the $\langle \texttt{task}_i \rangle \texttt{\_fork}/\texttt{\_join}$ components to be replicated for each `task`$_i$ in the `dynamicForkTasks` multiset. Thus, whenever the place `task`$_i$`_choice` is marked, the `task`$_i$ can either be executed or not, depending on the non deterministic choice of fire either $\langle \texttt{task}_i \rangle \texttt{\_fork}$ or $\langle \texttt{task}_i \rangle \texttt{\_skip}$. Whenever all the forked tasks complete their execution, the `Passenger_join` transition becomes enable to fire (*i.e.*, the output component of the translation pattern).

The final model, automatically derived from the translation process of CONDUCTOR2PN, formally defines the entire execution flow and can be used to perform different verification activities, such as simulation and model checking.

5 Formal Verification

Based on the TB net modeling formalism described in the previous sections, we are able to formally verify the requirements by essentially inspecting the *TRG* structure. In this Section, we describe some verifiable properties, by means of some significant examples upon the taxi-hailing application. The properties can be verified by using the CONDUCTOR2PN output directly fed into GRAPHGEN.

A very common property to check is *deadlock/livelock* freedom. If the property does not hold, all the paths leading to a deadlock state can be easily visualized. Livelock freedom has been proven on the taxi-hailing process flow. However, there exist potentially unwanted execution paths leading into deadlock states. For instance, since the *access control* microservice is not replicated, it represents a single point of failure. When, for some reason, it would not be reachable, the incoming requests would be partially handled and the process flow would not reach a final state. This scenario is represented by a feasible execution path, where the *non-urgent* transition `accessControl_P2C` never fires.

More generally, it is possible to formalize the requirements by using specific CTL/TCTL formulas [20, 21], in order to verify *invariant, safety, liveness* and *bounded-response time* properties [8, 16]. An example of a *safety* property is:

$$\neg EF(\texttt{payment\_inProgress} > 0 \wedge \texttt{payment\_timeout} > 0) \quad (1)$$

Formula (1) means that does not ($\neg$ operator) exists (E operator) a feasible path, where the argument eventually (F operator) holds. The argument is a state formula expressed as combination of conditions on the number of tokens in places: *i.e.*, an inconsistent state of the **payment** component, where both **inProgress** and **timeout** status coexist, a condition that we want to be sure it will never happen. An example of a *liveness* property is:

$$AG(\texttt{accessControl\_complete} > 0 \wedge \texttt{cache\_complete} > 0 \implies$$
$$AF(\texttt{Passenger\_schedule} > 0 \vee \texttt{Driver\_schedule} > 0 \vee \texttt{TripManagement\_schedule} > 0))$$
$$(2)$$

Formula (2) is used to verify that for all paths (A), globally (G), if a request has been handled, then a decision between **Driver**, **Passenger** and **Trip** management tasks is always (A), eventually (F) taken.

Bounded-response time properties can be used to perform timing analysis on the process flow. A simple example of this property is presented in Formula 3:

$$AG(\texttt{payment\_schedule} > 0 \implies EF_{\leq 2400}(\texttt{billing\_complete} > 0)) \quad (3)$$

This formula is used to verify that whenever a payment task is requested, it is possible to complete the billing process (without failures), within 2.4 s. Another example follows below:

$$AG(\texttt{APIGateway\_forking} > 0 \wedge \texttt{notification\_message} = 0 \implies$$
$$EF_{\leq 4800}(\texttt{notification\_message} > 0)) \quad (4)$$

Formula 4 is used to verify that whenever a user request is received, a final state (*i.e.*, a notification message has been enqueued), is reachable in 4.8 s.

6   Related Work

Orchestration [3] and choreography [22] are two well-established alternative approaches to define cooperation between services in order to provide arbitrary complex interactions and functionalities. Although, orchestration was more popular in SOA, this approach has recently seen a renewed interest due to its simplicity of use and easier ways to manage complexity. Moreover, peer task choreography, can lead to harder scalability with growing business needs [4]. The approach presented in this paper has been mainly influenced by different related lines of work aiming at reuse theoretical results from well-established models and techniques in formal methods. Recent proposed techniques try to connect choreographies and behavioral types to either logic-based formalisms, such as μ-calculus [23], linear logic [24], or automata-based formalisms, such as abstract machines and communicating automata [25]. Our translation approach is somehow inspired by previous studies that propose to map Business Process Execution Language (BPEL) for Web Services [26–28] to PNs. These techniques provide computer aided verification for SOA systems. However, these approaches are not directly applicable in the context of microservices, where new emerging languages and frameworks, such as JOLIE [29] and CONDUCTOR [4], are being adopted as major references for orchestration, from both industry and academia.

Our work represents the first attempt (to the best of our knowledge) to leverage the expressiveness of the TB nets to supply formal specification and verification of microservice based process flows defined via CONDUCTOR blueprints. TB nets also allows to easily map and analyze temporal aspects that can be of primary importance in different application contexts, at least to ensure a certain quality of service. The formalization process opens up the possibility to directly apply model checking, simulation, model-based testing, and runtime verification by means of powerful off-the-shelf tools, such as GRAPHGEN [8,14], MARDIGRAS [30] and MAHARAJA [31].

7   Conclusion and Future Work

In this paper we propose a formal semantics for process flows specified using CONDUCTOR, *i.e.,* an open source orchestration framework in use at Netflix, Inc. Our approach aims at mechanically producing a formal representation in terms of Time Basic Petri Nets. The translation process is fully automated by means of a JAVA software tool called CONDUCTOR2PN. The formal semantics is complete (*i.e.,* it covers all the language constructs of CONDUCTOR). The TB net model can be used to perform model checking, simulation, model-based testing, and runtime verification by means of powerful off-the-shelf tools. We demonstrated the use of the tool on a small taxi-hailing system, illustrating how to analyze the behavior of a CONDUCTOR blueprint by model-checking its translation.

We are interested in expanding on this work in different directions. CONDUCTOR2PN is currently a prototypal implementation and has been tested on a variety of small benchmarking examples. We are going to test it with more sophisticated real-world applications in order to evaluate the scalability of the proposed approach. Moreover, we want to expand the translation to stochastic formalisms to support both performance analysis and probabilistic model checking in presence of uncertainty. A suitable modeling formalism that nicely supports these features is Generalized Stochastic Petri Nets [32].

References

1. Lewis, J., Fowler, M.: Microservices: a definition of this new architectural term, March 2014. https://martinfowler.com/articles/microservices.html
2. Dragoni, N., Giallorenzo, S., Lafuente, A.L., Mazzara, M., Montesi, F., Mustafin, R., Safina, L.: Microservices: yesterday, today, and tomorrow. In: Mazzara, M., Meyer, B. (eds.) Present and Ulterior Software Engineering, pp. 195–216. Springer, Cham (2017). https://doi.org/10.1007/978-3-319-67425-4_12
3. Mazzara, M., Govoni, S.: A case study of web services orchestration. In: Jacquet, J.-M., Picco, G.P. (eds.) COORDINATION 2005. LNCS, vol. 3454, pp. 1–16. Springer, Heidelberg (2005). https://doi.org/10.1007/11417019_1
4. Netflix, Inc.: Conductor. https://netflix.github.io/conductor/. Accessed June 2017
5. The Netflix Tech Blog: Netflix conductor: a microservices orchestrator. https://medium.com/netflix-techblog/netflix-conductor-a-microservices-orchestrator-2e8d4771bf40, December 2016
6. Ghezzi, C., Morasca, S., Pezzè, M.: Validating timing requirements for time basic net specifications. J. Syst. Softw. 27, 97–117 (1994)
7. Peterson, J.L.: Petri nets. ACM Comput. Surv. 9(3), 223–252 (1977). https://doi.org/10.1145/356698.356702
8. Bellettini, C., Capra, L.: Reachability analysis of time basic Petri nets: a time coverage approach. In: Proceedings of the 2011 13th Internationl Symposium on Symbolic and Numeric Algorithms for Scientific Computing, Series, SYNASC 2011, pp. 110–117. IEEE Computer Society, Washington, DC (2011)
9. Camilli, M.: Petri nets state space analysis in the cloud. In: Proceedings of the 2012 International Conference on Software Engineering, Series ICSE 2012, Piscataway, NJ, USA, pp. 1638–1640. IEEE Press (2012)
10. Bengtsson, J., Yi, W.: Timed automata: semantics, algorithms and tools. In: Desel, J., Reisig, W., Rozenberg, G. (eds.) ACPN 2003. LNCS, vol. 3098, pp. 87–124. Springer, Heidelberg (2004). https://doi.org/10.1007/978-3-540-27755-2_3
11. Gurevich, Y.: Sequential abstract-state machines capture sequential algorithms. ACM Trans. Comput. Logic 1(1), 77–111 (2000)
12. Lee, W.J., Cha, S.D., Kwon, Y.R.: Integration and analysis of use cases using modular Petri nets in requirements engineering. IEEE Trans. Softw. Eng. 24(12), 1115–1130 (1998)
13. Iglesia, D.G.D.L., Weyns, D.: MAPE-K formal templates to rigorously design behaviors for self-adaptive systems. ACM Trans. Auton. Adapt. Syst. 10(3), 15:1–15:31 (2015)
14. Camilli, M., Bellettini, C., Capra, L., Monga, M.: Coverability analysis of time basic Petri nets with non-urgent behavior. In: Davenport, J.H., Negru, V., Ida, T., Jebelean, T., Petcu, D., Watt, S.M., Zaharie, D. (eds.) 18th International Symposium on Symbolic and Numeric Algorithms for Scientific Computing, SYNASC 2016, Timisoara, Romania, 24–27 September 2016, pp. 165–172. IEEE Computer Society (2016). https://doi.org/10.1109/SYNASC.2016.036
15. Alur, R., Courcoubetis, C., Dill, D.: Model-checking for real-time systems. In: Proceedings of the Fifth Annual IEEE Symposium on Logic in Computer Science, June 1990, pp. 414–425 (1990)
16. Camilli, M., Gargantini, A., Scandurra, P.: Specifying and verifying real-time self-adaptive systems. In: 2015 IEEE 26th International Symposium on Software Reliability Engineering (ISSRE), November 2015, pp. 303–313 (2015)
17. Uber Technologies, Inc.: https://www.uber.com/. Accessed June 2017

18. Merkel, D.: Docker: lightweight Linux containers for consistent development and deployment. Linux J. **2014**(239) (2014). http://dl.acm.org/citation.cfm?id=2600239.2600241
19. Amazon Simple Queue Service: https://aws.amazon.com/sqs/. Accessed June 2017
20. Alur, R., Courcoubetis, C., Dill, D.: Model-checking in dense real-time. Inf. Comput. **104**(1), 2–34 (1993)
21. Camilli, M., Bellettini, C., Capra, L., Monga, M.: CTL model checking in the cloud using MapReduce. In: 16th International Symposium on Symbolic and Numeric Algorithms for Scientific Computing, September 2014, pp. 333–340 (2014)
22. Peltz, C.: Web services orchestration and choreography. Computer **36**(10), 46–52 (2003)
23. Caires, L., Pfenning, F.: Session types as intuitionistic linear propositions. In: Gastin, P., Laroussinie, F. (eds.) CONCUR 2010. LNCS, vol. 6269, pp. 222–236. Springer, Heidelberg (2010). https://doi.org/10.1007/978-3-642-15375-4_16. http://dl.acm.org/citation.cfm?id=1887654.1887670
24. Wadler, P.: Propositions as sessions. In: Proceedings of the 17th ACM SIGPLAN International Conference on Functional Programming, Series, ICFP 2012, pp. 273–286. ACM, New York (2012). http://doi.acm.org/10.1145/2364527.2364568
25. Caires, L., Pérez, J.A.: Multiparty session types within a canonical binary theory, and beyond. In: Albert, E., Lanese, I. (eds.) FORTE 2016. LNCS, vol. 9688, pp. 74–95. Springer, Cham (2016). https://doi.org/10.1007/978-3-319-39570-8_6
26. Hinz, S., Schmidt, K., Stahl, C.: Transforming BPEL to Petri nets. In: van der Aalst, W.M.P., Benatallah, B., Casati, F., Curbera, F. (eds.) BPM 2005. LNCS, vol. 3649, pp. 220–235. Springer, Heidelberg (2005). https://doi.org/10.1007/11538394_15
27. Lohmann, N., Massuthe, P., Stahl, C., Weinberg, D.: Analyzing interacting WS-BPEL processes using flexible model generation. Data Knowl. Eng. **64**(1), 38–54 (2008). https://doi.org/10.1016/j.datak.2007.06.006
28. Ouyang, C., Verbeek, E., van der Aalst, W.M.P., Breutel, S., Dumas, M., ter Hofstede, A.H.M.: Formal semantics and analysis of control flow in WS-BPEL. Sci. Comput. Program. **67**(2), 162–198 (2007). https://doi.org/10.1016/j.scico.2007.03.002
29. Montesi, F., Guidi, C., Lucchi, R., Zavattaro, G.: JOLIE a Java orchestration language interpreter engine. Electr. Notes Theor. Comput. Sci. **181**, 19–33 (2007). https://doi.org/10.1016/j.entcs.2007.01.051
30. Bellettini, C., Camilli, M., Capra, L., Monga, M.: MARDiGRAS: simplified building of reachability graphs on large clusters. In: Abdulla, P.A., Potapov, I. (eds.) RP 2013. LNCS, vol. 8169, pp. 83–95. Springer, Heidelberg (2013). https://doi.org/10.1007/978-3-642-41036-9_9
31. Camilli, M., Gargantini, A., Scandurra, P., Bellettini, C.: Event-based runtime verification of temporal properties using time basic Petri nets. In: Barrett, C., Davies, M., Kahsai, T. (eds.) NFM 2017. LNCS, vol. 10227, pp. 115–130. Springer, Cham (2017). https://doi.org/10.1007/978-3-319-57288-8_8
32. Marsan, M.A., Balbo, G., Conte, G., Donatelli, S., Franceschinis, G.: Modelling with Generalized Stochastic Petri Nets, 1st edn. Wiley, New York (1994)

Towards a Taxonomy of Microservices Architectures

Martin Garriga[✉]

Dipartimento di Elettronica, Informazione e Bioingegneria,
Politecnico di Milano, Milan, Italy
martin.garriga@polimi.it

Abstract. The microservices architectural style is gaining more and
more momentum for the development of applications as suites of small,
autonomous, and conversational services, which are then easy to understand, deploy and scale. However, the proliferation of approaches leveraging microservices calls for a systematic way of analyzing and assessing
them as a completely new ecosystem: the first cloud-native architectural
style. This paper defines a preliminary analysis framework in the form of
a taxonomy of concepts, encompassing the whole microservices lifecycle,
as well as organizational aspects. This framework is necessary to enable
effective exploration, understanding, assessing, comparing, and selecting microservice-based models, languages, techniques, platforms, and
tools. Then, we analyze state of the art approaches related to microservices using this taxonomy to provide a holistic perspective of available
solutions.

1 Introduction

Microservices is a novel architectural style that tries to overcome the short-
comings of centralized, monolithic architectures [1,2], in which application logic
is encapsulated in big deployable chunks. In contrast, microservices are small
components, built around business capabilities [3], that are easy to understand,
deploy, and scale independently, even using different technology stacks [4]. Each
runs in a dedicated process and communicates through lightweight mechanisms,
often a RESTful API.

Several companies have recently migrated, or are considering migrating, their
existing applications to microservices [5], and new microservice-native applications and support tools are being conceived. While the adoption of this architectural style should help one address the typical facets of a modern software system:
for example, its distribution, coordination among parts, and operation, some
aspects are still blurred [6]. Like traditional developers, microservice adopters
would benefit from a comprehensive support for the whole microservices lifecycle. All in all, the increasing number of microservice-based approaches calls for a
systematic way to analyze and assess them as a completely new ecosystem: the
first cloud-native architectural style [7].

In this context, this paper defines a preliminary analysis framework that
captures the fundamental understanding of microservice architectures in the

© Springer International Publishing AG 2018
A. Cerone and M. Roveri (Eds.): SEFM 2017 Workshops, LNCS 10729, pp. 203–218, 2018.
https://doi.org/10.1007/978-3-319-74781-1_15

form of a taxonomy of concepts, encompassing the whole microservices lifecycle, as well as organizational aspects. This framework enables effective exploration, understanding, assessing, comparing, and selecting microservice-based models, languages, techniques, platforms, and tools. We carried out an analysis of state of the art approaches (28 in total) related to microservices using the proposed taxonomy to provide a holistic perspective of available solutions.

The rest of the paper is organized as follows. Section 2 defines microservices architectures. Section 3 details the proposed taxonomy, and the analysis of state of the art approaches according to it. Section 4 discusses open challenges distilled from the previous analysis. Section 5 concludes the paper.

2   Microservices Architectures

The most widely adopted definition of microservices architectures is "an approach for developing a single application as a suite of small services, each running in its own process and communicating with lightweight mechanisms, often an HTTP API" [1]. In contrast to monoliths, microservices foster independent deployability and scalability, and can be developed using different technology stacks [4].

However, this definition can be applied to traditional or RESTful services as well, which feeds the debate regarding microservices and SOA (Service-oriented Architectures). Although microservices can be seen as an evolution of SOA, they are inherently different regarding the sharing and reuse aspects. SOA is built on the concept of foster reuse: a share-as-much-as-possible architecture style, whereas microservices architecture is built on the concept of a share-as-little-as-possible style [8]. Given that service reuse has often been less than expected [9], instead of reusing existing microservices for new tasks or use cases, they should be "micro" enough to allow rapidly developing a new one that can coexist, evolve or replace the previous one according to the business needs [10].

3   A Taxonomy of Microservices Architectures

The first step to delineate the taxonomy comprised a literature review, following the guidelines for Systematic Literature Review (SLR) proposed in [11]. Although a SLR is outside the scope of this work, this helped us to organize the process of finding and classifying relevant literature. We searched for articles indexed in Scopus, Science Direct, IEEE Xplore, ACM Digital Library, SpringerLink, Google Scholar and Wiley Online. The search strings used were "microservice[s]", "microservice[s] architecture[s]", "cloud-native architecture[s]". The search comprised articles published up to 2016 (inclusive). Then, we applied snowballing [12], by looking for relevant references included in the works previously found, in order to identify other potential works. As microservices is a very recent topic, we considered journal, conference and workshop publications. Finally, we suppressed duplicated papers from the results, since the search engines and databases are overlapped to a certain extent. After these steps, the initial collection consisted of 64 potentially relevant works from which we performed a detailed, qualitative analysis in order to exclude different papers of the same authors/group, incrementally reporting their results, and certain works that used the term "microservices" with a different meaning.

From this analysis we refined a collection of 46 relevant work[1], classified as: primary studies, that is, literature investigating specifically the research question (using microservices, proposing microservice-oriented frameworks, tools or architectures); and secondary studies, that is, literature reviewing primary studies (surveys, reviews and comparative studies assessing microservices or microservice-based approaches).

The former group (28 approaches, summarized in Table 1) became the target of our analysis (discussed in Sect. 4), while the latter was used to identify the concepts (and disambiguate their definitions) that are potentially relevant for the taxonomy. Additionally, we enriched this taxonomy by leveraging our previous experience with classification frameworks in the context of SOA, both for traditional Web Services [39] and the most recent RESTful services [40]. Figure 1 presents the taxonomy of concepts, which are defined below. For most of the concepts it is not possible to provide an exhaustive list of values, due to the wide (and growing) variety of approaches. Thus, we included *other* as a possible value for completeness.

Design implies thinking about the boundaries of microservices that will maximize their upsides and avoid some of the potential downsides, focused on loose coupling and high cohesion as the two key principles of SOA. The architects face this set of decisions, together with the possible choices, at the earliest stage of the lifecycle. The design space can be represented in a textual or graphical form, by means of architectural concepts. Design encompasses the following sub-concepts:

- *Design approaches* means the preexistence (or absence) of legacy software that should be transitioned to a microservices architecture, constraining its design [2]. Possible values: brownfield, greenfield.
- *Design practices* to handle the complexity of microservices architectures into design time [41, 42]. Possible values: domain-driven design, design for failure, other.
- *Architectural support* describing the obligations/constraints to be fulfilled by the microservices system, and how to apply them into a dynamic context environment [43]. Possible values: reference architectures, model-driven design, other.

Implementation implies being aware of program complexity, due to the thousands of microservices running asynchronously in a distributed computer network: programs that are difficult to understand are also hard to write and modify [23]. Also, the implementation should allow continuous evolution, which is often required by the application domain. Although implementation decisions

---

[1] Due to the space limit, the full list can be found in: https://goo.gl/j5ec4A.

Table 1. Microservices primary approaches

Id	Reference	Key points
01	Kratzke et al. [13]	Tradeoffs of containerized microservices and Software Defined Networks (SDNs)
02	Balalaie et al. [4]	Experience report and migration patterns for migration to microservices and DevOps
03	Bogner et al. [14]	Microservices integration from the enterprise architectures point of view
04	Toffetti et al. [7]	Cloud-native applications definition, self-managing monitoring and scaling
05	Ciuffoletti [15]	Monitoring-as-a-service for microservices
06	Florio et al. [16]	Autonomic and self-adaptable containerized microservices
07	Gabbrielli et al. [17]	Self-reconfiguring microservices using the ad-hoc Jolie Redeployment Optimizer tool
08	Gadea et al. [18]	Reference architecture to propagate database changes through microservices
09	Guo et al. [19]	PaaS Architecture based on microservices and containers
10	Gysel et al. [20]	Systematic approach to decompose a monolith into microservices
11	Heorhiadi et al. [21]	Failure testing framework for microservices
12	Kecskemety et al. [22]	Methodology to split traditional SOA architectures in microservices
13	Liu et al. [23]	Agents-oriented language and IDE for developing microservices
14	Grieger et al. [24]	Model-driven integration of microservices and self-adaptation with models at runtime
15	Safina et al. [25]	Data-driven workflows based on microservices, defined in the ad-hoc language Jolie
16	Nikol et al. [26]	Multi-tenancy microservice composition by adapting traditional BPEL workflows
17	Rahman et al. [27]	Automated acceptance testing architecture for Behavior Driven Development (BDD)
18	Savchenko et al. [28]	A framework and platform for microservices validation and testing
19	Sousa et al. [29]	Multi-cloud architecture with automatic selection of cloud providers for microservices deployment
20	Stubbs et al. [30]	Fully decentralized solution to the microservices discovery problem using Docker, Serfnode and gossip protocol
21	Sun et al. [31]	Extension to container's network hypervisor, enabling flexible monitoring and policy enforcement for microservices
22	Villamizar et al. [32]	Infrastructure cost comparison using monolithic and different microservices deployments on the cloud
23	Yahia et al. [33]	Event-driven lightweight platform for microservice composition, based on a DSL for describing orchestration
24	Bak et al. [34]	Context- and location-based microservices for mobile and IoT
25	Levcovitz et al. [35]	Identification and extraction of candidate microservices in a monolith by dependency graphs of modules and database tables
26	Meinke et al. [36]	Learning-based testing to evaluate the functional correctness and robustness of distributed microservices
27	Viennot et al. [37]	Middleware model for heterogeneous data-driven microservices integration
28	Amaral et al. [38]	Comparison between two models to deploy containerized microservices: master-slave and nested-container

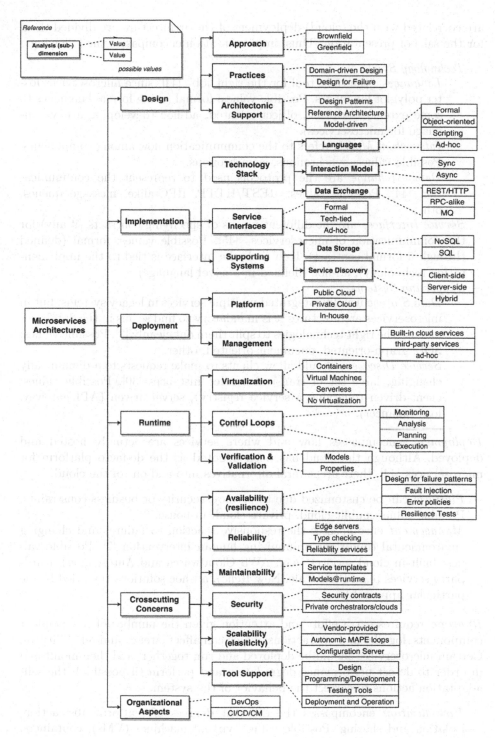

Fig. 1. Microservices taxonomy

are correlated with the (cloud) deployment of the architecture, we divided them for the sake of presentation. Thus, implementation encompasses the following:

- *Technology Stack*:
  Languages "the right tool for the right job" [44], since microservices foster polyglot languages. Possible values: formal (using formal languages to some extent), scripting, object-oriented, ad-hoc (developing a new language for microservices).
  Interaction Models refers to the communication flow among components. Possible values: synchronous, asynchronous.
  Data Exchange are the protocols used to represent the communication [44]. Possible values: REST/HTTP, RPC-alike, message queues, other.
- *Service Interfaces* are the different means of specifying contracts (if any) for the communication of microservices [45]. Possible values: formal (defined through a formal contract), tech-tied (the interface is tied to the implementation technology), ad-hoc (defined in a novel language).
- *Supporting Systems*:
  Data Storage usually integrated multiple services in legacy systems, but in microservices architectures it is mandatory to find seams in the databases and use the right technologies to split them out cleanly [3]. Possible values: SQL, graph-oriented, document-oriented, other.
  Service Discovery should allow clients to make requests to a dynamically changing, large set of transient service instances [30]. Possible values: client-driven (querying a service registry), server-driven (API gateway, load balancer).

Deployment encompasses how and where services are actually hosted and deployed. Although the cloud has been adopted as the de-facto platform for microservices [44], there are several alternatives into and out of the cloud.

- *Platform* can be customized due to privacy, security or business constraints. Possible values: public cloud, private cloud, in-house.
- *Management* encompasses the responsive reaction to failures and changing environmental conditions, minimizing human intervention [7]. Possible values: built-in cloud services (e.g., AWS Cloudwatch and Autoscaling), third-party services (e.g., Rightscale, New Relic), ad-hoc solutions (i.e., tied to the particular approach).

Runtime requires extra effort and attention given the number of independent components, log files and interactions, which can affect latency and reliability [3]. Certain microservices should be deployed and run together, and then monitored in order to detect performance degradation and perform (if possible), the self-adaptation actions to correct the behavior of the system.

- *Virtualization* encompasses the different degrees of platform abstraction, isolation and sharing. Possible values: virtual machines (VMs), containers, serverless (i.e., Functions-as-a-Service [46]), no virtualization.

- *Control loops* or MAPE loops (monitor-analyize-plan-execute) allow for different degrees of self-adaptation. This is challenging in a distributed setting since the overall system behavior emerges from the localized decisions and interactions. In our view, approaches can implement one or more stages of the control loop. Possible values: monitoring, analysis, planning, execution.
- *Verification & Validation* at runtime, concern the quality assessment of microservices throughout their lifecycle [47]. Possible values: models (at runtime), properties, other.

Crosscutting Concerns mostly regard QoS aspects that have to be tracked within the microservices lifecycle, supported by the infrastructure through specific artifacts and independent of individual microservices.

- *Availability and Resilience* imply handling both service-level and low-level failures that demand for persistence and recovery techniques [45]. Possible values: resilience patterns, fault injection, error-handling policies, resilience tests, other.
- *Reliability* refers to a system that is capable of perform well without halting, according to its requirements, and is fault-tolerant. This is particularly challenging for distributed microservices, threatened by integration and message passing mechanisms. Possible values: edge servers [4], type checking [25], reliability services [31,37], other.
- *Maintaintability* can be plainly defined by the premise "you build it, you run it" which claims for a better understanding of business capabilities, roles and operational details [48]. Possible values: service templates, models at runtime, other.
- *Security* vulnerabilities are those of SOA [45], plus the high distribution and network complexity that pose additional difficulty in debugging, monitoring, auditing and forensic [31]. Possible values: security contracts, private cloud, other.
- *Scalability* and elasticity refer to the capability to rapidly adjust the overall capacity of the platform by adding or removing resources, also minimizing human intervention [7]. Possible values: vendor-provided, autonomic MAPE loops, configuration servers, other.
- *Tool Support* should be provided given the program complexity, performance criticality and evolutive characteristics of microservices [3]. Possible values: design, programming/developing, testing, deployment/operation.

Organizational Aspects are crucial since organizations produce designs which are copies of their communication structures. Thus, a siloed organization will produce a siloed-system, while a DevOps one [4], with development and operations teams organized around business capabilities and collaboration (cross-functional teams) will be able to produce well-bounded microservices [1,8]. Although this concept is less technical when compared with the previous ones, it is important to understand the complex "organizational rewiring" scenarios that need to be faced when transitioning to microservices [49], which may imply continuously adapting both the organization and architecture, and understand or mediate new requirements and concerns. Possible values: DevOps, Continuous delivery/deployment/integration practices, other.

Tables 2 and 3 summarize the analysis of the 28 approaches according to the taxonomy in Fig. 1. The following section discusses the findings and implications of such an analysis.

Table 2. Characterization of microservice approaches (Part 1)

	Concept	Value	Approaches	Total
Design	Approach	Brownfield	02, 03, 04, 10, 12, 16, 21, 22, 25	9
		Greenfield	06, 07, 08, 13, 15, 23, 27	7
	Practices	DDD	10, 22	2
		Design for failure	11	1
		Other	17	1
	Architectonic support	Design patterns	02, 15	2
		Reference architecture	03, 05, 08, 09	4
		Model-driven design	13, 14, 16, 19, 27	5
		Other	10	1
Implementation	Tech./languages	Semi-formal	03,05,16,25	5
		Object-oriented	02, 05, 22	3
		Scripting	11, 23, 28	3
		Ad-hoc	07, 10, 12, 13, 14, 15, 17, 19, 21, 23	9
	Tech./interaction model	Synchronous	02, 05, 16, 22, 25, 27, 28	7
		Asynchronous	13, 23, 25	3
	Tech./data exchange	REST/HTTP	01, 02, 06, 08, 10, 11, 21, 22, 23, 24	10
		RPC-alike	05, 10, 21, 25	4
		Other	13, 20	2
		Message queues	26, 27	2
	Service interfaces	Formal	05, 08, 14, 16	4
		Tech-tied	02	2
		Ad-hoc	06, 07, 10, 11, 12, 18, 23	7
	Supp. syst./storage	SQL	02, 22, 24, 25, 27	5
		NoSQL	08, 27	2
		Graph-oriented	27	1
		Document-oriented	27	1
		Other	15, 27	2
	Supp. syst./discovery	Client-side (discovery registry)	02, 04, 05	3
		Server-side (APIgateway/LB)	13	1
		Hybrid	20	1
Deployment	Platform	Public cloud	04, 06, 07, 08, 11, 12, 19, 21, 24	9
		Private cloud	04, 06, 13, 18, 19	5
		In-house	09, 28	2
	Management	built-in cloud services	22	1
		third-party services	02, 18	2
		ad-hoc solution	04, 05, 06, 07, 08, 09, 12, 13, 14, 16, 19, 20, 23, 27	14

Table 3. Characterization of microservice approaches (Part 2)

	Concept	Value	Approaches	Total
Runtime	Virtualization	Virtual machines	01, 04, 07, 12, 13, 19, 21, 22, 28	9
		Containers	01, 02, 04, 05, 06, 07, 08, 09, 11, 12, 14, 16, 19, 20, 22, 28	16
		Serverless	22	1
		No virtualization	01, 07, 28	3
	Control loop (MAPE-K)	Monitoring	05, 06, 08, 14, 20, 21, 24, 26	8
		Analysis	06, 08, 14, 26	4
		Planning	06, 26	2
		Execution	06, 26	2
		Shared knowledge	06	1
	Verification & Validation	Models	03, 14, 19, 26	4
		Properties	15	1
		Other	05, 11, 17, 18, 24	5
Crosscutting Concerns	Availability (resilience)	Patterns	02,11,20	3
		Fault injection	11, 26	2
		Error-handling policies	23	1
		Resilience tests	11	1
		Other	04, 10, 27	3
	Reliability	Edge servers	02	1
		Type checking	15	1
		Reliability services	21, 27	2
		Other	04, 13	2
	Maintainability	Service templates	02	1
		Models@Runtime	14	1
		Other	15	1
	Security	Security contracts	21	1
		Private orchestrators	23	1
		Other	10	1
	Scalability (elasticity)	Vendor-provided	04, 21, 22, 27	4
		Auto. MAPE loop	06	1
		Configuration server	02, 07	2
		Other	02, 27	2
	Tool support	Design	03, 09, 10, 13, 16, 25	6
		Programming	09, 13, 15	3
		Testing tools	09, 11, 17, 18, 26, 28	6
		Deployment/operation	02, 05, 07, 09, 16, 19, 27	7
Organizational aspects		DevOps	02, 07, 24	3
		CD/CI/CM	02, 13, 18	3

4   Discussion and Open Research Challenges

Design approaches are equally distributed between brownfield (9) and greenfield (7). The design phase is mainly supported through reference architectures and model-driven design. However, despite the hype and business push towards microservitization, there is still a lack of academic efforts regarding the design practices and patterns [10]. Design for failure and design patterns could allow to early address challenges as to bring responsiveness (e.g. by adopting "let-it-crash" models), fault tolerance, self-healing and variability characteristics. Resilience patterns such as circuit-breaker and bulkhead seem to be key enablers in this direction. It is also interesting to understand whether the design using a stateless model [50] can affect elasticity and scalability as well [43].

Another problem at design time is finding the right granularity level of microservices, which implies a tradeoff between size and number of microservices [10]. Intuitively, the more microservices introduced into the architecture, the higher the level of isolation between the business functionalities, but at the price of increased network communications and distribution complexity. Addressing this tradeoff systematically is essential for assessing the extent to which "splitting" is beneficial regarding the potential value of microservitization.

Implementation approaches mostly define their own, ad-hoc languages (9) for programming microservices or defining different parts of their architecture (e.g., in the form of DSLs). Some of those provide semi-formal support, by embracing standards such as MOF (Meta Object Facility) [14] or OCCI (Open Cloud Computing Interface) [15]. Interestingly, microservices architectures are intuitively associated to lightweight, scripting languages such as JavaScript or Python, which is not reflected explicitly in the analyzed literature [44].

Regarding the interaction model, the vast majority choose the synchronous one (7) rather than the asynchronous (3). Interestingly, microservices are most suitable for asynchronous communication, bringing performance, decoupling and fault-tolerance, but the paradigm shift implied has not been overtaken yet in practice. Synchronous request-response model is still easier to understand and implement, and much common in monolith systems (brownfield) but hinders decentralization, availability and performance. The transition from synchronous to asynchronous models calls for further analysis.

RESTful HTTP communication is the most widespread data exchange solution (10), being the de-facto standard to implement microservices. Message queues is not as adopted as expected, in concordance with the lack of proposals adopting asynchronous interaction models. Regarding interfaces, their ad-hoc definition (7) is the rule. This suggests not only that microservices are being used in-house, with contracts negotiated between different teams/people inside the company, but also that they are not supposed to be reused but to be (re)developed entirely from scratch to fulfill new requirements. The recent efforts on standardizing RESTful APIs through OpenAPI specifications[2] seem interesting and also applicable to specify microservices [51].

---

[2] https://www.openapis.org/.

Finally, SQL is still the common choice for storage (5) even considering the benefits and hype for NoSQL databases (5 among the different options). This can be related to the fact that brownfield approaches inherit legacy databases and their migration is not straightforward. This also opens a question mark regarding the splitting and migration of data to fully exploit microservices advantages of data governance and data locality. Finally, discovery approaches are not so common (4), which suggests that more research is needed in this topic, given its importance in microservice architectures [30].

Deployment appears as a broadly discussed topic in the literature. Public cloud is the de-facto standard for deploying microservice applications (9) which confirms the increasing adoption of XaaS platforms. For deployment management, several approaches (14) propose their own ad-hoc solutions. There seems to be a mistrust regarding built-in services of cloud providers, which sometimes result too rigid [52] or cumbersome to configure and adjust [50]. However, these solutions are growing in variety and usability (e.g., AWS offering around 1000 new features per year[3]), and we believe that they will become the standard to deploy and manage cloud microservices in the near future.

Runtime shows that containers and microservices seems to be the perfect marriage (16). Even though, virtual machines are also widespread (9). However, only one approach considered serverless functions, also known as Functions-as-a-Service or FaaS[4]. FaaS appeared as a disruptive alternative that delegates the management of the execution environment of application functionality (in the form of stateless functions) to the infrastructure provider [46]. However these new solutions bring together new challenges[5], among others: determine the sweetspots where running code in a FaaS environment can deliver economic benefits; automatically profile existing code to offload computation to serverless functions; bring adequate isolation among functions; determine the right granularity to exploit data and code locality; and provide methods to handle state (given that functions are stateless by definition).

Only one approach provides the full control loop to manage microservice applications at runtime, while the vast majority provide monitoring facilities (8) with other purposes rather than self-adaptation (e.g., profiling, verification, service discovery). Verification & Validation at runtime is not yet widespread among microservices approaches, which calls for further research. Some approaches provide static V&V at model level (4), while a few provide dynamic testing and monitoring.

Crosscutting Concerns. Regarding availability and resilience, a few approaches (3) use resilience patterns[6] such as circuit breaker and bulkhead, while others provide their ad-hoc availability solutions [7]. Reliability is another aspect

---

[3] https://techcrunch.com/2016/12/02/aws-shoots-for-total-cloud-domination/.
[4] https://martinfowler.com/articles/serverless.html.
[5] https://blog.zhaw.ch/icclab/research-directions-for-faas/.
[6] http://microservices.io/patterns/.

that calls for coverage (4). The challenges regarding reliability come from the microservices integration mechanisms: network integration and message passing is unreliable [45]. Maintainability is not particularly addressed (3), even if in practice an abuse of the freedom of choice (polyglot languages and persistence) could result in a chaos in the system and make it even unmaintainable [4]. Consequently, it is important to investigate how standards, good practices, processes and frameworks can help to organize (and automate) microservices maintainability.

Security is not extensively addressed (3), even though the microservices ecosystem makes monitoring and securing networks very challenging due to the myriad of small, distributed and conversational components: microservices are often designed to completely trust each other, therefore the compromise of a single microservice may bring down the entire application [31]. The main ongoing trends in security are either monitoring techniques for SDNs inspired by their physical counterparts TAP (Test Access Point) and SPAN (Switch Port Analyzer), which can then be combined with a policy enforcement infrastructure [31]; or application-based security approaches[7], which gather information to build ad-hoc application profiles and then use them to detect anomalous patterns. Surprisingly, only a few approaches addressed scalability, with four of them relying in the cloud vendor to achieve it. Again, the adoption of serverless functions can go one step beyond on this concern, since once deployed, the cost and effort in operation, scaling and load balancing these functions are reduced to zero.

Finally, various approaches provided tool support for the different activities. A few of them for programming activities, mostly relying in well known IDEs as common solution. For the rest of the lifecycle, design activity (6) is supported, for example, through an ad-hoc PaaS [19], a decomposition tool based on cross-cutting concerns [20], and a design tool to define multi-tenant BPEL-based microservices [26]. Testing (6) is supported through a resilience testing framework [21], and a tool to generate and manage reusable acceptance tests [27]. Finally, Deployment/Operation (7) is supported through a reconfigurator for the ad-hoc language Jolie [17], and a tool for automatic setup of multi-cloud environments for microservices [29].

Organizational Aspects are not fully or explicitly addressed yet, with 3 approaches mentioning the adoption of DevOps (which implies an organizational rewiring, equivalent to the adoption of Agile methodologies) and other 3 adopting only certain key practices (Continuous Delivery, Integration, Management). It would be interesting to link more explicitly microservices with the DevOps movement. DevOps seems to be a key factor in the success of this architectural style [4], by providing the necessary organizational shift to minimize coordination among the teams responsible for each component and removing the barriers for an effective, reciprocal relationship between the development and operations teams.

---

[7] E.g., Netflix Fido – https://github.com/Netflix/Fido.

Additionally, the literature reports different socio-technical patterns to ease organizational rewiring [49], which can pave the ground for the transition towards microservices. For example, Sociotechnical-Risks Engineering, where critical architecture elements remain tightly controlled by an organization and loosely coupled with respect to outsiders; or Shift Left, where organizational and operational concerns (for example, development-to-operations team mixing) are addressed earlier ("left") in the life cycle toward architecting and development.

5   Conclusions

Microservices architectures are fairly new, but their hype and success is undeniable. This paper presented a preliminary analysis framework that captures the fundamental understanding of microservices architectures in the form of a taxonomy of concepts, encompassing the whole microservices lifecycle, as well as organizational aspects. This framework is necessary to enable effective exploration, understanding, assessing, comparing, and selecting microservice-based models, languages, techniques, platforms, and tools. We carried out an analysis of state of the art approaches related to microservices using the proposed taxonomy to provide a holistic perspective of available solutions.

Additionally, from the results of the literature analysis, we identified open challenges for future research. Among them, the early use of resilience patterns to design fault-tolerant microservice solutions, the standardization of interfaces, and the development of asynchronous microservices. Special attention should be given to the latent use of serverless architectures to deploy and manage microservices. They have the potential to become the next evolution of microservices [53], to event-driven, asynchronous functions, because the underlying constraints have changed, costs have reduced, and radical improvements in time to value are possible.

References

1. Lewis, J., Fowler, M.: Microservices (2014). http://martinfowler.com/articles/microservices.html
2. Fowler, M.: Monolith first (2015). http://martinfowler.com/bliki/MonolithFirst.html
3. Newman, S.: Building Microservices. O'Reilly Media Inc., Newton (2015)
4. Balalaie, A., Heydarnoori, A., Jamshidi, P.: Microservices architecture enables devops: migration to a cloud-native architecture. IEEE Softw. **33**(3), 42–52 (2016)
5. Richardson, C.: Microservices architecture (2014). http://microservices.io/articles/whoisusingmicroservices.html
6. George, F.: Challenges in implementing microservices (2015). http://gotocon.com/dl/goto-amsterdam-2015/slides/FredGeorge_ChallengesInImplementingMicroServices.pdf
7. Toffetti, G., Brunner, S., Blöchlinger, M., Spillner, J., Bohnert, T.M.: Self-managing cloud-native applications: design, implementation, and experience. In: Future Generation Computer Systems, vol. (2016, in Press)

8. Richards, M.: Microservices Service-Oriented Architecture. O'Reilly Media, Newton (2015)
9. Wilde, N., Gonen, B., El-Sheikh, E., Zimmermann, A.: Approaches to the evolution of SOA systems. In: El-Sheikh, E., Zimmermann, A., Jain, L.C. (eds.) Emerging Trends in the Evolution of Service-Oriented and Enterprise Architectures. ISRL, vol. 111, pp. 5–21. Springer, Cham (2016). https://doi.org/10.1007/978-3-319-40564-3_2
10. Hassan, S., Bahsoon, R.: Microservices and their design trade-offs: a self-adaptive roadmap. In: IEEE International Conference on Services Computing (SCC), pp. 813–818. IEEE (2016)
11. Kitchenham, B.: Guidelines for performing systematic literature reviews in software engineering. Technical report, Version 2.3 EBSE Technical Report. EBSE, sn (2007)
12. Wohlin, C.: Guidelines for snowballing in systematic literature studies and a replication in software engineering. In: Proceedings of the 18th International Conference on Evaluation and Assessment in Software Engineering, p. 38. ACM (2014)
13. Kratzke, N.: About microservices, containers and their underestimated impact on network performance. In: Proceedings of CLOUD COMPUTING 2015, pp. 165–169 (2015)
14. Bogner, J., Zimmermann, A.: Towards integrating microservices with adaptable enterprise architecture. In: 2016 IEEE 20th International Enterprise Distributed Object Computing Workshop (EDOCW), pp. 1–6, September 2016
15. Ciuffoletti, A.: Automated deployment of a microservice-based monitoring infrastructure. Procedia Comput. Sci. **68**, 163–172 (2015)
16. Florio, L., Di Nitto, E.: Gru: an approach to introduce decentralized autonomic behavior in microservices architectures. In: 2016 IEEE International Conference on Autonomic Computing (ICAC), pp. 357–362. IEEE (2016)
17. Gabbrielli, M., Giallorenzo, S., Guidi, C., Mauro, J., Montesi, F.: Self-reconfiguring microservices. In: Ábrahám, E., Bonsangue, M., Johnsen, E.B. (eds.) Theory and Practice of Formal Methods. LNCS, vol. 9660, pp. 194–210. Springer, Cham (2016). https://doi.org/10.1007/978-3-319-30734-3_14
18. Gadea, C., Trifan, M., Ionescu, D., Ionescu, B.: A reference architecture for real-time microservice API consumption. In: Proceedings of the 3rd Workshop on Cross-Cloud Infrastructures & Platforms, p. 2. ACM (2016)
19. Guo, D., Wang, W., Zeng, G., Wei, Z.: Microservices architecture based cloudware deployment platform for service computing. In: 2016 IEEE Symposium on Service-Oriented System Engineering (SOSE), pp. 358–363. IEEE (2016)
20. Gysel, M., Kölbener, L., Giersche, W., Zimmermann, O.: Service cutter: a systematic approach to service decomposition. In: Aiello, M., Johnsen, E.B., Dustdar, S., Georgievski, I. (eds.) ESOCC 2016. LNCS, vol. 9846, pp. 185–200. Springer, Cham (2016). https://doi.org/10.1007/978-3-319-44482-6_12
21. Heorhiadi, V., Rajagopalan, S., Jamjoom, H., Reiter, M.K., Sekar, V.: Gremlin: systematic resilience testing of microservices. In: 2016 IEEE 36th International Conference on Distributed Computing Systems (ICDCS), pp. 57–66. IEEE (2016)
22. Kecskemeti, G., Marosi, A.C., Kertesz, A.: The ENTICE approach to decompose monolithic services into microservices. In: 2016 International Conference on High Performance Computing & Simulation (HPCS), pp. 591–596. IEEE (2016)
23. Liu, D., Zhu, H., Xu, C., Bayley, I., Lightfoot, D., Green, M., Marshall, P.: CIDE: an integrated development environment for microservices. In: IEEE International Conference on Services Computing (SCC), pp. 808–812. IEEE (2016)

24. Derakhshanmanesh, M., Grieger, M.: Model-integrating microservices: a vision paper. In: Software Engineering (Workshops), pp. 142–147 (2016)
25. Safina, L., Mazzara, M., Montesi, F., Rivera, V.: Data-driven workflows for microservices: genericity in jolie. In: IEEE International Conference on Advanced Information Networking and Applications (AINA), pp. 430–437. IEEE (2016)
26. Nikol, G., Träger, M., Harrer, S., Wirtz, G.: Service-oriented multi-tenancy (SO-MT): enabling multi-tenancy for existing service composition engines with Docker. In: 2016 IEEE Symposium on Service-Oriented System Engineering (SOSE), pp. 238–243. IEEE (2016)
27. Rahman, M., Gao, J.: A reusable automated acceptance testing architecture for microservices in behavior-driven development. In: 2015 IEEE Symposium on Service-Oriented System Engineering (SOSE), pp. 321–325. IEEE (2015)
28. Savchenko, D.I., Radchenko, G.I., Taipale, O.: Microservices validation: mjolnirr platform case study. In: 2015 38th International Convention on Information and Communication Technology, Electronics and Microelectronics (MIPRO), pp. 235–240. IEEE (2015)
29. Sousa, G., Rudametkin, W., Duchien, L.: Automated setup of multi-cloud environments for microservices-based applications. In: 9th IEEE International Conference on Cloud Computing (2016)
30. Stubbs, J., Moreira, W., Dooley, R.: Distributed systems of microservices using docker and serfnode. In: International Workshop on Science Gateways (IWSG), pp. 34–39. IEEE (2015)
31. Sun, Y., Nanda, S., Jaeger, T.: Security-as-a-service for microservices-based cloud applications. In: 2015 IEEE 7th International Conference on Cloud Computing Technology and Science (CloudCom), pp. 50–57. IEEE (2015)
32. Villamizar, M., Garcés, O., Ochoa, L., Castro, H., Salamanca, L., Verano, M., Casallas, R., Gil, S., Valencia, C., Zambrano, A., et al.: Infrastructure cost comparison of running web applications in the cloud using AWS lambda and monolithic and microservice architectures. In: 2016 16th IEEE/ACM International Symposium on Cluster, Cloud and Grid Computing (CCGrid), pp. 179–182. IEEE (2016)
33. Ben Hadj Yahia, E., Réveillère, L., Bromberg, Y.-D., Chevalier, R., Cadot, A.: Medley: an event-driven lightweight platform for service composition. In: Bozzon, A., Cudre-Maroux, P., Pautasso, C. (eds.) ICWE 2016. LNCS, vol. 9671, pp. 3–20. Springer, Cham (2016). https://doi.org/10.1007/978-3-319-38791-8_1
34. Bak, P., Melamed, R., Moshkovich, D., Nardi, Y., Ship, H., Yaeli, A.: Location and context-based microservices for mobile and internet of things workloads. In: 2015 IEEE International Conference on Mobile Services (MS), pp. 1–8. IEEE (2015)
35. Levcovitz, A., Terra, R., Valente, M.T.: Towards a technique for extracting microservices from monolithic enterprise systems. In: 3rd Brazilian Workshop on Software Visualization, Evolution and Maintenance (VEM), pp. 97–104 (2015)
36. Meinke, K., Nycander, P.: Learning-based testing of distributed microservice architectures: correctness and fault injection. In: Bianculli, D., Calinescu, R., Rumpe, B. (eds.) SEFM 2015. LNCS, vol. 9509, pp. 3–10. Springer, Heidelberg (2015). https://doi.org/10.1007/978-3-662-49224-6_1
37. Viennot, N., Lécuyer, M., Bell, J., Geambasu, R., Nieh, J.: Synapse: a microservices architecture for heterogeneous-database web applications. In: Proceedings of the Tenth European Conference on Computer Systems, p. 21. ACM (2015)
38. Amaral, M., Polo, J., Carrera, D., Mohomed, I., Unuvar, M., Steinder, M.: Performance evaluation of microservices architectures using containers. In: 2015 IEEE 14th International Symposium on Network Computing and Applications (NCA), pp. 27–34. IEEE (2015)

39. Garriga, M., Flores, A., Cechich, A., Zunino, A.: Web services composition mechanisms: a review. IETE Tech. Rev. **32**(5), 376–383 (2015)
40. Garriga, M., Mateos, C., Flores, A., Cechich, A., Zunino, A.: Restful service composition at a glance: a survey. J. Netw. Comput. Appl. **60**, 32–53 (2016)
41. Evans, E.: Domain-Driven Design: Tackling Complexity in the Heart of Software. Addison-Wesley Professional, Boston (2004)
42. Homer, A., Sharp, J., Brader, L., Narumoto, M., Swanson, T.: Cloud Design Patterns: Prescriptive Architecture Guidance for Cloud Applications. Microsoft Patterns & Practices (2014)
43. Casale, G., Chesta, C., Deussen, P., Di Nitto, E., Gouvas, P., Koussouris, S., Stankovski, V., Symeonidis, A., Vlassiou, V., Zafeiropoulos, A., et al.: Current and future challenges of software engineering for services and applications. Procedia Comput. Sci. **97**, 34–42 (2016)
44. Schermann, G., Cito, J., Leitner, P.: All the services large and micro: revisiting industrial practice in services computing. In: Norta, A., Gaaloul, W., Gangadharan, G.R., Dam, H.K. (eds.) ICSOC 2015. LNCS, vol. 9586, pp. 36–47. Springer, Heidelberg (2016). https://doi.org/10.1007/978-3-662-50539-7_4
45. Dragoni, N., Giallorenzo, S., Lafuente, A.L., Mazzara, M., Montesi, F., Mustafin, R., Safina, L.: Microservices: yesterday, today, and tomorrow, arXiv preprint arXiv:1606.04036 (2016)
46. Roberts, M.: Serverless architectures (2016). http://martinfowler.com/articles/serverless.html
47. de Lemos, R., et al.: Software engineering for self-adaptive systems: a second research roadmap. In: de Lemos, R., Giese, H., Müller, H.A., Shaw, M. (eds.) Software Engineering for Self-Adaptive Systems II. LNCS, vol. 7475, pp. 1–32. Springer, Heidelberg (2013). https://doi.org/10.1007/978-3-642-35813-5_1
48. Bass, L.: Software Quality Assurance In Large Scale and Complex Software-intensive Systems, vol. 1. Morgan Kauffmann, San Francisco (2015). Ch. Forewords by Len Bass
49. Tamburri, D.A., Kazman, R., Fahimi, H.: The architect's role in community shepherding. IEEE Softw. **33**, 70–79 (2016)
50. Hendrickson, S., Sturdevant, S., Harter, T., Venkataramani, V., Arpaci-Dusseau, A.C., Arpaci-Dusseau, R.H.: Serverless computation with openlambda. Elastic **60**, 80 (2016)
51. Baresi, L., Garriga, M., De Renzis, A.: Microservices identification through interface analysis. In: De Paoli, F., Schulte, S., Broch Johnsen, E. (eds.) ESOCC 2017. LNCS, vol. 10465, pp. 19–33. Springer, Cham (2017). https://doi.org/10.1007/978-3-319-67262-5_2
52. Baresi, L., Guinea, S., Leva, A., Quattrocchi, G.: A discrete-time feedback controller for containerized cloud applications. In: ACM Sigsoft International Symposium on the Foundations of Software Engineering (FSE). ACM (2016, accepted for publication)
53. Cockroft, A.: Evolution of business logic from monoliths through microservices, to functions (2017). https://goo.gl/H6zKMn

Towards a Reference Dataset
of Microservice-Based Applications

Antonio Brogi, Andrea Canciani, Davide Neri,
Luca Rinaldi, and Jacopo Soldani[✉]

Department of Computer Science, University of Pisa, Pisa, Italy
{luca.rinaldi,soldani}@di.unipi.it

Abstract. The microservice-based architectural style is rising fast in
enterprise IT. Tools and solutions for supporting microservices-based
applications are proliferating. It is however often difficult to qualita-
tively/quantitatively assess and compare such tools and solutions, also
because of the lack of reference datasets of microservice-based applications. The objective of this paper is precisely to set the ground of a first
reference dataset of microservice-based applications.

1 Introduction

The microservice-based architectural style proposes to develop *"a single application as a suite of small services, each running in its own process and communicating with lightweight mechanisms, often an HTTP resource API"* [6]. Each
microservice implements a precise business capability, and it can be deployed and
scaled independently from all other microservices forming an application [9,18].

Microservices are already pervading enterprise IT [3]. Various companies are
already delivering their business services with microservice-based applications,
with Amazon and Netflix being the most prominent examples. As a consequence,
researchers and practitioners are rushing to provide an adequate support to such
companies. This resulted in a rapid proliferation of heterogeneous tools and
solutions (e.g., Docker Compose [4], Apache Mesos [16], Kubernetes [17]), which
aim at offering an enhanced support for developing, deploying, and/or managing
microservice-based applications [3].

It is however often difficult to assess and compare existing solutions, as well
as to show that a newly proposed solution is actually enhancing the support
already provided by its competitors (e.g., by supporting additional functionalities, or by running the same business with better performances). This is also
due to the lack of reference datasets of microservice-based applications. Such
datasets would indeed permit developing a set of repeatable experiments for
evaluating a solution (e.g., an orchestrator of microservice-based applications),
or for comparing it with other existing solutions [11].

The main objective of this paper is to set the ground of μSET, a first reference dataset of microservice-based applications. The μSET dataset will permit

A. Cerone and M. Roveri (Eds.): SEFM 2017 Workshops, LNCS 10729, pp. 219–229, 2018.
https://doi.org/10.1007/978-3-319-74781-1_16

assessing and evaluating a solution offering support for microservice-based applications. It will indeed provide a set of microservice-based applications, each permitting to evaluate a solution qualitatively (viz., by checking whether it supports one or more desired functionalities) and/or quantitatively (viz., by measuring its performances). We also present a first set of microservice-based applications that are already included in μSET.

Beside checking whether a solution supports desired functionalities with desired performances, the applications contained in μSET will be exploitable by practitioners and researchers in two other ways. On the one hand, μSET dataset will permit performing a systematic comparison of existing solutions. The latter will then ease the choice of the most appropriate solution for developing, or managing a microservice-based application. On the other hand, μSET dataset will permit developing a set of repeatable experiments, to show that a newly proposed solution actually enhances the support provided by its competitors.

The rest of the paper is organised as follows. Section 2 presents the design of μSET, as well as the microservice-based applications it already contains. Section 3 presents an example of evaluation based on the applications currently available in μSET. Sections 4 and 5 discuss related work and provide some concluding remarks.

2   The μSET Dataset

We hereby present the design of the μSET dataset of microservice-based applications. The main requirements driving the design and population of μSET are the following:

- All applications in μSET will be publicly available.
- μSET will contain applications easy to understand and manage, as this will simplify setting up repeatable experiments based upon them.
- All applications in μSET will permit evaluating a solution qualitatively (by checking whether it supports a desired functionality) or quantitatively (by measuring the performances of a solution).

To satisfy the first requirement, we implemented μSET as a public GitHub repository[1]. We also started populating the dataset with a first set of microservice-based applications that, much in the spirit of unit testing [13], we crafted "ad-hoc" to test the support of a specific functionality.

More precisely, we selected five functionalities that are crucial for supporting microservice-based applications. Namely, we selected the functionalities to support *communication* between microservices [6], *fault resilience* [10], *horizontal scalability* [6], *replaceability* of a microservice [9], and *extensibility* of a microservice-based application [9].

We then defined five categories of microservice-based applications (viz., *communication support, fault resilience, horizontal scalability, replaceability,* and

---

[1] https://github.com/di-unipi-socc/microset.

extensibility), one for each of the above mentioned functionalities. Each category will contain microservice-based applications aimed at "unit testing" whether/how a solution supports the corresponding functionality. For instance, an application in the *horizontal scalability* category can be used both to (qualitatively) check whether a solution supports horizontal scalability and to (quantitatively) measure the performances of such solution when scaling its microservices (e.g., time and resources needed to scale in/out a microservice).

We then developed one application for each category, each designed to be as simple as possible (but not simpler). We hereafter present such applications, by first explaining their rationale, by describing the applications themselves, and by finally showing an example of how they permit checking whether an orchestrator of microservice-based applications supports the corresponding functionalities.

2.1 Communication Support

Rationale. Microservices need to communicate each other via lightweight mechanisms, often being HTTP resource APIs. Any solution aiming to support microservice-based applications should hence provide functionalities to support communication between microservices.

Description. The `communication-support` application is composed by two microservices, viz., *backend* and *frontend* (Fig. 1). The *backend* microservice offers an HTTP API. The latter exposes just one operation, requiring no input parameters, and returning a JSON object containing a randomly generated number.

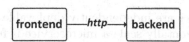

Fig. 1. Microservices in the `communication-support` application.

The microservice *frontend* offers an HTTP endpoint, through which it serves automatically generated HTML pages. Whenever a client connects to *frontend*, the latter invokes the API of *backend*. If *backend* answers to *frontend*, *frontend* returns an HTTP 200 response containing a HTML page rendering the information obtained from *backend*. Otherwise, *frontend* returns an HTTP 500 error.

Example of test. An orchestrator of microservice-based applications supports communication if it can deploy and interconnect *frontend* and *backend*, so that one can afterwards connect to *frontend*, and *frontend* returns an HTTP 200 response. If *frontend* instead returns an HTTP 500 error, this means that it is not able to communicate with *backend*.

222   A. Brogi et al.

2.2   Fault Resilience

Rationale. Microservice-based applications should be designed by taking into account that their microservices may fail. Any solution supporting microservices-based applications should hence manage failures by allowing to restart failed microservices.

Description. `fault-resilience` is composed by a single microservice (*app*), which can be used to check whether a solution is capable to manage a microservice failure (Fig. 2). *app* is designed to fail after a given period of time (10 s, by default).

Fig. 2. Failure behaviour of the microservice *app* in the `fault-resilience` application.

Example of test. An orchestrator of microservice-based applications supports failures if it can automatically restart *app* whenever it fails. This can be tested by checking whether *app* is running and responding right after the failure period is expired.

2.3   Horizontal Scalability

Rationale. Microservices are independently deployable and scalable by definition. Being able to horizontally scale a microservice is fundamental to improve the performances of a microservice-based application.

Description. `horizontal-scalability` is a microservice-based application designed to check whether a solution can deal with the horizontal scaling of a microservice. It is composed by two microservices, *consumer* and *producer*, communicating via HTTP.

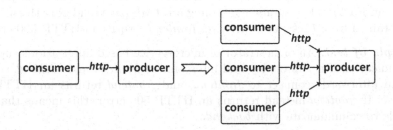

Fig. 3. An example of how to scale the number of microservices in the `horizontal-scalability` application.

The *producer* is a web service generating a finite stream of random numbers, and offering an endpoint to consume the numbers in the stream. The *consumer* is a script iteratively invoking the endpoint offered by the *producer*. Each time a *consumer* invokes such endpoint, the *producer* returns the next number available in the stream, until all numbers have been consumed.

The *producer* also records the time interval needed to consume all numbers and the amount of different *consumer*s that have required at least a number.

Figure 3 shows an example of how to scale the microservices in `horizontal-scalability`. Initially, only one *consumer* and one *producer* are running. The number of *consumer*s is then increased to three, to reduce the time needed to consume the stream.

Example of test. An orchestrator of microservice-based applications supports horizontal scalability if it permits changing the amount of running *consumer*s. This can be tested, for instance, by scaling the *consumer*s as in Fig. 3, and by checking that the *producer* returns 3 as the amount of different *consumer*s that consumed at least a number[2].

2.4   Replaceability

Rationale. Replaceability is the ability to replace a microservice with another microservice offering the same functionality. Solutions that aim to support microservice-based applications should hence permit replacing a microservice independently of the others.

Description. `replaceability` is a microservice-based application that permits checking whether a solution supports the replaceability of a microservice with another. It is composed by two microservices, viz., *frontend* and *backend* (Fig. 4).

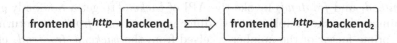

Fig. 4. Two consecutive configurations of `replaceability` application.

The *backend* microservice offers an HTTP API endpoint that returns a randomly generated number each time is called. It is available in two different implementations, namely *backend*₁ and *backend*₂. *backend*₁ returns only even random numbers, while *backend*₂ returns only odd numbers.

The *frontend* microservice serves HTML pages. Whenever a client connects to *frontend*, the latter invokes the API of the backend. If the backend answers to *frontend*, then *frontend* returns an HTTP 200 response containing an HTML page rendering the information obtained from backend. Otherwise, *frontend* returns an HTTP 500 error.

---

[2] The length of the stream can be configured so that all *consumer*s can consume at least one number.

Example of test. An orchestrator of microservice-based applications supports replaceability if, after deploying *frontend* with *backend₁*, it permits replacing *backend₁* with *backend₂* without restarting or reconfiguring the *frontend*. Moreover, when the *backend₁* is deployed, the *frontend* must return even numbers, while with *backend₂* the *frontend* must return odd numbers.

2.5   Extensibility

Rationale. Extensibility is the ability to add and integrate a new microservice in a microservice-based application independently of its other microservices. Solutions offering support for microservice-based applications should hence permit adding a new microservice in a existing application (without requiring to reconfigure the other microservices in such application).

Description. extensibility is a microservice-based application composed by three microservices, viz., *frontend₁*, *frontend₂*, and *backend* (Fig. 5). The *backend* microservice offers an HTTP API, which exposes one operation returning a JSON object containing a randomly generated number.

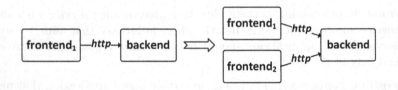

Fig. 5. Two consecutive configurations of the **extensibility** application.

frontend₁ and *frontend₂* invoke the API of *backend* to get a randomly generated number, but they implement two different operations. *frontend₁* returns the largest prime factor of the number received from the *backend*. *frontend₂* checks whether the number received from the *backend* is prime or not. Both *frontend₁* and *frontend₂* render the response in a HTML page.

Example of test. An orchestrator of microservice-based applications supports extensibility if, after deploying *frontend₁* and *backend*, it is possible to add *frontend₂* without touching the other components. Afterwards, both *frontend₁* and *frontend₂* must return an HTTP 200 response (when invoked), as this means that they can communicate with *backend*.

3   μSET at Work

In order to test whether a solution (e.g., an orchestrator of microservice-based applications) supports a functionality, it is first required to select an application from μSET that test such functionality and then build a test on top of it. The test should check whether the solution permits describing the application, running it and finally verifying that application behaves as expected. This testing approach can be iterated over all the functionalities which are considered by the μSET dataset consider, in order to determine the functionalities provided by a solution.

We now show how we used the above approach to check whether Docker Compose[3] supports all functionalities discussed in Sect. 2 (viz., *communication support, fault resilience, horizontal scalability, replaceability,* and *extensibility*)

We specified each microservice-based application of μSET in Docker Compose by means of a compose file (which combines the containers packaging the microservices forming an application). We then developed a set of test scripts, each executing the compose file of an application and checking whether the corresponding functionality is supported[4]. Below we provide some additional details on the test we developed, and we discuss the results we obtained.

Communication support. We created a compose file that specifies the two containers packaging *frontend* and *backend,* and the connection link from *frontend* to *backend*. We created a test script that runs such compose file (to build, start, and interconnect *frontend* and *backend*). It then performs a HTTP request to *frontend,* and it checks whether the latter returns a HTTP 200 response.

Docker Compose passed the test we created. This is because it deploys first the container of *backend* and then the container of *frontend,* and since it creates a bridge network allowing such containers to communicate.

Fault resilience. We created a compose file that defines a container packaging the *app* microservice, and we indicated that such container must be restarted whenever it exits with an error (by setting the option `restart` of the container of *app* to `on-failure`). We created a test script that runs the above mentioned compose file, and which checks whether the container of *app* is restarted by Docker Compose after its first failure (by invoking *app* and verifying that it returns an HTTP 200 response).

Docker Compose passed the above explained test. This is thanks to option `restart: on-failure` of the container of *app,* which instructs Docker Compose to automatically restart such container whenever it fails.

Horizontal scalability. We created a compose file that defines the two containers packaging *producer* and *consumer*. We also created a test script that exploits such compose file to first run one *producer* and one *consumer,* and which then scales the number of *consumer*s up to three (by using the `docker-compose scale` command). The script also verifies that three different *consumer*s actually interacted with the *producer.*

---

[3] Docker Compose is an engine which permits deploying and managing multi-container Docker applications. Docker Compose permits describing the components of an application by using a `compose file` (specification file written in YAML). It is possible to find more information at [14].

[4] All compose files and test scripts are available in the GitHub repository of μSET.

Docker Compose passed also this test. It indeed natively supports the horizontal scalability of the containers forming an application, which can be scaled out/in by executing the `docker-compose scale` command.

Replaceability. We created a compose file that defines the two containers packaging *frontend* and *backend*, by also indicating that the actual implementation of *backend* is $backend_1$. We then created a copy of such compose file, and we modified such copy by substituting the actual implementation of *backend* (from $backend_1$ to $backend_2$). Finally, we created a test script that first executes the initial compose file (hence running *frontend* and $backend_1$), and which checks that the actual implementation of *backend* can be changed from $backend_1$ to $backend_2$ by running the modified compose file.

Docker Compose passed also the above test. It can indeed detect the changes that occurred in the compose file describing a running application. Such changes are then processed by re-building and re-deploying only the containers they affect (without touching the other containers in the application).

Extensibility. We created a compose file describing the containers packaging $frontend_1$ and *backend*. We then created a copy of such compose file, and we modified such copy by adding the container packaging $frontend_2$. We created a test script that first executes the initial compose file (hence deploying $frontend_1$ and *backend*), and it then executes the modified compose file (to add $frontend_2$). Afterwards, the scripts checks whether $frontend_2$ is actually added to the application (without touching the other containers). Docker Compose passed the test we developed. It can indeed detect that new containers are added to the compose file describing a running application, which are processed by building and deploying only such containers.

Summary. We developed five tests, from which Docker Compose turned out to support all functionalities covered by the applications currently in μSET.

4   Related Work

The need for reference datasets allowing to set up repeatable experiments is widely recognised in computer science [8, 12]. For instance, SPEC (*Standard Performance Evaluation Corporation*) is working since 1988 to produce, establish, maintain, and endorse a standardised set of performance benchmarks for computer systems [15]. Concrete examples are the reference applications contained in SPEC CPU2006 and SPEC Cloud_IaaS 2016. The former are designed to provide performance measurements that can be used to compare compute-intensive workloads on different computer systems. The latter instead measure the performances IaaS platforms, by stressing provisioning and runtime aspects of a cloud using I/O and CPU intensive workloads.

Other examples are MiBench [7] and PARSEC [1] which provide reference applications for evaluating embedded systems and shared-memory systems, respectively. DataGov [19] instead offers hundreds of thousands of reference datasets for evaluating approaches for information retrieval/data mining.

A reference dataset allowing to evaluate solutions for supporting microservice-based applications is however, to the best of our knowledge, missing. There exist some demo applications (such as the Sock Shop [20], or those available on eventuate.io [5]), which could be used to compare different solutions based on their performances. Such applications are however designed to demonstrate specific solutions, and this makes them unsuitable to evaluate the actual performances of different and heterogeneous solutions.

The dataset we propose (viz., μSET) can hence provide a first reference for evaluating and comparing solutions offering support for microservice-based applications. μSET is indeed designed to permit evaluating different and heterogeneous solutions, both qualitatively (by allowing to check whether a solution supports a certain functionality) and quantitatively (by providing a reference to measure the performances of a solution).

Finally, there exists orthogonal approaches (e.g., [2]) that permit testing microservice-based applications. μSET, instead, permits testing solutions supporting the analysis/deployment/management of microservice-based applications.

5   Conclusions

Microservices are pervading enterprise IT, with various companies already delivering their business services with microservice-based applications. To provide an adequate support to these companies, researchers and practitioners are working day-by-day on enhancing the current support for developing, deploying and managing microservice-based applications. The result is an increasing number of heterogeneous solutions, offering similar functionalities in a different manner [3] (e.g., Docker Compose [4], Apache Mesos [16], Kubernetes [17]).

It is often difficult to choose the most appropriate solution fitting our needs, namely a solution offering the functionalities needed by our microservice-based applications with the desired performances. It is also difficult to give evidence that a newly proposed solution is actually enhancing the support provided by its competitors (e.g., by supporting additional functionalities, or by running the same business with better performances). This is because it is difficult to develop a set of repeatable experiments that can be used to evaluate a solution, and to compare its evaluation with respect to that of its competitors [11].

The μSET dataset proposed in this paper starts tackling this issue, by proposing an easy-to-use, reference dataset of microservice-based applications. Such dataset will indeed be exploitable to develop repeatable experiments evaluating solutions qualitatively and/or quantitatively. Its aim is indeed to provide microservice-based applications that permit checking whether a solution supports a desired functionality or measuring its performances (e.g., measuring the time and resources needed to add a new microservice to an already running application, to detect when a microservice fails, and to scale a microservice).

The population of μSET is currently ongoing. μSET already includes a first set of microservice-based applications, which are designed to "unit test" whether a solution provides some fundamental functionalities needed by microservice-based applications. It however requires to be extended to include other applications for checking functionality support (both for already selected functionalities and for functionalities yet to be selected), as well as more complex applications (crafted or taken from real deployments) that permit measuring the performances of a solution. We plan to continue extending μSET dataset as part of our immediate future work, and we are willing to involve other practitioners and researchers in this extension process.

Finally, it is worth noting that μSET can be used not only to evaluate a single solution, but also to perform a systematic comparison of existing solutions. Solutions can indeed be evaluated by exploiting the microservice-based applications that will be contained in μSET, and this would provide enough information to compare them based on the functionalities and performances they provide. Such a comparison would then be very useful when looking for the most appropriate solutions for a microservice-based application. We hence plan to exploit μSET to systematically compare existing solutions as part of our future work.

References

1. Bienia, C., Kumar, S., Singh, J.P., Li, K.: The PARSEC benchmark suite: characterization and architectural implications. In: Proceedings of the 17th International Conference on Parallel Architectures and Compilation Techniques, PACT 2008, pp. 72–81. ACM (2008)
2. de Camargo, A., Salvadori, I., Mello, R.D.S., Siqueira, F.: An architecture to automate performance tests on microservices. In: Proceedings of the 18th International Conference on Information Integration and Web-based Applications and Services, iiWAS 2016, pp. 422–429. ACM (2016)
3. Di Francesco, P., Malavolta, I., Lago, P.: Research on architecting microservices: trends, focus, and potential for industrial adoption. In: 2017 IEEE International Conference on Software Architecture (ICSA), pp. 21–30. IEEE Computer Society (2017)
4. Docker, Inc.: Docker-compose. https://docs.docker.com/compose/. Accessed 16 June 2017
5. Eventuate, Inc.: Eventuate example applications. http://eventuate.io/exampleapps.html. Accessed 16 June 2017
6. Fowler, M., Lewis, J.: Microservices. ThoughtWorks. https://martinfowler.com/articles/microservices.html. Accessed 16 June 2017
7. Guthaus, M.R., Ringenberg, J.S., Ernst, D., Austin, T.M., Mudge, T., Brown, R.B.: MiBench: a free, commercially representative embedded benchmark suite. In: Proceedings of the Workload Characterization, 2001. WWC-4. 2001 IEEE International Workshop, WWC 2001, pp. 3–14. IEEE Computer Society (2001)
8. Myers, G.J., Sandler, C.: The Art of Software Testing. Wiley, Hoboken (2004)
9. Newman, S.: Building Microservices. O'Reilly Media Inc., Sebastopol (2015)
10. Nygard, M.: Release It!: Design and Deploy Production-Ready Software. Pragmatic Bookshelf, Raleigh (2007)
11. Pahl, C., Jamshidi, P.: Microservices: a systematic mapping study. In: Proceedings of the 6th International Conference on Cloud Computing and Services Science, CLOSER 2016, vol. 1 and 2, pp. 137–146. SciTePress (2016)

12. Roper, M.: Software Testing. McGraw-Hill Inc., New York (1995)
13. Runeson, P.: A survey of unit testing practices. IEEE Softw. **23**(4), 22–29 (2006)
14. Smith, R.: Docker Orchestration. Packt Publishing, Birmingham (2017)
15. Standard Performance Evaluation Corporation (SPEC): Benchmarks. http://www. spec.org/benchmarks.html. Accessed 16 June 2017
16. The Apache Software Foundation: Mesos. http://mesos.apache.org/. Accessed 16 June 2017
17. The Kubernetes Authors: Kubernetes. https://kubernetes.io/. Accessed 16 June 2017
18. Thönes, J.: Microservices. IEEE Softw. **32**(1), 113–116 (2015)
19. U.S. Government: Data.Gov - The home of the U.S. Governments open data. https://www.data.gov. Accessed 16 June 2017
20. Weaveworks Inc.: Sock shop. https://microservices-demo.github.io. Accessed 16 June 2017

Towards a UML Profile for Domain-Driven Design of Microservice Architectures

Florian Rademacher[1]([⊠]) [iD], Sabine Sachweh[1], and Albert Zündorf[2]

[1] Institute for Digital Transformation of Application and Living Domains,
University of Applied Sciences and Arts Dortmund, Dortmund, Germany
{florian.rademacher,sabine.sachweh}@fh-dortmund.de
[2] Department of Computer Science and Electrical Engineering,
Software Engineering Research Group, University of Kassel, Kassel, Germany
zuendorf@uni-kassel.de

Abstract. Domain-driven Design (DDD) is a model-driven approach to software development that focuses on capturing the application domain, its concepts and relationships in the form of domain models for architecture design. Among others, DDD provides modeling means for decomposing a domain into Bounded Contexts and expressing the relationships between them. With the recent emergence of Microservice Architecture (MSA), DDD again gains broad attention because a Bounded Context naturally maps to a Microservice, which enables the application of DDD for MSA design.

However, DDD is not a formal modeling language. Instead, it leverages informal UML class diagrams to express domain models, which prevents model validation and transformation. In this paper we address this limitation by providing an initial UML profile for Domain-driven MSA Modeling. Together with a survey on the UML constructs used in DDD, the profile denotes a foundation for validating domain models and deriving Microservice code from them.

Keywords: Domain-Driven Design · Microservice architecture
UML profile

1 Introduction

Domain-driven Design (DDD) [3] is an approach to software development that focuses on the application domain, its concepts and their relationships as primary drivers for architecture design. Core principles of DDD comprise (i) capturing relevant domain knowledge in *domain models* that might comprise structural and behavioral aspects; (ii) collaborative modeling of domain experts and software engineers; (iii) fostering experimental design by strictly aligning model and implementation throughout the software development process as well as continuous model refinement; (iv) fostering communication between domain experts and software engineers by jointly defining an explicit *ubiquitous language*, which

© Springer International Publishing AG 2018
A. Cerone and M. Roveri (Eds.): SEFM 2017 Workshops, LNCS 10729, pp. 230–245, 2018.
https://doi.org/10.1007/978-3-319-74781-1_17

consists of relevant domain-specific terms and is used in both, domain models and implementation.

As a set of model-driven practices, techniques and principles for software design, DDD has been defined by Evans in 2004 [3]. With Microservice Architecture (MSA) as an architectural style for distributed, service-based software systems [9], that is gaining broad attention of both practitioners and scientists as of 2014 [13], the relevance of DDD recently increases. This is due to DDD providing various modeling patterns and techniques for the identification of coherent domain concepts and their encapsulation within conceptual boundaries that might serve as foundation for MSA-based service decomposition [9].

Thereby, Evans proposes to express domain models that capture structural domain knowledge in the form of UML class diagrams [3]. He therefore leverages a subset of standard UML elements, which are partially enriched with DDD-specific semantics to define *DDD patterns*. However, the pattern definitions lack a formal, UML-based foundation and sometimes differ in their notations. While the absence of a formal foundation leads to a high degree of freedom concerning syntaxes and semantics of DDD-specific modeling elements [3], it prevents structured model operations like validation [16] and transformation [8]. Hence, further usage of domain models next to being integral parts of stakeholder communication and domain documentation is hampered.

To overcome this limitation, we present an initial, twofold contribution towards a formalization of DDD for *Domain-driven MSA Modeling* (DDMM). First, we provide a survey regarding syntaxes, semantics and frequency of UML elements applied in DDD for capturing domain models. This defines a basic set of modeling constructs to consider when processing domain models for validation or transformation purposes. Second, we define a UML profile for DDMM and discuss its usage to model Microservices and derive interactions between them.

The remainder of the paper is organized as follows. Section 2 gives an overview of DDD and how it is applied for MSA. Section 3 presents the findings of a literature survey regarding syntaxes, semantics and occurrences of UML constructs in DDD domain models. In Sect. 4 we introduce the UML profile for DDMM. Section 5 presents related work and Sect. 6 concludes the paper.

2   Domain-Driven Design

In this section we elaborate on DDD as an approach to abstracting a domain in the form of *structural domain models* that describe structure and relationships of domain concepts [3]. We also describe the *Bounded Context pattern* that is commonly proposed for modeling services in MSA [9].

2.1   Structural Domain Models

In DDD, a *domain model* is a rigorously organized, selective abstraction of conceptual knowledge about a domain or relevant parts of it [3]. Basically, the notation to express domain models is not bound to a certain modeling language. However, Evans proposes to use UML class diagrams to capture *structural domain models*, which leverage UML classes, attributes and methods to model domain concepts, and UML associations, multiplicities and collection specifications to express concept relationships. Figure 1 shows a preliminary structural domain model for a cargo shipping system described in [3].

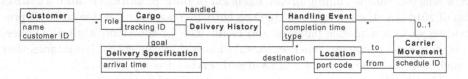

Fig. 1. Preliminary structural domain model for a cargo shipping system [3]

Each class represents a *domain object*, which in DDD is synonymous with "domain concept" [3]. The model contains the core domain objects and their relationships. For example, it shows that a `Cargo` has a `tracking ID` and is associated with a set of `Customers`, each distinguished by its `role`, e.g. "shipper" or "receiver". Assigned to a `Cargo` is a `Delivery History` that tracks cargo-related `Handling Events`, which might involve at most one `Carrier Movement` from a source to a target `Location`. Furthermore, a `Cargo` has a goal, i.e. a `Delivery Specification` with a destination `Location`.

On the basis of certain UML class diagram elements, DDD introduces a variety of patterns to enrich a structural domain model with further semantics for Model-driven Design [3]. These patterns and their definition by means of the UML 2.5 metamodel [12] are described in Table 1.

Figure 2 shows an excerpt of the cargo shipping model with refined associations and extended by a selection of DDD patterns [3].

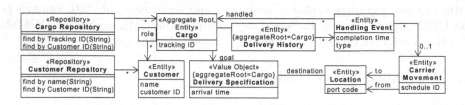

Fig. 2. Excerpt of refined cargo shipping model with additional DDD patterns [3]

All domain objects are annotated with pattern-specific stereotypes to identify them as Entities, Value Objects, Aggregate roots or Repositories [3]. For example, the Entity `Cargo` is also a root for the Aggregates `Delivery Specification` and `Delivery History`, which may only be accessed via the root object. The `Cargo Repository` models the retrieval of `Cargoes` by `tracking ID` and `customer ID`. While most domain objects are Entities, `Delivery Specification` is a Value Object to communicate that two `Cargoes` might share

Table 1. DDD patterns and their UML 2.5 metamodel [12] equivalents. Note: "Annotated" stands for any mechanism that allows to assign additional meaning to UML modeling elements, e.g. stereotypes or comments.

Pattern	UML metamodel equivalent	Description
Aggregate	Associated Classes with annotated root Class	Cluster of associated Entities and Value Objects. An Aggregate is treated as a whole when being accessed by referencing its root Entity
Closure of Operations	Annotated Operation	A Closure's return type is of the same type as its arguments and provides an interface without additional domain object dependencies
Entity	Annotated Class	An instance of the domain object is distinguished from other instances by its identity. Identity determination is domain-specific
Module	Annotated Package	Encapsulation mechanism whose primary goal is to reduce cognitive overload in domain models by partitioning cohesive sets of domain objects
Repository	Annotated Class with outgoing Associations to other Classes	Models access to persistent domain object instances via operations that perform instance selection based on given criteria
Service	Annotated Class containing only Operations	Services encapsulate processes or transformations that are not in the responsibility of Entities or Value Objects
Side-effect-free Function	Annotated Operation	Expresses that a domain object's Operation does not have any side effects on a system's state
Specification	Annotated Class depending on specified Class	Used to determine if a domain object instance fulfills a specification. Contains a set of Boolean Operations to perform specification checks
Value Object	Annotated Class	Typically immutable object without domain-specific identity. Might act as value container

the same `Delivery Specification`, but with most likely differing `Delivery Histories`. Otherwise the `Cargoes` would exhibit the same identity [3].

2.2 Domain-Driven Design for Microservice Architecture

In contrast to Service-oriented Architecture (SOA), MSA imposes explicit requirements on service granularity [14]. Each Microservice should realize exactly one capability of the software system that is clearly distinct from others. The goal of business-related service decomposition in MSA is to cluster related domain objects and functionalities in isolated *functional Microservices*.

For modeling functional Microservices and domain objects exchanged between these, i.e. *shared domain objects*, DDD's *Bounded Context* pattern is predestined [9] and has become a common means for determining and expressing MSA-based service granularity prior to service decomposition [2,4,5].

Next to Modules (cf. Table 1), Bounded Contexts are another encapsulation mechanism of DDD. While Modules solely structure domain objects in different namespaces, Bounded Contexts define *scopes* for enclosed domain objects, i.e. boundaries for object validity and applicability [3].

The boundaries of a Bounded Context typically impact team, code and application organization [3]. Only the team responsible for a context may change its internal structure. It is further responsible for context implementation and interface provisioning on the basis of shared domain object models. As these responsibilities correspond to those of a Microservice [9], a Bounded Context provides the foundation for the domain-specific implementation of a Microservice. Figure 3 shows a version of the cargo shipping model that has been decomposed into Bounded Contexts depicted as UML packages.

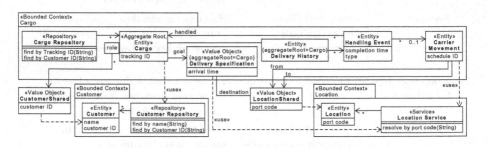

Fig. 3. Cargo shipping model decomposed into several Bounded Contexts

Relationships between the Bounded Contexts are expressed as shared Value Objects, i.e. instances of `CustomerShared` and `LocationShared` act as containers for exchanging values between contexts (cf. Table 1). Each shared object depends on the Entity it represents, i.e. `Customer` and `Location`. For the retrieval of shared object instances, `Cargo` uses the existing `Customer Repository`, while instances of `LocationShared` can be requested from the

Location context via the introduced Location Service (cf. Table 1). It dynamically resolves the port code from a given argument, i.e. Locations are not stored in a Repository.

3 Survey on UML Elements in Domain-Driven Design

In the following, we present an overview and characterization regarding syntaxes, semantics and frequency of UML elements used by DDD to model structural domain models. We identified the elements by surveying each of the 92 UML class diagrams in [3] representing real-world structural domain models. Thereby, we left out the 29 diagrams showing domain object interactions as they are (i) modeled with various notations differing in the degree of formality, e.g. object interaction, UML sequence and domain-specific diagrams; (ii) used to exemplify interactions between few selected objects rather than in a comprehensive architectural design; (iii) not applicable for identifying functional Microservices and their structural relationships (cf. Subsect. 2.2).

Together with the DDD patterns described in Sect. 2, the UML elements identified in our survey define a basic set of modeling constructs to be considered in UML-based DDMM, e.g. when validating domain models or deriving code.

Table 2 shows the results of our survey. It lists each UML element used in the domain models in [3] and classifies them on the basis of six categories representing basic UML concepts, i.e. "Associations", "Attributes", "Classes", "Constraints", "Methods" and "Multiplicities". We further state the occurrence count per element, that is the number of domain models comprising it at least once, as well as its representation with UML 2.5 metaclasses [12] to be considered in UML-based DDMM. Due to space limitations, we do not present survey results for modeling constructs used in DDD domain models that are not conform to UML 2.5 and hence might not be validly expressed leveraging its metamodel, e.g. abstract attributes or named extensions between classes. As only four out of 92 domain models (4.34%) comprise such elements, we view them as negligible.

Next, we describe category-specific characteristics of conform UML elements.

3.1 Classes

In structural domain models, DDD expresses domain objects as named Classes. Hence, every domain model contains at least one Class, which makes this element the predominant UML construct in DDD. Thereby, a Class might be modeled as being abstract to specify Methods (cf. Subsect. 3.5) that have to be realized by Sub-classes and enable polymorphism in domain model implementations. A special case of abstract classes are generalized Specifications (cf. Table 1) where different instances of a domain object need to satisfy different specifications, e.g. an Invoice for which two Specifications DelinquentInvoiceSpec and BigInvoiceSpec inheriting from a general InvoiceSpec are modeled, that specify a date or a threshold amount, respectively [3].

A DDD Class corresponds to the UML metaclass Classifier. For abstract Classes, Classifier.isAbstract is set to true.

Table 2. Results of surveying the 92 UML class diagrams in [3] for UML elements used in structural domain models. Table ordering is based on elements' occurrence count.

Element	Category	Occurrence Count
Class	Classes	92 (100%)

UML Metamodel Representation: `Classifier` with `name`. `Classifier.isAbstract` may be set to `true`.

Attribute	Attributes	72 (78.26%)

`Property` with `name`, `type` or both. `Property.isDerived` may be set to `true`. A `MultiplicityElement` may be used to specify that the `Property` value is optional.

Multiplicity	Multiplicities	67 (72.82%)

`MultiplicityElement` with `ValueSpecification` for `lowerValue` and `upperValue`.

Non-navigable Association	Associations	58 (63.04%)

`Association` with optional `name` and without specified navigability. `ownedEnd` comprises two possibly named `Properties`, of which one can have a `qualifier`. To add a collection specification, `ValueSpecification.isOrdered` of an assigned Multiplicity may be `true`.

Method	Methods	49 (53.26%)

`Operation` with `name` that may have `isAbstract` set to `true`. `ownedParameter` may contain `Parameters` with `name`, `type` or both and `direction` typically set to `in`. One `Parameter` may have it's `direction` set to `return`.

Unidirectional Navigable Association	Associations	36 (39.13%)

`Association` with optional `name` and one `Property` in `navigableOwnedEnd`. `ownedEnd` comprises two possibly named `Properties` with a possible `qualifier`. To specify a collection, `ValueSpecification.isOrdered` of an assigned Multiplicity may be `true`.

Non-navigable Aggregation	Associations	28 (30.43%)

`Association` without `name`. `ownedEnd` comprises two possibly named `Properties` with one having `aggregation` set to `shared` and a possible `qualifier`. To specify a collection, `ValueSpecification.isOrdered` of an assigned Multiplicity may be `true`.

"extends" Relationship (Inheritance)	Associations	23 (25%)

`Generalization` relationship between two `Classifiers` (single inheritance). The specific `Classifier` holds a `Generalization` with `general` pointing to the general `Classifier`.

Informal Constraint	Constraints	13 (14.13%)

Informal domain-specific constraints like "Itinerary must satisfy specification" may be specified as `names` of `Associations` or `Dependencies` where `client` constrains `supplier`.

Unidirectional Navigable Aggregation	Associations	11 (11.95%)

`Association` without `name`. `ownedEnd` comprises two possibly named `Properties`, with one being in `navigableOwnedEnd`, having `aggregation` set to `shared` and an optional `qualifier`. May have a collection specification like Non-navigable Aggregation.

Formal Constraint	Constraints	6 (6.52%)

Formal domain-specific constraints like "Bucket.contents <= Bucket.capacity" may be specified as (i) `body` of `Comment` with `annotatedElement` being `Classifier` or `Property`; (ii) `name` of `Dependency` whose `supplier` is an `Association` and `client` is a `Classifier`.

Semi-formal Constraint	Constraints	3 (3.26%)

Semi-formal domain-specific constraints like "sum of item <= approved limit" are specified as `names` of Unidirectional Navigable Associations or Aggregations.

Class Dependency	Associations	2 (2.17%)

`Dependency` without `name` and both `supplier` and `client` being `Classifiers`.

3.2 Associations

The elements in this category are applied in 87 of the 92 domain models (94.56%), which makes Associations the second most occurring UML construct in DDD. Associations are used to specify relationships between exactly two domain objects. A special form of Associations are Aggregations in the sense of UML *shared aggregations* [12], whose semantics depend on application area or modeler. Aggregations group together a set of assigned domain object instances.

Most Associations lack an explicit specification of navigability, which otherwise is always unidirectional. An Association end may exhibit an "ordered" collection specification and be qualifying to partition a set of assigned instances, e.g. Customers by their role (cf. Fig. 1).

Next to Associations, the category comprises Inheritance relationships and Dependencies. Both establish Associations between Classes and are applied corresponding to the UML specification of Generalization and Dependency.

3.3 Attributes

Attributes represent *structural features* of domain objects. For the majority of Attributes, no type is specified, which increases the level of modeling flexibility but complicates domain model processing. For example, when generating code from domain models, e.g. in an object-oriented language like Java, untyped Attributes might be assigned a generic type like Java's Object. However, this prevents type-safety and relies on the semantics of an Attribute being sufficiently communicated by its name. A facing issue is DDD possibly specifying unnamed Attributes that only have a type. The meaning of an Attribute may then remain unclear, especially when its type is not domain-specific, e.g. Double instead of MoneyAmount [3].

Attributes may be modeled as derived or optional. Thereby, a derivation specification is missing and optional Attributes' names are terminated by "(opt)".

Attributes correspond to the UML metaclass Property. For derived Attributes, Property.isDerived is set to true. Optional Attributes may be specified by assigning a MultiplicityElement to the Property with a lowerValue of 0 and an upperValue of 1 or *.

3.4 Multiplicities

All occurrences of Multiplicity specifications in domain models conform to UML. Typically, an Association or Attribute is provided with Multiplicities. Multiplicity specifications correspond to UML's metaclass MultiplicityElement, whose properties lowerValue and upperValue reference instances of ValueSpecifications that represent an Integer and an UnlimitedNatural, respectively.

3.5   Methods

DDD leverages Methods to model the interfaces of domain objects' *behavioral features*. Thus, concrete behavior specifications are omitted and Methods are only represented by their type signatures. Methods correspond to UML's meta-class `Operation`, possibly comprising a set of `Parameters`. Parameter names and types are mutually optional, which is conform to UML but raises the same issues as for unnamed and untyped Attributes (cf. Subsect. 3.3). `Parameters` are modeled as incoming or returning, i.e. with `direction` set to `in` or `return`.

3.6   Constraints

We classify Constraints used by DDD depending on their degree of formality.

Informal Constraints are formulated in natural language and modeled as names of Associations or Dependencies. In the latter case, the dependent domain object always constrains the independent object, e.g. a `Route Specification` depends on an `Itinerary` stating that it must satisfy the Specification (cf. [3] and Table 1). This semantically makes the dependency bidirectional, because logically `Itinerary` depends on `Route Specification`, which it otherwise could not satisfy. This can be resolved in that the direction of the modeled Dependency is reversed, i.e. the specified object depends on the Specification (cf. Sect. 4).

Semi-formal Constraints are stated in natural language mixed with formal notations. Like Informal Constraints, they are modeled as names of Associations.

Formal Constraints leverage a formal notation for their constraint expression. In DDD, they are modeled in the form of Class or Attribute Comments, or, in one occurrence, as name of a Dependency in which a domain object depends on the Association between two other domain objects to express that an `Overbooking Policy` (the dependent object) ensures that the sum of `Cargo` sizes does not exceed a `Voyage's` capacity by more than 10% [3].

Alternatively, all Constraint types could be modeled as UML `Constraints`. This would make their existence more explicit and allow to formally specify the Constraint's type. For example, to identify Informal and Semi-formal Constraints, an instance of `OpaqueExpression` with `language` set to "Natural language" could be assigned to `Constraint.specification`. Formal Constraints could analogously be expressed in the form of automatically evaluable expressions, e.g. by leveraging the Object Constraint Language (OCL) [11].

4   A UML Profile for Domain-Driven Microservice Architecture Design

This section presents an initial UML profile, which enables the expression of structural domain models as UML class diagrams by providing stereotypes and constraints for DDD patterns (cf. Sect. 2).

We decided to apply UML's profile mechanism [12] as *metamodeling technique* [15] for DDMM because (i) in [3], when introducing DDD, Evans expresses structural domain models as UML class diagrams because he perceived them to be well understandable by domain experts; (ii) it provides an approach for defining graphical modeling languages by extending UML's mature metamodel [17] and use complementary specifications, e.g. OCL [11] for profile-specific constraint specification (cf. Subsect. 4.2); (iii) UML is a common modeling language, even for the design of Microservice architectures [1]; (iv) it enables the usage of existing UML toolchains suitable for domain experts or software engineers for DDMM.

A UML profile comprises *extensions* of UML metaclasses like Class or Property in the form of *stereotypes* [12]. Instances of extended metaclasses might then be semantically enriched with profile-specific stereotypes. A UML profile might also define formal constraints that enable automatic validation of profile-based models, e.g. to verify that stereotypes have been used as intended.

Figure 4 shows all stereotypes of our UML profile for DDMM. The relationship between a stereotype and the metaclasses it extends is depicted as an arrow with filled arrowhead pointing from stereotype to metaclass [12].

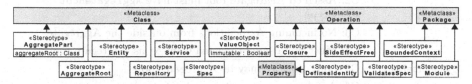

Fig. 4. Stereotypes of the DDMM UML profile as extensions of UML metaclasses

The profile provides stereotypes for all DDD patterns presented in Sect. 2, i.e. the ones listed in Table 1 as well as Bounded Contexts. It therefore extends the UML metaclasses Class, Operation, Package and Property. In the following, we discuss characteristics of the profile concerning differences between pattern definitions in DDD and the profile, constraints, mapping between profile-based models and MSA, and the profile's implementation.

4.1 Differences Between Pattern Definitions in Domain-Driven Design and UML Profile

While most of the profile's stereotypes correspond to their textual definition in [3], few of them were accompanied by additional stereotypes to formally enable their DDD-conform application. For example, the DefinesIdentity stereotype was added to specify which Attributes or Method of an Entity provide identity.

Moreover, the definition of an Aggregate involves the combined application of the AggregateRoot and AggregatePart stereotypes. The latter is necessary because in [3] the boundaries of an Aggregate are sketched informally by freehand drawings that enclose the Aggregate and its parts. When leveraging the profile for DDMM, the root of an Aggregate is annotated with AggregateRoot. Aggregate objects are then assigned to the root by means of the AggregatePart stereotype and specifying the Aggregate's root in the aggregateRoot property.

Another difference between its definition in DDD and in the profile exists for the Specification pattern. First, due to a name conflict with the UML metamodel [12], the profile's stereotype for Specifications is abbreviated as Spec. Second, all predicate-like validation Methods of a Specification [3] need to exhibit the stereotype ValidatesSpec.

4.2   Profile Constraints

To ensure consistency between profile application and DDD, we added constraints to the profile, i.e. restrictions that need to be satisfied by a profile-based structural domain model to be considered valid. Table 3 describes them in natural language.

Table 3. Stereotype constraints of the profile following DDD pattern definitions in [3]

Stereotype	Constraints based on UML metamodel
AggregatePart	C1: Only Entities and Value Objects may be Aggregate parts
	C2: Assigned Aggregate root must have AggregateRoot stereotype
	C3: No incoming Associations from outside the Aggregate
	C4: Must be in same Bounded Context as Aggregate root
AggregateRoot	C5: Only Entities may be Aggregate roots
	C6: Aggregate must contain at least one part
Entity	C7: One Operation or at least one Property defines the identity
Repository	C8: Class has no other stereotypes
	C9: Class contains only Operations and at least one
	C10: Outgoing Associations must point to Entities or Value Objects
Service	C11: Class has no other stereotypes
	C12: Class contains only Operations and at least one
Spec	C13: Class has no other stereotypes
	C14: Class contains at least one validation Operation
	C15: At least one domain object is specified
	C16: Validation Operation has Parameter typed as specified object
Closure	C17: Must not be specification validation or identity Operation
	C18: Return Parameter type must conform input Parameter type
DefinesIdentity	C19: Must not be specification validation Operation
	C20: May only be applied within Entities
SideEffectFree	C21: Operation must have a return Parameter
ValidatesSpec	C22: Must have Boolean-typed return Parameter
	C23: May only be applied within Specifications
BoundedContext	C24: Must not have Module stereotype
	C25: Must not be nested, i.e. part of another Package

According to [12], all constraints have been formalized by expressing them in OCL [11]. However, due to lack of space, we only present the OCL code for constraints C4 and C25 in Listings 1 and 2. The OCL expressions for the remaining constraints are part of the profile's implementation (cf. Subsect. 4.4).

```
let partPackage = self.base_Class.package in
let root = self.base_Class
    .extension_AggregatePart.aggregateRoot in
partPackage <> null and
root <> null and
partPackage.extension_BoundedContext <> null and
partPackage = root.package
```

Listing 1. OCL code to ensure Aggregate parts being in same context as root (C4)

```
let nestingPkg = self.base_Package.nestingPackage in
let pkgStereotypes = nestingPkg.getAppliedStereotypes() in
nestingPkg = null or
pkgStereotypes->isEmpty() and
nestingPkg.nestingPackage = null
```

Listing 2. OCL constraint preventing nested Bounded Contexts (C25)

4.3 Mapping of Profile-Based Structural Domain Models to Microservice Architecture

In the following, we present initial ideas on how to map structural domain models applying the profile to conceptual elements of MSA for DDMM. We thereby focus on coherences between modeled Bounded Contexts and Microservices [2, 4,5] for the purpose of transforming profile-conform domain models into code. While [3] describes the implementation of the DDD patterns listed in Table 1, a possibly automatic derivation of Microservice code from structural domain models remains an open question.

An important aspect of mapping a Bounded Context and its encapsulated domain objects to a Microservice implementation is the determination of the service interfaces on the basis of context relationships. For example, in Fig. 3 the Customer Bounded Context shares a reduced form of its Customer Entity, which is modeled as a shared Value Object named CustomerShared that depends on the Customer Entity and is outside the context. As the shared object is referenced from the Cargo context, a Microservice for the Customer context needs to provide an interface that exposes Customers as instances of CustomerShared.

Moreover, in the domain model in Fig. 3, the signatures of interface operations as well as service provider and requester may be identified on the basis of usage dependencies between Bounded Contexts. For example, Carrier Movement from the Cargo context uses the Location Service from the Location context, which has access to a set of Location Entities, to retrieve shared model instances of these. Thus, a service for the Location context needs to provide an interface to a Cargo service that adapts the signature of the Location Service.

While the described mappings of Bounded Context relationships to Microservice interfaces are intuitive, several questions arise when taking the potential informality of structural domain models in DDD into account. First, besides Bounded Context relationships in the form of Associations between fragmented, probably shared domain objects, none of the surveyed domain models comprises constructs that specify technical characteristics of context interfaces for subsequent service implementation (cf. Sect. 3). Among these are the assignment of protocols and message formats to prospective interface operations, as well as an approach for stating the type of action performed by an operation, e.g. read or update. Additionally, when modeling service calls as ≪use≫-Dependencies in which the supplier has more than one Operation that returns the same shared model type, it cannot be unambiguously determined, which of the Operations the client invokes for shared model instance retrieval, e.g. for the `Cargo` object in Fig. 3 `find by name` or `find by Customer ID` from `Customer Repository`.

Another open question concerns the handling of Associations between context-internal domain objects and shared models. For example, in Fig. 3 `Carrier Movement` is associated with `LocationShared`. However, as `Carrier Movement` is an Entity and probably gets persisted when a `Cargo` Microservice proceeds [3], an approach is needed for keeping `LocationShared` (and hence `Location`) and `Carrier Movement` instances persistently associated. This includes retrieval of shared model instances when `Carrier Movement` is reinstantiated, with considering that the `Location` might since have been deleted by a `Location` service.

Furthermore, DDD lacks a construct for specifying how a domain object is transformed into a shared model representation, e.g. in Fig. 3 `CustomerShared` does not comprise the `Customer`'s name. As an initial approach, a code generator for the UML profile could yield stubs for operations that transform domain object instances into their shared representations. However, then the consistency between model and code needs to be ensured for future model refinements.

A last aspect stems from DDD being a modeling technique focused on expressing core domain parts rather than achieving model completeness. In case two shared models of the same domain object are modeled, it cannot be unambiguously determined which shared representation a derived service interface returns when the retrieval operations of the underlying provider objects, e.g. Repositories or Services, do not specify a return type.

4.4   Implementation

We have implemented an initial version of the UML profile that comprises all stereotypes and constraints presented in Fig. 4 and Subsect. 4.2 on the basis of Eclipse and the Papyrus modeling environment[1]. The current version can be found on GitHub[2]. Figure 5 shows the `Cargo` context from Fig. 3 and its relationship to `LocationShared` modeled with Papyrus and applying the profile.

---

[1] https://www.eclipse.org/papyrus.
[2] https://github.com/SeelabFhdo/ddmm-uml-profile.

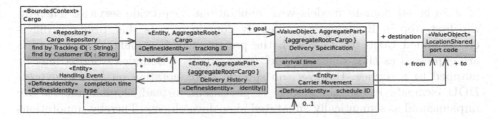

Fig. 5. Excerpt of the `Cargo` context modeled with Eclipse Papyrus and the profile

5 Related Work

We discuss work related to employing UML class diagrams for DDD as well as the design of service-based software systems leveraging UML profiles and DDD.

In [7], a DDD-based approach is presented that leverages *meta-attributes* (MAs) as annotation mechanism for UML class diagrams representing structural domain models with the goal to enable capturing domain-specific requirements. MAs reflect domain-specific abstractions that may be directly mapped to code by using built-in extension mechanisms of the programming language, e.g. Java annotations. They are modeled as classes with attributes, whose values correlate to property values of code annotations, and are associated with domain model elements. This approach differs from the application of our UML profile. First, MAs instead of stereotypes are used to annotate domain models. While this is UML-conform, extending domain models with additional MA classes enlarges their structure and may complicate understanding. This effect is mitigated when using a UML profile as its application might be flexibly hidden from a UML diagram [12]. Second, MAs do not enable constrained expression of DDD patterns (cf. Table 1). Instead, MAs map to UML metaclasses like `Classifier`. Third, to foster semantic understanding of domain experts, MAs partially capture information being already part of the model, e.g. the `name` Property of a `DAttr` MA specifies the name of a modeled domain object Attribute. Our approach assumes that domain experts are already able to read basic UML class diagrams. Fourth, existing UML tools may not semantically differentiate between MAs and domain objects as both are UML classes without specific stereotypes. This hampers automatic validation of annotated structural domain models.

SoaML [10] is a UML profile and metamodel from the OMG for model-driven engineering of service-based systems. It defines modeling elements to describe, e.g., services, interfaces and data exchange, and addresses SOA, which characteristically differs from MSA [14]. However, SoaML provides an extensive set of constructs for modeling service interfaces and interactions our profile might draw on (cf. Subsect. 4.3). Thereby, it would be crucial to balance the technical needs of MSA architects and developers with the profile's applicability for domain experts, which is central to DDD but not one of SoaML's primary goals.

In [6] the Romulus approach for the development of service-based software systems is presented. It integrates a metaframework that enables the enrichment of Java-based domain models with annotations to provide services. Thereby, the first step in Romulus is to identify domain objects that reside in different Bounded Contexts. Like with the presented UML profile, domain models are expressed as class diagrams and, conceptually, a Bounded Context may be mapped to a service. However, no specific UML notation on how to express DDD elements in domain models is presented. Instead, domain models are implemented as semantically annotated plain Java objects. Thereby, annotations do not express DDD concepts but complement a domain model with technical aspects like view representation and validation. MSA is not explicitly covered.

6   Conclusion and Future Work

In this paper we introduced an initial UML profile that aims at enabling the modeling of Microservice systems by leveraging Domain-driven Design [3]. Therefore, we first presented DDD and its patterns, with Bounded Context being central for modeling Microservice candidates (cf. Sect. 2). In Sect. 3, DDD was characterized by means of a literature survey, which comprised each of the 92 structural domain models in [3]. It identified syntaxes, semantics and occurrences of UML class diagram constructs used to capture domain models. Together with the DDD patterns, these UML elements define an initial set of modeling elements, which need to be considered in UML-based DDMM, e.g. for model validation or transformation purposes. In Sect. 4 we presented a UML profile for DDMM, which integrates constrained stereotypes for all mentioned DDD patterns. We also discussed initial thoughts on how to map profile-based domain models to Microservices with considering the findings of our survey (cf. Subsect. 4.3).

In future works we plan to implement a code generator for producing MSA code from profile-based domain models. We therefore focus on transforming Bounded Contexts into services with regard to deriving service interfaces from associations between domain objects of different contexts. With the code generator, we plan to evaluate the profile's applicability for both software engineers and domain experts, as well as the generators efficiency.

References

1. Alshuqayran, N., Ali, N., Evans, R.: A systematic mapping study in microservice architecture. In: Proceedings of the 9th International Conference on Service-Oriented Computing and Applications (SOCA), pp. 44–51. IEEE (2016)
2. Balalaie, A., Heydarnoori, A., Jamshidi, P.: Microservices architecture enables DevOps: migration to a cloud-native architecture. IEEE Softw. **33**(3), 42–52 (2016)
3. Evans, E.: Domain-Driven Design. Addison-Wesley, Boston (2004)
4. Gysel, M., Kölbener, L., Giersche, W., Zimmermann, O.: Service cutter: a systematic approach to service decomposition. In: Aiello, M., Johnsen, E.B., Dustdar, S., Georgievski, I. (eds.) ESOCC 2016. LNCS, vol. 9846, pp. 185–200. Springer, Cham (2016). https://doi.org/10.1007/978-3-319-44482-6_12

5. Hassan, S., Ali, N., Bahsoon, R.: Microservice ambients: an architectural meta-modelling approach for microservice granularity. In: Proceedings of the International Conference on Software Architecture (ICSA), pp. 1–10. IEEE (2017)
6. Iglesias, C.A., Fernández-Villamor, J.I., del Pozo, D., Garulli, L., García, B.: Combining domain-driven design and mashups for service development. In: Iglesias, C.A., Fernández-Villamor, J.I., del Pozo, D., Garulli, L., García, B. (eds.) Service Engineering, pp. 171–200. Springer, Vienna (2011). https://doi.org/10.1007/978-3-7091-0415-6_7
7. Le, D.M., Dang, D.H., Nguyen, V.H.: Domain-driven design using meta-attributes: a DSL-based approach. In: 8th International Conference on Knowledge and Systems Engineering (KSE), pp. 67–72. IEEE (2016)
8. Mens, T., Van Gorp, P.: A taxonomy of model transformation. Electron. Notes Theor. Comput. Sci. **152**, 125–142 (2006)
9. Newman, S.: Building Microservices. O'Reilly Media, Sebastopol (2015)
10. Object Management Group: Service oriented architecture modeling language (SoaML) specification version 1.0.1 (formal/2012-05-10) (2012)
11. Object Management Group: Object constraint language (OCL) version 2.4 (formal/2014-02-03) (2014)
12. Object Management Group: OMG unified modeling language (OMG UML) version 2.5 (formal/2015-03-01) (2015)
13. Pahl, C., Jamshidi, P.: Microservices: a systematic mapping study. In: Proceedings of the 6th International Conference on Cloud Computing and Services Science (CLOSER), pp. 137–146 (2016)
14. Rademacher, F., Sachweh, S., Zündorf, A.: Differences between model-driven development of service-oriented and microservice architecture. In: International Conference on Software Architecture Workshops (ICSAW), pp. 38–45 (2017)
15. Da Silva, A.R.: Model-driven engineering: a survey supported by the unified conceptual model. Comput. Lang. Syst. Struct. **43**, 139–155 (2015)
16. Seidewitz, E.: What models mean. IEEE Softw. **20**(5), 26–32 (2003)
17. Selic, B.: A systematic approach to domain-specific language design using UML. In: Proceedings of the 10th International Symposium on Object and Component-Oriented Real-Time Distributed Computing (ISORC), pp. 2–9. IEEE (2007)

A Framework for Modelling Variable Microservices as Software Product Lines

Moh. Afifun Naily[1](✉), Maya Retno Ayu Setyautami[1], Radu Muschevici[2], and Ade Azurat[1]

[1] Faculty of Computer Science, Universitas Indonesia, Depok, Indonesia
{afifunnaily,mayaretno,ade}@cs.ui.ac.id
[2] Department of Computer Science, Technische Universität Darmstadt, Darmstadt, Germany
radu.muschevici@cs.tu-darmstadt.de

Abstract. Microservices architecture is a software development style that divides software into several small, independently deployable services. Every service can be invoked by standard protocols such as HTTP, so it can be used on a variety of platforms (e.g. mobile, web, desktop). The diversity of users of microservices-based software causes an increased variation in software requirements. In order to accommodate this variability, we propose a framework for microservices-based software based on the Software Product Line Engineering (SPLE) approach. We call this framework *ABS Microservices Framework*, as it relies on the Abstract Behavioral Specification (ABS) language development platform that readily supports SPLE. The framework created in this research has shown more flexibility to accommodate software variability than other microservices frameworks. Hence, the ABS Microservices Framework can support the software industry to distribute variable software of high quality and reliability.

Keywords: Microservices · Framework
Software Product Line Engineering · Abstract Behavioral Specification

1 Introduction

Microservices are an emerging architectural style of software development. This style changes the development paradigm to creating an application as a set of (small) services instead of a single unit [4]. Each unit of system functionality is built as an independent service that can be accessed by other multi-platform applications. In this architectural style, an application could even be written using different programming languages for each service, while the data representation will be standardized as per Representational State Transfer (REST) and encoded in the JSON format.

As software evolves over its lifetime, requirement changes are all but inevitable. In microservices architecture, the impact of such changes – the effort

© Springer International Publishing AG 2018
A. Cerone and M. Roveri (Eds.): SEFM 2017 Workshops, LNCS 10729, pp. 246–261, 2018.
https://doi.org/10.1007/978-3-319-74781-1_18

to adapt the system to the new requirements – can be mitigated, as each service is modular. Of course, if a service is implemented with the help of several modules, all these might be subject to implementation changes. Requirement changes could also directly affect a whole range of services and necessitate complex implementation changes as a consequence. Thus, we argue that a more structured mechanism to manage requirement changes in microservices architecture is required.

The Software Product Line Engineering (SPLE) paradigm allows the development of multiple software products in a single development cycle by defining commonalities and differences between products [11]. To help do this systematically, SPLE uses *features* and expresses products as compositions of features. Delta Oriented Programming (DOP) [14] is a software design methodology aligned with the SPLE paradigm, where the features are implemented using *delta modules* (deltas). Deltas define the modification of a *core* module, which describes the system commonality. The Abstract Behavioral Specification (ABS) language [7] is an executable modeling and programming language that supports SPLE by implementing the DOP approach.

In this paper, we propose a new framework to build microservices-based software with the Software Product Line Engineering approach. We aim to minimize the effort in accommodating requirement changes by using the rigorous approach to variability management provided by SPLE. By using this approach, our framework offers *flexibility* to accommodate changes combined with the confidence that changes are always applied consistently, as specified by the variability model.

The paper is structured as follows: Sect. 2 provides background information on microservice architecture, software product line engineering, and the Abstract Behavioral Specification language; Sect. 3 describes the design of the framework; Sect. 4 explains how the framework works and details its implementation. We conduct analysis by comparing our framework with other microservice framework (Spring Boot) in Sect. 5. Section 6 discusses related work. Conclusions and some possible future work are presented in Sect. 7.

2   Background

2.1   Microservices Architecture

The microservices architecture was first discussed in 2011 at a workshop on software architecture in Venice, Italy [4]. The following year at the same event, a set of microservices terminology was defined. This was followed by a presentation by James Lewis on "Micro Services - Java, the Unix Way" at 33rd Degree in Krakow in 2013. In recent years microservices architecture has gradually become more popular, which is apparent from the number of forums and special conferences on this topic.

Being relatively new, there is no standard definition of microservices architecture. Martin Fowler defines microservices architecture as an approach for developing single applications into small services (microservice), where each service runs independently in different processes and can be called through simple communication mechanisms, such as the HTTP protocol [4]. According to microservices.io, microservice architecture is divided in four components [12]:

1. Presentation components, that is responsible for handling HTTP requests and responding with either HTML or JSON/XML (for web services APIs),
2. Business logic, that consist of application functionalities,
3. Database access logic, that is responsible to access persistent data,
4. Application integration logic, that is responsible for exchanging messages with other systems.

2.2 Software Product Line Engineering

Pohl et al. [11] defines Software Product Line Engineering (SPLE) as a paradigm for developing software applications using platform and mass customization. In SPLE context, platform is a common structure of software used to produce derived products efficiently. Mass customization is achieved through variability management, that is, the precise modelling of similarities and differences between applications, which enables the automatic derivation of customized software products.

The main concept of SPLE is to capture commonality and variability into software features [10]. Commonality is a property or features that can be shared and used by all applications (software) in a product line. Variability is the difference of features used by all or several applications in a product line.

The development process of SPLE is divided into two processes, domain engineering and the application engineering [11]. Domain engineering is a process to define or model commonality and variability in the product line, while application engineering is the process of building concrete products based on the model constructed in the domain engineering process.

2.3 Abstract Behavioral Specification (ABS)

ABS is a formal modeling language, executable, object oriented, concurrent and can model software with a high level of variability, such as software product lines [6]. ABS was developed by a European consortium since 2008 in a project called Highly Adaptable and Trustworthy Software (HATS). There are five language layers in the ABS model that together support SPLE [5]:

- Core ABS: provides functional and object-oriented programming constructs, used to specify the "core" product with functionality common to all products of the product line.
- Feature modeling: defines the SPL's features and dependencies among them.
- Delta modelling: defines the implementation of features. Delta Model modifies core model by adding, removing, or modifying classes, interfaces, attributes, or methods.

– Product line configuration: defines the connection between Delta Model and Feature Model. One delta can be used by many features and one feature can be implemented by many deltas. The configuration thus defines which deltas are applied for specific feature combinations.
– Product selection: defines products as sets of features and naming them for convenient reference.

3 Methodology

This section describes the methodology used in the paper, explaining how we design and construct our framework.

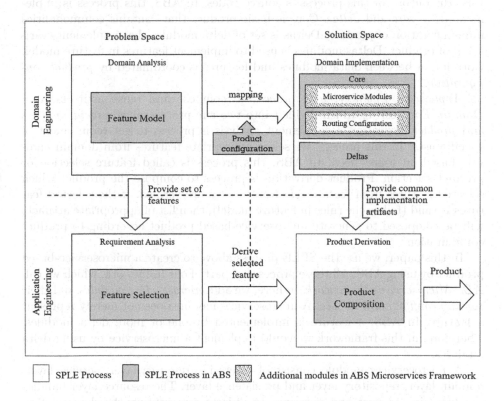

Fig. 1. SPLE Process in ABS Microservices Framework

Figure 1 shows an overview of the SPLE process in ABS Microservices Framework which adapted from [1]. Czarnecki and Eisenecker [3] distinguish between *problem space* and *solution space*. The problem space is the perspective of users. Problem space comprises domain-specific abstractions that describe the requirements on a software system and its intended behavior [8]. The solution space is the developers' perspective. Solution space comprises implementation-oriented abstractions, such as code artifacts [8].

According to [1], there are two engineering process, *Domain Engineering* and *Application Engineering*. Domain Engineering is a process to analyze potential requirement of application (commonalities and variants) and build reusable artifacts based that analysis. In this process, there two sub-process, *domain analysis* and *domain implementation*. Domain analysis takes place in problem space in domain engineering. Domain analysis is process to analyze scope and all possibility requirement of domain, the output from this process is set of features. In ABS, this process in called feature modeling, and it implemented in *feature model*. Domain implementation is solution space of domain engineering. Domain implementation is process to implement reusable artifact based on domain analysis, the output of this process is source codes. In ABS, this process is implemented by *core* and *deltas*. Core is basic product that contains commonalities implementation of product. Deltas is set of delta modules that implements variation of product. Deltas modules is used to implement features in feature model. Correlation between delta modules and features is coordinated by *product configuration*.

Application Engineering is process to compose and reuse artifacts from *Domain Engineering* which divided into two sub-process, *requirement analysis* and *product derivation*. Requirement analysis is process to get requirement of specific user. In this process, we select appropriate features from domain analysis based on users' need. In ABS, this process is called feature selection or product selection. Product derivation is process to compose the product which selected features from *feature selection* process are verified. If the selected features is valid (follow the rules in feature model), then list of appropriate artifacts will be composed to generate microservice-based product according to product configuration.

In this paper, we use the SPLE process above to create a microservice-based product by using ABS. All those process are part of our framework, which we call *ABS Microservices Framework*. In here, we add *microservices modules* and their *routing configuration* in core. A microservices module does not merely represent a feature. In ABS, a feature is implemented by one or more delta modules. Therefore, in this framework we could implement a microservice by using delta modules.

A microservices module consist of layers i.e. resource layer, service layer, domain layer, repository layer and persistence layer. The resource layer handles the incoming request and messages to objects representing the domain. Service layer contains logic implementation and coordinates across multiple domain activities. Domain layer represents model or entity that related with microservice. Repository layer provides a collection of operation to access persistent data through ORM. Persistence layer maps persistent data to domain. This structure is adapted from [2]. Figure 3 shows the structure and the connectivity between layers.

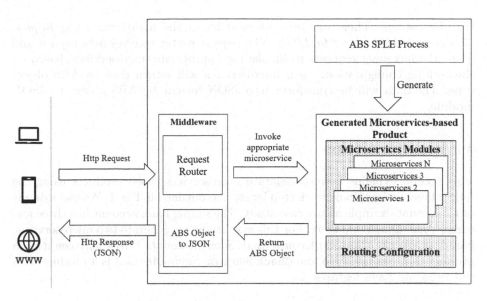

Fig. 2. Design of ABS Microservices Framework

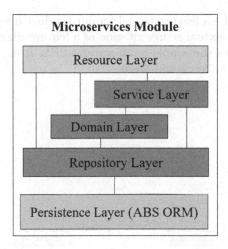

Fig. 3. The anatomy of microservices module in ABS Microservices Framework

Figure 2 shows the design of the ABS Microservices Framework that consists of three parts: ABS SPLE process, the generated microservice-based product and middleware. The ABS SPLE process is modeling part of the system using ABS modeling language as well as illustrated in Fig. 1. Furthermore, the generated microservice-based product is a product that produced from the ABS SPLE Process. The product contains the selected microservices module and its routing configuration. The middleware is a module that acts as an interface for the microservice modules so it can be accessed from the external system using the

HTTP protocol. There are two sub-modules in the middleware, the *Request Router* and *ABS Object to JSON*. The request router receives *http request* and maps the incoming requests to invoke the appropriate microservices, based on the routing configuration. Each microservices will return data as ABS object type. The data will be transform into JSON format by ABS object to JSON module.

4   Implementation

This section explains how to generate microservices-based products using the ABS Microservices Framework step by step, as outlined in Fig. 1. We use a simple bank account example as toy case study. The simple bank account has three features, Type, Check and Save. For this case study, we generate two microservices-based products, *CheckingAccount* and *SavingAccount*. *CheckingAccount* is a product that has the Type and Check features. *SavingAccount* is a product with the Type and Save features.

4.1   Feature Model

First we need to define a feature model for our product line. A feature model in ABS is essentially a textual representation of a feature diagram. Figure 4 shows the feature diagram of the simple bank account SPL. It has a Type feature that has two child features Check and Save.

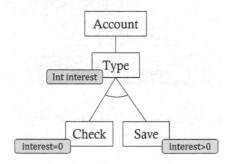

Fig. 4. Simple bank accountfeature diagram

If the Check feature is selected, the value of the interest attribute must be 0, whereas with the Save feature it must be greater than 0. The arc between Check and Save means that we only allow to choose one feature; in other words, the account can be either a checking or savings account. The corresponding ABS feature model of simple bank account is shown in the code below.

```
root Account {
  group allof {
    Type {
      Int interest;
      group oneof {
        Check { ifin: Type.interest == 0; },
        Save { ifin: Type.interest > 0; }
      }
    }
  }
}
```

4.2   Microservices Module

Microservices module is a module that contains the implementation of microservices. A microservices module implements one or more microservices. For example, in our bank account, we have `Account` module that contains two microservices i.e. `withdraw` and `deposit`. `Account` consists of `MAccountResource` as resource layer, `MAccountService` as service layer, `MAccountModel` as domain layer, `MAccountDbImpl` and persistence layer is implemented using a library called ABS ORM. In this paper, we just focus on the service layer.

The service layer implementation of the `Account` module provides two microservices, "withdraw" and "deposit". The implementation of "withdraw" is illustrated below. It performs a query on the database based on the account ID to get the account model. Then it calls the withdraw method on the account model and saves it back to the database. The deposit service follows the same pattern to perform the deposit operation.

```
class AccountServiceImpl implements AccountService {
  Account withdraw(String id, Int amount) {
    AccountDb orm = new local AccountDbImpl();
    String qry = "id=" + id;
    Account a = orm.findByAttributes("MAccountModel.AccountImpl_c", qry);
    a.withdraw(amount);
    orm.update(a);
    return a;
  }
}
```

4.3   Delta Modules

In the next step we create a delta module for each feature defined in the feature model; we name these deltas `DType`, `DSave` and `DCheck`. Below we show the implementation of delta `DSave`. It modifies class `AccountImpl` by removing its `interest` variable and re-adding it, initializing it with the value provided by the delta parameter `i`.

```
delta DSave (Int i);
  uses MAccountModel;
  modifies class AccountImpl {
    removes Int interest;
    adds Int interest = i;
}
```

4.4 Routing Configuration

Routing configuration is used to configure URL for each microservice. The routing configuration is defined by the following format:

```
"<URL>" => "<resource_class_name>@<method_name>"
```

URL defines address called by the users if they want to invoke a microservice. Resource class name is the name of class that has responsibility to handle request of microservice. Then, method name is the name of method that serves the microservice. The routing configuration of Simple Bank Account is shown in the following code. For example, /account/withdraw.abs is the URL to access withdraw microservices.

```
module ABS.Framework.Route;
class RouteConfigImpl implements RouteConfig {
  String route(String url) {
    String result = case url {
      "/account/withdraw.abs"
            => "MAccountResource.AccountResourceImpl@withdraw";
      "/account/deposit.abs"
            => "MAccountResource.AccountResourceImpl@deposit";
    }
    return result;
  }
}
```

4.5 Product Configuration

In this step we define the product configuration of the simple bank account. It is used to define the relationship between feature and delta modules. For example, delta module DType will be applied to Type feature, if it is selected.

```
productline Accounts;
  features Fee, Overdraft, Check, Save, Type;
  delta DType(Type.interest) when Type;
  delta DSave(Type.interest) after DType when Save;
  delta DCheck after DType when Check;
```

4.6 Product Selection

The next step is to define all products to be generated. In this case, we will generate two products i.e. **CheckingAccount** and **SavingAccount**. CheckingAccount is a product that have Type and Check features. SavingAccount is a product with Type and Save features.

```
product CheckingAccount (Type{interest=0},Check);
product SavingAccount (Type{interest=1},Save);
```

4.7 Generate and Run Product

If all the steps has been completed, next we generate the product by using the command `ant -Dabsproduct=<product_name> abs.deploy`. The product name is the name of product, that has been defined in product selection before. For example, if we want to generate CheckingAccount, we type `ant -Dabsproduct=CheckingAccount abs.deploy`.

After product generation has been successful, the next step is running the product by using `java -jar absserver.jar` command. By default, products run on `localhost` on port 8081. You could access this example in our repository at https://github.com/afifun51/abs-microservices-framework. You could try this example by yourself or create your own product line.

5 Analysis

For analysis, we compared the requirement changes handling between this framework and other framework. For comparison we used Spring Boot Framework - the most popular JAVA microservices framework-. We modified the requirement of microservices-based application that developed before by adding two features i.e. `Overdraft` and `Fee`. `Overdraft` is a feature that allowed Bank Account to withdraw money more than its balance and `Fee` is a feature to add fee to Bank Account every deposit. In this case, we generate three products:

1. AccountWithFee : product with feature `Type`, `Check` and `Fee`.
2. AccountWithOverdraft : product with feature `Type`, `Check` and `Overdraft`.
3. AccountWithFeeAndOverdraft : product with feature `Type`, `Check`, `Fee` and `Overdraft`.

After that, we applied the requirement changes to each frameworks. First, we simulate it in Spring Boot. Then, we simulate it in ABS Microservices Framework. We will compare how many changes that is done to overcome the requirement changes.

5.1   Simulation in Spring Boot

AccountWithFee Product - We create `FeeAccount` class that extends
`Account` class. `FeeAccount` class override `deposit` method of `Account`. And
then, we can see that we have to add its associate class in each layer (See Fig. 5a).

```
package com.rse.domain;
...
@Entity
public class FeeAccount extends Account {
  ...
  public int deposit(int x){
    Int result = x;
    if (x>=fee) { result = super(x-fee)};
    this.balance = result;
    return this.balance;
  }
}
```

AccountWithOverdraft Product - We create `OverdraftAccount` class that
extends `Account` class and override `withdraw` method of `Account` by removing
the mechanism of checking balance and the amount of withdrawal. And then,
we add its associate class in each layer (See Fig. 5b).

```
package com.rse.domain;
...
@Entity
public class OverdraftAccount extends Account {
  ...
  public int withdraw(int x){
    this.balance = this.balance - y;
    return this.balance;
  }
}
```

AccountWithFeeAndOverdraft Product - We do same as before. we create
`OverdraftFeeAccount` class that extends `Account` class and override `withdraw`
and `deposit` method of `Account`. And then, we add its associate class in each
layer (See Fig. 5c).

```
package com.rse.domain;
...
@Entity
public class OverdraftAccount extends Account {
  ...
  public int withdraw(int x){
    this.balance = this.balance - y;
    return this.balance;
  }
}
```

```
  public int deposit(int x){
    Int result = x;
    if (x>=fee) { result = super(x-fee)};
    this.balance = result;
    return this.balance;
  }
}
```

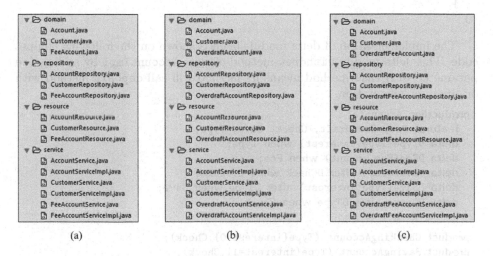

(a) (b) (c)

Fig. 5. Subclass for each product in every layer Spring Boot. (a) AccountWithFee product, (b) AccountWithOverdraft product and (c) AccountWithFeeAndOverdraft product.

5.2 Simulation in ABS Microservices Framework

Before we start to build product, we have to create delta module for `Overdraft` and `Fee`. We create delta module `DOverdraft` for `Overdraft` and delta module `DFee` for `Fee`. After that, we have to update our product configuration and add three products above to product selection.

```
delta DOverdraft;
uses MAccountModel;
modifies class AccountImpl {
  modifies Int withdraw(Int y) {
    balance = balance - y;
    return balance;
  }
}
```

The following snippet code is implementation of delta module DOverdraft, which modify withdraw method of class AccountImpl by removing balance checker.

```
delta DFee (Int fee);
uses MAccountModel;
modifies class AccountImpl {
  modifies Int deposit(Int x) {
    Int result = x;
    if (x>=fee) result = original(x-fee);
    return result;
  }
}
```

The implementation of delta module DFee is shown on the following snippet code. This delta modify withdraw method of class AccountImpl by adding fee parameter. original method means its method will call deposit method with original implementation.

```
productline Accounts;
  features Fee, Overdraft, Check, Save, Type;
  delta DType(Type.interest) when Type;
  delta DFee(Fee.amount) when Fee;
  delta DOverdraft after DCheck when Overdraft;
  delta DSave(Type.interest) after DType when Save;
  delta DCheck after DType when Check;
```

```
product CheckingAccount (Type{interest=0},Check);
product SavingAccount (Type{interest=1},Check);
product AccountWithFee (Type{interest=0},Check,Fee{amount=1});
product AccountWithOverdraft (Type{interest=0},Check,Overdraft);
product AccountWithFeeAndOverdraft (Type{interest=1},Save,Fee,Overdraft);
```

Finally, we generate (build) the products by executing the following commands on the console:

```
ant -Dabsproduct=AccountWithFee abs.deploy
ant -Dabsproduct=AccountWithOverdraft abs.deploy
ant -Dabsproduct=AccountWith FeeAndOverdraft abs.deploy
```

From both simulation above we found that in the Spring Boot, we have to do same effort for each product. We have to add new class in every layer. Otherwise, in ABS Microservices Framework, we can get three products on a single way. We just need to add delta module for each features, configure it, select it, and the last one generate the product. That simulation shows that in our framework, we need less effort to overcome the requirement changes than Spring Boot. In Sprint Boot, if there are requirement changes we have to modify each layer while in our framework only modify one layer (see Fig. 6).

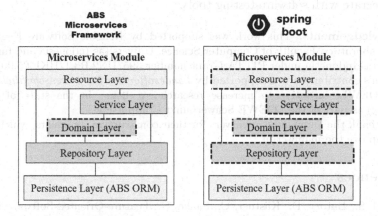

Fig. 6. The dash borderline box is modules that changed for handling requirement changes

6   Related Work

Our research is not the first effort to provide more structured support for microservices development. Safina et al. [13] extend Jolie, a programming language for the microservices paradigm, with a type system support for choices. While our framework is aimed more at managing evolution of microservices, by employing a programming language that provides broad support for variability, it could be also used to design a data-driven workflow. CIDE [9] is another microservices development environment that innovates in the domain of programming languages with an multi-agent-oriented programming style.

7   Conclusion and Future Work

The ABS Microservices Framework proposed in this research is a novel paradigm in microservices-based applications development; it's essential underlying idea is to structure related microservices as a software product line. It has been designed to be used in a similar way to other microservices frameworks such as Spring Boot, with the added benefit of more flexibility to handle requirements changes.

Future work will focus on finalising the framework design. For instance, the connection between features and microservices has not yet been fully explained. Furthermore, we need to add additional modules such as load balancer and security mechanism. This framework only support HTTP methods GET and POST, we have to add other methods, such as PUT and DELETE. In addition to JSON format data, we also can provide other data representations such as XML. Moreover, this framework have to be able to support multi-database and also integrate with software testing tools.

Acknowledgements. This work was supported by Reliable Software Engineering (RSE) Laboratory, Faculty of Computer Science, Universitas Indonesia and funded by Universitas Indonesia under PITTA Grant number 395/UN2.R3.1/HKP.05.00/2017.

Radu's contribution was supported by *Landesoffensive für wissenschaftliche Exzellenz* (LOEWE; initiative to increase research excellence in the state of Hessen, Germany) as part of the LOEWE Schwerpunkt CompuGene.

We thank the anonymous reviewers for their constructive comments, which helped us to improve the manuscript.

References

1. Apel, S., Batory, D., Kästner, C., Saake, G.: Feature-Oriented Software Product Lines. Springer, Heidelberg (2016). https://doi.org/10.1007/978-3-642-37521-7
2. Clemson, T.: Testing strategies in a microservice architecture (2014)
3. Czarnecki, K., Eisenecker, U.W., Czarnecki, K.: Generative Programming: Methods, Tools, and Applications, vol. 16. Addison Wesley Reading, Boston (2000)
4. Fowler, M., Lewis, J.: Microservices. ThoughtWorks (2014). http://martinfowler.com/articles/microservices.html. Accessed 17 Feb 2015
5. Hähnle, R.: The abstract behavioral specification language: a tutorial introduction. In: Giachino, E., Hähnle, R., de Boer, F.S., Bonsangue, M.M. (eds.) FMCO 2012. LNCS, vol. 7866, pp. 1–37. Springer, Heidelberg (2013). https://doi.org/10.1007/978-3-642-40615-7_1
6. Hähnle, R., Helvensteijn, M., Johnsen, E.B., Lienhardt, M., Sangiorgi, D., Schaefer, I., Wong, P.Y.H.: HATS abstract behavioral specification: the architectural view. In: Beckert, B., Damiani, F., de Boer, F.S., Bonsangue, M.M. (eds.) FMCO 2011. LNCS, vol. 7542, pp. 109–132. Springer, Heidelberg (2013). https://doi.org/10.1007/978-3-642-35887-6_6
7. Johnsen, E.B., Hähnle, R., Schäfer, J., Schlatte, R., Steffen, M.: ABS: a core language for abstract behavioral specification. In: Aichernig, B.K., de Boer, F.S., Bonsangue, M.M. (eds.) FMCO 2010. LNCS, vol. 6957, pp. 142–164. Springer, Heidelberg (2011). https://doi.org/10.1007/978-3-642-25271-6_8
8. Kästner, C., Apel, S.: Feature-oriented software development. In: Lämmel, R., Saraiva, J., Visser, J. (eds.) GTTSE 2011. LNCS, vol. 7680, pp. 346–382. Springer, Heidelberg (2013). https://doi.org/10.1007/978-3-642-35992-7_10
9. Liu, D., Zhu, H., Xu, C., Bayley, I., Lightfoot, D., Green, M., Marshall, P.: CIDE: an integrated development environment for microservices. In: 2016 IEEE International Conference on Services Computing (SCC), pp. 808–812 (2016)
10. Metzger, A., Pohl, K.: Software product line engineering and variability management: achievements and challenges. In: Proceedings of the on Future of Software Engineering, pp. 70–84. ACM (2014)

11. Pohl, K., Böckle, G., Van Der Linden, F.: Software Product Line Engineering: Foundations, Principles, and Techniques. Springer, Heidelberg (2005). https://doi.org/10.1007/3-540-28901-1
12. Richardson, C.: Pattern: Microservices architecture. Microservices. io.http://microservices.io/patterns/microservices.html. Accessed 17 February 2015 (2014)
13. Safina, L., Mazzara, M., Montesi, F., Rivera., V.: Data-driven workflows for microservices: genericity in Jolie. In: 2016 IEEE 30th International Conference on Advanced Information Networking and Applications (AINA), pp. 430–437 (2016)
14. Schaefer, I., Bettini, L., Bono, V., Damiani, F., Tanzarella, N.: Delta-oriented programming of software product lines. In: Bosch, J., Lee, J. (eds.) SPLC 2010. LNCS, vol. 6287, pp. 77–91. Springer, Heidelberg (2010). https://doi.org/10.1007/978-3-642-15579-6_6

CoSim-CPS 2017

CoSim-CPS 2017 Organizers' Message

The First Workshop on Co-Simulation of Cyber-Physical Systems (CoSim-CPS[1]) was a one-day event held in Trento, Italy, on September 5, 2017. The workshop was a satellite event of the 15th International Conference on Software Engineering and Formal Methods (SEFM 2017).

The focus of CoSim-CPS is the integrated application of formal methods and co-simulation technologies in the development of software for cyber-physical systems. Co-simulation is an advanced simulation technique that allows developers to generate a global simulation of a complex system by orchestrating and composing the concurrent simulation of individual components or aspects of the system. Formal methods link software specifications and program code to logic theories, providing developers with means to analyze program behaviors in a way that is demonstrably exhaustive. The two technologies complement each other. Using co-simulation, developers can create prototypes suitable to validate hypotheses embedded in formal models and for the formal properties of the software to be analyzed. This is fundamental to ensure that the right system is being developed. Using formal methods, developers can extend test results obtained with co-simulation runs, and ensure that the same results apply to all program states for all possible program inputs. This enables the early detection of latent design anomalies.

All papers submitted to this first edition of the CoSim-CPS workshop were carefully reviewed by at least three members of the Program Committee. The final program included 13 papers and a keynote talk by Claudio G. Gomes on the state of the art of co-simulation technologies.

We would like to thank all the authors who contributed to the success of this first edition of the CoSim-CPS workshop. Special thanks goes to the Program Committee members, for their support and considered reviews that helped the authors further improve their work. Finally, we would like to thank the SEFM workshop chairs and local organizers for their help.

October 2017

Cinzia Bernardeschi
Peter Gorm Larsen
Paolo Masci

---

[1] http://sites.google.com/view/cosimcps17.

Organization

CoSim-CPS 2017 - Program Committee

Stylianos Basagiannis	United Technologies Research Center, Ireland
Estela Bicho Erlhagen	Centro Algoritmi/Universidade do Minho, Portugal
David Broman	KTH Royal Institute of Technology, Sweden
Fabio Cremona	United Technologies Research Center, Italy
Marco Di Natale	Sant'Anna School of Advanced Studies, Italy
Andrea Domenici	University of Pisa, Italy
Adriano Fagiolini	University of Palermo, Italy
Camille Fayollas	IRIT/University of Toulouse 3, France
John Fitzgerald	Newcastle University, UK
Stefania Gnesi	ISTI/CNR, Italy
Temesghen Kahsai	NASA Ames/Carnegie Mellon University, USA
Mario Porrmann	Bielefeld University, Germany
Akshay Rajhans	MathWorks, USA
Steve Reeves	University of Waikato, New Zealand
Matteo Rossi	Polytechnic University of Milan, Italy
Sriram Sankaranarayanan	University of Colorado at Boulder, USA
Mirko Sessa	Fondazione Bruno Kessler, Italy
Neeraj Kumar Singh	IRIT-INPT-ENSEEIHT/University of Toulouse, France
Hans Vangheluwe	University of Antwerp/McGill University, Belgium/Canada
Yi Zhang	US Food and Drug Administration, USA

Co-simulation: State of the Art and Open Challenges (Keynote Talk)

Cláudio Gomes

Department of Mathematics and Computer Science,
University of Antwerp, Belgium

Co-simulation is a technique to couple multiple simulation tools, so that the interactions with, and within, a coupled system can be simulated through the cooperation of these tools.

As a response to the increasing complexity of engineered systems and the (entailed) specialization of supporting development tools, it has the potential to facilitate the virtualization of every major stage in the development of a system:

Design – the system can be designed entirely in a virtual setting, where each team is able to study the effects of its decisions directly in the designs of the other teams;

Assembly – the impact of externally supplied components can be measured without the physical components, using higher fidelity models produced by the suppliers themselves;

Operation – training and other human/machine interactions with the system can be made in an accurate and valid virtual environment;

Maintenance – virtual replicas of the system can be used to monitor the operation of the physical system, and diagnose/predict/prevent faults.

In all these scenarios, the ability to trust the results produced with co-simulation is of utmost importance.

In this presentation, co-simulation is introduced and a brief historical overview is given. The key events that helped shape the concept are then used to describe a vision of full virtualization. Finally, having a past and a vision, a research road map is proposed.

Some of the open challenges include:

- During a co-simulation, detecting and preventing violations of the physical assumptions embedded in the models.
- Accommodating uncertainty as a natural part of the engineering process and providing support for it in co-simulation.
- Computing bounds on the inaccuracies introduced due to communication constraints in a co-simulation.

Acknowledgments. This presentation was put together with the generous help of Casper Thule, Peter Larsen, David Broman, and Hans Vangheluwe.

A Refinement Approach to Analyse Critical Cyber-Physical Systems

Davide Basile[1,2]($\boxtimes$), Felicita Di Giandomenico[1], and Stefania Gnesi[1]

[1] I.S.T.I "A.Faedo", CNR Pisa, Pisa, Italy
davide.basile@isti.cnr.it
[2] Department of Information Engineering, University of Florence, Florence, Italy

Abstract. Cyber-Physical Systems (CPS) are characterised by digital components controlling physical equipment, and CPS are typically influenced by the surrounding environment conditions. Due to the stochastic continuous nature of the involved physical phenomena, for quantitative evaluation of non-functional properties (e.g. dependability, performance) stochastic hybrid model-based approaches are mainly used. In case of critical applications, it is also important to verify specific qualitative aspects (e.g. safety). Generally, stochastic hybrid approaches are not suitable to account for the co-existence of both qualitative and quantitative aspects. In this paper we address this issue by proposing a refinement approach for analysing stochastic hybrid systems starting from a verified discrete representation of their logic. Different formalisms are used and formally related. It is then possible to combine the quantitative assessment of stochastic continuous properties with the qualitative verification of logic soundness, thus improving the trustworthiness of the analysis results.

1 Introduction

Recently, Cyber-Physical Systems (CPS) [18] have been given attention from the research community and are characterised by digital components (e.g. transducers) interacting with continuous phenomena describing the surrounding physical environment. These systems can be thought as communication-based applications (CBA), where different cyber entities (e.g. sensors, actuators) communicate to realise the overall behaviour. CBA are generally error-prone and verifying them is not an easy task [7].

Dependability and efficiency aspects of CPS can be analysed through a stochastic model-based approach, because of the stochastic nature of the involved physical phenomena. When critical applications are considered, it is definitely not sufficient to concentrate the verification efforts on quantitative properties only, but the validation of qualitative properties such as safety aspects is paramount.

However, when stochastic continuous behaviours are introduced in the models, the verification of qualitative safety properties becomes undecidable [16].

A. Cerone and M. Roveri (Eds.): SEFM 2017 Workshops, LNCS 10729, pp. 267–283, 2018.
https://doi.org/10.1007/978-3-319-74781-1_19

Previously, in [5,8] we have analysed a cyber-physical system from the rail-way domain with a tailored approach, not reusable in other cyber-physical systems. In this paper we propose a general approach for validating CPS models based on modelling the system starting from its logical aspects (e.g. components interactions), to be refined and decorated to include dependability aspects. A key insight of this approach is to analyse fault-tolerant systems acting when dependability/performance aspects are threatened, to restore them to safe values. These aspects are related to stochastic hybrid quantities. However, the logic can be efficiently modelled and verified separately, by assuming that the conditions detecting threats hold. If it is not the case then the system can be assumed to operate safely. The verified logical aspects are automatically synthesised and embedded into the overall model. Then the cyber-physical model is (1) equipped with guarantees on the soundness of the implemented logic, and (2) provides a verified basis for detailing the stochastic continuous aspects of interest (e.g. related to performance, dependability) and analyse them.

Through the combination of quantitative assessment of stochastic continuous properties with the qualitative verification of interactions soundness, we aim at improving the trustworthiness of the obtained analysis results. To illustrate its application and the potential benefits, the proposed methodology will be applied to an industrial case study from the railway domain [5].

Structure of the paper. In Sect. 2 a motivating example is introduced that will be used throughout the paper. The proposed methodology is described in Sect. 3 and a brief description of contract automata and stochastic activity networks is in Sect. 3.1. The case study is modelled through contract automata in Sect. 4. The main results of the paper (i.e. the mapping from contract automata to activity networks) are in Sect. 5. The extension to include stochastic continuous aspects is detailed in Sect. 6, while related work and conclusions are in Sect. 7. All proofs and additional details can be found in [4].

2   Motivating Example

We start by introducing the case study, a rail road switch heating system [5], that will be used in the paper to explain our methodology. A rail road switch is a mechanism enabling trains to be guided from one track to another. Heaters are used so that the temperature of the rail road switches can be kept above freezing, to avoid possible disasters.

We will consider a dynamic power management policy for heating the switches, with parametric thresholds representing the temperatures triggering the activation/deactivation of the heating. In particular, the policy employed is based on two threshold temperatures: the *warning threshold* (T_{wa}) represents the lower temperature that the track should not trespass. If the temperature T is lower than T_{wa}, then the risk of ice or snow can lead to a failure of the rail road switch and therefore the heating system needs to be activated. The *working threshold* (T_{wo}) is the working temperature of the heating system. Once this temperature is reached (i.e. $T > T_{wo}$), the heating system can be safely turned off in order to avoid an excessive waste of energy. This is an example of a system reaction to threats, to guarantee required reliability while improving energy consumption. Indeed if $T_{wa} < T < T_{wo}$ then, respectively, the switch will not freeze and will not waste energy: in this case there is no threat to the reliability and energy consumption of the analysed system.

The control part of our system mainly consists of two components realising the logic described above: the *heater* and the *central coordinator*. A network of heaters is realised by composing the heater components, and their activation/deactivation is controlled by the central coordinator. The coordinator collects the requests of activation from the pending heaters, and it manages the energy supply according to a prioritised order. In particular, for each priority class, the first heater that asks to be turned on will be the first to be activated, according to a FIFO order. If there is no energy available, each request will be enqueued in the queue of pending heaters. The continuous aspects are related to the temperature of the rail road track. The induction heating will be modelled with a differential equation modelling the balance of energy. The stochastic aspects of the case study concern modelling the environment temperature (weather conditions) and the probabilistic time-to-failure when the freezing threshold is reached.

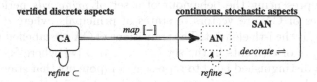

Fig. 1. The proposed framework for CPS based on CA, AN and SAN models

3   Modelling Cyber-Physical Systems

Our approach to model cyber-physical systems relies on the combined usage of the following formalisms and tools. *Contract automata* (CA) [6] are a recent formalism for modelling and verifying CBA, implemented in the *Contract Automata Tool* (CAT) [7]. An original facet of CA is the adoption of techniques from Control Theory to synthesise a controller enforcing safety properties (thus motivating our choice over this formalism). Stochastic Activity Networks (SAN) [20] are widely used for analysing CPS. They generalise Stochastic Petri Nets [10] and are equipped with a powerful tool, called Möbius [11], useful for evaluating quantitative properties under a given degree of confidence. However, despite their popularity, the formal verification of qualitative properties of SAN models has received low attention [1].

In Fig. 1 our modelling framework is depicted, which can be divided into three phases. In the first phase, the system logic will be modelled through the CA formalism and the verified control part will be synthesised. In the second phase, Activity Networks (AN) models are automatically generated through a mapping from CA models. Finally, in the third phase the SAN models will be obtained by properly extending the generated AN models to introduce the stochastic continuous physical aspects of the modelled system (e.g. differential equations and stochastic phenomena describing the surrounding physical environment), while identifying the point of interactions between logical and physical sub-modules. We remark that the CA are supported by mechanisms (e.g. controller synthesis) not available for AN and SAN, and this motivates the mapping from CA models to AN models. In all the phases it is possible to refine the abstract models to more concrete representations. The correspondence among the different models is guaranteed by formal results. In the following we will apply this modelling framework to our case study. The detailed formalization of the above phases is performed with the support of the case study introduced in Sect. 2. This makes the steps concrete, while exposing the developed theory at the basis of our approach. Before doing this we shortly present the adopted formalisms.

3.1   Background

Contract Automata and (Stochastic) Activity Networks are recalled below.

Contract Automata. A contract automaton (see Definition 1) is a finite state automaton representing the behaviour of a set of *principals* performing some *actions*. States of CA are vectors of states of principals, where $\vec{q}$ stands for a vector and $\vec{q}_{(i)}$ is the i-th element. The transitions of CA are labelled with *actions*, that are vectors of elements in the set $\mathbb{L} = \mathbb{R} \cup \mathbb{O} \cup \{\bullet\}$ where $\mathbb{R} \cap \mathbb{O} = \emptyset$, and $\bullet \notin \mathbb{R} \cup \mathbb{O}$ is a distinguished label to represent components that stay idle. Actions are as followed: *offers* (belonging to the set $\mathbb{O}$ and depicted as overlined labels on arcs, e.g. $\overline{ins}$), *requests* (belonging to the set $\mathbb{R}$ and depicted as non-overlined labels on arcs, e.g. *ins*), or *match* actions (i.e. handshake between a request and an offer). The goal of each principal is to reach an accepting (*final*) state where all its requests and offers are matched. We borrow the following definition from [6], where the *rank* is the number of principals inside the contract automaton.

Definition 1. *Given a finite set of states $\mathfrak{Q} = \{q_1, q_2, \ldots\}$, a contract automaton $\mathcal{A}$ of rank n is a tuple $\langle Q, \vec{q}_0, A^r, A^o, T, F \rangle$, where $Q = Q_1 \times \ldots \times Q_n \subseteq \mathfrak{Q}^n$ is the set of states, $\vec{q}_0 \in Q$ is the initial state, $A^r \subseteq \mathbb{R}, A^o \subseteq \mathbb{O}$ are finite sets (of requests and offers, respectively), $F \subseteq Q$ is the set of final states, $T \subseteq Q \times A \times Q$ is the set of transitions, where $A \subseteq (A^r \cup A^o \cup \{\bullet\})^n$ and if $(\vec{q}, \vec{a}, \vec{q'}) \in T$ then both the following conditions hold: (1) $\vec{a}$ is either a request or an offer or a match; (2) if $\vec{a}_{(i)} = \bullet$ then it must be $\vec{q}_{(i)} = \vec{q'}_{(i)}$.*

A *principal* is a contract automaton of rank 1 such that $A^r \cap co(A^o) = \emptyset$. A step $(w, \vec{q}) \xrightarrow{\vec{a}} (w', \vec{q'})$ occurs if and only if $w = \vec{a}w', w' \in A^*$ and $(\vec{q}, \vec{a}, \vec{q'}) \in T$. Let $\rightarrow^*$ be the reflexive, transitive closure of the transition relation $\rightarrow$. The language of $\mathcal{A}$ is denoted as $\mathscr{L}(\mathcal{A}) = \{w \mid (w, \vec{q}_0) \xrightarrow{w}{}^* (\varepsilon, \vec{q}), \vec{q} \in F\}$. A step is denoted as $\vec{q} \xrightarrow{\vec{a}}$ when w, w' and $\vec{q'}$ are irrelevant and $(w, \vec{q}) \rightarrow (w', \vec{q'})$ when $\vec{a}$ is irrelevant.

We now describe informally the composition operators of CA. The product automaton basically interleaves or matches the transitions of principals. Synchronisations are forced to happen when two contract automata are ready on their respective request/offer action and in a composed CA, states and actions are, respectively, vectors of states and actions of principals (i.e. the formalism is compositional). Moreover, a contract automaton admits *strong agreement* if it has at least one trace made only by match transitions; and it is *strongly safe* if all the traces are in strong agreement. Basically, strong agreement guarantees that the composition of services has a sound execution, while strong safety guarantees that *all* executions of the composition are sound.

An original facet of CA is the possibility of synthesising a controller; that is a non-empty sub-portion of a CA $\mathcal{A}$ that is strongly safe and convergent, i.e. from each reachable state it is possible to reach a final state. The *most permissive strong controller* (mpc) $\mathcal{KS}_A$ of $\mathcal{A}$ is such that all controllers $\mathcal{KS}'_A$ are included in the mpc, and it is unique up to language equivalence. Techniques for synthesising the mpc have been introduced in [6] and implemented in [7]. The *Contract Automata Tool* (CAT) [7] has been implemented for supporting the modelling and verification of CA. It provides functionalities for generating and composing different CA, and for checking if their composition is correct under different properties, for example strong agreement and strong safety.

Stochastic Activity Networks. Stochastic activity networks (SAN) [20] models are widely used for performance, dependability and performability evaluation of complex systems. The SAN formalism is a variant of Stochastic Petri Nets [10], and has similarities with Generalised Stochastic Petri Nets [3].

A SAN is composed of the following primitives: *places, activities, input gates* and *output gates.* Places and activities have the same interpretation as places and transitions of Petri Nets. Input gates control the enabling conditions predicate of an activity. Output gates define the change of marking upon completion of the activity. Each enabled activity may complete. Activities are of two types: *instantaneous* and *timed.* Instantaneous activities complete once the enabling conditions are satisfied. Timed activities take an amount of time to complete following a temporal stochastic distribution function. An enabled activity is aborted, i.e. it cannot complete, when the SAN moves into a new marking in which the enabling conditions of the activity no longer hold. Cases are associated with activities, and are used to represent probabilistic uncertainty about the action taken upon completion of the activity. Moreover, each input or output gate is connected to a single activity and to a unique place.

A stochastic activity network is formally defined as a tuple $\langle AN, C, F, G \rangle$ where AN is the underlying activity network, C and F are functions assigning probabilistic distribution to cases of activity and time (for timed activities), respectively, and G is the predicate of reactivation. In Sect. 5 we will provide a mapping from contract automata to activity networks (AN), hence their formalisation is introduced. Let P be the set of all places of the network and $S \subseteq P$. The marking of S is formally defined as $\mu : S \to \mathbb{N}$. Moreover, $M_S = \{\mu | \mu : S \to \mathbb{N}, S \subseteq P\}$ is the set of possible markings of S. In the following input gates are defined as triples (G, e, f) where $G \subseteq P$ is the set of input places, $e : M_G \to \{0, 1\}$ is the enabling predicate and $f : M_G \to M_G$ is the input function. Output gates are defined as pairs (G, f) where $G \subseteq P$ is the set of output places and $f : M_G \to M_G$ is the output function.

Definition 2. *An activity network (AN) is defined as* $\mathcal{N} = \langle P, A, I, O, \gamma, \tau, \iota, o \rangle$ *where:* P *is a finite set of places,* A *is a finite set of activities,* I *is a finite set of input gates,* O *is a finite set of output gates,* $\gamma : A \to \mathbb{N}^+$ *defines the number of cases for each activity, and* $\tau : A \to \{Timed, Instantaneous\}$ *specifies the type of each activity. Finally, the function* $\iota : I \to A$ *maps input gates to activities, and the function* $o : O \to \{(a, c) \mid a \in A \land c \in \{n \mid n \in \mathbb{N}^+, n \le \gamma(a)\}\}$ *maps output gates to pairs of activity and corresponding cases.*

Moreover, let $IP(a)$ and $OP(a)$ be the input and output gates of an activity a, respectively. A step $\mu \xrightarrow{a,c} \mu'$ denotes the completion of the activity a (enabled in μ) and selected case c that yields μ'. We will denote $\mu \xrightarrow{a} \mu'$ when the activity has a single case and $\mu \xrightarrow{w}{}^* \mu'$ for the reflexive transitive closure of $\to$, where $w \in A^*$. Moreover, we assume the existence of an initial marking μ_0 and a set of final markings $F = \{\mu_1, \ldots, \mu_n\}$. We introduce the notion of *convergent* AN, that is an AN always capable of reaching a final (successful) state.

Definition 3. *An activity network* $\mathcal{N}$ *is* convergent *iff* $\forall \mu . \mu_0 \to^* \mu, \exists \mu_f \in F . \mu \to^* \mu_f$, *and is* deadlock-free *iff* $\forall \mu . \mu_0 \to^* \mu, \exists \mu' . \mu \to \mu'$.

Note that convergence implies the absence of both deadlocks and livelocks.

4   Modelling the System Logic Through CA

The control part of our example is described below. In particular, following the general guidelines of our approach we firstly abstract the stochastic continuous behaviour related to the temperatures (assuming that the related conditions on temperatures are eventually satisfied) to efficiently verify the soundness of interactions (used to enforce reliability and energy saving when threatened). In particular, priorities are initially abstracted in the given CA, and will be enforced later on by the refinement operation of the controller.

Stochastic continuous aspects related to temperature can be introduced later on through model refinement to allow the evaluation of quantitative properties (e.g. performance, reliability), while preserving the soundness of interactions.

In Fig. 2 the contract automaton representing a rail road switch heater H is displayed, while the contract automaton of the central control unit Q is in Fig. 3.

Heater. In the initial state q_{H_0} the heater H is switched off and the internal temperature T is above T_{wa}. Once T goes below T_{wa}, H asks to be activated to the central control unit Q with the offer $\overline{ins}$ (i.e. insert). In state q_{H_1}, T is below T_{wa} and H is waiting for a notification from the Q to be turned on. When the message NI (i.e. notify in) is received, H is turned on, represented by the state q_{H_2}.

Fig. 2. H

From q_{H_2} two transitions are allowed: (1) $\overline{rem}$ (i.e. remove), H has $T > T_{wo}$, and communicates to Q the termination of the heating phase and switches to state q_{H_0}; (2) NO (i.e. notify out) a second heater H′ with higher priority asks to be turned on. The energy delivered to H is turned off and H is switched to state q_{H_0}, even though it has not yet reached a T above T_{wo} (however T could be above T_{wa}: if it is not the case there will be an instantaneous transition from q_{H_0} to q_{H_1} as previously described). The target state of both transitions is q_{H_0}, which is also the final state of H.

Central control unit. In the initial (and final) state q_{Q_0} the central control unit Q is waiting for a message from one of the heaters. Two messages can be received: (1) ins, a heater asks to be activated. This request can be rejected in case there is no available energy and the priority is not higher than those activated heaters, which is modelled by the inner loop (q_{Q_0}, ins, q_{Q_0}). In this case a notification of activation will be issued as soon as there is energy available (see below).

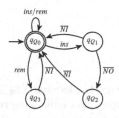

Fig. 3. Q

Otherwise, the request is accepted and the target state is q_{Q_1}. In state q_{Q_1} two transitions are allowed. In case there is enough available energy, the heater is activated with the message $\overline{NI}$. Otherwise, if there is no available energy but H has a priority higher than one of the activated heaters H′, firstly a message $\overline{NO}$ is issued to H′, which will be consequently turned off, and then the activation is notified to H with the message $\overline{NI}$. From state q_{Q_0} the second possible message is: (2) rem, a heater H notifies the deactivation. If there are no heaters H′ activated or waiting for being activated then no action is performed, modelled with the inner loop (q_{Q_0}, rem, q_{Q_0}). Otherwise, after receiving the message rem, one of the pending heater H′ is activated by issuing the message $\overline{NI}$ to H′.

Composition. The composition of the network of switches with the control unit is now introduced. The CA models over approximate the real behaviour of the system. For example, from state q_{Q_0} of Q different transitions can be chosen non deterministically. Indeed, priorities and energy available are not modelled in the CA, but they will be enforced by synthesising a controller such that all and only the behaviour satisfying these constraints will be obtained. Let nH be the number of heaters in the network. By composing (through the CA operators of composition) nH instances of the heater model H with the central control unit Q, it is possible to analyse the behaviour of the overall system against the property of *strong agreement* of the product automaton (i.e. composed system).

For displaying purposes, in our working example we will consider a network composed of two heaters and the central control unit. We remark that the case study scales to a higher number of heaters. Through CAT it is possible to compute automatically the mpc of the composed automaton $H_1 \otimes H_2 \otimes Q$ (subscript are used to identify an instance of H). In Fig. 4 $\mathcal{KS}_{H_1 \otimes H_2 \otimes Q}$ is displayed.

CAT provides further information on the interactions between the central control unit and the heaters that could lead to a deadlock/livelock (i.e. those

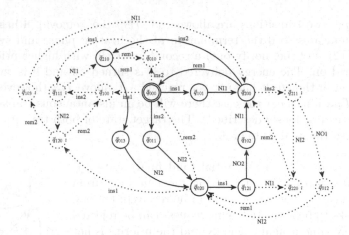

Fig. 4. The mpc $\mathcal{KS}_{\mathtt{H}\otimes\mathtt{H}\otimes\mathtt{Q}}$ (solid/dotted lines) and the controller $\mathcal{KS}' = \mathcal{KS}_{\mathcal{KS}_{spr}}$ (solid lines). For enhancing readability the labels are renamed as: $ins1 = (\overline{ins}, \bullet, ins)$, $ins2 = (\bullet, \overline{ins}, ins)$, $rem1 = (\overline{rem}, \bullet, rem)$, $rem2 = (\bullet, \overline{rem}, rem)$, $NI1 = (NI, \bullet, \overline{NI})$, $NI2 = (\bullet, NI, \overline{NI})$, $NO1 = (NO, \bullet, \overline{NO})$, $NO2 = (\bullet, NO, \overline{NO})$.

blocked by the controller). For this purpose, the *strongly liable* transitions in the composed automaton are checked, that are scenarios in which (1) no heater is activated (hence there is energy available) but Q refuses the activation, or (2) no heater is waiting for being activated (i.e. their temperatures are above the warning threshold), but Q issues a notification of activation.

We note that the liable transitions are due to non-deterministic behaviour of Q, because we are not explicitly modelling the available energy, the priorities and the queue of pending heaters. The synthesis of $\mathcal{KS}_{\mathtt{H}_1 \otimes \mathtt{H}_2 \otimes \mathtt{Q}}$ automatically removes these unwanted behaviours. Indeed, the conditions *"if no heater is active then accept a request of activation"* and *"if no heater is waiting for being activated then do not notify any activation"* are inferred automatically, without explicitly modelling the energy and the queue of pending heaters, which would increase the state-space of the system. However, $\mathcal{KS}_{\mathtt{H}_1 \otimes \mathtt{H}_2 \otimes \mathtt{Q}}$ still admits behaviours not expected in the system. For example, a notification of deactivation (i.e. $\overline{NO}$) should be emitted only if one of the heaters has a priority higher than the other, but the controller admits traces where the message $\overline{NO}$ is delivered to both heaters.

Refinement. As mentioned earlier, the enforcement of FIFO priorities and energy available constraints in the CA of the example is discussed. For this purpose, there is the need to refine the given composition of CA to a more concrete one. Indeed, the behaviour of a CA $\mathcal{A}$ (or its mpc) over-approximates that of the analysed application. We introduce here a notion of refinement of an mpc $\mathcal{KS}_{\mathcal{A}}$ to remove unwanted behaviours. From the supervisory control theory, any controller $\mathcal{KS}'_{\mathcal{A}}$ of $\mathcal{A}$ is a refinement (i.e. a sub-automaton) of the mpc $\mathcal{KS}_{\mathcal{A}}$ of $\mathcal{A}$.

In the following a set of "bad" states $Bad(Q)$ to be removed in the refinement of the mpc is identified.

Lemma 1. *Let $\mathcal{KS}_A$ be the mpc of A and $Bad(Q) \subseteq (Q_{\mathcal{KS}_A} \setminus F_{\mathcal{KS}_A})$. Moreover, let $\mathcal{KS}_{spr}$ be a CA obtained from $\mathcal{KS}_A$ by removing all states in $Bad(Q)$ and their incident transitions. The controller $\mathcal{KS}'_A = \mathcal{KS}_{\mathcal{KS}_{spr}}$ is a refinement of $\mathcal{KS}_A$.*

The refinement of the mpc of the example to a more concrete one is now discussed. The bad states representing behaviours to remove will be firstly declared as predicates ϕ_i and removed from the controller. Note that such bad states can be identified as those not satisfying one or more temporal logic formulae (e.g. CTL). In particular we will use four predicates to identify states $\vec{q} \in Q$ such that: $\phi_1(Q)$ – there are more active heaters than available energy; $\phi_2(Q)$ – the maximum number of active heaters has been reached, but a request of activation of a high/low priority heater has been wrongly accepted; $\phi_3(Q)$ – the maximum number of active heaters has been reached, but a request of activation of a high priority heater has been wrongly rejected, because there is an active low priority heater; $\phi_4(Q)$ – a request of activation of a heater has been wrongly rejected, because there is energy available. The set of bad states to be removed will be defined as the union of these four predicates, detailed below.

We assume that two priority classes are present in our system and each heater is uniquely identified by an index. Let $\mathbb{N}^{<n}$ be the set of positive natural numbers equal or smaller than n. Let $P1$ and $P2$ be respectively the (index) sets of high-priority and low priority heaters, such that $P1 \cap P2 = \emptyset$ and $P1 \cup P2 = \mathbb{N}^{<nH}$, and let $S = \mathcal{P}(\mathbb{N}^{<nH})$ be the power set of indexes. Moreover, $en \in \mathbb{N}^{<nH}$ is the maximum number of active heaters, i.e. the energy available to the system.

For example by assuming that H_1 has a priority higher than H_2 and only one heater can be active in a unit of time, we have $P1 = \{1\}, P2 = \{2\}, en = 1$. Let $\circ \in \{>, <, =\}$, and let $\phi_\circ(Q) = \{\vec{q} \in Q \mid \exists P \in S, |P| \circ en, \forall i \in P, j \in \mathbb{N}^{<nH} \setminus P :$ $\vec{q}_{(i)} = q_{H2} \wedge \vec{q}_{(j)} \neq q_{H2}\}$ be the predicate stating that the maximum number of active heaters has been, respectively, exceeded ($\circ$ equal $>$), not reached ($\circ$ equal $<$) and reached ($\circ$ equal $=$). The "bad" states of the mpc are $Bad(Q) = \{\vec{q} \in Q \mid \vec{q} \in \bigcup_{i \in \mathbb{N}^{<4}} \phi_i(Q)\}$, where $\phi_1(Q) = \{\vec{q} \in \phi_>(Q)\}$, $\phi_2(Q) = \{\vec{q} \in \phi_=(Q) \mid (\vec{q}_{(nH)} = q_{Q1}) \wedge ((\bigvee_{i \in P2} \vec{q}_{(i)} = q_{H1}) \vee (P \subseteq P1 \wedge (\bigvee_{i \in P1} \vec{q}_{(i)} = q_{H1})))\}$, $(\vec{q}_{(nH)} = q_{Q1}$ is the state of the coordinator that has accepted a request). Here a low priority heater cannot trigger the deactivation of another low priority heater, while for high priority heaters it is required $P \subseteq P1$ (all active heaters have high priority). Finally, $\phi_3(Q) = \{\vec{q} \in \phi_=(Q) \mid (\vec{q}_{(nH)} = q_{Q0}) \wedge (\bigvee_{i \in P2} \vec{q}_{(i)} = q_{H2}) \wedge (\bigvee_{i \in P1} \vec{q}_{(i)} = q_{H1})\}$ $(\vec{q}_{(nH)} = q_{Q0}$ states that the request of activation of the pending heater (q_{H1}) has been rejected), and $\phi_4(Q) = \{\vec{q} \in \phi_<(Q) \mid (\bigvee_{i \in \mathbb{N}^{<nH} \setminus P} \vec{q}_{(i)} = q_{H1}) \wedge (\vec{q}_{(nH)} = q_{Q0})\}$.

Let us assume that in our example H_1 has a priority higher than H_2 and only one heater can be active in a unit of time. We know that state $\vec{q}_{220} \in \phi_1(Q)$ (see Fig. 4), because both heaters are activated, $\vec{q}_{211} \in \phi_2(Q)$ since Q has accepted the request of activation of H_2 but no energy is available and its priority is low, $\vec{q}_{120} \in \phi_3(Q)$ because Q has rejected the request of activation of H_1 (high priority), and

$\vec{q}_{100}, \vec{q}_{010} \in \phi_4(Q)$ because Q has refused the request of activation of a heater but there is energy available. This removal operation leads to a spurious controller $\mathcal{KS}_{spr}$. By reapplying the synthesis step a controller $\mathcal{KS}' = \mathcal{KS}_{\mathcal{KS}_{spr}}$ is computed (see Fig. 4) where all dangling states and transitions are removed, e.g. $\vec{q}_{012}, \vec{q}_{103}$ and $\vec{q}_{111}$. Now the non-determinism has been removed from $\mathcal{KS}'$, and we have synthesised all and only sound interactions implementing the logic of the system (i.e. the policy of energy saving). Following Lemma 1, $\mathcal{KS}_{spr}$ is the automaton obtained from $\mathcal{KS}_{H_1 \otimes H_2 \otimes Q}$ by removing these states, and $\mathcal{KS}_{\mathcal{KS}_{spr}} = \mathcal{KS}'$ is the corresponding controller in Fig. 4.

5   Mapping from CA to AN

In this section we present the second phase of our approach, which is the core part of this paper: the formal mapping from CA to AN, together with a notion of refinement of AN. The mapping will be tailored to satisfy the property of strong agreement of CA.

We start by introducing some notation useful for defining the mapping. Let $id : \mathbb{O} \to \mathbb{N}^+$ be an injective function assigning a unique id to each offer. The set identifying all possible states $\vec{q}$ of $\mathcal{A}$ in which principal i in state $q = \vec{q}_{(i)}$ is ready to fire the offer $\bar{a}$ is denoted as: $S \uparrow_{q,i,\bar{a}} = \{\vec{q} \mid (\vec{q}, \vec{a}, \vec{q}') \in T, \vec{q}_{(i)} = q, \vec{a}_{(i)} = \bar{a}\}$. Conversely, the set of states $\vec{q}_1$ in which principal i in state $q = \vec{q}_{1(i)}$ is ready to perform the request a and principal j has performed the corresponding offer (i.e. $\vec{q}_{1(j)} = \vec{q}'_{(j)}$) is denoted as: $S \downarrow_{q,i,a} = \{\vec{q}_1 \mid (\vec{q}, \vec{a}, \vec{q}') \in T, \vec{q}_{(i)} = q, \vec{a}_{(i)} = a, \exists j.\vec{a}_{(j)} = \bar{a}, \forall z \neq j.\vec{q}_{(z)} = \vec{q}_{1(z)}, \vec{q}_{1(j)} = \vec{q}'_{(j)}\}$. According to the strong agreement property, a request will be fired only after the corresponding offer has been made. Moreover, the marking function is extended to vectors of states/places as: $\mu(\vec{q}) = 1$ if $\forall i.\mu(\vec{q}_{(i)}) = 1, \mu(\vec{q}) = 0$ otherwise. Note that there could be other places in the AN ignored by $\mu(\vec{q})$.

The mapping from CA to AN is informally described now, to help intuition. The states of principals are in one-to-one correspondence with places in the AN, plus an additional place act for storing the offer performed in the intermediate step. Activities are in one-to-one correspondence with transitions of principals. All activities are instantaneous and have only one case. The firing of activities will be in correspondence with match transitions fired in the composed CA: given a match transition t where a principal i performs an offer transition t_i and a principal j performs a request transition t_j then the order of firing of activities of the corresponding AN will be: first a_{t_i} (offer) and then a_{t_j} (request). According to the semantics of AN, for each action a_t firstly the function of the corresponding input gate $IG(a_t)$ will be executed, and then the function of the corresponding output gate $OG(a_t)$.

For each input gate, its guard ensures that the corresponding principal does not evolve autonomously but its behaviour adheres with the synthesised controller. In particular, for an activity in correspondence with an offer transitions t_o the guard checks that the place act is empty (i.e. there are no other pending offers waiting to be received), and that the overall marking of the network corresponds to a state of the CA where the (offer) activity can be fired (i.e. $\mu(\vec{q})$) such that $\vec{q} \in S \uparrow_{q,i,\bar{a}}$).

The marking changes (function f of, respectively, input and output gate) by setting to zero the marking of source place q of the principal i who is firing the offer and by adding one token in the target place and $id(o)$ tokens to place act, to record that the offer o has been fired. For an activity in correspondence with a request transition t_r, the guard checks if the marking of act codifies the corresponding offer (i.e. the offer has been fired), and if the overall marking of the network corresponds to a state of the automaton where the (request) activity can be fired (i.e. in $S \downarrow_{q,i,a}$). The marking changes by setting to zero the markings of the source place act (the offer has been received) and by adding a token in the target place.

The conditions on the gates allow to define the set of places of the AN as the union of states of principals. An alternative solution could be to consider as set of places the states of the product of principals (i.e. $Q_1 \times \ldots \times Q_n$), and avoiding the guards on input gates. However, the latter solution would generate a bigger state-space. In the following, $\Pi^i(\mathcal{A})$ is the projection operator of CA, extracting from a CA $\mathcal{A}$ of rank $n > 1$ the i-th principal with $1 \leq i \leq n$. The mapping is formally defined below.

Definition 4 (Mapping). *Let* $\mathcal{A} = \langle Q, \vec{q}_0, A^r, A^o, T, F \rangle$ *be a CA of rank* n *such that* $\forall i \in \mathbb{N}^{<n}$. $\Pi^i(\mathcal{A}) = \langle Q_i, \vec{q}_{0(i)}, A^r_i, A^o_i, T_i, F_i \rangle$. *The mapping function* $[\![-]\!] : C\mathcal{A} \to AN$ *is defined as* $[\![\mathcal{A}]\!] = \mathcal{N}$ *where* $\mathcal{N} = \langle P, A, I, O, \gamma, \tau, \iota, o \rangle$ *and:*

- $P = \bigcup_{i \in \mathbb{N}^{<n}} Q_i \cup \{act\}$, $A = \{a_t \mid t \in T_i, i \in \mathbb{N}^{<n}\}$,
- $I = \{IG(a_t) \mid a_t \in A\}$, *where* $\forall a_t \in A$ *s.t.* $t = (q, a, q') \in T_i, i \in \mathbb{N}^{<n}$

$$\textit{if } a \in \mathbb{O} \textit{ then } \begin{cases} IG(a_t) = (\bigcup_{\vec{q} \in S \uparrow_{q,i,a}} \{\vec{q}(1), \ldots, \vec{q}(n)\} \cup \{act\}, g, f) \\ g = ((\mu(act) == 0) \wedge (\bigvee_{\vec{q} \in S \uparrow_{q,i,a}} \mu(\vec{q}) == 1)), \\ f(\mu) = \{\mu' \mid \forall p \in P \setminus \{q\}.\mu'(p) = \mu(p), \mu'(q) = 0\} \end{cases}$$

$$\textit{if } a \in \mathbb{R} \textit{ then } \begin{cases} IG(a_t) = (\bigcup_{\vec{q} \in S \downarrow_{q,i,a}} \{\vec{q}(1), \ldots, \vec{q}(n)\} \cup \{act\}, g, f) \\ g = ((\mu(act) == id(\bar{a})) \wedge (\bigvee_{\vec{q} \in S \downarrow_{q,i,a}} \mu(\vec{q}) == 1)), \\ f(\mu) = \{\mu' \mid \forall p \notin \{q, act\}.\mu'(p) = \mu(p), \mu'(q) = \mu'(act) = 0\} \end{cases}$$

- $O = \{OG(a_t) \mid a_t \in A\}$ *s.t.* $\forall a_t \in A, t = (q, a, q') \in T_i, i \in \mathbb{N}^{<n}$. $OG(a_t) = (\{q', act\}, f)$ *where if* $a \in \mathbb{O}$ *then*
  $f(\mu) = \{\mu' \mid \forall p \in P \setminus \{q', act\}.\mu'(p) = \mu(p)\mu'(q') = 1, \mu'(act) = id(a)\}$
  else if $a \in \mathbb{R}$ *then* $f(\mu) = \{\mu' \mid \forall p \in P \setminus \{q'\}.\mu'(p) = \mu(p), \mu'(q') = 1$
- $\forall a \in A.\gamma(a) = 1, \tau(a) = Instantaneous, IG(a) = \{ig\}.\iota(ig) = a,$
- $\forall a \in A, OG(a) = \{og\}.o(og) = (a, 1)$.

The initial marking $[\![\mathcal{A}]\!]$ *is* $\mu_0(\vec{q}_0) = 1, \mu_0(act) = 0$ *and the set of final markings is* $\{\mu \mid \mu(\vec{q}) = 1, \vec{q} \in F, \mu(act) = 0\}$.

Example 1. In Fig. 5 the AN $\mathcal{N} = [\![\mathcal{KS}_{H_1 \otimes H_2 \otimes Q}]\!]$ computed through Definition 4 is depicted. For example, for the activity off_ins we have the input gate $ig11 = (P, g, f)$ where the places of the input gate are: $P =$

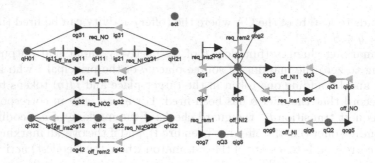

Fig. 5. The AN $[\![\mathcal{K}S_{H\otimes H\otimes Q}]\!]$.

$\{qH01, qH02, qQ0, \ qH12, qH11, act\}$; the guard is: $g = (\mu(act)\!=\!=\!0) \wedge (\mu(qH01)\!=\!=\!\mu(qH02)\!=\!=\!\mu(qQ0)\!=\!=\!1 \vee \mu(qH01)\!=\!=\!\mu(qH22)\!=\!=\!\mu(qQ0)\!=\!=\!1) \vee \mu(qH01)\!=\!=\!\mu(qH12)\!=\!=\!\mu(qQ0)\!=\!=\!1))$; and the change of marking is $f(\mu) = (\mu'(qH01) = 0, \forall p \in P \setminus \{qH01\}.\mu'(p) = \mu(p))$. Moreover, the output gate $og1 = (P, f)$ where its places are $P = \{qH11, act\}$ and the change of marking is $f(\mu) = \mu'(qH11) = 1, \mu'(act) = id(\overline{ins}), \forall p \in P\setminus \{qH11, act\}, \mu'(p) = \mu(p)$.

The following definition provides a mapping from transitions of CA to corresponding activities of AN, and will be useful in the following. Even though traces in strong agreement are only made by match transitions, we also consider offer and request transitions for a total mapping.

Definition 5. *The mapping from a transition t of a CA to the corresponding activity a_t of AN is defined as:*

$$[\![(\vec{q}, \vec{a}, \vec{q}')]\!] = \begin{cases} a_{(\vec{q}_{(i)}, \vec{a}_{(i)}, \vec{q}'_{(i)})} & \text{if } \vec{a} \text{ offer/request}, a_{(i)} \neq \bullet \\ a_{t1}a_{t2} & \text{if } \vec{a} \text{ match}, \vec{a}_{(i)} \in \mathbb{O}, \vec{a}_{(j)} \in \mathbb{R}, t1 = (\vec{q}_{(i)}, \vec{a}_{(i)}, \vec{q}'_{(i)}) \\ & t2 = (\vec{q}_{(j)}, \vec{a}_{(j)}, \vec{q}'_{(j)}) \end{cases}$$

The trace correspondence between the contract automaton $\mathcal{A}$ and the corresponding activity network $\mathcal{N}$ is proved below. Firstly, we need to define the notion of bisimulation between $\mathcal{A}$ and $\mathcal{N}$.

Definition 6. *Let $\mathcal{A}$ be a CA of rank n and $\mathcal{N}$ be an AN. We say that $\mathcal{A}$ and $\mathcal{N}$ are bisimilar, denoted $\mathcal{A} \sim \mathcal{N}$ iff there exists a binary relation $B \subseteq Q \times M_P$ such that $(\vec{q}_0, \mu_0) \in B$ and for any $(\vec{q}, \mu) \in B$ the following holds:*

1. *$\forall \vec{q} \xrightarrow{\vec{a}} \vec{q}'$ there exists $\mu \xrightarrow{[\![(\vec{q}, \vec{a}, \vec{q}')]\!]}{}_{,*}\mu'$ s.t. $(\vec{q}', \mu') \in B$, and*
2. *$\forall \mu \xrightarrow{a_{t1}a_{t2}}{}_{,*}\mu'$ there exists $\vec{q} \xrightarrow{\vec{a}} \vec{q}'$ s.t. $[\![(\vec{q}, \vec{a}, \vec{q}')]\!] = a_{t1}a_{t2}, (\vec{q}', \mu') \in B$*

The correspondence between a strongly safe controller of $\mathcal{A}$ and the corresponding activity network $\mathcal{N}$ is given below.

Lemma 2. *Let $\mathcal{K}S_{\mathcal{A}}$ be a (strongly safe) controller of $\mathcal{A}$ and $\mathcal{N} = [\![\mathcal{K}S_{\mathcal{A}}]\!]$ be the corresponding activity network, then: $\mathcal{K}S_{\mathcal{A}} \sim \mathcal{N}$.*

Example 2. In Sect. 2 we noted that the $\mathcal{KS}_{H_1 \otimes H_2 \otimes Q}$ over-approximates the behaviour of the analysed system, and so does $[\![\mathcal{KS}_{H_1 \otimes H_2 \otimes Q}]\!]$ by Lemma 2.

An important consequence of Lemma 2 is that an activity network computed through the mapping in Definition 4 is *convergent*.

Theorem 1. *Let $\mathcal{KS}_A$ be a (strongly safe) controller of the CA $\mathcal{A}$, and $\mathcal{N} = [\![\mathcal{KS}_A]\!]$ be the corresponding activity network, then $\mathcal{N}$ is convergent*

A refinement relation between two AN is introduced below. The refined network $\mathcal{N}'$ will have stricter conditions on guards of input gates, a subset or the same activities of $\mathcal{N}$ and a subset or the same set of places. Moreover, the functions of gates will be equal to the former network, except for the new places. Intuitively, $\mathcal{N}'$ will admit fewer behaviours (i.e. firing of activities) than $\mathcal{N}$.

Definition 7. *Let $\mathcal{N} = \langle P,\ A,\ I,\ O,\ \gamma,\ \tau,\ \iota,\ 0 \rangle$ and $\mathcal{N}' = \langle P',\ A',\ I',\ O',\ \gamma',\ \tau',\ \iota',\ 0' \rangle$ be two activity networks, then $\mathcal{N}'$ refines $\mathcal{N}$, written $\mathcal{N}' \preceq \mathcal{N}$, iff*

- *$P' \subseteq P;\ A' \subseteq A;$*
- *$ig = (P, g, f) \in I_{AP}, \iota(ig) = a$ implies $ig' = (P', g', f') \in I_{AP'}, \iota'(ig') = a$ where g' implies g and $\forall \mu, p \in P'.f(\mu)(p) = f'(\mu)(p)$ (written $ig' \preceq ig$);*
- *$og = (P, f) \in O_{AP}, o(og) = a$ implies $og' = (P', f') \in O_{AP'}, o'(og') = a$ and $\forall \mu, p \in P'.f(\mu)(p) = f'(\mu)(p)$ (written $og' \preceq og$);*
- *$\forall a \in A'.\gamma(a) = \gamma'(a), \tau(a) = \tau'(a), \forall ig \in IG(a), ig' \in IG'(a), ig' \preceq ig.\iota(ig) = \iota'(ig'), \forall og \in OG(a), og' \in OG'(a), og' \preceq og.o(og) = o'(og')$*
- *the initial marking μ'_0 of $\mathcal{N}'$ is s.t. $\forall p \in P'.\mu'_0(p) = \mu_0(p)$, and the final markings of $\mathcal{N}'$ are $\{\mu' \mid \mu$ final marking of $\mathcal{N} \wedge \forall p \in P'.\mu'(p) = \mu(p)\}$.*

Simulation between two AN is now introduced, and will be used in the following.

Definition 8. *Let $\mathcal{N}, \mathcal{N}'$ be two AN, then $\mathcal{N}$ simulates $\mathcal{N}'$, written $\mathcal{N}' \leq \mathcal{N}$ iff there exists a binary relation $R \subseteq M_{P'} \times M_P$ such that $(\mu'_0, \mu_0) \in R$ and for any $(\mu', \mu) \in R$ it holds: $\forall \mu' \xrightarrow{a} \mu'_1$ there exists $\mu \xrightarrow{a} \mu_1$ s.t. $(\mu'_1, \mu_1) \in R$.*

The next lemma shows that $\preceq$ does not introduce unwanted behaviours in $\mathcal{N}'$.

Lemma 3. *Let $\mathcal{N}$ be an AN and $\mathcal{N}'$ be s.t. $\mathcal{N}' \preceq \mathcal{N}$, then it holds $\mathcal{N}' \leq \mathcal{N}$.*

When refining networks it is possible to introduce deadlocks in the system, by disabling or removing all activities in a reachable marking. This could happen if, for example, we refine all predicates of input gates as $g' = g \wedge false$.

The following theorem uses a correspondence with the former mpc from which $\mathcal{N}$ was obtained and implies convergence of a refined network $\mathcal{N}' \preceq \mathcal{N}$.

Theorem 2. *Let $\mathcal{KS}_A, \mathcal{KS}'_A$ be respectively the mpc of $\mathcal{A}$ and the controller from Lemma 1. Moreover let $\mathcal{N} = [\![\mathcal{KS}_A]\!]$, $\mathcal{N}' = [\![\mathcal{KS}'_A]\!]$, then $\mathcal{N}' \preceq \mathcal{N}$.*

Example 3. The network $[\![\mathcal{KS}']\!] = \mathcal{N}'$ is, by Theorem 2, a refinement of $\mathcal{N}$, and is *convergent* by Theorem 1.

A commutative diagram explaining Theorem 2 is depicted below. Theorem 2 yields two procedures for generating a verified system that amounts to refine either the AN or the mpc. Both procedures start by (i) modelling the system as a composition of principals $\mathcal{A}$ in input, and (ii) compute the mpc $\mathcal{KS}_A$. The first procedure p1 refines the controller $\mathcal{KS}_A$ to a controller $\mathcal{KS}'_A$ (p1-i) and translates it to a network $\mathcal{N}' = [\![\mathcal{KS}'_A]\!]$ (p1-ii). Alternatively, the second procedure p2 generates the corresponding AN $[\![\mathcal{KS}_A]\!] = \mathcal{N}$ (p2-i), and refines $\mathcal{N}$ to a network $\mathcal{N}''$ with stricter guards on the input gates (p2-ii).

While p1 yields a convergent network by Theorem 2, p2 does it only if $(\mathcal{N}' \sim \mathcal{N}'')$ holds, that is both refinements of $\mathcal{N}$ and $\mathcal{KS}_A$ result in removing the same unwanted behaviours. Note that in general $\mathcal{N}' \neq \mathcal{N}''$ could hold, and we remark that the AN refinement is an optional step.

$$\begin{array}{ccc} \mathcal{KS}_A & \xrightarrow{\supseteq \mathscr{L}} & \mathcal{KS}'_A \\ {\scriptstyle[\![-]\!]}\downarrow & & \downarrow{\scriptstyle[\![-]\!]} \\ \mathcal{N} & \xrightarrow{\succeq} & \mathcal{N}' \end{array}$$

6 Stochastic Continuous Aspects

The stochastic continuous behaviour related to the temperatures of the rail road track to allow the analysis of quantitative properties is now considered. As depicted in Fig. 1, we will use the SAN formalism. Generally, for modelling CPS we need to add stochastic hybrid behaviour to the convergent network obtained either with p1 or p2. This can be obtained by extending the AN to a SAN model, as defined below. In the following let AN $\mathcal{N}'$ be a sub-network of $\mathcal{N}''$ only if $\mathcal{N}''$ contains all places and activities of $\mathcal{N}'$.

Definition 9. *Let $\mathcal{N}, \mathcal{N}', \mathcal{N}''$ be AN s.t. $\mathcal{N}' \preceq \mathcal{N}$ and $\mathcal{N}'$ is a sub-net of $\mathcal{N}''$, then given C, F, G the SAN $\mathcal{S} = \langle \mathcal{N}'', C, F, G \rangle$ is a decorated $\mathcal{N}$, written $\mathcal{S} \leftrightharpoons \mathcal{N}$.*

Example 4. The AN $\mathcal{N}$ will be decorated to a SAN $\mathcal{S}$ describing all stochastic continuous information related to the quantities that we want to evaluate, which in this case are the temperature of the rail road track and the weather conditions. In particular, an extended place $Temperature_i$ (i.e. the marking is a real number) describing the physical temperature of the rail road track is shared with the corresponding network H_i. Moreover a stochastic process modelling the weather conditions and a differential equation modelling the physical evolution of temperature through induction heating are added to the SAN model $\mathcal{S}$ (see [4] for technical details). This decoration is such that $\mathcal{S}$ preserves all the logic described in $\mathcal{KS}'$, and can be used to quantitatively analyse the measures of interest. The guards g of input gates of activities off_ins$_i$ are refined as $g' = g \wedge (Temperature_i < T_{wa})$. The guards g of input gates of activities off_rem$_i$ are refined as $g' = g \wedge (Temperature_i > T_{wo})$. All the guards g' imply the corresponding g, and the network *Cyber Module* is a correct refinement of $\mathcal{N}'$ and the corresponding SAN is a correct decoration.

Now each guard depends also on the (continuous stochastic) marking of place $Temperature_i$, and generally the model checking problem for complex stochastic hybrid systems is undecidable [16]. Nevertheless, through our methodology it is possible to guarantee: (1) by Lemma 3 that $\mathcal{N}'$ simulates the synthesised controller, i.e. no unwanted behaviour is introduced by the refinement; (2) by assuming that $(Temperature_i < T_{wa})$ and $(Temperature_i > T_{wo})$ eventually hold, the network $\mathcal{N}'$ such that $\mathcal{S} \leftrightharpoons \mathcal{N}'$ is convergent. We remark that if the above assumptions are not verified then the switches will never fail and will never waste energy. Hence, the overall behaviour of the system is guaranteed to be safe. If, for example, a higher consumption of energy is detected, then it is formally proved that this is not due to a wrong interaction between a heater asking to be deactivated and the central control unit not receiving the request, but can only be related to the physical parameters instantiated in $\mathcal{S}$ (e.g. too high T_{wo}).

Note that Definition 7 does not pose any restriction on places used in gates of the refined network. Indeed, in the extension the guards of $\mathcal{N}'$ could use newly added places. For a correct design, the new places and activities of $\mathcal{S}$ should model the stochastic hybrid behaviour, while all the discrete (verified) behaviours should be defined in the "embedded" network $\mathcal{N}'$.

7   Related Work and Conclusion

Related Work. Several approaches for the verification and validation of stochastic hybrid models have been proposed in the literature. In particular, model checking [12] is a widely-used and powerful approach for the verification of finite state systems. However, the continuous stochastic nature of CPS is not always captured by finite state systems, and models as hybrid automata [15], hybrid Petri net [14], stochastic activity network [20] have been proposed for modelling CPS, where the evolution of the continuous variables can be uniform or described by ordinary differential equations. Several tools have been proposed for their modelling, evaluation and verification, as for example UPPAAL [17], Kronos [21], Möbius [11]. When the continuous time behaviours of CPS are subject to complex and stochastic dynamics, the model checking problem is undecidable [16], and generally an approximation to more tractable models, as for example timed automata [2], is performed.

Statistical Model Checking (SMC) [19] uses results from statistics on top of simulations of a system to decide whether a given property is satisfied with some degree of confidence, and it represents a valid alternative to probabilistic model checking and testing, especially in the case of undecidability. UPPAAL-SMC [13] has been proposed as a tool that implements the above techniques. Compared to these previous works, we propose a hybrid qualitative and quantitative framework for analysing both critical quantitative properties and qualitative measures related to performance and dependability parameters, which is based on a formal relation between different formalisms to account for these analyses.

Conclusion. We have proposed a modular approach to efficiently design and verify models of cyber-physical systems. These models are thought of as composed of a cyber (discrete) and a physical (stochastic continuous) part, that are modelled through different formalisms: (1) contract automata models for the cyber module and (2) stochastic activity networks for the physical module. A correct mapping from CA to SAN has been formalised, where CA are firstly mapped to AN and then decorated to SAN. Refinement relations from abstract to more concrete representations have been defined for all these formalisms, while retaining the correctness of the mapping. The proposed methodology has been applied to a realistic case study from the railway industry: a system of rail road switch heaters. This case study has been analysed in [5] to evaluate indicators of reliability and energy consumption. In this paper critical aspects related to the interactions of components implementing a policy of energy consumption have been verified through our methodology, and the corresponding SAN models have been automatically synthesised with further guarantees on the correctness of the control.

We are planning to implement our methodology as a toolchain by using existing tools (e.g. Möbius tool, CAT [7]), for generating correct SAN models starting from CA descriptions of components interactions, and to extend the approach to consider other existing formalisms and techniques [9].

Acknowledgements. This work has been partially supported by the Tuscany Region project POR FESR 2014–2020 SISTER and H2020 2017–2019 S2R-OC-IP2-01-2017 ASTRail.

References

1. Abdollahi, M.A., Movaghar, A.: A modeling tool for a new definition of stochastic activity networks. IJST Trans. B **29**, 79–92 (2005)
2. Alur, R., Dill, D.L.: A theory of timed automata. Theor. Comput. Sci. **126**(2), 183–235 (1994)
3. Balbo, G.: Introduction to generalized stochastic Petri nets. In: Bernardo, M., Hillston, J. (eds.) SFM 2007. LNCS, vol. 4486, pp. 83–131. Springer, Heidelberg (2007). https://doi.org/10.1007/978-3-540-72522-0_3
4. Basile, D., Di Giandomenico, F., Gnesi, S.: A refinement approach to analyse critical cyber-physical systems: extended version. Technical report 2017-TR-005, ISTI-CNR (2017). http://puma.isti.cnr.it/rmydownload.php?filename=cnr.isti/cnr.isti/2017-TR-005/2017-TR-005.pdf
5. Basile, D., Chiaradonna, S., Di Giandomenico, F., Gnesi, S.: A stochastic model-based approach to analyse reliable energy-saving rail road switch heating systems. JRTPM **6**(2), 163–181 (2016)
6. Basile, D., Degano, P., Ferrari, G.L.: Automata for specifying and orchestrating service contracts. LMCS **12**(4), 1–51 (2016)
7. Basile, D., Degano, P., Ferrari, G.-L., Tuosto, E.: Playing with our CAT and communication-centric applications. In: Albert, E., Lanese, I. (eds.) FORTE 2016. LNCS, vol. 9688, pp. 62–73. Springer, Cham (2016). https://doi.org/10.1007/978-3-319-39570-8_5
8. Basile, D., Di Giandomenico, F., Gnesi, S.: Enhancing models correctness through formal verification: a case study from the railway domain. In: Amaretto, Modelsward (2017)

9. Basile, D., Di Giandomenico, F., Gnesi, S.: Statistical model checking of an energy-saving cyber-physical system in the railway domain. In: SAC (2017)
10. Bause, F., Kritzinger, P.S.: Stochastic Petri nets: an introduction to the theory. SIGMETRICS Perform. Eval. Rev. **26**(2) (1996)
11. Clark, G., Courtney, T., Daly, D., Deavours, D., Derisavi, S., Doyle, J.M., Sanders, W.H., Webster, P.: The möbius modeling tool. In: PNPM (2001)
12. Clarke Jr., E.M., Grumberg, O., Peled, D.A.: Model Checking. MIT Press, Cambridge (1999)
13. David, A., Larsen, K.G., Legay, A., Mikuăionis, M., Poulsen, D.B.: Uppaal SMC tutorial. Int. J. Softw. Tools Technol. Transf. **17**, 397–415 (2015)
14. David, R., Alla, H.: On hybrid Petri nets. Discret. Event Dynamic Syst. **11**(1–2), 9–40 (2001)
15. Henzinger, T.A.: The theory of hybrid automata. In: LICS 1996, p. 278. IEEE Computer Society (1996)
16. Henzinger, T.A., Ho, P.-H.: Algorithmic analysis of nonlinear hybrid systems. In: Wolper, P. (ed.) CAV 1995. LNCS, vol. 939, pp. 225–238. Springer, Heidelberg (1995). https://doi.org/10.1007/3-540-60045-0_53
17. Larsen, K.G., Pettersson, P., Yi, W.: Uppaal in a nutshell. Int. J. Softw. Tools Technol. Transf. **1**, 134–152 (1997)
18. Lee, E.A.: Cyber physical systems: design challenges. In: ISORC 2008. IEEE Computer Society (2008)
19. Legay, A., Delahaye, B., Bensalem, S.: Statistical model checking: an overview. In: Barringer, H., Falcone, Y., Finkbeiner, B., Havelund, K., Lee, I., Pace, G., Roşu, G., Sokolsky, O., Tillmann, N. (eds.) RV 2010. LNCS, vol. 6418, pp. 122–135. Springer, Heidelberg (2010). https://doi.org/10.1007/978-3-642-16612-9_11
20. Sanders, W.H., Meyer, J.F.: Stochastic activity networks: formal definitions and concepts. In: Brinksma, E., Hermanns, H., Katoen, J.-P. (eds.) EEF School 2000. LNCS, vol. 2090, pp. 315–343. Springer, Heidelberg (2001). https://doi.org/10.1007/3-540-44667-2_9
21. Yovine, S.: KRONOS: a verification tool for real-time systems. JSTTT **1**, 123–133 (1997). (kronos user's manual release 2.2)

Injecting Formal Verification in FMI-Based Co-simulations of Cyber-Physical Systems

Luís Diogo Couto[1], Stylianos Basagiannis[1(✉)], El Hassan Ridouane[1],
Alie El-Din Mady[1], Miran Hasanagic[2], and Peter Gorm Larsen[2]

[1] United Technologies Research Center, Cork, Ireland
{CoutoLD,BasagiS,RidouaE,MadyAA}@utrc.utc.com
[2] Aarhus University, Aarhus, Denmark
{miran.hasanagic,pgl}@eng.au.dk

Abstract. Model-based design tools supporting the Functional Mockup Interface (FMI) standard, often employ specification languages ideal for modelling specific domain problems without capturing the overall behavior of a Cyber-Physical System (CPS). These tools tend to handle some important CPS characteristics implicitly, such as network communication handshakes. At the same time, formal verification although a powerful approach, is still decoupled to FMI co-simulation processes, as it can easily lead to infeasible explorations due to state space explosion of continuous or discrete representations. In this paper we exploit co-modelling and co-simulation concepts combined with the injection of formal verification results indirectly in a model-based design workflow that will enable verification engineering benefits in a heterogeneous, multi-disciplinary design process for CPSs. We demonstrate the approach using a Heating, Ventilation and Air Conditioning (HVAC) case study where communication delays may affect the CPS system's analysis. We model discrete events based on the Vienna Development Method Real-Time dialect, Continuous Time phenomena using Modelica, and communications using PROMELA. Results are considered and inspected both at the level of constituent models and the overall co-simulation.

1 Introduction

One of the approaches to Cyber-Physical System (CPS) analysis is based nowadays on the availability of interoperable, precise, and efficient co-simulation frameworks. Starting from requirements definition of heterogeneous components of a CPS, designers are being challenged to trace and analyse correctly the requirements validity against intermediate system models. Moreover, the complexity of the cyber and physical aspects of the system makes it important to employ approaches based on model abstraction techniques. Those interactions will include shared parameters exchanged between Discrete Event (DE) and Continuous Time (CT) models in a contract based manner that will realise the CPS evolution. A well known approach that standardises co-simulation is the Functional Mockup Interface (FMI) standard [4].

© Springer International Publishing AG 2018
A. Cerone and M. Roveri (Eds.): SEFM 2017 Workshops, LNCS 10729, pp. 284–299, 2018.
https://doi.org/10.1007/978-3-319-74781-1_20

The INTO-CPS project [16] is developing a tool-chain to support model-based engineering of CPSs [9], based on FMI. In the INTO-CPS approach, the system configuration and CPU instruction execution is typically modelled within the DE models; in this case using the Overture tool [15] and the VDM-RT notation [17]. CT models describing physical phenomena (e.g. thermal, fluid or air flow dynamics) are modelled using notations and tools such as Modelica [8] or 20-Sim [13] in order to engage differential equation solvers to evaluate dynamic behaviour.

The INTO-CPS approach enables CPS developers to take advantage of the powerful domain-specific features and abstraction capabilities of various specialized modelling and simulation tools. This maps well onto the kinds of heterogeneous and multi-disciplinary teams that are necessary to carry out CPS design and development. On the other hand, the kinds of simulation tools employed in INTO-CPS and similar approaches often handle CPS characteristics like network communication protocols implicitly. Formal verification and especially model checking is a powerful tool that can complement these approaches but it is typically decoupled from the co-simulations, as it can easily lead to infeasible explorations due to state space explosion challenges.

In this work in progress paper, we seek to address the aforementioned issue by combining co-modelling and co-simulation with formal verification by means of injecting verification results in the co-simulations. The work does not focus on pruning the resulted state space; instead it uses the expressiveness power of PROMELA to model communications principles in interacting co-simulated objects using the FMI standard that previously could not be realized. In our case, we manually model the communication medium and protocol in Promela, in order to fully exploit synchronous or asynchronous communication packet exchange between our Heating, Ventilation and Air-Conditioning (HVAC) objects, using un-buffered (rendez-vouz) or buffered channels respectively [12]. This enables both verification engineers to be brought into a closer collaboration loop with the multi-disciplinary CPS team and results to be used to steer subsequent validation efforts including e.g. communication delays. We demonstrate our approach by means of a case study drawn from the HVAC domain.

The remainder of this paper is structured as follows: in Sect. 2, we present information about FMI co-simulation and the HVAC domain, necessary to follow the rest of the paper; we describe our approach to combining verification with co-simulation in Sect. 3 and instantiate it in Sect. 4; in Sect. 5, we present and discuss co-simulation results; finally, we conclude in Sect. 6 with remarks and next steps for the proposed approach.

2   Background

A CPS can be defined as an integration of computation with physical processes. According to literature, CPSs are considered to be a composition of networks of embedded devices that control physical processes, based on open or closed feedback loops where computations are being affected by physical phenomena [6].

Nowadays, CPS complexity has considerably increased the cyber-physical points of interaction to a state where system correctness and functional safety are a great challenge for validation. In addition to that, cyber-physical devices tend to be developed by multidisciplinary engineers, thus increasing the need for a common engineering framework where different engineers contribute common CPS models and concepts.

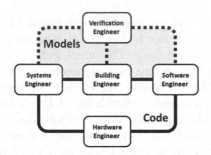

Fig. 1. Multidisciplinary engineer scheme for model-based design of CPS

In this paper, we present a CPS example derived from the HVAC domain. HVAC systems are in general cyber-physical systems composed by HVAC equipment controlling the temperature of areas through heating or cooling of air circulated in rooms by mastering a series of actuation devices (e.g. fans, water valves) and external physical phenomena (i.e. external temperature, air flow). Embedded devices on the HVAC equipment are typically executing control loop feedback mechanisms (e.g. PI controllers [22]), prognostics, health management and decision support functions that allow the device to handle mechanical components of the equipment. Currently the equipment considered for the HVAC case study consists of: 4 Fan Coil Units (FCUs) responsible for controlling temperature in a given area; 1 supervisory controller coordinating the FCUs; and 1 air handling unit heating or cooling the circulated air to the FCUs. In terms of necessary competencies for CPS development, as seen from Fig. 1, there are various engineers involved in the HVAC development cycle. For our example, we have identified the following: (a) A *system engineer* will be responsible for CPS system requirements and validation, (b) A *building engineer* for modelling the physical effects of the CPS, (c) A *software engineer* for modeling and realisation of the CPS software, (d) a *verification engineer* for extracting model verification and validation guaranties for high or low level requirements and (e) a *hardware engineer* for system realization on a target platform. Towards the CPS analysis, focus is given to:

- Artifacts (models or code) generated from each of the engineer
- The common CPS framework that would allow the multi-model interaction towards validation and verification of the system.

An effective way to involve multiple engineers through a common framework is by using co-simulation approaches such as the FMI standard [4]. FMI is a tool independent industry standard that supports the collaborative simulation (co-simulation) of models developed in different tools and notations. This makes it well suited for supporting model-based development of CPSs, whose nature is highly heterogeneous. In the FMI, the models to be co-simulated are exported by their tools as Functional Mockup Units (FMUs) – compiled C code and XML-based model descriptions that specify the inputs and outputs of the model, thus abstracting away the internal complexity and domain-specificity of the model. A master algorithm is responsible for executing the co-simulation by coordinating the exchange of data between FMUs and progressing overall co-simulation time. In the INTO-CPS project, the implementation of the master algorithm and execution of co-simulations are handled by a tool called co-simulation Orchestration Engine (COE) from the INTO-CPS project [16].

3 Approach

The method proposed in this paper indirectly captures the communication delays due to communication handling mechanisms that are imposed by the used protocol, including them in the FMI-based CPS co-simulation. Since the current engineer development process does not include the means (e.g. modelling tools) to capture these communication mechanism and reason about packet delays within the FMI context, we argue that the proposed approach could be of benefit especially where communication delays can affect the overall CPS correctness. Efforts have been recorded in the current bibliography that try to tackle network verification problems by using either executable formal models in network simulation [2,3] or extracting formal verification results with respect to communication delays [7,19]. The main difference highlighted in this work is the incorporation of verification results within the FMI-based co-simulation processes that currently handle communication delays implicitly.

We propose an experimental work flow that introduce the use of formal verification techniques to evaluate network communication requirements in an FMI-based co-simulation experiment. Figure 2 illustrates the work flow, instantiated in the HVAC case study with the INTO-CPS tool chain. The work flow consists of the following steps:

1. model the discrete aspects of the systems, including system deployment configuration and behaviour of the cyber components in VDM-RT
2. model physical phenomena of the system in Modelica
3. extract physical plant FMU using Dymola tool
4. model communication aspects of distributed components in Promela
5. verify desired properties using the Spin for VDM-RT time parameters
6. if verification is not successful, update the DE models (e.g. VDM-RT) by constraining the RT timing parameters compared to the initial ones verified in Spin, for communicating objects in VDM; rerun the verification till no errors found with the refined Linear Temporal Logic (LTL) properties

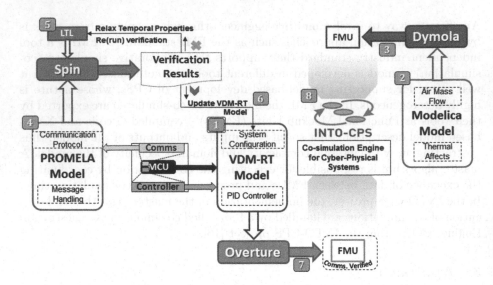

Fig. 2. Proposed experimental work flow

7. generate FMU for DE model with injected verification results using Overture tool. The new FMU will contain updated RT timing parameters that have been previously formally verified by Spin
8. launch a co-simulation experiment with the produced FMUs using the INTO-CPS COE and generate co-simulation results.

Spin model checking verification results are glued to the co-simulation by confirming that our VDM-RT timing parameters do take into account certain communication delays contributed to the communication overhead of the modelled protocol. For example if communication specifications for a UART protocol are being defined in Promela for the communicating objects i.e. number of data packets expected to be sent to a common bus in t msec reaching an object, we verify total time delays and packet loses for a network of objects mapped in Promela, equally as in our co-simulation. Total time delays and packet conflicts are defined in our customer requirements, depending on the use-case. Parameter t is being revised (e.g. decreased) in our VDM specification when model checking results can be produced. If verification is successful for the modelled communication protocol, timing parameters are acting as a guard to the VDM model enforcing the delays of the protocol in its generated FMU. Otherwise, the engineer will have to check its hardware characteristics to validate the constrained t value -whether it is supported- and re-run the verification, or to consider changing its hardware to support higher communication bandwidth.

In VDM, models consist of representations of the data on which a system operates and the functionality that is to be performed. In our case this will be the discrete aspects of the HVAC system which will include behavior of the control functionality residing in the FCU devices. Data in the VDM model includes the externally visible input or output and internal state data, which in our case will be the states of the FCUs. PROMELA and its expressiveness for modelling synchronous and asynchronous (buffered) communication channels, will help us 'quantify' communication conflicts and delays in the shared bus of the VDM-RT objects, represented on the discrete model. Since, those objects are co-simulated with the physical part (e.g. sensing the continuous-time environment temperature), each FCU controller expected behavior has to take into account communication conflicts such as lost messages, synchronization issues between master and slave as well as, jamming cases due to message overflow in the common bus due to malfunctions.

4   CPS Modelling

In this section, we describe the CPS modelling tasks necessary to combine co-simulation and verification. Our approach is instantantiated in a case study from the HVAC domain: temperature control in multiple rooms with supervision [10, 20]. Based on the INTO-CPS project [11], we carry out *Cyber* modelling using DE formalisms and *Physical* modelling using CT formalisms, leading to two kinds of constituent models. The verification model is created separately, and its results are subsequently injected in the co-simulation. For our case study, we have one DE model, and one CT model, mapped at an architecture level using SySML, and handling communication handshakes using a PROMELA model.

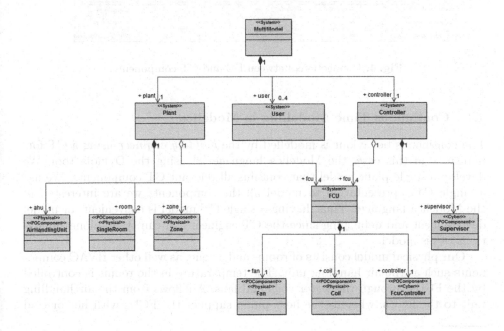

Fig. 3. Multi-model components for the HVAC case study.

SysML is used by the *system engineer* to describe the components of the CPS (which map onto the constituent models) and the connections between them, which are necessary to carry out co-simulations. The combination of the multiple constituent models and their connections is called *multi-model*. The components of the case study are shown in the INTO-CPS Architecture Diagram [1,5] of Fig. 3. Broadly speaking, the most relevant components are the controllers (which are parts of the DE model) and the various physical components such as rooms, encapsulated in a single CT plant model. The FCU component itself is abstract and represents the boundary between the CT and DE worlds, thus our system is inherently a hybrid system. The controllers and hardware of the FCU communicate via exchange of FMI signals across various ports, as shown in the INTO-CPS Connections Diagram of Fig. 4[1].

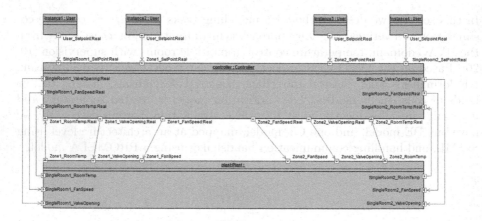

Fig. 4. Connections between DE and CT components.

4.1 Continuous Time Modelling in Modelica

The continuous behaviour is modelled by the *building engineer* using a CT formalism – in this case, the Modelica language [8] using the Dymola tool. We develop a single plant model that contains all relevant CT components. We use a single CT representation to model all the components we are interested in the Modelica language. Thus, having a single CT model is convenient for model development and debugging since the CT engineer can run stand-alone simulations of his model.

Our physical model consists of rooms and a zone, as well other HVAC components such as the air handling unit. The temperature in the rooms is controlled by the FCUs through the water coils and fans. Air flows from the air handling unit to the FCUs, whereas the heat pump supplies the FCUs with hot or cold

---

[1] The User component is a basic abstraction used only to enable requests to the system during co-simulation.

water. A PI controller regulates the fan speed and the rate of the water flow from the heat pump to the coil to maintain a constant temperature in the area in which the FCU is located. For space reasons, the Air Handling Unit descriptions modelled in DYMOLA is omitted from this paper.

The PI controller controls the actuation signals based on the sensor signals. This controller is present in both the CT and DE models. At the co-simulation level, the DE controller is used. The CT controller is primarily used to enable standalone simulation of the CT model.

The model is based on mass and energy balances in a given room/zone. Two major assumptions were used to simplify the model for a given zone: (a) zone air is uniformly distributed, and (b) long wave radiation exchange between surfaces is ignored. The energy balance equation of a zone can be described by:

$$m_{air\_zone}(C_{pa} + \omega_{zone}C_{pv})\frac{dT_{zone}}{dt} = \dot{m}_{air\_sa}C_{pa}(T_{sa} - T_{zone}) +$$
$$\dot{m}_{air\_sa}C_{pv}(\omega_{sa}T_{sa} - \omega_{zone}T_{zone}) + Q_{int} + \sum_{i}^{N_{surface}} Q_{structure\_i} +$$
$$\dot{m}_{inf}C_{pa}(T_{oa} - T_{zone}) + \sum_{i}^{N_{zone}} \dot{m}_i C_{pa}(T_{zone_i} - T_{zone}) + \dot{m}_v C_{pv}T_{zone}$$

The internal water vapour generation rate m_v is neglected since it is typically small in office buildings. The small heat transfer due to water vapor temperature difference between supply air flow and room air $m_air_{sa}C_{pv}(\omega_{sa}T_{sa} - \omega_{zone}T_{zone})$ is also neglected. The time rate of change of the zone air temperature is given by:

$$m_{air\_zone}C_{pa}\frac{dT_{zone}}{dt} = \dot{m}_{air\_zone}C_{pa}(T_{sa} - T_{zone}) + Q_{int} + \sum_{i}^{N_{surface}} Q_{structure\_i}$$
$$+ \dot{m}_{inf}C_{pa}(T_{oa} - T_{zone}) + \sum_{i}^{N_{zone}} \dot{m}_i C_{pa}(T_{zone_i} - T_{zone}) + \dot{m}_v C_{pv}T_{zone}$$

where: $m_{airZone}$ is air mass of room air [kg], C_{pa} is specific heat capacity of air [J/kg.°C], C_{pv} is specific heat capacity of water [J/kg.°C], T_{zone} is room air temperature (RAT) [°C], $\dot{m}_{air_{sa}}$ is the supply air mass flow rate [kg/s], $\dot{m}_{inf}$ is the infiltration mass flow rate [kg/s], $\dot{m}_v$ is the internal water vapor generation rate [kg/s], Q_{int} is the sum of the convective internal loads [W] (assumed to be constant), T_{isurf} is inside surface temperature [°C], T_{osurf} is outside surface temperature [°C], A is wall surface area [m^2], R_{wall} is thermal resistance of the wall [°C/W], C is capacity of the wall [J/°C] and T_{amb} is outside air temperature (OAT) [°C].

Profiling information on the complexity of the Modelica model, will report: 2087 components, 21278 variables, 979 constants, 11083 parameters, 9216 unknowns, 412 differentiated variables, 7028 equations, 5775 nontrivial. Modelica was also used to develop a simple model of the user behaviour. This model merely outputs different set point requests at predefined instances in time. Its primary purpose was to enable us to assess the performance of the models when users request changes in temperature.

4.2 Discrete Event Modelling Using VDM-RT

The discrete behaviour is modelled using a DE formalism by the *software engineer*. In the case of INTO-CPS, the real-time dialect of Vienna Development

Method (VDM) [23] is used. In our case study, we employ a single VDM-RT model that includes behavior of the PI controllers of the FCUs and the supervisor. This modelling choice provide us access to the rich set of VDM-RT features to specify distribution and to minimise the amount of DE-to-DE communication done through the FMI signals.

The model consists of four instances of PI controllers and a single supervisory controller. Each controller is allocated to an individual VDM-RT CPU and connected via a single VDM-RT bus. The role of the PI controllers is to execute a PI loop that regulates the temperature in the FCU's area. The role of the supervisor is to monitor the behavior of the PI controllers to ensure that desired higher level properties are exhibited. As an example, we show the supervisor operation that enforces that FCU set point stays within a given range by overriding the controller set points if they fall outside the range. A VDM post-condition ensures that the property must hold after the operation executes.

```
private setPointAdjust: Controller ==> ()
setPointAdjust (fcu) == (
  let sp = fcu.getSPValue(),
      target = if minTemp >= 0 and sp < minTemp
               then minTemp
               elseif maxTemp >= 0 and sp > maxTemp
               then maxTemp
               else sp
  in
    fcu.setSuperSetPoint(target)
)
post fcu.acquireSetPoint() <= maxTemp and
  fcu.acquireSetPoint() >= minTemp;
```

Listing 1.1. Supervisor property enforcing through set point adjustment.

Using the interpreter of the Overture tool, the model can be executed, enabling independent analysis of the behaviour of the discrete parts of the CPS. In this analysis, communication concerns are implicitly handled by VDM-RT by means of remote operation calls behind the scenes [23], as illustrated in Fig. 5. This figure shows the setPointAdjust operation where the getSPValue invocation is being sent across the bus that connects the CPUs of the supervisor and PI controller. In VDM-RT, communication times across the bus are implicitly calculated from the speed of the bus and size of arguments of the remote operation calls. We extend the model to allow for explicit control of communication duration, by making the bus connections instantaneous and prefixing them with parametrized delays. This is only an approximation – the delay occurs before executing the remote operation where the actual message passing takes place – but it allows us to inject timing result estimates extracted from the verification analysis. These results can them be further experimented with and analysed further in the DE model itself and, eventually, in a co-simulation.

It is worth noting that an important aspect of communication time to consider is the availability of the communication channel since this could affect the

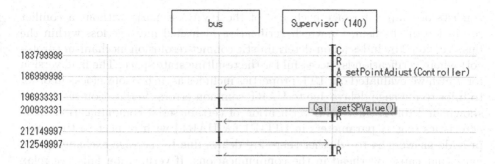

Fig. 5. Excerpt of Overture VDM-RT log viewer showing remote operation call.

communication time by introducing delays if the channel is not immediately available. Since we use an instant bus as channel, there are no communication delays in the DE model. Therefore, we have to account for them in the Promela model and the estimates extracted from it.

4.3 Communications Modelling in PROMELA

PROMELA (the input language of the Spin model checker [12]) is used by the *verification engineer* to model communication handshakes between the HVAC CPS entities in our use case. The PROMELA channel definition is ideal for describing distributed communication message exchange between multiple entities accessing a common bus. We model an arbitrary serial bus (UART), conflict resolution mechanism and 4 FCU entities as agents that will exchange messages with the supervisor, which controls the overall HVAC functionality.

Our objective is to identify the maximum time delays caused by UART conflicts by repetitive verification experiments for LTL formulae that will define serial channel properties. Particularly for our case, we are interested in verifying a certain degree of channel reliability with respect to errors found in the technical specifications of message transmission or receipt (i.e. Underrun or Framing errors [21]). As we would like to reason about all paths in the generated state space, we define LTL-P1 and LTL-P2 properties as follows:

LTL-P1: *Always if there is traffic in the bus, communication conflicts for all exchanged messages will be less than* $\gamma = 20\%$ *of total exchanges for total time t.*

$[\ ]((Exc_{msg} > 0\ \&\&\ Exch_{msg} \leq Total_{msg})\ \&\&\ Total_{time} < Time_{bound} \rightarrow (Total_{conflicts}) < Total_{msg} * (\gamma))$

LTL-P2: *An ACK message will be sent to the FCU before a PAYLOAD message has been received from the Supervisor*

$FCU_{(i)}[ACK_{rec} = TRUE] \rightarrow <> (FCU_{(i)}[PAYLOAD_{Sd} = TRUE]\ \&\&\ Time < 100)$

We developed 3 different versions of PROMELA models where the Spin model checker produced verification results, both for assertion statements within the models, as well as LTL properties defined as LTL-P1 and LTL-P2. Version 1 consists of simple message exchange of the HVAC scenario without a conflict resolution mechanism, for which verification identified message loss within the bus. Version 2 includes a non-deterministic conflict resolution mechanism (protocol) where verification is successful for the resulting state space. The final version for which we evaluated our LTL properties includes asynchronous clocks in order to infer to message delays due to UART common errors. Verification results are shown in Table 1. Successful verification of certain serial communication characteristics (e.g. γ parameters in LTL-P1 for UART) with respect to time, will provide answers as to whether there are delays due to message exchange problems that cause overhead in the communications. If verification fails, we relax the time constraints of the LTL property and rerun the experiment in order to produce a successful verification of the overall communications. Total relaxed time will create an additional delay overhead to the communication instructions executed, and thus force an update to our VDM-RT instruction execution duration parameters. For similar real-time model checking studies the reader can refer to [14].

Table 1. PROMELA model verification results using Spin model checker

Model version	States	Transitions	Memory	Exp. time	Result
Version 1	3031	6137	612 MB	0.05 sec	Fail
Version 2	44285	304015	611 MB	1.65 sec	Success
Final version	45706	866430	622 MB	4.4 sec	Success

5   Co-simulation Using the INTO-CPS Platform

In this section, we present the combination of co-simulation and formal verification. Co-simulation allows us to combine the capabilities of various domain-specific tools to validate more complex scenarios. As described in Sect. 3 and modelled in Sect. 4, our co-simulations results are based on a HVAC proof of concept use-case with FMUs extracted from Dymola and Overture tools (Fig. 6).

The timing estimates verified with Spin were taken and injected into the VDM-RT model. This model is then co-simulated with the Dymola model, using the INTO-CPS COE, a standalone tool for running FMI co-simulations with both fixed and variable step-size algorithms. Figure 7 shows co-simulation results for a scenario where the user requests set point changes outside the range allowed by the supervisor. We can see that, unlike the results shown from the standalone simulation, the supervisor steps in and ensures that the temperature is kept within the defined range – this is an example of the kinds of scenarios that co-simulation approaches can enable.

The results from Fig. 7 are not particularly sensitive to the timing estimates of the communication between supervisor and controllers. This is because temperature variations takes minutes to assert themselves, as described by the CT model,

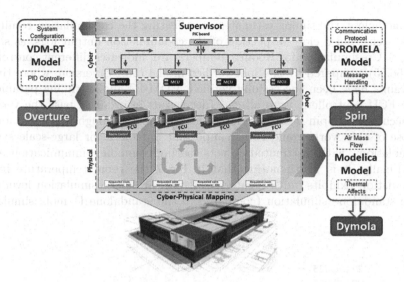

Fig. 6. HVAC proof of concept use case for proposed approach

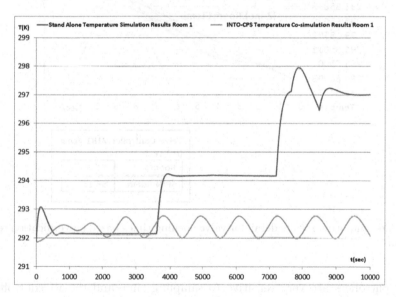

Fig. 7. Comparison between standalone simulation and INTO-CPS co-simulation results for Room 1 Temperature.

whereas the communications occur within milliseconds. Thus, even though the communication estimates from SPIN are significantly slower than the implicit times from VDM-RT – a supervisor loop takes 26 times longer to complete – the overall effect on the temperature is minimal.

Nonetheless, the timing estimates are affecting the co-simulation results, as can be seen from a close inspection of the co-simulation output logs, as shown in Fig. 8. Co-simulation for Room 1 temperature, indicates different control signals (56.55) compared to the Spin verified model (56.15) version, where timing constraints have been successfully verified. VDM-RT model timing parameters of the FCU controllers, were altered (decreased) in order to pass the verification occurred by Spin model checker. Such a result, although indicative for the purpose of this work, could reveal important outcomes for large-scale system co-simulations, with distributed objects sharing common communication mediums. Finally, it is worth noting that in Fig. 7 the room temperature in the co-simulation exhibits much greater oscillation at the co-simulation level than in the standalone simulation (compared to the standalone Dymola simulation result).

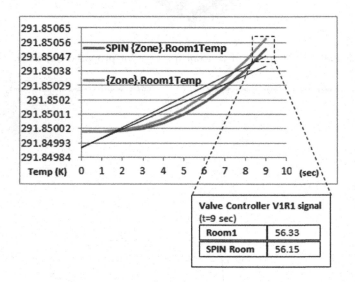

Fig. 8. Co-simulation results detail for valve opening times based on verification results injection.

PI controllers are very sensitive to sampling time and the PI controller in the co-simulation is modelled in VDM-RT (an imperative, DE notation) where sampling time is harder to control, particularly at the co-simulation level. In general, we have observed that this kind of DE formalism and tool is not ideal for modelling PI controllers. While this decision yielded significant benefits in terms of facilitating distributed discrete communication, the PI performance is a significant drawback.

6   Conclusions and Future Work

We have presented an approach for combining formal verification with co-simulation by means of results injection. This approach enables verification engineers to be brought into a closer collaboration loop with the multi-disciplinary teams that use co-simulation platforms to carry out CPS design and development. We have applied the approach to a case study from the HVAC domain, though we argue the approach is generic enough to be applied to other CPS domains – higher criticality domains may particularly benefit from it. This work will enable additional opportunities to extend it further based on evolving co-simulation results and INTO-CPS project features. We have identified two particularly interesting domains that include (a) code generation of the verified solution as well as, (b) model based testing of co-models. INTO-CPS code generators currently are being developed with a focus on distributed aspects, which will give us additional motivation to explore concurrency requirements. Capability of generating C code for a simplified version of the VDM-RT model is currently enabled, though future improvements to the generators will extend them to support the complete model for experimental hardware platforms. In the future, we will validate the code generators by deploying the code onto hardware platforms and performing Hardware-in-the-Loop co-simulations. Furthermore, model-based testing as an INTO-CPS plugin could be combined with our approach as an alternative to state space explosion cases.

Finally, we plan to address the performance verification of PI controllers in the co-simulation by increase our co-model heterogeneity. The PI controllers will be modelled in Simulink [18] and connected to the co-simulation as FMUs, while a supervisor model handling master-slave FCU policies will be still modelled in VDM-RT. This will bring additional challenges in terms of verifying communications between the supervisor and the controllers at the model level, but we expect again the PROMELA model to guide our model parameterization.

Acknowledgments. This work is supported by the INTO-CPS H2020 project: *Integrated Tool Chain for Model-based Design of Cyber-Physical Systems.* Funded by the European Commission-H2020, Project Number: 664047.

References

1. Amalio, N., Cavalcanti, A., Miyazawa, A., Payne, R., Woodcock, J.: Foundations of the SysML for CPS modelling. Technical report, INTO-CPS Deliverable, D2.2a, December 2016
2. Bernardeschi, C., Masci, P., Pfeifer, H.: Early prototyping of wireless sensor network algorithms in PVS. In: Harrison, M.D., Sujan, M.-A. (eds.) SAFECOMP 2008. LNCS, vol. 5219, pp. 346–359. Springer, Heidelberg (2008). https://doi.org/10.1007/978-3-540-87698-4_29
3. Bernardeschi, C., Masci, P., Pfeifer, H.: Analysis of wireless sensor network protocols in dynamic scenarios. In: Guerraoui, R., Petit, F. (eds.) SSS 2009. LNCS, vol. 5873, pp. 105–119. Springer, Heidelberg (2009). https://doi.org/10.1007/978-3-642-05118-0_8

4. Blochwitz, T.: Functional Mock-up Interface for Model Exchange and Co-Simulation, July 2014. https://www.fmi-standard.org/downloads
5. Brosse, E., Quadri, I.: SysML and FMI in INTO-CPS. Technical report, INTO-CPS Deliverable, D4.2c, December 2016
6. Derler, P., Lee, E.A., Sangiovanni-Vincentelli, A.L.: Addressing modeling challenges in cyber-physical systems. Technical report UCB/EECS-2011-17, EECS Department, University of California, Berkeley, March 2011. http://www.eecs.berkeley.edu/Pubs/TechRpts/2011/EECS-2011-17.html
7. Duflot, M., Kwiatkowska, M.Z., Norman, G., Parker, D.: A formal analysis of bluetooth device discovery. STTT **8**(6), 621–632 (2006)
8. Elmqvist, H., Mattsson, S.E.: An introduction to the physical modelling of language modelica. In: Proceedings of the 9th European Simulation Symposium, Technical report, October 1997
9. Fitzgerald, J., Gamble, C., Larsen, P.G., Pierce, K., Woodcock, J.: Cyber-physical systems design: formal foundations, methods and integrated tool chains. In: FormaliSE: FME Workshop on Formal Methods in Software Engineering, ICSE 2015, Florence, Italy, May 2015
10. Fitzgerald, J., Gamble, C., Payne, R., Larsen, P.G., Basagiannis, S., Mady, A.E.D.: Collaborative model-based systems engineering for cyber-physical systems - a case study in building automation. In: Proceedings of INCOSE International Symposium on Systems Engineering, Edinburgh, Scotland, July 2016
11. Fitzgerald, J., Gamble, C., Payne, R., Pierce, K.: Method Guidelines 2. Technical report, INTO-CPS Deliverable, D3.2a, December 2016
12. Holzmann, G.J.: The model checker SPIN. IEEE Trans. Softw. Eng. **23**(5), 279–295 (1997)
13. Kleijn, C.: Modelling and simulation of fluid power systems with 20-sim. Int. J. Fluid Power **7**(3), 57–60 (2006)
14. Lamport, L.: Real-time model checking is really simple. In: Borrione, D., Paul, W. (eds.) CHARME 2005. LNCS, vol. 3725, pp. 162–175. Springer, Heidelberg (2005). https://doi.org/10.1007/11560548_14
15. Larsen, P.G., Battle, N., Ferreira, M., Fitzgerald, J., Lausdahl, K., Verhoef, M.: The overture initiative - integrating tools for VDM. SIGSOFT Softw. Eng. Notes **35**(1), 1–6 (2010). https://doi.org/10.1145/1668862.1668864
16. Larsen, P.G., Fitzgerald, J., Woodcock, J., Fritzson, P., Brauer, J., Kleijn, C., Lecomte, T., Pfeil, M., Green, O., Basagiannis, S., Sadovykh, A.: Integrated tool chain for model-based design of cyber-physical systems: the INTO-CPS project. In: CPS Data Workshop, Vienna, Austria, April 2016
17. Larsen, P.G., Lausdahl, K., Battle, N., Fitzgerald, J., Wolff, S., Sahara, S., Verhoef, M., Tran-Jørgensen, P.W.V., Oda, T.: The VDM-10 language manual. Technical report TR-2010-06, The Overture Open Source Initiative, April 2010
18. MathWorks, October 2011. Simulink official website: http://www.mathworks.com/
19. Ölveczky, P.C., Thorvaldsen, S.: Formal modeling, performance estimation, and model checking of wireless sensor network algorithms in real-time maude. Theor. Comput. Sci. **410**(2–3), 254–280 (2009)
20. Ouy, J., Lecomte, T., Christiansen, M.P., Henriksen, A.V., Green, O., Hallerstede, S., Larsen, P.G., ger, C.J., Basagiannis, S., Couto, L.D., din Mady, A.E., Ridouanne, H., Poy, H.M., Alcala, J.V., König, C., Balcu, N.: Case Studies 2, Public Version. Technical report, INTO-CPS Public Deliverable, D1.2a, December 2016
21. Philips Semiconductors Corporation: SCC2691 UART data sheet. Technical report, May 2006

22. Timothy, S.: A survey of control technologies in the building automation industry. In: Proceedings of the IFAC 16th World Congress, Prague, Czech Republic, pp. 13–96 (2005)
23. Verhoef, M., Larsen, P.G., Hooman, J.: Modeling and validating distributed embedded real-time systems with VDM++. In: Misra, J., Nipkow, T., Sekerinski, E. (eds.) FM 2006. LNCS, vol. 4085, pp. 147–162. Springer, Heidelberg (2006). https://doi.org/10.1007/11813040_11

Integrated Simulation and Formal Verification of a Simple Autonomous Vehicle

Andrea Domenici[1](✉)(iD), Adriano Fagiolini[2](iD), and Maurizio Palmieri[3,1]

[1] Department of Information Engineering, University of Pisa, Pisa, Italy
{andrea.domenici,maurizio.palmieri}@ing.unipi.it
[2] Department of Energy, Information Engineering and Mathematical Models
(DEIM), University of Palermo, Palermo, Italy
fagiolini@unipa.it
[3] DINFO, University of Florence, Florence, Italy

Abstract. This paper presents a proof-of-concept application of an approach to system development based on the integration of formal verification and co-simulation. A simple autonomous vehicle has the task of reaching an assigned straight path and then follow it, and it can be controlled by varying its turning speed. The correctness of the proposed control law has been formalized and verified by interactive theorem proving with the Prototype Verification System. Concurrently, the system has been co-simulated using the Prototype Verification System and the MathWorks Simulink tool: The vehicle kinematics have been simulated in Simulink, whereas the controller has been modeled in the logic language of the Prototype Verification System and simulated with the interpreter for the same language available in the theorem proving environment. With this approach, co-simulation and formal verification corroborate each other, thus strengthening developers' confidence in their analysis.

1 Introduction

Simulation and formal verification are complementary techniques, both required in the development of complex, possibly safety-critical systems. Formal specification enables developers to deal with complexity using well-proven tools of logic and mathematics, providing strong assurance on compliance with requirements. On the other hand, it is always possible to correctly formalize wrong assumptions, or to prove wrong conclusions from wrong assumptions. It is also possible to produce simply wrong proofs, but this risk is mitigated by the use of automatic or interactive theorem proving. This given, simulation provides sanity checks at early stages of development, besides being a prototyping tool supporting the exploration of user interaction.

In the field of CPSs, simulation often takes the form of *co-simulation*, i.e., integrated simulation of different subsystems, each modeled with a specific formalism and simulated by a specific simulation engine. The need for co-simulation

© Springer International Publishing AG 2018
A. Cerone and M. Roveri (Eds.): SEFM 2017 Workshops, LNCS 10729, pp. 300–314, 2018.
https://doi.org/10.1007/978-3-319-74781-1_21

arises naturally from the fact that CPSs are usually composed of parts that follow different physical laws, or must be described under different aspects: For example, the rotor, stator, and winding of an electric motor are both electrical and mechanical systems.

A further motivation for using co-simulation stems from the previous considerations on the complementarity of simulation and verification, and also from the separation of controller and plant in a CPS: A model of the controller expressed in a logic language can be proved correct with respect to a model of the plant expressed in the same language, then the controller model can be simulated using an interpreter for that language, along with a simulation of a plant model built with an application-specific formalism, such as, e.g., a Simulink toolbox.

This paper illustrates the above approach to integrated co-simulation and verification with a simple case study from the field of autonomous vehicles. The case study concerns a single-axle vehicle, which moves at constant speed and whose turning speed can be controlled. The controller must be able to steer the vehicle until it reaches its assigned path, a straight line. The kinematics of the vehicle and the control law have been expressed in the higher-order logic language of the Prototype Verification System (PVS) [22]. Using the well-established methods of control theory, it has been proved that the target configuration (i.e., the vehicle following an assigned straight line) is an asymptotically stable state. Concurrently, a Simulink model of the vehicle's kinematics has been co-simulated with the PVS specification of the control law.

In the rest of the paper, Sect. 2 cites work related to the topics of this paper; Sect. 3 provides basic information on the PVS environment; Sect. 4 describes the case study; Sect. 5 reports on the verification of the considered system; Sect. 6 reports on its co-simulation; and Sect. 7 concludes the paper.

2   Related Work

Work on co-simulation of CPSs has produced a large body of literature that cannot be surveyed exhaustively within the limits of the present paper. Only a small number of recent works will be cited, while the reader is referred to more extensive reviews, such as [12].

The Vienna Development Method (VDM) [10] and the Bond-Graph notation [14] have been used in the Crescendo tool [16] to co-simulate discrete systems in VDM and continuous systems with Bond-Graphs.

In the approach proposed by Attarzadeh-Niaki and Sander [1], heterogeneous processes, executing models expressed in different modeling or programming languages, or even implemented in hardware, are organized hierarchically and coordinated by a framework that takes into account each process's *Model of Computation* [17] defining the time, synchronization, and communication models of the process.

Differential dynamic logic [24] is used with the KeYmaera X [11] theorem prover, developed for the verification of CPSs. Its language includes conditions, non-determinism, loops, composition, and continuous dynamics, i.e., behaviors defined by differential equations.

Another family of operational-style formalisms that produce executable models is the one of languages based on Petri Nets, such as *Stochastic Activity Networks* [25], used, e.g., to model FPGAs [2,3].

The PVS environment has been used in several application fields, such as hardware verification [23] or air traffic control [7]. Recently, it has been used to verify the specification and the implementation of a set of collision-avoidance algorithms for unmanned aircraft systems [20]. The authors of the present paper used the PVS environment to co-simulate an implantable pacemaker with a Simulink model of the heart [5]. The pacemaker was modeled by a PVS theory as a network of timed automata and executed in the PVSio-web framework [18,21], connected to a Simulink tool executing the heart model. The PVS language has also been used to verify a simple nonlinear hybrid control system [4].

3   Background on the PVS Environment

The PVS theorem prover is based on higher-order logic and the sequent calculus [26]. A PVS user writes *theories* containing definitions of types, constants, and variables. A function is a constant whose type is the function's signature. For example, the type expression '$[int \rightarrow real]$' denotes the type of functions from integers to reals. Variables may range over function types, and a function type may have other function types as domain and codomain.

A theory also contains statements of two kinds: *axioms*, assumed as valid by the prover, and *theorems* to be proved. A proved theorem can be used in further proofs. The language identifies statements with labels followed by the keywords *axiom* for axioms and *theorem*, *lemma*, or others, for theorems.

A theory may refer to other theories introduced by the *importing* declaration. A large number of pre-proved fundamental theories is collected in the *prelude* library and implicitly imported in all theories. Many other theories are available in several libraries, such as the NASA PVS Library (NASALIB) [9,13].

The PVS deduction system is based on sequent calculus. A *sequent* is an expression of the form $A_1, A_2, \ldots, A_n \vdash B_1, B_2, \ldots, B_m$, where formulae A_i's and B_i's are called the *antecedents* and the *consequents*, respectively.

The inference rules transform sequents, possibly introducing subgoals, generating a proof tree. A proof terminates successfully when all branches terminate with a sequent where either any formula occurs both as an antecedent and as a consequent, or any antecedent is false, or any consequent is true.

The PVS theorem prover offers inference rules that directly implement the basic rules of the sequent calculus, or combine them into powerful *strategies* that may often prove goals with a single prover command, such as *assert* or *grind*, that apply several substitutions and simplifications in one step.

The PVS language is purely declarative, but the PVSio extension [19] can compute the value of ground (i.e., fully instantiated) applications of a function. The PVSio ground evaluator, included in the PVS environment, can then be used as an interpreter for functions declared in a PVS theory. This feature makes it possible to use the PVS environment as a prototyping and co-simulation tool.

4   Case Study: A Two-Wheeled Vehicle

Let us consider an abstract representation of a terrestrial vehicle with a pair of wheels connected through an axle, moving on a flat surface. This representation abstracts away the workings of all subsystems, such as propulsion and steering mechanisms. In a rectangular Cartesian frame, its configuration can be defined by three state variables: the coordinates x and y of the axle's midpoint, and the orientation ψ (*yaw* angle) of the vehicle's instantaneous direction with the x axis (Fig. 1).

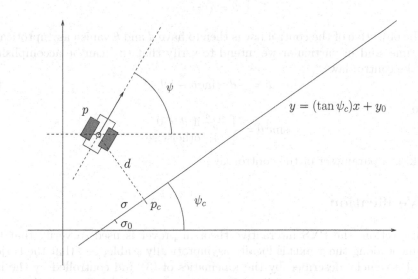

Fig. 1. Representation of the case study

Let us further assume that the vehicle's linear speed v is a constant V. The only controlled variable is then the yaw angle, which must satisfy the relation $\dot{\psi} = \omega$, where ω is the rotational speed around the vertical axis of the vehicle imposed by the controller. The kinematics of the vehicle in the Cartesian reference frame are then given by the following system:

$$\begin{cases} \dot{x} = \text{V} \cos \psi \\ \dot{y} = \text{V} \sin \psi \\ \dot{\psi} = \omega. \end{cases} \tag{1}$$

In this case study, the objective is to prove that a given control law is sufficient to lead the vehicle to move along an arbitrarily assigned target straight line. It is also required that the vehicle approaches the line smoothly, without oscillations.

Let the generic target line c be represented as

$$y = (\tan \psi_c)x + y_0. \tag{2}$$

If $p = (x, y)$ is the vehicle's position and p_c is the orthogonal projection of p on c, then $d = \mid p - p_c \mid$ and $\theta = \psi - \psi_c$ are, respectively, the distance from the vehicle to the target line and the difference between the vehicle's direction and the direction of the target line. It is convenient to adopt a mobile reference frame with p_c as its origin and σ and d as the spatial coordinates, where σ is the distance of p_c from a reference point σ_0 on c. In this new frame, we have

$$\begin{cases} \dot{\sigma} = \mathrm{V} \cos \theta \\ \dot{d} = \mathrm{V} \sin \theta \\ \dot{\theta} = \dot{\psi} = \omega. \end{cases} \tag{3}$$

The objective of the control law is then to have d and θ vanish asymptotically with time, and in particular we intend to verify that this can be accomplished with the control law

$$\omega = -dv \operatorname{sinc} \theta - k\theta, \tag{4}$$

where

$$\operatorname{sinc} \theta = \begin{cases} \frac{\sin \theta}{\theta} & \text{if } \theta \neq 0 \\ 1 & \text{otherwise} \end{cases}$$

and 'k' is a parameter of the control law.

5   Verification

In this section, the PVS interactive theorem prover is used to verify that the movement along the x-axis is locally asymptotically stable, i.e., that the trajectory of a vehicle, described by the kinematics of (3) and controlled by the law of (4), approaches the target line (2) as time approaches infinity, if the initial movement is contained within a "sufficiently small" neighborhood of the desired trajectory. Also, a condition on the control parameter k is found, guaranteeing that the movement is free of oscillation. The proof is very simple, and follows the common practice in control theory: The system is linearized at the desired state, the system's Jacobian is formulated, and the asymptotic stability of the state (without oscillations) is verified by showing that the eigenvalues are real and negative.

With the control law (4), the kinematics are given by this system of generating functions:

$$\begin{cases} \dot{\sigma} = f_\sigma(\sigma, d, \theta) & = \mathrm{V} \cos \theta \\ \dot{d} = f_d(\sigma, d, \theta) & = \mathrm{V} \sin \theta \\ \dot{\theta} = f_\theta(\sigma, d, \theta) & = -d\mathrm{V} \operatorname{sinc} \theta - k\theta, \end{cases} \tag{5}$$

whose partial derivatives are

$$\frac{\partial f_\sigma}{\partial \sigma} = 0 \qquad \frac{\partial f_\sigma}{\partial d} = 0 \qquad\qquad \frac{\partial f_\sigma}{\partial \theta} = -V\sin\theta$$

$$\frac{\partial f_d}{\partial \sigma} = 0 \qquad \frac{\partial f_d}{\partial d} = 0 \qquad\qquad \frac{\partial f_d}{\partial \theta} = V\cos\theta \qquad\qquad (6)$$

$$\frac{\partial f_\theta}{\partial \sigma} = 0 \qquad \frac{\partial f_\theta}{\partial d} = -V\operatorname{sinc}\theta \qquad \frac{\partial f_\theta}{\partial \theta} = -Vd(\frac{\theta\cos\theta - \sin\theta}{\theta^2}) - k.$$

The partial derivatives are expressed in the *intrinsic_kinematics* theory:

```
intrinsic_kinematics: THEORY BEGIN
IMPORTING sinc_th

t: VAR nnreal            % time
sigma(t): real           % sigma coordinate
d(t): real               % d coordinate
V: posreal               % linear velocity
k: posreal
theta(t): real           % angle between velocity and target line
omega(t): real           % turning speed

% partial derivatives of the generating functions
dfsigma_dsigma(sigma, d, theta: [nnreal -> real], t: real):
                                              real = 0
dfsigma_dd(sigma, d, theta: [nnreal -> real], t: real):   real = 0
dfsigma_dtheta(sigma, d, theta: [nnreal -> real], t: real):
                                     real = -V*sin(theta(t))
dfd_dsigma(sigma, d, theta: [nnreal -> real], t: real):   real = 0
dfd_dd(sigma, d, theta: [nnreal -> real], t: real):       real = 0
dfd_dtheta(sigma, d, theta: [nnreal -> real], t: real):
                                      real = V*cos(theta(t))
dftheta_dsigma(sigma, d, theta: [nnreal -> real], t: real):
                                              real = 0
dftheta_dd(sigma, d, theta: [nnreal -> real], t: real):
                                    real = -V*sinc(theta(t))
dftheta_dtheta(sigma, d, theta: [nnreal -> real], t: real):
                                                   real =
-V*d(t)*(cos(theta(t))/theta(t) - sin(theta(t))/(theta(t))^2) - k
END intrinsic_kinematics
```

In the above theory, the *importing* clause makes the *sinc_th* theory available, containing the definition of the 'sinc' function with an axiom defining its value at the origin. The initial declarations introduce t as the independent variable over non-negative reals (`nnreal`), σ, d, θ, and ω as real functions of t, and V and k as positive real (`posreal`) constants. The generating functions are then defined with four arguments: the three functions of time (of type [*nnreal* $\rightarrow$ *real*]) σ, d, and θ, and time t itself.

Another theory, *linearized_intrinsic*, defines the Jacobian that linearizes the system around the target configuration $d = 0$, $\theta = 0$:

$$J = \begin{bmatrix} \frac{\partial f_\sigma}{\partial \sigma} & \frac{\partial f_\sigma}{\partial d} & \frac{\partial f_\sigma}{\partial \theta} \\ \frac{\partial f_d}{\partial \sigma} & \frac{\partial f_d}{\partial d} & \frac{\partial f_d}{\partial \theta} \\ \frac{\partial f_\theta}{\partial \sigma} & \frac{\partial f_\theta}{\partial d} & \frac{\partial f_\theta}{\partial \theta} \end{bmatrix} = \begin{bmatrix} 0 & 0 & -V \sin \theta \\ 0 & 0 & V \cos \theta \\ 0 & -V \operatorname{sinc} \theta & -V d (\frac{\theta \cos \theta - \sin \theta}{\theta^2}) - k \end{bmatrix}. \quad (7)$$

In PVS, a matrix like this can be represented as a function of two natural numbers i and j, of the three state variables, and of time. The numbers i and j are the row and column indices of the matrix, which select one of the nine partial derivatives, which is then evaluated for the triple (σ, d, θ) and for the value t of time:

```
linearized_intrinsic: THEORY BEGIN
IMPORTING intrinsic_kinematics

% Jacobian
J(i, j: {n: posnat | n <= 3}, sigma, d, theta: [nnreal -> real], t)
                                                      : real =
    let idx = 3*(i - 1) + (j - 1)
    in cond
        idx = 0 -> dfsigma_dsigma(sigma, d, theta, t),
        idx = 1 -> dfsigma_dd(sigma, d, theta, t),
        ...
        idx = 7 -> dftheta_dd(sigma, d, theta, t),
        idx = 8 -> dftheta_dtheta(sigma, d, theta, t)
      endcond
```

In the above code, indices i and j are used to compute index idx, whose value is used in the *cond* clause to select one the nine elements of the Jacobian.

At the target configuration, the Jacobian reduces to

$$J_0 = \begin{bmatrix} 0 & 0 & 0 \\ 0 & 0 & V \\ 0 & -V & -k \end{bmatrix} \quad (8)$$

as stated in the *linearized_intrinsic* theory by the *J_0* predicate:

```
% Jacobian at desired configuration
J_0(sigma, d, theta: [nnreal -> real], t): bool =
    J(1, 1, sigma, d, theta, t) = 0 and
    ...
    J(2, 3, sigma, d, theta, t) = V and
    J(3, 1, sigma, d, theta, t) = 0 and
    J(3, 2, sigma, d, theta, t) = -V and
    J(3, 3, sigma, d, theta, t) = -k
```

The characteristic polynomial is

$$P(\lambda) = -\lambda^3 - k\lambda^2 - V^2\lambda, \tag{9}$$

whose eigenvalues are

$$\lambda_1 = -\frac{\sqrt{k^2 - 4V^2} + k}{2} \qquad \lambda_2 = \frac{\sqrt{k^2 - 4V^2} - k}{2} \qquad \lambda_3 = 0. \tag{10}$$

Accordingly, the theory has these declarations:

```
% characteristic polynomial of J_0
char_J(lam: real) : real = -lam^3 - k*lam^2 - (V^2)*lam

% eigenvalues
lam_1: real = - (sqrt(k^2 - 4*V^2) + k)/2
lam_2: real =   (sqrt(k^2 - 4*V^2) - k)/2
lam_3: real =   0
```

Note that in this theory the eigenvalues are *declared* to be reals, due to the requirement that the vehicle's approach to the target line be free of oscillations. The PVS theorem prover keeps record of each variable's type and uses this information to generate automatically *type-check conditions* that must be discharged to complete a proof.

The above listings are the axiomatic part of the theory, i.e., the declarations needed to formalize the problem at hand. The verification part involves writing lemmas to be proved, stating the desired properties. In this case, it must be proved that the three values proposed as eigenvalues are indeed roots of the characteristic polynomial, and that they are real and nonpositive.

The correctness of J_0 is expressed by this lemma:

```
J_0_lem: LEMMA
    d(t) = 0 and theta(t) = 0 implies J_0(sigma, d, theta, t)
```

which is proved introducing two simple lemmas on the values of the sine and cosine functions at zero and applying the *assert* rule.

From the form of the candidate eigenvalues λ_1 and λ_2, it is clear that k and V must satisfy $k \geq 2V$ for the eigenvalues to be real. We may note that if this constraint is overlooked (as might happen in a more complex case), interactive theorem proving can help discover it. In fact, let us try to prove the following:

```
eigenvals: LEMMA    % FIRST ATTEMPT
    char_J(lam_1) = 0 and char_J(lam_2) = 0 and char_J(lam_3) = 0
```

The proof does not succeed, but the failure shows clearly what is missing, since several steps in the attempted proof generate this unsolvable goal:

```
k*k >= 4*(V*V)
```

i.e., the condition on k and V required to have real-valued eigenvalues, which can then be introduced in the *eigenvals* lemma:

```
eigenvals: LEMMA k > 2*V implies
    char_J(lam_1) = 0 and char_J(lam_2) = 0 and char_J(lam_3) = 0
```

The above lemma is used as a step to prove the conclusive lemma on local stability (labeled as a theorem just to set it aside from the preliminary steps):

```
local_stability: THEOREM k > 2*V implies
    char_J(lam_1) = 0 and char_J(lam_2) = 0 and char_J(lam_3) = 0
    and lam_1 < 0 and lam_2 < 0
```

The proof of both lemmas is straightforward, relying mostly on basic sequent transformations, expansion of definitions, and algebraic manipulations. The latter play a major role in the proof, and are carried out with dedicated rules from the *manip* package [8], simple lemmas from the prelude or the NASALIB libraries, or *ad hoc* lemmas that are proved with the *grind* rule.

6   Co-simulation

In order to co-simulate the vehicle system, the control law has been expressed as a PVS theory executed by PVSio and the kinematics have been modeled and simulated with Simulink. The two simulations are coordinated by a module embedded in the Simulink model as an S-function, i.e., a user-defined block written in Matlab or, in this case, in C. More precisely, the Simulink model is composed of two subsystems: the vehicle kinematics and an S-function block that spawns the PVSio process executing the control law theory and then manages the communication between PVSio and Simulink.

6.1   Simulink Model of the Plant

Figure 2 shows the complete Simulink model, where the *controller* block produces the ω and v inputs to the *kinematics* block. The outputs of the latter are fed back to the controller, which also takes as input the parameters ψ_c and y_0 defining the target line.

The co-simulation is driven by the Simulink engine. At the beginning, the controller opens two Unix pipes for bidirectional communication with PVSio and spawns a PVSio process. At each subsequent simulation step, the controller block submits a request to evaluate a *step* function (explained below) for the current state. The interpreter's reply is parsed to extract the computed values of ω and v, which are returned to the Simulink engine.

The kinematics of the vehicle are modeled in Simulink as shown in Fig. 3. The turning speed ω is integrated to obtain the yaw angle ψ, which is fed to the blocks computing sine and cosine, their outputs are multiplied by the linear speed v, and the result is integrated to obtain the coordinates x and y.

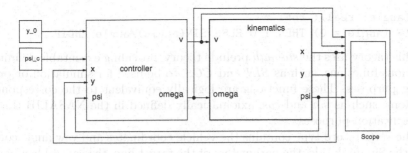

Fig. 2. Co-simulation model

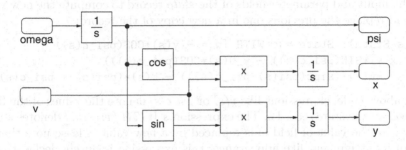

Fig. 3. Kinematics model in Simulink

6.2 PVS Model of the Controller

In the previous sections, the partial derivatives of the generating functions have been expressed directly in the PVS notation and used for verification. In order to *simulate* the behavior of the controller, i.e., to produce a sequence of values for ω corresponding to discrete instants, we must represent the controller as a transition system whose state changes at each step according to the specified control law. This is done by defining a *state* data structure containing the instantaneous values of all the variables, and a *step* function that updates the state.

At each simulation step, the *controller* Simulink block reads the values of x, y, and ψ from the *kinematics* block, composes a *state* record containing this information along with other parameters, and encodes the record into an application expression of the *step* function. The PVSio interpreter evaluates the new value of ω according to the control law, and inserts it in the updated state, which is returned to the *controller* block on the Simulink side.

The controller is defined by the *controller* theory:

```
controller: THEORY BEGIN
IMPORTING stdmath
State: TYPE = [#
    y: real, x: real, psi: real,      % inputs
    y_0: real, psi_c: real,           % target line
    k: real, v: real,                 % parameters
    w: real #]                        % output
```

```
sinc(angle: real): real =
    IF (angle = 0) THEN 1.0 ELSE SIN(angle)/angle ENDIF
```

This theory uses the *stdmath* prelude theory, providing executable definitions of various functions, such as *SIN* and *COS*, to be used for simulation or prototyping purposes. These functions are logically equivalent to the corresponding functions, such as *sin* and *cos*, axiomatically defined in the NASALIB theories for verification purposes.

The *state* record type contains the vehicle coordinates and yaw angle coming from the Simulink side, the parameters of the target line, the control law parameters, and the turning speed to be sent to the Simulink side. The *step* function uses the input and parameter fields of the *state* record to compute the new value of ω and replace the previous one in a new copy of the record:

```
step(s:State): State = s WITH [w:= -(y(s)*COS(psi_c(s))
    - x(s)*SIN(psi_c(s)) - y_0(s)*COS(psi_c(s)))
        *v(s)*(sinc(psi(s)-psi_c(s))) - k(s)*(psi(s) - psi_c(s))]
```

In the above code, expressions like *y(s)* or *psi_c(s)* denote the values of the fields *y* or *psi_c* of the state record *s*. The expression *s WITH [w:= ...]* denotes a copy of *s*, where the value of field *w* is replaced by a new value. Please note that, in spite of its assignment-like appearance, this expression is purely declarative: It is the PVSio ground evaluator that turns this declaration into executable code. The function applications produced by the Simulink *controller* block are similar to the following:

```
step((#y:=1,x:=0,psi:=0,y_0:=0,psi_c:=0,k:=0.5,v:=0.1,w:=0#));
```

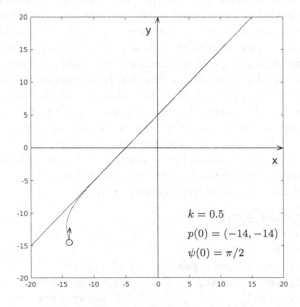

Fig. 4. Example simulation, $k = 0.5$

Such expressions are generated by the S-function in the Simulink model and sent to the PVSio interpreter, which returns a string with a similar syntax, sent back to Simulink and parsed by the S-function.

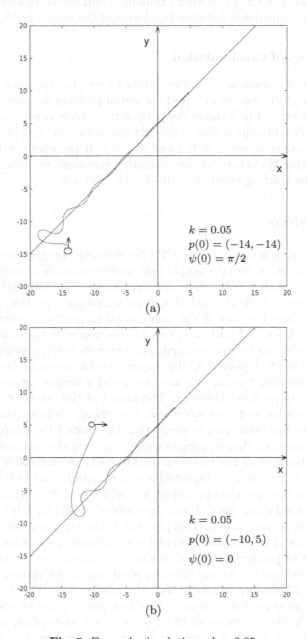

$$k = 0.05$$
$$p(0) = (-14, -14)$$
$$\psi(0) = \pi/2$$

(a)

$$k = 0.05$$
$$p(0) = (-10, 5)$$
$$\psi(0) = 0$$

(b)

Fig. 5. Example simulations, $k = 0.05$

It can be seen that the theory defining the controller is extremely simple. The relevant fact is that the controller theory used for co-simulation relies on the same control law as the one used for verification, without any need of translating it from one language (PVS) to another (Simulink), and therefore without any need of checking the equivalence between two forms of the same law.

6.3   Examples of Co-simulation

The co-simulation model has been exercised by varying the parameters of the target line and of the control law, and the initial position and orientation of the vehicle. For example, Fig. 4 shows the path of the vehicle starting at $(-14, -14)$ with $\psi(0) = \pi/2$ and approaching a straight line with $\psi_c = \pi/4$ and $y_0 = 5$. The control law parameters are $k = 0.5$ and $v = 0.2$. If parameter k is reduced to 0.05, the resulting trajectory has an oscillating transient, as shown in Fig. 5(a). In Fig. 5(b), the starting point is $(-10, 5)$ with $\psi(0) = 0$.

7   Conclusions

This paper proposes an approach to CPS development integrating co-simulation and formal verification, using a simple case study to provide a concrete example. The key concept is that both (co-)simulation and formal verification are necessary in this type of systems, and that both techniques can take advantage of environments where the same formalism is used to produce declarative models that can be both verified and executed. In this paper, it has also been shown how a PVS model can be co-simulated together with heterogeneous models.

In the case study reported in this paper, the higher-order language of the Prototype Verification System was used to model a simple autonomous vehicle and to specify its required behavior. The model of the vehicle consists in two parts: its kinematics and its control law. The theory defining the vehicle and its requirements has been used to verify that the control law complies with the requirements, provided that its parameters satisfy a relation needed in the proof. Concurrently, the control law has been used to build an executable model of the controller, which has been co-simulated with a Simulink model of the plant, i.e., the vehicle's kinematics, thus providing a validation of the verification results. For example, simulations have shown the system's behavior when the verification's assumptions are violated. This procedure has two useful consequences: (i) Using exactly the same controller model for verification and simulation avoids the effort both of producing two models of the same controller and of proving their equivalence; and (ii) having different plant models for verification and simulation makes it possible to cross-check the two models. This case study has convinced the authors that interactive theorem proving can be used effectively and efficiently in the development of CPSs. Another relevant aspect of the case study is the co-simulation framework. In this case, integration of PVSio and Simulink has been achieved quite simply by embedding the PVSio interpreter in the Simulink model, using the S-function feature and the operating system primitives for process management and communication. More general approaches can be used, such as, e.g., the Functional Mockup Interface standard [6] used in the INTO-CPS tool [15], or the PVSio-web framework [21].

References

1. Attarzadeh-Niaki, S.H., Sander, I.: Co-simulation of embedded systems in a heterogeneous MoC-based modeling framework. In: 2011 6th IEEE International Symposium on Industrial and Embedded Systems, pp. 238–247, June 2011. https://doi.org/10.1109/SIES.2011.5953667
2. Bernardeschi, C., Cassano, L., Domenici, A., Sterpone, L.: ASSESS: a simulator of soft errors in the configuration memory of SRAM-based FPGAs. IEEE Trans. Comput. Aided Des. Integr. Circ. Syst. **33**(9), 1342–1355 (2014). https://doi.org/10.1109/TCAD.2014.2329419
3. Bernardeschi, C., Cassano, L., Cimino, M.G., Domenici, A.: GABES: a genetic algorithm based environment for SEU testing in SRAM-FPGAs. J. Syst. Archit. **59**(10, Part D), 1243–1254 (2013). https://doi.org/10.1016/j.sysarc.2013.10.006
4. Bernardeschi, C., Domenici, A.: Verifying safety properties of a nonlinear control by interactive theorem proving with the Prototype Verification System. Inf. Process. Lett. **116**(6), 409–415 (2016). https://doi.org/10.1016/j.ipl.2016.02.001
5. Bernardeschi, C., Domenici, A., Masci, P.: A PVS-simulink integrated environment for model-based analysis of cyber-physical systems. IEEE Trans. Softw. Eng. **PP**(99), 1 (2017). https://doi.org/10.1109/TSE.2017.2694423
6. Blochwitz, T., Otter, M., Arnold, M., Bausch, C., Clauß, C., Elmqvist, H., Junghanns, A., Mauß, J., Monteiro, M., Neidhold, T., Neumerkel, D., Olsson, H., Peetz, J.V., Wolf, S.: The functional mockup interface for tool independent exchange of simulation models. In: Proceedings of the 8th International Modelica Conference, pp. 105–114. Linköping University Electronic Press (2011). https://doi.org/10.3384/ecp11063105
7. Carreño, V., Muñoz, C.: Aircraft trajectory modeling and alerting algorithm verification. In: Aagaard, M., Harrison, J. (eds.) TPHOLs 2000. LNCS, vol. 1869, pp. 90–105. Springer, Heidelberg (2000). https://doi.org/10.1007/3-540-44659-1_6
8. Di Vito, B.: Manip User's Guide, Version 1.3. http://shemesh.larc.nasa.gov/people/bld/ftp/manip-guide-1.3.pdf. Accessed 18 Aug 2015
9. Dutertre, B.: Elements of mathematical analysis in PVS. In: Goos, G., Hartmanis, J., van Leeuwen, J., von Wright, J., Grundy, J., Harrison, J. (eds.) TPHOLs 1996. LNCS, vol. 1125, pp. 141–156. Springer, Heidelberg (1996). https://doi.org/10.1007/BFb0105402
10. Fitzgerald, J.S., Larsen, P.G., Verhoef, M.: Vienna Development Method. Wiley, Hoboken (2007). https://doi.org/10.1002/9780470050118.ecse447
11. Fulton, N., Mitsch, S., Quesel, J.-D., Völp, M., Platzer, A.: KeYmaera X: an axiomatic tactical theorem prover for hybrid systems. In: Felty, A.P., Middeldorp, A. (eds.) CADE 2015. LNCS (LNAI), vol. 9195, pp. 527–538. Springer, Cham (2015). https://doi.org/10.1007/978-3-319-21401-6_36
12. Gomes, C., Thule, C., Broman, D., Larsen, P.G., Vangheluwe, H.: Co-simulation: state of the art. ACM Comput. Surv. (2017, to appear)
13. Gottliebsen, H.: Transcendental functions and continuity checking in PVS. In: Aagaard, M., Harrison, J. (eds.) TPHOLs 2000. LNCS, vol. 1869, pp. 197–214. Springer, Heidelberg (2000). https://doi.org/10.1007/3-540-44659-1_13

14. Karnopp, D., Rosenberg, R.: Analysis and Simulation of Multiport Systems; The Bond Graph Approach to Physical System Dynamics. M.I.T. Press, Cambridge (1968)

15. Larsen, P.G., Fitzgerald, J., Woodcock, J., Fritzson, P., Brauer, J., Kleijn, C., Lecomte, T., Pfeil, M., Green, O., Basagiannis, S., Sadovykh, A.: Integrated tool chain for model-based design of Cyber-Physical Systems: the INTO-CPS project. In: 2016 2nd International Workshop on Modelling, Analysis, and Control of Complex CPS (CPS Data), pp. 1–6, April 2016. https://doi.org/10.1109/CPSData.2016.7496424

16. Larsen, P.G., Gamble, C., Pierce, K., Ribeiro, A., Lausdahl, K.: Support for co-modelling and co-simulation: the crescendo tool. In: Fitzgerald, J., Larsen, P.G., Verhoef, M. (eds.) Collaborative Design for Embedded Systems. Co-modelling and Co-simulation, pp. 97–114. Springer, Heidelberg (2014). https://doi.org/10.1007/978-3-642-54118-6_5

17. Lee, E.A., Sangiovanni-Vincentelli, A.: A framework for comparing models of computation. IEEE Trans. Comput.-Aided Des. Integr. Circuits Syst. **17**(12), 1217–1229 (1998). https://doi.org/10.1109/43.736561

18. Masci, P., Oladimeji, P., Zhang, Y., Jones, P., Curzon, P., Thimbleby, H.: PVSio-web 2.0: joining PVS to HCI. In: Kroening, D., Păsăreanu, C.S. (eds.) CAV 2015. LNCS, vol. 9206, pp. 470–478. Springer, Cham (2015). https://doi.org/10.1007/978-3-319-21690-4_30

19. Muñoz, C.: Rapid prototyping in PVS. Technical Report, NIA 2003-03, NASA/CR-2003-212418, National Institute of Aerospace, Hampton, VA, USA (2003)

20. Muñoz, C., Narkawicz, A., Hagen, G., Upchurch, J., Dutle, A., Consiglio, M.: DAIDALUS: detect and avoid alerting logic for unmanned systems. In: Proceedings of the 34th Digital Avionics Systems Conference (DASC 2015) (2015)

21. Oladimeji, P., Masci, P., Curzon, P., Thimbleby, H.: PVSio-web: a tool for rapid prototyping device user interfaces in PVS. In: FMIS2013, 5th International Workshop on Formal Methods for Interactive Systems, London, UK, 24 June 2013. https://doi.org/10.14279/tuj.eceasst.69.963.944

22. Owre, S., Rajan, S., Rushby, J.M., Shankar, N., Srivas, M.: PVS: combining specification, proof checking, and model checking. In: Alur, R., Henzinger, T.A. (eds.) CAV 1996. LNCS, vol. 1102, pp. 411–414. Springer, Heidelberg (1996). https://doi.org/10.1007/3-540-61474-5_91

23. Owre, S., Rushby, J.M., Shankar, N., Srivas, M.K.: A tutorial on using PVS for hardware verification. In: Kumar, R., Kropf, T. (eds.) TPCD 1994. LNCS, vol. 901, pp. 258–279. Springer, Heidelberg (1995). https://doi.org/10.1007/3-540-59047-1_53

24. Platzer, A.: Logics of dynamical systems. In: Proceedings of the 2012 27th Annual IEEE/ACM Symposium on Logic in Computer Science, LICS 2012, pp. 13–24. IEEE Computer Society, Washington (2012). https://doi.org/10.1109/LICS.2012.13

25. Sanders, W.H., Meyer, J.F.: Stochastic activity networks: formal definitions and concepts*. In: Brinksma, E., Hermanns, H., Katoen, J.-P. (eds.) EEF School 2000. LNCS, vol. 2090, pp. 315–343. Springer, Heidelberg (2001). https://doi.org/10.1007/3-540-44667-2_9

26. Smullyan, R.M.: First-Order Logic. Dover Publications, New York (1995)

Co-simulation Between Trnsys and Simulink Based on Type155

Georg Engel$^{(\boxtimes)}$, Ajay Sathya Chakkaravarthy, and Gerald Schweiger

AEE - Institute for Sustainable Technologies, Feldgasse 19, Gleisdorf, Austria
g.engel@aee.at

Abstract. The interface between Trnsys and Matlab based on Type155 of Trnsys' standard library is used to construct a co-simulation between Trnsys and Simulink. The high flexibility of this interface is demonstrated, which includes its ability to provide a communication in strong and loose coupling schemes. A simplified use case including a compact thermal energy storage is considered to discuss accuracy and computational demands for various settings of the co-simulation. Loose coupling with constant and linear extrapolation of the input variables is presented, as well as an application of the strong coupling scheme to estimate the inaccuracies of the loose coupling co-simulation.

Keywords: Co-simulation · Trnsys · Simulink · Type155
Compact thermal energy storage

1 Introduction

1.1 Background

In recent decades, simulation-driven development has increasingly become established as a central method in academia and industry. This is leveraged by computational advances, like the recent emergence of equation-based modelling languages, which offers new possiblities compared to block diagram modelling using imperative programming languages.

Complex models are usually decomposed into subsystems, which reflects very often the structure of real systems. Classically, such systems are modelled in a single tool, which is refereed to as monolithic approaches. With the increased complexity of these systems and the need for linking several domains in one model, monolithic approaches have restrictions: Sometimes it is not possible to simulate a complex system in a single tool, but even if it is possible, very often there are more suitable tools available for different subsystems. Ideally, every subsystem is modelled in a tool that meets the particular requirements for the domain and the structure of the model. Different subsystems require, generally, different modelling approaches and differing solver algorithms. Thus, the need for coupling different tools is a pragmatic one. Co-simulation is an approach to enable a simulation of complex single or multi-domain systems that consists at

A. Cerone and M. Roveri (Eds.): SEFM 2017 Workshops, LNCS 10729, pp. 315–329, 2018.
https://doi.org/10.1007/978-3-319-74781-1_22

least two subsystems (modelled in different tools) which solve coupled (algebraic) differential systems of equations (Gomes et al. 2017). Co-simulation requires an exchange of data during runtime. Advantages of the co-simulation approach are: (i) it allows for the combination and reuse of existing tools and methods that are robust and well-suited for their particular domain, (ii) it facilitates cross-discipline and cross-company collaborations, (iii) the possibility to protect model intellectual property rights of subsystems and (iv) robust co-simulation frameworks can significantly shorten the innovation cycle (rapid prototyping) of novel system and control concepts.

The need for co-simulation in the field of energy systems arises from the goal of the energy transition: (i) existing systems must become more efficient, (ii) transition towards technologies that reduce emissions and (iii) as fluctuating energy sources such as wind and solar energy expand, other parts of the energy systems must become more flexible. There are a number of options for increasing energy system flexibility, including combining different energy domains, increasing supply and demand flexibility or integrating energy storage technologies (Lund et al. 2015; Schweiger et al. 2017b). Simulation-driven development is the method of choice in many applications and the simulation of specific solutions provides the necessary insights and information to support the transformation process towards sustainable energy systems. Similarly, in the automotive industry, the transition towards electric and hydrogen mobility poses a variety of challenges. Considering the lack of waste heat and the narrow temperature window required by the battery, a smart thermal management of vehicles including a thermal storage becomes increasingly important (Bandhauer 2011; Engel et al. 2017c). This leads to new requirements for simulation approaches and tools.

1.2   Co-simulation: State of the Art

Co-simulation approaches can be divided into three categories: discrete event, continuous time and hybrid co-simulations (Gomes et al. 2017). The standard is the Functional Mockup Interface (FMI) for continuous time co-simulations and High Level Architecture for discrete event ones, while no standard is yet available for hybrid co-simulation. A main drawback of co-simulation is that numerical stability problems may arise (Trcka et al. 2009), code optimizations within a particular tool may be lost (Wetter et al. 2015) and some co-simulation frameworks have inconvenient application programming interfaces so that such methods are inappropriate for engineering applications. An overview of co-simulation approaches and tools, research challenges, and research opportunities are presented e.g. in the references (Gomes et al. 2017; Trcka 2008; Atam 2017; Mathias et al. 2015).

The coupling between the different tools can be implemented either in a loose or strong coupling scheme (Trcka 2008). In loose coupling, the data exchange between simulators is realized only at certain points in time. There is no iteration between the coupled simulators. Strong coupling methods iterate the values needed from other partial systems in every time step. Generally, the strong coupling shows higher accuracy and higher stability at the costs of a higher computational demand. There are different numerical coupling approaches. The most common are parallel coupling ("Jacobi" scheme) and sequential coupling ("Gauss-Seidel" scheme). Parallel coupling is a straight forward approach, where the simulators exchange data once at the start of every time step. In sequential coupling approaches, the simulators are executed consecutively; a simulator uses the updated value of the other simulators in the same time step (Hafner et al. 2013).

A major issue for loose coupling co-simulations is a correct estimation of the error, which is in fact often omitted in engineering applications. Different methods to estimate the error that have been applied in co-simulation are listed in (Gomes et al. 2017). An error estimation for co-simulations based on classical Richardson extrapolation and a modified algorithm for a reliable communication step size control based on an extension of the step size control of classical time integration is presented in (Arnold et al. 2013). They conclude that the numerical efficiency of co-simulation algorithms may be improved by higher-order approximations of subsystem inputs. (Schmoll and Schweizer 2012) discusses how subsystem solvers influence the global error of the co-simulation. (Hoepfer 2011) shows that for dynamic models, the selection of the simulation time step is a crucial issue with respect to computational expense, simulation accuracy, and error control; a method to set a appropriate step size for co-simulations is described.

1.3   Tools and Interfaces

Trnsys and Matlab/Simulink are so called "general tools" in the category of multi-domain tools. The advantages of general tools, besides their flexibility, are that most of these tools are structured in libraries, that can be customized and extended. This enables an exchange of ideas and methods within the scientific community and industrial developments, which is a major advantage especially in interdisciplinary, rapidly evolving research areas. Another advantage is that some of these tools (e.g. Dymola, TRNSYS, Matlab) provide the possibility of co-simulation using the FMI standard (Schweiger et al. 2017a).

Trnsys is a state of the art commercial simulation tool for industry and academia in the field of buildings, HVACs and thermal energy systems, originally written in the Fortran programming language (Klein et al. 1976). Trnsys' standard library includes the Type155, which implements a direct link with Matlab. The connection uses the Matlab engine, which is launched as a separate process. The Fortran routine communicates with the Matlab engine through a COM interface. Type155 can be used in different calling modes (standard component called in each iteration or real-time controller called only after convergence). A particular methodology to export Trnsys models into the Simulink environment is presented in (Riederer et al. 2009). An tool to generate an FMU from a Trnsys model is available open source (Widl 2015).

Simulink is a widely used toolbox of Matlab for modeling, simulating and analyzing dynamic systems (Mathworks 2017). It can call Matlab routines and also itself be called from Matlab scripts. A library to import and export FMUs is commercially available by Modelon (Modelon 2017). Simulink is the state-of-the-art toolbox for controllers in industry and academia and therefore very interesting to couple to other simulation tools via co-simulation.

FMI (Blochwitz et al. 2009) is a tool independent standard that has been developed in the ITEA2 European Advancement project MODELISAR. FMI supports both model exchange and co-simulation of dynamic models using a combination of XML-files and compiled C-code. FMI is currently supported by 95 tools and is used by various industries and universities.

The Building Controls Virtual Test Bed (BCVTB) is a software environment developed at Lawrence Berkeley National Laboratory (Wetter 2011). It allows connecting different simulation tools to exchange data during the time integration. BCVTB is based on Ptolemy II, an open-source software framework supporting experimentation with actor-oriented design. BCVTB has interfaces to EnergyPlus, Dymola, FMU, Matlab and Simulink, Radiance, ESP-r, Trnsys and BACnet.

1.4   Motivation

The present paper discusses only the special case of a co-simulation between Trnsys and Simulink. In typical Trnsys thermal engineering applications, this is of high interest in particular in order to exploit the powerful Simulink library for controllers, but also its flexibility for rapid prototyping. So far, only particular loose-coupling interfaces like FMI and BCVTB with limited flexibility are available in this respect (Wetter 2011; Widl 2015; Modelon 2017). These interfaces are well established, but do not provide different types of input extrapolation functions, nor do they provide an estimation of the additionally introduced errors through the loose coupling communication, which is a major issue in loose coupling co-simulation performed in engineering sciences (compare Sect. 1.2).

The main contributions of this paper are as follows. It is shown how to construct a co-simulation between Trnsys and Simulink based on Trnsys' Type155, which is available free of charge. Only moderate Matlab scripting know-how is required for the construction. An open source release is planned (http://tes4set. at). Various properties of the interface are discussed considering a simplified use case in thermal engineering, which includes:

– Accuracy and computational demands for various settings.
– The high flexibility of the interface is demonstrated, in particular a simple switch between strong and loose coupling schemes.
– The flexibility allows also to easily implement different extrapolation schemes of the input variables, e.g., constant and linear extrapolation.
– The interface is compared with a common alternative free-of-charge interface based on BCVTB and FMI in various aspects, following the methodology presented in (Engel et al. 2017b).
– It is suggested to apply the strong coupling scheme to estimate the inaccuracies of the loose coupling co-simulation.

In the first section, the state of the art concerning co-simulation was discussed. Next, the construction of the interface is described and the method to determine the accuracy of different simulations is presented. Then, the use case is introduced, including its system design and the mathematical model. Results for the simulation of the use case are presented for various interface settings of the interface and finally conclusions are given.

2   Method

2.1   Construction of the Interface

Type155 establishes a communication between Trnsys and Matlab, its proforma is shown in Fig. 1. The parameter "callingMode" switches between calling Matlab in each Trnsys iteration ("callingMode = 0") or only after convergence ("callingMode = 10"), which is referred to as "standard iterative component" and "real-time controller", respectively. A generic Matlab-script was developed which correspondingly calls Simulink in each iteration or only after convergence. Individual Simulink simulations are executed at each call, making use of the built-in functions "SaveCompleteFinalState" and "LoadInitialState", where in each call the total Simulink simulation time matches one time step of the master Trnsys simulation. The input variables are communicated as global variables in the Matlab workspace to Simulink, while the output variables can be retrieved, e.g., from scope blocks. The initial values for the integrator blocks in Simulink can also be provided as global variables, where converged values from the last time step have been chosen (in each iteration, if "callingMode = iterative component").

Parameter	Input	Output	Derivative	Special Cards	External Files	Comment			
🔓	1	🔒	Mode		0		-		More...
ℹ	2	🔓	nInputs		2		-		More...
	3	🔓	nOutputs		2		-		More...
	4	🔓	callingMode		0		-		More...
	5	🔓	ignoreEngClose		◯ 0 ◉ 1		-		More...

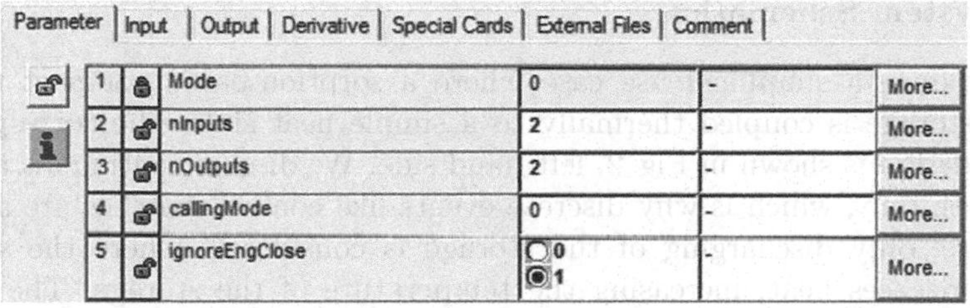

Fig. 1. The proforma of Trnsys' Type155. The parameter "callingMode" switches between calling Matlab in each Trnsys iteration or only after convergence.

In this setup, Type155 in "callingMode = real-time controller" implements a loose coupling scheme of sequential type, since Trnsys executes its various units in sequential order. Meanwhile, "callingMode = iterative component" implements a strong coupling scheme, provided implicit solvers are employed and time steps match. The setup for the strong coupling scheme comes with increased computational demand related to repeated Simulink simulations for each iteration. Its major strengths are the capability for a strong coupling scheme co-simulation with different solvers in the two simulation units, a high flexibility due to the custom Matlab-script, and a simple switch between loose and strong coupling provided in the very same interface. An open-source release of the corresponding Matlab-script is planned in the course of the project (http://tes4set.at).

2.2 Estimation of Accuracy and Computational Costs

The model is implemented as monolithic simulation also entirely in Trnsys, referred to as "reference simulation", employed with Trnsys' standard successive solver with improved solver parameters to ensure high accuracy results (time step of 0.1 s and solver tolerance of 10^{-7}). These serve to determine the accuracy of any other simulation, where a custom Python-script is set up to compare the corresponding time series. The variables communicated via the co-simulation interface (inlet and outlet temperature of the heat transfer fluid) as well as the temperatures of the heat storage and the body are compared to the corresponding time-series results obtained in the reference simulation. The maximum deviation is considered as a measure for accuracy. Results are shown in subsequent figures and listed in Table 1.

To discuss the computational costs, a batch-script is used to measure the overall simulation time (for details see Table 1). This includes overhead like starting Matlab etc., but this is in most cases the relevant timing for the user. Replica simulations serve to estimate the confidence interval.

3   Use Case

3.1   System Schematics

We introduce a simplified use case where a sorption-based compact thermal energy storage is coupled thermally to a simple heat sink. The corresponding system design is shown in Fig. 2, left hand side. We discuss continuous time co-simulation only, which is why discrete events like control switches are avoided. Therefore, only discharging of the storage is considered, where the sorption process releases heat, increasing the temperature of the storage. The heat is extracted by a heat transfer fluid and transported to the heat sink, which is represented by a simple body with one thermal node.

3.2   Heat Storage - Trnsys Model

The compact thermal energy storage is modelled in Trnsys as depicted in Fig. 2, right hand side. Type851 represents the sorption reactor, Type 852a the evaporator/condenser, Type39 a water reservoir and Type22 and an equation block which calculates the vapour pressure between the reactor and the evaporator/condenser. A more detailed description of the model is found in (Engel et al. 2017a). For the reference simulation, Type155 is replaced by a Type representing

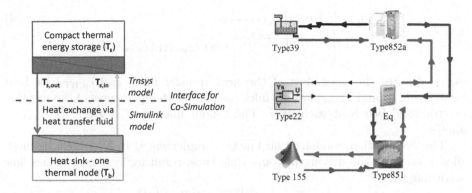

Fig. 2. Left: Schematics of the considered use case to discuss the co-simulation interface. A compact thermal energy storage is connected to a heat sink via a heat transfer fluid. The storage is modelled in Trnsys, while the heat sink is modelled in Simulink. The various temperatures of the model are indicated in the figure. Right: Model of the thermal energy storage in Trnsys including the interface based on Type155. For details refer to the main text.

a counter-flow heat exchanger with one thermal node at the secondary side. For an FMU-export, Type155 is replaced by Type6139a and Type6139b for input and output, respectively (Widl 2015).

The following system of ordinary differential equations, implemented in Type851, is used to model the inner states of the sorption store, i.e. store temperature T_s (energy balance, Eq. (1)) and water load of the sorption material x_s (mass balance, Eq. (2)) (Engel et al. 2017a):

$$C_{\text{tot}} \frac{dT_s}{dt} = \dot{Q}_{\text{HX}} + \dot{Q}_{\text{vap,in}} + \dot{Q}_{\text{ads}} + \dot{Q}_{\text{amb}} \qquad (1)$$

$$\frac{dx_s}{dt} = k_{\text{LDF}} \left[x_{s,\text{equ}}(p_{\text{vap}}, T_s) - x_s \right], \qquad (2)$$

where t denotes time, C_{tot} the total sensible heat capacity of the sorption store, and k_{LDF} the linear driving force parameter for adsorption and desorption, respectively (Glueckauf 1955). $x_{s,\text{equ}}(p_{\text{vap}}, T_s)$ is the equilibrium water load of the adsorbens, calculated for the current store temperature T_s and vapor pressure p_{vap}, e.g. by the Dubinin approach (Dubinin 1967),

$$x_{s,\text{equ}} = \rho(T) W_0 \exp \left[- \left(\frac{R_{\text{vap}} T}{E} \ln \frac{p_{\text{sat}}(T)}{p_{\text{vap}}} \right)^n \right], \qquad (3)$$

where W_0, E and n are material specific parameters, $\rho(T)$ is the water density, R_{vap} the gas constant of water vapor and $p_{\text{sat}}(T)$ the saturated vapour pressure. The different terms on the right hand side of Eq. 1 represent the heat flows for the sorption store. The heat flow via the heat exchanger (subscript "HX"), using the one-node approximation, i.e., constant temperature $T_s = $ const. over space, is calculated according to heat exchange theory by

$$\dot{Q}_{HX} = UA_{HX}\Delta T_{\log}(T_s, T_{s,in}) \tag{4}$$

$$= \left[1 - e^{\frac{-UA_{s,HX}}{\dot{m}_{HTF}c_{p,HTF}}} \right] \dot{m}_{HTF}\, c_{p,HTF}(T_{s,in} - T_s).$$

$\dot{m}_{HTF}$ denotes the mass flow of the heat transfer fluid, and $c_{p,HTF}$ its heat capacity. $T_{s,in}$ (and $T_{s,out}$) are the inlet (and outlet) temperatures of the sorption reactor fixed bed heat exchanger. The vapour mass flow is given by $\dot{m}_{vap} = m_0 \frac{dx_s}{dt}$.

The evaporation/condensation kinetics, implemented in Type852a, is modelled linearly in the driving pressure difference, resulting in a vapor mass flow according to

$$\dot{m}_{vap}(T_2) = \frac{(\beta A)\,(p_{vap} - p_{sat}(T_2))}{R_{vap}T_2}, \tag{5}$$

where βA is the mass transfer coefficient parametrizing the linearized kinetics. The vapour mass flow between the sorption store and the evaporator/condenser is finally determined using an additional iterative solver (Type22).

3.3   Heat Sink - Simulink Model

The heat sink is modelled as a simple body with one thermal node and a counter-flow heat exchanger by

$$\frac{dT_b}{dt} = \frac{\dot{m}_{HTF}\, c_{p,HTF}}{m_b c_{p,b}} \left[1 - e^{\frac{-UA_{HX}}{\dot{m}_{HTF}c_{p,HTF}}} \right] (T_{s,out} - T_b) \tag{6}$$

$$T_{s,in} = T_{s,out} - \left[1 - e^{\frac{-UA_{HX}}{\dot{m}_{HTF}c_{p,HTF}}} \right] (T_{s,out} - T_b). \tag{7}$$

T_b denotes the temperature of the body, m_b its mass and $c_{p,b}$ its heat capacity.

3.4   Co-simulation

The interface of the co-simulation is situated physically in the circuit of the heat transfer fluid. Correspondingly, the inlet and outlet temperatures $T_{s,in}$ and $T_{s,out}$ of the sorption reactor heat exchanger are the variables communicated via the interface between Trnsys and Simulink.

4   Results

We present results of the monolithic Trnsys simulation and subsequently results of various setups of the co-simulation based on Type155, and a comparison to a co-simulation based on BCVTB and FMI. Details concerning maximum deviation and computational costs are found in Table 1.

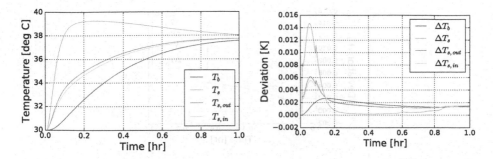

Fig. 3. Left: Results of the reference simulation for the temperatures of the heat sink T_b, the heat storage T_s, the outlet of the heat storage $T_{s,out}$ and the inlet of the heat storage $T_{s,in}$. Right: Deviation of the different temperatures of the monolithic Trnsys simulation with default parameters compared to the reference simulation.

4.1 Monolithic Simulation

The results produced by the reference simulation are shown in Fig. 3, left hand side. The enthalpy released by the reaction increases the temperature of the heat storage up to roughly $39\,°\mathrm{C}$, which is in the further progress cooled through the thermal coupling to the heat sink, until the various temperatures eventually converge.

To be able to evaluate the accuracies of the various co-simulation setups, we first discuss the accuracy of the monolithic simulation with default parameters. The deviation of the latter compared to the reference simulation (monolithic simulation with improved parameters) is shown in Fig. 3, right hand side. The initial peak in the deviation is related to the strong dynamics of the system in the initial phase where the state of charge of the storage is still high and hence the kinetics is sizeable. Parameters are given in Table 1.

4.2 Strong Coupling

In "callingMode = iterative component", Type155 calls a custom Matlab-script in each iteration. The script has been written such that Simulink is executed in each iteration, generating a strong coupling co-simulation.

Figure 4 shows the deviation of the results of the co-simulation based on Type155 in strong coupling scheme when compared to the results of the reference simulation. The deviation is of the same order as the one of the monolithic simulation itself. This is expected and verifies that the solver tolerances of the individual simulation tools are respected also by the co-simulation in this strong coupling scheme. This is valueable for an estimation of the accuracy of any co-simulation. Improvement of the accuracy has been investigated and was found to be possible to a high degree.

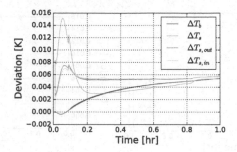

Fig. 4. Deviation of the different temperatures of the strong coupling scheme with default parameters compared to the reference simulation. The accuracy is of the same magnitude as the monolithic simulation, as expected for a strong coupling scheme.

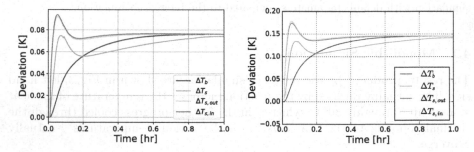

Fig. 5. Left: Deviation of the different temperatures of the loose coupling scheme with default parameters. Type155 is used in "callingMode = real-time controller", which corresponds to a sequential loose coupling scheme. Right: Deviation of the different temperatures of the co-simulation based on BCVTB and FMI. The parallel loose coupling scheme shows larger deviations than the sequential one.

4.3   Loose Coupling

In "callingMode = real-time controller", Type155 implements a loose coupling co-simulation. Figure 5, left hand side, shows the corresponding deviations of the results compared to the reference simulation. As expected, compared to the strong coupling scheme, the computational demands are lower while the accuracy becomes poorer.

As a comparison to another loose coupling co-simulation interface, we consider the same model implemented in Trnsys and Simulink coupled via BCVTB and FMI. A Trnsys-FMU is generated using an open source tool (Widl 2015) and integrated as such in BCVTB, while Simulink is integrated as "actor". This procedure implements a loose coupling scheme of parallel ("Jacobi") type, which allows a faster computation, however at the costs of a yet poorer accuracy. Figure 5, right hand side, shows the deviation of the results of the co-simulation based on BCVTB and FMI compared to the results of the reference simulation.

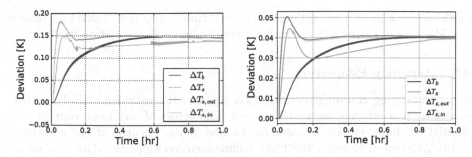

Fig. 6. Left: Like Fig. 5, but for the loose coupling scheme with parameters relaxed to match the accuracy of the BCVTB/FMI co-simulation. Right: Like Fig. 5, but including a linear extrapolation of the input values. The deviation is reduced by almost 50% compared to the constant extrapolation (compare Fig. 5, left hand side).

4.4 Loose Coupling: Modifications

In the following, various modifications of the interface are discussed. First, we consider how far the solver parameters of the sequential loose coupling (Type155) can be relaxed to match the accuracy of the parallel loose coupling (BCVTB/FMI) with default parameters. For the present use case, the time step can be increased by a factor of two, while the tolerance can be relaxed by a factor of a thousand. However, the computational demand still appears larger for the Type155-based co-simulation compared to the one based on BCVTB/FMI. The corresponding results are shown in Fig. 6, left hand side.

The flexibility of the interface based on Type155 can be exploited for various purposes. An intriguing extension is given by considering a linear extrapolation of the input values instead of a constant one. In the following, we sketch the main points of a possible corresponding construction. In a sequential loose coupling scheme, only one side of the communication requires extrapolation. This is represented by $T_{s,in}$, communicated from Simulink to Trnsys, in the present case. Since Type155 in "callingMode = real-time controller" calls the Matlab-script only after convergence of the Trnsys solver, it cannot be used to modify input values before convergence. Hence, the Matlab script is modified to mimic a "callingMode = real-time controller" behaviour, i.e., executing Simulink only after convergence even if called in each iteration, i.e., for Type155 in the setting "callingMode = iterative component". As a second step, values need to be stored to estimate the derivative and the extrapolation scheme has to be implemented. Finally, discontinuities like events should be accounted for to avoid sizeable extrapolation discrepancies. The deviation of the results of this loose coupling with linear extrapolation is shown in Fig. 6, right hand side. It is found that the deviation is reduced almost by a factor of two compared to the standard loose coupling scheme including a constant extrapolation of the input values (compare Fig. 5, left hand side). At the same time, the computational demand is increased by a factor of two (see Table 1), which, however, mainly originates in the mimicking of the "callingMode = real-time controller" behaviour (called but idle during the iterations) rather than the linear extrapolation itself.

4.5   Accuracy Estimation

Since the strong coupling co-simulation respects the user-defined solver tolerances, its inaccuracies are under control. The errors of any loose coupling co-simulation, however, are unkown in the first place, because of the additional errors introduced through the finite communication step size. This is a major drawback of loose coupling co-simulations, which are otherwise often preferred over strong coupling because of their lower computational demands, simplicity and better availability.

We suggest to make use of the strong coupling co-simulation to estimate the inaccuracy of the loose coupling one. In this respect, the flexibility of the interface based on Type155 is very valuable, as it allows to easily switch between strong and loose coupling. The deviation between the results of the loose coupling and the strong coupling co-simulation is shown in Fig. 7. Comparison to Fig. 5, left hand side, verifies that the errors are estimated to satisfactory precision. If required, the estimation of the error could be refined by choosing improved solver parameters for the strong coupling co-simulation, at the costs of a higher computational demand.

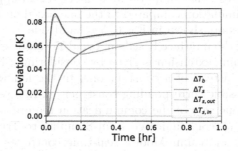

Fig. 7. Deviation of the different temperatures of the loose coupling scheme compared to the results of the strong coupling scheme (both in default setup). The curves differ only slightly from the ones shown in Fig. 5, left hand side, indicating that the strong coupling scheme can be used to estimate the accuracy of the loose coupling scheme.

5   Conclusions

A co-simulation interface between Trnsys and Simulink based on Type155 available in Trnsys' standard library was introduced and discussed regarding several aspects. Compared to the common alternative free-of-charge interfaces FMI and BCVTB, a high flexibility was demonstrated, requiring only moderate Matlab scripting know-how.

A thermal system involving a compact heat storage modelled in Trnsys and a heat sink modelled in Simulink has been employed as a use case to assess the interface. The accuracy and the computational demands for various settings of the interface have been investigated. The strong coupling scheme co-simulation was shown to achieve a similar accuracy as the monolithic simulation, while deviations of the sequential loose coupling are larger by a factor of 5 to 10, and the one of parallel loose coupling based on BCVTB/FMI by a factor of 10 to 30 (at otherwise matching solver parameters). The computational demand behaves in the opposite way, where clearly parallel loose coupling is the fastest choice.

The main strength of the interface based on Type155 is its flexibility to easily switch between a variety of different co-simulation setups, like loose and strong coupling, but also different input extrapolation functions or more exotic schemes. Up to now, it is the only implemented interface providing a strong coupling scheme between Trnsys and Simulink. The main weakness of the interface appears to be its inability for a parallel coupling scheme, which implies a larger computational demand.

Two specific examples have been discussed demonstrating the flexibility of the interface based on Type155. First, a sequential loose coupling co-simulatino with linear extrapolation of the input variables was implemented. This improves the accuracy almost by a factor of two compared to the co-simulation using constant extrapolation. Second, the simple switch between the loose and the strong coupling scheme can be exploited to estimate the inaccuracy of the loose coupling scheme, which is otherwise without control in the first place. The latter is very valuable in engineering applications, where the accuracy of loose coupling co-simulation is often left unchecked. The interface is scalable in terms of number of subsystems, exchange variables and domains. As many simulation tools provide an interface to Matlab, the approach described here may serve as a generic approach to construct interfaces from these tools to Simulink.

Acknowledgements. The research leading to these results has received funding from the Austrian FFG Programme Energieforschung under grant agreement no. 845020, and the Research Studio Austria no. 844732. The authors acknowledge valuable discussions with W. Glatzl, H. Schranzhofer, G. Lechner, I. Hafner and E. Widl.

Appendix: Detailed Settings and Results

The essential solver parameters used in this study are given in Table 1. In all cases discussed here, the Trnsys solver is the successive one (modified Euler) with a relaxation factor of 1. Table 1 also gives a comparison of the performance of the different co-simulation setups in terms of accuracy and computational costs.

Table 1. The parameter settings for the different simulations as well as performance indicators for the (co-)simulations for accuracy and computational demands are given. "Ref." denotes the reference simulation, "Monolithic" a Trnsys simulation without co-simulation, "default" the default parameter setting ($t_{step} = 1\,s$ and tol. $= 10^{-6}$), "lin. extrapol." the loose coupling with linear extrapolation of the input variables, "relaxed" the relaxed solver parameters (to match the accuracy of the BCVTB/FMI based co-simulation). t_{step} denotes the Trnsys time step; "call.Mode" abbreviates "callingMode", which is the parameter of the Type155 governing the commuication pattern; and "tol." gives the relative tolerance. ΔT_b, ΔT_s, $\Delta T_{s,out}$ and $\Delta T_{s,in}$ refer to the respective maximum deviation of these variables in units of Kelvin, and "comp." denotes the computational demand of the respective simulation. The simulations were executed on an Intel Xeon E5 6C/12T 2.2 GHz with 96 GB RAM.

	t_{step} [s]	call.Mode	tol.	ΔT_b	ΔT_s	$\Delta T_{s,out}$	$\Delta T_{s,in}$	comp. [s]
Ref	0.1	-	10^{-7}	-	-	-	-	31
Monolithic (default)	1	-	10^{-6}	0.003	0.015	0.006	0.006	4
Strong (default)	1	0	10^{-6}	0.005	0.015	0.008	0.007	1800
Loose (default)	1	10	10^{-6}	0.07	0.07	0.08	0.09	160
Loose (lin. extrapol.)	1	10	10^{-6}	0.04	0.04	0.05	0.05	330
Loose (relaxed)	2	10	10^{-3}	0.15	0.15	0.18	0.18	72
BCVTB/FMI	1	-	10^{-6}	0.15	0.14	0.17	0.18	22

References

Arnold, M., Clauss, C., Schierz, T.: Error analysis and error estimates for co-simulation in FMI for model exchange and co-simulation V2.0. Arch. Mech. Eng. **LX**, 75–94 (2013)

Atam, E.: Current software barriers to advanced model-based control design for energy-efficient buildings. Renew. Sustain. Energy Rev. **73**(August 2016), 1031–1040 (2017)

Bandhauer, T.M.: A critical review of thermal issues in lithium-ion batteries. J. Electrochem. Soc. **158**(3), R1 (2011)

Blochwitz, T., Otter, M., Arnold, M., Bausch, C., Clauß, C., Elmqvist, H., Junghanns, A., Mauss, J., Monteiro, M., Neidhold, T., Neumerkel, D., Olsson, H., Peetz, J.V., Wolf, S.: The functional mockup interface for tool independent exchange of simulation models. In: 8th International Modelica Conference 2011, pp. 173–184 (2009)

Dubinin, M.M.: Adsorption in micropores. J. Colloid Interface Sci. **23**(4), 487–499 (1967)

Engel, G., Asenbeck, S., Köll, R., Kerskes, H., Wagner, W., van Helden, W.: Simulation of a seasonal, solar-driven sorption storage heating system. J. Energy Storage **13**, 40–47 (2017a)

Engel, G., Chakkaravarthy, A., Schweiger, G.: A methodology to compare different co-simulation interfaces: a thermal engineering case study. In: Proceedings of the 7th International Conference on Simulation and Modeling Methodologies, Technologies and Applications, SIMULTECH 2017 (2017b)

Engel, G., Kohl, B., Girstmair, J., Hinteregger, M.: Sorption thermal energy storage for cooling the battery of a hybrid vehicle. In: International Conference on Renewable Energy Storage (2017c)

Glueckauf, E.: Theory of chromatography. Part 10. - Formulae for diffusion into spheres and their application to chromatography. Trans. Faraday Soc. **51**, 1540–1551 (1955)

Gomes, C., Thule, C., Broman, D., Larsen, P.G., Vangheluwe, H.: Co-simulation: state of the art. CoRR, abs/1702.0 (2017)

Hafner, I., Heinzl, B., Rössler, M.: An investigation on loose coupling co-simulation with the BCVTB. Simul. Notes Eur. **23**(1), 45–50 (2013)

Hoepfer, M.: Towards a comprehensive framework for co-simulation of dynamic models with an emphasis on time stepping. Ph.D. thesis (2011)

Klein, S.A., Beckman, W.A., Duffie, J.A.: TRNSYS: A Transient Simulation Program (1976)

Lund, P.D., Lindgren, J., Mikkola, J., Salpakari, J.: Review of energy system flexibility measures to enable high levels of variable renewable electricity. Renew. Sustain. Energy Rev. **45**, 785–807 (2015)

Mathias, O., Gerrit, W., Leon, U.: Life cycle simulation for a process plant based on a two-dimensional co-simulation approach. In: Computer Aided Chemical Engineering, vol. 37 (2015)

MathWorks (2017). https://de.mathworks.com/products/simulink.html

Modelon: FMI Toolbox for MATLAB/Simulink (2017)

Riederer, P., Keilholz, W., Ducreux, V., Antipolis Cedex, F.: Coupling of TRNSYS with SIMULINK - a method to automatically export and use TRNSYS models within SIMULINK and vice versa. In: Eleventh International IBPSA Conference Glasgow Scotland, pp. 1628–1633 (2009)

Schmoll, R., Schweizer, B.: Convergence study of explicit co-simulation approaches with respect to subsystem solver settings. In: Proceedings in Applied Mathematics and Mechanics, vol. 82, pp. 81–82 (2012)

Schweiger, G., Larsson, P.-O., Magnusson, F., Lauenburg, P., Velut, S.: District heating and cooling systems - framework for Modelica-based simulation and dynamic optimization. Energy (2017a, in press). https://doi.org/10.1016/j.energy.2017.05.115

Schweiger, G., Rantzer, J., Ericsson, K., Lauenburg, P.: The potential of power-to-heat in Swedish district heating systems. Energy (2017b, in press). https://doi.org/10.1016/j.energy.2017.02.075

Trcka, M., Hensen, J.L.M., Wetter, M.: Co-simulation of innovative integrated HVAC systems in buildings. J. Build. Perform. Simul. **2**(3), 209–230 (2009)

Trcka, M.: Co-simulation for performance prediction of innovative integrated mechanical energy systems in buildings. Ph.D. thesis (2008)

Wetter, M.: Co-simulation of building energy and control systems with the building controls virtual test bed. J. Build. Perform. Simul. **4**(3), 185–203 (2011)

Wetter, M., Fuchs, M., Nouidui, T.S.: Design choices for thermofluid flow components and systems that are exported as functional mockup units. In: 11th International Modelica Conference, no. iv, pp. 31–41 (2015)

Widl, E.: TRNSYS FMU Export Utility (2015). https://sourceforge.net/projects/trnsys-fmu/

Development of a Driverless Lawn Mower Using Co-simulation

Frederik F. Foldager[1]([✉]), Peter Gorm Larsen[2], and Ole Green[1]

[1] Agro Intelligence, Agro Food Park 13, 8200 Aarhus N, Denmark
{ffo,olg}@agrointelli.com
[2] Department of Engineering, Aarhus University, Aarhus, Denmark
pgl@eng.au.dk

Abstract. This work examines the use of co-simulation in the development and optimisation of a steering system for a driverless industrial size lawn mower. Initial models of the kinematics, dynamics and steering control system are co-simulated to investigate the performance of the controller in a virtual setting. The co-simulation consists of a Continuous-Time (CT) model of the lawn mower kinematics and dynamics and a Discrete-Event (DE) model of the steering controller modelled in VDM-RT. The models are co-simulated by the use of the Co-simulation Orchestration Engine which is a core tool of the INTO-CPS project. The CT model of the lawn mower is calibrated and verified experimentally. The result of co-simulation is in a similar fashion verified by comparing the simulated and measured trajectories.

Keywords: Co-simulation · Vehicle dynamics · VDM-RT · INTO-CPS

1 Introduction

Development of agricultural field equipment traditionally involves multiple prototypes and field tests. This study examines a simulation-aided development of the steering controller of an industrial size driverless lawn mower. The steering control is one component in the development of an automated system that manoeuvres an industrial lawn mower autonomously. The lawn mower consists of multiple interacting systems. The scope of this work is to develop and verify an initial model of the driverless lawn mower which allows for investigating the design space virtually and thereby reduce the number of field tests needed in the development of the steering system. Verification of the simulation results is crucial to the applicability of the simulation results using co-simulation [8]. Therefore, a calibration and a verification of the model is performed to ensure that mimicking of the model is satisfactory in relation to the physical system to aid the future development of the steering controller of the lawn mower.

The "Integrated Tool Chain for Model-based Design of Cyber-Physical Systems" (INTO-CPS) project supplies the majority of the technology used to

© Springer International Publishing AG 2018
A. Cerone and M. Roveri (Eds.): SEFM 2017 Workshops, LNCS 10729, pp. 330–344, 2018.
https://doi.org/10.1007/978-3-319-74781-1_23

develop the autonomous lawn mower [4,5,14]. This makes use of the Functional Mock-up Interface (FMI) version 2.0 standard for co-simulation [3]. It was decided to use FMI as the interface for the different simulation and testing tools, since it is a mature standard[1] created in the MODELISAR project [11] with an active community. The core FMI compliant tool of the INTO-CPS tool chain is a Co-simulation Orchestration Engine supporting both fixed and variable step size simulations.

The structure of this paper continues with an overview of the INTO-CPS technology in Sect. 2. Afterwards, Sect. 3 presents the underlying principles used for making the constituent models for this industrial application. Then Sect. 4 presents how the different constants have been calibrated and verified. This is followed by Sect. 5 describing the results of this work. Section 6 presents related scientific contributions. Finally, Sect. 7 provides a number of concluding remarks and points to directions for future work.

2   The INTO-CPS Technology

The overall workflow and services offered by the tool chain are illustrated in Fig. 1.

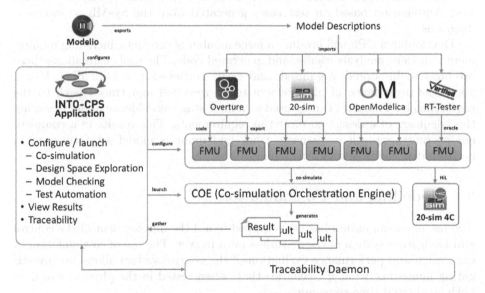

Fig. 1. Connections in the INTO-CPS tool chain

At the top level, the tool chain will allow requirements to be described using SysML using a new CPS profile made inside the Modelio tool [1]. This SysML profile allows the architecture of a CPS to be described, including both software and physical elements and based on this it is possible to automatically generate

---

[1] http://fmi-standard.org.

FMI model descriptions for each constituent model. It is also possible to automatically generate the overall connection between different Functional Mockup Units (FMUs) for a co-simulation[2].

Such FMI model descriptions can subsequently be imported into all the baseline modelling and simulation tools included in the INTO-CPS project. All of these can produce detailed models that can be exported as FMUs that each, as independent simulation units, can be incorporated into an overall co-simulation. The element models can either be in the form of Discrete Event (DE) models or in the form of Continuous-Time (CT) models combined in different ways. Thus, heterogeneous constituent models can then be built around this FMI interface, using the initial model descriptions as a starting point. A Co-simulation Orchestration Engine (COE) then allows these constitute models of a CPS to be evaluated through co-simulation. The COE will also allow real software and physical elements to participate in co-simulation alongside models, enabling both Hardware-in-the-Loop (HiL) and Software-in-the-Loop (SiL) simulation.

In order to have a user-friendly interface to manage this process, a web-based INTO-CPS Application has been produced. This can be used to launch the COE enabling multiple co-simulations to be defined and executed, and the results collated and presented automatically. The tool chain will allow these multiple co-simulations to be defined via Design Space Exploration (DSE) or through Test Automation based on test cases generated from the SysML requirement diagrams.

Developing a CPS will produce a large number of artefacts, including requirements, models, analysis results, and generated code. The tool chain allows these artefacts to be stored, organised, and easily retrieved at a later date. It will allow the provenance of all artefacts to be recorded and traced back to the requirements. This data can be used at a later stage as evidence in documenting the adequacy of a design to meet the requirements. This results in a complete engineering approach to manage, track and monitor model artefacts used in collaborative heterogeneous modelling.

3   Modelling and Co-simulation

The use of co-simulation has been applied to aid the development of the control and navigation system of the driverless lawn mower. The use of co-simulation in the design and performance evaluation of the control system allows for investigating numerous 'what if' scenarios that, when tested in the physical world, is both costly and time-consuming.

The co-simulation is constructed using a number of the baseline tools in the INTO-CPS Tool Chain as presented in Sect. 2. The structure of the co-simulation is visualised through the architecture diagram as shown in Fig. 2. The diagram is made within the Modelio tool [16]. The co-simulation of the driverless lawn mower consists of three FMUs. The FMUs are connected as shown in Fig. 3.

---

[2] These FMUs are produced using different tools as explained in the user manual for the INTO-CPS tool chain [2].

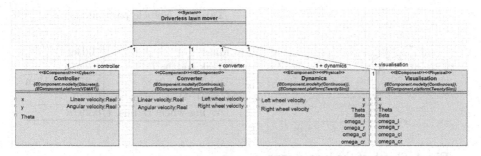

Fig. 2. Architecture diagram

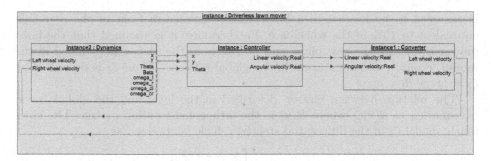

Fig. 3. Connection diagram of the co-simulation

The ports x, y, Theta in Fig. 2 illustrates the position and orientation of the driverless lawn mower in the global frame. These values are applied in the controller to calculate the desired motion towards the next point on the path. Beta is the relative angle of the caster wheels with respect to the orientation of the lawn mower which is depended on the direction that is driven [18]. The ports omega_l, omega_r, omega_cl, omega_cr describe the angular position of the driving wheels and the caster wheels. These values are used to visualise the motion of the driverless lawn mower.

The following subsections treat the development of the three FMUs in Fig. 2. First, a description of the dynamics of the driverless lawn mower is provided in Sect. 3.1, secondly, a description of the navigation and control system is provided in Sect. 3.2. Finally, Sect. 3.3 explains how the co-simulation was extended with a 3D simulation capability using the Unity game engine [21].

3.1 Vehicle Kinematics and Dynamics

The scope of the section is to derive the governing equations of the vehicle dynamics model which is included in the component Dynamics in Fig. 2.

The lawn mower is steered by controlling the velocity separately on the two driving wheels. A sketch of the vehicle is shown in Fig. 4. Vehicle specific parameters are shown in Table 1. The position of the Center of Gravity (COG)

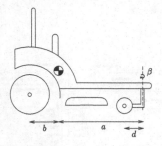

Fig. 4. Sketch of the lawn mower

Table 1. Vehicle parameters

Mass	700 kg
Track width, T	1.2 m
Dimension, (a,b)	1.35 m, 0.15 m
Caster wheel offset, d	0.1 m
Driving-wheel radius, r	0.29 m

is assumed to be located in a longitudinal distance in front of the rear axle equivalent to 10% of the wheelbase. Furthermore, it is assumed that the lawn mower is fixed in the yaw plane and no effects of the surface is included in the model. Position and orientation in the global reference frame ζ_I is described by $\zeta_I = [x \ y \ \theta]^T$.

The relation between motion described in the local and the global frame becomes $\dot{\zeta}_R = R(\theta)\dot{\zeta}_I$ where $R(\theta)$ is the orthogonal rotation matrix. The kinematic model $\dot{\zeta}_I$ of the differential steered vehicle is obtained as

$$\dot{\zeta}_I = R(\theta)^{-1} \begin{bmatrix} r\frac{\dot{\omega}_1}{2} + r\frac{\dot{\omega}_2}{2} \\ 0 \\ r\frac{\dot{\omega}_1}{2l} + r\frac{-\dot{\omega}_2}{2l} \end{bmatrix} \tag{1}$$

where r and $\dot{\omega}$ are the radius and rotational velocity of the driving wheels and l is the distance from the COG to each driving wheel. The caster wheels rotate freely around a vertical axis on the chassis of the vehicle. The relative orientation of the caster wheel β is obtained by numerically integrating the kinematic constraint equation of the caster wheel shown in Eqn. 2. A sketch of the chassis and caster wheels are shown in Fig. 5. The constraint equation of the caster wheel is presented in [18] as

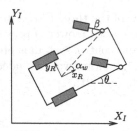

Fig. 5. Chassis and caster wheels

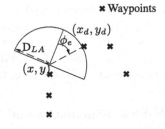

Fig. 6. Sketch of steering control, (x, y) is the current position of the lawn mower

$$0 = [\cos(\alpha_w + \beta) \ \ \sin(\alpha_w + \beta) \ \ d + l_c \sin(\beta)] \ R(\theta)\dot{\zeta}_I + d\dot{\beta} \tag{2}$$

where l_c is the distance from the centre of the lawn mower to the caster wheel hinge marked with dashed line in Fig. 5. d is the caster wheel offset from the chassis.

The dynamic response of the lawn mower is modelled by approximating the lateral forces acting from the caster wheels and the driving wheels. Furthermore the response of the steering mechanism is approximated as a first order system for each driving wheel by the solution to Eqn. 3.

$$\dot{s} = -k_\tau \cdot (s - s_{sp}) \tag{3}$$

where s_{sp} is the velocity set point, s is the velocity of the wheel and k_τ is the gain which is experimentally determined. The governing differential equations describing the physical systems is obtained by respectively evaluating the moment equilibrium and the lateral force equilibrium of the vehicle. The yaw-rate is described as the sum of a dynamic yaw distribution from the lateral forces of the tires and the kinematic yaw distribution which is determined from the third entry of Eqn. 1.

The orientation is obtained by integrating sum of the kinematic yaw distribution and the dynamic yaw distribution. The lateral force acting from the driving wheels on the chassis of the vehicle is determined for each tire $Fy_r = C_\alpha \tan(\alpha)$ where α is the slip angle and C_α is the cornering stiffness of the tire. The lateral force acting on the chassis from the caster wheels is approximated by the following relation

$$Fy_f = A_{Fy} \sin(\beta) \tag{4}$$

where the constant A_{Fy} is related to the tire properties of the caster wheels, the surface friction, joint friction, oct. A_{Fy} is determined experimentally. The determination of the constants k_τ and A_{Fy} is presented in Sect. 4.

The dynamic model of the lawn mower is obtained by numerically integrating the yaw-rate of Eqn. 5.

$$\ddot{\psi} = \frac{1}{I_{zz}} \left(Fy_f \cdot a - Fy_r \cdot b \right) \tag{5}$$

I_{zz} is the yaw moment of inertia, Fy_f and Fy_r is the lateral forces. The dynamic distribution is obtained by numerically integrating the moment equilibrium equation.

$$\theta = \int \int \ddot{\psi} \, dt + \frac{r}{2l} \left(\dot{\omega}_1 - \dot{\omega}_2 \right) \, dt \tag{6}$$

The position of the vehicle is obtained by numerically integrating the velocity components in x and y directions.

To extend the accuracy of the model and avoid performing the approximation of Eqn. 4 the slip angle of the caster wheels could be taken into account to estimate the tire forces from the caster wheels.

The model of the vehicle motion is developed and implemented in 20-sim. The model has the inputs and outputs as shown in architecture diagram in Fig. 2. The model contains the Eqns. (1, 2, 3, 4, 5 and 6). A standalone co-simulation FMU is generated of the model by the use of the built-in functionality of 20-sim [12].

In a similar fashion, a standalone co-simulation FMU is generated to convert the signals between the controller model and the dynamics model. This FMU simply converts the linear and angular velocities to left and right wheel rotation by evaluating the forward kinematics of the vehicle.

3.2   Steering Controller

The navigation and control system allows the lawn mower to move autonomously by performing intelligent route planning and obstacle avoidance. This case study surrounds the development and optimisation of the steering controller that manoeuvres the driverless lawn mower on the desired path. To evaluate the performance of the controller a path is specified to test and evaluate the control-system decoupled from the intelligent route planning and obstacle detection.

The path is discretized into a sequence of waypoints as shown in Fig. 6. The look-ahead distance determines how far ahead the controller evaluates the next waypoint which is crucial to the performance of the steering control system. The control signal is determined by comparing the current position and orientation (x_I, y_I, θ_I) of the lawn mower with a desired orientation towards the next waypoint within the look ahead distance. The error ϕ_e between the current orientation and the desired orientation is the counter clockwise angle between the solid and the dashed line in Fig. 6. The waypoint chosen has to meet two conditions. First the waypoint has to be in front of the vehicle, second the waypoint has to be at least the given look ahead distance from the vehicle. This is illustrated as an arc in Fig. 6.

To perform the co-simulation, a VDM-Real-Time (VDM-RT) [22] model of the steering controller is implemented in Overture [13]. The PD controller from the DTControl library of Crescendo is implemented [6]. The control parameter is the angular misalignment between the orientation of the vehicle and the orientation towards the next waypoint. The desired orientation is described as in Eqn. 7, from where the error ϕ_e is calculated as in Eqn. 8.

$$\phi_{des} = \text{atan2}\left((y_{WP} - y), (x_{WP} - x)\right) \tag{7}$$

$$\phi_e = \text{atan2}\left(\sin(\phi_{des} - \theta), \cos(\phi_{des} - \theta)\right) \tag{8}$$

The coordinate $\{x_{WP}, y_{WP}\}$ is the position of the waypoint of interest. In the simulation, the waypoints are specified in relative coordinates to the initial position of the vehicle.

The overall structure of the controller model can be seen in Fig. 7. Here the GuidanceController keeps track of its next waypoint in its planned route. It also contains a SteeringController that based on the calculated error steer after the desired angle. Input for this is based on the Global Navigation Satellite System (GNSS) and ActuatorSteering is used for setting the desired speed of the lawn mover at different points of time. The overall interface to the DE model is described in a special HardwareInterface class which is described in Listing 1.1 below.

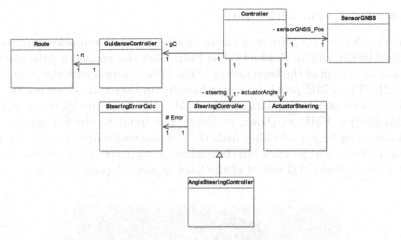

Fig. 7. Class diagram with the main controller classes

```
class HardwareInterface
values
    -- @ interface: type = parameter, name="speed_ref";
    public speed_ref : RealPort = new RealPort(1.0);
    -- @ interface: type = parameter, name="control_parameter";
    public control_parameter : RealPort = new RealPort(1.5);
    -- @ interface: type = parameter, name="look_ahead_dist";
    public look_ahead_dist : RealPort = new RealPort(1.0);

instance variables
    -- @ interface: type = input, name="pos_x";
    public pos_x : RealPort := new RealPort(0.0);
    -- @ interface: type = input, name="pos_y";
    public pos_y : RealPort := new RealPort(0.0);
    -- @ interface: type = input, name="pos_theta";
    public pos_theta : RealPort := new RealPort(0.0);
    -- @ interface: type = output, name="speed";
    public speed : RealPort := new RealPort(1.0);
    -- @ interface: type = output, name="ang_vel";
    public delta_f : RealPort := new RealPort(0.0);

end HardwareInterface
```

Listing 1.1. The HardwareInterface class

An FMU of the controller is generated with the interface from HardwareInterface and also shown in Fig. 2. The FMU is generated from Overture as a tool wrapper FMU.

3.3 3D Animation with Unity

During the INTO-CPS project, a custom FMU for 3D visualisation purposes are developed by Controllab Products. The FMU allows for connecting the governing equations of motion of the lawn mower to the 3D animation with the game engine Unity [21]. The FMU provides a user-friendly and structured set-up for direct visual feedback of the simulation. The FMU of the CT model is connected to the visualisation FMU as shown in Fig. 9. The input to the CT model of the lawn mower can be parsed either from the steering controller or a user input e.g. keyboard interface or joystick interface which is supported from 20-sim. Figure 8 shows a conceptual CAD model of the lawn mower adapted into Unity.

Fig. 8. Unity 3D animation

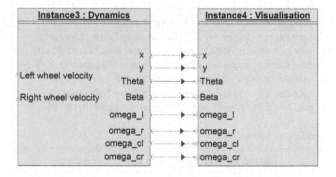

Fig. 9. Connection diagram for 3D support

4 Verification and Calibration

The scope of the calibration and verification is to experimentally identify the parameters k_τ and A_{Fy}. It is assumed that the steering mechanism follows the characteristics of Eqn. 3 where k_τ is a function of the settling time of the system. k_τ is determined experimentally by measuring the response of a steering input on the wheel encoder. k_τ is determined as $k_\tau = 15\,\text{s}^{-1}$.

The influence of the caster wheels on the orientation of the lawn mower is a function of several parameters as friction in the joints, tire properties and surface friction. Determination of these parameters is tedious and involves a certain amount of uncertainty. Hereby it is proposed to superimpose these parameters into the constant A_{Fy} that determines the impact of the caster wheels on the orientation of the vehicle. As a consequence, the orientation of the lawn mower becomes a function of the relative orientation of the caster wheel β as proposed in Eqn. 4. For low velocities, it is assumed that the motion of the caster wheels follows the motion described with the kinematic constraint equation in Eqn. 4. The constant A_{Fy} is determined experimentally by correlating experimental directional change of the chassis with the initial value of β for velocities between 0 m/s to 1 m/s. The value is determined as $A_{Fy} = 100\,N$. The test is performed by manually rotating the caster wheels to a position of $\beta = \pm 90°$ at $v = 0$, then initiating a forward motion on the each driving wheels. Due to the fact that $\beta \neq 0$ the vehicle is turning in the direction of the caster wheels while $\beta \to 0$. The angular displacement is measured when the yaw-rate and $\beta = 0$. This value is correlated to the initial value of β for low velocities.

5   Results

The co-simulation is conducted by the use of the COE. The co-simulation contains a model of the controller and a model of the kinematic and dynamic motion developed in 20-sim and exported as an FMU. The controller is developed in VDM-RT and exported as a tool wrapper FMU from Overture.

The co-simulation is applied to evaluate the influence of the look-ahead distance. Three simulations are conducted with varying distances of look-ahead. Simulation results are shown in Fig. 10. The initial conditions of the simulations are $[x, y, v_x, v_y] = [0\,\text{m}, 0\,\text{m}, 0\,\text{m/s}, 0\,\text{m/s}]$.

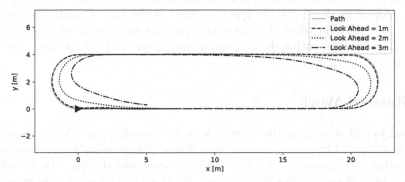

Fig. 10. Simulated trajectories for look-ahead distances: $\{1\,\text{m}, 2\,\text{m}, 3\,\text{m}\}$ and $v : 1\,\text{m/s}$

By evaluating the mean cross track error of the three simulations it can be concluded that the optimal look-ahead distance of the controller of the vehicle is 1 m. A field test has been conducted to verify the results of the co-simulation. The specified path of the field test is similar to the path applied in the initial simulations in Fig. 12. The simulations are performed with the corresponding control parameters of the field test. The results of the test are shown in Fig. 11. During the field test, a divergence from the path is observed within the first 10 m of the test. This divergence is believed to be the result of an uneven surface of the field which is not taken into account in the model. By comparing the results of the co-simulation with the measured trajectory of the lawn mower it can be concluded that the models mimic the physics of the systems satisfactorily.

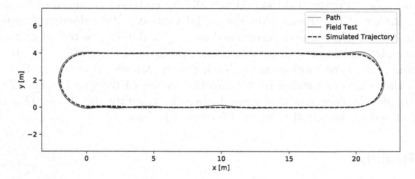

Fig. 11. Simulated and measured trajectories for v : 1 m/s and look-ahead distance : 1 m.

Due to the fact that the model is verified by the field test allows for the use of the co-simulation to numerically obtain valuable knowledge of the system applicable for the future development. The co-simulation is applied to evaluate the performance of the steering system with the same control parameters and look-ahead distance but with an increased forward velocity. The results of these simulations are shown in Fig. 12. It is shown that increased velocity increases the overshoot in the turns as expected. The capabilities of simulating the performance of the controller allow for optimising the parameters for different route segments across the path to be able to increase speed while maintaining the same accuracy.

6   Related Work

The subject of modelling the kinematic and dynamic properties of robots has been investigated by several researchers. Staicu [19] presents a derivation of the kinematics and dynamics of a mobile robot with two driving wheels and one caster wheel. Staicu applies the principle of virtual work to derive an expression of the torques of the two driving wheels to successfully control the motion of

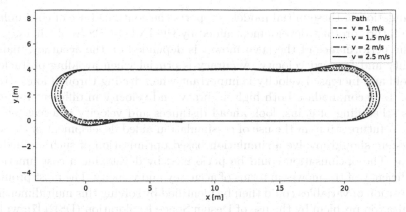

Fig. 12. Simulated trajectories for varying velocities: v: {1m/s, 1.5m/s, 2m/s, 2.5m/s} and look-ahead distance: 1m

the robot. Li et al. [15] derive a model of a wheeled mobile robot with powered caster wheels. The approach of deriving the equations of motion from a vehicle dynamics and stability point of view has been applied similarly to the approach of this work. Li et al. include the wheel-ground interaction to investigate dynamic effects caused by slip. Han et al. [9] presents an auto guidance system for navigating a tillage tractor. In similar fashion to the application of this study, their machine is navigated through a set of waypoints based on the heading of the vehicle relative to the waypoints. The state of the art in the field of co-simulation of vehicle-ground interaction is shown [17] by Serban et al. They simulate an off-road vehicle on soft soil. The co-simulation contains a description of the vehicle and suspension, a nonlinear FEA model of the deformable tires using the ANCF approach [10] and a model of the ground using the particle based DEM approach. This adds up to a system with millions of degrees of freedom. They propose an explicit force-displacement co-simulation framework based upon the multi-physics software package Chrono [20]. Similar approach could be applied in future projects to simulate traction forces between machine and surface.

7   Concluding Remarks

An initial study in the motion and steering control of a driverless lawn mower has been conducted by the use of the INTO-CPS Tool Chain. A co-simulation has been performed through the INTO-CPS application using the COE. A model of the physical system of the lawn mower has been developed in 20-sim and exported as an FMU, a model of the controller is modelled in VDM-RT and exported as an FMU from Overture. The CT model of the lawn mower has been calibrated experimentally. Finally, the co-simulation has been verified by comparing the simulation results with a field test. The simulations have revealed satisfactory results. The comparability between the results of the field test and the co-simulation of these initial models supports the continued use of co-simulation in the future product development aided by the INTO-CPS Tool Chain.

The performance of the lawn mower is depended on the accuracy, manoeuvrability and forward velocity. Accuracy is crucial when avoiding obstacles on the field and increased velocity is important when driving through long straight paths. To accommodate both high accuracy and velocity in different route segments scheduling of gains, look ahead distances and velocity is a feasible approach. A future study in the use of co-simulation aided development of the steering system should involve a simulation based optimisation of such a scheduling scheme. The optimisation could be performed by developing a cost function of the efficiency of the mower in terms of accuracy and velocity. The most promising composition of variables could then be identified by solving this multidimensional optimisation problem by the use of Design Space Exploration (DSE) [7], which is also a tool available in the INTO-CPS Application. Another suggestion of future work is related to the CT model of the dynamics of the vehicle. In this work, the lateral force of the caster wheels is assumed to follow a first order system. To increase the accuracy of the model, the tire properties and joint forces should be taken into account. This will additionally allow for representing the surface and thereby the contact forces between the surface and the tires in the model. Doing this allows for the possibility for optimising the model as a function of changing surface conditions such as moisture content and area density of the grass that is mowed. The initial model developed using the INTO-CPS Tool Chain has made it possible to simulate the influence of the different parameters in the system. The applicability of performing simulations reduces the number of physical tests needed, which are both costly in terms of resources and time. In comparison, a physical test requires a field, the machine and at least two persons to perform each test. Furthermore the use of simulations makes the development independent of external factors such as weather conditions.

Acknowledgments. The work presented here is partially supported by the INTO-CPS project funded by the European Commission's Horizon 2020 programme under grant agreement number 664047. The authors would also like to thank Nick Battle for his review comments on an earlier version of this paper.

References

1. Bagnato, A., Brosse, E., Quadri, I., Sadovykh, A.: The INTO-CPS cyber-physical system profile. In: DeCPS Workshop on Challenges and New Approaches for Dependable and Cyber-Physical System Engineering Focus on Transportation of the Future, Vienna, Austria, June 2017
2. Bandur, V., Larsen, P.G., Lausdahl, K., Thule, C., Terkelsen, A.F., Gamble, C., Pop, A., Brosse, E., Brauer, J., Lapschies, F., Groothuis, M., Kleijn, C., Couto, L.D.: INTO-CPS tool chain user manual. Technical report, INTO-CPS Deliverable, D4.2a, December 2016

3. Blochwitz, T., Otter, M., Arnold, M., Bausch, C., Clauß, C., Elmqvist, H., Junghanns, A., Mauss, J., Monteiro, M., Neidhold, T., Neumerkel, D., Olsson, H., Peetz, J., Wolf, S., Gmbh, G.I.T.I., Oberpfaffenhofen, D.L.R.: The functional mockup interface for tool independent exchange of simulation models. In: 8th International Modelica Conference, pp. 105–114, Munich, Germany, September 2011
4. Fitzgerald, J., Gamble, C., Larsen, P.G., Pierce, K., Woodcock, J.: Cyber-physical systems design: formal foundations, methods and integrated tool chains. In: FormaliSE: FME Workshop on Formal Methods in Software Engineering. ICSE 2015, Florence, Italy, May 2015
5. Fitzgerald, J., Gamble, C., Payne, R., Larsen, P.G., Basagiannis, S., Mady, A.E.D.: Collaborative model-based systems engineering for cyber-physical systems - a case study in building automation. In: Proceedings of INCOSE International Symposium on Systems Engineering, Edinburgh, Scotland, July 2016
6. Fitzgerald, J., Larsen, P.G., Verhoef, M. (eds.): Collaborative Design for Embedded Systems - Co-modelling and Co-simulation. Springer, Heidelberg (2014). http://link.springer.com/book/10.1007/978-3-642-54118-6
7. Gamble, C., Pierce, K.: Design space exploration for embedded systems using co-simulation. In: Fitzgerald, J., Larsen, P.G., Verhoef, M. (eds.) Collaborative Design for Embedded Systems, pp. 199–222. Springer, Heidelberg (2014). https://doi.org/10.1007/978-3-642-54118-6_10
8. Gomes, C., Thule, C., Broman, D., Larsen, P.G., Vangheluwe, H.: Co-simulation: state of the art. Technical report, February 2017. http://arxiv.org/abs/1702.00686
9. Han, X., Kim, H., Moon, H., Woo, H., Kim, J., Kim, Y.: Development of a path generation and tracking algorithm for a Korean auto-guidance tillage tractor. J. Biosyst. Eng. **38**, 1–8 (2013)
10. Hyldahl, P., Mikkola, A., Balling, O., Sopanen, J.: Behavior of thin rectangular ANCF shell elements in various mesh configurations. Nonlinear Dynamics **78**, 1277–1291 (2014)
11. ITEA Office Association: ITEA 3: project: 07006 MODELISAR, December 2015. https://itea3.org/project/modelisar.html
12. Kleijn, C.: Modelling and simulation of fluid power systems with 20-sim. Int. J. Fluid Power **7**(3), 57–60 (2006)
13. Larsen, P.G., Battle, N., Ferreira, M., Fitzgerald, J., Lausdahl, K., Verhoef, M.: The overture initiative - integrating tools for VDM. In: Zhang, M., Stolz, V. (eds.) Harnessing Theories for Tool Support in Software, pp. 9–19, November 2010
14. Larsen, P.G., Fitzgerald, J., Woodcock, J., Fritzson, P., Brauer, J., Kleijn, C., Lecomte, T., Pfeil, M., Green, O., Basagiannis, S., Sadovykh, A.: Integrated tool chain for model-based design of cyber-physical systems: the INTO-CPS project. In: CPS Data Workshop, Vienna, Austria, April 2016
15. Li, Y.P., Zielinska, T., Ang, M.H., Lin, W.: Vehicle dynamics of redundant mobile robots with powered caster wheels. In: Zielińska, T., Zieliński, C. (eds.) Romansy 16. CCL, vol. 487, pp. 221–228. Springer, Vienna (2006). https://doi.org/10.1007/3-211-38927-X_29
16. Quadri, I., Bagnato, A., Brosse, E., Sadovykh, A.: Modeling methodologies for cyber-physical systems: research field study on inherent and future challenges. ADA USER J. **36**(4), 246–253 (2015). http://www.ada-europe.org/archive/auj/auj-36-4.pdf
17. Serban, R., Olsen, N., Negrut, D., Recuero, A., Jayakumar, P.: A co-simulation framework for high-performance, high-fidelity simulation of ground vehicle-terrain interaction. In: Conference: NATO AVT-265 Specialists' Meeting, Vilnius, Lithuania (May 2017)

18. Siegwart, R., Nourbakhsh, I.R.: Introduction to Autonomous Mobile Robots. Bradford Company, Scituate (2004)
19. Staicu, S.: Dynamics equations of a mobile robot provided with caster wheel. Nonlinear Dyn. **58**, 237–248 (2009)
20. Tasora, A., et al.: Chrono: an open source multi-physics dynamics engine. In: Kozubek, T., Blaheta, R., Šístek, J., Rozložník, M., Čermák, M. (eds.) HPCSE 2015. LNCS, vol. 9611, pp. 19–49. Springer, Cham (2016). https://doi.org/10.1007/978-3-319-40361-8_2
21. Unity Technologies: Unity, December 2016. https://unity3d.com/
22. Verhoef, M., Larsen, P.G., Hooman, J.: Modeling and validating distributed embedded real-time systems with VDM++. In: Misra, J., Nipkow, T., Sekerinski, E. (eds.) FM 2006. LNCS, vol. 4085, pp. 147–162. Springer, Heidelberg (2006). https://doi.org/10.1007/11813040_11

Approximated Stability Analysis of Bi-modal Hybrid Co-simulation Scenarios

Cláudio Gomes[1]([✉]), Paschalis Karalis[2], Eva M. Navarro-López[2],
and Hans Vangheluwe[1,3,4]

[1] Department of Computer Science and Mathematics, University of Antwerp,
Antwerp, Belgium
{claudio.gomes,hans.vangheluwe}@uantwerp.be
[2] School of Computer Science, The University of Manchester, Manchester, UK
{paschalis.karalis,eva.navarro}@manchester.ac.uk
[3] McGill University, Montreal, Canada
[4] Flanders Make, Lommel, Belgium

Abstract. Co-simulation is a technique to orchestrate multiple simulators in order to approximate the behavior of a coupled system as a whole. Simulators execute in a lockstep fashion, each exchanging inputs and output data points with the other simulators at pre-accorded times.

In the context of systems with a physical and a cyber part, the communication frequency with which the simulators of each part communicate can have a negative impact in the accuracy of the global simulation results. In fact, the computed behavior can be qualitatively different, compared to the actual behavior of the original system, laying waste to potentially many hours of computation. It is therefore important to develop methods that answer whether a given communication frequency guarantees trustworthy co-simulation results.

In this paper, we take a small step in that direction. We develop a technique to approximate the lowest frequency for which a particular set of simulation tools can exchange values in a co-simulation and obtain results that can be trusted.

Keywords: Hybrid co-simulation · Hybrid systems
Lyapunov stability analysis · Coupled simulation · Hybrid automata

1 Introduction

As complexity in systems grows, and market pressure increases, system development is made by increasingly specialized teams, with tools tailored for each

This work has been done under the framework of the COST Action IC1404 – Multi-Paradigm Modelling for Cyber-Physical Systems (MPM4CPS), and partially supported by Flanders Make vzw, the strategic research centre for the manufacturing industry, and Ph.D. fellowship grants from the Agency for Innovation by Science and Technology in Flanders (IWT, dossier 151067).

© Springer International Publishing AG 2018
A. Cerone and M. Roveri (Eds.): SEFM 2017 Workshops, LNCS 10729, pp. 345–360, 2018.
https://doi.org/10.1007/978-3-319-74781-1_24

domain. Each team develops a part of the system, which is integrated with the remaining parts. Paradoxically, attaining innovative and multidisciplinary solutions requires that the development process is more integrated [22,24].

Modeling and simulation techniques improve the development of each part of the system (see, e.g., [8]), but face challenges when applied in holistic development processes. Co-simulation is a technique to overcome some of those challenges [25].

Co-simulation—the integration of multiple simulation tools, each specialized in the simulation of a particular kind of models, for the purpose of computing the global time behavior of the system—can be used to study system as a whole, when a single tool cannot. It is often required for systems whose models are best expressed in different formalisms [26].

During a co-simulation, each tool simulates the sub-model that pertains to its domain, and assumes that other tools will simulate the environment of the sub-model [10,21]. Therefore, underlying a particular co-simulation scenario – an assignment from outputs to inputs, of a set of simulation tools – there is an heterogeneous coupled model, which we denote as the original system.

To facilitate tool interaction, the Functional Mockup Interface (FMI) standard [3] was created, that defines an interface based on input and outputs.

An extra advantage of a standardized, modular coupling of tools, is that, in advanced stages of the development process, sub-models can be swapped by real-physical prototypes, interacting seamlessly in a (real-time) co-simulation with other tools – hardware-in-the-loop co-simulation.

Theoretically, any trajectory computed in a co-simulation should be the same as a solution to the original system [10]. In practice, just as with the simulation of systems described by differential equations, this is not the case. For example, it can happen that, while the behavior of the original system remains bounded over time, the trajectories computed by the co-simulation do not. This may be due to a delayed reaction of simulation tools to certain events, caused in turn by the frequency with which tools exchange inputs and outputs. It is therefore of utmost importance that co-simulation orchestration algorithms can tweak the communication frequency of the tools to ensure that system developers can trust the co-simulation results. However, more frequent communication entails a performance toll. Hence, a valid *research question* is: for a particular co-simulation scenario, what is the lowest frequency for which tools can exchange values, that still ensures that the computed trajectories are bounded? The question is not new: it has been studied for traditional simulation.

The *novelty of this paper* is that we reformulate the numerical stability of co-simulation scenarios as the stability of equilibrium points where the underlying original system is a hybrid system of a particular family.

Stability of hybrid systems has been studied extensively (see, for example, [9,12,14,20]). Most of the results define stability in the Lyapunov sense [13] (bounded trajectories, adapted from the continuous smooth case), and can be classified as: (i) the study of stability by using a common energy function for all the subsystems [14], or (ii) the use of multiple Lyapunov functions, one for each subsystem [4,12,19]. The consideration of multiple equilibria is not common in the hybrid systems literature, being typically focused on the study of systems with a unique equilibrium point for all the subsystems. Among very few results considering multiple equilibria are [19,20].

To the best of our knowledge, there is no work that applies these stability analysis techniques to study the effects of co-simulation in hybrid systems. Stability for co-simulation of original systems described by differential equations has been studied in [1,5,11,23] though. The dwell time approaches (e.g., [17]) can potentially be used, in the sense that they restrict the time that the system spends in each mode, as we do. However, our approach, spanning from the necessity to analyze co-simulation scenarios, does so by controlling the co-simulation step.

We contribute with a method for analyzing the stability of hybrid co-simulation scenarios and an algorithm to approximate the safe range of communication frequency between tools. To this end, we apply the stability results in [4] to a hybrid automaton representation of the co-simulation with multiple equilibria. The modeling of the co-simulation algorithm as a hybrid automaton – in a deterministic and non-deterministic versions – will be also one of the main contributions of our work. We use the hybrid-automaton modeling framework of hybrid systems (see, e.g., [16,18]).

The next section gives a brief introduction to hybrid automata, and describes the family of hybrid systems that our contribution applies to and how their stability can be studied. Sections 3 and 4 describe our contribution. Finally, in Sect. 5 we discuss the limitations of our approach and opportunities for future work.

2   Hybrid Systems

2.1   Hybrid Automaton Representation

Definition 1. *A hybrid automaton $\mathcal{H}$ is a collection*

$$\mathcal{H} = (Q, E, \mathcal{X}, Dom, \mathcal{F}, Init, G, R)$$

where: • $Q = \{q_1, q_2, \ldots\}$ *is a finite set of modes.* • $E \subseteq Q \times Q$ *is a finite set of edges called transitions.* • $\mathcal{X} \subseteq \mathbb{R}^n$ *is the continuous state space, for some natural n.* • $Dom \subseteq Q \to 2^{\mathcal{X}}$ *is the mode domain.* • $\mathcal{F} = \{f_{q_i}(x) : q_i \in Q\}$ *is a collection of time-invariant vector fields such that each $f_{q_i}(x)$ is Lipschitz continuous on $Dom(q_i)$ in order to ensure that the solution exists in q_i and is unique for a given initial state.* • $Init \subseteq Q \times \mathcal{X}$ *is a set of initial states.* • $G : E \to 2^{\mathcal{X}}$ *defines a guard set for each transition.* • $R : E \times \mathcal{X} \to 2^{\mathcal{X}}$ *specifies how the continuous state is reset at each transition.*

Intuitively, at any point in time t, $\mathcal{H}$ is in a mode $q_i \in Q$, with a continuous state $x(t)$. The continuous state evolves according to the Ordinary Differential Equation (ODE) $\dot{x}(t) = f_{q_i}(x(t))$ associated with mode q_i. $\mathcal{H}$ is allowed to stay in mode q_i as long as $x(t) \in Dom(q_i)$ holds. $\mathcal{H}$ *may* switch to mode q_j if $(q_i, q_j) \in E$ and $x(t) \in G((q_i, q_j))$. When such a mode switch happens at time t_s, the continuous state is reset to a new continuous state given by $R((q_i, q_j), x(t_s))$. The new state will be the initial state for the new mode ODE $\dot{x}(t) = f_{q_j}(x(t))$. Note that, for a given unique initial state, the behavior can still be non-deterministic.

It is common to represent a hybrid automaton as a directed graph with nodes depicting each mode, and edges depicting the transitions. The dynamics associated with each mode are represented inside the respective node, and the guards and reset map of each transition are represented near the edge corresponding to that transition. The guards are represented with conditions and the resets with assignments of the form $x := \dots$. When the state is not changed at the transition, that is $x := x$, we omit the assignment. We will often eliminate the time when writing the continuous state x for the sake of simplicity in the notation.

Example 1. Consider a system where a cart is connected to a spring/damper and a cord, illustrated in Fig. 1. The cord is connected to an actuator that stretches it whenever the cart crosses is to the left of the sensor, and loosens it when the cart is to the right of the sensor. The system is modeled as:

$$
\begin{array}{cc}
\boxed{\begin{array}{c} \dot{x}_1 = x_2 \\ \dot{x}_2 = \dfrac{1}{m}(-(c_s + c_c)x_1 - (d_s + d_c)x_2) \\ x_1 \leq l \end{array}}①
\xrightarrow{x_1 > l}
\boxed{\begin{array}{c} \dot{x}_1 = x_2 \\ \dot{x}_2 = \dfrac{1}{m}(-c_s x_1 - d_s x_2) \\ x_1 > l \end{array}}②
\end{array}
\qquad (1)
$$

$$x_1 \leq l$$

Mode 1 refers to the cord stretched and mode 2 to the cord loose, and: $l < 0$ is the sensor position, m is the mass of the cart, $x \in \mathbb{R}^2$ is the continuous state (position and velocity) of the cart, $c_s > 0$ is the stiffness coefficient of the spring, $d_s > 0$ the damping coefficient of the damper, and $c_c, d_c > 0$ the analogous coefficients of the cord. Figure 2 shows a trajectory of the cart position, for parameters $l = 10^{-4}, m = 1, c_s = 1, d_s = 0.5, d_c = 10^{-4}, c_c = 10^3$, and initial mode 2 and state $\begin{bmatrix} 1 & 0 \end{bmatrix}^T$.

2.2 Bi-modal Hybrid Automaton

We restrict our study to bi-modal hybrid automata defined as follows.

Definition 2. *A bi-modal hybrid automaton is represented as:*

$$
\begin{array}{cc}
\boxed{\begin{array}{c} \dot{x} = f_1(x) \\ x \in X_1 \\ X_1 = \{x \in \mathbb{R}^n | g(x) \leq 0\} \end{array}}①
\xrightarrow{g(x) > 0}
\boxed{\begin{array}{c} \dot{x} = f_2(x) \\ x \in X_2 \\ X_2 = \{x \in \mathbb{R}^n | g(x) > 0\} \end{array}}②
\end{array}
\qquad (2)
$$

$$g(x) \leq 0$$

with a given initial state $x(t_0) = x_0$. *The initial mode is inferred from* x_0.

The sets X_1 and X_2 define the invariant set of each mode and the dot denotes the time derivative. Throughout this paper, we make the following assumptions:

1. the switching surface $\mathscr{S} = \{x \in \mathbb{R}^n : g(x) = 0\}$ is a smooth hyper surface in $\mathbb{R}^n$;
2. the system has a single equilibrium point $x_{\mathrm{eq}} = \bar{0} \in \mathbb{R}^n$ common to all modes, i.e., $f_{q_i}(x_{\mathrm{eq}}) = \bar{0}$ for all $q_i \in \{1, 2\}$, not at the switching surface $(g(x_{\mathrm{eq}}) \neq 0)$;
3. the system trajectory does not enter a sliding motion on $\mathscr{S}$;
4. the continuous state is kept the same across mode transitions $(x := x)$.

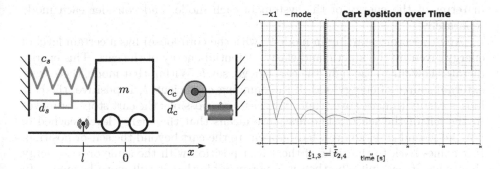

Fig. 1. Cart example.   **Fig. 2.** Cart position over time.

The cart system, defined in 1, is an example of a bi-modal hybrid automaton. It has one equilibrium point, at the origin.

In general, a solution of System (2) has two components: a continuous state evolution $x(t)$ in $\mathbb{R}^n$, and a piecewise constant function of time $\sigma(t) \in \{1, 2\}$, called switching sequence. At any time t, $\dot{x}(t)$ is given by $f_{\sigma(t)}(x(t))$.

For mode $q_i \in \{1, 2\}$, we denote the sequence of times at which mode q_i is switched on as $\{\bar{t}_{q_i,k}\}$ with $\bar{t}_{q_i,k} \leq \bar{t}_{q_i,k+1}$, and the set at which q_i is switched off as $\{\underline{t}_{q_i,k}\}$ with $\underline{t}_{q_i,k} \leq \underline{t}_{q_i,k+1}$. For example, if the system starts in mode $q_i = 1$, then $\bar{t}_{1,1} = 0 \in \{\bar{t}_{1,k}\}$. Note that $\bar{t}_{q_i,k} \leq \underline{t}_{q_i,k}$ is always the case, so $[\bar{t}_{q_i,k}, \underline{t}_{q_i,k}]$ represents the interval during which the system is in mode q_i for the k-th time. Figure 2 shows an example. To link these definitions with System (2), note that $\forall t \in [\bar{t}_{1,k}, \underline{t}_{1,k}] \implies g(x(t)) \leq 0$.

2.3   Stability

We use the term stability to refer to the fact that any solution to System (2), starting arbitrarily close to $x_{\mathrm{eq}} = \bar{0}$, will remain close to it as time advances [13].

Definition 3. *Given any* $\varepsilon > 0$, *the equilibrium point* $\bar{0}$ *is stable if and only if one can always find a* $\delta(\varepsilon) > 0$, *such that,*

$$\|x(0)\| < \delta(\varepsilon) \implies \|x(t)\| < \varepsilon, \forall t \geq 0$$

The equilibrium point is asymptotically stable *if it is stable and* $\lim_{t \to \infty} x(t) = \bar{0}$.

We will often assume that the initial conditions of System (2) belong to a known domain X_0, thereby relaxing the condition $\varepsilon > 0$ to have an upper bound. It is only within this domain of initial conditions that we are interested in studying the stability of x_{eq}.

The trajectory of System (1), plotted in Fig. 2, suggests that the equilibrium point $\bar{0}$ is stable. To formally prove this, we can formulate the stability property in terms of the energy of the system in each mode, and consider each mode separately.

Any trajectory starting in mode 2 (with the cord loose) has a certain level of energy given by the kinetic and elastic potential energy of the cart. This energy dictates how far to the right the cart can go, say b. Within that mode, there is no external source of energy and, if the damping coefficient d_s is positive, the cart looses energy (kinetic) over time. Two cases are possible: the cart stops, or moves to the left of the sensor. The first case means that the energy level reached 0. For the second case, ignore what happens to the cart beyond the sensor position. If it comes back to the right of the sensor position with the same or less energy than what it had initially, then it is not possible that it will move beyond b. In fact, if $d_s > 0$ then it will move less and less to the right, as it re-enters mode 2, eventually coming to a rest.

If the above argument applies to the system starting in mode 1 as well, then $\bar{0}$ is stable. And if one of the damping coefficients is positive, then it is asymptotically stable. This is essentially the result described in [4], applied to the cart example.

Without loss of generality, we will always assume that the stability analysis is made for the equilibrium point in mode 1. We now enumerate the formal conditions that need to be met to show the stability of the equilibrium point of System (2).

Suppose we have two continuous differentiable energy functions $V_1(x)$ and $V_2(x)$, and let Σ be a given set of possible switching sequences for solutions of System (2). If for each switching sequence $\sigma(t) \in \Sigma$, the following conditions are satisfied,

Condition 1. $V_{q_i}(x) > 0$, for all $x \in X_{q_i} \setminus \{\bar{0}\}$;

Condition 2. $V_1(\bar{0}) = 0$;

Condition 3. $\dot{V}_{q_i}(x) \leq 0$, for all $x \in X_{q_i} \setminus \{\bar{0}\}$;

Condition 4. $V_{q_i}(x(\bar{t}_{q_i,k+1})) \leq V_{q_i}(x(\bar{t}_{q_i,k})), \forall k$;

where $\bar{t}_{1,k}, \bar{t}_{1,k+1}$ are two consecutive switch-on instants and $q_i \in \{1,2\}$, then the equilibrium point at the origin of System (2) is stable.

In addition, if the following condition is satisfied,

Condition 5. $\dot{V}_q(x) < 0$, for all $x \in X_q \setminus \{\bar{0}\}$;

then the equilibrium point at the origin is asymptotically stable.

It is important to note that, in proving Condition 4, only the trajectories that re-enter mode q_i are of interest. For example, in System (1), not all trajectories starting in mode 1, will re-enter mode 1 after being in mode 2. Below a given level of energy, the cart cannot reach the sensor, and will thus stay in mode 2.

To relate these formal conditions with the intuitive argument given above, note that $V_{q_i}(x)$ is the energy level when the cart is in state x, and that $\dot{V}_{q_i}(x) \leq 0$ means that the energy is decreasing along the state trajectory, because $\dot{V}_{q_i}(x) = \frac{\partial V_{q_i}}{\partial x}\dot{x}$. Hence, as long as the cart is obeying the dynamics associated with mode q_i, its energy does not increase.

To exemplify the application of these conditions, we show the stability of the zero equilibrium point of the cart, in mode 2, using the energy functions:

$$V_1\left(\begin{bmatrix} x_1 & x_2 \end{bmatrix}^T\right) = \frac{1}{2}mx_2^2 + \frac{1}{2}(c_s + c_c)x_1^2; \qquad V_2\left(\begin{bmatrix} x_1 & x_2 \end{bmatrix}^T\right) = \frac{1}{2}mx_2^2 + \frac{1}{2}c_sx_1^2$$

Conditions 1–3 are easy to satisfy, so we prove Condition 4 for mode $q_i = 1$ only. For mode 2 the proof is analogous.

Let $x(\bar{t}_{1,k})$ be the state at the k-th switch on instant of mode 1 (stretched cord). Then we know that $x(\bar{t}_{1,k}) = \begin{bmatrix} x_1(\bar{t}_{1,k}) & x_2(\bar{t}_{1,k}) \end{bmatrix}^T = \begin{bmatrix} l & v \end{bmatrix}^T$, for some $v < 0$. Over the interval $\bar{t}_{1,k} \leq t \leq \underline{t}_{1,k}$, $x_1(t) \leq l$ and $\dot{V}_1(x) < 0$, hence $V_1(x(\underline{t}_{1,k})) \leq V_1(x(\bar{t}_{1,k}))$. Similarly, over the next interval $\bar{t}_{2,k} \leq t \leq \underline{t}_{2,k}$, $x_1(t) \leq l$ while in mode 2, we have $\dot{V}_2(x) < 0$, hence $V_2(x(\underline{t}_{2,k})) \leq V_2(x(\bar{t}_{2,k}))$. Now, note that since $V_1\left(\begin{bmatrix} x_1 & x_2 \end{bmatrix}^T\right) = V_2\left(\begin{bmatrix} x_1 & x_2 \end{bmatrix}^T\right) + \frac{1}{2}c_cx_1^2$, we have:

$$V_2(x(\bar{t}_{1,k+1})) = V_1(x(\bar{t}_{1,k+1})) - \frac{1}{2}c_cl^2 < V_2(x(\underline{t}_{1,k})) = V_1(x(\underline{t}_{1,k})) - \frac{1}{2}c_cl^2 \Leftrightarrow$$
$$V_1(x(\bar{t}_{1,k+1})) \leq V_1(x(\underline{t}_{1,k})) \leq V_1(x(\bar{t}_{1,k}))$$

The next section shows how the co-simulation of a stable System (2) can yield unstable trajectories, and the steps that can be taken to prevent so.

3 Hybrid Co-simulation

Co-simulation can be seen as a relaxation of the coupling constraints of a de-coupled hybrid system, introduced by the need for a finite frequency of communication between simulators. A particular realization of System (2) can be made with two coupled sub-systems: a software controller, and a plant. During a simulation, the controller reads the state $x(t_i)$ of the plant at a designated communication time t_i, and outputs $\sigma(t_i) \in \{1, 2\}$ which decides the mode that the plant should be in, until the next communication time $t_i + H$, with $H > 0$ denoting the communication time step. Figure 3 shows an example where the controller decides to change mode at time t_i because the plant state is above the $g(x)$ surface. This co-simulation approach, often denoted as Jacobi [10], fits most co-simulation scenarios that include software controllers and continuous sub-systems, with a fixed communication step size H.

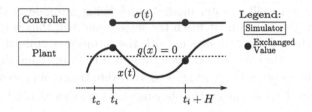

Fig. 3. Co-simulation approach under study.

Due to the fact that the two simulators do not communicate in between communication points, there is a variable delay in the reaction of the controller. As illustrated in Fig. 3, the plant has crossed the switching surface at time t_c, before the controller detects that change, at time t_i. This is known as the state event location, or zero crossing detection, problem [27]. We assume that the simulators do not know the exact moment that the plant crosses the surface. This is a reasonable assumption since employing state event location techniques in co-simulation is technically demanding (e.g., it requires the modification of existing simulation tools), has a performance penalty, and there is no standardized interface to communicating switching surfaces between simulators yet (e.g., see [2,7] for proposals).

Fortunately, as we show here, it is possible to select an appropriate communication step size H, that ensures that the co-simulation preserves the stability properties of the original system. To achieve this, we follow an approach that has also been followed for the study of numerical techniques in general simulation (see, e.g., [6]): we model the co-simulation of the original system as a dynamical system.

Figure 4 compares a trajectory approximated by the co-simulation algorithm illustrated in Fig. 3, with the analytical solution of System (1) (position and mode). The communication step size is $H = 0.05$ s and all other parameters are as in Fig. 2. While the original trajectory is asymptotically stable, the co-simulation is not. The co-simulation keeps alternating between mode 1 and mode 2 while the original trajectory settles in mode 2 after about 33 s. For a $H = 0.001$ s, the co-simulation at the origin seems to be asymptotically stable, as Fig. 5 suggests.

These experimental results hint that H plays an important role in making sure that the co-simulation has the same qualitative behavior as the original system it is intended to represent. Our research questions follows: for a given

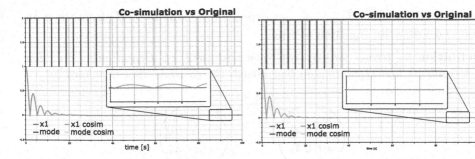

Fig. 4. Co-simulation with $H = 0.05$.   **Fig. 5.** Co-simulation with $H = 0.001$.

original system, with a given range of valid initial conditions, what is the *safe* range of communication step sizes that ensures that the co-simulation preserves the stability properties of the original system?

4   Stability Analysis

In order to study the stability of the co-simulation of an original system, we want to apply Conditions 1–4. For that, we need a hybrid automaton that represents the co-simulation algorithm applied to the original system.

Consider the co-simulation algorithm in Fig. 3. When there is no mode switch, the reaction delay does not affect the trajectory of the plant, since the plant will anyhow assume the most recently communicated mode. It is only when the plant crosses the switching surface, that the controller reaction delay can affect the co-simulation trajectory. For example, in the figure, the reaction delay at t_i is $t_i - t_c$. Obviously, the reaction delay is bounded by H, as shown at $t_i + H$ in the figure. The distance travelled by the plant before the controller reacts is also finite and depends on the reaction delay.

Therefore, in any co-simulation of a bi-modal system, a mode switch can happen anywhere in time between the moment that the plant crosses the switching surface (zero reaction delay), and *at most* H units of time after the plant crossed the surface. We can build a non-deterministic automaton that captures this behavior.

4.1   Non-deterministic Hybrid Model of Co-simulation

To build such hybrid automaton, we take the original system mode invariants ($x \in X_1$ and $x \in X_2$) in Eq. (2), and define new *relaxed* mode invariants, as functions of H, that capture the worst case reaction delay in each mode.

Definition 4. *For a given original invariant set X_{q_i} with $q_i \in \{1, 2\}$, the co-simulation and the communication step size H induce a relaxed mode invariant set $\tilde{X}_{q_i}$, defined as the reachable set [15] in H units, starting in X_{q_i}:*

$$\tilde{X}_{q_i}(H) = \left\{ \tilde{x}(t) \mid 0 \le t \le H \text{ and } \tilde{x}(t) \text{ satisfies the ODE } \dot{\tilde{x}} = f_{q_i}(\tilde{x}); \ \tilde{x}(0) \in X_{q_i} \right\}$$

Note that $\lim_{H \to 0} \tilde{X}(H)_{q_i} = X_{q_i}$, as expected. We will drop (H) from the notation and just write $\tilde{X}_{q_i}$ from now on.

Definition 5. *Using the relaxed invariant sets of Definition 4, the non-deterministic hybrid automaton that models the co-simulation is defined as:*

$$
\begin{array}{c}
g(x) > 0 \\
\left(\begin{array}{c} \dot{x} = f_1(x) \\ x(t) \in \tilde{X}_1 \end{array}\right) \qquad \left(\begin{array}{c} \dot{x} = f_2(x(t)) \\ x(t) \in \tilde{X}_2 \end{array}\right) \\
g(x) \leq 0
\end{array}
\tag{3}
$$

Due to the non-determinism of hybrid automata, the state $x(\bar{t}_{q_i,k})$ at switch-on instant $\bar{t}_{q_i,k}$ of mode q_i can be anywhere in the region $\tilde{X}_{q_j} \setminus X_{q_j}$, with $q_j \neq q_i$ being the other state. The region $D_{q_j} = \tilde{X}_{q_j} \setminus X_{q_j}$ will be called the danger zone of q_j.

Definition 6. *The danger zone of each mode is defined as:*

$$
D_1(H) = \left\{ \tilde{x}(t) \mid 0 \leq t \leq H \text{ and } \tilde{x}(t) \text{ is a solution to } \dot{\tilde{x}} = f_1(\tilde{x}); \ g(\tilde{x}(t)) \geq 0 \right\}
$$
$$
D_2(H) = \left\{ \tilde{x}(t) \mid 0 \leq t \leq H \text{ and } \tilde{x}(t) \text{ is a solution to } \dot{\tilde{x}} = f_2(\tilde{x}); \ g(\tilde{x}(t)) \leq 0 \right\} \tag{4}
$$

For $H = 0$, the danger zone D_{q_i} coincides with the switching surface of the original system. Furthermore, by definition, $0 < H_r \leq H_s$, implies that $D_{q_i}(H_r) \subseteq D_{q_i}(H_s)$.

Definition 6 allows us to approximate D_{q_i}, for a given H, by solving simultaneously a set of ordinary differential equations, whose initial value is a point in the switching surface. Continuity ensures that this set can be approximated with arbitrary accuracy. However, D_{q_i} is unbounded if the set of points in the surface (solutions to $g(\tilde{x}) = 0$) is unbounded. In that case, we construct D_{q_i} for a bounded set of points, that make sense in the physics of the original system. For example, in the cart system, the set of solutions to the surface equation $x_1 - l = 0$ is unbounded (all speeds at the sensor position are possible), but it is reasonable to assume that $|x_2| < 100$.

4.2 Stability Analysis

We are interested in studying the stability of System (3), assuming that the original system is stable (or asymptotically stable). We therefore assume that the energy functions V_1 and V_2 are given, so we do not need to build new ones for the co-simulation hybrid automaton. With these, we essentially restrict H until any solution to System (3) satisfies each of the Conditions 1–4.

Condition 1 needs to be satisfied for all $x \in \tilde{X}_{q_i} \setminus \{\bar{0}\}$. However, it suffices to show it for all $x \in D_{q_i} \setminus \{\bar{0}\}$. This can be done operationally by iteratively approximating the danger zone $D_{q_i}(H)$ for increasingly large values of H, as long as:

$$
D_{q_i} \subseteq \{x \in \mathbb{R}^n : V_{q_i}(x) > 0\} \Leftrightarrow D_{q_i} \setminus \{x \in \mathbb{R}^n : V_{q_i}(x) > 0\} = \emptyset
$$

Condition 2 is always satisfied by the co-simulation.

Condition 3 is checked by the same procedure as Condition 1: approximate the danger zone D_{q_i} for increasingly large values of H, as long as:

$$D_{q_i} \subseteq \left\{ x \in \mathbb{R}^n : \dot{V}_{q_i}(x) \leq 0 \right\} \Leftrightarrow D_{q_i} \setminus \left\{ x \in \mathbb{R}^n : \dot{V}_{q_i}(x) \leq 0 \right\} = \emptyset$$

To find the largest value H that proves Condition 4, we must understand how the co-simulation influences the energy of the system. Without loss of generality, we focus on studying the condition for mode $q_i = 1$. The analysis for mode 2 follows the same steps.

Figure 6 sketches the case where $H = 0$, that is, where the co-simulation behaves exactly as the original system, which satisfies the condition by assumption. In the figure, the notation $V_{q_i,k} = V_{q_i}(x(\bar{t}_{q_i,k}))$. The trajectory shown in grey violates the condition because it re-enters mode 1 with a level of energy higher than $V_{1,k}$.

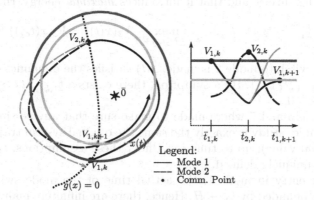

Fig. 6. Co-simulation trajectory for $H = 0$.

For $II - \varepsilon > 0$, the point $x(\bar{t}_{1,k}) \in D_2$, and $x(t)$ crosses the switching surface at some time $t_{c_1} \leq \bar{t}_{1,k}$, before switching from mode 2 to mode 1. Following the definition of System (3), $x(t)$ obeys:

$$\dot{x}(t) = f_2(x(t)) \text{ with } t_{c_1} \leq t \leq \bar{t}_{1,k} \text{ for some } \bar{t}_{1,k} \leq t_{c_1} + H \tag{5}$$

where $x(t_{c_1})$ is any given value that satisfies $g(x(t_{c_1})) = 0$.

The value $\bar{t}_{1,k}$ is uncertain, but bounded by $t_{c_1} + H$. It can be the case that $\bar{t}_{1,k} > t_{c_1}$ and $V_1(x(t_{c_1})) < V_1(x(\bar{t}_{1,k}))$, which means that the co-simulation, due to a switch that is delayed by $\bar{t}_{1,k} - t_{c_1}$ units of time, can introduce extra energy into the system, compared to the original system (this is essentially what happened in Fig. 4, where the co-simulation introduces just enough energy for the cart to always leave mode 2 again). However, the energy change caused by the co-simulation is always finite, as the functions f_1, f_2 are known to be continuous;

further, it is known that, as H approaches zero, and the co-simulation approaches the behaviour of the original system, the change in energy also approaches zero.

In the following paragraphs, to facilitate the explanation, we assume that

$$\bar{t}_{1,k} = t_{c_1}, \quad \min_{t_{c_1} \le t \le t_{c_1} + H} V_1(x(t)) = V_1(x(t_{c_1})),$$

$$\max_{t_{c_1} \le t \le t_{c_1} + H} V_1(x(t)) = V_1(x(t_{c_1} + H)) \tag{6}$$

In other words, V_1 is minimal under the dynamics of mode 2 at the switching surface, maximal away from the surface after H units of time, and the co-simulation has made the switch to mode 1 at the surface, introducing at that moment, a minimal amount of energy (compared to the original system).

After the switch to mode 1 is made, the co-simulation trajectory $x(t)$ satisfies the dynamics of mode 1 in the interval $[\bar{t}_{1,k}, \underline{t}_{1,k}]$. Furthermore, by assumption, there exists a t_{c_2} such that $\bar{t}_{1,k} < t_{c_2} \le \underline{t}_{1,k}$ and $g(x(t_{c_2})) = 0$.

For the sake of the argument, assume that the co-simulation switches right at the switching surface and that it introduces *maximal* energy, that is:

$$\underline{t}_{1,k} = \bar{t}_{2,k} = t_{c_2}, \quad \max_{t_{c_2} \le t \le t_{c_2} + H} V_2(x(t)) = V_2(x(t_{c_2})) \tag{7}$$

After the switch to mode 2 is made, $x(t)$ satisfies the dynamics of mode 2 in the interval $[\underline{t}_{1,k}, \bar{t}_{1,k+1}]$. By assumption, there exists a $\underline{t}_{1,k} < t_{c_3} \le \bar{t}_{1,k+1}$ such that $g(x(t_{c_3})) = 0$.

Assumptions 6 and 7 where made to make sure that any co-simulation trajectory $x(t)$ under study is exactly the same the original system trajectory (with the same initial value), up to time t_{c_3}. Under these assumptions, $\bar{t}_{1,k} = t_{c_1}$ and $\underline{t}_{1,k} = t_{c_2}$ are uniquely defined.

For the re-entry in mode 1, the actual time of the mode switch $\bar{t}_{1,k+1}$ is uncertain but bounded by $t_{c_3} + H$. Hence, there are infinitely many trajectories that re-enter mode 1 at each time between t_{c_3} and $t_{c_3} + H$, starting from the same initial value $x(t_{c_1})$. Figure 7 shows three of these possible trajectories satisfying the above equations. Two of those trajectories satisfy Condition 4 but the third one, in gray, does not. The notation $V_{q_i,c_i}^{max} = \max_{t_{c_i} \le t \le t_{c_i} + H} V_{q_i}(x(t))$. It stays in mode 2 for too long, increasing the energy level of the system beyond the limit $V_1(x(\bar{t}_{1,k}))$.

As Fig. 7 suggests, for a given initial value $x(t_{c_1})$, we do not need to consider all possible trajectories. It suffices to make sure H is small enough so that the condition is satisfied for the $x(t)$ where $V_1(x(\bar{t}_{1,k+1}))$ is maximal, so that the grey trajectory can never happen. Any other trajectory will then satisfy the condition as well. Formally, we consider $x(t)$ such that $V_1(x(\bar{t}_{1,k+1})) = \max_{t_{c_1} \le t \le t_{c_1} + H} V_1(x(t))$.

The above result is incomplete because we made Assumptions 6 and 7, to give the intuition. Relaxing these assumptions, we have the following general result. It suffices to check the trajectories $x(t)$ for which:

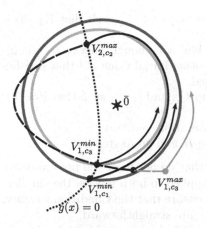

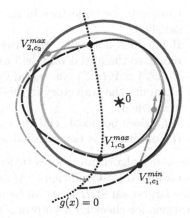

Fig. 7. Co-simulation effect in trajectories with Assumptions 6 and 7.

Fig. 8. Co-simulation effect in general trajectories.

1. The initial entry in mode 1 *minimizes* the added energy to the system. That is, $\bar{t}_{1,k}$ is such that

$$V_1(x(\bar{t}_{1,k})) = \min_{t_{c_1} \leq t \leq t_{c_1}+H} V_1(x(t)) \tag{8}$$

2. The intermediate entry in mode 2 *maximizes* the energy added to the system. That is, $\underline{t}_{1,k}$ is such that

$$V_2(\underline{t}_{1,k}) = \max_{t_{c_2} \leq t \leq t_{c_2}+H} V_2(x(t)) \tag{9}$$

3. The re-entry in mode 1 *maximizes* the energy added to the system. Formally, $\bar{t}_{1,k+1}$ satisfies

$$V_1(x(\bar{t}_{1,k+1})) = \max_{t_{c_1} \leq t \leq t_{c_1}+H} V_1(x(t)) \tag{10}$$

These trajectories represent essentially the worst case scenario in terms of energy distortion, caused by $H > 0$. Note that maximizing the energy at the intermediate entry in mode 2 increases the maximum energy when re-entering mode 1 later. Figure 8 shows a sketch of three trajectories, only one of which satisfies the stability condition. The grey ones do not.

Based on the above result, we can compute a safe H as follows:

1. Start with an initial $H \leftarrow H_0$.
2. Pick a range of values $x^{[s]} \in \mathbb{R}^n$ that are in the switching surface, that is, $g(x^{[s]}) = 0$.
3. For each $x^{[s]}$ in the switching surface:
    (a) Solve Eq. (5), with $x(t_{c_1}) = x^{[s]}, t_{c_1} = 0$ and find the $\bar{t}_{1,k}$ that satisfies Eq. (8).

(b) Compute the trajectory in mode 1, find t_{c_2} and $\underline{t}_{1,k}$ such that Eq. (9) is satisfied.

(c) If t_{c_2} does not exist, the trajectory has not enough energy to change mode, so the initial value $x^{[s]}$ and any other initial value $x^{[r]}$ that satisfies $V_1(x^{[r]}) < V_1(x^{[s]})$ can be safely ignored.

(d) Compute the trajectory in mode 2, find t_{c_3}, and $\bar{t}_{1,k+1}$ such that Eq. (10) is satisfied.

(e) If t_{c_3} does not exist, end the current iteration.

(f) If Condition 4 is not satisfied, decrease H and go to step 3a.

The above algorithm ignores trajectories that do not meet the pre-requisites to be considered for Condition 4. After it is applied to both modes, the smallest H is the largest safest H that can be used to ensure that the Condition 1 is met. Adaptations for checking asymptotic stability are straightforward.

The algorithm terminates because, even when the range of initial values in the switching surface is infinite: (1) there is a lower limit to the level of energy of the points in the surface that need to be considered; (2) not all initial values are physically meaningful.

An application of this algorithm to the cart example is available for download[1]. The result is $H < 0.039$ for mode 2, and $H < 0.0027$ for 1. Therefore the overall safest $H < 0.0027$.

5   Conclusion

This work presents an analysis procedure, and a conservative algorithm, to compute a safe range of communication step sizes which ensures that the co-simulation preserves the stability properties of the original system. As part of the analysis, we show how to model a co-simulation as a non-deterministic hybrid automaton, and how to satisfy the stability conditions presented in [4].

This is only a baby step in the analysis of co-simulation applied to hybrid systems, and the following are some of the important limitations: (i) it applies only to bi-modal hybrid automata that have at most one equilibrium in each mode, at the origin; (ii) only the Jacobi orchestration approach is considered. (iii) the current implementation of the algorithm is slow and requires insight about the physics of the original system; (iv) we require access to the equations of the original system, or at least, we need to be able to simulate them.

Ongoing and future work aims at addressing these limitations. For example, we are researching into how to generalize the analysis for multi-modal systems, with multiple equilibria, such as the ones studied in [19, 20]. Furthermore, we are exploring the possibility of using the FMI standard to simulate the original system in multiple modes, thus avoiding the need to disclose important information (such as intellectual property) about its dynamics.

With this and future work, we wish that system integrators running co-simulations can trust their results, thus enhancing the development of complex systems.

---

[1] http://msdl.cs.mcgill.ca/people/claudio/projs/AnalysisCart.zip.

References

1. Arnold, M.: Stability of sequential modular time integration methods for coupled multibody system models. J. Comput. Nonlinear Dyn. **5**(3), 9 (2010)
2. Bertsch, C., Ahle, E., Schulmeister, U.: The Functional Mockup Interface-seen from an industrial perspective. In: 10th International Modelica Conference (2014)
3. Blockwitz, T., Otter, M., Akesson, J., Arnold, M., Clauss, C., Elmqvist, H., Friedrich, M., Junghanns, A., Mauss, J., Neumerkel, D., Olsson, H., Viel, A.: Functional Mockup Interface 2.0: the standard for tool independent exchange of simulation models. In: 9th International Modelica Conference, pp. 173–184. Linköping University Electronic Press, Munich, November 2012
4. Branicky, M.: Multiple Lyapunov functions and other analysis tools for switched and hybrid systems. IEEE Trans. Autom. Control **43**(4), 475–482 (1998)
5. Busch, M.: Continuous approximation techniques for co-simulation methods: analysis of numerical stability and local error. ZAMM - J. Appl. Math. Mech. **96**(9), 1061–1081 (2016)
6. Cellier, F.E., Kofman, E.: Continuous System Simulation. Springer Science & Business Media, New York (2006). https://doi.org/10.1007/0-387-30260-3
7. Cremona, F., Lohstroh, M., Broman, D., Di Natale, M., Lee, E.A., Tripakis, S.: Step revision in hybrid co-simulation with FMI. In: 14th ACM-IEEE International Conference on formal Methods and Models for System Design, Kanpur, India (2016)
8. Friedman, J., Ghidella, J.: Using model-based design for automotive systems engineering - requirements analysis of the power window example. SAE Technical Paper, April 2006
9. Goebel, R., Sanfelice, R.G., Teel, A.R.: Hybrid Dynamical Systems: Modeling, Stability and Robustness. Princeton University Press, Princeton (2012)
10. Gomes, C., Thule, C., Broman, D., Larsen, P.G., Vangheluwe, H.: Co-simulation: state of the art. Technical report, February 2017. arXiv:1702.00686
11. Kalmar-Nagy, T., Stanciulescu, I.: Can complex systems really be simulated? Appl. Math. Comput. **227**, 199–211 (2014)
12. Karalis, P., Navarro-López, E.M.: Feedback stability for dissipative switched systems. In: Proceedings of 20th IFAC World Congress. IFAC, Toulouse (2017, to appear)
13. Khalil, H.K.: Nonlinear Systems. Prentice-Hall, Upper Saddle River (1996)
14. Liberzon, D.: Switching in Systems and Control. Springer Science & Business Media, Boston (2012). https://doi.org/10.1007/978-1-4612-0017-8
15. Lygeros, J., Johansson, K., Simic, S., Zhang, J., Sastry, S.: Dynamical properties of hybrid automata. IEEE Trans. Autom. Control **48**(1), 2–17 (2003)
16. Lygeros, J.: Lecture notes on hybrid systems (2004). https://robotics.eecs.berkeley.edu/~sastry/ee291e/lygeros.pdf
17. Mitra, S., Liberzon, D., Lynch, N.: Verifying average dwell time of hybrid systems. ACM Trans. Embed. Comput. Syst. **8**(1), 1–37 (2008)
18. Navarro-López, E.M., Carter, R.: Hybrid automata: an insight into the discrete abstraction of discontinuous systems. Int. J. Syst. Sci. **42**(11), 1883–1898 (2011)
19. Navarro-López, E.M., Carter, R.: Deadness and how to disprove liveness in hybrid dynamical systems. Theoret. Comput. Sci. **642**, 1–23 (2016)
20. Navarro-López, E.M., Laila, D.S.: Group and total dissipativity and stability of multi-equilibria hybrid automata. IEEE Trans. Autom. Control **58**(12), 3196–3202 (2013)

21. Ni, Y., Broenink, J.F.: Hybrid systems modelling and simulation in DESTECS: a co-simulation approach. In: Klumpp, M. (ed.) 26th European Simulation and Modelling Conference, pp. 32–36. EUROSIS-ETI, Ghent (2012)
22. Nielsen, C.B., Larsen, P.G., Fitzgerald, J., Woodcock, J., Peleska, J.: Systems of systems engineering: basic concepts, model-based techniques, and research directions. ACM Comput. Surv. **48**(2), 18:1–18:41 (2015)
23. Schweizer, B., Li, P., Lu, D.: Explicit and implicit cosimulation methods: stability and convergence analysis for different solver coupling approaches. J. Comput. Nonlinear Dyn. **10**(5), 051007 (2015)
24. Tomiyama, T., D'Amelio, V., Urbanic, J., ElMaraghy, W.: Complexity of multidisciplinary design. CIRP Ann. - Manuf. Technol. **56**(1), 185–188 (2007)
25. Van der Auweraer, H., Anthonis, J., De Bruyne, S., Leuridan, J.: Virtual engineering at work: the challenges for designing mechatronic products. Eng. Comput. **29**(3), 389–408 (2013)
26. Vangheluwe, H., De Lara, J., Mosterman, P.J.: An introduction to multi-paradigm modelling and simulation. In: AI, Simulation and Planning in High Autonomy Systems, pp. 9–20. SCS (2002)
27. Zhang, F., Yeddanapudi, M., Mosterman, P.: Zero-crossing location and detection algorithms for hybrid system simulation. In: IFAC World Congress, pp. 7967–7972 (2008)

Towards Resilience-Explicit Modelling and Co-simulation of Cyber-Physical Systems

Mark Jackson$^{(\boxtimes)}$ and John S. Fitzgerald

Newcastle University, Newcastle upon Tyne, UK
{M.Jackson3,John.Fitzgerald}@newcastle.ac.uk

Abstract. The resilience of Cyber-Physical Systems (CPSs) is of major public concern, but is an ill-defined property that is challenging to engineer, given the complexity and multi-disciplinarity of CPSs. Co-simulation techniques are therefore attractive options, permitting cross-domain analysis of cyber and physical failures, as well as their prevention, detection and tolerance. We propose the use of a multi-attribute resilience profile as a basis for assessment and trade-off analysis in CPSs. We propose augmentations to the INTO-CPS methods that explicitly use this profile to analyse resilience by means of co-simulation at several design stages. A small pilot study shows how such methods may help the CPS engineer to identify and evaluate new resilient designs.

1 Introduction

... we may expect "failures to be the norm in CPS". It seems evident that resilience will become a much-sought-after capability within society in the near future.

Reimann, Rückriegel, et al. [1]

Cyber-Physical Systems (CPSs) are a natural evolution of embedded devices in networked environments [2], ranging in scale from medical devices and automotive control systems, to "smart" infrastructures in areas such as road traffic management and energy grids [1]. In principle, such digitalisation should offer more efficient and reactive control with greater autonomy than is delivered by individual embedded or centralised architectures. However, combining cyber networks and their complex behaviours with physical systems is risky. As the 2017 Road2CPS [1] report indicates, there is a growing need for *resilience* to threats and vulnerabilities. We argue that this entails treating resilience as an explicit property in CPS design. Given the range of facets of resilience that are important in different application sectors, it is apparent that a nuanced characterisation of resilience is needed to facilitate disciplined engineering. We recognise that CPSs have a considerable human factor, however the tools and techniques used in this work do not account for stochastic human behaviour.

Model-based systems engineering methods offer considerable promise, but are challenged by the independence and heterogeneity of CPS constituents. Several

© Springer International Publishing AG 2018
A. Cerone and M. Roveri (Eds.): SEFM 2017 Workshops, LNCS 10729, pp. 361–376, 2018.
https://doi.org/10.1007/978-3-319-74781-1_25

of these challenges are addressed by multidisciplinary co-simulation technology such as that advanced in INTO-CPS[1]. It is therefore legitimate to ask whether such techniques and tools can help to deliver dependably resilient CPSs. In our previous work [3], we described *resilience profiling* – an approach to the explicit description of resilience characteristics, and discussed how this might be realised in a co-simulation framework. In this paper, we propose a more systematic utilisation of the resilience profile, and its implementation within the INTO-CPS methods and tools.

We discuss background and related work on resilience in Sect. 2. We recap our extended resilience profile briefly in Sect. 2.2. We consider how the INTO-CPS methods and tools could be made *resilience-explicit* in a workflow discussed in Sect. 3 and demonstrated on a standard INTO-CPS pilot-study (the line-following robot) in Sect. 4. We evaluate progress to date and future directions in Sect. 5.

2   Background and Related Work

We aim to provide usable methods and tools for engineering dependably resilient CPSs. In this section, we describe the scope and background to our work. We briefly indicate what we mean by a CPS, explain why we focus on model-based techniques and introduce our baseline tools. We then examine in more detail the existing work on resilience profiling in CPS-related contexts.

2.1   Multidisciplinary Model-Based Design for CPSs

A CPS integrates computational and physical processes [4]. CPS engineering should therefore address the integration of methods and tools from different (discrete and continuous) domains and disciplines [2]. The focus of much current work, including our own, is on systems of networked computing elements, including "smart" devices, that together deliver emergent properties on which reliance is placed. This adds to the mix important Systems-of-Systems (SoS) aspects, including the need to integrate independently owned and managed systems, the ability to reason about the composition of the contractual interfaces between them, and the ability to deal with dynamically evolving structures over the life of the CPS [5].

Collaborative and multi-paradigm Model-Based Design (MBD) techniques have been proposed as a means of evaluating alternative architectures and functionality, and providing early identification of defects in CPSs [6]. Realising the value of such approaches requires a semantic basis for linking models given in diverse notations, the ability to compose abstract descriptions of interfaces between system elements, and the ability to describe architectures explicitly. Much research builds on hybrid systems as a common semantic framework for CPSs [7]. Rather than work with a single formalism, we aim at an extensible framework able to integrate the diverse formalisms used in practice.

---

[1] http://into-cps.au.dk/.

INTO-CPS offers an integrated tool chain for the comprehensive MBD of CPSs. The tool chain supports multidisciplinary, collaborative modelling of CPSs from requirements through design, down to realisation in hardware and software. INTO-CPS provides a *multi-modelling* approach, allowing co-simulation of executables (Functional Mockup Units - FMUs) derived from multiple modelling tools [8] by means of a co-simulation orchestration engine. Techniques included in the INTO-CPS tool chain include Requirements Engineering (RE), Architectural Modelling (AM) and co-simulation. It leverages Unifying Theories of Programming (UTP) to permit extensible and reusable semantics [9]. Crucially for our work, the approach allows the direct modelling of causal chains across the cyber-physical boundary.

2.2 Resilience

Resilience is important in many fields [10]. In materials science it is "the ability of a material to absorb energy when deformed elastically and to return it when unloaded" [11]. In IT and organisational contexts, a resilient control system has been characterised as "one that maintains state awareness and an accepted level of operational normalcy in response to disturbances, including threats of an unexpected and malicious nature" [12]. In socio-ecological systems, Carpenter et al. argue that an assessment of system resilience must be qualified by specifying which system configuration and disturbances are of interest (resilience 'of what, to what, and under what conditions') [13]. It is open to debate whether resilience might be defined in terms of properties such as fault avoidance, detection, tolerance and recovery [14], but the term is often used in a broader sense to include "the ability of assets and networks to anticipate, absorb, adapt to and recover from disruption" [15]. Recent European research calls on crisis management see resilience as the ability to reduce the impact of disruptive events and the recovery time [16].

Together, the approaches in the literature reflect the idea that resilience is a composite property: a system cannot simply be said to either be resilient or not, but may be said to shown some characteristics of resilience in response to a certain set of faults or attacks under certain circumstances. There is a also a trade space here: for example, a system may be show resilience to a certain set of attacks, but at the expense of becoming less resilient to others, or at the price of slower recovery. Again, being able to trace cause and effect as they go across the cyber-physical boundary is critical to effective model-based engineering of resilience.

To analyse resilience in model-based CPS design, we need a working intuitive characterisation of resilience. We adopt some of the terminology of faults, errors and failures [14] in that we regard a failure as the deviation of a delivered service from correct service. An error occurs when the state of the system deviates from those required to deliver a correct service. A fault is the adjudged or hypothesized cause of an error. An error does not necessarily cause a failure, but it is possible one or more errors may. In our case study a failure denotes a fault–error–failure casual chain.

Rather than identify a single resilience metric, we treat resilience as a multi-attribute property defined in what we will call a *resilience profile*. The idea of a multifaceted definition of resilience is not new. Jackson [17] proposes a representation of resilience composed of four attributes:

Capacity: the ability of a system to absorb or adapt to a disturbance without a total loss of performance or structure.
Tolerance: the exhibition of graceful degradation near the boundary of a system's performance.
Flexibility: the system's ability to restructure itself in response to disruptions.
Inter-element Collaboration: collaborations, or communication and cooperation between human elements of a system.

Jackson also introduced three different phases for resilience: avoidance - the preventive aspects of system resilience, survival - the system continues to function when experiencing a disturbance, and recovery - surviving a major disturbance with reduced performance. Pflanz [18] extends Jackson's characterisation, applying it to command and control systems. Although Pflanz does not consider inter-element collaboration, he subdivides the first three of Jackson's attributes into the constituent facets listed in Fig. 1.

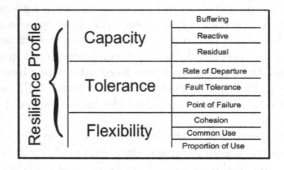

Fig. 1. Outline of Pflanz's resilience profile.

Pflanz also implemented Jackson's avoidance, survival and recovery notions as temporal phases. Pflanz's work focuses on the survival phase, where capacity, tolerance and flexibility provide means of analysing resilience in this phase alone. However, there is only limited further discussion of ways in which to characterise recovery. In [3] we extend the existing resilience profile with additional features that characterise the recovery phase, and demonstrate that it is possible to assess this aspect of resilience on CPS co-models using the Crescendo tool[2].

---

[2] http://crescendotool.org/.

2.3 Systems Modelling Language (SysML)

The INTO-CPS techniques and tools have been realised using the well-established System Modeling Language SysML[3] for requirements engineering and design modelling activities. Within SysML, a set of *diagrams* provide symbolic representations of parts of a system model. A *view* is typically a diagram that includes specific system facets. A SysML *profile* is a collection of extensions to basic SysML that support the needs of a particular domain. INTO-CPS offers a SysML profile that comprises diagrams for defining *cyber* and *physical* components, and also components representing *environment* and *visualisation* elements (see [19] for an example of the profile's use). In Sect. 3, we show the use of one of these views (the connections view) in our approach which augments the basic INTO-CPS views in helping to manage resilience.

3 Resilience-Explicit Modelling and Co-simulation

Our resilience profile allows us to define resilience as a first class property at different stages of a CPS design life cycle. How does this play out in practice? In this section we consider how a resilience-explicit approach might affect the following INTO-CPS design activities: Requirements Engineering (Sect. 3.1), Architectural Modelling (Sect. 3.2), co-simulation (Sect. 3.3). Finally, we consider how these activities might form a simple resilience-explicit workflow.

3.1 Requirements Engineering (RE)

INTO-CPS proposes a systematic approach to CPS requirements engineering based on the SoS-ACRE (System of Systems Approach to Context-based Requirements Engineering) implemented in SysML within the COMPASS[4] project on Systems-of-Systems (SoSs). The approach focuses on the identification of CPS needs, component interactions and stakeholders, enabling the identification and reasoning about requirements across constituent systems of a SoS and understanding multi-stakeholder contexts [20].

In our resilience-explicit approach, resilience is a first-class property: requirements may refer to properties from the resilience profile, for example. Requirements are also context-dependent, being related to specific scenarios. Where resilience is concerned, we look to characterise and identify these scenarios, and derive specific requirements for them. A *resilience scenario* describes a specific casual chain in which avoidance, survival and recovery can be observed and simulated. *Avoidance* refers to the preventive aspects of system resilience. *Survival* refers to the system's actions to mitigate the consequences of disruption, ensuring that the system continues to function at some level when experiencing a disturbance. *Recovery* refers to the ability to return to a known – if diminished – level of performance following disturbance itself [17].

---

[3] See http://www.omgsysml.org/.
[4] http://www.compass-research.eu.

Resilience Scenario Requirements (RSRs) identify, for a given scenario, the lowest acceptable level of performance: they are effectively the functional requirements in the context of a resilience scenario under a stated *failure condition*. The aim of an RSR is to ensure an acceptable level of performance after a failure has occurred. We adapt the current INTO-CPS approach to RE by explicitly stating RSRs as functional requirements in a resilience scenario. Section 3.3 outlines approaches to evaluating a CPS against its RSRs in the recovery phase of a resilience scenario.

3.2   Architectural Modelling (AM)

In order to restore performance within a resilience scenario, a system will either use capabilities already available within the system, or introduce new capabilities that are not inherent in the system. We aim to focus the engineer's attention during architectural modelling on connections in the CPS architectural model that contribute to a CPS's capability to meet a requirement. To this end, we introduce an Abstract Connections View Diagram (ACVD), which encourages the developer to identify information used to create resilient designs from the architecture of a CPS using SysML. The purpose of an ACVD is to highlight data connections in the CPS architecture that will help in the derivation of a resilient design. An ACVD abstracts the connections view of our CPS, and shows blocks that are connected to each other regardless of number of inputs and outputs. We do this so we can clearly identify data connections that contribute to a CPS capability. It is worth noting failures may occur at the system level, outside of the analysis used in this Section. However in this Section we propose an augmentation of the AM techniques used in the INTO-CPS tool chain only, described using SysML.

To derive an ACVD for a given resilience scenario, we identify any *fault blocks*, which are blocks in the SysML model that together define a behaviour observable at their output ports that causes a disruption to the CPS in a resilience scenario. We assume that we are able to identify the class of behaviours observable at the fault block's output ports that contribute to a failure.

Consider a block diagram as a directed graph $\langle B, \xrightarrow{l} \rangle$ of blocks B, and a labelled connection relation $\rightarrow: B \times L \times B$. We write $b_1 \xrightarrow{l} b_2$ to indicate that block b_1 has a labelled connection l to b_2, and $b_1 \rightarrow b_2$ if there exists an l such that $b_1 \xrightarrow{l} b_2$. We denote the transitive closure of the connection relation as $\rightarrow^*$. Consider a fault block fb. We wish to focus the engineer's attention on the "upstream" blocks that lead to fb. These form a sub-diagram $\langle B_{fb}, \xrightarrow[fb]{l} \rangle$ in which

$$b_1 \xrightarrow[fb]{l} b_2 \Leftrightarrow b_1 \xrightarrow{l} b_2 \wedge (b_2 = fb \vee b_2 \rightarrow^* fb)$$

We write $U(fb)$ to denote this upstream sub-diagram leading to fb. Further, if we have access to the internals of fb we can limit consideration to the sub-graph generating the inputs contributing to the disruptive output flows from the block. The engineer can now consider the elements of the upstream sub-graph to provide some capability that will help to meet system requirements, aiding recovery, or introduce new data connections that emulate the capability of the output paths that violated the requirements initially. Following this methodology we can reason about new designs, create multi-models, and then co-simulate. We co-simulate the design to see if we meet our RSRs, and use the calculations in Sect. 3.3 to evaluate our design in the recovery phase of our scenario.

3.3   Evaluating Resilience Through Co-Simulation

We can explore resilience properties by analysing co-simulation results against the resilience profile. Recovery is concerned with a CPS returning to a state in which its capabilities are performing within requirements. It is possible to evaluate properties such as the level to which a measurable capability has recovered, the rate at which it has recovered, how many RSRs have been met by the end of the co-simulation, etc. It is worth noting that boolean requirements such as "the lap time must be less than 60 s" may not produce enough data to be evaluated using these equations. We must be able to monitor the requirement over the course of the simulation. In this case we could consider substituting a related requirement i.e. "the average speed must be less than 0.01 m/s".

We will say that Potential Recovery Rec_{PR} is the level to which a capability can recover in comparison to ideal performance. $Rec_{PR}$is calculated as:

$$Rec_{PR} = |C_{max} - C_{min}| \tag{1}$$

where C_{max} is the maximum value achieved by the CPS under no failure, and C_{min} is the value at the start of the recovery phase.

Actual Recovery Rec_{AR} is the level to which a capability has recovered, as a proportion of the Rec_{PR}. Rec_{AR} is calculated as:

$$Rec_{AR} = \frac{C_{last} - C_{min}}{Rec_{PR}} \tag{2}$$

where C_{last} is the last recorded value of the capability at the end of the simulation. C_{min} is the value at the start of the recovery phase. Rec_{PR} is the potential recovery.

Recovery Rate Rec_{RR} is the rate at which a capability progresses towards the limit given by the RSR. Rec_{RR} is calculated as:

$$Rec_{RR} = \frac{C_{min} - C_{req}}{T_{min} - T_{end}} \tag{3}$$

where C_{min} is the value at the start of the recovery phase. C_{req} is the limit given by the RSR. T_{min} is the time at the start of the recovery phase. T_{end} is the time at the end of the recovery phase. T_{end} is obtained via co-simulation when we observe at what time the capability is performing within range.

Overall Performance Rec_{OP} is how many RSRs have been met. Rec_{OP} is calculated as:

$$Rec_{OP} = \frac{\sum_{i=1}^{T} r_i}{T} = \frac{r}{T} \tag{4}$$

where T is the total number of RSRs and r is the number of RSRs that have been met.

3.4   Towards a Resilience-Explicit Workflow

INTO-CPS does not propose the wholesale restructuring of development processes. Instead, it offers a set of integrated but adaptable design activities that can be composed into (perhaps fragmentary) workflows, according to user needs [20]. We can imagine that the activities outlined above could be composed into such workflows. For example, the resilience scenarios are first derived, and then RSRs are derived. The SysML architectural model of the CPS is analysed with the aid of ACVDs, and a modified architectural design may be proposed based on the identification of faults, compromised capabilities, and resources that could potentially be used to aid recovery. This leads to a new architectural design. The RSRs are the limits of acceptable performance in the given resilience scenario. Once we have a new design, we can create a multi-model and simulate our CPS to evaluate resilience in the recovery phase.

4   Pilot Study - Line Following Robot (LFR)

In this section we describe a pilot study using the resilience-explicit augmentations described in Sect. 3. The purpose of this study is to assess the potential advantages and disadvantages of using these techniques in contributing towards the discovery, evaluation and trade-off of a resilient CPS designs. We first give an example resilience scenario and derive RSRs. We then analyse the architectural model of our CPS using the approach described in Sect. 3.2, and propose two new architectural designs. We generate multi-models from our new designs, and use the INTO-CPS application to co-simulate our models. We provide outputs from our co-simulation in which we then analyse and evaluate using the proposed equations from Sect. 3.3.

4.1   The Line Following Robot

The R2-G2P Line Following Robot (LFR) example is a standard pilot study in INTO-CPS. R2-G2P (Fig. 2) is a small two-wheeled device that can be configured to follow a black line on a white surface. In our study the LFR is programmed to follow a circular track. Two infra-red sensors at the front of the robot allow it to detect the reflectivity of surfaces, and this sensed data can be used to guide the two independently controlled wheels. Both sensors are connected to a shared Sensor Processing Unit (SPU).

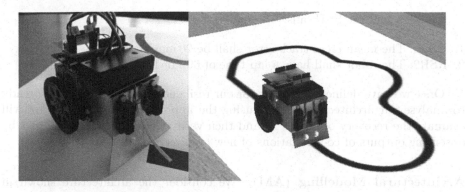

Fig. 2. The Line Following Robot.

Our pilot study assumes that we already have a working multi-model of the LFR, and that we have access to source code of all the constituent models in the LFR example, as well as modelling/simulation software needed to edit all aspects of the multi-model.

4.2 Resilience-Explicit Techniques

In this subsection we follow the resilience-explicit workflow proposed in Sect. 4. We first describe an example resilience scenario. We then derive RSRs from the original example requirements. We analyse the CPS architectural model using the approach in Sect. 3.2. From this we reason a new architectural design and generate a new multi-model configuration for co-simulation. We verify RSRs and evaluate the recovery of our designs by monitoring values during and after a co-simulation.

Resilience Scenario. A failure in the SPU of the LFR has prevented sensor readings from reaching the controller. Both sensors are connected to the SPU, making it a shared resource. This means the LFR has no sensor readings to use in the controller logic which determines the LFR's movement.

Requirements Engineering (RE). We give the following original requirements (ORs) to the LFR:

1. OR1. The mean cross track error shall be 7 mm or less.
2. OR2. The robot shall have a lap time of 30 s or less.

The deviation from a desired path, referred to as the cross track error, is the distance the robot moves from the line of the map. We then simulate the failure and identify our lowest acceptable performance for the ORs in the failure and create RSRs. These RSRs are a degraded performance version of the ORs and only apply under the condition of the failure:

Condition: If the SPU fails:

1. RSR1. The mean cross track error shall be 20 mm or less.
2. RSR2. The robot shall have a lap time of 60 s or less.

Once we have defined our RSRs for our resilience scenario we are now ready to analyse our architectural model using the approach from Sect. 3.2. We will evaluate the recovery of the LFR, and then verify the RSRs have been met by observing outputs of co-simulations of new architectural designs.

Architectural Modelling (AM). We consider the architecture shown in Fig. 3 D1. This is the current connections diagram view of the LFR architecture described in SysML. Following the approach in Sect. 3.2 we must identify the fault blocks as well as inputs and outputs of these fault blocks.

In our scenario the *sp* block is the fault block. We coalesce all data connections from D1 that terminate at a common output. This results in ACVD1. The four data connections from *b* connected to *sLeft* become one single data connection between *b* and *sLeft* (we do the same to *sRight*). We also notice that the two data connections from *sp* connected to *c* have been coalesced into one data connection. We position the fault block toward the bottom of ACVD1 so we can identify inputs to *sp* more easily.

We assume the engineer knows the functionality of each block in the SysML architecture. The engineer can then identify two inputs paths of the fault block: i_1 which contains blocks *c*, *b*, *sLeft* and *sp*, and i_2 which contains *c*, *b*, *sRight* and *sp*. Knowing the functionality of the fault block the engineer is able to establish whether i_1 or i_2 contribute to its observable outputs. In the current example i_1 and i_2 give sensor readings from *sLeft* and *sRight* respectively, and thereby provide a capability that is utilised by the fault block. This information allows the engineer to consider a revised design.

ACVD1. The purpose of creating an ACVD and following the approach in Sect. 3.2 is to aid us in the discovery of resilient designs. We highlight data connections in the CPS architecture that will be used to deliver some capability to meet requirements. In our example we integrate a failure into the SPU of the LFR in which the sensor readings do not change. We identify the output of the SPU to the controller, which under the resilience scenario does not provide the readings to the controller, and the LFR can no longer follow the line. We are able to identify which outputs from the failure block are responsible for the violation of requirements due to our knowledge of the failure itself. Recalling from Sect. 3.2 we must now consider if we can:

1. use i_1 or i_2 to provide enough capability to meet requirements. (ACVD2)
2. introduce new data connections that emulate the capability of the observable outputs of the failure block. (ACVD3).

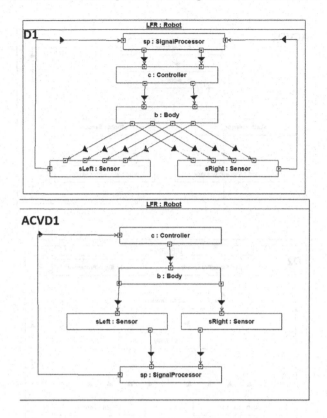

Fig. 3. Connections Diagram D1 with ACVD1.

This workflow does **not** necessarily provide solutions to failures. The ACVD can help direct a design engineer to new solutions. ACVD2 shows how we could use fault block inputs, ACVD3 shows us how we could introduce new data connections.

ACVD2 - Extra SPU. We propose that input paths i_1 **OR** i_2 can individually provide capability to meet requirements. We propose that i_1 **OR** i_2 would allow the LFR to follow the line using 1 sensor. This would require a change in the architecture to remove the dependency between the inputs and observable outputs of the fault block. We would also need to change the controller of the robot to accommodate a single follow algorithm. ACVD2 shows the new design which introduces an extra SPU. We then derive D2 which shows the connections view of our new architecture. We create a multi-model configuration and co-simulate this new design in the INTO-CPS app (Fig. 4).

ACVD2 - Failure Analysis. We only analyse RSR1. RSR2 is given in terms we cannot evaluate using the calculations in Sect. 3.3 due to its boolean nature.

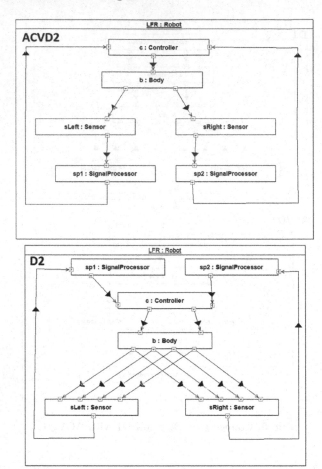

Fig. 4. ACVD2 and Connections Diagram D2.

Figure 6 shows the mean cross track error of ACVD2 vs the LFR using two sensors and no failure. A simulation time of 60 s results in a mean cross track error of 19 mm and lap time of 50 s. Recalling our calculations from Sect. 3.3. Rec_{OP} is 2/2 - both RSRs have been met. For RSR1: Rec_{PR} potential recovery is 45 mm. Rec_{AR} actual recovery is 30/45 mm, 67%. The recovery phase begins at 10 s, the LFR recovers at 59.4 s, $T_{min} - T_{end}$ is approximately 49 s. The LFR recovers to the threshold (RSR1) of 20 mm (67%) over 49 s therefore Rec_{RR} (rate of recovery) is 1.4% a second.

ACVD3 - Backup Sensor. We propose that we can introduce a new data connection that will provide some capability of input paths i_1 **OR** i_2. We propose a backup sensor and SPU that would allow the LFR to follow the line with one sensor. This would again require a change in the architecture to introduce a new

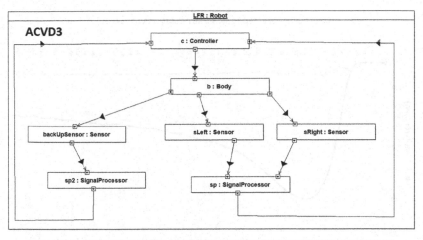

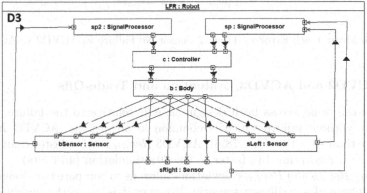

Fig. 5. ACVD3 and Connections Diagram D3.

data connection. We would also need to change the controller of the robot to accommodate a single follow algorithm. ACVD3 shows the new design which introduces the backup sensor and new SPU. We then derive D3 which shows the connections view of our new architecture We create a multi-model configuration and co-simulate this new design in the INTO-CPS app (Fig. 5).

ACVD3 - Failure Analysis. Figure 6 shows the mean cross track error of ACVD3 vs the LFR using two sensors and no failure. Mean cross track error is 17 mm and the lap time is 45 s. Rec_{OP} is 2/2 - both RSRs have been met. For RSR1: Rec_{PR} potential recovery is 45 mm. Rec_{AR} actual recovery is 35/45 mm, 78%. The recovery phase begins at 10 s, the LFR recovers at 46.2 s, $T_{min} - T_{end}$ is approximately 36 s. The LFR recovers to the threshold (RSR1) of 20 mm (67%) over 36 s therefore Rec_{RR} (rate of recovery) is 1.9% a second.

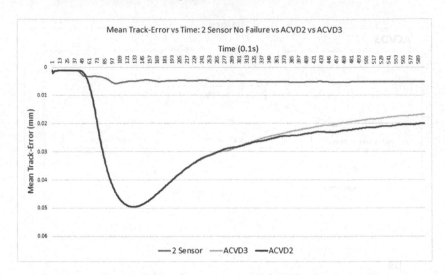

Fig. 6. Mean Track-Error vs Time: 2 Sensor No Failure vs ACVD2 vs ACVD3.

4.3   ACVD2 and ACVD3 Evaluation and Trade-Offs

Rec_{PR} is the same across both designs as it is relative to the failure, and the capability without failure which is common in all designs. ACVD3 Rec_{AR} is 11% more than ACVD3 (67%–78%). ACVD3 Rec_{RR} is 0.5% faster than ACVD2 (1.4%–1.9%), recovering 13 s faster in the 60 s simulation (46 s–59 s).

Rec_{PR}, Rec_{AR} and Rec_{RR} calculations allow us to compare two designs in the recovery phase of a resilience scenario. However it is up to the design engineer to further evaluate resilient designs in terms of costs elsewhere. For example, ACVD3 performs better in regards to Rec_{PR}, Rec_{AR} and Rec_{RR} calculations in the resilience scenario, however implementing the design ACVD3 is more costly than ACVD2.

5   Evaluation and Further Work

We have proposed a resilience-explicit approach to discovering and evaluating CPS designs. We have done this by augmenting existing INTO-CPS techniques for requirements engineering, architectural modelling and co-simulation. In RE we proposed the derivation of RSRs which present functional requirements that are specific to a resilience scenario. In AM we propose an approach that aims to focus the engineer's attention on connections in the CPS architectural model, that contribute to a CPS capability that has been removed due to a failure. In co-simulation we propose calculations that enable us to evaluate the RSRs of our CPS in the recovery phase of a resilience scenario, this also allows for the trade-off between resilient designs. We have presented a small pilot study in which we identify a resilience scenario and derived RSRs, and then analysed the architectural model of the CPS to produce an ACVD, which focussed attention on two new designs evaluated using the resilience profile characteristics proposed in Sect. 3.3. We finally discussed the trade-offs between designs.

Obviously this is a preliminary exploration of techniques that require full integration with co-simulation technology in real development environments. However, there does appear to be some merit in helping to uncover new designs that provide resilience that is engineered, rather than being merely fortuitous. Nevertheless, this is a further complicating factor in an already challenging design environment. We identify two aspects of particular importance. First, have we arrived at a "good" resilient solution? Design Space Exploration (DSE) techniques, which have been implemented in INTO-CPS offer the ability to sweep over design parameters to determine the best parameter combination against pre-determined criteria: an open question remains as to what criteria express desirable resilience properties. In our resilience-explicit workflow we could exploit DSE to generate the lowest limits of performance for RSRs, or to aid us in optimising an already resilient design. Second, there is a clear need to define the traceability structures that will allow engineers to manage the evolution of this complex design set in future. INTO-CPS offers some traceability and provenance structures that may be exploited here.

Acknowledgements. The work presented here is partially supported by the INTO-CPS project funded by the European Commission's Horizon 2020 programme under grant agreement number 664047.

References

1. Reimann, M., Rückriegel, C., Mortimer, S., et al.: Road2CPS: Priorities and Recommendations for Research and Innovation in Cyber-Physical Systems. Steinbeis edn. (2017)
2. Broy, M.: Engineering cyber-physical systems: challenges and foundations. In: Aiguier, M., Caseau, Y., Krob, D., Rauzy, A. (eds.) Complex Systems Design & Management, pp. 1–13. Springer, Heidelberg (2013). https://doi.org/10.1007/978-3-642-34404-6_1
3. Jackson, M., Fitzgerald, J.: Resilience profiling in the model-based design of cyber-physical systems. In: Larsen, P.G., Plat, N., Battle, N. (eds.) 14th Overture Workshop: Towards Analytical Tool Chains, Technical Report ECE-TR-28, pp. 1–15. Aarhus University, April 2016
4. Lee, E.A.: CPS foundations. In: Proceedings of 47th Design Automation Conference, DAC 2010, pp. 737–742. ACM, New York (2010)
5. Hellinger, A., Heinrich, S.: Cyber-physical systems driving force for innovation in mobility, health, energy and production. Technical report, acatech - National Academy of Science and Engineering (2011)
6. Brooks, C., Cheng, C.P., Feng, T.H., Lee, E.A., Von Hanxleden, R.: Model engineering using multimodeling. Technical report, DTIC Document (2008)
7. Alur, R., Courcoubetis, C., Halbwachs, N., Henzinger, T.A., Ho, P.-H., Nicollin, X., Olivero, A., Sifakis, J., Yovine, S.: The algorithmic analysis of hybrid systems. Theoret. Comput. Sci. **138**(1), 3–34 (1995)

8. Larsen, P.G., Fitzgerald, J., Woodcock, J., et al.: Integrated tool chain for model-based design of cyber-physical systems: the INTO-CPS project. In: Proceedings of 2nd International Workshop on Modelling, Analysis, and Control of Complex CPS (CPS Data), pp. 1–6, April 2016

9. Larsen, P.G., Fitzgerald, J., Woodcock, J., Nilsson, R., Gamble, C., Foster, S.: Towards semantically integrated models and tools for cyber-physical systems design. In: Margaria, T., Steffen, B. (eds.) ISoLA 2016. LNCS, vol. 9953, pp. 171–186. Springer, Cham (2016). https://doi.org/10.1007/978-3-319-47169-3_13

10. Hollnagel, E., Woods, D.D., Leveson, N.: Resilience Engineering: Concepts and Precepts. Ashgate Publishing Ltd., Aldershot (2007)

11. Mitchell, S.M.: Resilient engineered systems: the development of an inherent system property. Ph.D. thesis, Texas A&M University (2007)

12. Rieger, C.G., Gertman, D.I., McQueen, M.A.: Resilient control systems: next generation design research. In: 2nd Conference on Human System Interactions, HSI 2009, pp. 632–636. IEEE (2009)

13. Carpenter, S., Walker, B., Anderies, J., Abel, N.: From metaphor to measurement: resilience of what to what? Ecosystems 4(8), 765–781 (2001)

14. Avizienis, A., Laprie, J.-C., Randell, B., Landwehr, C.: Basic concepts and taxonomy of dependable and secure computing. IEEE Trans. Dependable Secur. Comput. 1, 11–33 (2004)

15. Summary of the 2015–16 sector resilience plans. United Kingdom Cabinet Office, April 2016

16. Council of the European Communities: Disaster resilience: safeguarding and securing society, including adapting to climate change

17. Jackson, S.: Architecting Resilient Systems: Accident Avoidance and Survival and Recovery from Disruptions, vol. 66. Wiley, New York (2009)

18. Pflanz, M.: On the resilience of command and control architectures. Ph.D. thesis, George Mason University (2011)

19. Fitzgerald, J., Gamble, C., Payne, R., Larsen, P.G., Basagiannis, S., Mady, A.E.-D.: Collaborative model-based systems engineering for cyber-physical systems, with a building automation case study. In: INCOSE International Symposium, vol. 26, no. 1, pp. 817–832 (2016)

20. Fitzgerald, J., Gamble, C., Payne, R., Pierce, K.: INTO-CPS Method Guidelines 2. Technical report Deliverable D3.2a (2016). INTO-CPS: http://into-cps.au.dk

Features of Integrated Model-Based Co-modelling and Co-simulation Technology

Peter Gorm Larsen[1]([⊠]), John Fitzgerald[2], Jim Woodcock[3], Carl Gamble[2], Richard Payne[4], and Kenneth Pierce[2]

[1] Department of Engineering, Aarhus University, Aarhus, Denmark
pgl@eng.au.dk
[2] School of Computing Science, Newcastle University, Newcastle upon Tyne, UK
{john.fitzgerald,carl.gamble,kenneth.pierce}@ncl.ac.uk
[3] Department of Computer Science, University of York, York, UK
jim.woodcock@york.ac.uk
[4] The Nine Software Company, Hebburn, UK
richard.payne@ninesoftware.co.uk

Abstract. Given the considerable ongoing research interest in collaborative multidisciplinary modelling and co-simulation, it is worth considering the features of model-based techniques and tools that deliver benefits to cyber-physical systems developers. The European project "Integrated Tool Chain for Model-based Design of Cyber-Physical Systems" (INTO-CPS) has developed a well-founded tool chain for CPS design, based on the Functional Mock-up Interface standard, and supported by methodological guidance. The focus of the project has been on the delivery of a sound foundation, an open chain of compatible and usable tools, and a set of accessible guidelines that help users adapt the technology to their development needs.

Keywords: Co-simulation · CPS engineering · Tool chain
Methodology · Foundations

1 Introduction

In Cyber-Physical Systems (CPSs), computing and physical processes interact closely. Their effective design therefore requires methods and tools that bring together the products of diverse engineering disciplines. Without such tools it would be difficult to gain confidence in the system-level consequences of design decisions made in any one domain, and it would be challenging to manage trade-offs between them. How, then, can we support such multidisciplinary design with semantically well-founded approaches in a cost-effective manner?

In the INTO-CPS project we start from the view that disciplines such as software, mechatronic and control engineering have evolved notations and theories that are tailored to their needs, and that it is undesirable to suppress this diversity by enforcing uniform general-purpose models [15,31] Our goal is to

© Springer International Publishing AG 2018
A. Cerone and M. Roveri (Eds.): SEFM 2017 Workshops, LNCS 10729, pp. 377–390, 2018.
https://doi.org/10.1007/978-3-319-74781-1_26

achieve a practical integration of diverse formalisms at the semantic level, and to realise the benefits in integrated tool chains. In order to demonstrate that the technology works industrially it has been applied in very different application domains (e.g., [12,17,19,30,34,38]).

To the CPS engineer, the system of interest includes both computational and physical elements, so the foundations, methods and tools of CPS engineering should incorporate both the Discrete-Event (DE) models of computational processes, and the continuous-value and Continuous-Time (CT) formalisms of physical dynamics engineering. Our approach is to support the development of collaborative models (*co-models*) containing DE and CT elements expressed in diverse notations, and to support their analysis by means of co-simulation based on a reconciled operational semantics of the individual notations' simulators [18]. This enables exploration of the design space and allows relatively straightforward adoption in businesses already exposed to some of these tools and techniques. The idea is to enable co-simulation of extensible groups of semantically diverse models, and at the same time the semantic foundations are extended using Unifying Theories of Programming (UTP) to permit analysis using advanced meta-level tools that are primarily targeted towards academics and thus not considered as a part of the industrial INTO-CPS tool chain.

Given the considerable interest in model-based CPS engineering, we believe that it is useful to consider what the *Unique Selling Points* (USPs) are for integrated tool chains. In this paper, we first provide an overview of what we consider the main USPs of the INTO-CPS technology from the perspective of industry use (Sect. 2). We then describe the open INTO-CPS tool chain (Sect. 3). In order to realise the benefits of the tools it is important to develop guidance for their use in collaborative modelling, and this is described in Sect. 4. We discuss our approach to providing integrated semantic foundations needed to underpin such co-modelling (Sect. 5) before looking forward (Sect. 6).

2   The Unique Selling Points

In our work on INTO-CPS, we have sought to deliver the following distinctive features, relevant to the industrial use of co-modelling and co-simulation technology. We see the main USPs as:

1. **Faster route to market for engineering CPSs:** In a highly active CPS marketplace, getting the right solution first time is essential. We believe that the interoperability of tools in the INTO-CPS tool suite enables a more agile close collaboration between stakeholders with diverse disciplinary backgrounds.
2. **Avoiding vendor lock-in by open tool chain:** Some commercial solutions provide at least a part of the functionality provided by the INTO-CPS tool chain with a high level of interoperability. However, in particular for Small and Medium-sized Enterprises (SMEs), there is a risk of being restricted in the choice of specialist tools.

3. **Exploring large design spaces efficiently:** CPS design involves making design decisions in both the cyber and physical domains. Trade-off analysis can be challenging. Co-simulation enables the systematic exploration of large design spaces in the search for optimal solutions.
4. **Limiting expensive physical tests:** CPS development often relies on the expensive production and evaluation of a series of physical prototypes. Co-simulation enables users to focus on testing different models of CPS elements in a virtual setting, gaining early assessment of CPS-level consequences of design decisions.
5. **Enabling traceability for all project artefacts:** In both documenting the coverage and quality of analysis and in managing the consequences of design change, there is a need to support the maintenance of traceable links between the many diverse artifacts produced during CPS development. We have sought to provide a basis for delivering levels of design traceability.

Tools as described in Sect. 3 will not, on their own, deliver these features. Methods guidance is needed to ensure that users get the greatest benefit from integrating co-modelling in their own development contexts. Firm semantic foundations are required in order to build confidence in the analyses that they deliver. To these ends, we have worked on methodological and semantic integration, discussed in Sects. 4 and 5, respectively.

3   The INTO-CPS Tool Chain

We have developed an open *integrated tool chain* to allow n-ary co-simulation of a wider range of model types. In order to facilitate this, we have developed an extensible semantic foundation using UTP. Figure 1 gives a graphic overview of the tool chain, which has been developed in the INTO-CPS project.

In the INTO-CPS tool chain, requirements and CPS architectures may be expressed using SysML. We have defined a special CPS SysML profile that allows cyber and physical system elements to be identified such that each of these elements corresponds to a constituent model [1,3]. From each element, we generate an interface following the Functional Mockup Interface (FMI) standard[1]. In our approach the tools in which the constituent models are developed can then import these interfaces and export conformant executable *Functional Mockup Units (FMUs)* following version 2.0 of the FMI standard for co-simulation.

Heterogeneous system models can be built around the FMI interfaces, permitting these heterogeneous *multi-models* to be co-simulated, and to allow static analysis, including model checking (of appropriate abstractions). A Co-simulation Orchestration Engine (COE) manages the co-simulation of multi-models and is built by combining existing co-simulation solutions. The COE has also been used with FMUs produced with other tools including Modelon[2],

---

[1] FMI essentially defines a standardised interface to be used in computer simulators to develop complex CPSs.

[2] http://www.modelon.com/.

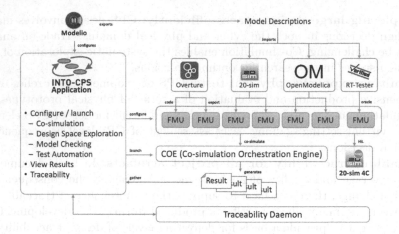

Fig. 1. The INTO-CPS Tool Chain

Dymola[3], 4diac[4] and SimulationX[5]. In addition a special 3D FMU capability has been enabled using the Unity game engine[6]. This also enables incorporation of 3D glasses such as Oculus Rift enabling a special experience with new CPSs in a virtual setting, before the CPSs are implemented[7]. The COE permits hardware-in-the-loop and software-in-the-loop analysis [19] and it is possible to use it in a distributed fashion. Thus, interoperability in relation to simulation of complex models of CPSs divided up in constituent models expressed using different formalisms and different tools is ensured. This is an important part of USP 1.

Results of multiple co-simulations can be collated, permitting systematic Design Space Exploration (DSE), and allowing test automation based on test cases generated from the SysML requirement diagrams [39]. The ability of both carrying out exploratory experiments as well as systematic testing a combination of constituent models leads to USP 3 since these features enable exploration of very large candidate design spaces. In particular the ability of visualising the results of co-simulations using the 3D FMU described above with the DSE capability (described further in Sect. 4.3) leads to USP 4 limiting the number of physical tests that needs to be carried out, which in particular is important whenever these are expensive to carry out or difficult to monitor the results of.

CPS SysML profile has been demonstrated in Modelio[8]. FMI-conformant constituent models have been produced in Overture from VDM-RT, and the

---

[3] https://www.3ds.com/products-services/catia/products/dymola.
[4] https://eclipse.org/4diac/.
[5] https://www.simulationx.com/.
[6] https://unity3d.com/.
[7] https://www.oculus.com/rift/.
[8] http://www.modelio.org/.

Continuous-Time (CT) formalisms 20-sim and OpenModelica [23][9]. A graphical front-end for the entire INTO-CPS tool chain called the INTO-CPS Application has been developed based on the cross-platform Electron technology [14]. This is developed as a desktop application, but using web technologies to enable a smoother transition to delivering this as an on-line web service should this be desirable in the future.

Multidisciplinary co-modelling and co-simulation naturally generate many design artifacts, including co-models, co-simulation inputs and outputs, requirements, code, etc. Such large design sets are expected to evolve as smart systems are developed by gradual integration of existing elements, and as elements change. The interrelationships between them are vital for allowing validation and third-party assurance. We have used the PROV[10] model to record the temporal relations between activities, entities and agents within a process (which we term *provenance*), and traceability has been supplied based on the Open Services for Lifecycle Collaboration (OSLC) standard[11]. In INTO-CPS, we have regarded it as a priority to lay foundations for provenance and traceability support in the tool chain; all the baseline tools have been extended with such OSLC support [32]. The openness resulting from the combination of FMI and OSLC contributes significantly to USP 2, giving freedom to choose the tools that best fit the purpose of each individual aspect of a CPS.

4   The INTO-CPS Methodology

Our work on methods aims to develop concrete guidelines, frameworks, and patterns for co-modelling and co-simulation that can be adapted to existing development processes, rather than defining a single workflow. Specifically, we focus on model-based CPS requirements engineering, architectural modelling in SysML, traceability and provenance, and DSE.

We support model-based systems engineering approaches because of their potential to enable early detection of potential bottlenecks and defects before commitment is made to physical prototypes (USPs 1 and 4). We advocate the use of *architectural models* that define the major elements of a system, their relationships and interactions. The bulk of our architectural modelling work uses SysML, which allows us to describe both digital interfaces between components in terms of the properties or functionality *provided* or *required*, and physical interfaces in terms of physical flows (e.g. material) between components.

An *architecture diagram* is a symbolic representation of part of an architectural model. An *architectural view* is typically an architecture diagram that includes specific system facets. An *architectural framework* is a set of architectural views defined to support a task, role, or industry [26]. A SysML *profile* is a collection of extensions to SysML that support a particular domain. We have developed a SysML profile consisting of diagrams for defining *cyber*, *physical*

---

[9] https://www.openmodelica.org/.
[10] http://www.w3.org/TR/prov-overview/.
[11] http://open-services.net/.

components, as well as components representing *environment* and *visualisation* elements (the delivering graphical presentation of co-simulation outputs).

4.1 Requirements Engineering

CPSs share important characteristics with Systems-of-Systems (SoSs) [35]. Cyber and physical elements can be independently owned and managed, evolve over time, and are distributed [40]. CPSs add the challenge of differing domain contexts [47]. In developing model-based requirements engineering approaches for CPSs, we have therefore extended a systematic approach to SoS requirements engineering, the *SoS Approach to Context-based Requirements Engineering (SoS-ACRE)* [27]. SoS-ACRE provides several views that encourage the systematic consideration of requirement context, sources and stakeholders.

A survey of our industry collaborators showed that a wide range of tools were used for requirements management and modelling, ranging from Microsoft Word to IBM Rational DOORS. It was therefore important to develop an approach that, while it could be supported by specialist notations like SysML, could also be adopted using document-based tools. This is a key facet of providing an open tool chain (USP 2). For example, SoS-ACRE can be adapted to these CPS needs as follows:

Source Element View (SEV) which identifies the sources from which requirements are derived. This could be represented as a SysML block definition diagram, an Excel table or a Word document, or by simply referring to source documents using OSLC traces.

Requirement Description View (RDV) defines the requirements. This could be a SysML requirements diagram, or in tabular form, or in DOORS.

Context Definition View (CDV) identifies interested stakeholders and points of context, including customers, suppliers and system engineers themselves. These could be SysML block definition diagrams, Excel tables or Word documents, and can be used to identify the CT/DE elements of a system.

Requirement Context View (RCV) defined for each constituent system context identified in CDVs. A *Context Interaction View (CIV)* is then defined to understand the overlap of contexts and any common/conflicted views on requirements. In SoS-ACRE, RCVs and CIVs are both defined with SysML use case diagrams. Excel could be used if unique identifiers are defined for contexts and requirements as described earlier.

Given that we aim to support the integration of co-simulation into established development processes, we realise the SoS-ACRE views using a range of combinations of SysML with other tools. For example, a single SysML model for both requirements engineering and architectural modelling will contain all SoS-ACRE views (SEV, RDV, CDV, RCV and CIV), in addition to diagrams defined using the INTO-CPS profile for the CPS composition and connections. Modelling in this way enables trace links to be defined inside a single SysML model, using <<trace>> relationships (e.g., Fig. 2). By contrast, one might combine URIs for the source elements with an Excel document for the RDV, CDV,

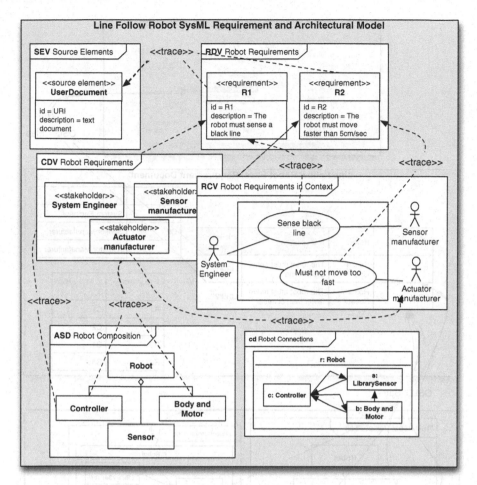

Fig. 2. Single SysML model – model overview

RCV and CIV. As above, SysML can be used to define the architecture in a single model. Trace links using OSLC may then be used to link source elements, rows of Excel documents (with internal tracing using unique identifiers referenced between sheets), and architectural elements of the SysML architectural model. Figure 3 presents an example with URI, Excel and SysML models and OSLC links between the artifacts.

4.2   Traceability and Provenance

USP 5 deals with the need to support engineers navigating the complexities of CPS design sets. INTO-CPS considers two tool-supported methods for recording design rationale. *Traceability* associates one model element (e.g. requirements, design artifacts, activities, software code or hardware) to another. *Requirements*

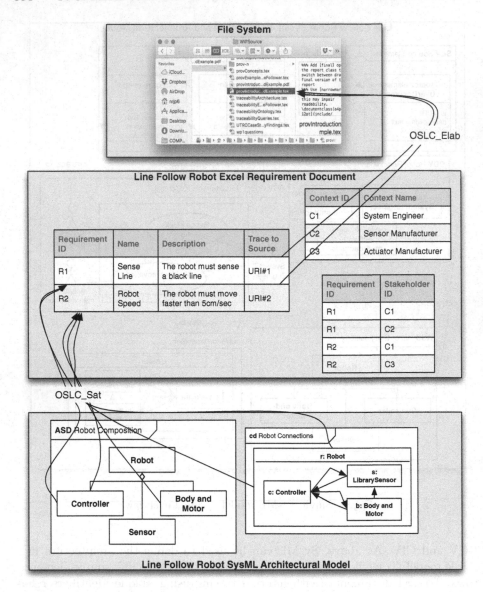

Fig. 3. URI, Excel and SysML – model overview

traceability "refers to the ability to describe and follow the life of a requirement, in both a forwards and backwards direction" [24]. *Provenance* "is information about entities, activities, and people involved in producing a piece of data or thing, which can be used to form assessments about its quality, reliability or trustworthiness" [33].

4.3 Design Space Exploration

USP 3 is the ability to sweep over the design space to identify optimal combinations of parameters with respect to evaluation criteria. A *design parameter* is a property of a model that varies the behaviour described, but remains constant during a simulation; a *variable* is a property that may change during a simulation. Where two or more models represent different solutions to the same problem, these are considered *design alternatives*. In INTO-CPS, design alternatives are defined using either a range of parameter values or different multi-models.

Designing DSE experiments can be complex and depends closely on the multi-model being analysed. Engineers need, therefore, to be able to model at an early stage of design how the experiments relate to the model architecture, and where possible trace from requirements to the analysis experiments. We have defined a SysML profile for modelling DSE experiments in a consistent and traceable way. The profile comprises five diagrams for defining *parameters*, *objectives* and *rankings*. Based on a requirements analysis (e.g. an RDV coming out of the processes described in Sect. 4.1), we identify objectives, and use the SysML profile for DSE to define the parameters, objectives and ranking function, traced to the requirements.

We use the INTO-CPS tool chain to simulate each design alternative. Whilst exhaustively seaching the design space, evaluating and ranking each design is acceptable on small-scale studies, it quickly becomes infeasible as the design space grows. For example, varying n parameters with m alternative values produces a design space of m^n alternatives. We have therefore implemented genetic approaches [16].

5 The Underlying Unified Semantic Approach

Since CPSs are networks of computational devices interacting with the world through their sensors and actuators, CPS models must combine discrete computational models with continuous physical environmental models. CPS engineering necessarily involves a wide range of modelling and programming paradigms [13], including concurrency, real-time, mobility, continuous variables, differential equations, object orientation, and diagrammatic languages. Practical CPS engineering uses a variety of domain-specific and general-purpose languages, such as Simulink, Modelica, SysML, Java, and C, and engineering trustworthy CPS requires that semantic models for these languages are integrated in a consistent way, which then enables reasoning about an entire CPS[12].

In practice, semantic integration is often achieved using the FMI standard [6], mentioned above, which describes a CPS using a network of FMUs to simulate components and their solvers and simulators. Each FMU has observable discrete and continuous variables that can be observed and modified, as well as an interface to drive the simulation engine in various ways. In a co-simulation

---

[12] For SysML we have only formalised the subset we need in a co-simulation setting [1].

a master algorithm manages stepping the individual FMUs forward, and distributing information in between time steps. In this way, FMI describes heterogeneous multi-models in different notations with different underlying semantics integrated through a common operational interface[13].

FMI provides a way of experimenting with the combined operational interfaces to heterogeneous models, and so it is useful for validation; but it does not provide the basis for verifying CPS properties. To do that, we need to be able to verify properties, both at the model level and at the multi-model level. One way of doing this is to explore the links between the different semantics. To do this, we use Hoare and He's *Unifying Theories of Programming* (UTP) [10,25,48] to describe different computing paradigms and their formal connections. We treat the various semantic aspects of a heterogeneous multi-model as individual theories that characterise a particular abstract modelling paradigm. Hoare and Jifeng [25] show how the mathematics of the alphabetised relational calculus can be used to construct a hierarchy of such theories, including an assertional approach to hybrid imperative parallel programming and control of continuous physical phenomena. Within this hierarchy, there are theories of real-time programming [45], object-oriented programming [43], security and confidentiality [4], mobile processes [44], probabilistic modelling [7], and hybrid systems [20]. The FMI API itself has been given a UTP-based semantics [11,49] that can be used as an interface to the semantic model of individual FMUs.

Our approach to practical CPS verification in the meta-tools is based on the theorem prover for UTP built on Isabelle/HOL [36], which we call *Isabelle/UTP* [21,22]. Isabelle is a powerful automated proof assistant that was used, for example, in the seL4 microkernel verification project [29]. Isabelle include recent work on formalising the integral and differential calculus, real analysis, and Ordinary Differential Equations (ODEs) [28], work that we are applying to verification of hybrid systems[14].

Crucial to all of these developments is the ability to integrate external tools into Isabelle that can provide decision procedures for specific classes of problems. Isabelle is well suited to such integrations due to its architecture based on the ML and Scala programming languages, both of which can be used to implement plugins. Isabelle is sometimes referred to as the *Eclipse* of theorem provers [46]. The `sledgehammer` tool [5], for example, integrates a host of first-order automated theorem provers and SMT solvers, which often shoulder the burden of proof effort. `Sledgehammer` has been used both at the theory engineering level, for constructing an algebraic hierarchy of verification logics (Kleene algebras), and also at the verification level, where it is used to discharge first-order proof obligations [2]. For verification of hybrid systems, it is necessary to integrate Isabelle with computer algebra systems like Mathematica, MATLAB, and SageMath, to provide solutions to differential equations, an approach that has been previously well used by the KeYmaera tool [41,42].

---

[13] FMI-based co-simulation with a black-box approach does have limitations [8,9] and we do not claim to repair those issues in any way in this work.

[14] This library can be viewed at github.com/isabelle-utp/utp-main.

Our vision is the use of Isabelle and UTP to provide the basis for CPS verification through formalisation of the fundamental building-block theories of CPS multi-modelling, and the integration of tools that implement these theories for coordinated verification.

6   Concluding Remarks

Integrated modelling such as that presented in this paper is essential to efficient engineering of CPSs. We believe that openness of the tool chain using different standards, the methodology supporting it and the underlying unified semantic approach jointly enable stakeholders with different disciplinary backgrounds to collaborate in the development of CPSs. This is by no means the only scientific approach by which such systems can be developed, but we think that it is a promising candidate that has future extension possibilities as well.

In the current version of the FMI standard there are a number of limitations. This includes that it is not able to cope with the modelling of the network communication in a natural manner and it is incapable of modelling dynamic reconfigurations. Thus, in a future extension it would be ideal if it would be possible to enable such capabilities for example to be able to appropriately model and develop constituents with their own independent behaviour. This could mean integration of machine learning capabilities as well as software agents including potentially incorporation of human-in-the-loop. Initial work with humans included have already started [37] but it is easy to imagine that it would be advantageous to combine this further in the future with human centered design ideas. We envisage great capabilities for the future that would bring additional USPs to the table.

Acknowledgment. The work presented here is partially supported by the INTO-CPS project funded by the European Commission's Horizon 2020 programme under grant agreement number 664047. We would like to thank all the participants of those projects for their efforts making this a reality.

References

1. Amálio, N., Payne, R., Cavalcanti, A., Woodcock, J.: Checking SysML models for co-simulation. In: Ogata, K., Lawford, M., Liu, S. (eds.) ICFEM 2016. LNCS, vol. 10009, pp. 450–465. Springer, Cham (2016). https://doi.org/10.1007/978-3-319-47846-3_28
2. Armstrong, A., Gomes, V., Struth, G.: Building program construction and verification tools from algebraic principles. Form. Asp. Comput. **28**(2), 265–293 (2015)
3. Bagnato, A., Brosse, E., Quadri, I., Sadovykh, A.: The INTO-CPS cyber-physical system profile. In: DeCPS Workshop on Challenges and New Approaches for Dependable and Cyber-Physical System Engineering Focus on Transportation of the Future. Vienna, Austria, June 2017
4. Banks, M.J., Jacob, J.L.: Unifying theories of confidentiality. In: Qin, S. (ed.) UTP 2010. LNCS, vol. 6445, pp. 120–136. Springer, Heidelberg (2010). https://doi.org/10.1007/978-3-642-16690-7_5

5. Blanchette, J.C., Bulwahn, L., Nipkow, T.: Automatic proof and disproof in Isabelle/HOL. In: Tinelli, C., Sofronie-Stokkermans, V. (eds.) FroCoS 2011. LNCS (LNAI), vol. 6989, pp. 12–27. Springer, Heidelberg (2011). https://doi.org/10.1007/978-3-642-24364-6_2

6. Blochwitz, T., Otter, M., Arnold, M., Bausch, C., Elmqvist, H., Junghanns, A., Mauss, J., Monteiro, M., Neidhold, T., Neumerkel, D., Olsson, H., Peetz, J.V., Wolf, S., Clau, C.: The functional mockup interface for tool independent exchange of simulation models. In: Proceedings of 8th International Modelica Conference, pp. 105–114 (2011)

7. Bresciani, R., Butterfield, A.: A UTP semantics of pGCL as a homogeneous relation. In: Derrick, J., Gnesi, S., Latella, D., Treharne, H. (eds.) IFM 2012. LNCS, vol. 7321, pp. 191–205. Springer, Heidelberg (2012). https://doi.org/10.1007/978-3-642-30729-4_14

8. Broman, D., Brooks, C., Greenberg, L., Lee, E.A., Masin, M., Tripakis, S., Wetter, M.: Determinate composition of FMUs for co-simulation. In: 13th International Conference on Embedded Software (EMSOFT), Montreal, September 2013. http://chess.eecs.berkeley.edu/pubs/1002.html

9. Broman, D., Greenberg, L., Lee, E.A., Masin, M., Tripakis, S., Wetter, M.: Requirements for hybrid cosimulation standards. In: Proceedings of 18th ACM International Conference on Hybrid Systems: Computation and Control (HSCC), pp. 179–188. ACM (2015)

10. Cavalcanti, A., Woodcock, J.: A tutorial introduction to CSP in *Unifying Theories of Programming*. In: Cavalcanti, A., Sampaio, A., Woodcock, J. (eds.) PSSE 2004. LNCS, vol. 3167, pp. 220–268. Springer, Heidelberg (2006). https://doi.org/10.1007/11889229_6

11. Cavalcanti, A., Woodcock, J., Amálio, N.: Behavioural models for FMI cosimulations. In: ICTAC (2016, in press)

12. Couto, L.D., Basagianis, S., Mady, A.E.D., Ridouane, E.H., Larsen, P.G., Hasanagic, M.: Injecting formal verification in FMI-based co-simulation of cyber-physical systems. In: Cerone, A., Roveri, M. (eds.) SEFM 2017 Workshops. LNCS, vol. 10729, pp. 282–297. Springer, Cham (2017)

13. Derler, P., Lee, E.A., Sangiovanni-Vincentelli, A.: Modeling cyber-physical systems. Proc. IEEE (special issue on CPS) **100**(1), 13–28 (2012)

14. The Electron website. http://electron.atom.io/ (2016)

15. Fitzgerald, J., Gamble, C., Larsen, P.G., Pierce, K., Woodcock, J.: Cyber-physical systems design: formal foundations, methods and integrated tool chains. In: FormaliSE: FME Workshop on Formal Methods in Software Engineering. ICSE 2015, Florence, Italy, May 2015

16. Fitzgerald, J., Gamble, C., Payne, R., Lam, B.: Exploring the cyber-physical design space. In: Proceedings of INCOSE International Symposium on Systems Engineering, Adelaide, Australia, vol. 27, pp. 371–385 (2017). http://dx.doi.org/10.1002/j.2334-5837.2017.00366.x

17. Fitzgerald, J., Gamble, C., Payne, R., Larsen, P.G., Basagiannis, S., Mady, A.E.D.: Collaborative model-based systems engineering for cyber-physical systems, with a building automation case study. In: INCOSE International Symposium, vol. 26, no. 1, pp. 817–832 (2016)

18. Fitzgerald, J., Larsen, P.G., Verhoef, M. (eds.): Collaborative Design for Embedded Systems - Co-modelling and Co-simulation. Springer, Berlin (2014). http://link.springer.com/book/10.1007/978-3-642-54118-6

19. Foldager, F., Larsen, P.G., Green, O.: Development of a driverless lawn mower using co-simulation. In: Cerone, A., Roveri, M. (eds.) SEFM 2017 Workshops. LNCS, vol. 10729, pp. 328–342. Springer, Cham (2017)
20. Foster, S., Thiele, B., Cavalcanti, A., Woodcock, J.: Towards a UTP semantics for Modelica. In: Proceedings of 6th International Symposium on Unifying Theories of Programming, June 2016 (to appear)
21. Foster, S., Zeyda, F., Woodcock, J.: Isabelle/UTP: a mechanised theory engineering framework. In: Naumann, D. (ed.) UTP 2014. LNCS, vol. 8963, pp. 21–41. Springer, Cham (2015). https://doi.org/10.1007/978-3-319-14806-9_2
22. Foster, S., Zeyda, F., Woodcock, J.: Unifying heterogeneous state-spaces with lenses. In: Sampaio, A., Wang, F. (eds.) ICTAC 2016. LNCS, vol. 9965, pp. 295–314. Springer, Cham (2016). https://doi.org/10.1007/978-3-319-46750-4_17
23. Fritzson, P.: Principles of Object-Oriented Modeling and Simulation with Modelica 2.1. Wiley-IEEE Press, January 2004
24. Gotel, O.C., Finkelstein, A.C.: An analysis of the requirements traceability problem. In: Proceedings of 1st International Conference on Requirements Engineering, pp. 94–101, April 1994
25. Hoare, T., Jifeng, H.: Unifying Theories of Programming. Prentice Hall, Upper Saddle River (1998)
26. Holt, J., Ingram, C., Larkham, A., Stevens, R.L., Riddle, S., Romanovsky, A.: Convergence report 3. Technical report, COMPASS Deliverable, D11.3, September 2014
27. Holt, J., Perry, S., Payne, R., Bryans, J., Hallerstede, S., Hansen, F.O.: A model-based approach for requirements engineering for systems of systems. IEEE Syst. J. 9(1), 252–262 (2015). https://doi.org/10.1109/JSYST.2014.2312051
28. Immler, F.: Formally verified computation of enclosures of solutions of ordinary differential equations. In: Badger, J.M., Rozier, K.Y. (eds.) NFM 2014. LNCS, vol. 8430, pp. 113–127. Springer, Cham (2014). https://doi.org/10.1007/978-3-319-06200-6_9
29. Klein, G., et al.: seL4: Formal verification of an OS kernel. In: Proceedings of 22nd Symposium on Operating Systems Principles (SOSP), pp. 207–220. ACM (2009)
30. Larsen, P.G., Fitzgerald, J., Woodcock, J., Lecomte, T.: Chapter 8: Collaborative modelling and simulation for cyber-physical systems. In: Trustworthy Cyber-Physical Systems Engineering. Chapman and Hall/CRC, Boca Raton (2016). ISBN 9781498742450
31. Larsen, P.G., Fitzgerald, J., Woodcock, J., Nilsson, R., Gamble, C., Foster, S.: Towards semantically integrated models and tools for cyber-physical systems design. In: Margaria, T., Steffen, B. (eds.) ISoLA 2016. LNCS, vol. 9953, pp. 171–186. Springer, Cham (2016). https://doi.org/10.1007/978-3-319-47169-3_13
32. Mengist, A., Pop, A., Asghar, A., Fritzson, P.: Traceability support in openmodelica using open services for lifecycle collaboration (OSLC). In: Kofránek, J., Casella, F. (eds.) Proceedings of 12th International Modelica Conference, pp. 823–830. Modelica Association and Linköping University Electronic Press, 15–17 May 2017
33. Moreau, L., Groth, P.: PROV-overview. Technical report, World Wide Web Consortium (2013). http://www.w3.org/TR/2013/NOTE-prov-overview-20130430/
34. Neghina, M., Zamfirescu, C.B., Larsen, P.G., Lausdahl, K., Pierce, K.: A discrete event-first approach to collaborative modelling of cyber-physical systems. In: Fitzgerald, J., Tran-Jørgensen, P.W.V., Oda, T. (ed.) 15th Overture Workshop: New Capabilities and Applications for Model-based Systems Engineering, Newcastle, UK, September 2017

35. Nielsen, C.B., Larsen, P.G., Fitzgerald, J., Woodcock, J., Peleska, J.: Model-based engineering of systems of systems. ACM Comput. Surv. **48**(2) (September 2015). http://dl.acm.org/citation.cfm?id=2794381

36. Nipkow, T., Wenzel, M., Paulson, L.C.: Isabelle/HOL: A Proof Assistant for Higher-Order Logic. LNCS, vol. 2283. Springer, Heidelberg (2002). https://doi.org/10.1007/3-540-45949-9

37. Palmieri, M., Bernardeschi, C., Masci, P.: Co-simulation of semi-autonomous systems: the Line Follower Robot case study. In: Cerone, A., Roveri, M. (eds.) SEFM 2017 Workshops. LNCS, vol. 10729, pp. 421–435. Springer, Cham (2017)

38. Pedersen, N., Lausdahl, K., Sanchez, E.V., Larsen, P.G., Madsen, J.: Distributed co-simulation of embedded control software with exhaust gas recirculation water handling system using INTO-CPS. In: Proceedings of 7th International Conference on Simulation and Modeling Methodologies, Technologies and Applications (SIMULTECH 2017), Madrid, Spain, pp. 73–82, July 2017. ISBN 978-989-758-265-3

39. Peleska, J.: Industrial-strength model-based testing - state of the art and current challenges. In: Petrenko, A.K., Schlingloff, H. (eds.) Proceedings Eighth Workshop on Model-Based Testing, MBT 2013. EPTCS, Rome, Italy, vol. 111, pp. 3–28, 17 March 2013. http://arxiv.org/abs/1303.0379

40. Penzenstadler, B., Eckhardt, J.: A requirements engineering content model for cyber-physical systems. In: RESS, pp. 20–29 (2012)

41. Platzer, A.: Differential-algebraic dynamic logic for differential-algebraic programs. J. Log. Comput. **20**(1), 309–352 (2010)

42. Platzer, A.: Logical Analysis of Hybrid Systems. Springer, Heidelberg (2010). https://doi.org/10.1007/978-3-642-14509-4

43. Santos, T., Cavalcanti, A., Sampaio, A.: Object-orientation in the UTP. In: Dunne, S., Stoddart, B. (eds.) UTP 2006. LNCS, vol. 4010, pp. 18–37. Springer, Heidelberg (2006). https://doi.org/10.1007/11768173_2

44. Tang, X., Woodcock, J.: Travelling processes. In: Kozen, D. (ed.) MPC 2004. LNCS, vol. 3125, pp. 381–399. Springer, Heidelberg (2004). https://doi.org/10.1007/978-3-540-27764-4_20

45. Wei, K.: Reactive designs of interrupts in *Circus Time*. In: Liu, Z., Woodcock, J., Zhu, H. (eds.) ICTAC 2013. LNCS, vol. 8049, pp. 373–390. Springer, Heidelberg (2013). https://doi.org/10.1007/978-3-642-39718-9_22

46. Wenzel, M., Wolff, B.: Building formal method tools in the isabelle/isar framework. In: Schneider, K., Brandt, J. (eds.) TPHOLs 2007. LNCS, vol. 4732, pp. 352–367. Springer, Heidelberg (2007). https://doi.org/10.1007/978-3-540-74591-4_26

47. Wiesner, S., Gorldt, C., Soeken, M., Thoben, K.-D., Drechsler, R.: Requirements engineering for cyber-physical systems. In: Grabot, B., Vallespir, B., Gomes, S., Bouras, A., Kiritsis, D. (eds.) APMS 2014. IAICT, vol. 438, pp. 281–288. Springer, Heidelberg (2014). https://doi.org/10.1007/978-3-662-44739-0_35

48. Woodcock, J., Cavalcanti, A.: A tutorial introduction to designs in unifying theories of programming. In: Boiten, E.A., Derrick, J., Smith, G. (eds.) IFM 2004. LNCS, vol. 2999, pp. 40–66. Springer, Heidelberg (2004). https://doi.org/10.1007/978-3-540-24756-2_4

49. Zeyda, F., Ouy, J., Foster, S., Cavalcanti, A.: Formalised cosimulation models. In: Cerone, A., Roveri, M. (eds.) SEFM 2017 Workshops. LNCS, vol. 10729, pp. 451–466. Springer, Cham (2017)

A Tool Integration Language to Formalize Co-simulation Tool-Chains for Cyber-Physical System (CPS)

Jinzhi Lu[1(✉)], Martin Törngren[1], De-Jiu Chen[1], and Jian Wang[2(✉)]

[1] KTH Royal Institute of Technology, Brinellvägen 83, 100 44 Stockholm, Sweden
{jinzhl,martint}@kth.se, chen@md.kth.se
[2] University of Electronic Science and Technology of China,
Xiyuan Ave, West Hi-Tech Zone, Chengdu 611731, China
wangjian3630@uestc.edu.cn
https://www.kth.se/en/itm/inst/mmk/avdelningar/mda

Abstract. Co-simulation has grown from point-to-point between simulation tools for specific purposes to complex tool-chains which often require additional functionalities, e.g., process management, data management and tool integration. With these additional functionalities, the related design activities could be controlled and implemented by unified platforms to improve efficiency and effectiveness. Due to increasing complexity and size of co-simulation tool-chains, a systematic approach is needed to formalize their evolution in order to analyze functionalities and evaluate their structures before development. In this paper, we extend a proposed domain specific language, - named Tool Integration Language (TIL) - to describe co-simulation tool-chain architectures on a high abstraction level aiming to promote the efficiency and effectiveness of co-simulation tool-chain development by the use of Model-based System Engineering (MBSE). We introduce how the extended TIL formalizes structures and present two industrial cases of co-simulation tool-chain from previous experiences and describe them using the TIL. Finally, we conclude this paper and introduce future work - a further extension of TIL supporting MBSE tool-chain development.

Keywords: Domain specific language · Tool integration
Co-simulation · Tool-chain development

1 Introduction

Co-simulation is a term used for creating combined simulations across multiple domains. A typical example where co-simulation is strongly motivated is in Cyber-Physical Systems (CPS), involving domains such as embedded systems, controls and computing and so on. It makes use of domain models and hardware, e.g. executing programs [4], hydraulic models [23] and multibody dynamics

© Springer International Publishing AG 2018
A. Cerone and M. Roveri (Eds.): SEFM 2017 Workshops, LNCS 10729, pp. 391–405, 2018.
https://doi.org/10.1007/978-3-319-74781-1_27

models [9] to support verification and validation of integrated system from system views. These models and hardware represent dynamic behaviors of specific subsystems and are integrated by a co-simulation environment.

Co-simulation is thus a natural technique in order to deal with the increasing complexities of CPS [12] to support concurrent, distributed and collaborative design during CPS development. It has the potential to resolve the problems of isolation among hardware and models from different tools and allows subsystem developers to build specific models using their own tools. System developers implement co-simulation to make use of such models to predict global behaviors in the initial phase of concept design.

Co-simulation for CPS has made progress through the introduction of the FMI, a tool independent standard that supports both model exchange and co-simulation [25]. However, the increasing complexity poses additional challenges both within and beyond co-simulation:

☐ **Technical challenges to co-simulation** - concentrates on the technical issues of co-simulation. In [13], the author provides several challenges which could influence *accuracy* and *robustness* of co-simulation implementations.

☐ **Information challenges** - focuses on the system aspects of CPS and integration of data, model, tool and information. Increasing CPS complexities with more complex requirements, system structures and verification & validation activities results in more requirements, such as *traceability* [2] and *consistency* [33]. The increasing number of stakeholders participating in the CPS design process leads to more design elements required, - e.g. tools, models and data -, which means tool-chains need more functionalities to manage and integrate such design elements.

☐ **Process challenges** -refers to the challenges of process management of co-simulation.

☐ **Social challenges** -refers to integration of stakeholders' social network. For example, during large-scale system development, different platforms supporting co-simulation for subsystems also need to be integrated in a unified framework or architecture in order to develop more complex large-scale system.

These challenges lead tool-chain developers to extend the co-simulation tool-chains' functionalities, which results in increasing complexity of tool-chains. This in turn challenges developers to analyze functionalities of co-simulation tool-chains and to make decisions about the techniques used to realize functionalities in tool-chain development. Traditional approaches for co-simulation tool-chains cannot satisfy the demand of stakeholders to develop co-simulation tool-chains in an efficient and effective way. The reasons include:

– Document based requirements are insufficient for formalizing the functionalities needed in co-simulation tool-chains due to the increasing complexities.
– In each simulation tool, adapters used for co-simulation, - referring to a software supporting simulation tools generating their co-simulation interfaces with other tools, are often developed by their developers themselves which increases R&D cost of the co-simulation tool-chains.

– Traditional tool-chain development used for developers is to obtain requirements from their customers by meetings and documents and validate their
tool-chains using industrial practices of their customers. However, this approach takes a long time and changes during validation could cause risks for
exceeding R&D cost and project delay.

In order to deal with the increasing complexity of co-simulation tool-chains,
we proposed a methodology [16] that aims to make use of a model-based approach to formalize their architectures based on a system engineering approach,
-called Model-based Systems Engineering (MBSE). It could support developers
in analyzing and making decisions about co-simulation tool-chains' functionalities during development. In our methodology, we adopt and extend a domain
specific language, - called Tool Integration Language (TIL) [5] -, to represent
the architectures of a co-simulation tool-chain at a high level of abstraction. The
original TIL aims to formalize tool-integration of tool-chains. We adopt and
extend it, formalizing architectures of co-simulation tool-chain using IEEE 1471
[15][1] and supporting improved description of the co-simulation features of tool-
chains. Based on the extended TIL, developers can formalize the co-simulation
tool-chains to analyze their functionalities and evaluate their structures before
development.

This paper is structured as follows. Section 2 introduces a basic concept of
tool integration during co-simulation. Based on the analysis, we highlight possibilities to formalize the co-simulation tool-chains by the use of an extended TIL
which is presented in Sect. 3. In Sect. 4, we illustrate how to use TIL on two case
studies from previous research. We conclude and suggest future work in Sect. 5.

2   Tool Integration for Co-simulation

2.1   A Systems Engineering Approach to Developing Co-simulation
Tool-Chains

In previous research [16], we proposed a systems engineering approach for MBSE
tool-chain development. We make use of IEEE 1471 to describe the architectures
of MBSE tool-chains. Stakeholders of co-simulation tool-chains are surveyed to
obtain viewpoints from the social layer, process layer, information layer and technical layer. These viewpoints then are used to construct the views to address the
functionalities of tool-chain. These views are realized by techniques, - combined
with environment policy constraints to select tools and tool interactions -, in
co-simulation tool-chains. In closing, tools and tool interactions construct co-
simulation tool-chains.

In order to make use of an MBSE approach to analyze dependencies [28]
and tool-integration of co-simulation tool-chains, two kinds of references models

---

[1] IEEE 1471 is the predecessor of ISO/IEC 42010 [30]. We use IEEE 1471 in this
paper, because IEEE 1471 is light weight and its overview of architecture description
is sufficient to describe co-simulation tool-chain development.

are provided in Table 1. The reference models are based on IEEE 1471 and support tool-chain development which propose a generic method to describe the dependencies of tool-chain development (From stakeholders to MBSE tool-chains' structure). The tool integration reference models are proposed to describe logic flows of co-simulation tool-chains.

Table 1. References model for dependency and tool integration

Dependency	
Reference model	Description
Stakeholders	Refer to people related to co-simulation tool-chains, e.g., users, developers
Viewpoints	Refer to a specifications of rulers to cover stakeholders' concerns about co-simulation tool-chains
Views	Refer to functional requirements of co-simulation tool-chains from the perspective of a related set of viewpoints
Technique	Refer to technical solutions used for realizing views
Environmentrules	Refer to environment rules and constraints of tool-chain development
Tool&Tool interactions	Refer tools and tool interactions used in co-simulation tool-chains
Tool integration	
Reference model	Description
Technique Space	Refer to a unified representation of data, tool operations, co-simulation models
Tool adapter	Refer to integrated tools or interfaces exposing both functionalities and data. It includes *tool interface* [5], *integration interface* [5] and logic that translates between the interfaces

In this paper, we extend TIL to formalize the co-simulation tool-chains' structure and identify further work to extend TIL to the reference models in Table 1. After first identifying the basic elements occurring during tool integration of co-simulation, we propose several approaches to identify high-level abstractions in the structures. We then use the high-level abstractions, which are common to all integration styles to construct the tool integration language.

2.2   Definitions and Scope

This section defines important terms used throughout the paper. Based on the definition of the MBSE tool-chain proposed in our previous paper, [16], we specified a definition of the **co-simulation tool-chain:** more than one modeling tool and hardware that, when combined, can support and implement a co-simulation workflow. Tool integration of co-simulation tool-chains has several dimensions; in this paper, we concentrate on:

☐ **Control integration** - focuses on the ability of tools to perform notifications and activate the tools under program control, [38].

☐ **Data integration** - refers to ensuring that all the development information in the design environment is managed as a consistent whole, [31].

☐ **Co-simulation** - refers to run-time communication between software and hardware or between software during co-simulation [29,39]. We extend this definition in TIL in order to describe the co-simulation features.

In related work on co-simulation (see further Sect. 2.3), tool integration is generally described in the following three ways: (a) **Control-centric approaches** focus on of service invocations, application programming interfaces (API) and tool operations. (b) **Data-centric approaches** which can be specified in two ways: (b.1) Development information exchange and reuse by transferring data between tools. (b.2) Linking and tracing of development information without operations of data. (c) **Co-simulation approaches** focus on run-time communications between simulation tools or between simulation tools and hardware for dynamic behavior analysis.

In our proposed methodology in [16], we define a MBSE tool-chain development process as a mission in IEEE 1471. The system in the architecture is the target MBSE tool-chains. In IEEE 1471, at least four kinds of stakeholders and their viewpoints need to be considered: developers, users, maintainers and acquirers.

2.3   Tool Integration Method

A considerable number of methods for tool integration have been used in co-simulation environments. In order to analyze these methods and identify high-level abstractions, we analyze literature reviews in [13] and classify the methods with examples:

☐ **Integrated Data model:** Authors designed data models, -ontology, in specific tools which could be mapped to elements in the co-simulation process to control execution [2, 36, 37].

☐ **Integrated Process:** Tools are used to describe the workflow of co-simulations [32, 41].

☐ **Service-oriented approach:** In [35], a web based HLA federate was developed.

☐ **Tool-centric:** Specific tools are used to control and orchestrate co-simulation process. In our previous researches [20, 21], we developed a platform to manage co-simulation between AMESim [40], Flowmaster [34], Saber [8], Matlab/Simulink [26] and LMS Motion [27].

☐ **Co-simulation between hardware and software:** Hardware and software communicate with each other in order to implement real-time simulation [14, 19].

☐ **Co-simulation between software:** Different simulation tools use their tool adapters to communicate with each other during run-time co-simulation. The authors developed local/remote tool adapters for each tool to support run-time communication between them during co-simulation execution [1, 10, 11, 18].

Based on the findings from the literature review, we categorize tool integration into three types: (A) Control integration (B) Data integration (C) Co-simulation integration. In the following section we discuss suitable abstractions for these types of integration.

2.4 High-Level Abstractions in Control Integration

Control integration refers to tool operations which allow tool-chain users and tools some element of control including notifying users, activating tools, calling specific tool operations in other tools and triggering co-simulation and data exchanges or transformations. We make use of *technical space* for control integration referring to a common representation of tool operations, which allows unified access. *Notification* refers to tool operations whereby tools or users can communicate, for example sending an e-mail. *Activation* refers to tool operations that launch a tool with inputs and models. *Calling functionalities* refers to those tool operations where some function(s) of a tool can be triggered. *Trigger co-simulation* refers to tool operations where stakeholders or tools trigger co-simulation execution (e.g., system engineers press the button to start co-simulation). Generally, data exchange is needed between tools, but some tools cannot support data exchange directly. Therefore a transformation is needed to change the format so that tools can assess the data *Trigger data exchange or transformations* can be used to trigger both data exchange and transformations.

In this paper, *control integration* refers to one type of tool-interactions from the dependency view. During control integration, a *tool* has one or more *tool adapters* used for control integration. *Technical space for control integration* refers to *Technical Space* to unify tool-operation allocation formats.

2.5 High-Level Abstractions in Data Integration

As presented in [6], there are two purposes of data integration: (a) Dealing with different *concrete syntax* [24] in the data model; and (b) Unifying *abstract syntax* and semantics, in different data models. Therefore, it could be said that three elements are needed: (1) A least two *tools* with one or more *tool adapters* used for data integration; (2) Tool interactions, data exchange directly between tools and data transformation. (3) A common representation of data referring to *TechniqueSpace* from tool-integration views.

2.6 High-Level Abstractions in Co-simulation

Compared to previous research in [6], we extend new high-level abstractions in co-simulation integration to describe co-simulation features. Co-simulation allows *tools* to communicate with each other by using *tool adapters* as specific interfaces. During co-simulation, tool adapters execute data exchange between themselves and their host tools at each communication time step point. In Fig. 1, there are three types of API operations: (a) *Development API*; (B) *Configuration API*; and (C) *Runtime API*. Before co-simulation execution, *Development API* is used for developing models to support co-simulation. *Development API1* is used to create a co-simulation model, for example, linking interface to blocks. *Development API2* is used to insert an interface for co-simulation in models. *Development API3* is used to generate execution files for co-simulation interface. *Development API4* is used to transform models into a common representation

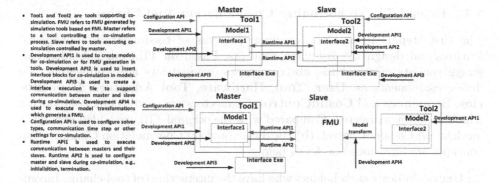

- Tool1 and Tool2 are tools supporting co-simulation. FMU refers to FMU generated by simulation tools based on FMI. Master refers to a tool controlling the co-simulation process. Slave refers to tools executing co-simulation controlled by master.
- Development API1 is used to create models for co-simulation or for FMU generation in tools. Development API2 is used to insert interface blocks for co-simulation in models. Development API3 is used to create a interface execution file to support communication between master and slave during co-simulation. Development API4 is used to execute model transformations which generate a FMU.
- Configuration API is used to configure solver types, communication time step or other settings for co-simulation.
- Runtime API1 is used to execute communication between masters and their slaves. Runtime API2 is used to configure master and slave during co-simulation, e.g., initialization, termination.

Fig. 1. API types during co-simulation

of co-simulation models, *technical space for co-simulation*, which allows unified access of exchange model format of co-simulation. *Configuration API* is used to configure tools for co-simulation, e.g., setting communication time step and setting solver types.

In general, co-simulation involves communication between executing softwares or between software and hardware and communication between executing softwares or between software and hardware by *technical space for co-simulation*, such as FMUs [25]. During co-simulation, *Runtime API1* is used for communication between co-simulation interfaces which is generated by adapters or FMUs (Functional Mockup Unit generated based on FMI) to exchange data between different models, e.g. send and get data from interface block. *Runtime API2* is used to control models or FMUs, e.g. initialize or terminate.

Abstraction Proposal : As with co-simulation, we propose that three elements are needed: (1) At least one *tool* with one or more *tool adapters* which support co-simulation. During co-simulation, tools include *masters* and *slaves* [25]. (2) Co-simulation either directly between tools, between hardware and software or through *technical space for co-simulation*. (3) A common representation of model referring to *Technique Space* from tool-integration views.

3   Extending TIL to Describe Co-simulation Tool-Chains

We extend TIL [5] to formalize co-simulation tool-chains in order to be able to describe them using a model-based approach. TIL is a domain specific language to describe tool integration solutions and thus is limited to describing co-simulation features in a tool integration scenario. Therefore we adopt additional meta models to describe the co-simulation features in order to use them in describing the structure of a co-simulation tool-chain.

3.1   Extend TIL to Formalize Co-simulation Tool-Chains

The first step is to find the common patterns of co-simulation tool-chains' features and design the language concepts. Based on TIL, our extended language consists of two basic abstract types: components and connectors. We define components as: **User, Tool, Hardware, Tool Adapters, Repositories, Sequences** and **CosimControl**. Connectors are used to link components which are always directed. Compared with the original TIL, we added new meta models: (a) Co-simuControl, (b) Hardware, and (c) Co-simulation Channel. The concepts are introduced in detail below:

☐ **Users** - indicate stakeholders who have the interactions of tool-chains. Incoming **Control Channels** refer to a notification of users, e.g. by e-mail or notices in system messages. Outcoming **Control channels** refer to actions or tool operations triggered by the *Users*.

☐ **Tools** - refers to components that expose both functionalities and data of software or tools. **Tools** provide functional services to tools and hardware exposing tool functionalities, data exchange and co-simulation by the use of **Tool adapters**.

☐ **Hardware** - refer to components that expose hardware used in co-simulation tool-chains.

☐ **Tool Adapters** - refer to components used to integrate tool functionalities and data or implement co-simulation. Capable of transforming, receiving data from tools or implementing co-simulation, e.g. code generation and co-simulation interface, it consists of two interfaces and the logic used to translate or communicate between them: (a) *Tool Interface* used to interact or communicate with the tool; and (b) *Integration Interface* for interacting with or communicating other integrated tools, integration platform or integration framework. In short, it could provide services that expose the functionalities of tools. For example, COM interface [3] is provided by Flowmaster to control Flowmaster execution [20].

☐ **Repositories** - refer to components that provide storage of tool data. Repositories accept data and model in specific formats. The inputs and outputs of **Repositories** are **Data Channels** referring to data or models import and export.

☐ **Sequencers** - refer to components executing multiple functional services of tools and tool adapters. They have incoming and outcoming **Control channels**. The incoming **Control channels**, - originating from any user or component - refer to the triggers of execution of sequences. The outcoming **Control channels** can activate a **Data channel** or components in a predefined order.

☐ **CosimControls** - refer to components mastering and controlling co-simulation of tools. They have incoming **Control channels, Data channels** and outcoming **Co-simulation channels**. The incoming **Control**

channels, - originating from any user or component -, refer to the triggers of executions of co-simulations. The incoming **Data channels** represent data input. The outcoming **Co-simulation Channels** can present run-time communication with other tools or tool adapters during co-simulation. **Sequences** can control and trigger **CosimControls** to execute co-simulations.

☐ **Data Channels** - refer to directed connections transferring data between components to deal with the heterogeneous source components and target components and data transmission without transformation. They connect source components to target components. There are three types of data channels: (a) Explicit transformation, attached with a transformation to deal with structural heterogeneities between tool metamodels. (b) Implicit transformation, the data needed by target components is different to source components, e.g. the Data Channels between Meta-Edit and Matlab/Simulink in [22] (Introduced in Case Study 2); and (c) Data transmission without transformation, for example, users use a tool to open a source model in repositories or copy the model to repositories.

☐ **Control Channels** - refer to directed edges between a source component and a target component or channel. The source component activates the target components or invokes a functional service of the target components. For instance, if the **Control channel** points at a **Data channel** or a **Co-simulation channel**, it means the **Data channel** or the **Co-simulation channel** is activated.

☐ **Trace Channels** - describe traceability links of data between different components.

☐ **Co-simulation Channels** -refer to real-time data exchange between components. For example, **Co-simulation channel** could connect tool to hardware which means they communicate with each other during co-simulation. The co-simulation channels need to be linked to **CosimControls**. The **Co-simulation channel** can be activated by **Control channels**.

3.2   Concrete Syntax of Extended TIL

In this paper, TIL is implemented in MetaEdit+ [2]. OPRR concepts (Object, Point, Relationship and Role) represent a method used in MetaEdit+ to implement a domain specific model. The concrete syntax for describing co-simulation tool-chains is shown in Fig. 2. The extended TIL includes the components and connectors in Table 2. Currently, it is used to formalize the structure of the tool-chains. We use two existing industrial co-simulation platform case studies to illustrate the potential of the extended TIL.

---

[2] We make use of MetaEdit+ to proof the concept of TIL and one of the further work to select a tool to support TIL.

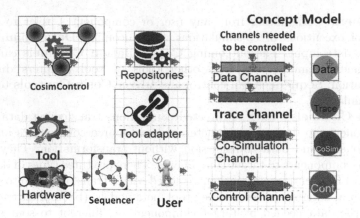

Fig. 2. Concept model of TIL

Table 2. Abstract syntax in extended TIL

Meta model in MetaEdit+	OPRR concepts [17]	Description
User	object	Refers to stakeholders who use tools
Tool	object	Refers to tools used in tool-chains
Tooladapter	object	Refers to tool adapters used in tool-chains. (It will be used in the future work).
Sequencer	object	Refers to sequencers used in tool-chains
Respositories	object	Refers to respositories used in tool-chains
CosimControl	object	Refers to cosimcontrol used in co-simulations
Hardware	object	Refers to hardware used in co-simulations
DataChannel	object	Refers to data channel controlled by a control channel
TraceChannel	object	Refers to trace channel controlled by a control channel
Co − simulationChannel	object	Refers to co-simulation channel controlled by a control channel
ControlChannel	object	Refers to control channel controlled by a control channel
Data	Relationship	Refers to data channel
Trace	Relationship	Refers to trace channel
CoSim	Relationship	Refers to co-simulation channel
Cont	Relationship	Refers to control channel

4   Case Study

4.1   Case Study 1

In [21], we proposed a co-simulation tool-chain used for mechatronics system design. This project was implemented in 2010, and aimed to integrate subsystem models into a unified platform for integrated system design. In the customer's department, they had different organizational groups for subsystem design. In each design group, they had their own simulation tools: (A) Fuel system designers used Flowmaster to simulate dynamics behaviors of fuel system. (B) Hydraulic system designers used AMESim to simulate dynamic behaviors of hydraulic systems. (C) Control system designers used Simulink to analyze control systems.

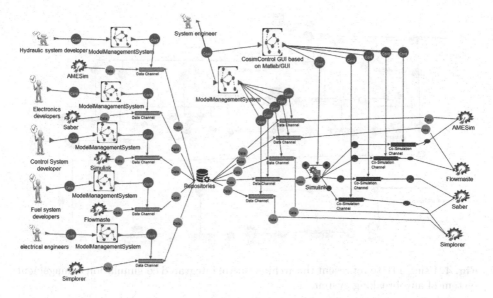

Fig. 3. Using TIL to represent the architecture of integrated co-simulation management system of mechatronics

(D) Electronics designers used Saber and Simplorer to analyze the electrical and electronic systems. This isolation of tools meant that an overall analysis of system performance could not be implemented. We designed a platform for our customers and its architecture is represented using extended TIL in Fig. 3.

As Fig. 3 shows, the various developers (hydraulic system, electronics, control system, fuel system and electrical) use a *ModelManagementSystem* to upload their models to *repositories*. Then the system engineers use the *ModelManagementSystem* to download the models and apply a home-made *co-simulation control GUI* (developed based on Matlab/GUI) to insert the co-simulation interfaces. At short, the system engineers use *co-simulation control GUI* to trigger Matlab/Simulink to execute simulations.

4.2 Case Study 2

In [22], we devised a modeling environment for domain specific models to support co-simulation between Simulink, Carmaker and FMUs generated from Modelica models. It was used to analyze an autobreaking system through simulations in Simulink, co-simulations between Simulink and Carmaker and co-simulations between Simulink, Carmaker and FMUs. Domain specific models were built in MetaEdit+.

Figure 4 represents the tool-chain's architecture. Mechanical engineers use MWorks [7] to build Modelica models for mechanical patterns of an autobraking system. Then they transform the Modelica models to FMUs and update them to *repositories*. System engineers build domain specific models in MetaEdit+,

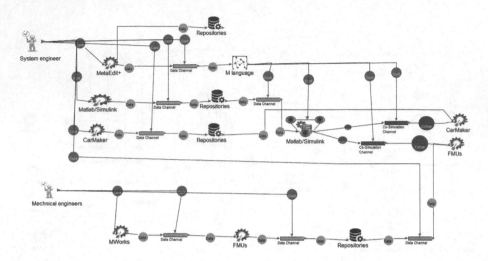

Fig. 4. Using TIL to represent the architecture of integrated co-simulation management system of autobreaking system

Simulink model library and Carmaker. They upload these models to *repositories* and transform the domain specific models to M language - used for Simulink operation, interface generation, Simulink model generation and Simulink execution. The co-simulation is triggered by the M language and executed by Simulink.

5   Evaluation and Future Work

In this paper, we have represented the need for MBSE to design co-simulation tool-chain solutions. We analyze the possibilities to formalize the co-simulation's architectures. We extended TIL, a high level domain specific modeling language to describe structures of co-simulation tool-chains. The industrial case studies illustrate how the TIL works. From the case study analysis, we summarize that:

☐ Systems engineering approaches could help stakeholders to capture the viewpoints and views of co-simulation tool-chains during design of the tool-chains' architectures.

☐ Model-based representation could provide visual architectures of co-simulation tool-chains in order to enhance the stakeholders' understanding and communication of tool-chain development.

☐ The model-based approach could be used as a potential extended method to achieve design automation for MBSE tool-chains.

In our methodology, we have used domain specific models (extended TIL) to represent tool-chain architecture. The conceptual model is now in its first version and is a work in progress. In the future, we plan to adopt IEEE 1471 to formalize the functional requirements of MBSE tool-chains firstly. Then dependencies between stakeholders and MBSE tool-chains, - presented in [16] as an initial plan -, would aim to concentrate on how views conformations work to confirm the functionalities of MBSE tool-chains by using extended TIL. At last, another main point of future work is to evaluate the proposed TIL and to investigate analysis and synthesis capabilities.

6 Conclusion

Our methodology allows for the description of tool-chain's architecture in current status and has potentials to formalize MBSE tool-chain development and support its functional synthesis. We still need to analyze where a functional synthesis is possible. On the other hand, we have adopt service oriented approaches to develop MBSE tool-chains to support co-simulation. We will investigate whether methodology proposed in this paper can support code generation for java-based tool adapters. In closing, we feel our methodology has real potential to increase the efficiency of co-simulation tool-chain development.

References

1. Al-Hammouri, A.T.: A comprehensive co-simulation platform for cyber-physical systems. Comput. Commun. **36**(1), 8–19 (2012)
2. Mengist, A., Pop, A., Fritzson, P.: Traceability support in openmodelica using open services for lifecycle collaboration (OSLC). In: Modelica 2017: Proceedings of 12th International Modelica Conference, 15th and 16th May. Citeseer (2017)
3. Baier, T., Neuwirth, E.: Excel :: COM :: R. Comput. Stat. **22**(1), 91–108 (2007)
4. Becker, D., Singh, R.K., Tell, S.G.: An engineering environment for hardware/software co-simulation. In: Proceedings of 29th ACM/IEEE Design Automation Conference, pp. 129–134. IEEE (1992)
5. Biehl, M., El-Khoury, J., Loiret, F., Törngren, M.: A domain specific language for generating tool integration solutions. In: 4th Workshop on Model-Driven Tool & Process Integration (MDTPI2011) at the European Conference on Modelling Foundations and Applications (ECMFA 2011), 6 June 2011 (2011)
6. Biehl, M., Sjöstedt, C.J., Törngren, M.: A modular tool integration approach: experiences from two case studies (2010)
7. Chen, X., Wei, Z.: A new modeling and simulation platform-MWorks for electrical machine based on Modelica. In: International Conference on Electrical Machines and Systems, ICEMS 2008, pp. 4065–4067. IEEE (2008)
8. Chwirka, S.: Using the powerful saber simulator for simulation, modeling, and analysis of power systems, circuits, and devices. In: The 7th Workshop on Computers in Power Electronics, COMPEL 2000, pp. 172–176. IEEE (2000)
9. Dietz, S., Hippmann, G., Schupp, G.: Interaction of vehicles and flexible tracks by co-simulation of multibody vehicle systems and finite element track models. Veh. Syst. Dyn. **37**(Suppl. 1), 372–384 (2002)
10. Eker, J., Janneck, J.W., Lee, E.A., Liu, J., Liu, X., Ludvig, J., Neuendorffer, S., Sachs, S., Xiong, Y.: Taming heterogeneity-the ptolemy approach. Proc. IEEE **91**(1), 127–144 (2003)

11. Fitzgerald, J., Larsen, P.G., Pierce, K., Verhoef, M., Wolff, S.: Collaborative modelling and co-simulation in the development of dependable embedded systems. In: Méry, D., Merz, S. (eds.) IFM 2010. LNCS, vol. 6396, pp. 12–26. Springer, Heidelberg (2010). https://doi.org/10.1007/978-3-642-16265-7_2

12. Fitzgerald, J., Larsen, P.G., Verhoef, M.: From embedded to cyber-physical systems: challenges and future directions. In: Fitzgerald, J., Larsen, P.G., Verhoef, M. (eds.) Collab. Des. Embed. Syst., pp. 293–303. Springer, Heidelberg (2014). https://doi.org/10.1007/978-3-642-54118-6_14

13. Gomes, C., Thule, C., Broman, D., Larsen, P.G., Vangheluwe, H.: Co-simulation: State of the art, February 2017. arXiv:1702.00686

14. Hoffman, A., Kogel, T., Meyr, H.: A framework for fast hardware-software co-simulation. In: Proceedings of the Conference on Design, Automation and Test in Europe, pp. 760–765. IEEE Press (2001)

15. ISO/IEC: Systems and software engineering - Recommended practice for architectural description of software-intensive systems, vol. 2007 (2007)

16. Lu, J., Chen, D.-J., Gürdür, D., Törngren, M.: An investigation of functionalities of future tool-chain for aerospace industry. In: INCOSE International Symposium. Wiley Online Library (2017, in press)

17. Kelly, S., Lyytinen, K., Rossi, M.: MetaEdit+ a fully configurable multi-user and multi-tool CASE and CAME environment. In: Constantopoulos, P., Mylopoulos, J., Vassiliou, Y. (eds.) CAiSE 1996. LNCS, vol. 1080, pp. 1–21. Springer, Heidelberg (1996). https://doi.org/10.1007/3-540-61292-0_1

18. Li, S., He, L.: Co-simulation study of vehicle ESP system based on ADAMS and MATLAB. J. Softw. 6(5), 866–872 (2011)

19. Li, W., Joós, G., Bélanger, J.: Real-time simulation of a wind turbine generator coupled with a battery supercapacitor energy storage system. IEEE Trans. Industr. Electron. 57(4), 1137–1145 (2010)

20. Lu, J.: Co-simulation for heterogeneous simulation system and application for aerospace. Master dissertation, Huazhong University of Science and Technology, Wuhan, China (2013)

21. Lu, J., Ding, J., Zhou, F., Gong, X.: Research of tool-coupling based electro-hydraulic system development method. In: Qi, E. (ed.) Proceedings of the 6th International Asia Conference on Industrial Engineering and Management Innovation, pp. 213–224. Atlantis Press, Paris (2016). https://doi.org/10.2991/978-94-6239-148-2_21

22. Lu, J., Chen, D., Törngren, M., Loiret, F.: A model-driven and tool-integration framework for whole vehicle co-simulation environments. In: 8th European Congress on Embedded Real Time Software and Systems (ERTS 2016) (2016)

23. Lynn, A., Smid, E., Eshraghi, M., Caldwell, N., Woody, D.: Modeling hydraulic regenerative hybrid vehicles using AMESIM and MATLAB/Simulink. In: Defense and Security, pp. 24–40. International Society for Optics and Photonics (2005)

24. Mierlo, S.V., Tendeloo, Y.V., Meyers, B., Vangheluwe, H.: The Handbook of Formal Methods in Human-Computer Interaction. Human-Computer Interaction Series. Springer International Publishing, Cham (2017). https://doi.org/10.1007/978-3-319-51838-1

25. Modelica Association Project "FMI": Functional Mock-up Interface for Model Exchange and Co-Simulation (07006), pp. 1–120 (2013)

26. Ong, C.M.: Dynamic Simulation of Electric Machinery: Using MATLAB/ SIMULINK. Prentice Hall, Upper Saddle River (1998)

27. Ong, E.P., Spann, M.: Robust multiresolution computation of optical flow. In: 1996 IEEE International Conference on Acoustics, Speech, and Signal Processing, ICASSP-1996. Conference Proceedings, vol. 4, pp. 1938–1941. IEEE (1996)
28. Qamar, A.: Model and dependency management in mechatronic design. Ph.D. thesis, KTH Royal Institute of Technology (2013)
29. Rowson, J.A.: Hardware/software co-simulation. In: 31st Conference on Design Automation, pp. 439–440. IEEE (1994)
30. International Standard: INTERNATIONAL STANDARD ISO/IEC/IEEE Systems and Software Engineering - Engineering 2011 (2011)
31. Thomas, I., Nejmeh, B.A.: Definitions of tool integration for environments. IEEE Softw. 9(2), 29–35 (1992)
32. Trappey, C.V., Trappey, A.J., Huang, C.J., Ku, C.: The design of a JADE-based autonomous workflow management system for collaborative SoC design. Expert Syst. Appl. 36(2), 2659–2669 (2009)
33. Trčka, M., Hensen, J.L., Wetter, M.: Co-simulation for performance prediction of integrated building and HVAC systems–an analysis of solution characteristics using a two-body system. Simul. Model. Pract. Theory 18(7), 957–970 (2010)
34. Tu, Y., Lin, G.: Dynamic simulation of aircraft environmental control system based on flowmaster. J. Aircr. 48(6), 2031–2041 (2011)
35. Tu, Z., Zacharewicz, G., Chen, D.: Developing a web-enabled HLA federate based on portico RTI. In: Proceedings of the 2011 Winter Simulation Conference (WSC), pp. 2289–2301. IEEE (2011)
36. Van Rompaey, K., Bolsens, I., De Man, H., Verkest, D.: Coware-a design environment for heterogenous hardware/software systems. In: Proceedings of Conference on European Design Automation, pp. 252–257. IEEE Computer Society Press (1996)
37. Wang, B., Baras, J.S.: Hybridsim: a modeling and co-simulation toolchain for cyber-physical systems. In: Proceedings of 2013 IEEE/ACM 17th International Symposium on Distributed Simulation and Real Time Applications, pp. 33–40. IEEE Computer Society (2013)
38. Wasserman, A.I.: Tool integration in software engineering environments. In: Long, F. (ed.) Software Engineering Environments. LNCS, vol. 467, pp. 137–149. Springer, Heidelberg (1990). https://doi.org/10.1007/3-540-53452-0_38
39. Wetter, M.: Co-simulation of building energy and control systems with the building controls virtual test bed. J. Build. Perform. Simul. 4(3), 185–203 (2011)
40. You-Guan, Y., Guo-fang, G., Guo-Liang, H.: Simulation technique of AMESim and its application in hydraulic system. Hydraul. Pneum. Seals 3, 28–31 (2005)
41. Zitney, S.E.: Process/equipment co-simulation for design and analysis of advanced energy systems. Comput. Chem. Eng. 34(9), 1532–1542 (2010)

A Framework for Analyzing Adaptive Autonomous Aerial Vehicles

Ian A. Mason[1], Vivek Nigam[2,3(✉)], Carolyn Talcott[1], and Alisson Brito[2]

[1] SRI International, Menlo Park, USA
{iam,clt}@csl.sri.com
[2] Federal University of Paraíba, João Pessoa, Brazil
alisson@ci.ufpb.br
[3] fortiss, Munich, Germany
vivek.nigam@gmail.com

Abstract. Unmanned aerial vehicles (UAVs), a.k.a. drones, are becoming increasingly popular due to great advancements in their control mechanisms and price reduction. UAVs are being used in applications such as package delivery, plantation and railroad track monitoring, where UAVs carry out tasks in an automated fashion. Devising how UAVs achieve a task is challenging as the environment where UAVs are deployed is normally unpredictable, for example, due to winds. Formal methods can help engineers to specify flight strategies and to evaluate how well UAVs are going to perform to achieve a task. This paper proposes a formal framework where engineers can raise the confidence in their UAV specification by using symbolic, simulation and statistical and model checking methods. Our framework is constructed over three main components: the behavior of UAVs and the environment are specified in a formal executable language; the UAV's physical model is specified by a simulator; and statistical model checking algorithms are used for the analysis of system behaviors. We demonstrate the effectiveness of our framework by means of several scenarios involving multiple drones.

1 Introduction

Unmanned aerial vehicles (UAVs), a.k.a. drones, have gained much attention in recent years not only for entertainment purposes, but also being used to carry out non-trivial tasks [22,24,36]. For example, UAVs are being used to autonomously deliver packages, monitor railroad tracks [6] and electricity lines, precision agriculture [10], automating inventory checking in large warehouses [31], and even air taxis [11]. The main reason for this increased interest derives from reduced costs and from the great improvement of UAV's control and flight mechanisms/algorithms.

Despite these successful applications, less attention has been given to how to devise a strategy for a UAV that is going to (autonomously) carry out a task. The current practice is, before UAVs are deployed and test flights are performed, to use simulators such as ArduPilot/SITL [33] to carry out simulations in order

© Springer International Publishing AG 2018
A. Cerone and M. Roveri (Eds.): SEFM 2017 Workshops, LNCS 10729, pp. 406–422, 2018.
https://doi.org/10.1007/978-3-319-74781-1_28

to check whether the strategy devised to accomplish the given task is sensible. While simulators implement reasonably faithful physical models of UAVs, including energy consumption, velocity and acceleration, etc., simulations many times do not take into account the unpredictable effect of winds and failures, such as GPS or equipment failures. Moreover even when such aspects are included in the simulation, only a few simulations are carried out, rather than systematic sampling of possibilities. This leads to very low coverage of the situations that might be encountered using the proposed strategy, possibly resulting in the discovery of failure in later stages of development such as during flight test, or worse during operation, when failures are more costly.

On the other hand, executable symbolic models, have been proposed [15] for analysing such systems. These models have been used to verify whether systems satisfy properties such as whether it is possible to carry out a task (realizability) or whether it is never possible for the UAV to fail to carry out a task (survivability). These models typically abstract from details of the physical environment, making simplifications that may be unrealistic, such as deterministic winds and no real account for the physical properties of the drone, such as energy consumption behavior, movement lag, etc.

This paper proposes bridging worlds allowing specifiers to design and specify strategies, analyse them symbolically, and by using the same specifications carry out these analyses using realistic models of the physical behavior of UAVs. Our framework has three main components (detailed in Sect. 2):

- **Executable Formal Specification of UAV Behavior:** The central piece of our framework is the executable formal specification of UAV behavior. The same specification can be used to carry out a number of analysis (as we describe below). For this paper, we use Soft Agents Framework recently proposed [34,35], but it should also be possible to use other formal agent specification languages. Soft agent strategies are specified symbolically as executable rewrite theories in Maude. An approximate UAV physics including energy consumption model, winds, (de-)accelaration, etc. is also specified as a rewrite theory;
- **UAV Simulator:** An interactive simulator implementing realistic UAV physical models is used to increase the precision of the analysis. For this paper, we use Ardupilot/SITL (or simply SITL) which is an open-source UAV simulator implementing many features, such as realistic UAV physical models (energy consumption, movement behavior, etc.), of different types of UAVs, such as copters or airplanes.
- **Statistical Model Checker:** In order to verify systems with uncertainty, our framework also includes a statistical model checker. For this paper, we ported a number of statistical algorithms for statistical reachability analysis [21,23, 32]. This simplified carrying out experiments, but in principle it is possible to use existing tools, such as PVeStA and MultiVeStA.

We call our framework $\mathcal{SA}^2$. $\mathcal{SA}^2$ allows combining the three components listed above to carry out different types of analyses of UAV flight strategies (see Sect. 3):

- **Purely Symbolic:** By using the abstract UAV physics specified in Maude, purely symbolic analyses (without uncertainty) can be carried out to determine (symbolically) whether the specified strategy satisfies properties such as *realizability*, *i.e.*, the goal can be achieved, and *survivability*, *i.e.*, the goal is always achieved [15]. Such analysis can help to find flaws in early stages of development.
- **Simulations:** $\mathcal{SA}^2$ can also simulate the UAV behavior specified as a soft agent system in Maude using SITL. SITL provides a more realistic modeling of UAV physics as opposed to the symbolic (discrete) Maude physics, and supports interaction with external components to receive commands and provide UAV status information (sensor readings);
- **Statistical Model Checking:** It is possible to add uncertainty to the environment model, such as winds, sensor failure, etc. Then, by applying the implemented statistical model checking algorithms, specifiers can obtain a quantitative evaluation of how well UAVs performed with a specified confidence. For example, what is the minimum energy that UAVs reached before landing; how many were able to return back home, or how much of the goal was achieved.

Our main contribution (Sects. 2 and 3) is thus to demonstrate how different verification methods (symbolic, simulation and SMC) can be integrated and used to carry out different analysis in different stages of UAV development. We discuss related work in Sect. 4 and point to future work in Sect. 5.

Running Example: Consider as running example, a set of n drones that start from possibly distinct home bases. Each drone d is assigned a set of points $\mathcal{P}_d$. Their goal is to visit their set of points and return close to home without running out of energy.

2 Soft Agents Squared ($\mathcal{SA}^2$)

As already mentioned our framework has three key components: (1) a formalism for executable symbolic specification of UAV behavior; (2) a UAV simulator;

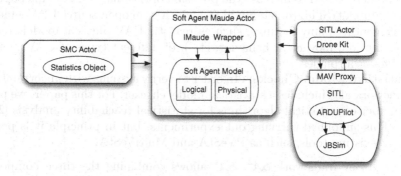

Fig. 1. $\mathcal{SA}^2$'s architecture

and (3) Statistical Model Checking (SMC) algorithms/tools. As we show in more detail in Sect. 3, the combination of these three components allows specifiers to develop and test UAV strategies in different development stages thus increasing the confidence in the proposed UAV strategies for accomplishing some task. In this paper, we report experience using a specific instance of the framework called Soft Agents Squared (SA^2). This instance uses the Soft Agents framework [34,35] as the executable specification language implemented in Maude [7], Ardupilot/SITL [33] for the UAV simulator, and SMC algorithms ported from [21,23,32]. We expect that other tools could be used to instantiate the framework as well. As shown in Fig. 1 the components are integrated by message passing. For this we use the IOP (InterOPerability) framework [26] which is based on the actor model. [1]Each component in embedded in an actor that coordinates its interactions with the other components. The SMC actor is responsible for managing interactions with the statistical model checking algorithms, the Maude Soft Agent actor coordinates interactions with Soft Agent specifications, and the SITL actor manages creation and interaction with ArduPilot/SITL drone instances.

2.1 Combining Symbolic Reasoning, Simulation, and Statistical Model Checking

Our framework supports analysis from different perspectives useful at different stages of system design and operation: Soft Agents alone, Soft Agents + SMC, SITL alone, Soft Agents + SITL, or Soft Agents + SITL + SMC.

At the center is the executable specification. Soft Agents alone can be used to carry out symbolic analysis. For example, the Maude search engine can be used for reachability analysis, looking for executions satisfying or violating given properties. This is useful in early stages to see that proposed strategies at least work under ideal conditions. Uncertainty can be added to the environment model (for example wind, GPS or motor failure ...), and Soft Agents + SMC can be used to evaluate the probability of successful behavior under different unpredictable environment, sensor and actuator models. SMC can be tuned to achieve increasing precision/confidence at the cost of more time/executions. Our framework allows users to carry out executions of scenarios specified as Soft Agents dwhere the effects of commands are computed by SITL's more realistic simulation, rather than using the abstract logical model. STIL also supports visualization of drone trajectories useful for identifying certain problems. Finally, all three components can be used together (Soft Agents + SITL + SMC) in order to analyze scenarios with uncertainty using more realistic physical models.

Figure 2 depicts the protocols used to communicate between the Maude (Soft Agents), SITL and SMC actors in the different combinations. In each case the Maude actor initiates the analysis. Figure 2(a) shows the interaction of the Maude actor and the SMC to carry out statistical model checking for a specific scenario. The Maude actor sends a message (create object with params) to SMC

[1] IOP binaries and documentation are available at https://jlambda.com/~iop/.

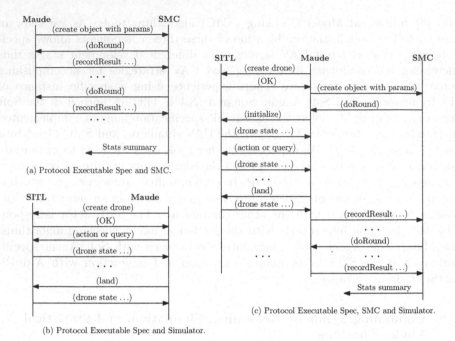

(a) Protocol Executable Spec and SMC.

(b) Protocol Executable Spec and Simulator.

(c) Protocol Executable Spec, SMC and Simulator.

Fig. 2. Messages exchanged used between the executable specification, simulator and statistical model checker (SMC).

to create a statistics object for the desired statistical algorithm. Params include the algorithm identifier, error bounds, and confidence levels. SMC then sends a message (doRound) to the Maude actor to execute the scenario being analyzed. When the execution finishes, Maude sends a (recordResult ...) message to SMC containing the results of the execution (energy remaining, number of points visited, ...) to be recorded by the statistics object. The (doRound,recordResult) loop is repeated until the statistics object determines that enough rounds have been done. At this point the Stats summary is reported. The result summary is also available by programatic query to the SMC actor.

Figure 2(b) shows the interactions of the Maude and SITL actors to execute a scenario. The Maude actor initiates the execution by sending a (create drone) message to the SITL actor for each drone in the scenario. In the figure we consider a scenario with a single drone. Once the drone object has been created and initialized, SITL replies to Maude with an (OK) message. Now Maude starts the execution. This consists of a series of (action or query) messages from Maude to SITL followed by (drone state ...) messages from SITL to Maude. The action messages control the drones motion during the scenario. The drone state sent by SITL includes the drone's energy level and position. A scenario parameter determines the frequency at which messages are sent to SITL, typically every 1–3 s. A scenario ends with a (land) message to SITL to land the drone followed by a final (drone state ...) report from SITL to Maude.

Figure 2(c) shows the messages exchanged when the three components are combined to carry out statistical model checking using the simulated drone physics. The message exchange is basically a merge of the diagrams of the pairwise combinations shows in Fig. 2(a,b). Again we consider messages for a single drone scenario. The Maude actor initializes the analysis by sending a (create drone) message to SITL, and once SITL confirms (OK) the creation of the drone object, Maude initializes the SMC with the configuration parameters (create object with params) for the statistics algorithm. As for the Soft Agent + SMC scenario, the SMC actor then proceeds to drive the analysis, by sending a (doRound) message to Maude. In response Maude initializes SITL (initialize), (re) starting the drone with its initial parameters. Then Maude executes the scenario as in the SoftAgents + SITL combination, sending (action or query) messages and receiving (drone state ...) updates. When the execution is complete (land, drone state ...) Maude sends a (recordResult ...) message to SMC and the (doRound, recordResult) process is repeated until the statistics object determines that the analysis is done. At this point, the SMC displays the result summary.

Although, for simplicity, illustrated the interactions for single drone scenarios, in general there can be mulitple drones. We note that system analysis can be sped up by using a concurrent version of the SMC actor that runs multiple simulations in parallel. In addition to the parameters for the simulation system one only needs to specify the number of parallel subsystems to be started. This can be used for Soft Agent-SMC analyses or for Maude-SITL-SMC combinations. This is particularly useful when SITL is used, as it is does much more computation and hence is much slower than Maude.

In the remainder of this section we provide brief overviews of the specific components we are using.

2.2   Soft Agents

Soft Agents is a rewriting logic framework for specifying and analysing (autonomous) agents. The core framework is specified in the rewriting logic language Maude [7]. It provides generic data structures for representing system state (cyber and physical), interface sorts and functions to be used to specify the environment, agent capabilities and effects of actions (physical), and agent behavior (cyber). The semantics, how a system evolves, is given by a small number of rewrite rules defined in terms of these sorts and functions. Details can be found in [34,35]. Figure 3 depicts the general architecture of a soft agent. A soft agent has a local knowledge base which may include, e.g., its perceived location, energy status, velocity and other data obtained from sensing information. Using the local knowledge base, it decides which action to perform according to its concerns specified as a soft constraint problem [5]. For example, if its energy has reached some low level, activating the energy concern, it may decide to go back home. There may be several possible actions equally preferred in which case one is selected non-deterministically. As soft constraints subsume other constraint

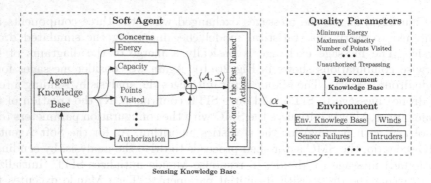

Fig. 3. A Soft Agent uses its sensing knowledge and its policies to decide which actions it will take. Here, $\mathcal{A}$ is the set of possible actions that a soft agent can perform, $\preceq$ is a pre-order on the set $\mathcal{A}$, and $\alpha \in \mathcal{A}$ is the selected action according to the specified concerns. The quality parameters indicate how well a soft agent has performed.

systems, *e.g.*, probabilistic, fuzzy, or classical constraint systems [5], it is possible to specify a wide range of decision algorithms.

For our running example, we consider two simple strategies for picking the next point to visit to illustrate the types of analysis enabled by our framework. More advanced features, such as collision avoidance algorithms and its verification can also be specified using Soft Agents.

- **Waypoint Strategy:** A drone d visits the points in $\mathcal{P}_d$ in some pre-specified order;
- **Closest Point Strategy:** A drone d chooses (non deterministically) the next point in $\mathcal{P}_d$ to visit from the set of points it has not yet visited that are closest to its current location.

In both strategies, however, if a drone's energy level reaches some particular caution level, *caution*, the drone heads back home regardless if it has visited all assigned points. Moreover, if its energy level reaches some critical value *critical* < *caution*, typically 5% of its battery level, the drone lands regardless of whether it is close to its home base. We specify such strategies by defining the concern "Points Visited" and combining it with concern "Energy". The "Energy" concern overrides the "Points Visited" concern whenever a drone's energy level reaches *caution*. Other examples of Soft Agent specifications can be found in [34].

An action's physical effects, *i.e.*, how it changes the position, energy, etc., of a drone, are also specified in the Soft Agent Framework in Maude. For example, the following equation specifies how much energy per time unit a drone consumes depending on its speed:

```
eq costMv(v) = (if v < 3.0 then 1.04 else 1.19 fi) .
```

If the drone's speed is less than 3.0, then it consumes 1.04% of energy per time unit, otherwise 1.19%. There are similar equations specifying a drone's moving model, *e.g.*, (de-)acceleration, top speed. The values in these equations will depend on the particular physical properties of the considered drone. For instance, the values used in the equation above were calibrated to correspond *roughly* to the energy model used by SITL's copter.

Once an action is selected, execution updates the environment's knowledge base, *e.g.*, the actual position of all drones, their energy, speed according to the specified physics. It may happen due to uncertainties that the perceived local knowledge base does not match the actual values stored in the environment knowledge base. Such uncertainties may be caused by non-malicious factors, such as winds and sensor failures, or by malicious intruders. This paper only considers non-malicious factors. (Scenarios with malicious intruders is still subject of intensive research [28].)

Finally, a soft agent system is a collection of soft agents, each one with its own local knowledge base and concerns, interacting with the same environment. They may share knowledge whenever some specified conditions are satisfied.

2.3   Ardupilot/SITL

ArduPilot SITL (Software In The Loop) [33] is a simulator that allows one to simulate a Plane, Copter or Rover without any actual hardware. Ardupilot [1] is a C/C++ autopilot software package for controlling a variety of vehicle systems ranging from conventional airplanes, multirotors, and helicopters,to boats and even submarines. The physics of the simulation is provided by the JSBSim software package [14]. We use the python library DroneKit-SITL to communicate to a ArduPilot SITL instance. The communication uses a MavProxy process that forwards MavLink commands [27] over the local IP network.

The SITL API provides many features that are usually available in actual UAV devices. It is possible to specify the direction, yaw, and velocity of a drone, and to monitor the energy levels, and GPS position of a vehicle and set their operational *modes*, which determine the level of assistance provided by its control mechanisms. (In fact, it is possible to simulate any command available in an normal UAV remote controller.)

SITL also provides an interface with maps and controller information that allow one to easily monitor a vehicle's location and state during a simulation.

2.4   Statistical Model Checking

Our statistical model checker (SMC) supports reachability/counting analysis. It draws on ideas and algorithms from Vesta [32] and XTune [21] (see Sect. 4). The core of our SMC is the notion of Statistics Object (implemented as an abstract Java class). Each concrete class implements a specific statistical algorithm for computing the expected value of a variable from a sampled set of measurements. A statistics object is created with parameters depending on the underlying algorithm, that generally include some measure of desired precision and/or confidence. It has a method to record the results of a run, the value whose expected value/average is being estimated. This could be as simple as 0 or 1 representing some notion of failure or success, or a tuple of quality parameters. A statistics object also has a method to inquire if the analysis is done (enough runs have been recorded) and to provide a summary of the results, which includes the number of runs recorded, the average of the recorded values, and possibly other information. We have ported the 5 algorithms provided in the NCPS framework [17,18], that builds on the XTune architecture ideas. For simplicity we focus here on the algorithm called GenericApproximation [23]. The parameters are ϵ (the error parameter, using additive approximation) and δ (the confidence parameter). The algorithm computes the number of rounds needed to achieve the precision and confidence specified by these parameters assuming a Bernoulli distribution. In our experiments, we set ϵ and δ to 0.25. Although these confidence/error levels are laughable in usual cases, given the uncertain drone behavior and small number of drones, as we discuss in Sect. 3, they allow us to get some idea of the range of behaviors in a modest amount of time.

3   Analyses

This section illustrates the main types of analyses that can be carried out within $\mathcal{SA}^2$ using different combinations of its components. The table in Fig. 4 summarizes the main (qualitative) properties of the possible analyses.

Recall our example where drones are assigned a set of points and should visit these points and return to home base without running out of energy. Moreover, we consider two different strategies of how to accomplish this task: *Waypoint Strategy* and *Closest Point Strategy*. These strategies come with two parameters *caution* and *critical* which specify when a drone should head back home and when it should land (see Sect. 2).

It is certainly possible to improve both strategies by adding more soft agent concerns and while this is an interesting research question, it is not the purpose of this paper. Our goal is to illustrate the types of analysis one can carry out in

Combination	Result	Speed	System Size	Physics	Type
SA	yes/no	fast	≤ 10 drones	no uncertainty	Symbolic
SA + SMC	quantitative	fast	≤ 60 drones	possibly uncertain	Statistical
SA + SITL	yes/no	slow	≤ 10 drones	possibly uncertain	Simulation
SA + SMC + SITL	quantitative	slow	≤ 4 drones	possibly uncertain	Statistical

Fig. 4. Qualitative comparison of the analyses available by using different combinations of the components of $\mathcal{SA}^2$. Here **SA** and **SMC** stand, respectively, for soft agents and statistical model checker. Speed is fast if runs take time much smaller (circa 1000 times faster) than actual flight time and slow if runs take time similar to (circa 3 times faster than) actual flight time. The system size is based on experiments carried out using a virtual machine built on top of 2.7 GHz ei5 processor with 8 GB of memory. It should be possible to analyse larger systems with more powerful hardware.

$\mathcal{SA}^2$. We use a small scenario with two drones and 8 points. In order to illustrate the analyses with uncertainty, we considered scenarios with varying chances of wind and intensity.

Finally, while we also describe how the different types of analyses available in $\mathcal{SA}^2$ scale with the number of drones, these results should be taken with a grain of salt as they are preliminary. There are many optimizations that should be investigated and implemented, *e.g.*, how to maximize the number of executions running in parallel. Nevertheless, our preliminary results are promising.

3.1   Soft Agents (Purely Symbolic)

By using Maude's built-in rewrite and search engines, we can analyse scenarios using the physics specified in Maude without uncertainty. Using this machinery is useful in early stages of development as specifiers can early on check whether some fail state can be reached (even without uncertainty), *e.g.*, drones not being able to visit all points or landing far from home or even running out of energy while flying and thus crashing. If so, specifiers may consider using more drones or drones with more energy or rethink the assignment of points.

For our running example, we can specify the following functions in Maude:

- success(C): The configuration C is a success if all drones were able to land back home and visit all assigned points;
- hardFail(C): The configuration C is a hard fail if at least one drone crashed, *i.e.*, ran out of energy during flight, or a drone landed very far away from its home base;
- softFail(C): The configuration C is a soft fail if it is not a hard fail and if all drones were able to reach back home, but at least one point was not visited.

Clearly a hard fail is worse than a soft fail.

Using the Soft Agent machinery, it is possible to check if drones can realize the assigned task by executing the following command where I is the initial configuration:

```
search I =>* C such that success(C)
```

Similarly, we can check whether hard or soft fail configurations can be reached.

Indeed while developing the Waypoint and Closest Point strategies, we initially assigned too many points (8 points) to each drone. Then, by using Maude's machinery, we quickly determined that two drones were not able to visit all the assigned points. Therefore, we reduced the number of assigned points to four per drone. If we did not perform this check early on, it is very likely that we would have spent a great deal of time further developing the strategies tuning the "Energy" and "Visited Points" concerns without realizing that it is not possible for the drones to visit so many points.

For small systems such as our running example, Maude can rapidly (less than 20 s) return yes/no answers. However, as state space increases exponentially, for larger systems (with more than 10 drones), Maude takes much longer times (more than 2 h) to traverse the whole search tree.

3.2   Soft Agents and SMC

Combining soft agents and the statistical model checker (SMC) enables users to analyze much larger systems (up to 60 drones) and analyze systems against uncertainties, *e.g.*, changing winds. Moreover, users can also obtain quantitative information on how their system performed. For example:

- **Back home** (H): How many drones on average were able to return back home?
- **Minimum Energy** (E): What is the minimum energy remaining for drones that were able to land (at home or not)?
- **Points Visited** (V): How many points on average were visited by the drones?

The combination of such quality parameters and the soft agents concern-based architecture turns out to be powerful: If the SMC returns low values for minimum energy, the specifier may consider to calibrate the "Energy" concern by increasing *caution*. On the other hand, if the average of number of points visited is low, the specifier can change "Points Visited" concern by assigning less points to a drone and increasing the number of drones or decrease *caution*.

As described in Sect. 2.4, statistical confidence and other parameters (ϵ and δ) can be configured. Analyses requiring higher confidence take more time as more runs have to be carried out. This does not mean, however, that lower confidence results are not useful for a specifier. They can be used to quickly find problems in the flight strategy and make corrections or fine tuning before running $\mathcal{SA}^2$ for higher confidence results.

For example, setting ϵ and δ set to 0.25, only 17 runs are needed which takes the $\mathcal{SA}^2$ Soft Agents + SMC only 8 s. In contrast setting ϵ and δ to 0.05 requires 738 runs taking 500 s and returning higher confidence results. As the results below illustrate, lower confidence results can still be useful for tuning flight strategies. When analyzing our running scenario using the Closest Point Strategy and *caution* = 40 in an environment with 25% chance of wind we get values for H, E, V described above:

$$\text{with } \epsilon = \delta = 0.25 : \quad H = 2.0, E = 28, V = 7.0$$
$$\text{with } \epsilon = \delta = 0.05 : \quad H = 2.0, E = 29, V = 6.96$$

This means that both drones were able to make it back home with more than 25% energy remaining and were able to visit on average 7 of 8 points. This result suggests to a specifier that in such an environment, drones can adopt a less conservative strategy by reducing their *caution* level. Running the same scenario with *caution* = 20, we get:

$$\text{with } \epsilon = \delta = 0.25 : \quad H = 2.0, E = 20, V = 8.0$$
$$\text{with } \epsilon = \delta = 0.05 : \quad H = 1.97, E = 20, V = 7.99$$

where the drones are able to return home and visit practically all points without reaching dangerously low energy levels. It is possible to carry out such analyses with different *caution* levels and scenarios with different chances of winds. We postpone due to space restriction showing the results of such analyses to Sect. 3.4 (see Fig. 6) when we use all three components Soft Agents, SMC and SITL.

In practice, a specifier may consider carrying out lower confidence, but still meaningful experiments to quickly find ways to tune strategies and then run higher confidence experiments to further fine tune their strategies. For the example above, the specifier could consider increasing caution slightly in order for both drones to return back home and not 1.97 as the higher confidence results indicate.

Scalability. The combination of Soft Agents and SMC does not require many computational resources. This not only means that for small scenarios users obtain results quickly, but also scales well to larger scenarios. For example, while using only soft agents we are able to analyze symbolically scenarios with up to 10 drones, by combining soft agents with the SMC, we are able to analyze scenarios with up to 60 drones. The time for running the analysis is depicted in Fig. 5 taking around 3000 s with a scenario with 60 drones.

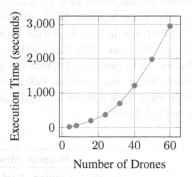

Fig. 5. Execution time for analyzing scenarios with soft agents and the SMC using $\epsilon = \delta = 0.25$.

Running higher confidence results would take much longer, but may be turned tractable by executing runs in parallel. Such optimizations are left to future work.

3.3 Soft Agents and SITL

As described in Sect. 2, SITL provides faithful physical models of several types of drone along with useful features like Google-like maps and the console with further drone information, *e.g.*, AirSpeed, Battery Level, etc. These features can be helpful in further finding bugs in particular those bugs due to mismatches between the Soft Agents discrete physical model and the more faithful SITL model.

For a concrete example, after analyzing our strategies using SA and the SMC, we ran the same strategies, but using SITL. By observing the map provided by SITL, we noticed that when a drone reached close to an assigned point it would be circling around it not being able to visit it. Such flaw was not noticed using the discrete SA's physical model as the drones were moving discretely from one grid point to the next. In SITL, where drones are not guaranteed to be located at discrete points, the same actions might cause a drone to overshoot a target point. Then, continuing at the same speed it tries to turn and correct, which can result in circling around the point and never reaching it.

Therefore, we needed to modify both flight strategies: whenever a drone is close to a point that it is attempting to visit, it should reduce its speed in order to allow it to make a more careful approach and ultimately be able to visit the point.

The downside of using SITL is that while one simulation using Maude only took seconds, one simulation using SITL takes time similar to the actual flight of drones. (It is possible to increase speed up to be 3 to 4 times faster than actual flight, but simulations still take some minutes.)

3.4   Soft Agents, SITL and SMC

Finally, it is possible to use all of $\mathcal{SA}^2$'s components in order to obtain similar results as described in Sect. 3.2, but instead of using the discrete physical model, use the more realistic SITL drone model.

The table in Fig. 6 contains some of the results obtained by using soft agents in combination with the statistical model checker and SITL. We varied wind chance and considered several values for *caution*. The results for each choice of wind chance and caution takes around 900 s, *i.e.*, it is around 110 times slower than using Soft Agents and SMT alone. This is expected as runs take time similar to actual flight.

		Waypoint Strategy (Closest Point Strategy)		
Wind	Caution	Back Home	Minimum Energy	Points Visited
	20	1.3 (2,0)	0.0 (36.1)	8.0 (8.0)
12.5% chance	30	2.0 (2.0)	11.3 (36.1)	8.0 (8.0)
	40	2.0 (2.0)	17.6 (40.3)	8.0 (7.6)
	20	0.6 (1.9)	0.0 (31.1)	8.0 (7.9)
25% chance	30	1.3 (2.0)	0.0 (33.5)	8.0 (7.6)
	40	2.0 (2.0)	18 (36.8)	8.0 (7.1)
	20	0.6 (1.6)	0.0 (8.4)	7.3 (6.3)
50.0% chance	30	1.3 (1.6)	3.0 (5.11)	6.3 (4.9)
	40	1.3 (1.8)	3.6 (14.5)	5.6 (4.5)
	20	0.0 (0.3)	0.0 (0.0)	3.6 (3.2)
62.5% chance	30	0.3 (0.5)	0.0 (0.1)	2.0 (3.0)
	40	0.6 (0.8)	0.0 (2.0)	2.0 (2.6)

Fig. 6. Experiments using Soft Agents, SITL and SMC. $\epsilon = \delta = 0.25$.

We observe that, as expected, when increasing the wind chance the performance of the drones deteriorates. While with low chances of wind (12.5%), the drones are able to visit most of the points and safely return home, with higher chances of wind (62.5%) drones visit less than 4 of the 8 assigned points and they fail to return home. Moreover, by increasing the caution level, more drones are able to return to home with higher energy levels, but then the number of visited points reduce.

When comparing the two strategies, in scenarios with less wind the Waypoint Strategy seems to perform better than the Closest Point Strategy in terms of visited points, but at the expense of drones using more energy, even reaching dangerously low levels. This is also reflected in the number of drones that are able to return back home, especially when there is a greater wind chance. On the other hand, the Closest Point Strategy seems more conservative in terms of energy consumption, accomplishing in many cases the task of visiting all eight points and still having high level of energy (above 30%) at the end. This is also reflected in the number of drones returning home.

Given these results, specifiers can further tune the specified strategies. For example, one could set the Closest Point Strategy to be less conservative by tuning the "Energy Concern" as it seems over-conservative.

4 Related Work

Formal executable models can provide valuable tools for exploring system designs, testing ideas, and verifying aspects of a systems expected behavior. Executable models are often cheaper and faster to build and experiment with than physical models, especially in early stages as ideas are developing. For example, [8,9] illustrates the value of using formal executable models in the process of designing and deploying network defenses.

The notion of soft agent system is similar to the notion of *ensemble* that emerged from the Interlink project [12] and that has been a central theme of the ASCENS (Autonomic Service-Component Ensembles) project [2]. In [13] a mathematical system model for ensembles is presented. Similar to soft agents, the mathematical model treats both cyber and physical aspects of a system. A notion of fitness is defined that supports reasoning about level of satisfaction. Adaptability is also treated. While the soft agent framework provides an executable model, the ensembles system model is denotational.

A closely related area is work on Collective Adaptive Systems (CAS) [16]. CAS consist of a large number of spatially distributed heterogeneous entities with decentralized control and varying degrees of complex autonomous behavior that may be competing for shared resources, even when collaborating to reach common goals. CARMA (Collective Adaptive Resource-sharing Markovian Agents) [25] is a language and tool set for modeling CAS. CARMA complements the soft agent framework, focusing on quantitative analysis by simulation, and abstracting from details of agent behavior specification.

XTune [19–21] is a framework for designing, analyzing, testing and deploying cross-layer optimization policies. The goal is to find robustly optimal solutions to constraints, possibly conflicting, representing concerns/objectives of different system components. The framework supports analysis of design tradeoffs by a combination of formal methods, simulation, and testing in deployed systems. Formal specifications are analyzed using statistical model checking and statistical quantitative analysis, to determine the impact of resource management policies for achieving desired end-to-end timing/QoS properties. XTune has been applied to the adaptive provisioning of resource-limited distributed real-time systems using a multi-mode multimedia case study.

The Real-Time Maude tool [29,30] has been integrated into the Ptolemy II Discrete Event (DE) modeling system [3]. Real-Time Maude models are automatically synthesized from Ptolemy II design models, enabling Real-Time Maude verification of the synthesized model within Ptolemy II. This enables a model-engineering process that combines the convenience of Ptolemy II DE modeling and simulation with formal verification in Real-Time Maude. Formal verification of Ptolemy II models has been illustrated with several case studies [3].

In our previous work [15,34,35] we considered an ideal (symbolic) model without uncertainties. We introduced and studied a number of purely symbolic problems, such the complexity of the Reachability and Survivability Problems.

Recently [4], we also studied using Ptolemy instead of the soft agent model in conjunction with SITL for analysing flight strategies for visiting a set of points. We did not consider in that work the use of statistical model checking algorithms, but only analyse systems using simulations.

5   Conclusions

This paper introduces $\mathcal{SA}^2$ a framework for analysing drone flight strategies. Drones are specified in the soft agent framework, allowing the drone physics to be modeled logically or using a simulation engine such as ArduPilot/SITL (or simply SITL). $\mathcal{SA}^2$ allows users to carry out a number of analyses, such as symbolic model checking, simulation, and statistical model checking to explore behavior of different flight strategies, identify limitations and improve designs.

There are a number of directions for future work that we are investigating. Until now our system only supports SITL copters. It is possible, however, to support other types of drones, such as SITL airplanes or rovers. It is possible in principle to use other simulators to model other types of vehicles. We plan to carry out experiments using more powerful hardware to analyse larger scenarios using more realistic flight strategies. We are also interested in analyzing scenarios that require communication and co-operation/coordination among different drones, for example to carry out multi-step tasks or for fault tolerance. Furthermore, we would like to go a step further and investigate how our analyses correspond to the results obtained by using drones on the field. Finally, we are also investigating malicious environments with faulty sensors or where intruders try to trick drones, e.g., to think they visited some point, but they actually did not.

Acknowledgments. Nigam was partially supported by Capes and CNPq. This work has been partially developed under contracting of Diehl Aerospace GmbH and Airbus Defense GmbH. Talcott and Mason were partially supported by ONR grant N00014-15-1-2202. Nigam and Talcott were partially supported by Capes Science without Borders grant 88881.030357/2013-01.

References

1. Arduplane, arducopter, ardurover. https://github.com/ArduPilot/ardupilot
2. Ascens: Autonomic service-component ensembles. http://www.ascens-ist.eu
3. Bae, K., Ölveczky, P.C., Feng, T.H., Lee, E.A., Tripakis, S.: Verifying hierarchical ptolemy II discrete-event models using real-time maude. Sci. Comput. Program. **77**(12), 1235–1271 (2012)
4. Barros, J., Brito, A., Oliveira, T., Nigam, V.: A framework for the analysis of UAV strategies using co-simulation. In: SBESC (2016)
5. Bistarelli, S., Montanari, U., Rossi, F.: Semiring-based constraint satisfaction and optimization. J. ACM **44**(2), 201–236 (1997)
6. Why BNSF railway is using drones to inspect thousands of miles of rail lines. http://fortune.com/2015/05/29/bnsf-drone-program/
7. Clavel, M., Durán, F., Eker, S., Lincoln, P., Martí-Oliet, N., Meseguer, J., Talcott, C.: All About Maude: A High-Performance Logical Framework. Springer, Heidelberg (2007). https://doi.org/10.1007/978-3-540-71999-1
8. Dantas, Y.G., Lemos, M.O.O., Fonseca, I.E., Nigam, V.: Formal specification and verification of a selective defense for TDoS attacks. In: Lucanu, D. (ed.) WRLA 2016. LNCS, vol. 9942, pp. 82–97. Springer, Cham (2016). https://doi.org/10.1007/978-3-319-44802-2_5
9. Dantas, Y.G., Nigam, V., Fonseca, I.E.: A selective defense for application layer DDos attacks. In: JISIC (2014)
10. Das, J., Cross, G., Qu, A.M.C., Tokekar, P., Mulgaonkar, Y., Kumar, V.: Devices, systems, and methods for automated monitoring enabling precision agriculture. In: CASE (2015)
11. Autonomous taxi drones. https://www.forbes.com/sites/parmyolson/2017/02/14/dubai-autonomous-taxi-drones-ehang/#54543d934702
12. Hölzl, M., Rauschmayer, A., Wirsing, M.: Engineering of software-intensive systems. In: Software-Intensive Systems and New Computing Paradigms (2008)
13. Hölzl, M., Wirsing, M.: Towards a system model for ensembles. In: Agha, G., Danvy, O., Meseguer, J. (eds.) Formal Modeling: Actors, Open Systems, Biological Systems. LNCS, vol. 7000, pp. 241–261. Springer, Heidelberg (2011). https://doi.org/10.1007/978-3-642-24933-4_12
14. The JSBSim flight dynamics model. http://www.jsbsim.org
15. Kanovich, M., Ban Kirigin, T., Nigam, V., Scedrov, A., Talcott, C.: Timed multiset rewriting and the verification of time-sensitive distributed systems. In: Fränzle, M., Markey, N. (eds.) FORMATS 2016. LNCS, vol. 9884, pp. 228–244. Springer, Cham (2016). https://doi.org/10.1007/978-3-319-44878-7_14
16. Kernbach, S., Schmickl, T., Timmis, J.: Collective adaptive systems: challenges beyond evolvability. In: Fundamentals of Collective Adaptive Systems. European Commission (2009)
17. Networked cyber physical systems. http://ncps.csl.sri.com
18. Kim, M., Stehr, M.-O., Kim, J., Ha, S.: An application framework for loosely coupled networked cyber-physical systems. In: EUC (2010)
19. Kim, M., Stehr, M.-O., Talcott, C., Dutt, N., Venkatasubramanian, N.: Combining formal verification with observed system execution behavior to tune system parameters. In: Raskin, J.-F., Thiagarajan, P.S. (eds.) FORMATS 2007. LNCS, vol. 4763, pp. 257–273. Springer, Heidelberg (2007). https://doi.org/10.1007/978-3-540-75454-1_19

20. Kim, M., Stehr, M.-O., Talcott, C., Dutt, N., Venkatasubramanian, N.: A probabilistic formal analysis approach to cross layer optimization in distributed embedded systems. In: Bonsangue, M.M., Johnsen, E.B. (eds.) FMOODS 2007. LNCS, vol. 4468, pp. 285–300. Springer, Heidelberg (2007). https://doi.org/10.1007/978-3-540-72952-5_18

21. Kim, M., Stehr, M.-O., Talcott, C., Dutt, N., Venkatasubramanian, N.: XTune: a formal methodology for cross-layer tuning of mobile embedded systems. Trans. Embed. Comput. Syst. (2011)

22. Knightscope. http://www.knightscope.com

23. Lassaigne, R., Peyronnet, S.: Probabilistic verification and approximation schemes. Ann. Pure Appl. Log. **152**(1–3), 122–131 (2008)

24. Liquid robotics. http://liquidr.com

25. Loreti, M., Hillston, J.: Modelling and analysis of collective adaptive systems with CARMA and its tools. In: Bernardo, M., De Nicola, R., Hillston, J. (eds.) SFM 2016. LNCS, vol. 9700, pp. 83–119. Springer, Cham (2016). https://doi.org/10.1007/978-3-319-34096-8_4

26. Mason, I.A., Talcott, C.L.: IOP: the interoperability platform and IMaude: an interactive extension of maude. In: WRLA 2004 (2004)

27. MAVLink micro air vehicle marshalling/communication library. https://github.com/ArduPilot/mavlink.git

28. Nigam, V., Talcott, C., Aires Urquiza, A.: Towards the automated verification of cyber-physical security protocols: bounding the number of timed intruders. In: Askoxylakis, I., Ioannidis, S., Katsikas, S., Meadows, C. (eds.) ESORICS 2016. LNCS, vol. 9879, pp. 450–470. Springer, Cham (2016). https://doi.org/10.1007/978-3-319-45741-3_23

29. Ölveczky, P.C., Meseguer, J.: Abstraction and completeness for real-time maude. In: WRLA (2007)

30. Ölveczky, P.C., Meseguer, J.: Semantics and pragmatics of real-time maude. High.-Order Symb. Comput. **20**(1–2), 161–196 (2007)

31. Inventory robotics. http://www.pinc.com/inventory-robotics-cycle-counting-drones

32. Sen, K., Viswanathan, M., Agha, G.A.: VESTA: a statistical model-checker and analyzer for probabilistic systems. In: QEST (2005)

33. SITL (2016). http://python.dronekit.io/about/index.html

34. Talcott, C., Nigam, V., Arbab, F., Kappé, T.: Formal specification and analysis of robust adaptive distributed cyber-physical systems. In: Bernardo, M., De Nicola, R., Hillston, J. (eds.) SFM 2016. LNCS, vol. 9700, pp. 1–35. Springer, Cham (2016). https://doi.org/10.1007/978-3-319-34096-8_1

35. Talcott, C., Arbab, F., Yadav, M.: Soft agents: exploring soft constraints to model robust adaptive distributed cyber-physical agent systems. In: De Nicola, R., Hennicker, R. (eds.) Software, Services, and Systems. LNCS, vol. 8950, pp. 273–290. Springer, Cham (2015). https://doi.org/10.1007/978-3-319-15545-6_18

36. Drone swarms: The buzz of the future. https://www.vlab.org/events/drone-swarms/

Co-simulation of Semi-autonomous Systems: The Line Follower Robot Case Study

Maurizio Palmieri[1,2], Cinzia Bernardeschi[2], and Paolo Masci[3(✉)]

[1] Dipartimento di Ingegneria dell'Informazione, University of Florence,
Florence, Italy
[2] Dipartimento di Ingegneria dell'Informazione, University of Pisa, Pisa, Italy
[3] HASLab/INESC TEC, Universidade do Minho, Braga, Portugal
paolo.masci@inesctec.pt

Abstract. Semi-autonomous systems are capable of sensing their environment and perform their tasks autonomously, but they may also be supervised by humans. The shared manual/automatic control makes the dynamics of such systems more complex, and undesirable and hardly predictable behaviours can arise from human-machine interaction. When these systems are used in critical applications, such as autonomous driving or robotic surgery, the identification of conditions that may lead the system to violate safety requirements is of main concern, since people actually entrust their life on them. In this paper, we extend an FMI-based co-simulation framework for cyber-physical systems with the possibility of modelling semi-autonomous robots. Co-simulation can be used to gain more insights on the system under analysis at early stages of system development, and to highlight the impact of human interaction on safety. This approach is applied to the Line Follower Robot case study, available in the INTO-CPS project.

1 Introduction

Cyber-Physical Systems (CPS) are complex physical systems operated by digital controllers. The physical part (the *plant*) may be an entirely engineered system (e.g., a chemical plant) as in traditional control system, but can also be a natural system (e.g., a patient) as in medical applications. From the computational point of view, the existence of digital and physical components requires the use of different kinds of mathematical formalisms, e.g., discrete logic-based models for controllers, and continuous models based on differential equations for plants. In addition, the physical parts of a same CPS may need to be modelled with different languages and tools. Because of this, an efficient way of simulating CPS is by using co-simulation frameworks, which enable integrated simulation of heterogeneous models using multiple tools.

Semi-autonomous systems are a particular kind of CPS. In these systems, the user interface of the system has an important role, as it allows an operator to interact with the system, e.g., to override its autonomous behaviour when

A. Cerone and M. Roveri (Eds.): SEFM 2017 Workshops, LNCS 10729, pp. 423–437, 2018.
https://doi.org/10.1007/978-3-319-74781-1_29

desired or necessary. A common example is a car's cruise control that automatically adjusts the speed of the car. The driver can take over control at any time just by pressing either the brake or the accelerator pedal. Another example is robotic-assisted surgery, where a surgeon console registers the hand's gestures of a surgeon and translates them into micro-movement of robotic arms.

Simulation and prototyping are important technologies for early detection of design problems in user interfaces of CPS, as they facilitate the discussion of scenarios and design aspects in a multi-disciplinary team of developers, human factors specialists, and domain experts. In critical application domains such as automotive and healthcare, however, simulation and prototyping alone may not be sufficient to ensure that the system meets the safety levels required by regulatory frameworks—they can be used to explore only a finite set of scenarios and user input sequences. Formal verification technologies can be used to extend simulation results and reach the necessary safety level. They are based on mathematical proofs, and allow developers to gain additional confidence that a system meets given safety requirements. It is therefore desirable to integrate as much as possible formal verification with simulation and prototyping frameworks, to make the overall development process more efficient.

In our previous work [2], we developed a CPS co-simulation framework that integrates the Prototype Verification System (PVS) [24] and Simulink[1]. PVS is used for modelling, simulation, and verification of critical CPS software components. Simulink is used for modeling and simulation of continuous aspects of the CPS. Ad-hoc APIs were used to execute two models in lockstep and for time synchronization. In the present work, we enhance this PVS-based co-simulation framework with a Functional Mockup Interface (FMI), a tool-independent co-simulation interface that is becoming a de-facto industry standard.

Contribution. This paper reports on our work on developing an FMI-compliant interface for the Prototype Verification System (PVS) [24] that includes the capability of a GUI and enables human-in-the-loop co-simulation. An example based on a semi-autonomous vehicle is used to demonstrate the utility and capabilities of the developed interface. A controller is modelled and verified in PVS; the PVSio-web [19] toolkit is then used to connect the verified PVS model with a realistic interactive dashboard prototype; a co-simulation is then carried out by using the developed FMI interface to integrate the PVS model and dashboard with the rest of the system components (vehicle's mechanics, sensors, and environment) simulated with other tools.

Structure. Section 2 presents related work on simulation and verification of CPS. Section 3 illustrates background concepts and tools used in this work. Sections 4 and 5 present the main contributions of this work, i.e., the development of an FMI-compliant interface for PVS, and an example application based on a semi-autonomous system. Section 6 concludes the paper.

---

[1] http://www.mathworks.com/products/simulink.

2   Related Work

In [7], an approach is presented, based on expressing the discrete-event model in the Vienna Development Method (VDM) [8] and the continuous-time model in the Bond-Graph notation [14]. The simulation environment Overture [16] for VDM and the simulation environment 20-sim [5] for Bond-Graphs are integrated into the Crescendo tool [17]. The information needed to co-ordinate the two models, including shared parameters, variables, and events are identified in a contract listing. Synchronization and data exchange is managed by a co-simulation engine.

In [23], the ForSyDe modelling framework [25] is extended to support heterogeneous co-simulation. A ForSyDe model is a hierarchical set of processes, where each process may belong to a Model of Computation (MoC) [18]. A MoC represents the underlying time, synchronization, and communication model assumed by a process. The framework enables processes with different MoCs to co-execute. This framework has been extended with wrapper processes interacting with external simulators or hardware components.

The INTO-CPS project [13] created an integrated tool chain for comprehensive Model-Based Design of CPS based on the Functional Mockup Interface (FMI) standard [3,4]. The core of INTO-CPS is an FMI-compliant Co-simulation Orchestration Engine that enables a coordinated simulation of heterogeneous models in a distributed environment. Even if many challenges are still open, such as establishing the correctness of the co-simulation of mix continuous and discrete behaviour [6], there are efforts to apply this standard in industry.

Other works address the problem of simulating CPS by using only one specification formalism for both continuous and discrete systems (like for example, HybridSim [27]) or extend original languages to new features, for example, in [12,26] the integration of MATLab/Simulink with UML is proposed. For a recent survey of co-simulation technologies for cyber-physical systems, readers may refer to [10].

A complementary approach to the analysis of CPS is formal verification. In this respect, KeYmaera [9] is a theorem prover for differential dynamic logic. It has been applied successfully for proving correctness of automotive, avionics and medical CPS. Our work differs from KeYmaera in that we aim to integrate formal verification by theorem proving in PVS (see for example [1]) with the possibility of performing co-simulation of the system. Our aim is ultimately to facilitate the introduction of formal verification technologies in development processes that routinely use simulation and prototyping.

3   Background

3.1   The Functional Mockup Interface

The Functional Mockup Interface (FMI) [3,4] is a tool-independent standard to support both model exchange and co-simulation of dynamic models. Co-simulation is performed by a number of *Functional Mockup Units* (FMUs), each responsible for simulating a single sub-model. An FMU contains a sub-model represented in the native formalism of the tool that created it, and the information or tools needed for its execution. That is, an FMU may carry a whole simulation environment, or just information needed by an FMI-compliant host environment to simulate the model contained in the FMU. An FMI-compliant host environment provides a *master* program that communicates with the FMUs acting as *slaves*. The FMI defines a standard API for the FMUs and standard methods of deployment for them.

The FMU's APIs include functions called at the initialization phase, functions to trigger one simulation step (`fmi2DoStep()`), and functions to exchange data. The latter have a standard signature `fmi2Get<`*TYPE*`>` and `fmi2Set<`*TYPE*`>`, where `<`*TYPE*`>` is a concrete type name, e.g., *Integer* or *Real*. These functions are used to transmit data from and to the FMUs, respectively. Other two functions, `fmi2Termminate` and `fmi2FreeInstance`, can be used to terminate simulation and release resources. Figure 1 shows the communication pattern for these functions.

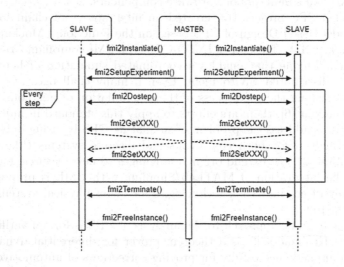

Fig. 1. FMI communication schema.

3.2   INTO-CPS

INTO-CPS [15] is a EU-funded project that is finalizing the development of an integrated tool-chain for model-based design of CPS based on FMI-compliant co-simulation. The tool-chain currently supports simulation of models produced by various tools, including OpenModelica, 20-sim, and Overture. SysML is used to specify the overall architecture of the system to be simulated, by representing the interconnections among the sub-models.

In this work, we embrace the INTO-CPS tool-chain and a case study developed in the INTO-CPS project (the Line Follower Robot[2]), and use them to

---

[2] https://github.com/into-cps/case-study_line_follower_robot

demonstrate the FMI extensions we have developed for PVS (additional details on the case study are in Sect. 5).

3.3   The Prototype Verification System (PVS)

The Prototype Verification System (PVS) [24] is an interactive theorem proving environment for higher-order logic. The PVS specification language provides basic types, such as Booleans, naturals, integers, reals, and others, and type constructors to define more complex data-types (e.g., *records*) and *subtypes*. The mathematical properties of each type are defined axiomatically in a set of fundamental theories, called the *prelude*. New types are declared using the TYPE keyword. A *record* type is a tuple whose elements are referred to by their respective *field* name. For example, given the declarations:

```
Wheels: TYPE = [# left: real, right: real #]
axle: Wheels = (# left := 1.0, right := 0.5 #)
```

the expressions left(axle) and right(axle) denote the speeds of the left and right wheels of axle, respectively. Equivalent notations are axle'left and axle'right. The *override* expression WITH [..] can be used for in-line redefinition of record field values. For example, for the declarations above, the expression axle WITH [left := -1.0] denotes the record value (# left := -1.0, right := 0.5 #). An example PVS subtype is the following:

```
Speed: TYPE = { x: real | x >= -1 AND x <= 1 }
```

which defines type Speed as a subtype of real numbers in the interval $[-1, 1]$. Subtypes can be used in function definitions to define safety constraints and limits that shall be checked. We will use these feature in Sect. 5, to verify that, e.g., the velocity commanded by the controller does never exceed the robot's mechanical specifications.

3.4   PVSio and PVSio-Web

PVSio [22] is a ground evaluator that computes the value of ground (variable-free) expressions. The PVSio evaluator acts as an interactive interpreter for the logic language of PVS, and can be used by developers to simulate a PVS model. At the PVSio prompt, the user types a ground PVS expression (which is equivalent to a function call of imperative languages) and PVSio returns the result of the evaluation. For example, if a PVS theory contains the following function definition

```
compute_velocity(v:real, a:real, t:real): real = v + a*t
```

then its value for a particular triple of arguments can be computed with the following function application: compute_velocity(3.5, 1.8, 3.0);

PVSio-web [19] is an open source toolkit that extends PVSio with functions for creating and executing realistic user interface prototypes based on PVS models. Using PVSio-web, developers can define the visual appearance of the prototype, as well as capture user actions over input widgets, and render feedback on displays and other output widgets on the user interface. These functionalities are used in Sect. 5 to create an interactive dashboard for driving a Line Follower robot.

4 Development of an FMI-Compliant Interface for PVS

We developed an FMI-compliant interface for PVS by creating a C wrapper module that implements the FMI interface and spawns a PVSio process. At the beginning of the co-simulation, the wrapper starts a PVSio instance, loads a given PVS model in PVSio, creates a server module to exchange commands with interactive GUI, and waits for input. In more detail, the wrapper performs the following two actions at each simulation step:

- Translates calls to FMI functions into appropriate commands for PVSio;
- Receives replies from PVSio and stores them into appropriate buffers.

Communication between the wrapper and PVSio relies on standard Unix pipes, and communication between the wrapper and GUI uses the WebSocket[3] protocol. This latter choice allows us to have a loose coupling between the FMU and the GUI, which promotes separation of concerns between the visual appearance of the user interface from its functional behaviour (Model-Controller-View architectural pattern). The overall architecture is summarized in Fig. 2.

4.1 Implementation of the FMU

The FMU module implements four core functions: fmi2Instantiate, which initializes the FMU; fmi2DoStep, which executes a simulation step; and a battery of fmi2Get/fmi2Set functions for data exchange. To use a PVS model in the FMU, the model needs to provide at least two functions: init, that initializes the PVS model to the initial state (where the state is represented using a PVS record type); and step, that performs a simulation step.

The initialization function (fmi2Instantiate) starts the PVSio interpreter, redirects the PVSio standard I/O towards a Unix pipe, invokes the init function of the PVS model, and stores the result of the evaluation in a variable of the FMU. Finally, a WebSocket server necessary for communication with a PVSio-web prototype is created.

The fmi2DoStep function sends PVSio a string encoding a call to the PVS function step. A function argument is included, representing the current state of the system. The result of the evaluation is stored in a variable in the FMU.

---

[3] https://www.websocket.org.

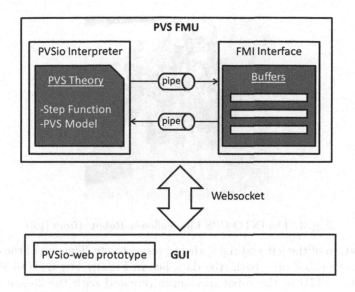

Fig. 2. Architecture of the FMU module for PVS.

4.2   Implementation of the PVSio-Web Prototype

The PVSio-web prototype is a JavaScript module executed in a web browser. The prototype builds on the PVSio-web communication architecture to open a Websocket connection to Websocket server executed in the PVS FMU. A picture is used as a basis to create the visual appearance of the prototype (e.g., to create the remote dashboard controller prototype illustrated in Sect. 5, we used a photo of a joypad and a smartphone—see left side of Fig. 4). Control and display elements in the prototype are created using a library of input and output widgets provided by PVSio-web. Button widgets capture user actions on certain areas of the prototype (e.g., pressing a button) and translate these actions into commands for the FMU. Display widgets are used for rendering visible state attributes of the system, using an appropriate visualization style (e.g., the velocity of a vehicle can be rendered with speedometer gauges). The FMU, in turn, translates these commands into calls to functions defined in the PVS model. State updates are periodically sent by the FMU to the PVSio-web prototype, to keep the user interface updated with the actual system state.

5   Case Study

Our case study is based on the Line Follower Robot example provided by the INTO-CPS European project. In the original example, an autonomous robot (see Fig. 3) has the goal of following a line painted on the ground. The controller of the robot receives the readings from two light sensors placed on the front of the robot, and sends commands to the left and right motors which are in charge

Fig. 3. The INTO-CPS Line Follower Robot (from [13]).

of the rotation of the left and right wheels, respectively. The aim of the controller is to keep the robot on a path (the dark line in Fig. 3). The INTO-CPS project provides the FMU of the robot mechanics (created with the 20-sim tool), the FMU of the sensors (created with 20-sim and OpenModelica), and the FMU of the controller (created with the Overture tool). It also provides a SysML model necessary to link these components.

In the present work, we replaced the original controller of the robot with a more advanced controller developed in PVS. The new controller allows a driver to override the automatic line following control of the robot, and operate the robot manually, using controls on a dashboard. The sensors and the mechanics of the robot are unaltered with respect to the original INTO-CPS example.

The prototype of the dashboard (see left side of Fig. 4) provides a navigation display with the trajectory of the robot, two speedometer gauges to monitor the velocities of the wheels, a speedometer gauge to monitor the velocity of the robot, and various control buttons to allow a driver to *accelerate* or *brake*, change direction of the robot (*turn right*, *turn left*), and change gear (*drive*, *reverse*). There is also a command (*home*) to switch control mode from manual back to automatic. Velocity and trajectory shown on the dashboard mirror sensor data communicated to the dashboard through the FMI interface. The original SysML model has been modified to include these new communication links.

In the following sub-section, a description of the PVS controller and the PVSio-web prototype of the dashboard are presented. The full example, including the PVS theory and the PVSio-web prototype, can be downloaded from our repository on github[4].

5.1 PVS Theory of the New Controller

Theory `advanced_controller` defines the characteristics and functionalities of the new controller. The initial part of the theory defines the structure of the controller state (lines 9–13), and the data-types of the state attributes:

---

[4] https://github.com/PaoloMasci/pvsioweb-fmi-extensions.

```
1  advanced_controller: THEORY BEGIN
2    \%-- type definitions
3    LSR: TYPE = { x: nonneg_real | x <= 255 }
4    LightSensors: TYPE = [# left: LSR, right: LSR #]
5    Speed: TYPE = { x: real | x >= -1 AND x <= 1 }
6    MotorSpeed: TYPE = [# left: Speed, right: Speed #]
7    ControlMode: TYPE = { AUTO, MANUAL }
8    \%-- controller state
9    State: TYPE = [#
10     lightSensors: LightSensors,
11     motorSpeed: MotorSpeed,
12     gear: Gear,
13     cm: ControlMode #]
14   \%-- ...more definitions omitted for brevity
15 END advanced_controller
```

Field `lightSensors` in the state of the controller (line 10 in the snippet above) holds the input values received from the light sensors, ranging from 0 to 255, according to the robot's sensors specifications; `motorSpeed` holds the rotation speed of the robot wheels, ranging from -1 to 1, according to the robot's mechanical specifications; `gear` is an extension used to represent possible gears of a car-like system. It can be `DRIVE` or `REVERSE`; `cm` stores the control mode, which can be either `AUTO` or `MANUAL`.

The `step` function called at every simulation step updates the rotation speed of the left and right motors when `cm` is in mode `AUTO`.

```
1  step(st: State): State =
2    IF cm(st) = AUTO
3    THEN st WITH [
4      motorSpeed := (#
5        left := update_left_motor_speed(st),
6        right := update_right_motor_speed(st)
7      #) ] ELSE st ENDIF
```

Function `update_left_motor_speed` (`update_right_motor_speed`) in the snippet above updates the left (right) motor speed using a simple control algorithm based on a threshold and the current light sensors reading. The same algorithm was also used in the Overture model of original controller of the robot.

```
1  update_left_motor_speed(st: State): Speed =
2    LET ls = lightSensors(st)
3    IN COND ls'right < 150 AND ls'left < 150 -> 0.4,
4            ls'right > 150 AND ls'left < 150 -> 0.5,
5            ls'right < 150 AND ls'left > 150 -> 0.1,
6            ELSE -> motorSpeed(st)'left ENDCOND
```

In the snipped above, the LET-IN construct introduces local definition that can be used in the expressions following IN. The COND-ENDCOND expression is a many-way switch composed of clauses of the form *condition* $\rightarrow$ *expression*, where all conditions must be mutually exclusive and must cover all possible combinations of their truth values (an ELSE clause provides a catch-all). The PVS type checker verifies that these constraints are satisfied.

For each control provided on the dashboard, the PVS theory provides a matching function. For example, the *accelerate* button is associated with the PVS function accelerate, which is defined as follows:

```
1  accelerate(st: State): State = st WITH [
2    cm := MANUAL,
3    motorSpeed := (#
4      left := COND
5        gear(st) = DRIVE
6          -> inc_CW_speed(motorSpeed(st)'left, ACC_STEP),
7        gear(st) = REVERSE
8          -> inc_CCW_speed(motorSpeed(st)'left, ACC_STEP),
9        ENDCOND,
10     right := COND
11       gear(st) = DRIVE
12         -> inc_CCW_speed(motorSpeed(st)'right, ACC_STEP),
13       gear(st) = REVERSE
14         -> inc_CW_speed(motorSpeed(st)'right, ACC_STEP),
15       ENDCOND #)]
```

When function accelerate is executed, cruise control is automatically changed to MANUAL (line 2 in the snippet above). The speed of the robot is increased by updating the rotation speed of the left and right motors of the robot by an acceleration step ACC_STEP. The specific direction of rotation of the motors (clockwise, or counter-clockwise) depends on the *gear* selected by the driver, and on which wheel the motor controls (e.g., to move the robot forward, the left motor needs to rotate clockwise, but the right motor needs to rotate counter-clockwise). When the gear is DRIVE (lines 5–6 and 11–12) the rotation speed of the left and right motors is set to move the robot forward. When the gear is REVERSE (lines 7–8 and 13–14) the rotation speed of the left and right motors is set to move the robot backwards.

For the developed theory, the PVS type-checker automatically generated 22 proof obligations to ensure correct use of types, coverage of conditions, and disjointness of conditions. All proof obligations were automatically verified by the PVS theorem prover in just 0.29 s on a standard laptop (Intel Core i7-5500U, 8 GB RAM). This ensures that the developed model does not have bugs such as division by zero, or logic errors such as erroneous control definitions that overshoot the robot's motors specifications.

5.2   PVSio-Web Prototype of Dashboard

We developed a dashboard prototype in PVSio-web (see Fig. 4) to allow a driver to interact with the PVS controller and, by doing so, operate the robot and monitor its speed and position. The prototype is based on a joypad: directional arrows are used to steer the robot, and a number of buttons can be used to effect

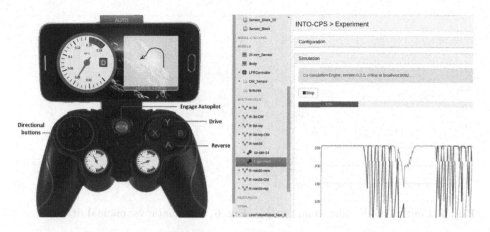

Fig. 4. Screenshot taken during a co-simulation run. The dashboard prototype is on the left. The output of the INTO-CPS co-simulation window is on the right.

actions of the robot. For example, if the robot had a mechanical arm, some of the buttons could be used to move the arm, or if the robot represents a car-like vehicle, as in our case, they can simulate a gear shift control.

The developed dashboard prototype uses directional arrows to control the direction and accelerate/brake. The *home* button at the centre for the joypad can be used to activate automatic control mode. These interactive controls were created by overlaying the picture of the joypad with transparent interactive areas that can detect button presses. Gears can be shifted using the joypad buttons *Y* (drive), and *A* (brake). This is the standard approach used in PVSio-web to create interactive controls.

A smartphone mounted at the top of the joypad is used to render speedometer with the current speed of the robot and the current gear, and a navigation display with the current position and direction of the robot on a map. A frameless display at the top of the smartphone shows the control mode (auto/manual). Two additional gauge displays are placed at the bottom of the joypad, to monitor the current rotation speed of the wheels. All these display elements were created by overlaying the picture of the joypad with digital displays available in the PVSio-web distribution. An external JavaScript library (d3-gauge-plus[5]) is used to render gauges. The navigator display is implemented using HTML5 Scalable Vector Graphics (SVG). The gauge and navigator displays are part of a new domain-specific library for the PVSio-web, which will be released with the next version of the toolkit.

5.3 Results

Several co-simulation runs were performed by connecting the PVS FMU to the INTO-CPS Co-Simulation Engine. All experiments were configured with a fixed

---

[5] https://github.com/gimbo/d3-gauge-plus.

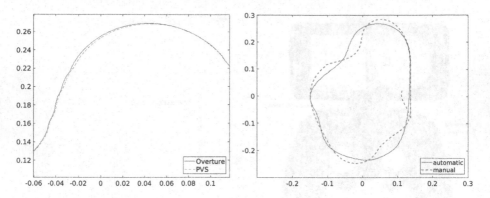

Fig. 5. Control mode validation.   **Fig. 6.** Automatic vs. manual drive.

simulation step of 0.01 s, and a duration of 35 s of simulated time. Figure 4 shows a screen-shot from an ongoing simulation. On the left side, the image shows the joypad prototype displaying the trajectory and speed of the robot. On the right side, the image shows the INTO-CPS application window hosting the co-simulation.

As a first experiment, we checked that the behaviour of the new PVS controller in automatic control mode was the same of that produced by the original Overture controller developed in the INTO-CPS project. As shown in Fig. 5, this check was successful: the trajectory of the robot is identical in the two cases (modulo small differences due to mathematical approximation).

Other experiments were then performed to check that the robot was following the commands given by a driver with the dashboard prototype. In one experiment, we tried to use the manual drive to follow the same path as the automatic controller, obtaining the result in Fig. 6 (manual driving is shown with a dashed line). The plot shows that it is possible to approximately follow the same path. The low accuracy in some sections of the track are mainly due to the relatively high speed used by the driver to move the robot, which did not allow an accurate control of the robot's direction.

Finally, experiments were also performed to check the robot behaviour when switching control mode from automatic to manual, and vice-versa. Switching from manual to automatic mode highlighted some interesting scenarios where the robot had an unexpected behaviour. For example, the robot was sometimes overshooting the path so much that a U-turn was then necessary to get back on track (see Fig. 7). This happened, e.g., when the control of the robot was initially set to *manual*, the driver accelerated the robot to its maximum speed, and then switched to automatic control mode. When switching from manual to automatic control mode, the robot keeps the same speed set by the driver until a direction adjustment is needed. Because of this, when the robot encounters the line painted on the track, the speed is too high and the directional change issued by the controller is not enough to perform the necessary sharp turn.

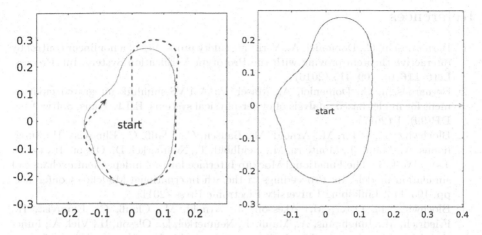

Fig. 7. U-turn due to high speed.   **Fig. 8.** Missed turn.

Another example abnormal situation is shown in Fig. 8, where the robot under automatic control mode does not perform the directional change necessary to bring the robot on track. This seems to be a boundary case of the cruise control algorithm: when the robot reaches the path perpendicularly, both sensors return the same value, and the control algorithm decides not to turn.

6 Conclusions

We have presented the implementation of the FMI-compliant interface for the PVS system. This allows us to use PVS in FMI-based frameworks, such as the INTO-CPS tool-chain. An example based on a semi-autonomous vehicle was developed. The example builds on the Line Follower Robot case study of the INTO-CPS project. We extended the example by developing a new controller that allows an operator to drive manually the robot using a joypad-like controller. The logic of operation of the new controller is entirely specified in PVS, which allows the use of the PVS theorem prover to verify use-related safety properties of the human-machine interface of the system, e.g., consistency of response to user actions, visibility of operating modes, and predictability of response to user commands (see also [11, 20, 21]).

Acknowledgments. We would like to thank the INTO-CPS team for their support with the INTO-CPS tool-chain and the Line Follower Robot example. Paolo Masci's work is financed by the ERDF (European Regional Development Fund) through the Operational Programme for Competitiveness and Internationalisation – COMPETE 2020 Programme, within the project POCI-01-0145-FEDER-006961, and by National Funds through the Portuguese funding agency, FCT (Fundação para a Ciência e a Tecnologia) as part of the project UID/EEA/50014/2013.

References

1. Bernardeschi, C., Domenici, A.: Verifying safety properties of a nonlinear control by interactive theorem proving with the Prototype Verification System. Inf. Process. Lett. **116**(6), 409–415 (2016)
2. Bernardeschi, C., Domenici, A., Masci, P.: A PVS-simulink integrated environment for model-based analysis of cyber-physical systems. IEEE Trans. Softw. Eng. **PP**(99), 1 (2017)
3. Blochwitz, T., Otter, M., Arnold, M., Bausch, C., Clauß, C., Elmqvist, H., Junghanns, A., Mauß, J., Monteiro, M., Neidhold, T., Neumerkel, D., Olsson, H., Peetz, J.-V., Wolf, S.: The Functional Mockup Interface for tool independent exchange of simulation models. In: Proceedings of the 8th International Modelica Conference, pp. 105–114. Linköping University Electronic Press (2011)
4. Blochwitz, T., Otter, M., Åkesson, J., Arnold, M., Clauß, C., Elmqvist, H., Friedrich, M., Junghanns, A., Mauß, J., Neumerkel, D., Olsson, H., Viel, A.: Functional Mockup Interface 2.0: the standard for tool independent exchange of simulation models. In: Proceedings of the 9th International Modelica Conference, pp. 173–184. The Modelica Association (2012)
5. Broenink, J.F.: Modelling, simulation and analysis with 20-sim. J. A **38**(3), 22–25 (1997)
6. Cremona, F., Lohstroh, M., Broman, D., Tripakis, S., Lee, E.A., Masin, M.: Hybrid co-simulation: it's about time. Technical report UCB/EECS-2017-6, University of California, Berkeley, April 2017
7. Fitzgerald, J., Larsen, P.G., Pierce, K., Verhoef, M., Wolff, S.: Collaborative modelling and co-simulation in the development of dependable embedded systems. In: Méry, D., Merz, S. (eds.) IFM 2010. LNCS, vol. 6396, pp. 12–26. Springer, Heidelberg (2010). https://doi.org/10.1007/978-3-642-16265-7_2
8. Fitzgerald, J.S., Larsen, P.G., Verhoef, M.: Vienna Development Method. Wiley, Hoboken (2007)
9. Franchetti, F., Low, T.M., Mitsch, S., Mendoza, J.P., Gui, L., Phaosawasdi, A., Padua, D., Kar, S., Moura, J.M.F., Franusich, M., Johnson, J., Platzer, A., Veloso, M.M.: High-assurance spiral: end-to-end guarantees for robot and car control. IEEE Control Syst. **37**(2), 82–103 (2017)
10. Gomes, C., Thule, C., Broman, D., Larsen, P.G., Vangheluwe, H.: Co-simulation: state of the art. arXiv:1702.00686 (2017)
11. Harrison, M.D., Masci, P., Campos, J.C., Curzon, P.: Verification of user interface software: the example of use-related safety requirements and programmable medical devices. IEEE Trans. Hum.-Mach. Syst. (2017, to appear)
12. Hooman, J., Mulyar, N., Posta, L.: Coupling simulink and UML models. In: Schnieder, B., Tarnai, G. (eds.) Proceedings of Symposium FORMS/FORMATS, Formal Methods for Automation and Safety in Railway and Automotive Systems, pp. 304–311 (2004)
13. INTO-CPS: Integrated Tool Chain for Model-based Design of Cyber-Physical Systems®, Horizon H2020 project. Grant #644047 (2015)
14. Karnopp, D., Rosenberg, R.: Analysis and Simulation of Multiport Systems; the Bond Graph Approach to Physical System Dynamics. M.I.T. Press, Cambridge (1968)

15. Larsen, P.G., Fitzgerald, J., Woodcock, J., Fritzson, P., Brauer, J., Kleijn, C., Lecomte, T., Pfeil, M., Green, O., Basagiannis, S., Sadovykh, A.: Integrated tool chain for model-based design of cyber-physical systems: the INTO-CPS project. In: 2016 2nd International Workshop on Modelling, Analysis, and Control of Complex CPS (CPS Data), pp. 1–6 (2016)
16. Larsen, P.G., Battle, N., Ferreira, M., Fitzgerald, J., Lausdahl, K., Verhoef, M.: The overture initiative integrating tools for VDM. SIGSOFT Softw. Eng. Notes 35(1), 1–6 (2010)
17. Larsen, P.G., Gamble, C., Pierce, K., Ribeiro, A., Lausdahl, K.: Support for co-modelling and co-simulation: the Crescendo tool. In: Fitzgerald, J., Larsen, P.G., Verhoef, M. (eds.) Collaborative Design for Embedded Systems, pp. 97–114. Springer, Heidelberg (2014). https://doi.org/10.1007/978-3-642-54118-6_5
18. Lee, E.A., Sangiovanni-Vincentelli, A.: A framework for comparing models of computation. IEEE Trans. Comput.-Aided Des. Integr. Circuits Syst. 17(12), 1217–1229 (1998)
19. Masci, P., Oladimeji, P., Zhang, Y., Jones, P., Curzon, P., Thimbleby, H.: PVSioweb 2.0: joining PVS to HCI. In: Kroening, D., Păsăreanu, C.S. (eds.) CAV 2015. LNCS, vol. 9206, pp. 470–478. Springer, Cham (2015). https://doi.org/10.1007/978-3-319-21690-4_30
20. Masci, P., Rukšenas, R., Oladimeji, P., Cauchi, A., Gimblett, A., Li, Y., Curzon, P., Thimbleby, H.: The benefits of formalising design guidelines: a case study on the predictability of drug infusion pumps. Innov. Syst. Softw. Eng. 11(2), 73–93 (2015)
21. Masci, P., Zhang, Y., Jones, P., Curzon, P., Thimbleby, H.: Formal verification of medical device user interfaces using PVS. In: Gnesi, S., Rensink, A. (eds.) FASE 2014. LNCS, vol. 8411, pp. 200–214. Springer, Heidelberg (2014). https://doi.org/10.1007/978-3-642-54804-8_14
22. Muñoz, C., Rapid prototyping in PVS. Technical report NIA 2003–03, NASA/CR-2003-212418, National Institute of Aerospace, Hampton, VA, USA (2003)
23. Attarzadeh Niaki, S.H., Sander, I.: Co-simulation of embedded systems in a heterogeneous MoC-based modeling framework. In: 2011 6th IEEE International Symposium on Industrial and Embedded Systems, pp. 238–247, June 2011
24. Owre, S., Rushby, J.M., Shankar, N.: PVS: a prototype verification system. In: Kapur, D. (ed.) CADE 1992. LNCS, vol. 607, pp. 748–752. Springer, Heidelberg (1992). https://doi.org/10.1007/3-540-55602-8_217
25. Sander, I., Jantsch, A.: System modeling and transformational design refinement in ForSyDe. IEEE Trans. Comput.-Aided Des. Integr. Circuits Syst. 23(1), 17–32 (2004)
26. Sjöstedt, C.-J., Törngren, M., Shi, J., Chen, D.-J., Ahlsten, V.: Mapping simulink to UML in the design of embedded systems: investigating scenarios and transformations. In: OMER4 Post-proceedings, pp. 137–160 (2008). QC 20100810
27. Wang, B., Baras, J.S.: HybridSim: a modeling and co-simulation toolchain for cyber-physical systems. In: 2013 IEEE/ACM 17th International Symposium on Distributed Simulation and Real Time Applications (DS-RT), pp. 33–40 (2013)

A Framework for the Co-simulation of Engine Controls and Task Scheduling

Paolo Pazzaglia$^{(\boxtimes)}$, Marco Di Natale, Giorgio Buttazzo, and Matteo Secchiari

Scuola Superiore Sant'Anna, Pisa, Italy
{paolo.pazzaglia,marco.dinatale,giorgio.buttazzo}@sssup.it,
msecchiari@gmail.com

Abstract. To evaluate the impact of scheduling latency and task design on the performance of engine control applications, we developed a co-simulation framework, based on Simulink and an extension of the T-Res scheduling simulator tool. The objective of the research and the tool development is to provide a better characterization of the very popular problem of scheduling and analysis of Adaptive Variable Rate Tasks (AVR) in engine control. The purpose of the tool is to go beyond the simplistic model that assumes hard deadlines for all tasks and to study the impact of scheduling decisions (and possibly missed deadlines) with respect to the functional implementations of the control algorithms and the engine performance. The developments include a co-simulation framework and a set of models for the engine components in order to evaluate the performance with respect to fuel efficiency, consumption, soot and NOx emissions.

1 Introduction

The study of the schedulability conditions for engine control tasks (denominated as adaptive variable rate - AVR [1]) has become popular in the real-time research community because of the novel nature of the problem, which applies to the concept of Cyber-physical systems; the special activation conditions that apply to some of the system tasks and the adaptive nature of the computations.

Several engine control tasks are not periodic or sporadic, but are activated by the rotation of the engine crankshaft (a parameter of the physical controlled system). In addition, to compensate for the increased CPU load at high rotation speeds (and more frequent activation times), the code implementation of these tasks is defined in such a way that at given speed boundaries, the implementation is simplified and the execution time is reduced. A typical engine control application consists of time-driven periodic tasks with fixed periods, typically between a few milliseconds and 100 ms (see [2], p. 152), and angular tasks triggered at specific crankshaft angles.

The activation rate of such angular tasks varies with the engine speed (variable-rate tasks). For example, for speeds from 500 to 6500 revolutions per minute (RPM), the interarrival times of the angular tasks range from about 10 to 120 ms (assuming a single activation per cycle).

© Springer International Publishing AG 2018
A. Cerone and M. Roveri (Eds.): SEFM 2017 Workshops, LNCS 10729, pp. 438–452, 2018.
https://doi.org/10.1007/978-3-319-74781-1_30

With respect to the set of activation instants, the dependency from a physical phenomenon characterizes this problem as truly belonging to the class of problems in cyber-physical systems (CPS). However, in many papers the dependency of the timing and scheduling problem from the physics of the controlled system is restricted to the set of activation events and every other concern is hidden under the typical assumption of hard deadlines.

In reality, this problem (as many others) is representative of a class of control systems in which deadlines can be missed without catastrophic consequences, and the problem should actually be defined as a design optimization, where the objective is to select the controls implementations and the scheduling policy in such a way that a set of engine performance functions are optimized (including power, emissions, noise, pollution). These performance functions depend in complex ways from timing parameters, such as jitter and latency. Informally, the objective of the scheduler is not to miss too many deadlines or produce actuation signals that are too much delayed.

Formally, the problem is quite complex and extremely unlikely to be solved in a simple, closed analytical form or even with a general procedure for expressing the dependency of the performance from scheduling. This is the reason for the investigation of alternative approaches that are based on the simulation of the three system components in a joint environment:

- A model of the engine combustion process (the physical system or plant)
- A model of the engine controls
- A model of the task configuration and execution and of the scheduler.

In this work we describe the framework that was developed for this task; the components developed for modeling the AVR tasks and the engine subsystems of interest; and the early results obtained from simulations. This framework significantly improves our previous work [3], especially in the combustion modeling and control parts. The co-simulation framework is based on the popular Simulink tool from the Mathworks and a simulator of real-time scheduling and task execution for single-and multicore platforms: the T-Res framework.

In the following sections, the problem is introduced (in Sect. 2). Then, in Sect. 3 we outline the main components and functionality of the framework, and in Sect. 4 we briefly introduce the T-Res framework. The extensions to the TRes custom components are outlined in Sect. 5. The Engine model and controller components are described in Sect. 6. The preliminary analysis results are in Sect. 7, and the related work is in Sect. 9.

2   The Problem

One of the main objectives of a fuel injection system is to determine the point(s) in time and the quantity of fuel to be injected in the cylinders of an engine, relative to the position of each piston, which is in turn a function of the angular position of the crankshaft. In a reciprocating engine, a common reference is the *top dead centre* (TDC), that is, the position in which one of the pistons is nearest to the crankshaft (Fig. 1). In a four-cylinder engine, the pistons are paired in phase opposition, so that, when two of them are in a TDC, the others are in the bottom dead center or BDC. The TDC is the typical reference point for the functions and actions that need to take place within the rotation. These action include (among others) computing the phase (time relative to the TDC) of the injection and the quantity of fuel to be injected, but also checking whether the combustion occurred properly.

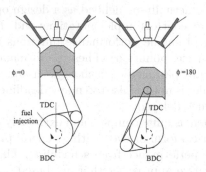

Fig. 1. Relationship among engine phases and reference points in the crankshaft rotation period. In a 4-cylinder engine, cylinder pairs are in phase opposition.

The time between two activations (at the TDC) is not constant, nor arbitrary, but depends on the rotation speed of the engine, which can vary within given ranges with a given maximum acceleration. At low revolution rates, the time interval between two reference points (the TDC for a set of cylinders) is large and allows the execution of sophisticated controls and possibly multiple fuel injections. The same algorithm cannot be executed at higher revolution rates, because it would lead to an overload, generating several deadline misses. Therefore, the implementation is adapted using a simplified algorithm that reduces the (worst-case) execution time (i.e., the functions to be executed) when the rotation speed falls within pre-defined ranges. For most cars, the rotation speed typically varies between 600 and 6000 revolutions per minute (rpm), which maps to activation intervals between 100 and 10 ms. The model proposed to describe such a type of engine control tasks is referred to as *Adaptive Variable Rate* task model, or AVR-model [1].

The analysis of the schedulability conditions for AVR tasks has been conducted by assuming that tasks have hard deadlines, often implicit, meaning that each task must complete before its next activation. This is not necessarily true. Besides evidence gathered from the common industrial practice, an indication that this is indeed the case is that the AUTOSAR automotive standard (and its predecessor OSEK) allow system configurations in which multiple instances of the same task are active at the same time.

If deadline misses are allowed, it is important to understand what are the consequences of a late task and what action (if any) should be performed by the scheduler. In our model, we assume that control tasks program a TPU (Time Processing Unit) that is in charge of actuating the fuel injectors. In this case, the effect of a missed deadline is that the TPU remains programmed with the parameters (angle of injection and duration of the injection) computed in the previous cycle.

An additional objective of our framework is to explore scheduling options, including the use of the Earliest Deadline First scheduling policy in the context of applications of this type. Finally, we aim at verifying the conjecture that the engine performance functions can be fit with an exponential function. This assumption was used to derive an algorithm for computing the optimal mode switching speeds in [4]. Overall, the parameters of interest that are meant to be captured by the model are (i) the engine thermodynamic efficiency, (ii) the NOx emissions and (iii) the soot emissions.

3   The Simulation Framework for the Performance Analysis of Controls and Scheduling Design

To explore the impact of scheduling on the engine performance we constructed a co-simulation framework in which the master simulation engine is Simulink. The engine model has been defined as a Simulink model, which will be presented in detail in Sect. 6. Next, we leveraged the T-Res cosimulation environment for the co-simulation of the task execution and scheduling [5]. An introduction to T-Res is presented in Sect. 4, while some extensions of the framework are described in Sect. 5.

For the development of the engine model we leveraged information from several sources, including engine models for the steady state and event-based models as described in [6] and other empirical models found online.

The engine controls have been incrementally defined and now include several components that allow to simulate individual cylinders, with injectors, the turbocharger, the intake and exhaust manifolds, and the gas recirculation. The desired angle of injection and the injection time are defined by calibration tables obtained from the literature.

4   The T-Res Cosimulation Framework

The T-Res (Time and Resource-aware simulator) framework is the result of a project that aims at integrating in Simulink the effect of code execution latencies and scheduling delays. T-Res consists of a set of custom Simulink blocks representing tasks and kernels and allows to interface the Simulink simulation engine, acting as master, with a scheduling simulator in a co-simulation environment (see Fig. 2). The scheduling simulator (we use RTSim [7], but the backend simulation engine can be changed) computes the scheduling delays and holds the output valuess of the corresponding tasks until their simulated completion time. This allows to simulate delays in the production of output values and the corresponding impact on the control function.

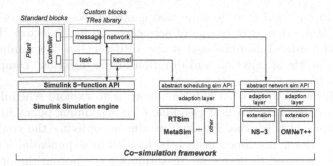

Fig. 2. The TRes cosimulation architecture.

T-Res provides a custom block for representing the kernel and its scheduler (left side of Fig. 3). The block is configured with the selection of the scheduling policy and the behavior in case of deadline (period) overrun. The possible options are to drop the task or to let it execute until its late completion. The kernel block provides a set of activation signals as output for the tasks it manages.

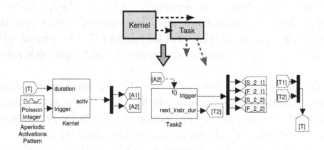

Fig. 3. The custom block for schedulers in T-Res.

These activation signals go to instances of the second type of custom blocks, representing tasks (right side of Fig. 3). Each task receives an activation signal from the kernel (indicating when the task begins or resumes execution), and is characterized by an execution time estimate (a configuration parameter), and a signal going back to the kenel and providing the amount of time that is still required by the task at each point in time. The execution time of a task is defined in T-Res as a sequence of instructions of predefined execution (constant or computed from a distribution) using a simple language and assigned as one of the task block parameters. The task block produces as output a set of activation and latch signals for all the functional subsystems that are executed by the task. With respect to the activation, sporadic tasks are characterized by an activation event going as input to the kernel block, or a periodic activation specification, provided as a configuration parameter to the kernel (for details, refer to [5]).

5 Extending T-Res for Modeling AVR Tasks

For the purpose of this project we extended the task model block and the timing information associated with it to allow the representation of Adaptive Variable Rate tasks.

For what concerns the activations, the AVR task can be treated as a particular case of an aperiodic task. The task block in T-Res includes a signal for the explicit activation in case the task is event-triggered. This signal is used to define the activation in correspondence to given angular positions of the engine crankshaft, by using a simple trigger block activated at specific angles. For what concerns the execution, an *ad-hoc* AVR task block must be created for handling the mode switching: this AVR task block has a dedicated *mode* input that is referred to the active mode index, as presented in Fig. 4. The mode input is used here to select which control functionality must be executed. For the engine control system, each execution mode represent different execution times, associated with different control strategies: the most complex and complete control tasks (which are time-consuming) are activated at low speeds, while the simpler (and time-saving) ones are used at higher speeds.

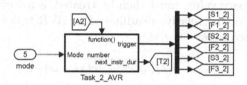

Fig. 4. A custom block for modeling an AVR task.

The AVR block triggers an arbitrary number of pairs of segment-latch blocks, each implementing an executable segment of the functionality and the delay caused by its execution time. The subsystem block contains the control instructions and it is triggered at the start of *execution* of the job. The latch block holds the previous data until it is triggered at the *completion* of the job.

For each modality it is possible to specify which pairs of blocks are executed or skipped, and also specify different execution times. The implementation of the AVR segment-latch blocks that has been used for this paper is presented in Fig. 5. This implementation has been created for modelling a multiple injection control system: the first segment block computes the main injection parameters, the second the post-injection and the third the pre-injection parameters. The strength of this approach is that the activation of the second and third pair can be selectively disabled when the injection mode is changed.

The mode index is provided by an external block called *mode selector* which senses the current engine speed and selects the execution modality that is required, according to a user-defined map. Each mode is activated when the engine speed value lies in a specific interval. The optimal selection of the switching speeds is a non-trivial process, and a performance-based analysis on the topic

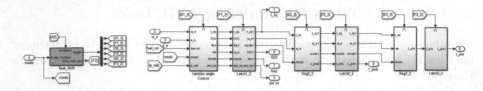

Fig. 5. An example of AVR task modelled with TRES, implementing the multiple injection control

has been provided in [4]. The mode selector supports also hysteresis between the switching, in order to avoid potentially dangerous oscillations when the engine operates near the switching speeds.

5.1 Variable Deadline Implementation

In order to correctly test the system under EDF scheduling, the deadline of the AVR task must be changed at every job activation, accordingly to its activation rate. The deadline value, which in the original TRes implementation is statically defined as a workspace value, must then be treated as a variable.

A formulation for the relative deadline of an AVR task has been calculated in [8] and is reported here:

$$D_i(\omega) = \delta_i\left(\sqrt{\omega^2 + 2\Theta_i\alpha} - \omega\right)/\alpha, \tag{1}$$

where ω is the engine speed, δ_i a fraction of angular period ($\delta \in [0,1]$), Θ_i the angular period and α the engine acceleration, supposed constant during the angular interval Θ_i. If the formula is implemented "as is", it implies iteratively solving on-line calculations, which could increase the scheduler overhead. The possible solutions for this problem are: (i) creating a sufficiently detailed look-up table for different (ω, α) combinations, or (ii) using an approximated computation. In order to reduce the number of inputs in the Kernel block (thus reducing the overall complexity of the scheduler) we decided to use an approximate computation, where the deadline at every iteration k has the value:

$$\begin{cases} D_i(0) = \delta_i T_0 \\ D_i(k) = \delta_i\left(t_{act}(k) - t_{act}(k-1)\right) \end{cases} \tag{2}$$

where T_0 is the (precomputed) interval between two activations at the starting speed, and $t_{act}(k)$ is the absolute time of the k-th job activation. The deadline is then directly provided to the external scheduler RTSIM at the job arrival.

6   Simulink Models of the Engine and the Control Tasks

Figure 6 shows the model of the engine and the control functionality in Simulink. The blocks in the upper part of the figure represent the engine subsystems that are currently considered and include a turbocharger, compressor manifold, inter-cooler, intake and exhaust manifolds and the model of the engine cylinders. The subsystem on the bottom part of the figure wraps our model of the engine controller, with its outputs: the injection angle and duration and the VGT.

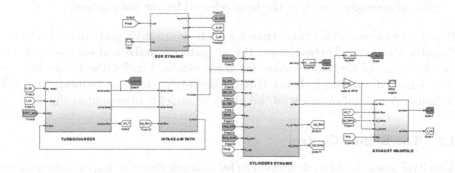

Fig. 6. Physical part of the engine model implemented in Simulink

The framework has been improved with respect to the one presented in our previous work [3], both in the physical and control parts. The engine now supports the simulation of multiple cylinders, properly phased, instead of a mean-modelling with a single cylinder.

6.1   The Engine Model

The main improvements of the physical model are related to the cylinder dynamics and the analysis of the effect of multiple injections in the same cycle. A generic cylinder block has been created, containing all the mechanical and combustion dynamics, as a Simulink library block, with the possibility to consider a large number of status variables of the internal dynamics. An arbitrary number of cylinders can then be easily added to the model, by only changing the initial conditions and angular phasing. The equations used for this framework have been carefully implemented using the state-of-the-art models, mainly from the work of Kiencke and Nielsen [9]. In detail, the block is composed by:

- valves dynamics, modelled as variable area flow restrictions, in order to have a more realistic model of the intake and exhaust flow through the cylinders;
- injector dynamics, controlling directly the timing of the nozzle opening and the rail pressure, in order to manage multiple-injection strategies;
- energy release of combustion using the zero-dimensional Chmela model proposed in [10], which assures a good sensitivity to the shape of the fuel injection profile, while maintaining low computational requirements;
- piston dynamics as a crankshaft-rod mechanism;
- pressure and temperature dynamics, with equations of energy balance, wall losses and flow exchanges

- NOx formation dynamics, modelled using the semi-empirical equation from the work of Guardiola et al. [11];
- soot formation, with both formation (Hiroyasu model [12]) and oxidation (Nagle and Strickland-Constable model [13]) dynamics;
- thermodynamic efficiency of the entire combustion cycle, computed as the ratio of generated work to the heat released by the combustion;

The model presents also the dynamics of the crankshaft and engine friction, a Variable Geometry Turbocharger, the air path of intake and exhaust gas, and the dynamics of the temperature for these blocks. Finally, the model has also been enriched with an Exhaust Gas Recirculation block for reducing the NOx emission. A general overview of the physical model is presented in Fig. 6.

6.2   The Engine Control

A control block has been developed to take care of the most important dynamics of the engine. The control uses data from sensors (engine speed, acceleration, intake air flow, boost pressure, exhaust pressure and pedal input) to compute the actuation signals. The control variables are the turbine palettes orientation and a mix of injection-related variables: rail pressure, injection angles, injection duration and fraction of fuel. The control laws are implemented using both lookup tables and classic controllers such as PID blocks.

For what concerns the injection control, three strategies have been implemented: triple injection (pre-main-post), double injection (either pre-main or main-post) and single injection. The reason behind this choice is that splitting the injection provides better results in terms of combustion of fuel and reduction of pollutants. In particular, pre-injections provide a better initial mixture and a more uniform combustion, while post-injection are typically used to burn the residual fuel.

The framework is able to capture changing of performance in NOx, soot and thermodynamic efficiency by varying a great number of parameters, such as the starting angle of injection, the duration of the injections, the fraction of fuel for each injection, and the relative angle between splits.

The model consists of a kernel, and seven tasks. One of the seven tasks is an AVR, three are periodic controllers and two represents other computations.

As the modelled engine has 4-cylinders and the injection must be performed once every two cycles for each cylinder, the AVR task is activated every half rotation. The TPU is actuated after 180° of the AVR task activation, and that instant corresponds also to the AVR deadline.

7   Objective and Status

A detailed modeling of the control function is necessary to better understand the impact of deadline misses or long latencies. Depending on the implementation of the control function, a deadline miss may result in a late actuation, or a missed actuation or even an actuation with old data. In our controls implementation, the AVR task computes the phase and duration of the injection and passes them to the task that simulates the injection actuators. Hence, a missed deadline results in actuating the injectors with the values computed in the previous cycle with a likely error in phase and duration with respect to the ideal values.

The objective of our framework is multifold:

- To understand the effect of the scheduling on the engine performance and to use the environment for analyzing the impact of scheduling policies and parameters, such as evaluating fixed priority vs EDF or different possible priority assignments and task configurations.
- To analyze the timing parameters of interest for evaluating the performance of the engine and possibly attempt a characterization that isolates the attributes of interest. This includes, among others, the evaluation of schemes like m-k deadline misses, or overload management (maximum lateness).
- To better characterize the design problem consisting in the optimal selection of the transition speeds for AVR tasks.

The final application goal of this work is to create a tool for testing different strategies of control and scheduling before implementing them in real cars, which can be particularly useful especially for automotive companies. However, currently the scope of the analysis is relatively limited, due to the huge complexity of both the physical model and the real software implementation. The difference among the engine control laws at different speeds (one for each possible execution mode of the AVR tasks) mostly consists in the possibility of defining one, two or three fuel injections. We assume at low speeds three injections are possible, while at high rotation speeds there is only enough computation time available to compute the angle and duration of a single injection.

The current engine model is capable of simulating several performance functions of interest for a variable number of injections. Figure 7 shows the simulated amount of NOx pollutants produced for simulation runs in which one (green line), two (red) or three (blue line) injections are performed during the cycle. The figure shows the benefit on the pollutant emissions that can be obtained by using multiple injections in the cycle.

Similarly, the graph in Fig. 8 shows the quantity of soot produced in the simulated runs under the hypothesis of one, two or three injections for each cycle.

8 Studying the Effects of Deadline Misses on Performance

In Diesel engine control, the injector actuation is managed by the Time Processing Unit (TPU), or by its most recent version called Enhanced Time Processing Unit (eTPU). The TPU is a co-microprocessor which works in synchronous modality, driven by both an internal clock and an Angle Clock that is based on the crankshaft angular position. Among all its functions, it generates the voltage signal for the injectors, using the control data provided by the CPU. This

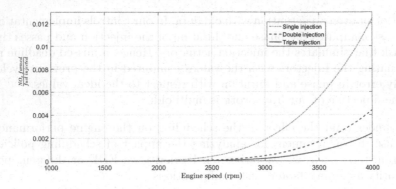

Fig. 7. Decrease in NOx emission with multiple injections (Color figure online)

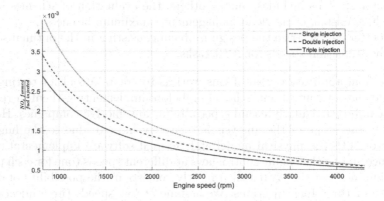

Fig. 8. Decrease in soot production with multiple injections

action is done with high precision at very specific angles, synchronized with the crankshaft rotation.

The function computing the control of the injection should provide the computed values before the TPU injection process is activated. For this reason, this instant is defined as the deadline of the AVR task: if the AVR task misses its deadline and cannot provide new data to the TPU, the TPU uses the old data. This may result in errors in the timing of the injection (i.e., the starting angle) and the quantity of fuel injected, if the old data are not suitable for the current cycle, for example if the engine suddenly accelerates, then the errors can be significant and worsen the combustion performance. Thus, in order to minimize the emissions of pollutants and the wear of the engine components, a system model helps understand how scheduling delays are related to the performance.

Currently, within the assumptions of our model, the simulation is able to show how the scheduling delays result in errors in the angle/duration of the injection actuation and the corresponding loss in performance (for each selected metric). Our objective is to relate the errors in phase and duration of the injection to a possible loss of efficiency or an increase in pollutants, providing ways to analyze the impact of scheduling with respect to the first performance function of interest. Figure 9 shows the results of an example run in which the task execution times have been defined to have one or two deadline misses on each cycle (for one or two cylinders) under a throttle input consisting of a ramp (to force a variation in the engine rpm and the ideal injection conditions).

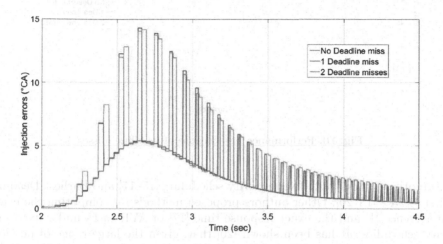

Fig. 9. Angular error because of deadline misses (Color figure online)

In the figure graph, the vertical axis shows the phase error in the actuation of the injection for a sample manoeuvre consisting of a sudden acceleration and a corresponding increase in the engine rotation speed from low to high values. Three graphs are plot in the figure. The graph in blue (dark) color shows the angle error when the execution time of the AVR task does not generate any deadline miss. When forcing a single miss (red line) or two misses on each cycle (green line) the injection angle error grows to almost 15°.

The angular error in the injection is related to a variation (loss) in the power performance of the engine. Figure 10 shows the corresponding effect of the deadline misses imposed on the system (in the same experiment configuration) on the thermodynamic efficiency. The graph clearly shows how deadline misses result in a loss of efficiency. Similar results are obtained for the performance that relate to the pollutants NOx and soot.

9   Related Work

The presentation of the task model in which engine control tasks are implemented with a variable computational requirements for increasing speeds is in [14]. These tasks are also referred to adaptive variable-rate (AVR). Analyzing the schedulability of tasks sets consisting of both periodic and AVR tasks is a difficult problem that has been addressed by several authors under various simplifying

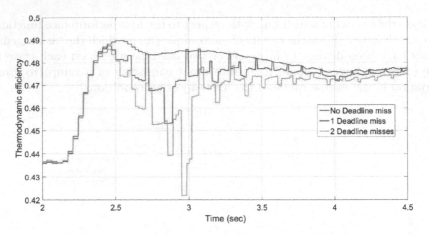

Fig. 10. Performance loss because of deadline misses

assumptions, under both fixed priority scheduling [15–17] and Earliest Deadline First (EDF) [18–20]. Other authors proposed methods for computing the exact interference [1] and the exact response time [17] of AVR tasks under fixed priority scheduling. It has been shown [20] that, given the large range of possible interarrival times of an AVR task, fixed priority scheduling is not the best choice for engine control systems since, while EDF exhibits a nearly optimal scheduling performance. Based on this fact, Apuzzo et al. [21] provided an operating system support for AVR tasks under the Erika Enterprise kernel [22].

All the papers considered above, however, focus on the schedulability analysis of task sets consisting of periodic and AVR tasks, without any concern on engine performance. A performance-driven design approach has been addressed in [23] for finding the transition speeds that trigger the mode changes of an AVR task.

A very large number of projects target the evaluation of scheduling policies and the analysis of task implementations. A necessarily incomplete list includes Yartiss [24], ARTISST [25], Cheddar [26], and Stress [27].

Finally, TrueTime [28] is a *freeware*[1] Matlab/Simulink-based simulation tool that has been developed at Lund University since 1999. It provides models of multi-tasking real-time kernels and networks that can be used in simulation models for networked embedded control systems. TrueTime is used by many research groups worldwide to study the (simulated) impact of lateness and deadline misses on controls. In TrueTime, the model of task code is represented by *code functions* that are written in either Matlab or C++ code. Several research works investigate the consequences of computation (scheduling) and communication delays on controls. An overview on the subject can be found in [29].

---

[1] http://www3.control.lth.se/truetime/LICENSE.txt.

10   Conclusions and Future Work

The co-simulation framework is in its early developing stages and starts producing results of interest. However, to better characterize the performance impact of scheduling delays, a better model of the control tasks and of some engine characteristics is still needed. In the context of the project we also aim at the evaluation of different task allocation strategies on multicore platforms.

References

1. Biondi, A., Melani, A., Marinoni, M., Natale, M.D., Buttazzo, G.: Exact interference of adaptive variable-rate tasks under fixed-priority scheduling. In: Proceedings of the 26th Euromicro Conference on Real-Time Systems (ECRTS 2014), Madrid, Spain, 8–11 July 2014
2. Guzzella, L., Onder, C.: Introduction to Modeling and Control of Internal Combustion Engine Systems. Springer Science & Business Media, Heidelberg (2009). https://doi.org/10.1007/978-3-642-10775-7
3. Pazzaglia, P., Biondi, A., Di Natale, M., Buttazzo, G.: A simulation framework to analyze the scheduling of AVR tasks with respect to engine performance (2016)
4. Biondi, A., Di Natale, M., Buttazzo, G.: Performance-driven design of engine control tasks. In: Proceedings of the 7th International Conference on Cyber-Physical Systems, p. 45. IEEE Press (2016)
5. Cremona, F., Morelli, M., Di Natale, M.: Tres: a modular representation of schedulers, tasks, and messages to control simulations in simulink. In: Proceedings of the 30th Annual ACM Symposium on Applied Computing, Salamanca, Spain, 13–17 April 2015, pp. 1940–1947 (2015)
6. Guzzella, L., Onder, C.: Introduction to Modeling and Control of Internal Combustion Engine Systems. Springer, Heidelberg (2010). https://doi.org/10.1007/978-3-642-10775-7
7. Palopoli, L., Lipari, G., Abeni, L., Natale, M.D., Ancilotti, P., Conticelli, F.: A tool for simulation and fast prototyping of embedded control systems. In: Hong, S., Pande, S. (eds.) LCTES/OM, pp. 73–81. ACM (2001)
8. Biondi, A., Buttazzo, G.: Engine control: task modeling and analysis. In: Design, Automation and Test in Europe Conference and Exhibition (DATE), pp. 525–530. IEEE (2015)
9. Kiencke, U., Nielsen, L.: Automotive Control Systems: for Engine, Driveline, and Vehicle (2000). https://doi.org/10.1007/b137654
10. Chmela, F.G., Orthaber, G.C.: Rate of heat release prediction for direct injection diesel engines based on purely mixing controlled combustion. Technical report, Sae Technical Paper (1999)
11. Guardiola, C., López, J., Martin, J., Garcia-Sarmiento, D.: Semiempirical in-cylinder pressure based model for NOX prediction oriented to control applications. Appl. Thermal Eng. 31(16), 3275–3286 (2011)
12. Hiroyasu, H., Kadota, T.: Models for combustion and formation of nitric oxide and soot in direct injection diesel engines. Technical report, SAE Technical Paper (1976)
13. Nagle, J., Strickland-Constable, R.: Oxidation of carbon between 1000–2000 c. In: Proceedings of the Fifth Carbon Conference, vol. 1, no. 1, p. 154. Pergamon Press, London (1962)

14. Buttle, D.: Real-time in the prime-time. In: Keynote Speech at the 24th Euromicro Conference on Real-Time Systems, Pisa, Italy, 12 July 2012 (2012)
15. Kim, J., Lakshmanan, K., Rajkumar, R.: Rhythmic tasks: a new task model with continually varying periods for cyber-physical systems. In: Proceedings of the Third IEEE/ACM International Conference on Cyber-Physical Systems (ICCPS 2012), Beijing, China, April 2012, pp. 28–38 (2012)
16. Davis, R.I., Feld, T., Pollex, V., Slomka, F.: Schedulability tests for tasks with variable rate-dependent behaviour under fixed priority scheduling. In: Proceedings of 20th IEEE Real-Time and Embedded Technology and Applications Symposium, Berlin, Germany, April 2014 (2014)
17. Biondi, A., Natale, M.D., Buttazzo, G.: Response-time analysis for real-time tasks in engine control applications. In: Proceedings of the 6th International Conference on Cyber-Physical Systems (ICCPS 2015), Seattle, Washington, USA, 14–16 April 2015 (2015)
18. Buttazzo, G., Bini, E., Buttle, D.: Rate-adaptive tasks: model, analysis, and design issues. In: Proceedings of the International Conference on Design, Automation and Test in Europe, Dresden, Germany, 24–28 March 2014 (2014)
19. Biondi, A., Buttazzo, G.: Engine control: task modeling and analysis. In: Proceedings of the International Conference on Design, Automation and Test in Europe (DATE 2015), Grenoble, France, 9–13 March 2015, pp. 525–530 (2015)
20. Biondi, A., Buttazzo, G., Simoncelli, S.: Feasibility analysis of engine control tasks under EDF scheduling. In: Proceedings of the 27th Euromicro Conference on Real-Time Systems (ECRTS 2015), Lund, Sweden, 8–10 July 2015 (2015)
21. Biondi, V.A.A., Buttazzo, G.: OSEK-like kernel support for engine control applications under EDF scheduling. In: Proceedings of the 22nd IEEE Real-Time and Embedded Technology and Applications Symposium (RTAS 2016), Vienna, Austria, 11–14 April 2016 (2016)
22. ERIKA enterprise: an OSEK compliant real-time kernel. http://erika.tuxfamily. org/drupal/
23. Biondi, A., Di Natale, M., Buttazzo, G.: Performance-driven design of engine control tasks. In: Proceedings of the 7th International Conference on Cyber-Physical Systems (ICCPS 2016), Vienna, Austria, 11–14 April 2016 (2016)
24. Chandarli, Y., Fauberteau, F., Masson, D., Midonnet, S., Qamhieh, M., et al.: Yartiss: a tool to visualize, test, compare and evaluate real-time scheduling algorithms. In: Proceedings of the 3rd International Workshop on Analysis Tools and Methodologies for Embedded and Real-time Systems, pp. 21–26 (2012)
25. Decotigny, D., Puaut, I.: ARTISST: an extensible and modular simulation tool for real-time systems. In: Proceedings. Fifth IEEE International Symposium on Object-Oriented Real-Time Distributed Computing: (ISORC 2002), pp. 365–372. IEEE (2002)
26. Singhoff, F., Legrand, J., Nana, L., Marcé, L.: Cheddar: a flexible real time scheduling framework. In: ACM SIGAda Ada Letters, vol. 24, no. 4, pp. 1–8. ACM (2004)
27. Audsley, N.C., Burns, A., Richardson, M.F., Wellings, A.J.: STRESS: a simulator for hard real-time systems. Softw.: Practice Experience 24(6), 543–564 (1994)
28. Cervin, A., Henriksson, D., Lincoln, B., Eker, J., Årzén, K.-E.: How does control timing affect performance? IEEE Control Syst. Mag. 23(3), 16–30 (2003)
29. Astrom, K.J., Wittenmark, B.: Adaptive Control. Prentice Hall, Upper Saddle River (2016)

Formalising Cosimulation Models

Frank Zeyda[1](✉), Julien Ouy[2], Simon Foster[1], and Ana Cavalcanti[1]

[1] Department of Computer Science, University of York, York YO10 5GH, UK
{frank.zeyda,simon.foster,ana.cavalcanti}@york.ac.uk
[2] ClearSy, Les Pléiades III — Bât. A, 320 Avenue Archimède,
13857 Aix-en-Provence Cedex 3, France
julien.ouy@clearsy.com

Abstract. Cosimulation techniques are popular in the design and early testing of cyber-physical systems. Such systems are typically composed of heterogeneous components and specified using a variety of languages and tools; this makes their formal analysis beyond simulation challenging. We here present work on formalised models and proofs about cosimulations in our theorem prover Isabelle/UTP, illustrated by an industrial case study from the railways sector. Novel contributions are a mechanised encoding of the FMI framework for cosimulation, simplification and translation of (case-study) models into languages supported by our proof system, and an encoding of an FMI instantiation.

1   Introduction

Cosimulation techniques are popular in the design of cyber-physical systems (CPS) [11]. Such systems are typically specified using a variety of languages and tools that adopt complementary modelling paradigms, such as physics-related models, control laws, and sequential, concurrent and real-time programming. The industrial standard FMI (Functional Mock-up Interface) [7] addresses the challenge of coupling different simulators and simulations. It defines an API used to implement master algorithms that mitigate issues of interoperability.

Our aim is to complement cosimulation with proof-based techniques. Simulation is useful in helping engineers to understand modelling implications and spot design issues, but cannot provide universal guarantees of correctness and safety. This is due to the complexity of CPS in considering continuous behaviours as well as real-world interactions, and the impracticality of running an exhaustive number of simulations. It is moreover often not clear how the evidence provided by simulations is to be qualified, since simulations depend on parameters and algorithms, and are software systems (with possible faults) in their own right.

Challenges in analysing heterogeneous CPS *formally* are multifarious. Firstly, we have to consider the semantics of various modelling approaches and languages. Secondly, we have to consolidate those semantic models to enable us to reason about the system as a whole. And thirdly, realistic industrial systems are often difficult to tackle by formal approaches due their complexity and level of detail. A key challenge remains to find abstractions that make the system tractable for

A. Cerone and M. Roveri (Eds.): SEFM 2017 Workshops, LNCS 10729, pp. 453–468, 2018.
https://doi.org/10.1007/978-3-319-74781-1_31

formal analysis, and, at the same time, not forfeit fidelity, so that formal analysis can justify and support claims about the real system under inspection.

In this paper, we outline our approach to address the above challenges using an industrial application from railways. The example is a system developed by ClearSy and involves control models of trains in 20-sim [21] and an implementation of the interlocking system in VDM-RT [17]. We first show how the initial models of the industrial example can be simplified and expressed in notations for which we have a precise formal semantics: Modelica for dynamic systems and VDM-RT for concurrent real-time programming. We then present work towards encoding the models in our theorem prover Isabelle/UTP [10]. Part of this is also a mechanised reactive and timed model of the FMI framework, which we formulate in the *Circus* [2] process algebra for state-rich reactive systems.

Our contributions in this paper are summarised as follows. Firstly, we simplify an industrial railways application and case study and reformulate it in notations which we have embedded into our Isabelle/UTP theorem prover; secondly, we encode the FMI framework for cosimulation in Isabelle/UTP; and thirdly, we encode key parts of the railways model together with examples of proofs.

The rest of the paper is organised as follows. In Sect. 2, we review preliminary material: Modelica and VDM-RT, and the *Circus* language. FMI and its mechanisation are described in Sect. 3. Then, Sect. 4 discusses the railways case study and our simplified FMI model of it, and Sect. 5 details our encoding in Isabelle/UTP. Lastly, in Sect. 6 we conclude and outline future work.

2   Preliminaries

We proceed by reviewing preliminary material.

2.1   Modelica and VDM-RT

Modelica [18] is a language that targets continuous systems modelling, although discrete-time systems are well supported within it too. It is applicable to a large spectrum of domains, including physical, electrical, and control systems. Various tools exist that provide simulation support for Modelica models.

Modelica allows control models to be expressed either in explicit equational form or as control laws (meaning diagrams). Continuous behaviours are described by virtue of Differential Algebraic Equations (DAE) [20]. We may also define discontinuous state changes when some condition (guard) becomes true.

An example of a Modelica *control law* relevant to our railways example is given in Fig. 1. The control law models the deceleration of a moving body—in our case the braking of a train. The model consists of two integrators, *Velocity* and *Position* that calculate the velocity and travelled distance of the body. We introduce a control switch to set its acceleration to a fixed value of $-1.4\,\text{ms}^{-2}$ when the velocity is greater than zero, and otherwise to $0\,\text{ms}^{-2}$.

We can simulate this model to confirm that the body stops after $v_{init}^2/(2a)$ metres, where v_{init} is a particular initial speed of the body and a the deceleration.

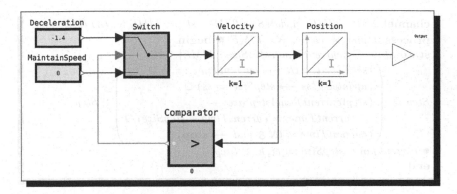

Fig. 1. Modelica control law of a decelerating moving object.

However, simulation cannot prove that this is indeed the case in every scenario. A safety concern is that a train must always be able to stop in time to not overrun a red signal or wrongly-set switch. We discuss a more realistic train model in Sect. 4 that enables us to examine such proofs in the context of a cosimulation with two trains moving independently on a given track layout.

Control laws such as the one in Fig. 1 are interpreted as equational systems in Modelica and flattened into a single large system of simultaneous equations, some of which correspond to connecting wires of the control diagram, and others to the specification of subcomponents. Modelica also provides limited support for `algorithms` formulated in sequential statements. Yet, their semantics does not account for execution time, concurrency, and effects on data sharing. Support for those features is provided by VDM-RT, which we briefly discuss next.

VDM-RT [17] is a real-time extension of the VDM language [16], which supports sequential program development from model-based specifications. It has a precise semantics that enables correctness proofs. Verification of implementations is supported by tools such as Overture [6]. Beyond VDM, VDM-RT has features to model execution time and concurrency. It also adds system entities that correspond to clocks, CPUs, threads and communication buses.

Our technique to reason about Modelica and VDM-RT specifications is based on a unifying semantic framework, the Unifying Theories of Programming (UTP) of Hoare and He. We have mechanised the UTP inside the Isabelle/HOL theorem prover [10], and within that mechanisation also encoded the semantics of various languages for CPS modelling and design, including Modelica [9], Simulink and VDM-RT [8]. Our Modelica semantics considers flat Modelica models only, after index reduction. We give meaning to a core subset of Modelica constructs, using hybrid relational programs [9]. Mechanisation of that semantics in Isabelle/UTP enables us to prove properties and laws about these constructs.

The encoding of particular Modelica models has to be done by hand for now, although automation of the encoding step is envisaged as future work.

A third language is used as a front-end to the UTP to tie our models together: the process algebra *Circus* [2]. We summarise it next.

$$
\begin{array}{l}
\textbf{channel } setT : TIME;\ updateSS : TIME;\ step : TIME \times NZTIME;\ end; \\
\textbf{process } Timer \;\hat{=}\; ct, hc, tN : TIME \;\bullet\; \textbf{begin} \\
\textbf{state } State \;\hat{=}\; [\,currentTime, stepSize : TIME\,] \\
\qquad
Step \;\hat{=}\;
\left(
\begin{array}{l}
(setT?t : t < tN \longrightarrow currentTime := t)\ \square \\
(updateSS?ss \longrightarrow stepSize := ss)\ \square \\
(step!currentTime!stepSize \longrightarrow \\
\quad currentTime := currentTime + stepSize)\ \square \\
(currentTime = tN\ \&\ end \longrightarrow \textbf{stop})
\end{array}
\right)
\;;\ Step \\
\bullet\; currentTime, stepSize := ct, hc\;;\ Step \\
\textbf{end}
\end{array}
$$

Fig. 2. Timer process of the *Circus* FMI specification.

2.2 The *Circus* Language

Circus is a process algebra similar to CSP [13], but with additional support for defining data operations and state. *Circus* inherits many of its process operators from CSP, including sequential $(A\ ;\ B)$ and parallel $(A \parallel B)$ composition, input $(c?x \to A(x))$ and output $(c!e \to A)$ communications on a channel c, external choice $(A \square B)$, interrupt $(A \triangle B)$, guards $(p\ \&\ A)$ and recursion. A summary of *Circus* constructs relevant to our models is included in Appendix A.

To define a process state (**state** paragraph), a *Circus* process declares a record whose fields define a data model. Data operations can either be written as Z operation schemas [22] or constructs from Morgan's refinement calculus [19], such as specification statements, assignment, conditionals and iteration.

An example of a *Circus* process *Timer* is included in Fig. 2. It is part of the FMI model that we discuss in more detail in the next section. The process defines a state record *State* that introduces two variables *currentTime* and *stepSize* of type *TIME* (which model simulation time). It also includes a local action *Step*.

The main action after the '•' at the bottom prescribes the behaviour of the process. In our example, it first initialises the state variables and then proceeds by calling *Step*. For initialisation, we refer to the variables *ct* and *hc*, which are parameters of the process. *Step* is an external choice (operator □) that offers communication on the channels *setT*, *updateSS*, *step* and *end*. These channels are declared (with their types) by the **channel** construct above the process.

The channel events here are used by simulation (master) algorithms to model the progression of time during cosimulation steps. The environment can change *currentTime* and *stepSize* through communication on the channels *setT* and *updateSS*, respectively. When a *step* event occurs, modelling a cosimulation step, both these values are communicated and *currentTime* is increased by *stepSize*. Lastly, an *end* event may occur only if *currentTime* = *tN*, where *tN* is a process parameter specifying the simulation end time. The **stop** action that follows effectively refuses any further interaction. Otherwise, the *Step* action behaves recursively, repeating the previously described behavioural pattern.

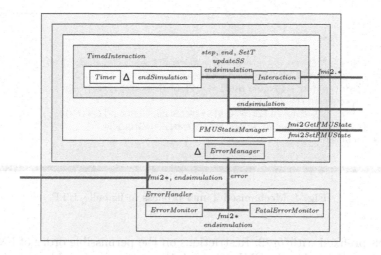

Fig. 3. Overview of the abstract *Circus* model for master algorithms.

3   FMI and Its Mechanisation

The conceptual view of an FMI cosimulation entails a master algorithm (MA) to orchestrate the cosimulation, and several Functional Mock-up Units (FMUs) that wrap tool and vendor-specific simulation components. The FMI standard [1] not only specifies the API by which MAs must communicate with the FMUs, but also how control and exchange of data must be realised. Typically, the master algorithm reads outputs from all FMUs and then forwards them to the FMUs that require them as inputs. After this, the MA notifies the FMUs to concurrently compute the next simulation step. Some master algorithms assume a fixed step size while others enquire the largest step size that the FMUs are cumulatively willing to accept. MAs sometimes also perform roll-backs of already performed simulation steps, and suitably deal with errors raised during cosimulations.

Our model of FMI formalises a cosimulation (including the MA and FMUs) as a collection of *Circus* processes. There exist processes that specify the interaction of master algorithms with FMUs, as well as processes that describe the behaviour of *particular* master algorithms. For illustration, the top-level abstract architecture of master algorithms is depicted in Fig. 3. Each box corresponds to a *Circus* process and the **thick** red lines between them highlight internal and external communications. The basic (non-composite) processes of the *Circus* model are *Timer*, *Interaction*, *FMUStatesManager*, *ErrorManager*, *ErrorMonitor* and *FatalErrorMonitor*. Their surrounding boxes denote parallel compositions.

The *Timer* process has already been discussed in Sect. 2.2: its purpose is to ensure that simulation time increases in accordance with the current time and step size. More complex is the *Interaction* process, which determines the order in which FMI functions that initialise FMUs, read their outputs (fmi2Get), set their inputs (fmi2Set), and invoke the next simulation step (fmi2DoStep) must be called. Function calls are modelled by communication events on special

```
definition
"process Timer(ct::TIME('τ), hc::NZTIME('τ), tN::TIME('τ)) ≜ begin
   Step =
      (tm:setT?(t : «t ≤ tN») →c (<currentTime> := «t») ;; Step) □
      (tm:updateSS?(ss) →c (<stepSize> := «ss») ;; Step) □
      (tm:step![out₁]($<currentTime>)![out₂]($<stepsize>) →c
         (<currentTime::'τ> :=
            minu(&<currentTime> + §(&<stepSize::'τ pos>), «tN»)) ;; Step) □
      ((&<currentTime> =u «tN») &u tm:endc →c Stop)
   • (<currentTime>, <stepSize> := «ct», «hc») ;; Step
end"
```

Fig. 4. Mechanised Timer process in Isabelle/UTP.

channels prefixed with *fmi2*. Restrictions on the permissible order of FMI function calls, as defined in the FMI standard [1], are thus captured by the *observable event traces* in our process model. For instance, the *Interaction* process includes local actions *TakeOutputs* and *DistributeInputs* that correspond to phases of the control cycle of a master algorithm, whereas *FMUStatesManager* prescribes the use of functions `fmi2GetFMUState` and `fmi2SetFMUState` to obtain and set FMU states during roll-back. An in-depth discussion of the *Circus* model can be found in [3]; in the remainder of the section, we report on its mechanisation.

In essence, we translate *Circus* notations into corresponding operators in our embedding of *Circus* in Isabelle/UTP. To give an example, a mechanised version of the *Timer* process from Fig. 2 is presented in Fig. 4. We note, however, that this (and other) mechanised processes do not have a *State* definition, since the process state is implicit in the variables used within actions.

One challenge that we faced is the encoding of mixed prefixes of inputs and outputs on the same channel. These, we translate into a single input communication. This solution requires us to supply an input variable for each output (`out1` and `out2` in Fig. 4). That variable is, however, preconditioned to only accept a particular value, thereby emulating the behaviour of an output. Another challenge is the encoding of recursive actions, such as `Step` in Fig. 4. In general, our tool rewrites local actions into a chain of HOL `let` statements, and fixed-point predicates are used to encode single-recursive actions. Parameters are dealt with via hidden stack variables, which allows for an elegant treatment of scopes.

To give another example, the mechanised encoding of the `TakeOuputs` action of the *Interaction* process in Fig. 3 is recaptured below.

```
TakeOutputs = <rinp::(port × VAL) list> := () ;;
   (;; out : outputs •
      fmi:fmi2Get.[out₁](«FMU out»).[out₂](«name out»)?(v)?(st) →c
         (;; inp : pdg out • <rinp> := &<rinp> ^u ((«inp», «v»)u)))
```

It reads the outputs of all FMUs (first iterated sequence ;;) and stores them in the state component `rinp` of the process, so that they can subsequently be forwarded to the FMUs requiring them, prior to initiating the next simulation step. The HOL type of `rinp` is a list of pairs whose first component is an FMU port, and whose second component is a permissible FMI value.

We note that `pdg` is a global constant that determines the port-dependency relationships between the input and output ports of FMUs. Our mechanised model introduces it via an Isabelle **constant** definition, alongside other global constants to determine the identifiers of FMUs, their parameters, initial values, and so on. Isabelle **constants** are uninterpreted, so that concrete FMI instantiations can define suitable values for these constants. An example of this is given later on in Sect. 5, where we consider our railways case study.

The complete mechanised FMI model can be found in [23]. Our contribution is that (a) we embedded the syntax and semantics of *Circus* into Isabelle/UTP on top of its UTP CSP model, and (b) achieved a direct correspondence between *Circus* notations and Isabelle constructs of the mechanisation.

4   The Railways Case Study

Our case study considers an existing tramway station. Its railway layout is presented in the diagram of Fig. 5. Trains enter the interlocking at the points Q2, Q3 and V1, and then issue a telecommand to request a route. Telecommand stations are denoted by the green dots, and possible routes through the railway network are Q2→V2, Q3→V2, V1→Q1, V1→Q2 and V1→Q3.

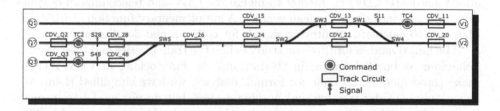

Fig. 5. Railway interlocking layout of the case study.

Access to the interlocking is controlled by the signals S28, S48 and S11. They are initially set to red causing trains arriving on the tracks CDV_Q2, CDV_Q3 and CDV_11 to stop and wait. When a telecommand is issued by a train, the control logic of the interlocking allocates a free route, if available, and then gives the respective train a green light to go ahead. No other train is allowed to proceed meanwhile. This guarantees that no collision can occur due to multiple trains passing through the same track segment. The control logic also caters for the setting of track points (SW1-5) so that trains move on their allotted paths.

The inputs of the interlocking controller are the CDV and telecommand boolean vectors. The CDV is a bit vector whose elements register the presence of a train on a particular track segment. Telecommand requests are likewise encoded by bit vectors where each bit corresponds to a particular route request.

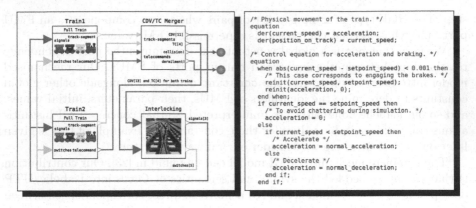

```
/* Physical movement of the train. */
equation
    der(current_speed) = acceleration;
    der(position_on_track) = current_speed;

/* Control equation for acceleration and braking. */
equation
    when abs(current_speed - setpoint_speed) < 0.001 then
        /* This case corresponds to engaging the brakes. */
        reinit(current_speed, setpoint_speed);
        reinit(acceleration, 0);
    end when;
    if current_speed == setpoint_speed then
        /* To avoid chattering during simulation. */
        acceleration = 0;
    else
        if current_speed < setpoint_speed then
            /* Accelerate */
            acceleration = normal_acceleration;
        else
            /* Decelerate */
            acceleration = normal_deceleration;
        end if;
    end if;
```

Fig. 6. FMI cosimulation (left) and train control equations (right).

Outputs (actuators) of the interlocking are signals and track point switches that control the paths of trains when they proceed through the interlocking.

A high-level view of the system as a cosimulation is given in the left diagram of Fig. 6. There are four FMU components. Two of them, Train1 and Train2, simulate the physical behaviour of the trains, which includes the actions of the train driver in setting the speed of the trains. A third FMU (Interlocking) encapsulates the physical plant and the software that controls it. Lastly, we require an additional FMU CDV/TC Merger to merge the CDV and telecommand outputs of both trains into single boolean vectors. A supplementary function of CDV/TC Merger is to calculate monitoring signals for collision and derailment.

The initial models for this case study define the train physics and their control behaviour as bond diagrams in 20-sim, and the interlocking in VDM-RT. To make those models tractable for formal analysis, we have simplified them. We hence only consider traction and braking actions but do not model train mass and gravity, and neither smooth acceleration and braking curves (jerk). This simplification is justified because the influence of the more precise model does not alter the fundamental system behaviour and is negligible in its real-world impact. The 20-sim train model has been encoded in Modelica, for which—unlike 20-sim bond diagrams—we have a (mechanised) formal semantics.

The kinematics and speed control of both trains is encoded by the equations in the right-hand diagram of Fig. 6. The first equation block captures motion: acceleration is the derivative of velocity (der(_) operator), and velocity the derivative of position. While an accurate physics model of the train would be expressed in terms of traction and braking forces, the assumption of constant train mass and Newton's law entitles us to consider acceleration alone.

The second equation block realises a simplified control algorithm: train acceleration is set to either 0, normal_acceleration or normal_deceleration, depending on whether the current speed is equal, below or above the set-point speed of the train, set by the driver. The latter two are suitable constants of the model. A special case is added by the when statement that simultaneously

```
algorithm
  setpoint_speed := 0;
  if current_track > 0 then
    signalID := Topology.signal_tab[current_track];
    if signalID <> NONE then
      if signals[signalID] == GREEN then
        setpoint_speed := max_speed;
      else
        setpoint_speed := 0;
      end if;
    else
      setpoint_speed := max_speed;
    end if;
  end if;
```

Fig. 7. Modelica function (body) for calculating the set-point speed.

sets the train speed to the set-point speed and acceleration to zero if we are close to the set-point speed. This is to avoid chattering during simulation and can also be thought of as 'engaging the brakes' when the train approaches zero speed while decelerating. We note that this equational characterisation is partly equivalent to the control law in Fig. 1, with the added feature of considering not merely braking but also up-regulation of the train speed. For formal analysis, the explicit version in Fig. 6 is more suitable as it is formulated in terms of derivatives rather than integrals, making the conversion into an ODE or DAE easier.

The behaviour of the driver is captured by the following equation:

```
equation
  setpoint_speed = CalculateSpeed(track_segment, signals, max_speed);
```

The computation is carried out by the function `CalculateSpeed` which expects the current track segment (`current_track`), signal values (`signals`), and maximum permissible speed (`max_speed`) as arguments. It then sets the set-point speed (`setpoint_speed`) to `max_speed` if there is either a green or no signal on the current track; otherwise, it sets it to zero (see Fig. 7).

Encapsulation of algorithmic behaviours into Modelica functions, where possible, is a deliberate refactoring. Our encoding profits from this as those functions can be naturally encoded as HOL functions into the proof system. This kind of engineering has a modularising ripple-on effect on subsequent proofs.

A last aspect of the train model considers equations for the discontinuous variable changes that occur when the train reaches the end of a track and enters the next track. The Modelica equations for this are given below.

```
equation
  when position_on_track > pre(track_length) then
    track_segment = NextTrack(pre(track_segment), pre(switches), direction);
    reinit(position_on_track, 0);
  end when;

equation track_length =
  (if track_segment > 0 then track_length_tab[track_segment] else 0);
```

The NextTrack() function calculates the next track segment when the train's relative position on the current track, given by the position_on_track variable, reaches the track_length. The function requires the current track, state of track points (switches), and travel direction as inputs, and its output is equated with the newly entered track segment after the discontinuity. Simultaneously, it also reinitialises position_on_track back to zero.

In addition to the above, we also need an equation that generates telecommand signals when the train is on a track equipped with a telecommand station, but we omit its straightforward definition here.

As already mentioned, the VDM-RT interlocking has also been simplified from its production code in hardware. Its initial model is actually an automaton whose functional behaviour was defined in *ladder logic*. Ladder models are graphical representations tailored for relay-based hardware implementations, and here gave rise to approximately 3,000 lines of VDM-RT code that, to a large part, deals with the safe interface between software and actuators.

To capture its essential behaviour, we introduce a variable Relay to record the state for relay switches that, in real hardware, record the locking of a particular route for a train that requests it. Below is an extract of the sequential program logic that performs the locking.

```
-- Relay Activation
if TC(4) and not TC(3) and not Relay(2) and not Relay(3) and CDV(4) and CDV(5)
    then Relay(1) := true;
if TC(3) and not TC(4) and not Relay(1) and not Relay(3) and not Relay(4)
    and not Relay(5) and CDV(4) and CDV(8) and CDV(9) and CDV(10) and CDV(1)
    then Relay(2) := true;
...
```

For locking to occur, a telecommand must have been issued that requests the respective route; this is achieved by the condition on the bit vector TC that cumulatively records the telecommands issued by all three telecommand stations. The constraints on Relay ensure that locked routes are non-intersecting, so that trains can pass without crossing each others' paths. Lastly, we have additional constraints on the CDV signal that ensure that the track segments of the route to be locked are not still occupied by a previous train.

While our software implementation retains the core logic of the hardware realisation, it does not consider time delays incurred by the latency of relay and point actuators. The rationale for this is to keep it simple in order to illustrate the *feasibility* of our approach. Although those delays can potentially impact on a safety analysis, refining our models to incorporate them is left as future work.

5   Encoding in Isabelle/UTP

We consider two aspects of the encoding here: the mechanised FMI system model (Sect. 5.1) and the continuous train FMUs (Sect. 5.2). All our Isabelle theories are available online: https://github.com/isabelle-utp/utp-main.

5.1   FMI System Model

The FMI system model introduces concrete definitions for uninterpreted constants of the abstract FMI model described in Sect. 3. These constants determine the names of the FMUs, their input and output ports, initial values and parameters, and graphs that capture internal and external port dependencies. The latter two are relevant to establish the absence of algebraic loops within the cosimulation architecture. Instantiation of the model for a particular cosimulation is realised by an `axiomatization` in Isabelle/UTP, as shown below.

```
axiomatization
  train1 :: "FMI2COMP" and train2 :: "FMI2COMP" and
  merger :: "FMI2COMP" and interlocking :: "FMI2COMP" where
  fmus_distinct : "distinct [train1, train2, merger, interlocking]" and
  FMI2COMP_def : "FMI2COMP = {train1, train2, merger, interlocking}"
```

Here, we introduce the constants `train1`, `train2`, `merger` and `interlocking` of a given (abstract) type `FMI2COMP`, together with axiomatic constraints that ensure that (a) the constants are distinct, and (b) they enumerate the type.

An extract of the port dependency graph of our system is sketched below:

```
definition pdg :: "port relation" where
"pdg = {
  (* External Dependencies *)
  ((train1, $track_segment:{int}ᵤ), (merger, $track_segment1:{int}ᵤ)),
  ((train2, $track_segment:{int}ᵤ), (merger, $track_segment2:{int}ᵤ)), ...,
  (* Internal Dependencies *)
  ((merger, $track_segment1:{int}ᵤ), (merger, $CDV:{int}ᵤ)),
  ((merger, $track_segment2:{int}ᵤ), (merger, $CDV:{int}ᵤ)), ...
}"
```

External dependencies correspond to connection arrows in Fig. 6, and internal dependencies arise from direct signal feed-through within FMUs. Above, we can see that a direct internal dependency exists between the inputs and outputs of the `merger` block. There is, however, no such dependency between inputs and outputs of the `train` FMUs due to integration (see Fig. 1). For this reason, our feedback system does not contain an algebraic loop. We have proved this by using Isabelle's evaluation tactic; it amounts to showing that `pdg` is acyclic. The mechanised proof of this can be found in the report [23], too.

5.2   Continuous Train Model

Continuous and hybrid behaviour is given a semantics in terms of the hybrid relational calculus (HRC) [12]. We have mechanised this calculus in Isabelle/UTP using the Multivariate Analysis and HOL-ODE theory libraries [14].

The hybrid relational calculus extends the UTP with continuous variables, which are encoded using timed traces. A timed trace, as illustrated in Fig. 8, is a partial function $\mathbf{tt} : \mathbb{R}_{\geq 0} \nrightarrow \Sigma$, such that $\text{dom}(\mathbf{tt}) = [0, \ell)$, for some $\ell : \mathbb{R}_{\geq 0}$, and $\mathbf{tt}$ is piecewise continuous. Type Σ is a topological space that defines the entire

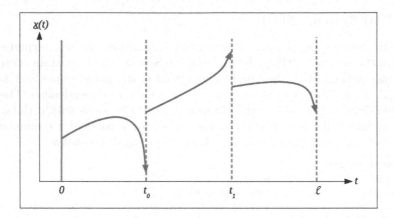

Fig. 8. Piecewise continuous function modelling a timed trace.

continuous state type, accommodating all continuous variables. Typically, Σ is associated with a vector space of type $\mathbb{R}^n$.

A continuous variable is decorated with an underscore $\underline{x}$ to distinguish it from a discrete variable. Like timed traces, continuous variables are functions on time. A key feature of the hybrid relational calculus is the ability to perform discrete assignments to continuous variables. This is achieved by pairing each continuous variable $\underline{x}$ with an assignable discrete copy variable x, such that $x = \underline{x}(0)$ holds for the before state, and $x' = \lim_{t \to \ell} \underline{x}(t)$ holds for the after state, for any $\ell > 0$.

Hybrid relations are constructed using common programming operators, such as assignment and sequential composition, plus various operators to specify continuous evolutions. For instance, we adopt the interval operator $\lceil P \rceil$ from the Duration Calculus [4] in order to specify constraints on the continuous variables during evolution, such that P must be satisfied at every instant.

With the above, we define evolution operator $\underline{x} \leftarrow f(x_0, t) \mathrel{\widehat{=}} \lceil \underline{x} = f(x_0, t) \rceil$. It specifies that continuous variable $\underline{x}$ evolves according to the function f, whose parameters are the initial values x_0 and time t, for any evolution duration ℓ. We also have $\underline{x} \leftarrow_n f(x_0, t)$, which presumes a definite duration $\ell = n$. Lastly, we define the pre-emption operator $P \; \mathbf{until}_h \; b$ that permits evolution according to P until the condition b becomes true; it thus imposes constraints on the possible durations ℓ after which control passes to the next hybrid computation.

The Multivariate Analysis package [14] of Isabelle provides a precise encoding of real numbers as Cauchy sequences and several operators from the integral and differential calculus. We use that package and our interval operator to encode ordinary differential equations (ODEs) in the hybrid relational calculus. Namely, $\langle \dot{x} = f(t, x) \rangle$ specifies that the derivative of $x(t)$ is given by $f(t, x(t))$— a function of the current time and continuous state. Using Immler's HOL-ODE package [14] we can certify symbolic solutions to initial value problems, and thus reduce $\langle \dot{x} = f(t, x) \rangle$ to a function evolution $x \leftarrow g(x_0, t)$ where g is the solution to $\dot{x}(t) = f(t, x(t))$ with initial condition x_0. Our abstract Modelica semantics in Isabelle/UTP makes use of all of the aforementioned constructs.

We next describe part of the Modelica train model from Sect. 4 in the hybrid relational calculus. We focus on the situation when the train is stopping due to an approaching red signal. The other behaviours can be encoded in a similar way. We formalise this situation using shorter variable names *acc*, *vel* and *pos* for *acceleration*, *current-speed* and *position-on-track*. We note that *normal-deceleration* below is negative and determines the rate at which the train reduces its speed as a result of braking forces being applied.

$$
Braking\,Train \;\widehat{=}\; \left(
\begin{array}{l}
acc := normal\text{-}deceleration\,; \\
vel := max\text{-}speed\,; \\
pos := 0\,; \\
\left\langle \begin{pmatrix} \dot{acc} \\ \dot{vel} \\ \dot{pos} \end{pmatrix} = \begin{pmatrix} 0 \\ acc \\ vel \end{pmatrix} \right\rangle \; \mathbf{until}_h \; (vel \le 0)\,; \\
acc := 0
\end{array}
\right)
$$

We first assign initial values to the continuous variables, and this effectively creates initial conditions for the ODE. We then evolve the continuous variables, according to the ODE, until the velocity reaches 0. After this, we set the acceleration to 0, so that the train halts and does not start moving backwards.

The above hybrid relation encodes the kinetic and control equations in the right diagram of Fig. 6, albeit only considering deceleration. For the complete train model, we require an additional variable for the set-point speed and equations for calculating it from the signal vector. Those, however, are not differential equations and can likewise use the interval operator previously described.

We have encoded the example in Isabelle/UTP and mechanised a proof (see Fig. 9) that the train stops before the track ends, that is, $\lceil pos < 44 \rceil$ holds, where 44 m is the track length of CDV_Q2 in Fig. 5. For the sake of brevity, we elide details of the proof, other than the first four steps. The proof proceeds as follows.

1. Solve the ODE *symbolically* to obtain a function evolution statement. This requires us to show Lipschitz continuity of the ODE so that, via the Picard Lindelöf theorem, there is precisely one such solution;
2. Use the assigned values to obtain the set of initial conditions;
3. Calculate the precise time at which the velocity reaches zero; here, that is approximately after 2.97 s;
4. Prove that the position at every earlier instant is less than 44 m.

Step (4) requires to solve the polynomial inequality $(104/25) * t - (7/10) * t^2 < 44$ which includes the solution for the position derivative. In Isabelle, this can be done using the lesser-known *approximate* tactic, which safely employs a floating-point approximation to prove the conjecture with respect to the reals, including support for transcendental functions like *sin*, *cos* and square root.

Our analysis has proceeded directly at the level of the Modelica train model, and our next aim shall be to transfer this result to the FMI cosimulation model

```
definition
"BrakingTrain =
    c:accel, c:vel, c:pos := «normal_deceleration», «max_speed», «0» ;;
    ({&accel,&vel,&pos} • «train_ode»)ₕ untilₕ ($vel´ ≤ᵤ 0) ;; c:accel := 0"

theorem braking_train_pos_le:
  "($c:accel´ =ᵤ 0 ∧ ⌈$pos´ <ᵤ 44⌉ₕ) ⊑ BrakingTrain" (is "?lhs ⊑ ?rhs")
proof -
  -- {* Solve ODE, replacing it with an explicit solution: @{term train_sol}. *}
  have "?rhs =
    c:accel, c:vel, c:pos := «-1.4», «4.16», «0» ;;
    {&accel,&vel,&pos} ←ₕ «train_sol»(&accel,&vel,&pos)ₐ(«time»)ₐ untilₕ ($vel´ ≤ᵤ 0) ;;
    c:accel := 0"
  by (simp only: BrakingTrain_def train_sol)
  -- {* Set up initial values for the ODE solution using assigned variables. *}
  also have "... =
    {&accel,&vel,&pos} ←ₕ «train_sol(-1.4,4.16,0)(time)» untilₕ ($vel´ ≤ᵤ 0) ;; c:accel := 0"
  by (simp add: assigns_r_comp usubst unrest alpha, literalise, simp)
```

Fig. 9. The braking train scenario encoded in Isabelle/UTP.

of the entire system. For this, the train models are wrapped into *Circus* processes corresponding to the train FMUs in the left diagram of Fig. 6. This is on-going work; our initial results provide evidence that our semantic theories and reasoning framework is up to the challenge of proving properties in this context.

6   Conclusion

We have reported on some initial results in formalising and mechanising FMI cosimulations in our theorem prover Isabelle/UTP. Our contribution entails a novel mechanisation of *Circus* and the FMI in Isabelle/UTP, as well as the train FMUs of the railways case study, which we encoded for proof-based analysis.

The relevance of our project is to enable proofs about cosimulated systems, as well as the cosimulation itself. Such proofs may, for instance, entail behavioural correctness and safety properties, such as trains cannot collide. We also envisage proofs that validate the suitability of simulations to observe faults or—vice versa—provide tangible evidence for their absence. While the details of how this can be done touches upon open research problems, the models and their encoding described here are a first important step into this direction.

A collateral contribution is to provide an encoding of the *Circus* language, as this was required to mechanise the semantics of the FMI framework. While our proof system currently offers support for CSP, the *Circus* language poses further challenges related to the representation of *Circus* processes and actions, dynamic channel declarations, and specialised *Circus* operators.

Related work is Broman's formalisation of the FMI [5]. It proposes a functional model that is sufficiently expressive to enable proofs of determinacy and termination of master algorithms. A more general approach is by Iugan et al. who present a conceptual framework for cosimulation not confined to FMI [15]. That work uses the DEVS formalism together with timed automata, and the UPPAAL model checker for validation. Their focus is, however, on rigorous tool design.

Future work will address the completion of our models and investigate proof strategies and laws to reason about the cosimulation as a whole. In addition, we aim to elicit and verify properties of master algorithms that hold independently of the simulators and structure of the simulated model as an FMI system.

Acknowledgement. We would like to thank the anonymous reviewers for their valuable comments. The work was funded by the INTO-CPS EC grant 644047.

A *Circus* Constructs

Summary of *Circus* constructs used in our models in the Figs. 2 and 4.

Table 1. Overview of relevant *Circus* operators on actions.

Name	Syntax	Description
Sequence	$A \ ; \ B$	Execute A and B in sequence
Parallelism	$A \llbracket cs \rrbracket B$	Execute A and B in parallel, synchronising on the channels in the channel set cs
External choice	$A \square B$	The environment decides whether A or B is executed; communication resolves the choice
Input prefix	$c?x \to A(x)$	Input a value on a typed channel c
Output prefix	$c!e \to A$	Output a value e on a typed channel c
Guarded action	$g \ \& \ A$	Proceed with A only if g is true
Assignment	$x := e$	Assignment to a state component x
Stop	**stop**	Stop and refuse any further communication

References

1. Modelica Association: Functional Mock-up Interface for Model Exchange and Co-Simulation. Technical Report Document Version 2.0, Linköping University (Sweden), July 2014. http://fmi-standard.org/downloads/
2. Cavalcanti, A., Sampaio, A., Woodcock, J.: A refinement strategy for *Circus*. Form. Asp. Comput. **15**(2), 146–181 (2003)
3. Cavalcanti, A., Woodcock, J., Amálio, N.: Behavioural models for FMI co-simulations. In: Sampaio, A., Wang, F. (eds.) ICTAC 2016. LNCS, vol. 9965, pp. 255–273. Springer, Cham (2016). https://doi.org/10.1007/978-3-319-46750-4_15
4. Chaochen, Z., Hoare, T., Ravn, A.P.: A calculus of durations. Inf. Process. Lett. **40**(5), 269–276 (1991)
5. Broman, D., et al.: Determinate composition of FMUs for co-simulation. In: Proceedings of EMSOFT 2013, pp. 2:1–2:12. IEEE Press, September 2013
6. Larsen, P.G., et al.: Tutorial for Overture/VDM-RT. Technical Report TR-005, September 2015. http://overturetool.org/documentation/tutorials.html

7. Blochwitz, T., et al.: The functional mockup interface for tool independent exchange of simulation models. In: Proceedings of the 8th International Modelica Conference (2011)

8. Foster, S., Cavalcanti, A., Canham, S., Pierce, K., Woodcock, J.: Final Semantics of VDM-RT. Deliverable 2.2b, INTO-CPS Project, H2020 Grant 644047, December 2016. http://projects.au.dk/fileadmin/D2.2b_Final_VDM-RT_Semantics.pdf

9. Foster, S., Thiele, B., Cavalcanti, A., Woodcock, J.: Towards a UTP semantics for modelica. In: Bowen, J.P., Zhu, H. (eds.) UTP 2016. LNCS, vol. 10134, pp. 44–64. Springer, Cham (2017). https://doi.org/10.1007/978-3-319-52228-9_3

10. Foster, S., Zeyda, F., Woodcock, J.: Isabelle/UTP: a mechanised theory engineering framework. In: Naumann, D. (ed.) UTP 2014. LNCS, vol. 8963, pp. 21–41. Springer, Cham (2015). https://doi.org/10.1007/978-3-319-14806-9_2

11. Gomes, C., Thule, C., Broman, D., Larsen, P.G., Vangheluwe, H.: Co-simulation: state of the art. ArXiv e-prints, arXiv:1702.00686, February 2017

12. Jifeng, H., Qin, L.: A hybrid relational modelling language. In: Gibson-Robinson, T., Hopcroft, P., Lazić, R. (eds.) Concurrency, Security, and Puzzles. LNCS, vol. 10160, pp. 124–143. Springer, Cham (2017). https://doi.org/10.1007/978-3-319-51046-0_7

13. Hoare, T.: Communicating Sequential Processes. Prentice-Hall, Upper Saddle River (1985)

14. Immler, F., Hölzl, J.: Numerical analysis of ordinary differential equations in Isabelle/HOL. In: Beringer, L., Felty, A. (eds.) ITP 2012. LNCS, vol. 7406, pp. 377–392. Springer, Heidelberg (2012). https://doi.org/10.1007/978-3-642-32347-8_26

15. Iugan, L.G., Boucheneb, H., Nicolescu, G.: A generic conceptual framework based on formal representation for the design of continuous/discrete co-simulation tools. Des. Autom. Embed. Syst. **19**(3), 243–275 (2015)

16. Jones, C.B.: Systematic Software Development using VDM. Prentice-Hall, Upper Saddle River (1990)

17. Lausdahl, K., Verhoef, M., Larsen, P.G., Wolff, S.: Overview of VDM-RT constructs and semantic issues. In Proceedings of the 8th Overture Workshop, CS-TR, vol. 1224, pp. 57–67, September 2010

18. Modelica Association: Modelica® – A Unified Object-Oriented Language for Systems Modeling, Language Specification, Version 3.4, April 2017. https://www.modelica.org/documents/

19. Morgan, C.: Programming from Specifications. Prentice-Hall, Upper Saddle River (1996)

20. Petzold, L.: Differential/algebraic equations are not ODEs. SIAM J. Sci. Stat. Comput. **3**(3), 367–384 (1982)

21. van Amerongen, J., Kleijn, C., Gamble, C.: Continuous-time modelling in 20-sim. In: Fitzgerald, J., Larsen, P.G., Verhoef, M. (eds.) Collaborative Design for Embedded Systems, pp. 27–59. Springer, Heidelberg (2014). https://doi.org/10.1007/978-3-642-54118-6_3

22. Woodcock, J., Davies, J.: Using Z: Specification, Refinement, and Proof. Prentice-Hall, Upper Saddle River (1996)

23. Zeyda, F., Foster, S., Cavalcanti, A.: Mechanisation of the FMI. Technical report, University of York, UK, June 2017. https://github.com/isabelle-utp/utp-main/blob/master/fmi/fmi_report.pdf

FOCLASA 2017

FOCLASA 2017 Organizers' Message

Modern software systems are distributed, concurrent, mobile, and often involve composition of heterogeneous components and stand-alone services. Service coordination and self-adaptation constitute the core characteristics of distributed and service-oriented systems. Coordination languages and formal approaches to modeling and reasoning about self-adaptive behavior help to simplify the development of complex distributed service-based systems, enable functional correctness proofs, and improve the reusability and maintainability of such systems.

The 15th International Workshop on Foundations of Coordination Languages and Self-Adaptative Systems (FOCLASA 2017) was held in Trento, Italy, on September 5, 2017. It was colocated with the 15th International Conference on Software Engineering and Formal Methods (SEFM 2017). The goal of FOCLASA is to put together researchers and practitioners to share and identify common problems, and to devise general solutions in the context of coordination languages and self-adaptive systems

FOCLASA 2017 received 16 full submissions. Papers underwent a rigorous review process, and each paper received three reviews. After a careful discussion phase, the international Program Committee decided to select seven research papers for presentation during the workshop and inclusion in the proceedings. The workshop also featured one invited talk by Gianluigi Zavattaro (University of Bologna, Italy), who presented recent results on the automatic deployment of cloud applications.

We would like to thank the local Organizing Committee for taking care of all the local arrangements, the workshop chairs (Antonio Cerone and Marco Roveri) for guiding us during the workshop organization, Gianluca Barbon for acting as publicity chair, and Alejandro Perez Vereda for acting as Web master.

We assembled an exciting technical program that would not have been possible without the excellent work of the Program Committee during the review process and discussions, and the participation of the external reviewers in the review process. Last, but not least, we thank all the authors for submitting papers to the workshop, our invited speaker for taking the time to travel to Trento and for giving us an excellent talk, and all the participants (speakers or not) who attended the workshop in Trento. All these people contributed to the success of the 2017 edition of FOCLASA.

September 2017

Carlos Canal
Gwen Salaün

Organization

FOCLASA 2017 - Steering Committee

Farhad Arbab	CWI, The Netherlands
Antonio Brogi	University of Pisa, Italy
Carlos Canal	University of Málaga, Spain
Jean-Marie Jacquet	University of Namur, Belgium
Ernesto Pimentel	University of Málaga, Spain
Gwen Salaün	University of Grenoble Alpes, France

FOCLASA 2017 - Program Committee

Pedro Alvarez	Universidad de Zaragoza, Spain
Farhad Arbab	CWI, The Netherlands
Simon Bliudze	EPFL, Switzerland
Radu Calinescu	University of York, UK
Javier Camara	Carnegie Mellon University, USA
Flavio De Paoli	University of Milan, Italy
Schahram Dustdar	TU Wien, Austria
Jean-Marie Jacquet	University of Namur, Belgium
Nima Kaviani	IBM, USA
Alberto Lluch Lafuente	Technical University of Denmark
Sun Meng	Peking University, China
Hernan C. Melgratti	University of Buenos Aires, Argentina
Mohammad Mousavi	Halmstad University, Sweden
Marc Oriol	Universitat Politècnica de Catalunya, Spain
Pascal Poizat	Université Paris Ouest, France
Jose Proenca	INESC TEC and Universidade do Minho, Portugal
Michael Sheng	University of Adelaide, Australia
Marjan Sirjani	Reykjavik University, Iceland
Carolyn Talcott	SRI International, USA
Massimo Tivoli	University of L'Aquila, Italy
Lina Ye	CentraleSupélec, France
Gianluigi Zavattaro	University of Bologna, Italy

FOCLASA 2017 - Additional Reviewers

Marco Autili	University of L'Aquila, Italy
Antonio Bucchiarone	FBK, Italy

Saverio Giallorenzo	University of Bologna, Italy
Ali Jafari	Reykjavik University, Iceland
Sung-Shik Jongmans	Open University of The Netherlands
Fatemeh Ghassemi	University of Tehran, Iran
Narges Khakpour	Royal Institute of Technology, Sweden
Ehsan Khamespanah	University of Tehran, Iran
Alfons Laarman	Leiden University, The Netherlands
Stefano Mariani	University of Bologna, Italy
George Mason	University of York, UK
Anastasia Mavridou	Vanderbilt University, USA
Morteza Mohaqeqi	Uppsala University, Sweden
Colin Paterson	University of York, UK

A Foundational Study of Automatic Cloud Applications Deployment

(Keynote Talk)

Jacopo Mauro[1] and Gianluigi Zavattaro[2]

[1] Department of Computer Science, University of Oslo, Norway

[2] Department of Computer Science and Engineering, University of Bologna, Italy

Modern software systems are based on a large number of interconnected software components that must be deployed on a pool of (virtual) machines. We have formally investigated this deployment problem by defining the *Aeolus* model, in which the classical notion of component, seen as a black-box that exposes (resp. requires) functionalities via provide-port (resp. require-) ports, is extended with a finite state automaton describing the component configuration life-cycle. Moreover, Aeolus allows for the specification of conflicts among component types and for the quantification of upper (resp. lower) bounds on the number of connections on provide- (resp. require-) ports. The deployment problem consists of checking, given a universe of component types, the possibility to configure at least one component of a given type in a given target state.

The main results we have obtained are: the deployment problem is undecidable in its general version, it is non-primitive recursive if we remove conflicts, and it is poly-time if we remove also numerical constraints. In the light of these results, and noting that violating conflicts and numerical constraints while systems are deployed is tolerable, we have proposed a novel approach for automatic deployment: first compute a correct final configuration abstracting away from the configuration automata (this can be done by exploiting constraint solving technology) and then synthesize a deployment plan considering the configuration automata, but abstracting away from conflicts and numerical constraints. This is particularly suited for the blue green continuous deployment strategy where a new system (green) is deployed from scratch and replaces the old system (blue).

Towards the Performance Analysis of Elastic Systems with e-Motions

Patrícia Araújo de Oliveira, Francisco Durán$^{(\boxtimes)}$, and Ernesto Pimentel

University of Málaga, Málaga, Spain
{patricia,duran,ernesto}@lcc.uma.es

Abstract. We use graph transformation to define an adaptive component model, what allows us to carry on predictive analysis of dynamic architectures through simulations. Specifically, we build on an e-Motions definition of the Palladio component model, and then specify adaptation mechanisms as generic adaptation rules. We show how the simulation-based analysis available in such a static definition can be extended in order to use the collected information on metrics such as response time, throughput and resource usage to adapt to the workload of the system and the environmental conditions. We illustrate our approach with rules modeling the scale in and out of servers, fired in response to the violation of specified constraints on the usage of resources. We evaluate this scenario by analyzing its performance, and discuss on its consequences in practice.

1 Introduction

Different approaches have been proposed for the predictive analysis of systems, including techniques based on queue networks, Petri nets and statistical methods. However, current predictive analysis tools present serious limitations to deal with dynamic architectures, in general, and to manage elasticity in cloud environments, in particular. The main limitations exhibited by most current tools come from the fact that they operate on static structures, which cannot be modified along the analysis process. This is the case, for instance, of the Palladio tool [1], one of the currently more successful predictive analysis frameworks, and widely used both in industry and academia. Although the Palladio Simulator can be used to predict QoS properties (performance and reliability) from software architecture models, Palladio does not provide support for systems that dynamically adapt to context changes, which is the case in state-of-the-art technologies, such as cloud or IoT scenarios. Despite recent efforts, as we explain in Sect. 6, neither Palladio-based proposals in [2–4], nor other alternative approaches such those in [5–7], provide satisfactory solutions to the problem.

With the objective of extending Palladio's predictive capabilities to support dynamic systems, we propose to use the e-Motions implementation of the Palladio Component Model (PCM) described in [8], and use the graph rewriting approach used there to also model the elastic behavior of systems. Given

A. Cerone and M. Roveri (Eds.): SEFM 2017 Workshops, LNCS 10729, pp. 475–490, 2018.
https://doi.org/10.1007/978-3-319-74781-1_32

the metamodel of Palladio and its operational semantics expressed in terms of graph-transformation rules, this implementation allows to analyze (static) systems modeled in Palladio Bench. However, the relevance of this e-Motions specification is the capability of integrating new adaptation rules, which extend the behavior of Palladio, making feasible the analysis of dynamic systems, and increasing its expressiveness [9]. The facilities for the analysis of different metrics, including response time, resource usage and throuhtput, and the facilities for the extension of the language, present an optimal setting for the definition of the adaptation mechanisms and the analysis of the performance of elastic systems thus defined.

The diagram in Fig. 1 depicts the main elements in our proposal. In e-Motions, a Domain Specific Language (DSL) is specified by its syntax (a metamodel) and a behavior (an operational semantics described as a set of graph transformation rules). The systems to be analyzed are specified using Palladio, and specifically the Palladio Component Model (PCM). Models conforming to the PCM are composed of four different submodels, which correspond to respective views of the system. The Palladio language is specified in e-Motions by taking an extended PCM, denoted PCM*, which includes definitions for tokens and dynamics of systems, and its behavior. As presented in [8], static systems defined in the Palladio Bench (models M_{app} conforming to the PCM) can be loaded and analyzed in e-Motions using the DSL PCM* + $Beh_{Palladio}$. In this work, to deal with adaptive systems, the behavior to be used is extended with adaptation mechanisms, specified as additional e-Motions transformation rules, $Beh_{Adaptation}$. Then, a specific model M_{app} can be used to analyze the performance of the described elastic system using the DSL PCM* + ($Beh_{Palladio}$ + $Beh_{Adaptation}$).

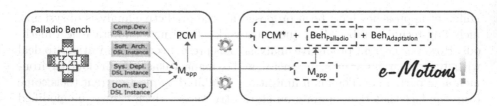

Fig. 1. Architecture

The remainder of this paper is structured as follows. Section 2 provides some background on the Palladio and e-Motions frameworks, also introducing a motivating example to illustrate our approach. Section 3 presents how adaptive rules were defined in e-Motions and shows how they are woven with the Palladio system to enrich its capabilities to analyze dynamic systems. Section 4 presents some experimental results and a discussion on them. Section 5 presents some related work. We wrap up with some conclusions and future work in Sect. 6.

2   Palladio and e-Motions

This work is based on the Model-Driven Engineering (MDE) frameworks Palladio and e-Motions. We use Palladio [1] for the system modeling, and e-Motions [10] to specify Palladio's operational semantics and the adaptation of Palladio systems over time, what allows us to simulate and analyze Palladio-like adaptive systems. In this section, we provide some background on both frameworks to ground the discussion that will follow. We introduce our motivational example to illustrate the main ideas of Palladio, and illustrate the use of e-Motions on its definition of Palladio. Although very simple, it will allow us to introduce the different models involved and the possibilities of our approach.

2.1   The Palladio Component Model

The metamodel of Palladio—its language description—is provided by the Palladio Component Model (PCM) [11]. The semantics of the models, and of the non-functional properties to be analyzed, is encapsulated in respective transformations to different languages and formalisms in which the analysis is carried out.

Palladio assumes a Component-Based Software Engineering (CBSE) development process, in which component developers specify and implement parametric descriptions of components and their behavior. These descriptions are organized in four different views [12]: component developers provide component specifications, software architects provide assembly models, system developers provide allocation models, and business domain experts provide usage models. To illustrate the Palladio views, we present a very simple scenario with a single server and a load balancer structure (depicted in Fig. 2). Then, in Sect. 3, we will use our adaptation rules to add and remove nodes when necessary from this initial scenario.

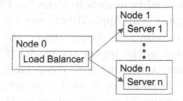

Fig. 2. Structure of the example

Figure 3(a) shows the component repository for our example. It depicts two components and their corresponding interfaces: ApplicationServer implements IApplicationServer and LoadBalancer implements ILoadBalancer. There is one Requires relations from the LoadBalancer component to the IApplication-Server interface, that offers the processRequest() operation. As we can see in

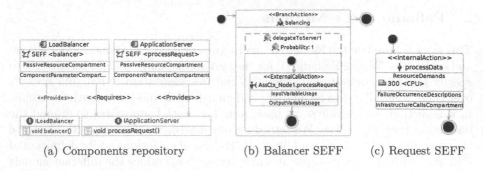

(a) Components repository   (b) Balancer SEFF   (c) Request SEFF

Fig. 3. Component model

the assembly model in Fig. 4(a), the front-end node, containing the LoadBalancer component, will invoke the processRequest() operation provided by the IApplicationServer interface. Components' services are described by service effect specifications (SEFF), which abstractly model the externally visible behavior of a service with resource demands and calls to required services. Figure 3(c) shows the SEFF of the processRequest service, which models the behavior of the server component. Such processing is very simple in our example, it just consists in an internal action that consumes 300 units of CPU (CPU cycles). Figure 3(b) shows the SEFF of the balancer() operation, which models the control flow in the LoadBalancer component as a probabilistic branching. In our example, the system starts with one server, we will see in the coming sections how the dynamic extensions is in charge of adding and removing nodes as needed. Since there is only one branch in this initial Palladio definition, the probabilistic branching initially has one single branch, with probability 1, which has an external call action to the single node of the model. As new nodes are added to the architecture, new branches will be added to this action, thus modeling the distribution of works between the existing servers handled by the load balancer.

Software architects assemble components from the repository to build applications, represented by assembly models in Palladio. Figure 4(a) shows how the services of the LoadBalancer and ApplicationServer components are composed. The biggest square surrounding the boxes represents the entire environment. For each 'provides' relation in the repository model (Fig. 3(a)), a provided role is created for the container containing such component.

Allocation models are provided by system deployers, who model the resource environment and the allocation of components from the assembly model to different resources of the resource environment. Figure 4(b) shows the allocation model for our initial model, where we can see how each of the components is allocated in a different node.

Finally, usage models are provided by domain experts, who specify a system's usage in terms of workload, user behavior, and parameters. Given the usage model definition in Fig. 4(c), in our case study, tasks will arrive following an exponential probability distribution with rate parameter 4.9 time units (Exp(4.9)).

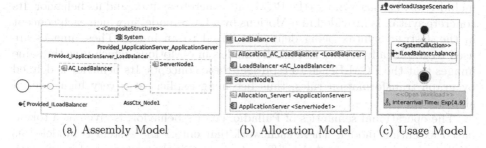

(a) Assembly Model   (b) Allocation Model   (c) Usage Model

Fig. 4. Allocation, usage and assembly models

2.2 Palladio Specification in the e-Motions System

The e-Motions system [10] is a graphical framework that supports the specification, simulation, and formal analysis of real-time systems. It provides a way to graphically specify the dynamic behavior of DSLs using their concrete syntax, making this task very intuitive. The abstract syntax of a DSL is specified as an Ecore metamodel, which defines all relevant concepts and their relations in the language. Its concrete syntax is given by a GCS (Graphical Concrete Syntax) model, which attaches an image to each language concept. Then, its behavior is specified with (graphical) in-place model transformations.

The e-Motions language provides a model of time, supporting features like duration, periodicity, etc., and mechanisms to state action properties. From a DSL definition, the e-Motions tool generates an executable Maude [13] specification which can be used for simulation and analysis. For instance, we can perform reachability analysis, model checking, and statistical model checking of the DSLs defined using e-Motions (see [14,15]).

The in-place model transformations used to specify the behavior of systems are defined by rules, each of which represents a possible *action* of the system. These rules are of the form [NAC]* × LHS → RHS, where LHS (left-hand side), NAC (negative application conditions) and RHS (right-hand side) are model patterns that represent certain (sub-)states of the system. The LHS and NAC patterns express the conditions for the rule to be applied, whereas the RHS represents the effect of the corresponding action if its conditions are satisfied. Thus, the action described in RHS can be applied, i.e., a rule can be triggered, if a match of the LHS is found in the model and none of its NAC patterns occurs. An LHS may also have positive conditions, which are expressed, as any expression in the RHS, using OCL (Object Constraint Language). If several matches are found, one of them is non-deterministically chosen and applied, giving place to a new model where the matching objects are substituted by the appropriate instantiation of its RHS pattern. The transformation of the model proceeds by applying the rules on sub-models of it in a non-deterministic order, until no further transformation rule is applicable.

Palladio is a DSL, and has been specified in [8] using the visual facilities of the e-Motions system [10]. As for any DSL, the e-Motions definition of Palladio includes its abstract syntax (the PCM), its concrete syntax, and its behavior. Its concrete syntax is provided in e-Motions by a GCS model in which each concept in the abstract syntax being defined is linked to an image. These images are used to graphically represent Palladio models in e-Motions, which uses the same images that the PCM Bench to represent these concepts. Its behavior is defined by graph transformation rules, thus becoming explicit at a very high level of abstraction.

The operational semantics of Palladio, i.e., its behavior, is given as a token-based execution model, where each work that enters the system is modeled as a token that moves around the different services of the system, and inside each service description, around the different tasks (start, stop, branch, loop, etc.) in its SEFF descriptions. Each of the actions that may occur in the system are then specified by e-Motions transformation rules. For example, Fig. 5 shows the e-Motions rule that specifies the execution of an InternalAction, like the one shown in Fig. 3(c). This rule represents a generic execution of an internal activity by a component service, possibly using some resources, like HDD or CPU. In Palladio, these executions present a high-level of abstraction, and the resource demands are expressed as stochastic expressions. In the e-Motions rule, the LHS indicates that if there is an internal action not completed in the system, the RHS will execute in time rTime. The duration of this action depends on the corresponding Palladio elements, specifically on the Parameter Resources Demanded (PRD) and on the Processing Resource Specified (PRS). For example, a PRS may have an initial specification of 300 work units per second (PRS.processingRate) and 1 CPU replica (PRS.numberOfReplicas). Tokens are served following an FCFS (First Come First Served) strategy by using a queue associated to each resource type. Only the first PRS.numberOfReplicas tokens in the queue PRT.queue get to be executed. Once an internal action is executed, its token is removed from the queue (PRT.queue→excluding(t)), and marked as completed, being then 'moved' to the following task in the service description.

The behavior of Palladio's core features has been specified by time-aware in-place transformation rules, corresponding to the possible model changes. Once the whole DSL has been defined, and given a model as initial state, it may be simulated by applying the rules describing its behavior. However, this model does not collect information on non-functional properties (NFPs), and therefore is not ready for performance analysis. For this, an observer mechanism [16] is used to measure the non-functional properties of each of the components in the system. The PCM metamodel is extended with a family of observer classes, and their semantics is defined by appropriate definitions in the rules defining the behavior of Palladio. In the rule of the Fig. 3(c), the rus object collects information about PRS resource at run-time, which can then be used for quality informations both during the simulation or for post-simulation analysis. Since the PCM is used as metamodel in the e-Motions definition of Palladio, models developed using the Palladio Bench can be directly loaded into the e-Motions tool. The complete e-Motions definition of the Palladio DSL is available at http://atenea.lcc.uma.es/e-Motions.

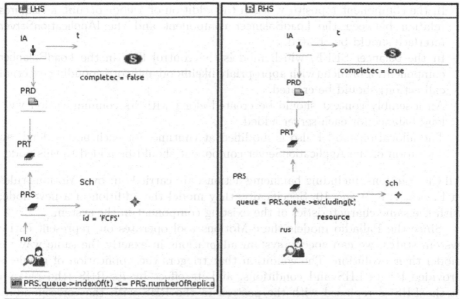

Fig. 5. Internal action SEFF rule

3   Adaptation Mechanisms for e-Motions Palladio Models

In our approach, the different adaptation mechanisms are defined as transformation rules on the model of the system under analysis. Thus, given monitoring information on the different metrics under observation, systems may adapt in different ways by performing different operations, like scale up/down (increase/decrease of the amount of resources like computation capacity, memory, etc.), scale in/out (adding/removing computation or storage nodes), etc. As usual, the monitoring of metrics is stored in the observer objects, which allows us to consult current values, windows of values of certain length, and complete histories of data. To illustrate how our approach works, we focus on one of the most challenging of these operations: the scale out associated to a load balancer as the one in our example, scaling out when the average usage of CPU in the last time window goes over 65%. The analysis in Sect. 4 will use rules for both scale in and out.

Adaptation rules operate on the structure defined in the Palladio models, which are indeed used to provide the initial models for the simulations. The addition of a node in any state of the system (see Fig. 2) will imply the modification of the models of the different views in the Palladio description:

– In the component repository, when the addition of a node occurs, a Requires relation between the LoadBalancer component and the IApplicationServer interface should be created.
– In the balancer SEFF, which models the control flow in the LoadBalancer component, a branch (with appropriate likelihood and corresponding external call action) should be created.
– An assembly context should be created along with its communication with load balance for each server added.
– The allocation model also is modified at runtime: for each node added, an allocation of the ApplicationServer component should be added to this node.

All these actions, including balancing actions, are carried out by e-Motions rules in Figs. 6, 7, 8, 9 and 10. Specifically, they model the addition of a new node, with the same characteristics of the existing component in the system.

Since the Palladio models the e-Motions tool operates on, represent entire system states, we can specify system adaptations in exactly the same way we model their evolution. The condition that triggers the application of a rule is provided by its LHS and conditions, and its effect by its RHS (the pattern in the LHS is replaced with the pattern in the RHS with the corresponding substitution).

The Add Node Rule (Fig. 6) is the main one firing the addition of the node. It is in charge of creating action tokens that will fire and guide the execution of the subsequent rules. The Add Node Rule is triggered when the attribute usPerc of the observer ob indicates that the current value of the average resource usage in the time window is over 65%. The RHS of the rules specifies that the action to perform to react to such an event consist in the creation of a new node nNode in the environment recEnv; in addition, a link is established with the computing lan center linkRes, a token indicating the creation of a new node tNnode and a token of the resource specification spec. After this rule, and fired by the reception of these tokens, four additional rules are in charge of configuring and inserting the node in the existing context. Figure 7 shows the rule that creates the resource specification of the new node, which is triggered when there is a token resource specification spec linked to a node object nNode, the resource type rType and the scheduling policy sPolicy (both values in the token specification spec) is in the model. In such a situation, this rule creates the indicated specification for the new rule, removing the token specification spec when the action is performed.

Figure 8 shows the establishment of the context of the new node. The action is triggered when there is a new node token tNnode linked with a node object nNode. The rule uses the context of the component to allocate the new node, associated to the signature sign, Resource Demanding SEFF seffRD, Application Server reBasComp (Basic Component), Operation Provided Role prov and Operation Interface reOpInterface. When applied, the rule allocates the component to the new node, creating a new assembly context for it. Figures 9 and 10 are executed to conclude the process, creating a connection with the Load Balancer component lbResBasComp and a new probabilistic branch transition to the new node seffProbBranchTrans, respectively.

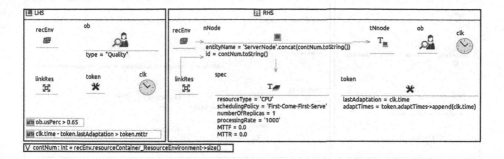

Fig. 6. Add node rule

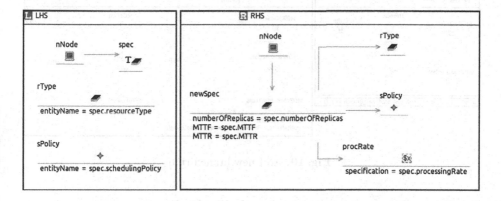

Fig. 7. Resource specification new node rule

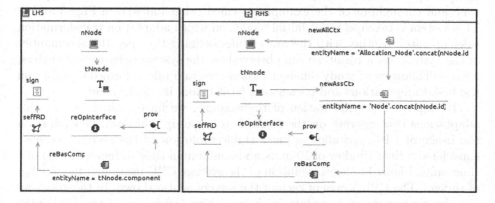

Fig. 8. Context new node rule

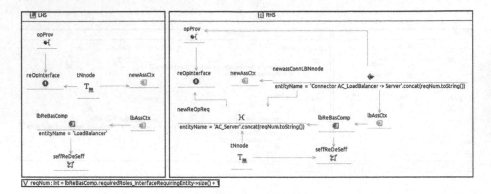

Fig. 9. Load balancer and new node connection rule

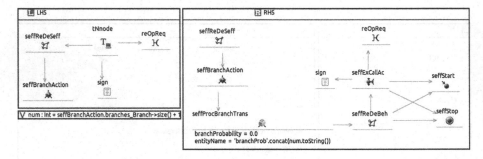

Fig. 10. Add new branch rule

4   Some Experimentation and Analysis

As for static systems, we can now carry on performance analysis of system designs. Specifically, we discuss here the analysis of the resource usage, response time and throughput of the example specified using Palladio in Figs. 3 and 4. This system is taken as input initial model, on which adaptation transformation rules operate, together with the rest of rules defining the operational semantics of the system. As a result we can observe how the system behaves and evolves, what will allow us to study different parameters, and take informed decisions on the best configurations and parameters for it before its deployment.

To improve the presentation of the example, we have limited the possible adaptations that operate on the example to scale up and down depending on the usage of CPU. To allow a more stable evolution of the system, we have considered a time window of 10 units and a minimum time to repair (TBA) of 5 time units. Figure 11 shows evolution of the average CPU usage and the number of servers. The CPU usage of each of the servers is also shown. In the graph we can observe how the system starts with one servers (initial model provided in the Palladio specification), and although the average CPU usage is 100% (the rate of incoming works clearly overrates the capacity of the only server), a second server is not created until time 5 (the application of the first scale-out adaptation occurs at time 5.07). We can observe an immediate drop in the average resource usage after the creation of this second server. However, it is not quick enough, after 5 time units a new adaptation occurs, and after 5 more a third adaptation leaves the system with 4 servers (at times 10.19 and 15.27). This configuration with 4 servers goes on until time 68.32, where the average CPU usage goes below 35%, the threshold for a scale in. The works in the queues produce a new scale out some time later, and one more scale in after some more time. After this last adaptation the average CPU usage of the servers stays within the established thresholds and the system stays with 3 servers.

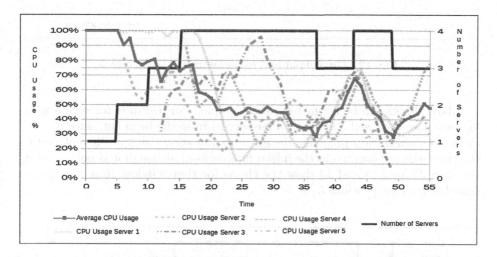

Fig. 11. CPU usage correlation with the number of servers scaled: TW 5, TBA 5

The scale in operation is quite similar to the scale out one described in Sect. 3. In this case, the node is removed, the references to it are removed, and the probabilities of the remaining nodes are redistributed. However, although no further works are submitted to a node being removed, it is kept in operation until all the jobs in its execution queue are processed. This explains the non-abrupt ending lines for nodes being destroyed.

The chart in the Fig. 12 shows the throughput (defined as the number of works processes per time unit) and response time values compared with the adaptations that have occurred over time. We can see the increase in the throughput as the number of servers increases. The impact on the response time can be noticed from time 10. Notice however that after the first server is added, in the time 5.07, there are some works with response times above 4 time units and others with response time below 1 time unit. This of course happens because the works are distributed between different servers, and the server that has just been added can handle new works immediately until it gets saturated. The response time stabilizes after some time, staying below 2 time units after time 15.

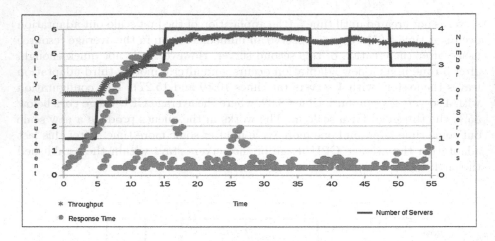

Fig. 12. Throughput and response time: TW 5, TBA 5

Many things can be learnt from these graphs. For instance, for such a workload we may very well start with three servers from the begining, since it seems to be its stabilization point for the given parameters. Using a different size for the time window may avoid the initial fluctuations, although it is not necessary the case. Figures 13 and 14 show the charts for time window 10 and minimum time between adaptations 5.

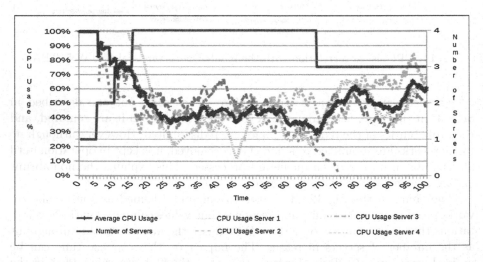

Fig. 13. CPU usage correlation with the number of servers scaled: TW 10, TBA 5

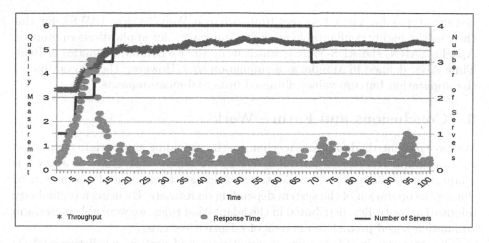

Fig. 14. Quality metrics impact: TW 10, TBA 5

5 Related Work

In this section, we discuss other approaches that use predictive strategies, most of them for performance prediction at runtime or at design time.

Huber et al. propose in [2] a DSL to describe the behavior of self-adaptive systems based on strategies, tactics and actions. This work is part of the Descartes project, which uses Palladio PCM for their design time phases. However, they focus on runtime performance analysis, not in predictive analysis of applications at design time.

SimuLizar [3] is an extension of Palladio for the performance analysis of self-adaptive systems at design time. However, the simulation scope is limited to only a set of rules that are triggered between the static environment models, which prevents from testing all possible reachable states of the systems. This proposal has been recently extended in [4]. However, only scale up/down is supported in this approach, and specifically the change in the number of replicas and the computation capacity of a node.

D-Klaper [5] is a tool for model-driven performance engineering which can be applied to self-adaptive systems. It uses an intermediate language to provide software design models, which can then be analyzed. However, the D-Klaper language does not support the modeling of adaptation rules, nor the transformation of input models.

MEDEA [6] is an approach that proposes the performance prediction at the beginning of its life cycle for this, modeled the workloads with the resource consumption, capturing the CPU, memory and disks, and this is used to generate executable code for real hardware and middleware deployments. The results of the executions are presented to the expert through specific context views that indicate whether the design meets the performance requirements.

Johnsen et al. present in [7] an approach model-based prediction to compare the effect, in terms of performance and accumulated cost, of selecting different instance types for virtual servers from Amazon Web Services (AWS), for this their used a highly configurable modeling framework for applications running on Apache YARN, the ABS-YARN, which using the executable semantics of Real-Time ABS, defined in Maude, as a simulation tool. However, they do not model the application but use values obtained from real measurements.

6   Conclusions and Future Work

We have presented adaptations mechanisms by providing appropriate adaptation rules as graph transformation rules. We used a simple case study to apply our adaptation rules developed in e-Motions to change the amount of resources used during the operation of the system depending on its state. By using a preliminary adaptation controller distributed in the adaptation rules, we were able to perform simulation-based predictive analysis of adaptive systems.

Our approach is able to operate simulations and perform predictive analysis taking into account different adaptation mechanisms. In this work, we have presented the scale out mechanism, although the scale in was also used in the experiments presented. For our case study we observed the response time, throughput at resource usage of the system in order to show the feasibility of the approach. Building on the knowledge we have gathered so far, we will specify other mechanisms of adaptation available for cloud systems in more ambitious case studies. We will consider other QoS metrics in addition to the metrics used in this paper, including not only performance metrics, but also others related to feasibility, costs, and security.

To perform the analysis of a dynamic system, it is necessary to consider their capacity to process and manage different workflows, react through variations of the usage, and to carry on the necessary changes when components have assigned different workloads. Following standard techniques, we will model workloads based on real uses of systems, and will use this information to perform our simulations.

We will evaluate our proposal modeling real applications running in real cloud environments, and will verify that the results produced by our predictive analysis match the actual behavior of the real system executed in the cloud.

With this work, we try to offer the techniques and tools to allow the modeling of self-adaptive systems, and specifically cloud infrastructure, and their analysis, so that a better estimation of the satisfaction of the requirements of systems can be carried on, supporting a better selection of resources and a better calibration of the operational parameters.

The prediction of QoS metrics is one of the most relevant issues when gathering knowledge of applications and their environments, compared to other solutions presented in the literature [17]. However, existing prediction methods do not consider specific cloud metrics and, therefore, they are not capable of managing other particular cloud features, such as self-provisioning on demand, measured usage, network access, resource pooling, and elasticity. Properties related to scalability, elasticity and efficiency are essential to achieve a dynamic adaptation in a cloud scenario, specifically for resource allocation and pay-per-use.

Thus, we need to take into account these new metrics [18], and also a taxonomy of different sources of uncertainty present in the models of self-adaptive systems and the different ways of managing them [19].

Acknowledgements. This work has been partially supported by MINECO/FEDER projects TIN2014-52034-R and TIN2015-67083-R, by Universidad de Málaga, Campus de Excelencia Internacional Andalucía Tech, and by funding agency CNPq of the Ministry of Science and Technology (MCT), Brazil.

References

1. Happe, J., Koziolek, H., Reussner, R.: Facilitating performance predictions using software components. IEEE Softw. **28**(3), 27–33 (2011)
2. Huber, N., van Hoorn, A., Koziolek, A., Brosig, F., Kounev, S.: S/T/A: meta-modeling run-time adaptation in component-based system architectures. In: 9th International Conference on e-Business Engineering (ICEBE), pp. 70–77. IEEE (2012)
3. Becker, M., Becker, S., Meyer, J.: SimuLizar: design-time modeling and performance analysis of self-adaptive systems. Softw. Eng. **213**, 71–84 (2013)
4. Becker, S., Brataas, G., Lehrig, S.: Engineering Scalable, Elastic, and Cost-Efficient Cloud Computing Applications. Springer, Heidelberg (2017). https://doi.org/10.1007/978-3-319-54286-7
5. Grassi, V., Mirandola, R., Randazzo, E.: Model-driven assessment of QoS-aware self-adaptation. In: Cheng, B.H.C., de Lemos, R., Giese, H., Inverardi, P., Magee, J. (eds.) Software Engineering for Self-Adaptive Systems. LNCS, vol. 5525, pp. 201–222. Springer, Heidelberg (2009). https://doi.org/10.1007/978-3-642-02161-9_11
6. Falkner, K., Szabo, C., Chiprianov, V.: Model-driven performance prediction of systems of systems. In: Proceedings of the ACM/IEEE 19th International Conference on Model Driven Engineering Languages and Systems, p. 44. ACM (2016)
7. Johnsen, E.B., Lin, J.-C., Yu, I.C.: Comparing AWS deployments using model-based predictions. In: Margaria, T., Steffen, B. (eds.) ISoLA 2016. LNCS, vol. 9953, pp. 482–496. Springer, Cham (2016). https://doi.org/10.1007/978-3-319-47169-3_39
8. Moreno-Delgado, A., Durán, F., Zschaler, S., Troya, J.: Modular DSLs for flexible analysis: an e-Motions reimplementation of Palladio. In: Cabot, J., Rubin, J. (eds.) ECMFA 2014. LNCS, vol. 8569, pp. 132–147. Springer, Cham (2014). https://doi.org/10.1007/978-3-319-09195-2_9
9. de Oliveira, P.A., Moreno-Delgado, A., Durán, F., Pimentel, E.: Towards the predictive analysis of cloud systems with e-Motions. In: XX Ibero-American Conference on Software Engineering (CIbSE) (2017)
10. Rivera, J.E., Durán, F., Vallecillo, A.: A graphical approach for modeling time-dependent behavior of DSLs. In: 2009 IEEE Symposium on Visual Languages and Human-Centric Computing (VL/HCC), pp. 51–55. IEEE (2009)
11. Becker, S., Koziolek, H., Reussner, R.: Model-based performance prediction with the Palladio component model. In: 6th International Workshop on Software and Performance (WOSP). ACM (2007)
12. Becker, S., Koziolek, H., Reussner, R.: The Palladio component model for model-driven performance prediction. J. Syst. Softw. **82**(1), 3–22 (2009)

13. Clavel, M., Durán, F., Eker, S., Lincoln, P., Martí-Oliet, N., Meseguer, J., Talcott, C.L.: All About Maude. LNCS, vol. 4350. Springer, Heidelberg (2007). https://doi.org/10.1007/978-3-540-71999-1
14. Rivera, J.E., Durán, F., Vallecillo, A.: Formal specification and analysis of domain specific models using Maude. Simulation **85**(11–12), 778–792 (2009)
15. Durán, F., Moreno-Delgado, A., Álvarez-Palomo, J.M.: Statistical model checking of e-Motions domain-specific modeling languages. In: Stevens, P., Wąsowski, A. (eds.) FASE 2016. LNCS, vol. 9633, pp. 305–322. Springer, Heidelberg (2016). https://doi.org/10.1007/978-3-662-49665-7_18
16. Troya, J., Vallecillo, A., Durán, F., Zschaler, S.: Model-driven performance analysis of rule-based domain specific visual models. Inf. Softw. Technol. **55**(1), 88–110 (2013)
17. Chinneck, J., Litoiu, M., Woodside, M.: Real-time multi-cloud management needs application awareness. In: Proceedings of the 5th ACM/SPEC International Conference on Performance Engineering, ICPE 2014, pp. 293–296. ACM (2014)
18. Becker, M., Lehrig, S., Becker, S.: Systematically deriving quality metrics for cloud computing systems. In: 6th International Conference on Performance Engineering, pp. 169–174. ACM (2015)
19. Pérez-Palacín, D., Mirandola, R.: Uncertainties in the modeling of self-adaptive systems: a taxonomy and an example of availability evaluation. In: 5th International Conference on Performance Engineering (ICPE), pp. 3–14. ACM (2014)

From (Incomplete) TOSCA Specifications to Running Applications, with Docker

Antonio Brogi, Davide Neri, Luca Rinaldi, and Jacopo Soldani[✉]

Department of Computer Science, University of Pisa, Pisa, Italy
soldani@di.unipi.it

Abstract. Cloud applications typically consist of multiple interacting components, each requiring a virtualised runtime environment providing the needed software support (e.g., operating system, libraries). In this paper, we show how TOSCA and Docker can be effectively exploited to orchestrate multi-component applications, even if their (runtime) specification is incomplete. More precisely, we first propose a TOSCA-based representation for multi-component applications, and we show how to use it to specify only the components forming an application. We then present a way to automatically complete TOSCA application specifications, by discovering Docker-based runtime environments that provide the software support needed by the application components. We also discuss how the obtained specifications can be automatically orchestrated by existing TOSCA engines.

1 Introduction

Cloud computing permits running on-demand distributed applications at a fraction of the cost which was necessary just a few years ago [1]. This has revolutionised the way applications are built in the IT industry, where monoliths are giving way to distributed, component-based architectures. Modern cloud applications typically consist of multiple interacting components, which (compared to monoliths) permit better capitalising the benefits of cloud computing [8].

At the same time, the need for orchestrating the management of multi-component applications across heterogeneous cloud platforms has emerged [14]. The deployment, configuration, enactment and termination of the components forming an application must be suitably orchestrated. This must be done by taking into account all the dependencies occurring among the components forming an application, as well as the fact that each application component must run in a virtualised environment providing the software support it needs [10].

Developers and operators are currently required to manually select and configure an appropriate runtime environment for each application component, and to explicitly describe how to orchestrate such components on top of the selected environments [16]. Such process must then be manually repeated whenever a developer wishes to modify the virtual environment actually used to run an application component (e.g., because the latter has been updated and it now needs additional software support).

© Springer International Publishing AG 2018
A. Cerone and M. Roveri (Eds.): SEFM 2017 Workshops, LNCS 10729, pp. 491–506, 2018.
https://doi.org/10.1007/978-3-319-74781-1_33

The current support for developing cloud applications should be enhanced. In particular, developers should be required to describe only the components forming an application, the dependencies occurring among such components, and the software support needed by each component [2]. Such description should be fed to tools capable of automatically selecting and configuring an appropriate runtime environment for each application component, and of automatically orchestrating the application management on top of the selected runtime environments. Such tools should also allow developers to automatically modify the virtual environment running an application component whenever they wish.

In this paper, we present a solution geared towards providing such an enhanced support. Our solution is based on TOSCA [18], the OASIS standard for orchestrating cloud applications, and on Docker, the de-facto standard for cloud container virtualisation [19]. The main contributions of this paper are indeed the following:

- We propose a TOSCA-based representation for multi-component applications, which can be used to specify the components forming an application, the dependencies among them, and the software support that each component requires to effectively run.
- We present a tool that automatically completes TOSCA application specifications, by discovering and including Docker-based runtime environments providing the software support needed by the application components. The tool also permits changing –when/if needed– the runtime environment used to host a component.

The obtained application specifications can then be processed by orchestration engines supporting TOSCA and Docker (such as TosKer [4], for instance). Such engines will automatically orchestrate the deployment and management of the corresponding applications on top of the specified runtime environments.

The rest of the paper is organised as follows. Section 2 illustrates an example further motivating the need for an enhanced support for orchestrating the management of cloud applications. Section 3 provides some background on TOSCA and Docker. Section 4 shows how to specify application-specific components only, with TOSCA. Section 5 then presents our tool to automatically determine appropriate Docker-based environments for hosting the components of an application. Sections 6 and 7 discuss related work and draw some concluding remarks, respectively.

2   Motivating Scenario

Consider the open-source web-based application *Thinking*[1], which allows its users to share their thoughts, so that all other users can read them. *Thinking* is composed by three interconnected components (Fig. 1), namely (i) a *MongoDB*

---

[1] The source code of *Thinking* is publicly available on GitHub at https://github.com/di-unipi-socc/thinking.

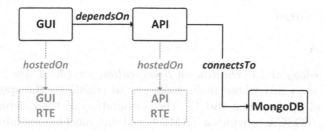

Fig. 1. Running example: the application *Thinking*.

storing the collection of thoughts shared by end-users, (ii) a Java-based REST *API* to remotely access the database of shared thoughts, and (iii) a web-based *GUI* visualising all shared thoughts and allowing to insert new thoughts into the database. As indicated in the documentation of the *Thinking* application:

(i)   The *MongoDB* component can be obtained by directly instantiating a standalone Docker-based service, such as mongo[2], for instance.

(ii) The *API* component must be hosted on a virtualised environment supporting maven (version 3), java (version 1.8) and git (any version). The *API* must also be connected to the *MongoDB*.

(iii) The *GUI* component must be hosted on a virtualised environment supporting nodejs (version 6), npm (version 3) and git (any version). The *GUI* also depends on the availability of the *API* to properly work (as it sends GET/POST requests to the *API* to retrieve/add shared thoughts).

Docker containers work as virtualised environments for running application components [19]. However, we have currently to manually look for the Docker containers offering the software support needed by *API* and *GUI* (or to manually extend existing containers to include such support). We have then to manually package the *API* and *GUI* components within such Docker containers, and to explicitly describe the orchestration of all the Docker containers in our application. In other words, we have to identify, develop, configure and orchestrate all components in Fig. 1, including those not specific to the *Thinking* application (viz., the lighter nodes *API RTE* and *GUI RTE*).

Our effort would be much lower if we were provided with a support requiring us to describe our application only, and automating all remaining tasks. More precisely, we should only be required to specify the thicker nodes and dependencies in Fig. 1. The support should then be able to automatically complete our specification, and to exploit the obtained specification to automatically orchestrate the deployment and management of the application *Thinking*. In this paper, we show a TOSCA-based solution geared towards providing such a support.

---

[2] https://hub.docker.com/_/mongo/.

3   Background

3.1   TOSCA

TOSCA (*Topology and Orchestration Specification for Cloud Applications* [18]) is an OASIS standard whose main goals are to enable (i) the specification of portable cloud applications and (ii) the automation of their deployment and management. TOSCA provides a YAML-based and machine-readable modelling language that permits describing cloud applications. Obtained specifications can then be processed to automate the deployment and management of the specified applications. We hereby report only those features of the TOSCA modelling language that are used in this paper[3].

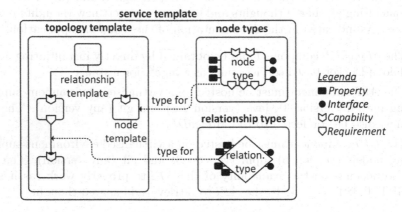

Fig. 2. The TOSCA metamodel [18].

TOSCA permits specifying a cloud application as a service template, which is in turn by a topology template, and by the types needed to build such a topology template (Fig. 2). The topology template is essentially a typed directed graph, which describes the topological structure of a multi-component cloud application. Its nodes (called node templates) model the application components, while its edges (called relationship templates) model the relations occurring among such components.

Node templates and relationship templates are typed by means of node types and relationship types, respectively. A node type defines the observable properties of a component, its possible requirements, the capabilities it may offer to satisfy other components' requirements, and the interfaces through which it offers its management operations. Requirements and capabilities are also typed, to permit specifying the properties characterising them. A relationship type instead describes the observable properties of a relationship occurring between two application components. As the TOSCA type system supports inheritance,

---

[3] A more detailed, self-contained introduction to TOSCA can be found in [2,7].

a node/relationship type can be defined by extending another, thus permitting the former to inherit the latter's properties, requirements, capabilities, interfaces, and operations (if any).

Node templates and relationship templates also specify the artifacts needed to actually perform their deployment or to implement their management operations. As TOSCA allows artifacts to represent contents of any type (e.g., scripts, executables, images, configuration files, etc.), the metadata needed to properly access and process them is described by means of artifact types.

TOSCA applications are packaged and distributed in so-called CSARs (*Cloud Service ARchives*). A CSAR is essentially a zip archive containing an application specification along with the concrete artifacts realising the deployment and management operations of its components.

3.2 Docker

Docker (https://docker.com) is a Linux-based platform for developing, shipping, and running applications through container-based virtualisation. Container-based virtualisation [22] exploits the kernel of the operating system of a host to run multiple isolated user-space instances, called *containers*.

Each Docker container packages the applications to run, along with whatever software support they need (e.g., libraries, binaries, etc.). Containers are built by instantiating so-called Docker *images*, which can be seen as read-only templates providing all instructions needed for creating and configuring a container. Existing Docker images are distributed through so-called Docker *registries* (e.g., Docker Hub—https://hub.docker.com), and new images can be built by extending existing ones.

Docker containers are volatile, and the data produced by a container is (by default) lost when the container is stopped. This is why Docker introduces *volumes*, which are specially-designated directories (within one or more containers) whose purpose is to persist data, independently of the lifecycle of the containers mounting them. Docker never automatically deletes volumes when a container is removed, nor it removes volumes that are no longer referenced by any container.

Docker also allows containers to intercommunicate. It indeed permits creating virtual networks, which span from bridge networks (for single hosts), to complex overlay networks (for clusters of hosts)[4].

4 Specifying Applications Only, with TOSCA

Multi-component applications typically integrate various and heterogeneous components [10]. We hereby propose a TOSCA-based representation for such components (Sect. 4.1). We also illustrate how it can be used to specify only the components that are specific to an application, and to constrain the Docker containers that can be used to actually host such components (Sect. 4.2).

---

[4] A more detailed introduction to Docker can be found in [15, 20].

4.1   A TOSCA-Based Representation for Applications

We first define three different TOSCA node types[5] to distinguish Docker containers, Docker volumes, and software components that can be used to build a multi-component application (Fig. 3).

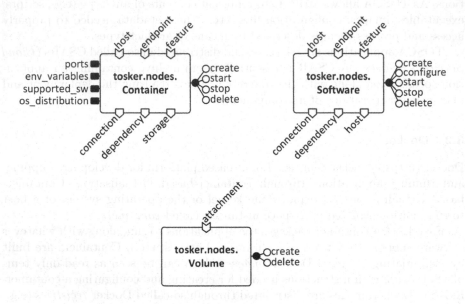

Fig. 3. TOSCA node types for multi-component, Docker-based applications, viz., *tosker.nodes.Container*, *tosker.nodes.Software*, and *tosker.nodes.Volume*.

tosker.nodes.Container permits representing Docker containers, by indicating whether a container requires a *connection* (to another Docker container or to an application component), whether it has a generic *dependency* on another node in the topology, or whether it needs some persistent *storage* (hence requiring to be attached to a Docker volume). *tosker.nodes.Container* also permits indicating whether a container can *host* an application component, whether it offers an *endpoint* where to connect to, or whether it offers a generic *feature* (to satisfy a generic *dependency* requirement of another container or application component). It also lists the operations to manage a container (which correspond to the basic operations offered by Docker [15]).

   To complete the description, *tosker.nodes.Container* provides placeholder properties for specifying port mappings (*ports*) and the environment variables (*env_variables*) to be configured in a running instance of the corresponding Docker container. It also provides two properties (*supported_sw* and *os_distribution*) for indicating the software support provided by the corresponding Docker container and the operating system distribution it runs.

---

[5] The actual TOSCA definition of all node types discussed in this section is publicly available on GitHub at https://github.com/di-unipi-socc/tosker-types.

tosker.nodes.Volume permits specifying Docker volumes, and it defines a capability *attachment* to indicate that a Docker volume can satisfy the *storage* requirements of Docker containers. It also lists the operations to manage a Docker volume (which corresponds to the basic operations offered by the Docker platform [15]).

tosker.nodes.Software permits indicating the software components forming a multi-component application. It permits specifying whether an application component requires a *connection* (to a Docker container or to another application component), whether it has a generic *dependency* on another node in the topology, and that it has to be *hosted* on a Docker container or on another component[6]. *tosker.nodes.Software* also permits indicating whether an application component can *host* another application component, whether it provides an *endpoint* where to connect to, or whether it offers some *feature* (to satisfy a generic *dependency* requirement of a container/application component). Finally, *tosker.nodes.Software* indicates the operations to manage an application component (viz., *create, configure, start, stop, delete*).

The interconnections and interdependencies among the nodes forming a multi-component application can then be indicated by exploiting the TOSCA normative relationship types [18]. Namely, *tosca.relationships.AttachesTo* can be used to attach a Docker volume to a Docker container, *tosca.relationships.ConnectsTo* can indicate interconnections between Docker containers and/or application components, *tosca.relationships.HostedOn* can be used to indicate that an application component is hosted on another component or on a Docker container, and *tosca.relationships.DependsOn* can be used to indicate generic dependencies between the nodes of a multi-component application.

4.2   Specifying Application-Specific Components Only

The TOSCA types introduced in the previous section can be used to specify the topology of a multi-component application. We hereby illustrate, by means of an example, how to specify in TOSCA only the fragment of a topology that is specific to an application (by also constraining the Docker containers that can be used to actually host the components in such fragment).

Example. Consider again the application *Thinking* in our motivating scenario (Sect. 2). The components specific to *Thinking* (viz., *MongoDB, API,* and *GUI*) can be specified in TOSCA as illustrated in Fig. 4:

– *MongoDB* is obtained by directly instantiating a Docker container `mongo` (modelled as a node of type *tosker.nodes.Container*). The latter is attached to a Docker volume where the shared thoughts will be persistently stored[7].

---

[6] The *host* requirement is mandatory for nodes of type *tosker.nodes.Software*, as we assume that each application component must be installed in another component or in a Docker container.

[7] The documentation of `mongo` explicitly states that a `mongo` container must be attached to a Docker volume to persistently store data.

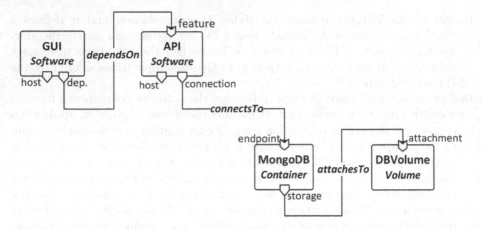

Fig. 4. A specification of our running example in TOSCA (where nodes are typed with *tosker.nodes.Container, tosker.nodes.Volume,* or *tosker.nodes.Software,* while relationships are typed with TOSCA normative types [18]).

- *API* is a software component (viz., a node of type *tosker.nodes.Software*). *API* requires to be connected to the back-end *MongoDB*, to remotely access the database of shared thoughts.
- *GUI* is a software component (viz., a node of type *tosker.nodes.Software*). *GUI* depends on the availability of *API* to properly work (as it sends HTTP requests to the *API* to retrieve/add shared thoughts).

Please note that the requirements *host* of both *API* and *GUI* are left pending (viz., there is no node satisfying them). This is because the actual runtime environment of *API* and *GUI* is not specific to the application *Thinking*, and it should be automatically determined among the many possible (as we will discuss in Sect. 5). The only effort required to the developer is to specify constraints on the configuration of the Docker containers that can effectively host *API* and *GUI* (e.g., which software support they have to provide, which operating system distribution they must run, which port mappings they must expose, etc.).   □

TOSCA natively supports the possibility of expressing constraints on the nodes that can satisfy requirements left pending [18], through the clause **node_filter** that can be indicated within a requirement. **node_filter** permits specifying the type of a node that can satisfy a requirement, and it permit constraining the properties of such node.

We can hence exploit **node_filter** to indicate that the software components in an application must be hosted on Docker containers (viz., on nodes of type *tosker.nodes.Container*). We can also indicate constraints on the software support to be provided by such containers, on the operating system distribution they must run, and on how to configure them (e.g., which port mappings they must expose, or which environment variables they should define).

Example (cont.). Consider again the multi-component application *Thinking*, modelled in TOSCA as in Fig. 4. The pending requirements *host* of *API* and *GUI* must constrain the nodes that can actually satisfy them.

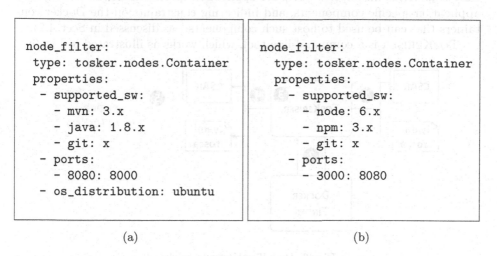

```
node_filter:                      node_filter:
  type: tosker.nodes.Container      type: tosker.nodes.Container
  properties:                       properties:
    - supported_sw:                   - supported_sw:
      - mvn: 3.x                        - node: 6.x
      - java: 1.8.x                     - npm: 3.x
      - git: x                          - git: x
    - ports:                          - ports:
      - 8080: 8000                      - 3000: 8080
    - os_distribution: ubuntu
```

(a)   (b)

Fig. 5. Constraints on the Docker containers that can effectively run the software components (a) *API* and (b) *GUI* (specified within their requirements *host*).

The requirement *host* of *API* can express the constraints on the Docker containers that can effectively host it with the `node_filter` in Fig. 5(a). The latter indicates that *API* needs to run on a Docker container, viz., a node of type *tosker.nodes.Container*, which supports maven (version 3), java (version 1.8) and git (any version). It also indicates a port mapping to be configured in the hosting container and that such container must be based on a Ubuntu distribution[8].

Analogously, the requirement *host* of *GUI* can constrain the Docker containers for hosting it with the `node_filter` in Fig. 5(b). The latter prescribes that *GUI* must run on a Docker container supporting node (version 6), npm (version 3) and git (any version). It also requires the hosting container to expose the indicated port mapping.   □

---

[8] Constraining the operating system distribution is particularly useful when the artifacts implementing the management operations of a software component require to perform distribution-specific system calls (e.g., a *.sh* script performing a command `apt-get`, which is supported only in Ubuntu-based distributions).

5   Completing TOSCA Specifications, with Docker

We hereby present TosKERISER, an open-source prototype tool[9] that automatically completes "incomplete" TOSCA application specifications (describing only application-specific components, and indicating constraints on the Docker containers that can be used to host such components—as discussed in Sect. 4.2).

TosKERISER is a command-line tool, which works as illustrated in Fig. 6:

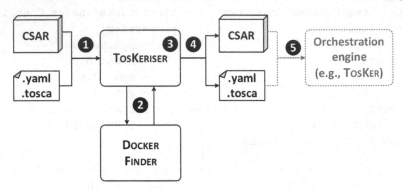

Fig. 6. How TosKERISER works.

❶ TosKERISER inputs a (CSAR or YAML) file containing a TOSCA application specification. It then parses the application topology, and it identifies the set of software components whose requirement *host* has to be fulfilled (according to the constraints indicated in the clause `node_filter` of such requirement).

❷ For each of such components, it invokes DOCKERFINDER[10] to identify a Docker container providing the needed support (viz., satisfying the constraints concerning the `supported_sw` and the `os_distribution`).

❸ The discovered containers are then included in the application topology. More precisely, TosKERISER satisfies the pending requirements *host* by connecting them to new nodes of type *tosker.nodes.Container*. Each of the newly introduced nodes is configured to satisfy the constraints indicated by the software components it hosts (e.g., if a software component is requiring some port mappings, then the newly introduced container that hosts it will have the property *port* set accordingly).

❹ TosKERISER outputs the (CSAR or YAML) file containing the automatically completed TOSCA application specification.

---

[9] The Python sources of TosKERISER are publicly available on GitHub at https:// github.com/di-unipi-socc/toskeriser (under MIT license). TosKERISER is also available on PyPI, and it can be directly installed on Linux hosts by executing the command `pip install toskeriser`.

[10] DOCKERFINDER [3] is a tool allowing to search for Docker containers based on multiple attributes, including the software distributions they support and the operating system distribution they are based on.

5 The obtained file can then be passed to an orchestration engine supporting TOSCA and Docker (e.g., TOSKER [4]), which will automatically deploy and manage the actual instances of the specified application.

TOSKERISER can be actually run by executing the following command[11]:

```
$ toskerise FILE [COMPONENTS] [OPTIONS]
```

where FILE is the (YAML or CSAR) file containing the TOSCA application specification to be completed. COMPONENTS is an optional list, which permits restricting the completion process to a subset of the software components contained in the input application specification (by default, the completion process is applied to all software components). OPTIONS is instead a list of additional options, which permit further customising the execution of TOSKERISER. Among all options that can be indicated, the following are the most interesting:

--constraints The option --constraints permits customising the discovery of Docker images by indicating additional constraints (e.g., by allowing to search for images whose size is lower of 200MB).

--policy This option allows to indicate which images of Docker containers to privilege, among all those that can satisfy the requirement *host* of a software component. The policy top_rated (default) privileges images best rated by Docker users, while policies size and most_used privilege smallest images and most pulled images, respectively.

--interactive (or -i) This option allows users the manually select the image of the Docker container to be used for satisfying the *host* requirement of a software component, from a list that contains only the best images (according to the privileging policy—see --policy).

--force (or -f) The option --force instructs TOSKERISER to search for a new Docker container for each considered component (even if the requirement *host* of such component is already satisfied).

Example. Consider again the application *Thinking* in our motivating scenario, whose corresponding TOSCA representation is displayed in Fig. 4. The CSAR file (thinking.csar) containing the TOSCA application specification of *Thinking* is publicly available on GitHub[12]. Such file can be automatically completed by executing the following command:

```
$ toskerise thinking.csar --policy size
```

The above will generate a new CSAR file (thinking.completed.csar). Such file contains the TOSCA specification of *Thinking*, whose topology is completed by including two new Docker containers, namely *APIContainer* and *GUIContainer*

---

[11] The help of TOSKERISER can be displayed by executing toskerise --help|-h, while its actual version can be displayed by executing toskerise --version|-v.

[12] https://github.com/di-unipi-socc/TosKeriser/blob/master/data/examples/thinking-app/thinking.csar.

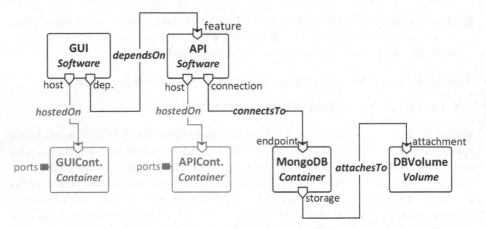

Fig. 7. Application topology obtained by completing the partial topology of the application *Thinking* (Fig. 4). Lighter nodes and relationships are those automatically included by TosKeriser.

(Fig. 7, lighter nodes). Such nodes provide the software support and the port mappings needed by *API* and *GUI*, respectively. We can then run such file with TosKer [4] (or with another orchestration engine supporting both TOSCA and Docker), which will be capable of automatically deploying and managing actual instances of the specified application.

Please note that we run TosKeriser with the option `--policy size`. The latter instructs TosKeriser to concretely implement *APIContainer* and *GUI-Container* with the images of Docker containers having the smallest size (among all images of containers providing the needed software support). Suppose now that we wish to change the containers used to host *GUI* and *API*, e.g., because we now wish to select the containers are most used by Docker users. We can run again TosKeriser on the obtained specification, by setting the option `-f` to force TosKeriser to change the actual implementation of the Docker containers it previously created:

```
$ toskerise thinking.completed.csar -f --policy most_used
```

This will result in changing the actual implementation of *APIContainer* and *GUIContainer* by selecting (among all images of Docker containers that can provide the software support needed by *API* and *GUI*) those images that are most used by Docker users.   □

6   Related Work

We presented a solution for automatically completing TOSCA specifications, which is much in the spirit of [13]. The latter indeed inputs TOSCA specifications containing only the components specific to an application, and it can automatically determine their runtime environments. However, the approach presented in [13] only checks type-compatibility between nodes and runtime environments, while we also allow developers to impose additional constraints on the nodes that can be used to host a component (e.g., by allowing to indicate that an application component requires a certain software support on a certain operating system distribution).

Other approaches worth mentioning are [5,6,21], as they also propose solutions that can be used to automatically determine the runtime environment needed by the components of TOSCA applications. They indeed allow to abstractly specify desired nodes, and they can determine actual implementations for such nodes by matching and adapting existing TOSCA application specifications. [5,6,21] however differ from our approach as they look for type-compatible solutions, without constraining the actual values that can be assigned to a property (hence not allowing to indicate the software support that must be provided by a Docker container, for instance).

If we broaden our view beyond TOSCA, we can identify various other efforts that have been recently oriented to try devising systematic approaches to adapt multi-component applications to work with heterogeneous cloud platforms. For instance, [9,12] propose two approaches to transform platform-agnostic source code of applications into platform-specific applications. In contrast, our approach does not require the availability of the source code of an application, and it is hence applicable also to third-party components whose source code is not available nor open.

[11] proposes a framework allowing developers to write the source code of cloud applications as if they were "on-premise" applications. [11] is similar to our approach, since, based on cloud deployment information (specified in a separate file), it automatically generates all artefacts needed to deploy and manage an application on a cloud platform. [11] however differs from our approach, as artefacts must be (re-)generated whenever an application is moved to a different platform, and since the obtained artefacts must be manually orchestrated on such platform. Our approach instead produces portable TOSCA application specifications, which can be automatically orchestrated by engines supporting both TOSCA and Docker (e.g., TosKer [4]).

In general, most existing approaches to the reuse of cloud services support a from-scratch development of cloud-agnostic applications, and do not account for the possibility of adapting existing (third-party) components. To the best of our knowledge, ours is the first approach for adapting multi-component applications to work with heterogeneous cloud platforms, by relying on TOSCA [18] and Docker to achieve cloud interoperability, and by supporting an easy (re)use of third-party components.

On the one hand, TOSCA is proved to allow automating the orchestration of a multi-component application, thanks to the fact that deployment and management plans can be directly inferred from the topology of an application [2,17]. On the other hand, Docker can standardise the virtual runtime environment of application components to a Linux-based environment [19], hence allowing to implement their deployment and management operations as artefacts supported by such environment.

7 Conclusions

Cloud applications typically consist of multiple heterogeneous components, whose deployment, configuration, enactment and termination must be suitably orchestrated [10]. This is currently done manually, by requiring developers to manually select and configure an appropriate runtime environment for each component in an application, and to explicitly describe how to orchestrate such components on top of the selected environments.

In this paper, we have presented a solution for enhancing the current support for orchestrating the management of cloud applications, based on TOSCA and Docker. More precisely, we have proposed a TOSCA-based representation for multi-component applications, which allows developers to describe *only* the components forming an application, the dependencies among such components, and the software support needed by each component. We have also presented a tool (called TOSKERISER), which can automatically complete the TOSCA specification of a multi-component application, by discovering and configuring the Docker containers needed to host its components.

The obtained application specifications can then be processed by orchestration engines supporting TOSCA and Docker, like TOSKER [4], which can process specifications produced by TOSKERISER, to automatically orchestrate the deployment and management of the corresponding applications.

TOSKERISER is integrated with DOCKERFINDER [3], and it produces specifications that can be effectively processed by TOSKER [4]. TOSKERISER, DOCKERFINDER and TOSKER are all open-source tools, and their ensemble provides a first support for automating the orchestration of multi-component applications with TOSCA and Docker. We plan to further extend this ensemble, to pave the way towards the development of a full-fledged, open-source support for orchestrating multi-component applications with TOSCA and Docker.

In this perspective, an interesting direction for future work is to investigate whether existing approaches for reusing fragments of TOSCA applications (e.g., TOSCAMART [21]) can be included in TOSKERISER. This would permit completing TOSCA specifications by hosting the components of an application not only on single Docker containers, but also on software stacks already employed in other existing solutions.

TOSKERISER currently relies only on DOCKERFINDER [3] to search for existing images of Docker containers. If there is no image providing the software support and the operating system distribution needed by an application component, TOSKERISER cannot complete the corresponding TOSCA specification of the application containing such component. This could be avoided by supporting the creation of ad-hoc images (configured from scratch, if necessary). The development of a tool allowing to build ad-hoc images, as well as its integration with TOSKERISER, is in the scope of our immediate future work.

References

1. Armbrust, M., Fox, A., Griffith, R., Joseph, A.D., Katz, R., Konwinski, A., Lee, G., Patterson, D., Rabkin, A., Stoica, I., Zaharia, M.: A view of cloud computing. Commun. ACM **53**(4), 50–58 (2010)
2. Binz, T., Breitenbücher, U., Kopp, O., Leymann, F.: TOSCA: portable automated deployment and management of cloud applications. In: Bouguettaya, A., Sheng, Q., Daniel, F. (eds.) Advanced Web Services, pp. 527–549. Springer, New York (2014). https://doi.org/10.1007/978-1-4614-7535-4_22
3. Brogi, A., Neri, D., Soldani, J.: DockerFinder: multi-attribute search of Docker images. In: 2017 IEEE International Conference on Cloud Engineering (IC2E), pp. 273–278. IEEE (2017)
4. Brogi, A., Rinaldi, L., Soldani, J.: TosKer: orchestrating applications with TOSCA and Docker (2017, submitted for publication)
5. Brogi, A., Soldani, J.: Matching cloud services with TOSCA. In: Canal, C., Villari, M. (eds.) ESOCC 2013. CCIS, vol. 393, pp. 218–232. Springer, Heidelberg (2013). https://doi.org/10.1007/978-3-642-45364-9_18
6. Brogi, A., Soldani, J.: Finding available services in TOSCA-compliant clouds. Sci. Comput. Program. **115**, 177–198 (2016)
7. Brogi, A., Soldani, J., Wang, P.W.: TOSCA in a nutshell: promises and perspectives. In: Villari, M., Zimmermann, W., Lau, K.-K. (eds.) ESOCC 2014. LNCS, vol. 8745, pp. 171–186. Springer, Heidelberg (2014). https://doi.org/10.1007/978-3-662-44879-3_13
8. Buyya, R., Yeo, C.S., Venugopal, S., Broberg, J., Brandic, I.: Cloud computing and emerging IT platforms: vision, hype, and reality for delivering computing as the 5th utility. Future Gener. Comput. Syst. **25**(6), 599–616 (2009)
9. Di Martino, B., Petcu, D., Cossu, R., Goncalves, P., Máhr, T., Loichate, M.: Building a mosaic of clouds. In: Guarracino, M.R., Vivien, F., Träff, J.L., Cannatoro, M., Danelutto, M., Hast, A., Perla, F., Knüpfer, A., Di Martino, B., Alexander, M. (eds.) Euro-Par 2010. LNCS, vol. 6586, pp. 571–578. Springer, Heidelberg (2011). https://doi.org/10.1007/978-3-642-21878-1_70
10. Fehling, C., Leymann, F., Retter, R., Schupeck, W., Arbitter, P.: Cloud Computing Patterns: Fundamentals to Design, Build, and Manage Cloud Applications. Springer, Vienna (2014). https://doi.org/10.1007/978-3-7091-1568-8
11. Guillén, J., Miranda, J., Murillo, J.M., Canal, C.: A service-oriented framework for developing cross cloud migratable software. J. Syst. Softw. **86**(9), 2294–2308 (2013)
12. Hamdaqa, M., Livogiannis, T., Tahvildari, L.: A reference model for developing cloud applications. In: Leymann, F., Ivanov, I., van Sinderen, M., Shishkov, B. (eds.) CLOSER 2011 - Proceedings of the 1st International Conference on Cloud Computing and Services Science (2011)
13. Hirmer, P., Breitenbücher, U., Binz, T., Leymann, F.: Automatic topology completion of TOSCA-based cloud applications. In: 44. Jahrestagung der Gesellschaft für Informatik e.V. (GI), vol. 232, pp. 247–258. Lecture Notes in Informatics (LNI) (2014)
14. Leymann, F.: Cloud computing. It—Information Technology, Methoden und innovative Anwendungen der Informatik und Informationstechnik **53**(4), 163–164 (2011)
15. Matthias, K., Kane, S.P.: Docker: Up and Running. O'Reilly Media, Sebastopol (2015)

16. Newman, S.: Building Microservices. O'Reilly Media Inc., Sebastopol (2015)
17. OASIS: Topology and Orchestration Specification for Cloud Applications (TOSCA) Primer (2013). http://docs.oasis-open.org/tosca/tosca-primer/v1.0/tosca-primer-v1.0.pdf
18. OASIS: Topology and Orchestration Specification for Cloud Applications (TOSCA) Simple Profile in YAML, Version 1.0 (2016). http://docs.oasis-open.org/tosca/TOSCA-Simple-Profile-YAML/v1.0/TOSCA-Simple-Profile-YAML-v1.0.pdf
19. Pahl, C., Brogi, A., Soldani, J., Jamshidi, P.: Cloud container technologies: a state-of-the-art review. IEEE Trans. Cloud Comput. (in press). https://doi.org/10.1109/TCC.2017.2702586
20. Smith, R.: Docker Orchestration. Packt Publishing, Birmingham (2017)
21. Soldani, J., Binz, T., Breitenbücher, U., Leymann, F., Brogi, A.: ToscaMart: a method for adapting and reusing cloud applications. J. Syst. Softw. **113**, 395–406 (2016)
22. Soltesz, S., Pötzl, H., Fiuczynski, M.E., Bavier, A., Peterson, L.: Container-based operating system virtualization: a scalable, high-performance alternative to hypervisors. In: SIGOPS Operating Systems Review, vol. 41, no. 3, pp. 275–287 (2007)

Combining Trust and Aggregate Computing

Roberto Casadei[1(✉)], Alessandro Aldini[2], and Mirko Viroli[1]

[1] Alma Mater Studiorum—Università di Bologna, Cesena, Italy
{roby.casadei,mirko.viroli}@unibo.it
[2] Università di Urbino Carlo Bo, Urbino, Italy
alessandro.aldini@uniurb.it

Abstract. Recent trends such as the Internet of Things and pervasive computing demand for novel engineering approaches able to support the specification and scalable runtime execution of adaptive behaviour of large collections of interacting devices. Aggregate computing is one such approach, formally founded in the field calculus, which enables programming of device aggregates by a global stance, through a functional composition of self-organisation patterns that is turned automatically into repetitive local computations and gossip-like interactions. However, the logically decentralised and open nature of such algorithms and systems presumes a fundamental cooperation of the devices involved: an error in a device or a focused attack may significantly compromise the computation outcome and hence the algorithms built on top of it. We propose *trust* as a framework to detect, ponder or isolate voluntary/involuntary misbehaviours, with the goal of mitigating the influence on the overall computation. To better understand the fragility of aggregate systems in face of attacks and investigate possible countermeasures, in this paper we consider the paradigmatic case of the *gradient* algorithm, analysing the impact of offences and the mitigation afforded by the adoption of trust mechanisms.

Keywords: Aggregate computing · Computational fields
Collaborative P2P systems · Security · Safety · Trust

1 Introduction

The last decades have been feeding a process where large numbers of interconnected computing devices get deployed in our environments. Such technological and social movements seem to imply a future of increasing pervasiveness and interconnection, where dense networks of computer-like nodes are overlaid on and tightly interacting with our physical world and humans in it. Exploiting such computational fabric is appealing but it does challenge current methods and tools in a paradigmatic way: the large-scale, situated and complex nature of this kind of systems makes open-loop approaches unfeasible and pushes forward the need to endow such systems with self-* properties, but hence a whole set of new challenges arises.

© Springer International Publishing AG 2018
A. Cerone and M. Roveri (Eds.): SEFM 2017 Workshops, LNCS 10729, pp. 507–522, 2018.
https://doi.org/10.1007/978-3-319-74781-1_34

The field of collective adaptive systems is devoted to the study of systems where large groups of entities jointly seek to reach their goals in a dynamic environment. The main issues include (i) how to provide an effective specification of the self-organising and goal-oriented behaviour of the system and (ii) how to turn that program into resilient and efficient execution. Moreover, it should be noted that these scenarios are not only interesting from a scientific point of view, but also from the engineering side—where trade-offs have to be taken and limited resources need to be coped with. Additionally, given this complex setting and the impracticality of in-field tests, it would be crucial to have ways to obtain certain guarantees on the correctness of implementations; for this purpose, both formal methods and simulations are invaluable.

Aggregate computing [2], which we recall in Sect. 2, is one promising approach for the engineering of (possibly large-scale) distributed systems that need to resiliently adapt to local, environmental conditions. It takes an abstract, global stance in which one programs the desired collective behaviour, through a composition of self-organising and coordination patterns, and lets the platform deal with the proper unfolding of the computation at the micro-level in a complex set of repetitive, weaved interactions and calculations. The field calculus [7], which builds on the idea of computational fields, provides the formal underpinnings of aggregate computing and gives a concrete shape to the approach: in this framework, programs at the aggregate level are represented as functional compositions of dynamic fields that map devices to computational values in space-time. In practice, an aggregate system consists of a collection of networked devices where each device computes the same aggregate program and interacts with a subset of other devices known as its neighbourhood. That is, computation unwinds in a logically decentralised way based on locally sensed information and data received through peer-to-peer, gossip-like communications.

Among the various challenges behind the design and development of successful collective and adaptive systems, trust represents a fundamental aspect in a setting in which the rapid and continuous exchange and propagation of information is a key feature. The need for cooperation is typically accompanied by the growth of potential (insider) security threats, which may depend on selfish or malicious behaviors of nodes, either in isolation or in collusion. From the viewpoint of a node issuing a request to another node, which may refer to the communication of a simple detected value or the delivery of a complex paid service, trust can be defined as the belief perceived by the former node about the capability, intention, honesty, and reliability of the latter node in satisfying the request. Over the last decades, a lot of research was done to promote the effective use of computational notions of trust allowing to estimate such a belief perception and simplify related decision making processes. Such an effort ranges from formal specification approaches [11] and verification methods [1,10,14,20] to the development of distributed trust management systems [6,8,13,16] and the analysis of threats and vulnerabilities [15,24].

Starting with these considerations, this paper develops on the combination of trust and aggregate computing, providing the following contributions:

- an overview of the security issues in aggregate computing (see Sect. 3);
- the applicability of classical trust management techniques in this framework (see Sect. 4);
- an empirical study of the effectiveness of trust fields in mitigating or avoiding at all the consequences of (deliberate or not) misbehaviours of nodes in a gradient computation (see Sect. 5).

2 Aggregate Computing

Aggregate computing [2] is an approach for the engineering of systems where coordinated adaptation plays a major role. It is built around three interrelated core ideas.

The first idea is *working at the macro-level while letting the platform deal with the micro-macro bridging*: the target of programming is not an individual element of the system but rather the whole system itself, which can be seen as a distributed computational body, i.e., a programmable aggregate. This partial inversion of the point of view is what relieves the programmer of solving the local-to-global mapping problem by herself, i.e., what supports the steering of a self-organising process by declaring the desired outcome from the favoured intermediate position between the micro and the macro levels.

Secondly, the approach is *compositional*, in that it enables complex behaviours to be built out of simpler ones. There is a number of general coordination operators, building blocks and patterns that can be used in concert to specify a sort of global-state flow graph. The point is having one adaptive behaviour (of predictable dynamics) feed another one and so on until the proper chain of system transformations is in place.

The third idea relates to *abstraction*, namely, leaving some pieces of information unspecified, for achieving declarativeness and driving run-time adaptation. More specifically, the logic and the correctness of an aggregate program may be quite independent from a set of conditions such as the topology of the network and the density of the devices situated in some region. In addition, this generality provides some valuable flexibility at the platform-side: though the approach encourages a fully decentralised mindset, there is large freedom with respect to which concrete execution strategy can operate an aggregate system [22]—ranging from completely peer-to-peer to centralised (server- or cloud-based), up to hybrid and adaptive ones (e.g., according to available infrastructure).

2.1 Fields and Aggregate Computations

The key concept that allows us to put this conception into practice is that of *computational field*. This is an abstraction that maps every device to a computational value over time. If, as often is the case, devices are situated in some space, fields can also be thought of as functions from space-time points to the values produced by the devices at those locations; this gives the primary interpretation, the digital-physical correspondence that makes this framework amenable to programming situated collective adaptive systems. The time-wise nature of fields is what accounts for dynamics, whereas the spatial dimension provides a foundation for context and local interaction. Also note that a field can be interpreted both punctually and globally, opening the way for bridging individual and aggregate behaviour.

The principal formal framework for working with fields is known as the *field calculus* [7,23]. It provides the basic constructs for transforming and combining field computations together. Hence, an aggregate program can be represented as a field expression, deployed to a set of networked devices geared with middleware aggregate support, and executed according to the operational semantics of the field calculus. A system enacting field computations has also to operate in accordance with an abstract execution model where devices iteratively run their program and communicate with one another in order to cooperate in building the local contexts and driving micro-level activity. Each device repeatedly runs the same aggregate program (which might branch differently throughout the nodes, though), alternating sleep periods so that computation locally proceeds at discrete rounds of execution. From a global point of view, computation is usually fair and partially synchronous, though these assumptions may change or be relaxed on a case-specific basis. At any round, a device (i) builds its up-to-date local context by collecting previous computation state, sensor values, and messages received from other devices, (ii) runs the aggregate program, which produces both a result value as well as a description of the just-performed computation that is known as the *export*, (iii) shares its export, e.g., through a broadcast, to its neighbour devices, as defined by an application-specific notion of neighbourhood, which typically relies on physical distance, and finally (iv) executes the actuators as specified by the program. The export is a tree-like descriptor of an aggregate computation that is communicated and used by devices to safely interact with one another. In fact, in this framework, a device is allowed to interact – at a given point of the computation, namely at a given point in the export tree that is currently being built – only with the set of its *aligned* neighbours. This process, which is known as "alignment," is a key mechanism in that it supports consistent execution of aggregate computations and also provides the means for splitting computations (fields) into completely separated branches (field partitions).

2.2   SCAFI and the Field Calculus Constructs

SCAFI [5] (Scala Fields) is an open-source framework[1] for aggregate computing. It provides a Scala-internal Domain-Specific Language (DSL) for expressing and running aggregate computations according to the field calculus; it gives access to aggregate programming features[2] together with the type system and all the

---

[1] https://bitbucket.org/scafiteam/scafi.
[2] The semantics of the field calculus has been implemented in a slightly different but largely equivalent way with respect to the "standard" one, due to design choices as well as technicalities involved in the DSL embedding.

amenities that can be found in a mainstream programming language supporting imperative, object-oriented and functional paradigms.

The core constructs for working with fields are reified as plain, generic methods[3]; they are defined in the following Scala interface.

```scala
trait Constructs {
  // Key constructs
  def rep[A](init: => A)(fun: A => A): A
  def aggregate[A](f: => A): A
  def nbr[A](expr: => A): A
  def foldhood[A](init: => A)(acc: (A, A) => A)(expr: => A): A

  // Contextual, but foundational
  def mid(): ID
  def sense[A](name: LSNS): A
  def nbrvar[A](name: NSNS): A
}
```

In Scala, methods are introduced with the `def` keyword, have their return type specified at the end of the method signature, can be generic (type parameters are specified within square brackets) and can be defined in curried form by providing multiple parameter lists; when invoked, 1-element parameter lists can be equivalently specified with round or curly brackets (in the latter case, it visually emulates block-like structures, which is nice for DSLs); syntax `(T1,T2)` denotes a 2-element tuple type (and there is coherent syntactic sugar for tuple values); syntax `A=>R` denotes a function type (and there is similar syntactic sugar for lambdas); and syntax `=> R` denotes a call-by-name parameter which is passed unevaluated to the method body (as a thunk) and in there gets (re-)evaluated at each use (basically it is a syntactic shorthand over nullary functions).

When discussing the field constructs, as well as when reading and writing aggregate programs, two complementary perspectives can be adopted: the local, device-centric one (which relates to the operational semantics) and the global, field-centric one. For example, expression 5 can be thought of as either a single number calculated by a specific device or a field of fives.

Construct `rep(init)(fun)` yields an `init` field that evolves over time according to the given state transformation `function`. Note that such a progressive transformation is not atomic nor necessarily homogeneous, as it depends on when the devices that make up the field actually fire. For example,

```scala
rep(0)(x => x + 1)
```

produces a field counting the number of rounds performed (point-wise).

Construct `aggregate(f)` is used to wrap the body expression `f` of a function that has to be interpreted according to the aggregate semantics, which means that it must work as a unit for alignment; in other words, an aggregate function

---

[3] Actually, fields do not explicitly appear in the method signatures: there are no "first-class" fields in ScaFi; rather, that notion (which still can be used while reasoning about code) has been replaced with that of *neighbour-dependent expression*.

expresses a subcomputation which restricts the domain of the field to only the devices that are executing that very subcomputation. For example, consider how this foundational feature can be used to implement a building block `branch` that splits the domain of computation according to a Boolean field `cond` (here, `mux` is a purely functional multiplexer; moreover, notice how Scala functions can be directly used to wrap aggregate code and hence enable code reuse in a conventional way):

```
def branch[A](cond: => Boolean)(th: => A)(el: => A): A =
  mux(cond)(() => aggregate{ th })(() => aggregate{ el })()
```

The code works by first creating a field of (anonymous) functions out of the `condition` field, and then using the function application operator () to continue the computation at the two branches. The nodes that follow the `then`-branch (or the `else`-branch, likewise) will be able to interact only with the nodes that followed the same path; i.e., the field gets split into two completely separated parts.

In the field calculus, communication is achieved through neighbouring fields. A neighbouring field can be thought of as a field of fields; point-wise, every device is mapped to a field that consists of the information shared by its neighbours. Now, construct `foldhood(init)(acc)(expr)` is what allows you to accumulate the neighbouring field `expr` (using `init` as the identity field for operation `acc`) into a flat field (or to a single value in the device-centric interpretation). `nbr(expr)` is the basic operator that supports communication of information among devices[4], i.e., the creation of neighbouring fields. For example,

```
foldhood(false)(_ || _)(nbr { sense[Boolean]("alarm") })
```

denotes the field of all the devices that sensed an alarm or that are nearby someone who did. In general, `sense[T]("name")` represents the field of readings of a value of type `T` from a sensor called `"name"` (which is assumed to be in place); punctually, it corresponds to a query to a local sensor (it is a matter of the platform to bridge these logical sensors to physical ones, in case). Moreover, there are a special kind of sensors, known as neighbouring sensors and read through `nbrvar`, that, similarly to `nbr`, produce neighbouring fields; they are of use for mapping each neighbour set to platform-level readings. A common one is `nbrRange`, that yields the (second-order) field of distances from neighbours:

```
def nbrRange = nbrvar[Double]("NBR_RANGE")
```

Just like `nbr`, it has to be used in a `foldhood` expression.

Example: the gradient field. Now we show a simple example that will also be used in the security-related experiments of Sect. 5. It is known as the *gradient* and represents the field of minimum distances from source nodes (Fig. 1). This is

---

[4] Note that the actual communication between devices is matter of the platform and is usually performed through export broadcasting (and not during program execution).

a fundamental pattern that is used extensively in many applications; for instance, it can be applied to drive escape to security exits by following the shortest paths to them, or to propagate information up to a given area of interest. In SCAFI, it can be implemented as follows:

```
def gradient(source: Boolean): Double =
  rep(Double.PositiveInfinity){ distance =>
    mux(source) { 0.0 } {
       foldhood(Double.PositiveInfinity)(Math.min)(nbr{distance}+nbrRange)
    }
  }
}
```

When the source field is true, the gradient is zero; otherwise, the new gradient estimate is built by taking the minimum value among the neighbour estimates augmented by the corresponding node-to-node distance. The outer rep is necessary to keep track of the estimated distance from one round to the next. Note that this gradient algorithm is self-healing, i.e., it reacts to perturbations (e.g., as triggered by mobility or change of sources) by starting a process that steers the field towards the correct shape.

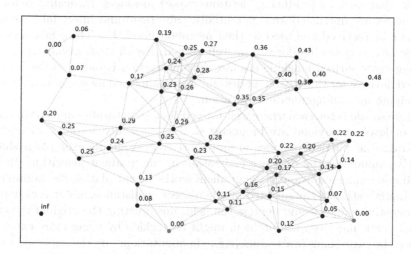

Fig. 1. Snapshot of a stabilised gradient field from a simulation in SCAFI. Devices are represented by bold dots; the red ones denote the sources from which the gradient is computed. The grey lines represent neighbouring links: connected nodes exchange their exports. The nodes are labelled with the string representation of the result value of the local computation. (Color figure online)

3   Aggregate Computing and Security

Aggregate computing systems are susceptible to the security threats that naturally arise from distribution and situatedness. In particular, attacks may target physical devices, the aggregate computing platform, and/or the application logic. At the level of the physical device, sensors may be impaired, networking may be interrupted, and so on. At the platform level, examples of attacks include Denial of Service (DoS), fake messages, and traffic analysis—just to name a few.

The decentralised nature as well as the peculiar characteristics of adaptivity of the approach make aggregate systems resilient to intermittent or prolonged failure of some nodes—especially for self-stabilising computations like the gradient [21]. However, the actual impact of node malfunctioning depends on many factors, such as the topology of the network or how dense it is (i.e., the extent of "spatial redundancy"): network partitions may prevent information to reach significant regions of a collective, and sparseness increases the relevance of individuals. Also crucial is the role a node plays in the application: for example, behaviours building on the gradient algorithm (Sect. 2.2) may be ruined if the source nodes fail and the other nodes at some point get rid of the past export[5], though not necessarily in short time, as it also depends on the frequency of round execution and the transitory phase of the particular gradient algorithm in action.

In this paper, we are most interested in attacks at the application-level, i.e., in attacks that work by producing factitious export messages. Basically, we assume that nodes are untrusted and, potentially, can create and inject fake messages that can be received and used by their neighbourhood [17]. These fake messages can be of two types: malformed or well-formed. Recall that, in our framework, the aggregate virtual machine ensures that interaction is only possible between aligned devices; for this reason, nodes emitting malformed messages cannot really participate into an aggregate application.

More subtle is the case where well-formed (i.e., structurally-aligned) messages with malevolent payload are broadcasted. This basically accounts to injecting forged data at particular nodes in an export tree. A simple example is sharing negative values for the distance estimation in the gradient algorithm. In fact, the simple implementation of the gradient works by calculating the minimum of neighbours' estimates augmented by the respective distance, and it is easy to see how negative values would depress the field, misdirecting the original intention. In this particular case, the problem might be tackled by using more expressive types or by expressing constraints (e.g., via annotations) on the expected values, letting the platform deal with it; but in general, it might not be that easy.

The misbehaviour enacted by a given malevolent entity can be more or less sophisticated. Its choices include (i) what kind of factitious data has to be generated, (ii) when, and (iii) who is the recipient. In fact, data can be randomly generated or suitably forged; also, an attacker may alternate good and bad communications (on-off misbehaving), and may limit bad communications to only a few targets (selective misbehaving) [6,15]. Obviously, the complexity and the potential of attacks can escalate when, instead of limiting ourselves to individual attackers, we also consider coordinated attacks by malevolent collectives.

---

[5] The amount of time that neighbour exports are retained depends on the platform configuration for a particular application.

At the heart of the problem is the fundamentally cooperative nature of aggregate applications: each device of an aggregate system, while preserving some autonomy with respect to mobility, sensing and actuation, is required to appropriately participate in the distributed aggregate computing process—which means executing the same program and not cheating. Of course, a proper security strategy would require the application of countermeasures across the whole aggregate computing stack—from humans and physical devices up to the programs. In the next sections, we consider the problem at the code-level and propose the use of trust mechanisms to deal with malicious payload.

4   Trust

In the setting of distributed systems, in which it is not possible nor convenient to rely on centralised trusted third parties managing a trustworthiness infrastructure, trust relations rely on direct observations (and potentially recommendations) gathered by every node when interacting with its neighbours. For instance, in trustworthy crowdsourcing and sensor networks, a computational notion of trust derives from the exchange and aggregation of information disseminated by the participating nodes [3,8,9,16,24].

Then, trust-based decision-making policies rely typically on the comparison between the trust estimated by a node, called trustor, about the expected behaviour of another node, called trustee, and a trust threshold value tth, which may depend on several factors, like, e.g., the initial willingness of the trustor to cooperate with the trustee.

Several trust metrics are based on a Bayesian approach. In essence, the trustor assumes that there exists an unknown parameter θ used to predict probabilistically the future good/bad behavior of the trustee, and the related outcome is drawn independently for each interaction between them. In order to model the uncertainty about θ, a given *prior* distribution is used to draw it, which is updated as new interactions between the parties occur. In the setting of trust, among the various probability prior distributions proposed in the literature, the beta distribution received particular attention [3,8,12,19]. Such a distribution is fed with two parameters, α and β, which count the number of positive and negative observations experienced by the trustor when interacting with the trustee, respectively. The evaluation of the observation depends on the context, e.g., in the setting of data relaying, a packet sent from the trustor that is forwarded (resp., discarded) by the trustee is considered as a positive (resp., negative) cooperation. Then, trust is estimated as the statistical expectation E of a beta distribution Beta parameterized with respect to α and β, as follows:

$$E(Beta(\alpha, \beta)) = \frac{\alpha}{\alpha + \beta}.$$

If initially $\alpha = \beta = 0$, then we have to compute the expectation of Beta($\alpha + 1, \beta + 1$), so that the estimated trust expresses a situation of total uncertainty in the absence of any prior interaction between the parties.

Different techniques based on such a Bayesian approach differ for the way in which (*i*) observations are weighted, e.g., depending on their age, and (*ii*) recommendations gathered via the neighbours are combined with the parameters discussed above.

4.1 Application to Aggregate Computing

The proposed idea consists of applying the approach described above to the aggregate computing framework. For the sake of simplicity, we consider the case in which nodes compute locally on the base of numerical values exchanged with the neighbours, as in the case, e.g., of the gradient. The basic principle we follow is that at each round every node receives from its neighbourhood a set of new estimates of the gradient, which, if all the nodes are cooperative, shall not be too much different from each other, up to certain fluctuations that may depend on several factors, like, e.g., the topology of the network. Hence, if the value received from a node differs too much from the others, then such an observation is used to impair negatively the trust towards that node. In other words, unexpected perturbations of the gradient against the overall trend are considered as a potential attack to the system.

In order to implement such an idea, we estimate trust by following the Bayesian approach in such a way that every gradient estimate received from a node is compared with the average of all the estimates received for each round. The detected difference is then used to evaluate the observation and update the trust parameters. In particular, as the mean square deviation represents a standard way to predict differences among values, we use it as the tolerance threshold for the evaluation of the difference above.

Formally, each node maintains locally the pair of parameters (α_i, β_i) for each neighbour i. Their initial value is zero. At each round, every node performs the following operations:

1. The node computes the mean $\bar{x}$ of the values x_i, $1 \leq i \leq N$, read from the N neighbours that have a value to communicate and then, assumed the deviation $\xi_i = x_i - \bar{x}$, computes the mean square deviation:

$$s = \sqrt{\frac{\sum_{i=1}^{N} \xi_i^2}{N}}.$$

2. For each neighbour i, if $|x_i - \bar{x}| > s$ then $\beta_i = \beta_i + 1$, else $\alpha_i = \alpha_i + 1$.
3. For each neighbour i, if $\mathrm{E}(\mathrm{Beta}(\alpha_i + 1, \beta_i + 1)) < tth$ then x_i is discarded.
4. The node computes its local value on the base of the non-discarded x_i.

Notice that in order to preserve the nature of aggregate computing, each node computes locally and makes decisions deriving from the knowledge of its neighbourhood. The novelty is the application of a mechanism used in trust systems to monitor the neighbourhood and detect potential suspicious behaviours. Obviously, s and tth are two threshold parameters that deserve empirical evaluation as they characterize the attitude of the node to trust perturbed values and other nodes sharing perturbed values, respectively. Finally, the generalization to non-numeric field domains is possible without changing the nature of the approach and by adapting the semantics of the functions and operators used in the algorithm above.

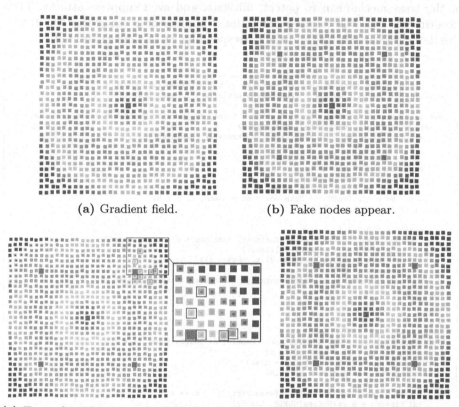

(a) Gradient field.   (b) Fake nodes appear.

(c) Trust algorithm at work while the gradient is partially corrupted.   (d) Fakes are mistrusted and the gradient field is recovered.

Fig. 2. Phases of the experiment. The hued squares denote the trust-based gradient field; the fuchsia squares denote fake nodes issuing random distance estimates; the little hued circles visible within the squares, e.g. in the zoomed section of (c), denote the plain gradient field which does not consider fakes (the ideal situation against which the error is calculated). Note, in (c), the corrupted gradient shape, especially at the corners (e.g., the presence, on a light square, of a darker dot means the fake is punctually creating an unwanted depression). The blue squared contours identify the nodes which are mistrusted by at least one of their neighbours. (Color figure online)

5   Analysis

In order to study the trust algorithm proposed in Sect. 4.1, we have applied it to the case of a gradient computation. We have arranged a set of experiments to exercise the SCAFI implementation of a gradient which makes use of the trust mechanism to detect, mitigate, and even suppress attacks. These experiments take the form of simulations[6] implemented using the ALCHEMIST simulator framework [18] and the corresponding SCAFI incarnation [4].

```
class TrustGradient extends AggregateProgram with ScafiAlchemistSupport {
  override def main(): Double = trustedGradient(isSrc, isFake, useTrust)

  def gradient(src: Boolean, fake: Boolean = false, applyTrust: Boolean = false): Double = {
    rep(Double.PositiveInfinity){ distance =>
      def nbrDist = nbr { branch(!fake){ distance }{ fakeValue() } }

      var n, xmean, s = 0.0
      branch(applyTrust){
        n = countHood(nbrDist)
        xmean =  sumHood(nbrDist) / n
        s = Math.sqrt(sumHood{ Math.pow(dist - xmean, 2) } / n)
      }{ /* do nothing */ }

      mux(src) { 0.0 } {
        foldhoodPlus(Double.PositiveInfinity)(Math.min){ // except myself
          val isTrusted = branch(applyTrust){
            trustable(calculateTrust(dist, xmean, s))
          } else { true }
          mux(isTrusted){ nbr{dist}+nbrRange }{ Double.PositiveInfinity }
        }
      }
    }
  }

  def calculateTrust(x: => Double, mean: Double, s: Double): Double = {
    val (nbrId, nbrVal) = nbr(mid(), x)
    val deviation = Math.abs(nbrVal - mean)
    val maxError = Math.max(s, errorLB)

    val obss = rep(MutableField[AlfaBetaHistory]()){ m =>
      val history = m.getOrElse(nbrId, List())
      val obs = if(nbrVal.isFinite){
        if(deviation > maxError) (0.0, 1.0) else (1.0, 0.0)
      } else { (0.0,0.0) }
      m.put(nbrId, (obs :: history).take(observationWindow))
      m
    }.getOrElse(nbrId, List())
    val (a,b) = obss.foldRight((1.0,0.0))((t,u)=>(t._1+u._1, t._2+u._2))
    beta(a+1,b+1)
  }

  def beta(a: Double, b: Double): Double = (a)/(a+b)

  def trustable(trustValue: Double): Boolean = trustValue >= tth

  // ...
}
```

Fig. 3. Implementation of the trust-based gradient algorithm in SCAFI.

---

[6] The experimental setup is available at the following repository: https://bitbucket.org/metaphori/trusted-ac-experiments.

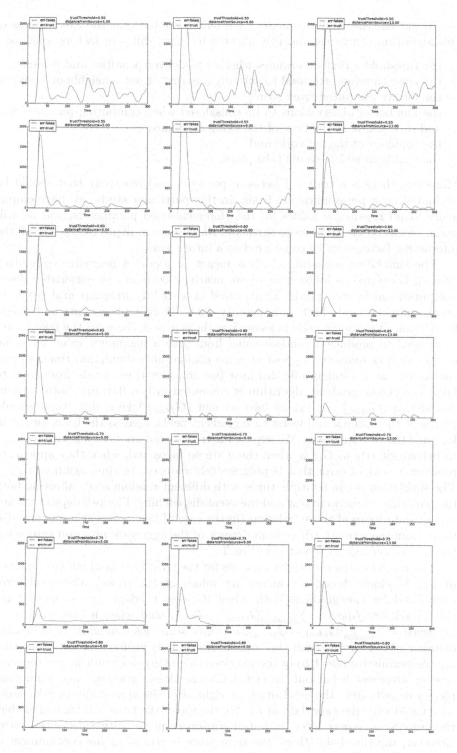

Fig. 4. Sensitivity analysis for the trust threshold. (Color figure online)

To put the theory into practice, it should be noted that the effectiveness of this algorithm can be significantly affected by many different factors, such as:

- the threshold s that determines whether to deliver penalties and rewards;
- the trust threshold tth used to actually mistrust or not a neighbour based on the locally computed trust score;
- the number of observations to be considered when computing parameters α and β, which is at the base of the aging mechanism;
- the topology of the network; and
- the timing in which events take place.

Moreover, there is a trade-off between prudence and reactivity that should be evaluated on a per-application basis. In this particular study, we have empirically found reasonable values for the aforementioned parameters, and we will mainly focus on the trust score threshold tth; a more in-depth analysis of all the interacting factors can be considered as a future work.

The simulation scenario, which is meant to model a pervasive computing system, is defined as follows: there are nearly 1000 nodes (a reasonably dense computational fabric), randomly arranged in a slightly irregular grid (so as to break simmetry and check functionality with different placements and neighbourhoods); the source node is located at the centre of the grid; the fake nodes, configured to produce a random value from 0 to a maximum value set equal to the network diameter, appear at some configurable simulation time, around the source, at a configurable distance (we consider three levels from near to far). The classic gradient algorithm is computed in two flavours: both without considering (G_{ideal}) and taking into account (G_{fake}) fake nodes—these should represent the optimal and worst-case gradient fields, used as the basis for calculation of the relative errors. We expect the trust-based gradient algorithm G_{trust} to behave exactly as G_{ideal} when there are no fakes and, when they appear, to produce a peak of error that is progressively reduced, tending again to G_{ideal}. The simulation is run multiple times with different random seeds affecting both the particular scenario to test and the event dispatching. Figure 2 depicts the key events and phases of the simulation (in the case of fake nodes at a medium distance from the source), whereas an excerpt of the aggregate program expressing the simulation logic is reported in Fig. 3.

The results of the sensitivity analysis for the trust threshold tth are reported in Fig. 4, which shows, for increasing values of tth (rows), the total error committed by the gradient both when it doesn't adopt any form of trust (blue line), $err\text{-}fakes = \sum_{nodes} |G_{ideal} - G_{fake}|$, and when it does (red line), $err\text{-}trust = \sum_{nodes} |G_{ideal} - G_{trust}|$, for three scenarios (columns) of increasing distance of fake nodes from the source. There, it is visible how attitudes that are too permissive (low tth) or too cautious (high tth) can result in greater error or even divergent behaviour. In fact, while the classic `gradient` algorithm completely departs from the ideal situation right after the appearance of fake nodes (simulated with the `fake` flag) at $t = 20$, the use of the trust mechanism enables the system to recover after an initial transitory phase with substantial error. However, the threshold tth on the trust score is crucial in the containment of the deviation: an excessive eagerness to trust neighbours ($tth = 0.50$) leads to accepting too many suspicious messages; up to $tth = 0.70, 0.75$, things improve with the additional severity, but once the circumspection reaches paranoid levels ($tth = 0.80$), too many nodes get distrusted and the system becomes unable to precisely isolate and resolve the problem. Moreover, notice how lower values of tth (i.e., an indulgent attitude) lead to greater noise (higher error fluctuations).

6 Conclusion and Future Work

In this paper, we have for the first time considered security-related aspects in the context of aggregate computing. Though many vulnerabilities are inherent to the distributed nature of aggregate systems, and though the framework is resilient against many temporary sources of failure, the often large attack surface, the suitability of the approach for safety-critical applications (e.g., crowd management and tactical networks), and the fundamental assumption of cooperation on the nodes involved just make the problem worth to be investigated. In particular, our study has focused on attacks based on the diffusion of well-formed, factitious messages and we have proposed the use of trust mechanisms to make algorithms resistant to them.

Future works include a more in-depth analysis of the factors that affect the trust algorithm applied in this paper, a study of the response of the algorithm when considering a recommendation infrastructure among nodes and when tackling more insidious attacks, as well as a more extensive investigation of the vulnerabilities of the full aggregate computing stack.

References

1. Aldini, A.: Modeling and verification of trust and reputation systems. J. Secur. Commun. Netw. 8(16), 2933–2946 (2015)
2. Beal, J., Pianini, D., Viroli, M.: Aggregate programming for the internet of things. IEEE Comput. 48(9), 22–30 (2015)
3. Buchegger, S., Boudec, J.Y.L.: A robust reputation system for peer-to-peer and mobile ad-hoc networks. In: 2nd Workshop on the Economics of Peer-to-Peer Systems, P2PEcon (2004)
4. Casadei, R., Pianini, D., Viroli, M.: Simulating large-scale aggregate mass with alchemist and scala. In: 2016 Federated Conference on Computer Science and Information Systems (FedCSIS), pp. 1495–1504. IEEE (2016)
5. Casadei, R., Viroli, M.: Towards aggregate programming in scala. In: 1st Workshop on Programming Models and Languages for Distributed Computing, p. 5. ACM (2016)
6. Cho, J.H., Swami, A., Chen, I.R.: A survey on trust management for mobile ad hoc networks. Commun. Surv. Tutor. 13(4), 562–583 (2011)
7. Damiani, F., Viroli, M., Beal, J.: A type-sound calculus of computational fields. Sci. Comput. Program. 117, 17–44 (2016)
8. Ganeriwal, S., Balzano, L.K., Srivastava, M.B.: Reputation-based framework for high integrity sensor networks. ACM Trans. Sens. Netw. 4(3), 1–37 (2008)

9. Han, G., Jiang, J., Shu, L., Niu, J., Chao, H.C.: Management and applications of trust in wireless sensor networks: a survey. J. Comput. Syst. Sci. **80**(3), 602–617 (2014). Special Issue on Wireless Network Intrusion
10. Huang, J.: A formal-semantics-based calculus of trust. Internet Comput. **14**(5), 38–46 (2010)
11. Jøsang, A.: A logic for uncertain probabilities. Int. J. Uncertain. Fuzziness Knowl.-Based Syst. **9**(3), 279–311 (2001)
12. Jøsang, A., Ismail, R.: The beta reputation system. In: 15th Bled Conference on Electronic Commerce (2002)
13. Li, J., Li, R., Kato, J.: Future trust management framework for mobile ad hoc networks. IEEE Commun. Mag. **46**(4), 108–114 (2008)
14. Li, Z., Shen, H.: Game-theoretic analysis of cooperation incentives strategies in mobile ad hoc networks. Trans. Mob. Comput. **11**(8), 1287–1303 (2012)
15. Marmol, F.G., Perez, G.M.: Security threats scenarios in trust and reputation models for distributed systems. Comput. Secur. **28**(7), 545–556 (2009)
16. Mousa, H., Mokhtar, S.B., Hasan, O., Younes, O., Hadhoud, M., Brunie, L.: Trust management and reputation systems in mobile participatory sensing applications: a survey. Comput. Netw. **90**, 49–73 (2015)
17. Perrig, A., Szewczyk, R., Tygar, J., Wen, V., Culler, D.: SPINS: security protocols for sensor networks. Wirel. Netw. **8**(5), 521–534 (2002)
18. Pianini, D., Montagna, S., Viroli, M.: Chemical-oriented simulation of computational systems with ALCHEMIST. J. Simul. **7**(3), 202–215 (2013)
19. Priayoheswari, B., Kulothungan, K., Kannan, A.: Beta reputation and direct trust model for secure communication in wireless sensor networks. In: International Conference on Informatics and Analytics, ICIA 2016, pp. 1–5. ACM (2016)
20. Trcek, D.: A formal apparatus for modeling trust in computing environments. Math. Comput. Model. **49**(1–2), 226–233 (2009)
21. Viroli, M., Beal, J., Damiani, F., Pianini, D.: Efficient engineering of complex self-organising systems by self-stabilising fields. In: IEEE 9th International Conference on Self-Adaptive and Self-Organizing Systems (SASO), pp. 81–90. IEEE (2015)
22. Viroli, M., Casadei, R., Pianini, D.: On execution platforms for large-scale aggregate computing. In: Proceedings of the 2016 ACM International Joint Conference on Pervasive and Ubiquitous Computing: Adjunct, pp. 1321–1326. ACM (2016)
23. Viroli, M., Damiani, F., Beal, J.: A calculus of computational fields. In: Canal, C., Villari, M. (eds.) ESOCC 2013. CCIS, vol. 393, pp. 114–128. Springer, Heidelberg (2013). https://doi.org/10.1007/978-3-642-45364-9_11
24. Yu, Y., Li, K., Zhoub, W., Lib, P.: Trust mechanisms in wireless sensor networks: attack analysis and countermeasures. J. Netw. Comput. Appl. **35**(3), 867–880 (2012)

Reasoning About Sensing Uncertainty
in Decision-Making for Self-adaptation

Javier Cámara$^{(\boxtimes)}$, Wenxin Peng, David Garlan, and Bradley Schmerl

School of Computer Science, Institute for Software Research,
Carnegie Mellon University, Pittsburgh, PA 15213, USA
{jcmoreno,garlan,schmerl}@cs.cmu.edu, wenxinp@andrew.cmu.edu

Abstract. Self-Adaptive systems are expected to adapt to unanticipated run-time events using imperfect information about their environment. This entails handling the effects of uncertainties in decision-making, which are not always considered as a first-class concern. This paper contributes a formal analysis technique that explicitly considers uncertainty in sensing when reasoning about the best way to adapt, possibly executing uncertainty reduction operations to improve system utility. We illustrate our approach on a Denial of Service (DoS) attack scenario and present some preliminary results that show the benefits of uncertainty-aware decision-making with respect to using an uncertainty-ignorant approach.

Keywords: Self-adaptation · Decision-making · Uncertainty
Stochastic games

1 Introduction

Complex software-intensive systems are increasingly relied on in our society to support tasks in different contexts that are typically characterized by a high degree of *uncertainty*. Self-adaptation [12,22] is regarded as a promising way to engineer in an effective manner systems that are *resilient* to run time changes despite the different uncertainties derived from their execution environment (e.g., resource availability, interaction with human actors), goals, or even in the system itself (e.g., faults).

The information and models employed for decision-making in self-adaptive systems are also subject to different types of uncertainty (e.g., sensor readings may be inaccurate, some important aspect of the domain may be abstracted away in models). However, despite the fact that these uncertainties can have a noticeable impact on run-time system behavior, many approaches to engineering self-adaptation do not model the uncertainties that affect the system explicitly or as as first-class entity [20]. Moreover, some types of adaptation tactics can reduce uncertainty at run time (e.g., introducing a CAPTCHA in a web system can reduce the uncertainty about potentially malicious clients controlled by bots accessing the website). These tactics often come at a cost (e.g., CAPTCHA

© Springer International Publishing AG 2018
A. Cerone and M. Roveri (Eds.): SEFM 2017 Workshops, LNCS 10729, pp. 523–540, 2018.
https://doi.org/10.1007/978-3-319-74781-1_35

can increase the annoyance of legitimate clients accessing the website, whose sessions are disrupted). So, it is also important to enable systems to reason about the trade-offs of enacting such tactics, quantifying the benefits of uncertainty reduction and balancing them against its cost when trying to achieve system goals.

One of the most popular patterns for building self-adaptation into software-intensive systems is IBM's MAPE-K [23], which integrates activities to monitor, analyze, plan, and execute adaptations in close-loop control over a managed software (sub)system. Furthermore, a central knowledge base that typically includes models about the managed system, its environment, and adaptations, informs the different MAPE activities.

According to categorizations carried out by different authors [17,24,25], uncertainty occurs in all activities associated with the MAPE-K loop. In this paper, we focus on the aleatoric uncertainties (i.e., due to the randomness of events) induced by inaccuracies in sensor readings (i.e., deviations from the ideal reading of the sensor), and how its explicit representation and incorporation into reasoning mechanisms can improve decision-making in self-adaptation.

Concretely, we investigate two research questions: **(RQ1)** The extent to which explicit representation and reasoning about sensing uncertainty improves the quality of adaptation decisions, and **(RQ2)** the circumstances under which uncertainty awareness improves the quality of decisions (subject to RQ1 being true).

To motivate our approach, we consider a simple scenario illustrated in Fig. 1(a), where the system/environment state space is divided into regions A and B. We assume that the sensors employed to monitor some of the variables that form the system/environment state are not very accurate, and therefore the monitoring infrastructure cannot determine the exact system/environment state (which could be any point in the circle).

Figure 1(b) introduces the concept of *reward*, which is an indicator of how well the system is meeting its goals (e.g., minimizing malicious users or maximizing requests served). Every time a system takes some action, it can be rewarded based on how this action impacts the state of the system (and how well the new

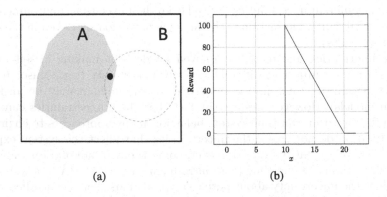

(a)   (b)

Fig. 1. Simple model scenario.

state aligns with system goals). The higher the reward, the better the decision is. In other words, we assume that the system's target in this scenario is to accumulate as much reward as possible over time by taking a series of actions.

In this simple scenario, we assume that reward is only associated with metric x, as shown in Fig. 1(b). When x is below 10, there is no reward; when x is equal to 10, the reward is at its maximum, and decreases as x moves away from 10. Thus, the entire state space of this model is effectively divided into two regions:

Region A : $x < 10$ **Region B** : $x \geq 10$

Suppose that this system can perform a single action to reduce the value of x by an integral amount. Hence, when the system determines that the current state lies within region B (according to the *observed* value of x), it should try to decrease the value of x to maximize reward, making it as close as possible to 10 (but without going below 10). However, the sensor that monitors the value of x is not very accurate and the system has to make the best possible decision under the uncertainty that arises due to the inaccuracy of the sensing process. In particular, if the sensor indicates that the value of x is higher than it really is in states close to $x = 10$, there is a risk that the system will reduce the value of x below 10, incurring in a high penalty (due to the fact that no further reward will be accrued).

There is a need to enable formal reasoning mechanisms for self-adaptation to reduce such risks. In this paper, we contribute a formal analysis technique that enables us to quantify the potential benefits of explicitly considering sensing uncertainty in models and decision-making mechanisms for self-adaptation, and produce adaptation decisions with worst-case guarantees. The formal underpinnings of our proposal are based on model checking of stochastic multiplayer games (SMGs) [10]. The main idea behind the approach is analyzing the interplay of a self-adaptive system and its environment in a game. System and environment are modeled as players with independent behaviors (reflecting the fact that processes in the environment – in this case, sensing – cannot be controlled by the system). System and environment players compete against each other, providing a theoretical setup for worst-case scenario analysis.

The remainder of this paper first presents some background on SMG in Sect. 2, used by a description of our approach in Sect. 3 illustrated on the simple scenario that we have introduced. Next, Sect. 4 introduces a more complex self-protecting systems scenario and discusses some results on comparing uncertainty-aware vs. uncertainty-ignorant decision making. Section 5 discusses some related work. Section 6 presents some conclusions and points at directions for future work.

2   Background: Model Checking of Stochastic Multiplayer Games

Automatic verification techniques for probabilistic systems have been successfully applied in a variety of application domains including security [14,26] and communication protocols [21]. In particular, techniques such as probabilistic model checking provide a means to model and analyze systems with stochastic behavior, and enable quantitative reasoning about probability and reward-based properties (e.g., resource usage, time).

Competitive behavior may also appear in systems when some component cannot be controlled, and could behave according to different or even conflicting goals with respect to other components in the system. Self-adaptive systems are a good example of systems in which the behavior of some components that are typically considered as part of the environment (non-controllable software, network, human actors) cannot be controlled by the system. In such situations, a natural fit is modeling a system as a game between different players, adopting a game-theoretic perspective.

Our approach to analyzing self-adaptation builds upon a recent technique for modeling and analyzing stochastic multi-player games (SMGs) extended with rewards [10]. In this approach, systems are modeled as turn-based SMGs, meaning that in each state of the model, only one player can choose between several actions, the outcome of which can be probabilistic. Players in the game can follow strategies for choosing actions in the game, cooperating in coalition to achieve a common goal, or competing to achieve their own goals. These strategies are guaranteed to achieve optimal expected rewards for the kind of cumulative reward structures that we use in our models.[1]

Reasoning about strategies is a fundamental aspect of model checking SMGs, which enables checking for the existence of a strategy that is able to optimize an objective expressed as a property in a logic called rPATL. Concretely, rPATL can be used for expressing quantitative properties of SMGs, and reasoning about the ability of a coalition of players to collectively achieve a particular goal (e.g., ensuring that the probability of an event's occurrence or an expected reward measure meets some threshold).

rPATL is a CTL-style branching-time temporal logic that incorporates the coalition operator $\langle\langle C \rangle\rangle$, combining it with the probabilistic operator $P_{\bowtie q}$ and path formulae from PCTL [2]. Moreover, rPATL includes a generalization of the reward operator $R^r_{\bowtie x}$ from [19] to reason about goals related to rewards. An extended version of the rPATL reward operator $\langle\langle C \rangle\rangle R^r_{max=?}[F \ \phi]$ enables the quantification of the maximum accrued reward r along paths that lead to states satisfying state formula ϕ that can be guaranteed by players in coalition C, independently of the strategies followed by the rest of the players. An example of the typical usage of combining the coalition and reward maximization operators is $\langle\langle sys \rangle\rangle R^{utility}_{max=?}[F^c \ end]$, meaning "value of the maximum utility reward accumulated along paths leading to an end state that a player sys can guarantee, regardless of the strategies of other players".

---

[1] See Appendix A.2 in [10] for details.

3   Approach

In this section, we describe our approach to analyzing uncertainty-aware self-adaptation, illustrating it on the simple scenario described in the introduction. First, we introduce the definition of the formal model for the game, including a description of how reward is collected. The section finishes by describing the analytical process followed to quantify the difference between uncertainty-aware and uncertainty-ignorant decision-making.

3.1   Formal Model Definition

The purpose of this model is to compare uncertainty-aware adaptation, i.e., decision-making that considers explicitly uncertainty information (in this case induced by inaccuracies in sensing), against uncertainty-ignorant adaptation that assumes that there is no uncertainty in the information it employs for decision-making. The model is implemented using PRISM-Games [9], a tool capable of model checking rPATL properties on stochastic multiplayer games.

The model encodes a game played by an environment and a system player, and it can be instantiated in two variants: one in which the system player is uncertainty-aware, and another in which the system is uncertainty-ignorant. The details of how these different variants are used are explained in Sect. 3.2.

Defining the Players. There are two players in this model: Environment (*env*) and System (*sys*). These two players take turns to take actions. As shown in Listing 1, the turn is controlled by the global variable *turn*. There are two other global variables: *real_x* represents the real value of x at any given time, whereas *obs_x* represents the value of x observed by the system (i.e., the value obtained by the inaccurate sensor).

```
1   player sys target_system,[act],sensor,[sense] endplayer
2   player env environment,[generate] endplayer
3   const ENV_TURN, SYS_TURN;
4   global turn:[ENV_TURN..SYS_TURN] init ENV_TURN; // Used to alternate between players
5   global obs_x, real_x:[0..20];
```

Listing 1. Player definition.

The game is played in alternating turns by the system and the environment players. A typical cycle of the game works in the following way:

1. The environment generates the real value of x (*real_x* - see Listing 2, line 4).

```
1   const INIT_X, error, MAX_TURNS;
2   module environment
3     t : [-1..MAX_TURNS] init 0;
4     [] (t>=0 & t<MAX_TURNS) & (turn=ENV_TURN) -> // 1.Generate value of real x
5         (t'=t+1) & (turn'=SYS_TURN) & (real_x'=INIT_X);
6   endmodule
```

Listing 2. Simple environment model definition.

2. The system senses the value obs_x (Listing 3, line 2). The uncertainty in the sensing process is modeled by a simple probability distribution, in which there is 0.5 probability that the sensor reads the value accurately (i.e., $obs\_x = real\_x$), and 0.5 probability the reading exceeds the real value of x by a constant $error$ (i.e., $obs\_x = real\_x + error$).

```
1   module sensor
2      [sense] true −> 0.5:(obs_x' = real_x) + 0.5:(obs_x' = real_x+error);
3   endmodule
```

Listing 3. Sensor definition.

3. After obtaining the observed value obs_x, the system (Listing 4, line 7) can choose to: (a) do nothing (line 11), or (b) reduce the value of $real\_x$, subtracting the value of s_step from $real\_x$ (lines 8-10). s_step is just the saturated value of a constant $step$ supplied as parameter to the model, which represents the maximum magnitude of the modification that the system's effector can carry out on the value of x. For example, if $step = 3$, s_step can take values in $\{1, 2, 3\}$.

```
1    const step;
2    formula s_step = obs_x−step >= 10 | obs_x < 10 ? step : obs_x − 10;
3
4    module target_system
5    expected_x:[0..20] init 0;
6    new_info:[0..1] init 0;
7       [sense] (new_info=0) & (turn=SYS_TURN) −> (new_info'=1); // 2. Sense
8       [act] (new_info=1) & (turn=SYS_TURN) −> // 3.a. Act
9          (real_x'=real_x−s_step>=0?real_x−s_step:0) & (new_info'=0)
10       & (expected_x'=obs_x−s_step>=0?obs_x−s_step:0) & (turn'=ENV_TURN);
11       [] (new_info=1)&(turn=SYS_TURN) −> // 3.b. Do nothing
12          (expected_x'=obs_x) & (turn'=ENV_TURN) & (new_info'=0);
13   endmodule
```

Listing 4. Simple system model definition.

Note that in the listing above, $expected\_x$ encodes the expected value of x from the perspective of the system after its turn is completed (the expected value of x is built on the value of obs_x).

The cycle repeats until the maximum number of turns played by the system and the environment is reached. However, we assume in the rest of the discussion a single-turn game for the sake of clarity (i.e., the game ends after the environment, and then the system, play one turn each).

Collecting Reward. There are three types of rewards in this model. We use each one of them to emulate different types of adaptation (Listing 5):

1. rU: reward collected if the system has the accurate information to make a decision, i.e., when system knows $real\_x$.
2. rEU: reward collected if the system can only sense obs_x and the system is unaware of the uncertainty, i.e., the system assumes that obs_x is an accurate reading.
3. rEU_uncertain: reward collected if the system can only see obs_x, but is aware of the uncertainty. In this case, the system knows that there is a 0.5

probability that *obs_x* is not accurate and it calculates the reward factoring in this probability.

```
1    formula rU = (real_x<10? 0:200−10*real_x);
2    formula rEU = (expected_x<10? 0:200−10*expected_x);
3    formula rEU_uncertain = 0.5*rEU+0.5*rU;
4
5    rewards "rEU_uncertain" // Expected instantaneous utility reward (uncertainty−aware adaptation)
6        (turn=ENV_TURN) & (t>=1) :rEU_uncertain;
7    endrewards
8
9    rewards "rEU" // Expected instantaneous utility reward (uncertainty−ignorant adaptation)
10       (turn=ENV_TURN) & (t>=1) : rEU;
11   endrewards
12
13   rewards "rU" // Real Instantaneous utility reward
14       (turn=ENV_TURN) & (t>=1) : rU;
15   endrewards
```

Listing 5. Simple model reward structure definition.

3.2 Analytical Approach

To compare the uncertainty-aware vs. uncertainty-ignorant adaptation, we use rPATL specifications that enable us to analyze:

1. R_{real}: The maximum utility that the system can obtain when it has the accurate information (in our scenario, when the system tries to maximize the reward based on *real_x*). We can get this value by generating a strategy for the property:

$$\langle\langle sys \rangle\rangle R^{rU}_{max=?}[F^c \ t = MAX\_TURNS] \qquad (1)$$

2. $R_{u-ignorant}$: The maximum utility that adaptation is able to obtain without factoring uncertainty. To obtain this value, we proceed in two steps:
   (a) First, we generate a strategy using the following property that quantifies the maximum expected accrued reward that the system "believes" it can guarantee based on its beliefs (there is no uncertainty in the expected value of x because the value of *obs_x* is accurate):

$$\langle\langle sys \rangle\rangle R^{rEU}_{max=?}[F^c \ t=MAX\_TURNS] \qquad (2)$$

   (b) We verify Property 1 under the generated strategy for Property 2. This quantifies the real utility achieved (based on the value of *real_x*), under the strategy generated based on the beliefs of the system (i.e., the value of x is *obs_x*, and it coincides with the real one).
3. $R_{u-aware}$: The maximum utility that the adaptation is able to obtain when considering uncertainty. To quantify this value, we proceed in two steps:
   (a) First, we generate a strategy using the following property that quantifies the maximum expected accrued reward that the system "believes" it can guarantee based on its beliefs. However, in this case the system is aware

that the probability of $real\_x = obs\_x$ is only 0.5, so the strategy generated already accounts for the possibility of inaccurate readings. This is encoded in the reward $rEU\_uncertain$ in Listing 5 (line 5).

$$\langle\langle sys \rangle\rangle R_{max=?}^{rEU\_uncertain} [F^c \ t=MAX\_TURNS] \tag{3}$$

(b) We verify Property 1 under the generated strategy for Property 3. This quantifies the real reward under the strategy for uncertainty-aware decision-making.

Experiment and observations for the simple scenario. For our experiment, we collected the value of reward for uncertainty-aware and uncertainty-ignorant adaptation with both sensor *error* and actuator impact *step* taking values in $\{1, 3\}$. The range of values for x explored is $\{0, \ldots, 20\}$.

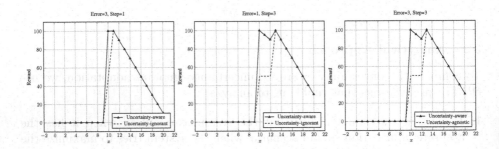

Fig. 2. Simple model scenario results.

Figure 2 compares the reward obtained by uncertainty-aware and uncertainty-ignorant adaptation (i.e., $R_{u-aware}$ and $R_{u-ignorant}$, respectively). Looking at the results, we can make the following observations:

1. *When in a "safe" region, uncertainty does not matter.* When the value of x is in region A ($x \geq 10$), and not close to the threshold $x = 10$, the reward obtained is not affected by uncertainty in any way, since there is no risk that the system will modify the value below the threshold, leading to a loss of reward. In practice, both uncertainty-aware and ignorant adaptations will choose to reduce the value of x to obtain more reward. This can be observed in Fig. 2, where the reward obtained by both adaptation variants converge as x moves to higher values, away from the threshold $x = 10$. Similarly, when the system is in region B ($x < 10$) uncertainty does not make any difference, since there is nothing that the system can do to collect more reward. So, both adaptation variants will behave in the same way.
2. *When close to the boundary between regions, uncertainty-aware adaptation performs better.* When the system is in region A, but in values that are close to the boundary between regions A and B, there is a chance that the system will make a sub-optimal decision due to the uncertainty in sensing. Concretely,

in the uncertainty-ignorant variant of adaptation, the system can determine that it is safe to reduce the value of x by a given amount based on the value of obs_x (when in reality, the value of x will go below 10 and reward will not be collected). This penalizes uncertainty-ignorant adaptation with respect to the uncertainty-aware variant, which is already accounting for the likelihood of an undesirable outcome, and is more conservative when choosing to reduce the value of x. Figure 2 shows how the different choices of adaptation variants lead to increased rewards in uncertainty-aware adaptation when the value of x is close to the boundary between regions.

3. *The difference between adaptation approaches is greater when sensor error is paired with actuator impact.* As sensor error increases, we would expect to see uncertainty-ignorant adaptation's reward progressively decrease. However, this is only true if sensor error is paired with higher actuator impact values, since otherwise the limited scope of the actuator mitigates the potentially detrimental effects that making the wrong choice would have on reward. For instance, if $error = 3$, but step=1, the plot in Fig. 2 (left) shows that there is little performance difference between the two variants of adaptation. This is because, even if the system makes the wrong choice under uncertainty-ignorant adaptation, e.g., when $x = 12$, the actuator can at most reduce x to a value 11, incurring only a light penalty, compared to uncertainty-aware adaptation. However, if we consider the same value of $x = 12$ when $step = 3$ (center, right), the difference in reward between approaches is much more pronounced because in situations in which reducing x is the wrong choice, it is more likely that x will go under the threshold $x = 10$, incurring a higher penalty.

4 Case Study: Denial of Service Attack (DoS)

In this section, we describe our approach on a more complex scenario where an enterprise web infrastructure similar to the Znn.com system experiences a DoS attack [26]. When web infrastructure experiences unusually high traffic, the cause of the high traffic might be malicious (e.g., the system is experiencing a DoS attack) or legitimate (some content has suddenly become popular - e.g., the slashdot effect). Treating legitimate users as DoS attackers by mistake, applying strategies like blocking their requests for accessing the website could be harmful to the business. Thus, uncertainty about such situations should be considered when applying defensive adaptation strategies to the system, evaluating carefully the benefit and cost of different adaptation choices, possibly including actions that can reduce uncertainty.

To facilitate the understanding of the DoS scenario, we structure our model in a similar way to the simple model described earlier and make the following assumptions:[2]

---

[2] A full listing of the PRISM-Games model can be found in [5].

1. *The entire space is divided into two regions:* (i) *DoS*, in which we assume that the system is experiencing an attack, and (ii) *Normal*, in which the system does not experience any anomalous activity that indicates a DoS attack.
2. *Regions are associated with specific metrics.* The system's state is determined by a single metric that captures the estimated *percentage of malicious clients* accessing the system (*mc*). This metric is an abstract concept used as proof of concept. We assume that if *mc* is above a given threshold, the system is in the *DoS* region of the state space; otherwise the system is considered to be in the *Normal* region.
3. *The system does not know the real value of metrics.* The observable value of the metric *mc* may not reflect its real value.
4. *Uncertainty in sensing is represented by a probability distribution.* We employ a normal distribution to model the observed percentage of malicious clients *mc*.
5. *The uncertainty-aware version of the system has knowledge about the probability distribution function that captures uncertainty in sensing.* To simplify the problem, we assume that the system has knowledge of the probability distribution function that represents how observed values are generated during the sensing process. In the real world, this knowledge may be obtained from historical data, for instance.

The two main extensions with respect to the simple scenario presented earlier are: (i) a richer set of actions or *tactics* that the system can carry out to influence state variables including those that reduce uncertainty, and (ii) a more sophisticated notion of reward that factors in metrics along more than one dimension of concern.

– *Tactics.* In the simple previous example, the system can either do nothing or *act* on the value of x by decreasing it. In the real world, a system may have a richer variety of adaptation actions, or *tactics*, to respond to run-time events. In this model, we divide tactics into two kinds:
  • *Uncertainty Reduction Tactics.* This kind of tactic can reduce uncertainty (in our scenario the uncertainty associated with the sensing of system metrics). This type of tactic often comes at a cost. For example, introducing CAPTCHA[3] can reduce uncertainty about the maliciousness of clients accessing the system (by determining which ones are controlled by bots), but it will increase the annoyance of legitimate users, who find their activities disrupted by the CAPTCHA.
  • *Non Uncertainty Reduction Tactics.* Tactics that do not reduce uncertainty like *blackholing* clients (i.e., dropping their incoming requests) do not provide any new information (e.g., about who is controlling the clients). Decisions of whether to exercise these tactics are therefore highly dependent on the quality of the information available to the system (i.e., the observed values of metrics).

---

[3] CAPTCHA is a type of challenge-response test used in computing to determine whether or not the user is human (https://en.wikipedia.org/wiki/CAPTCHA).

– *Reward Model.* In the simple scenario, the reward was related only to one dimension. However, in this scenario there are two dimensions of concern: security and user experience, and we assume them to be of equal importance. Security is directly related to the metric percentage of malicious clients mc (lower is better). User experience is also affected by system's choice of applying different tactics. For example, introducing CAPTCHA will increase the difficulty of legitimate users accessing system services and therefore increase their annoyance. We consider therefore user annoyance (ua) as an additional metric for the user experience dimension of concern.

4.1   Formal Model Definition

This section provides a high-level description of the game model for the DoS scenario. The scenario is modeled as a stochastic game involving two players that represent the system (sys) and the environment (env):

– The system player consists of two processes or *modules* that represent the *target system* and the *gauge* that collects observed values of the mc metric. These two modules are synchronized by a shared action $gaugeMc$.
– The environment player consists of the *generator* and *environment* modules, which are synchronized via the $generateMc$ shared action.

When the game starts, the environment player first generates the real value of the mc ($generateMc$), and it yields the turn to the system player. Next, the system player gauges mc ($gaugeMc$), producing its observed value. The system player then infers the region of the state space (DoS or Normal) based on the observed system metric, chooses one of the available tactics to execute (*blackHole*, *captcha*, or chooses not to do anything), and returns the turn to the environment.

The game contains three global variables: (i) $real\_mc$ is the real percentage of malicious clients, ranging from $[0,100]$, represents the real system metric, (ii) obs_mc is observed percentage of malicious clients, and (iii) std_mc is the standard deviation associated with the perceived percentage of malicious clients. Note that obs_mc and std_mc together describe the uncertainty function for the observed system metric.

Generating the Real Value of Metric. *Generator* is a module that is responsible for generating the real value of metric ($real\_mc$) during every turn of the environment.

Gauging Information. The *gauge* module is responsible for gauging information. This process is crucial to our scenario model because it encodes how observed values of mc are generated from the real values of the variable (i.e., it captures the source of aleatoric uncertainty in the sensing process). Concretely, the observed value of metric can be captured as the function:

$$P(x) = \frac{1}{std\_mc\sqrt{2\pi}} e^{-(x-obs\_mc)^2/2std\_mc^2} \quad or \quad f(x) = P[X = x]$$

This probability density function is actually a conditional probability distribution of the observed value of the metric, given a real value ($P(obs\_mc|real\_mc)$). In this scenario, we encode this function using six points to simulate this normal distribution.

Selecting and Applying Tactics. After the system obtains the information about system metrics, it can choose a tactic for execution (or do nothing). The model has two variants that capture two alternative selection strategies:

1. *Uncertainty-ignorant.* The system does not have knowledge about the real value of the metric mc. It is also oblivious to the fact that there is uncertainty in the gauging process and therefore treats the observed value as the real information, selecting tactics based on this information.
2. *Uncertainty-aware.* The system has no knowledge of the real value of mc. However, the system has knowledge about the uncertainty in the gauging process and evaluates the expected result considering the probability distribution over different system states and selects tactics based on that.

The adaptation decision is evaluated for the selection strategies based on the value of the following set of variables:

1. *real_mc*: Real value of metric mc.
2. *emc*: Expected percentage of malicious client after executing a tactic, assuming that $obs\_mc = real\_mc$.
3. *ua*: Real value for the metric user annoyance.
4. *eua*: Expected user annoyance after executing a tactic assuming $obs\_mc = real\_mc$
5. *eua_dos*: Expected user annoyance after executing a tactic if the system is currently at the DoS region.
6. *eua_normal*: Expected user annoyance after executing a tactic if the system is currently at the Normal region. This variable and *eua_dos* are used to calculate the expected reward when the system is aware of the uncertainty.

These six variables are used to calculate three types of reward (real, expected by uncertainty-aware, and expected by uncertainty-ignorant decision-making). By maximizing different types of reward, we can employ our formal model to generate adaptation decisions for: (a) adaptation based on real information, (b) uncertainty-ignorant adaptation, and (c) uncertainty-aware adaptation.

Table 1 summarizes the effect of exercising different tactics at different system states. For example, blackholing in both regions (DoS and Normal) reduces the *real_mc* by 30% but it increases user annoyance by 50% if the system is not in DoS, and by 10% if it is (reflecting the assumption that most clients will correspond to malicious users[4]).

---

[4] In this model, we assume that the effect of tactics is deterministic.

Collecting Reward. Rewards are calculated based on both user annoyance and the percentage of malicious clients. In this case, the reward we employ for our game encodes a simple utility function in which both metrics contribute to the overall utility calculation with a weight of 0.5. We employ three types of rewards to analyze uncertainty-aware and uncertainty-ignorant decision-making.

Table 1. Simple impact specification of tactics in a DoS adaptation scenario.

real_mc	Normal	DoS
IntroduceCAPTCHA	−10	−10
Blackhole	−30	−30

ua	Normal	DoS
IntroduceCAPTCHA	+10	+10
Blackhole	+50	+10

1. rIU (real utility): This reward is calculated based on the real value of the percentage of malicious clients (*real_mc*).
2. rEIU (expected utility for uncertainty-ignorant decision making): Is calculated based on the observable information about the percentage of malicious clients (*obs_mc*), and it is unaware of the uncertainty in sensing.
3. rEIU_uncertain (expected utility for uncertainty-aware decision making): Is also calculated based on the observed value of the metric *mc* (*obs_mc*). However, this alternative considers the uncertainty in sensing, since it draws the values for reward calculation based on all the possibilities captured in the probability distribution.

The calculation of *rEIU_uncertain* is the key of this model. When collecting reward in uncertainty-aware adaptation, we derive all the potential real values of metric *mc*, based on its observed value, and calculate the expected reward based on the probability distribution of these real values. In other words, *the system must have knowledge of the probability distribution of real values of the metric conditioned to its observed value* $P(real\_mc \mid obs\_mc)$ *to calculate rEIU_uncertain.*

The observed value (*obs_mc*) is normally distributed given a real value (*real_mc*), based on the joint probability mass function of two discrete random variables:

$$P(X = x, Y = y) = P(Y = y \mid X = x) * P(X = x) = P(X = x \mid Y = y) * P(Y = y)$$

4.2 Experiments and Observation

To compare uncertainty-aware with uncertainty-ignorant adaptation, we use the analytical process described in Sect. 3. For our experiment, we collected the value of reward for uncertainty-aware and uncertainty-ignorant adaptation with a DoS threshold value of 60, and different sensor standard deviations in the distribution that captures sensing uncertainty for mc $\sigma_{obs\_mc} \in \{10, 20\}$. The range explored for mc is $\{0, \ldots, 100\}$.

Figure 3 shows the result of our experiments. From these results, we can draw the following observations (which are consistent with the earlier example):

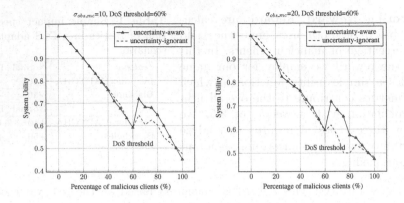

Fig. 3. DoS scenario results.

1. *When far from region boundary, uncertainty does not matter.* When the value of mc is in region DoS or Normal ($mc \geq 60$), and moves away from the threshold, the utility obtained both by uncertainty-aware and ignorant adaptations is similar.
2. *When close to the boundary between regions, uncertainty-aware adaptation performs better.* When the system is in region DoS, but in values that get close to the boundary between regions DoS and Normal, there is a chance that the system will make a sub-optimal decision due to uncertainty. Concretely, uncertainty-ignorant adaptation can determine that it is safe to blackhole clients based by the value of obs_mc and might incur in penalties for blackholing potentially legitimate clients.
3. *The difference between adaptation approaches is greater when standard deviation is higher.* As the standard deviation in sensor inaccuracies increases, we can see how the utility obtained by uncertainty-ignorant adaptation decreases. If we observe the plots, focusing on the range 60%- 90% of percentage of malicious clients, there is a noticeable drop in the utility obtained by the uncertainty-ignorant approach in the plot on the right, in which the standard deviation σ_{obs_mc} is doubled with respect to the one on the left.

5   Related Work

Uncertainty management has been studied by many authors in the field of self-adaptive systems, but not so far in managing sensing uncertainty. Possibility theory has been mainly used in approaches that deal with uncertainty in objectives, helping to assess the positive and negative consequences of uncertainty [1,16,27]. Other approaches employ probabilistic verification and estimates of the future environment and system behavior for optimizing the system's operation. These proposals target the mitigation of uncertainty due to *parameters over time* [3,4,15].

Although these approaches have shown promising results in dealing with different types of uncertainty they do not cover uncertainty that is directly caused by the information that is used as sensing input to the decision-making agent. Such uncertainty is especially important when the self-adaptive system is managing a cyber-physical system. In this case, attackers may exploit compromised sensors and effectors to steer a system into unsafe states that not only have an impact on the software, but ultimately on the physical context of the system.

The work in [18] is concerned with the estimation and control of linear systems when some of the sensors or actuators are corrupted by an attacker. The authors of [13] tackle a similar problem, with a stronger focus on sensing and state estimation in continuous-time linear systems, for which an attacker may have control over some of the sensors and inject (potentially unbounded) additive noise into some of the measured outputs. To characterize the resilience of a system against such sensor attacks, the authors introduce a notion of "observability under attacks" that addresses the question of whether or not it is possible to uniquely reconstruct the state of the system by observing its inputs and outputs over a period of time, with the understanding that some of the available system's outputs may have been corrupted by the attacker. The authors of [11] study CPS subject to dynamic sensor attacks, relating them to the system's strong observability. This work identifies necessary and sufficient conditions for an attacker to create a dynamically undetectable sensor attack and relates them to system dynamics.

Our approach can be regarded as complementary to these works, since it would enable us to potentially exploit the information provided by these approaches to improve decision-making and provide worst-case scenario guarantees. In [7] we reported on an analogous application of this technique to quantify the benefits of employing information about the latency of tactics for decision-making in proactive adaptation, comparing it against approaches that make the simplifying assumption of tactic executions not being subject to latency.

6   Conclusions and Future Work

This paper has described an analysis technique based on model checking of stochastic multi-player games that enables us to quantify the benefits in adaptation performance of factoring sensing uncertainty explicitly into decision-making. Our results show that although uncertainty-aware adaptation is not guaranteed to perform better than uncertainty-ignorant adaptation in all cases, *it does perform at least comparably in all cases* (RQ1), and *performs better in boundary regions of the state space in which the dynamics of the system may change* (RQ1 and RQ2). This is a relevant finding, because systems that exhibit variability in the effects of adaptation tactics that depend on specific run-time conditions may obtain a remarkable benefit in terms of improved reliability and performance by factoring uncertainty into decision-making.

With respect to future work, we plan on extending decision-making under uncertainty to reason only with partial knowledge about the uncertainty function. The current version of our approach assumes that information about

$P(observed\ value\ |\ real\ value)$ is known to the system, so it can derive $P(real\ value\ |\ observed\ value)$. A next logical step is to study how systems can gradually improve their ability to estimate the real state of the system, i.e. by automatically refining throughout subsequent system executions the knowledge that the system has about $P(real\ value\ |\ observed\ value)$. A second avenue for future work will investigate reasoning about uncertainty reduction and uncertainty-aware decision-making in human-in-the-loop adaptation, where human operators may provide information that is inaccurate, continuing the line started in [6,8].

Acknowledgments. This material is based on research sponsored by AFRL and DARPA under agreement number FA8750-16-2-0042 and by the Department of Defense under Contract No. FA8721-05-C-0003 with Carnegie Mellon University for the operation of the Software Engineering Institute, a federally funded research and development center. The U.S. Government is authorized to reproduce and distribute reprints for Governmental purposes notwithstanding any copyright notation thereon. The views and conclusions contained herein are those of the authors and should not be interpreted as necessarily representing the official policies or endorsements, either expressed or implied, of the AFRL, DARPA, ONR or the U.S. Government. References herein to any specific commercial product, process, or service by trade name, trade mark, manufacturer, or otherwise, does not necessarily constitute or imply its endorsement, recommendation, or favoring by Carnegie Mellon University or its Software Engineering Institute. This material has been approved for public release and unlimited distribution.

References

1. Baresi, L., Pasquale, L., Spoletini, P.: Fuzzy goals for requirements-driven adaptation. In: 18th Requirements Engineering Conference (RE 2010), pp. 125–134 (2010)
2. Bianco, A., de Alfaro, L.: Model checking of probabilistic and nondeterministic systems. In: Thiagarajan, P.S. (ed.) FSTTCS 1995. LNCS, vol. 1026, pp. 499–513. Springer, Heidelberg (1995). https://doi.org/10.1007/3-540-60692-0_70
3. Calinescu, R., Kwiatkowska, M.Z.: Using quantitative analysis to implement autonomic IT systems. In: ICSE (2009)
4. Calinescu, R., et al.: Dynamic QoS management and optimization in service-based systems. IEEE Trans. Software Eng. **37**(3), 387–409 (2011)
5. Cámara, J., Garlan, D., Kang, W.G., Peng, W., Schmerl, B.: Uncertainty in self-adaptive systems: categories, management, and perspectives. Technical report CMU-ISR-17-110, Institute for Software Research, Carnegie Mellon University (2017)
6. Cámara, J., Garlan, D., Moreno, G.A., Schmerl, B.: Evaluating trade-offs of human involvement in self-adaptive systems. In: Managing Trade-Offs in Self-Adaptive Systems (2016)
7. Cámara, J., Moreno, G.A., Garlan, D.: Stochastic game analysis and latency awareness for proactive self-adaptation. In: 9th International Symposium on Software Engineering for Adaptive and Self-Managing Systems, SEAMS, pp. 155–164 (2014)
8. Cámara, J., Moreno, G.A., Garlan, D.: Reasoning about human participation in self-adaptive systems. In: 10th International Symposium on Software Engineering for Adaptive and Self-Managing Systems, SEAMS, pp. 146–156 (2015)

9. Chen, T., Forejt, V., Kwiatkowska, M., Parker, D., Simaitis, A.: PRISM-games: a model checker for stochastic multi-player games. In: Piterman, N., Smolka, S.A. (eds.) TACAS 2013. LNCS, vol. 7795, pp. 185–191. Springer, Heidelberg (2013). https://doi.org/10.1007/978-3-642-36742-7_13

10. Chen, T., Forejt, V., Kwiatkowska, M.Z., Parker, D., Simaitis, A.: Automatic verification of competitive stochastic systems. Form. Methods Syst. Des. **43**(1), 61–92 (2013)

11. Chen, Y., Kar, S., Moura, J.M.F.: Cyber-physical systems: dynamic sensor attacks and strong observability. In: 2015 IEEE International Conference on Acoustics, Speech and Signal Processing (ICASSP), pp. 1752–1756 (2015)

12. Cheng, B.H.C., et al.: Software engineering for self-adaptive systems: a research roadmap. In: Cheng, B.H.C., de Lemos, R., Giese, H., Inverardi, P., Magee, J. (eds.) Software Engineering for Self-Adaptive Systems. LNCS, vol. 5525, pp. 1–26. Springer, Heidelberg (2009). https://doi.org/10.1007/978-3-642-02161-9_1

13. Chong, M.S., Wakaiki, M., Hespanha, J.P.: Observability of linear systems under adversarial attacks. In: 2015 American Control Conference (ACC), pp. 2439–2444, July 2015

14. Deshpande, T., Katsaros, P., Smolka, S., Stoller, S.: Stochastic game-based analysis of the dns bandwidth amplification attack using probabilistic model checking. In: Dependable Computing Conference (EDCC), 2014 Tenth European, pp. 226–237, May 2014

15. Epifani, I., et al.: Model evolution by run-time parameter adaptation. In: ICSE. IEEE CS (2009)

16. Esfahani, N., Kouroshfar, E., Malek, S.: Taming uncertainty in self-adaptive software. In: Proceedings of the 19th ACM SIGSOFT Symposium and the 13th European Conference on Foundations of Software Engineering. pp. 234–244. ESEC/FSE 2011, ACM (2011)

17. Esfahani, N., Malek, S.: Uncertainty in self-adaptive software systems. In: de Lemos, R., Giese, H., Müller, H.A., Shaw, M. (eds.) Software Engineering for Self-Adaptive Systems II. LNCS, vol. 7475, pp. 214–238. Springer, Heidelberg (2013). https://doi.org/10.1007/978-3-642-35813-5_9

18. Fawzi, H., Tabuada, P., Diggavi, S.: Secure estimation and control for cyber-physical systems under adversarial attacks. IEEE Trans. Autom. Control **59**(6), 1454–1467 (2014)

19. Forejt, V., Kwiatkowska, M., Norman, G., Parker, D.: Automated verification techniques for probabilistic systems. In: Bernardo, M., Issarny, V. (eds.) SFM 2011. LNCS, vol. 6659, pp. 53–113. Springer, Heidelberg (2011). https://doi.org/10.1007/978-3-642-21455-4_3

20. Garlan, D.: Software engineering in an uncertain world. In: Future of Software Engineering Research (FoSER), pp. 125–128 (2010)

21. He, K., Zhang, M., He, J., Chen, Y.: Probabilistic model checking of pipe protocol. In: Theoretical Aspects of Software Engineering (TASE), pp. 135–138 (2015)

22. Huebscher, M.C., McCann, J.A.: A survey of autonomic computing - degrees, models, and applications. ACM Comput. Surv. **4**(3) (2008). Article no. 7

23. Kephart, J.O., Chess, D.M.: The vision of autonomic computing. Computer **36**, 41–50 (2003)

24. Mahdavi-Hezavehi, S., Avgeriou, P., Weyns, D.: A classification of current architecture-based approaches tackling uncertainty in self-adaptive systems with multiple requirements. In: Managing Trade-offs in Adaptable Software Architectures. Elsevier (2016)

25. Ramirez, A.J., Jensen, A.C., Cheng, B.H.C.: A taxonomy of uncertainty for dynamically adaptive systems. In: 7th International Symposium on Software Engineering for Adaptive and Self-Managing Systems, SEAMS, pp. 99–108 (2012)
26. Schmerl, B.R., Cámara, J., Gennari, J., Garlan, D., Casanova, P., Moreno, G.A., Glazier, T.J., Barnes, J.M.: Architecture-based self-protection: composing and reasoning about denial-of-service mitigations. In: Symposium on the Science of Security, HotSoS, p. 2 (2014)
27. Whittle, J., Sawyer, P., Bencomo, N., Cheng, B., Bruel, J.: Relax: incorporating uncertainty into the specification of self-adaptive systems. In: 2009 17th IEEE International Requirements Engineering Conference, RE 2009, pp. 79–88, Aug 2009

Lightweight Preprocessing for Agent-Based Simulation of Smart Mobility Initiatives

Carlo Castagnari[1], Jacopo de Berardinis[1(✉)], Giorgio Forcina[1], Ali Jafari[3], and Marjan Sirjani[2,3]

[1] Division of Computer Science, Smart Mobility Lab, University of Camerino, Via Madonna delle Carceri 9, 62032 Camerino, MC, Italy
`jacopo.deberardinis@unicam.it`
[2] School of Innovation, Design and Engineering, Malardalen University, Hogskoleplan 1, 72123 Vasteras, Sweden
[3] School of Computer Science, Reykjavik University, Menntavegur 1, Reykjavik 101, Iceland

Abstract. Understanding the impacts of a mobility initiative prior to deployment is a complex task for both urban planners and transport companies. To support this task, Tangramob offers an agent-based simulation framework for assessing the evolution of urban traffic after the introduction of new mobility services. However, Tangramob simulations are computationally expensive due to their iterative nature. Thus, we simplified the Tangramob model into a Timed Rebeca (TRebeca) model and we designed a tool-chain that generates instances of this model starting from the same Tangramob's inputs. Running TRebeca models allows users to get an idea of how mobility initiatives affect the system performance, in a short time, without resorting to the simulator. To validate this approach, we compared the output of both the simulator and the TRebeca model on a collection of mobility initiatives. Results show a correlation between them, thus demonstrating the usefulness of using TRebeca models for unconventional contexts of application.

Keywords: Agent-based simulations
Actor-based modeling languages

1 Introduction

Being part of a continuously growing population, which is expected to shift from 7.3 billion to 9.6 billion inhabitants by 2050 [14], urges us to re-think urban mobility. Such an unbridled demographic growth is worsened by an increasing urbanization trend, as people living in urban areas will rise from 54% to 66% in the next 30 years. If poorly managed, these phenomena will jeopardize the quality

The work of the 4th and a part of that of the 5th author are supported by "Self-Adaptive Actors: SEADA" (project nr. 163205-051) from Icelandic Research Fund.

© Springer International Publishing AG 2018
A. Cerone and M. Roveri (Eds.): SEFM 2017 Workshops, LNCS 10729, pp. 541–557, 2018.
https://doi.org/10.1007/978-3-319-74781-1_36

of life of citizens, accentuating many problems like traffic congestion, high cost of personal mobility, land use inefficiencies as well as the environmental impacts.

Urged by these threats, urban planners are now shifting their attention to Smart Mobility, defined as "a complex set of projects and actions, different in goals, contents and technology intensity" [2] focused on mobility issues. Examples of smart mobility services range from carsharing and bikesharing services to more advanced ones like self-driving taxis and dynamic ridesharing systems.

Nevertheless, given a certain urban context, how can we evaluate the ability of a Smart Mobility Initiative (SMI), i.e. a number of smart mobility services, to meet the actual mobility needs of the population prior to its deployment? It turns out that estimating the impacts of a mobility initiative is one of the most crucial concerns in urban planning. In fact, the current approach of using heuristics and best-practises might end up being risky for decision makers, since the resulting mobility initiatives may be unaccepted by the population [6,9].

Driven by these motivations, *Tangramob* [4] offers a simulation environment for mobility assessment. This open source tool allows urban planners and transport companies to understand if the effects of the simulated mobility initiatives are expected to be in line with their objectives and plans. The peculiarities of this simulator are: the adaptability to different geographical contexts; the support of multimodal trips and mobility services; the ability to reproduce real-life scenarios. Tangramob relies on an Agent-Based Model (ABM) in which every citizen is given the ability to experience with the newly introduced mobility services in order to understand which is the best way to travel daily. Following a Reinforcement Learning (RL) strategy, a simulation is organized as a series of iterations, so that a single day is simulated multiple times: this approach allows citizens to accumulate experience so as to come up with better mobility decisions. At the end of a simulation, we will be able to understand how the mobility initiative is accepted by the population and how it affects both citizens and urban system.

However, the iterative nature of Tangramob simulations makes them computationally expensive in case of complex scenarios, i.e. when either or both the population under study is large and the number of new smart mobility services is substantial. On the other hand, a Tangramob user is interested in performing multiple experiments with the simulator, that is, evaluating different smart mobility initiatives so as to find out the most promising ones. For instance, a user can change the configuration of a mobility service by either increasing or decreasing the number of vehicles. Nonetheless, running as many simulations as the number of smart mobility initiatives to investigate might be time-consuming.

To address this obstacle, we reduced the complexity of the Tangramob's ABM in order to derive a Timed Rebeca (TRebeca) [10] model in which the RL-based learning process and the representation of traffic were both simplified. Together with the ability of modeling persons as packets, made possible by the actor-based modeling paradigm of TRebeca, the resulting model allows to run experiments faster with the cost of loosing the microscopic detail of Tangramob simulations. In addition, to improve its usability, we developed a tool chain that generates instances of the TRebeca model from the same input files of Tangramob scenarios. Despite the many simplifications, comparing the results obtained from the two models on different mobility initiatives for the same scenario shows that the TRebeca model behaves similarly to Tangramob. This correlation makes it possible for users to exploit the TRebeca model as a tool for getting first results of a SMI without simulating it. In particular, the experimenter can use this model to understand which initiatives are more in line with his expectations, so as to simulate them later with Tangramob to get more details.

The structure of this paper is as follows: Sect. 3 gives an overview of Tangramob, as well as a brief description of its ABM. In Sect. 4 we introduce the Rebeca and Timed Rebeca modeling languages and we present the simplified Timed Rebeca model derived from the original one. Section 4.3 details on how we performed the derivation process, focusing on the different assumptions and heuristics adopted in order to approximate the learning process of the simulator. In Sect. 5 we describe how we designed the experiment to prove both the similarity among the two models and the utility of the simplified TRebeca model. Finally, in Sect. 6 we show the experimental results and we discuss about their implications in order to confirm the former hypothesis.

2   Related Work

To the best of our knowledge, Tangramob is the first simulator supporting intermodality and multimodality in a context-independent architecture. This section thus provides the reader with an overview of common approaches aimed at handling large-scale scenarios within reasonable computational time. Indeed, this is one of the most faced challenges in Agent-Based (AB) traffic simulations. The state of the art provides different solutions to this problem, which can be classified into two groups: *technical approaches* and *model-based ones*.

The first group collects all those alternatives which keep the integrity of the AB traffic model, whereas trying to decrease the computational complexity by means of some expedients, such as: reducing the input dimension and optimizing the available computational resources. For instance, in [7] the practice is to scale down the model, i.e. instead of modeling the 100% of a city's population, only a representative portion is considered. It is thus possible to get comparable system dynamics with a 10% population if the transport system capacities are scaled down proportionally. Another approach is to harvest the computational power of Graphical Processing Units (GPU). For instance, [13] achieved a speedup of up to 67 times by means of a CUDA re-implementation of MATSim.

On the other hand, the second group comprises alternative approaches to model traffic at a more coarse-grained level, often resulting in loss of details. Indeed, microscopic traffic simulations are much computational demanding than other models, since they track the movement of each vehicle as well as the interactions among vehicles competing for roads. In contrast, macroscopic models aggregate vehicles, and traffic is described as a continuum. For instance, [3] introduces MacroSim, a MATSim's module for macroscopic mobility simulations. In MacroSim, agents are handled sequentially and decoupled from each other, as well from the environment, over the simulation. Their interactions are thus represented at a higher abstraction level by means of constraints in capacity and speed on each road of the network, expressed by volume-delay functions. With MacroSim, the simulation approach changes from a system-based to an individual-based one, allowing a more efficient parallelization of the mobility simulation (7–50 times faster). Another modeling approach is given by [5] in which, instead of performing a microscopic traffic simulation along fixed time steps, an event based model is used, performing only discrete actions which are relevant to the model (i.e. entering and leaving roads).

Although scaling the model to a smaller yet representative population is certainly helpful to save time, this approach is still not enough to cope with both large-scale scenarios and shared mobility services. Concerning the exploitation of GPU computing, it is worth considering that a CUDA implementation requires considerable design efforts since Tangramob is developed in Java. Moreover, the dependencies among agents and the environment, typical of macroscopic simulations, make it difficult to reach a good parallelization of the model.

For what concerns model-based approaches, shifting from a micro to a macroscopic model by means of abstractions is useful in some contexts. However, Tangramob aims at modeling both intermodal trips, which follow different traveling patterns than usual ones, and the acceptance of a mobility initiative for every single person of a sample population. This last consideration is due to the fact that an urban planner should be able to find a good balance of mobility resources for a certain district according to the actual mobility needs of the nearby citizens. Thus, it turns out that a macroscopic modeling approach is not suitable for our purposes. On the other hand, the event-based approach suggested in [5] can be even improved by modeling other traffic dynamics as messages.

3   The Tangramob Simulator

Tangramob [4] is an agent-based simulation framework supporting urban planners and transport companies in shaping Smart Mobility Initiatives (SMIs) within urban areas. Users can thus assess whether introducing a SMI can improve the traveling experience of the citizens, as well as the urban transport system. In order to consider people's acceptance, Tangramob returns an estimation of how a mobility initiative can impact on local communities, so as to figure out beforehand if a SMI can potentially succeed or not. Technically, a Tangramob simulation requires the following inputs:

- **road network** of the urban area under study, represented as a weighted graph with nodes denoting intersections and edges standing for streets;
- **mobility agendas** of a sample population (i.e. people's mobility habits),
- **smart mobility initiative** to be simulated, i.e. a list of geographically located containers of one or more smart mobility services, called *tangrhubs*. Each smart mobility service belongs to a *tangrhub* and it comes with a number of mobility resources (e.g. vehicles), as well as a service charge.

Once the above inputs are provided, Tangramob can start a simulation which returns several output files in order to provide users with a list of measures concerning how the mobility habits of citizens are expected to change after the introduction of the SMI. In particular, the following output variables are returned for each person, and then added together: *traveled distance*, *traveled time*, CO_2 *emissions*, *mobility costs* and whether he has accepted the mobility initiative or not. Tangramob will also provide a measure of the resulting *urban traffic levels*, as well as a metric on the *use of mobility resources*. From the analysis of such parameters, a user can realize if the simulated initiative is in line with his expectations. If not, he can change the configuration of the SMI (e.g. relocate/add/remove *tangrhubs*, change a mobility service) and run new experiments.

The detailed description of Tangramob is out of the scope of this work; nevertheless, in order to present the ABM as well as the derivation process for the TRebeca model, we introduce the following key concepts to the reader: *tangrhub*, *smart mobility initiative* and *commuting pattern*.

A **tangrhub** is a geo-located container of mobility services (e.g. carsharing, bikesharing), each of which in turn manages a fleet of vehicles (e.g. cars, bikes). A **Smart Mobility Initiative (SMI)** is thus about placing a number of *tangrhubs* within the urban area of interest, adding one or more mobility services to each of them, and providing a characterization for each service. In particular, to define a smart mobility service for a *tangrhub*, the user has to specify the service type (i.e. intra-hub or inter-hub), the initial number of vehicles and the service charge (i.e. cost per km, per hour and fixed cost). Each mobility service m_i provided by a *tangrhub* th_j must belong either to one of these service types:

- *intra-hub* services, used for moving people *to* and *from* th_j thereby serving first mile trips, e.g. from a commuter's home-place to th_j and viceversa;
- *inter-hub* services, moving people from th_j to another *tangrhub* th_k.

A **commuting pattern** is the intermodal representation of how a person moves from an origin location to his destination. Such a trip can be either simple, e.g. the commuter directly travel from origin to destination by either walking or car; or more complex, e.g. the commuter will use more than one means of transport, for instance: walking to the closest bus station, travel by bus, then reach a metro line and so on. A clear example of a commuting pattern is the route provided by the trip planner of Google Maps. However, how will the commuting patterns of citizens change as the smart mobility initiative is introduced? In Tangramob, the complexity of commuting patterns is limited to three schemes: direct path, 2-trip path and 3-trip path (shown in Figs. 1, 2, 3, respectively). In particular, nodes O and D represent respectively the commuter origin and destination; whereas nodes TH, TH_O and TH_D depict respectively a generic *tangrhub*, and the nearest *tangrhubs* to O and D. This is possible thanks to both the concept of *tangrhub* and interconnection among *tangrhubs* via inter-hub mobility services. The resulting architecture looks similar to a computer network, in which *tangrhubs* play the role of routers, mobility services are cables and commuters can be seen as packets.

Fig. 1. Direct path   **Fig. 2.** 2-trip path   **Fig. 3.** 3-trip path

3.1   Tangramob Agent-Based Model (ABM): An Overview

This section introduces the formalization of Tangramob, that will be helpful to understand the translation of the original agent-based model into the simplified TRebeca one (presented in Sect. 4.2).

The Tangramob ABM has two different agent types: *commuter* and *tangrhub*. A commuter agent, from now on commuter, is the computational counterpart of a person of the population. Every commuter has his own mobility agenda, i.e. a sequence of daily activities (e.g. home, work) interleaved by legs, each of which tells how the commuter moves from one activity location to the next one (e.g. car, bike). Instead, a *tangrhub* agent acts as a local mobility service provider.

Both agents live and operate, with different perceptions, in a composite environment made of three different spaces: the temporal one, the geographical one and the smart mobility services' state space. The geographical space is the core of the transport simulation, since the physical limitations of the road network can create bottlenecks and delays as people move with a certain pace.

As depicted in Fig. 4, every time a commuter needs to move from one place to another, an interaction with the surrounding *tangrhubs* takes place as follows: *tangrhubs* are expected to collaborate with each other in order to provide the commuter with a number of traveling alternatives for taking him to destination (a traveling alternative can be thought of as a combination of one up to three legs, each of which can involve a smart mobility service and it is based on the Tangramob commuting patterns). Next, the commuter will perform a decision-making process to select the traveling alternative that is expected to optimize his performance criteria. Once an alternative is chosen, the involved *tangrhubs* will reserve the required mobility services so that the commuter can start his journey. Finally, once the commuter has reached his destination, he will be asked to leave a feedback for each smart mobility service involved in the chosen alternative.

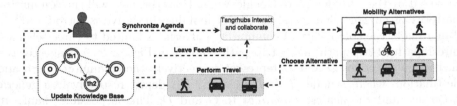

Fig. 4. Commuter-Tangrhub interaction loop

Each feedback quantifies the traveling experience of a commuter using a specific mobility service. This value is computed by means of a scoring function which takes into account some performance criteria of the commuter, such as travel time, traveled distance and travel comfort. The use of a feedback is dual: on one hand, it allows a person to make more informed decisions in the future; on the other hand, it enables *tangrhubs* to improve their mobility services.

To do this, following a Reinforcement Learning approach, Tangramob simulations are iterative: each iteration corresponds to a typical day in which commuters try the new mobility services and record their experience.

At the end of a simulation, commuters may change their original mobility habits in favour of those mobility services that can better accommodate their needs. In case the simulated SMI does not suit some commuters, those agents will then restore their initial traveling habits (e.g. traveling by private car).

4   From Tangramob ABM to TRebeca

In this section, we introduce Rebeca and TimedRebeca modeling languages, showing their features and the motivations behind their involvement in our work. Afterwards, we present the simplified TRebeca model, and we argue about its derivation process from the Tangramob ABM.

4.1   Rebeca and Timed Rebeca

Reactive Object Language (Rebeca) [11] is an actor-based language designed to connect practical software engineering domains and formal verification methods. In short, Rebeca is a language for modeling event-based distributed systems. Moreover, it represents an interpretation of the actor model adopting a Java-like syntax which is supported by verification tools. The semantics of Rebeca is presented by Labeled Transition System (LTS). Systems are modeled by concurrently executing reactive objects called *rebecs* which can interact with one another by asynchronous message passing. In particular, a Rebeca model consists of the definition of reactive classes, each of which corresponds to a specific actor type of the system. Technically, a reactive class comprises three parts: known rebecs (i.e. the other rebecs with which it can communicate), state variables (like attributes in object-oriented languages) and message server definitions, defining the behaviour of the actor itself (like methods in object-oriented languages). Each message server has a name, an optional list of parameters and its body, which can be described as the actual behaviour of the rebec once such kind of message is received; it includes a number of statements, i.e. assignments, sending of messages, and selections. The computation of a Rebeca model is event-driven [11], since messages can be seen as events. Each rebec takes a message from its message queue and executes the corresponding message server atomically. Communication among rebecs takes place by asynchronous message passing as follows: the sender rebec sends a message to the receiver rebec and continues its work; the message is put in the message queue of the receiver and it stays there until the receiver serves it. The behaviour of a Rebeca model is hence defined as the parallel execution of the released messages of the rebecs.

Timed Rebeca (TRebeca) [8,10,12] is a timed extension of Rebeca language with timing primitives. TRebeca supports the modeling and verification of distributed systems with timing features and its semantic is presented in Timed Transition System. Time is represented in terms of discrete time steps.

As it emerges from its features, TRebeca is the right modeling language for our purposes, since it allows to capture timing features, as well as to represent the interactions between the ABM's agents. In fact, timing is needed for organizing the actions performed by commuters during the course of a 24-h day.

4.2 The Simplified Tangramob Model in TRebeca

Tangramob is a very complex and fine-grained framework capable of simulating millions of events and interactions between agents and the environment. For this reason, it is prohibitive to reproduce the AB model as it is into a TRebeca model, since its executions would result into an unmanageable state explosion. Thus, the designed TRebeca model is simplified, but still keeping the core features. In detail, the TRebeca model is composed of the two following rebecs: *CommuterGenerator* and *Tangrhub*. In the simplified model, commuters do not have a rebec counterpart. They are modeled as packets to be delivered within a network. Each commuter is characterized by a data structure representing its daily mobility agenda (introduced in Sect. 3.1). This data structure holds the following information: the commuter identifier (id), the nearest tangrhub to his home (th_h), the time units to elapse before leaving home ($time_{h,w}$), the time units for walking from home to th_h ($time_{fm}$), the nearest tangrhub to its workplace (th_w), the time units spent working ($time_{work}$) and the time units for walking from th_w to his workplace ($time_{lm}$).

Modeling the so-described "commuter", required many assumptions. Indeed, a careful reader may notice that providing each commuter with two tangrhubs, implies that all of them are only expected to travel by inter-hub mobility services, thus adopting the 3-path commuting pattern (Fig. 3). Therefore, with this simplification, in the TRebeca model commuters have two commuting patterns:

$$home \rightarrow th_h \rightarrow th_w \rightarrow work \quad \text{and} \quad work \rightarrow th_w \rightarrow th_h \rightarrow home$$

Another strict assumption regards the fixed time units associated to each sub-trip: traveling times are always the same and traffic congestion is just emulated by adding random delays during the model-generation phase (Sect. 4.3).

Differently from the commuter, the tangrhub agent has been translated into a rebec named *Tangrhub*. Its behavior is similar to the one designed for the ABM, i.e. managing its mobility services and providing commuters with vehicles. Additionally, since commuters are modeled as messages in the TRebeca model, each *Tangrhub* has the responsibility of delivering commuters to the next *Tangrhub*. Every time this occurs, an available mobility service resource (i.e. a vehicle) is released to a commuter which will use it for reaching the next *Tangrhub*. Instead of letting commuters select a mobility service, in the TRebeca model this decision-process is made by *Tangrhubs*. Every time a commuter is scheduled, a *Tangrhub* releases a vehicle of the selected service with the best trade-off between its current fleet and its priority value. In particular, we associate each service with a priority value, which is meant to represent people's preferences: the higher the value, the more the service will be preferred.

Concerning the other rebec, the *CommuterGenerator* is in charge of monitoring the progress of commuters and their scheduling. In particular, it checks whether commuters are leaving home or they have just performed the last subtrip. Moreover, this rebec is notified every time a commuter experienced a service disruption, i.e. it did not find any available service for an inter-hub sub-trip.

In order to describe how actors interact in the simplified TRebeca model, we provide the reader with its event graph (Fig. 5), which gives an intuitive and highly abstracted view of events and their causality relations. The model showed in this graph is composed of labeled nodes which represent events and their owner rebec. Edges show the causality relations among vertices, and can be either conditional (thick edges) or mandatory (thin edges).

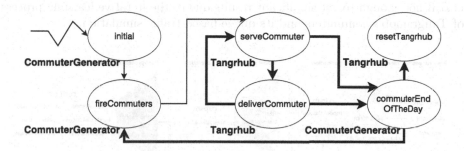

Fig. 5. Event Graph of the TRebeca Model

As shown in Fig. 5, the *CommuterGenerator* starts the run by sending a message to itself that triggers the *fireCommuters* event (message server). At this point, the *CommuterGenerator* evaluates the mobility agenda of commuters and sends a *serveCommuter* message to every th_h after a specific time unit, which is computed as follows: $time_{h,w} + time_{fm} + randomDelay$. When a *Tangrhub* receives such a message, one of the following three actions is possible:

1. it sends a message to the next *Tangrhub* (i.e. th_w), in case there is an available mobility service and the commuter is reaching his workplace,
2. it sends a message to the *CommuterGenerator*, which informs it that the commuter is coming back home,
3. it sends a message to the *CommuterGenerator*, which informs it that the commuter did not find an available mobility service (i.e. service disruption).

The first message triggers a deliverCommuter event, which represents the travel of a commuter by means of a mobility service. Then, a message is delivered to the next Tangrhub for informing it about the following commuter trip, triggering again a *serveCommuter* event. On the other hand, messages 2 and 3 will trigger a commuterEndOfTheDay event. Every time this event occurs, the *CommuterGenerator* updates the number of arrived commuters (i.e. the ones who finished their activities), and eventually registers a service disruption. In case the number of arrived commuters is equal to the total number of commuters, the *CommuterGenerator* restores the initial state of the system by sending a *resetSmarthub* message to each *Tangrhub* and restarts the run of the scenario by sending a fireCommuters message to itself.

The pseudo-code of the TRebeca model, together with a complete runnable example model, can be found at [1].

4.3   ToolTRain: Infer, Generate, Run, Infer and Collect

Since we aim at using the TRebeca model as a lightweight simulation tool, we should be able to generate new instances of the model from given scenarios, so as to collect similar output data of Tangramob after the model run. However, this is still not enough to get significant results due to the iterative learning process of Tangramob's commuters and its queue-based traffic simulation.

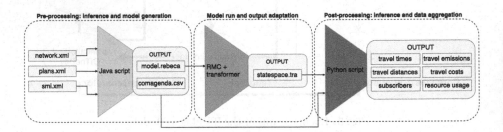

Fig. 6. The architecture of ToolTRain

For this purpose, we implemented ToolTRain: a tool-chain specifically designed for generating a TRebeca model from the simulator's input files according to some abstraction rules; running the resulting model; and inferring the output from the model run. Figure 6 shows the 3 building blocks of ToolTRain:

Model Inference and Generation. Starting from the input files of Tangramob (Sect. 3), a TRebeca model is generated according to the following points:

– A subset of the input population is selected as potential users of the new mobility services. The remaining commuters, i.e. those who live or work too far to the tangrhubs, are assumed to travel by car or walk.

- For each potential user, from now on *potential subscriber*, the tangrhubs closest to his home and to his workplace are chosen, and the corresponding 3-path commuting pattern (Fig. 3) is fixed for him.
- First mile trips (traveling towards a tangrhub) and last mile trips (traveling from a tangrhub to the destination) are performed by walk, thus the travel distance of such trips is computed as euclidean distance from point to point. This is done for all the daily trips of each commuter, since travel time is derived from travel distance according to a reference walk speed.
- Recalling the graph-like nature of the road network input, distances among tangrhubs are computed with the Dijkstra's shortest path algorithm. These values are expected to determine the travel time of inter-hub trips, depending on the characteristics of the vehicles provided by the new mobility services.
- Random delays are generated for all trips in order to emulate urban traffic.

Model Run. The so-generated TRebeca model is run with Rebeca Model Checker (RMC), a tool for direct model checking of TRebeca models. In particular, running a Rebeca model in RMC results in the generation of the whole state space of the model. Next, in ToolTRain, the so-generated statespace is converted into a tinier representation in which only a list of pre-defined state variables are reported for each state for further analysis. Therefore, it is worth remarking that we actually use RMC for performance evaluation rather than correctness.

Data Inference and Aggregation. Since we are interested in the results of a smart mobility initiative, the converted statespace is fed into a post-processing script to collect the observed variables at the very last reached state, which corresponds to the end of a day. Next, in order to emulate people's acceptance of a mobility initiative, all those commuters who encountered a service disruption (i.e. no vehicles available at a *tangrhub*) during the model run are selected and treated differently. In particular, as similarly done in the pre-processing step, those commuters are assumed to travel by car or by walk, and their travel metrics are computed accordingly. Finally, once every potential subscriber has been processed, all the progressively-collected travel metrics are aggregated in order to generate the same output files of Tangramob.

4.4   Comparing the Two Models

All the previously outlined abstraction rules are meant to simplify the original AB model, thereby removing its computationally-expensive features at the cost of loosing the microscopic detail of Tangramob simulations. Thus, traffic is emulated with random delays, whereas the Reinforcement Learning iterative process, used for modeling people's acceptance, is replaced by decision-rules. These rules are both encoded in the TRebeca model and achieved by the commuter filtering process of ToolTRain. Nevertheless, even though we pay in model expressiveness, a complete pass of ToolTRain is much faster than a Tangramob simulation. Indeed, as shown in Sect. 6.3, it turns out that running the TRebeca model can drastically reduce the computational burden of Tangramob, and this is a considerable gain if one needs to try many SMIs.

Concerning the modeling techniques, Tangramob lies on an agent-based model which is conceptually similar to the actor-based one of the TRebeca counterpart. Agent's perceptions can be thought of as triggering message forwarding in actor-based models: an actor receiving a message can be seen as an agent perceiving a change in the environment. This similarity makes it possible to translate the agent-based model into an actor-based one, keeping its conceptual integrity.

For what concerns the analysis capabilities, both models allow to observe the same information, with an exception made for traffic levels. In particular, as previously mentioned, we did not model traffic dynamics in the TRebeca model, thus it is not possible to have a measure of the road occupancy during the day.

Finally, if we look at the usability of the models, we can notice that both require the same input files to perform a model run/simulation. Therefore, considering that the output data is also presented in the same way (graphs and tables), using the TRebeca model is as intuitive as using Tangramob.

5   Experimental Design and Setup

So far, we outlined the ABM of Tangramob and the simplification process for the derivation of the corresponding TRebeca model. However, using ToolTRain as lightweight preprocessing for Tangramob requires us to prove this hypothesis:

H 1. *Given a network, a population and a SMI, ToolTRain can approximate Tangramob, i.e. there is a positive correlation between their outputs.*

Because Tangramob returns several output files, testing H1 is equivalent to testing different sub-hypothesis, one for each output variable of the simulator. Therefore, with the exception of urban traffic, which is not represented in the TRebeca model, we need to show that ToolTRain can return similarly to Tangramob:

- travel times
- travel distances
- CO_2 emissions

- mobility costs
- number of subscribers
- mobility resource usage

To test the positive correlation between the output variables of both these approaches, we propose a comparative experiment which also allows us to appreciate the usefulness of ToolTRain. First, we choose 9 smart mobility initiatives to evaluate and we partition them into 3 groups, according to the number of Vehicles Per-Capita (VPC) of each one. In particular, we defined the following partitions: *light-SMIs* (VPC ≤ 0.05); *medium-SMIs* ($0.05 \leq$ VPC ≤ 0.10); *massive-SMIs* (VPC ≥ 0.10). Each group thus represents a kind of intervention that the urban planner can evaluate on the basis of his/her goals.

Then, we feed each SMI into ToolTRain, together with a fixed set of input variables described later. Once the computation is over, we can observe how the output variables mentioned above differ for each SMI. Such analysis allows us to get a coarse-grained idea of the impacts of a mobility initiative on the urban system. Therefore, for each group we select the most promising SMI, i.e. the one that minimizes travel times, traveled distances, travel costs, CO_2 emissions and the number of unused vehicles while maximizing the number of subscribers. The selected SMIs are then simulated with Tangramob and their results are compared with the ones returned by ToolTRain. This allows to test H1.

Table 1. Cost and priority values per mobility service

	Cost per hour	Cost per km	Fixed Cost	Priority (only for ToolTRain)
Bikesharing	0.5 €	0 €	0.01 €	30
Carsharing	13 €	0.1 €	0.01 €	40
Scootersharing	2.5 €	0.1 €	0.01 €	35

For this experiment, we chose a subarea of Ascoli Piceno (Italy), a mid-sized town of 50 K inhabitants, and we scaled down the scenario in order to deal with 2068 commuters. The 9 SMIs to be investigated, outlined in Table 2, share the same number and location of *tangrhubs*, each of which is provided with the same type of mobility services. Charges are also fixed for each service type (Table 1). A more detailed description of the experimental setup is provided in [1].

Table 2. The investigated smart mobility initiatives (SMIs)

Tangrhub	Service type	light-SMIs			medium-SMIs			massive-SMIs		
		SMI-1	SMI-2	SMI-3	SMI-4	SMI-5	SMI-6	SMI-7	SMI-8	SMI-9
TH 0	bikesharing	0	2	2	2	2	4	5	10	25
	carsharing	2	2	6	2	4	4	5	5	25
	scootersharing	0	0	1	2	2	2	5	5	25
TH 1	bikesharing	0	2	2	2	4	4	5	5	25
	carsharing	2	2	5	2	2	2	5	10	25
	scootersharing	0	0	1	2	2	4	5	5	25
...	...	...	...	...	...	...	...	...	...	...
TH 8	bikesharing	0	0	2	5	5	5	10	10	25
	carsharing	2	2	3	3	3	5	10	15	25
	scootersharing	0	2	2	3	5	5	10	10	25
total fleet		22	44	68	101	119	140	338	333	675

6   Experimental Results

In this section, we first show the results of the 9 SMIs runs with ToolTRain, then we select 3 of them. Afterwards, to test H1, we compare the output variables of the selected SMIs with the ones returned by Tangramob on the same setup. A comparison of the computational times of the 3 SMIs is also provided.

6.1 9 SMIs Experimental Results

The output variables that we are going to discuss, presented in Sect. 5, can be gathered into three categories: (i) number of subscriptions, (ii) commuters' travel performance measures and (iii) mobility resources usage.

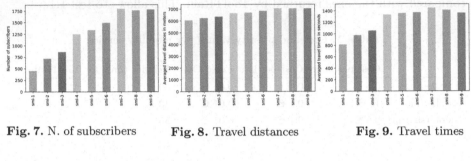

Fig. 7. N. of subscribers   **Fig. 8.** Travel distances   **Fig. 9.** Travel times

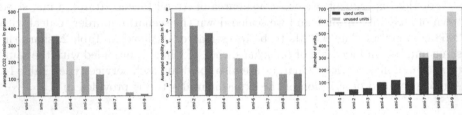

Fig. 10. CO2 emissions   **Fig. 11.** Mobility costs   **Fig. 12.** Mobility fleet usage

A Subscriber is a person who, at the end of the simulation, is expected to change his traveling habits in favour of the new mobility services. Thus, the number of subscribers is a measure of people acceptance of an SMI. Figure 7 shows that light-SMIs can attract between 20% and 42% of the whole population; the medium-SMIs could involve from 60% up to 72%; whereas the massive ones could interest around 85% of the population. These results show that the number of subscribers grows with the number of vehicles provided, both in the light and medium SMIs. However, when the number of subscriber is close to the total number of citizens, such as in the massive-SMIs, increasing the number of vehicles is not sufficient anymore. For instance, SMI-7 is more successful than SMI-9, even though the total amount of vehicles is less than half the other.

Commuters' Performance Measures are related to the number of subscribers. Concerning travel times and travel distances (Figs. 8 and 9), their averages grow as the number of subscribers of the SMI increases. These trends are due to the fact that subscribers will extend their trips since they pass through two *tangrhubs* instead of making a direct trip. Moreover, subscribers perform their first-mile and last-mile trips by walk, which is considerably time-consuming.

Even mobility costs and CO2 emissions (Figs. 10 and 11) follow the trend of subscribers, but in an inverse relationship: the higher the number of subscribers, the lower the average CO_2 emissions and mobility costs. Specifically, the CO_2 decrease is due to the fact that all the *tangrhubs* are provided with green vehicles. Thus, when the amount of subscribers is around 85% (smi-7, smi-8 and smi-9), the carbon footprint of a commuter is almost zero. Concerning the mobility costs decrease with the subscriptions growth, this is due to the fact that commuters are just paying for the time spent traveling. The fixed costs of owning a vehicle are thus shared with the community. Indeed, in smi-1 the average daily cost of travelling is just less than €8 per commuter; in smi-7 it is 4 times less.

Mobility Resources Usage. Figure 12 shows how vehicles are daily used. Light and medium SMIs are well configured, since there are no unused vehicles. Conversely, as the number of subscribers is close to 100%, the distribution of resources becomes tougher. Indeed, all the massive-SMIs have unused vehicles.

6.2   ToolTRain vs Tangramob: Comparing the 3-SMIs

The selection process of a light and a medium SMI is not trivial, since their performance is quite similar in scale. Thus, for each of these SMIs groups we selected the SMI with the lowest deployment of resources, i.e. smi-1 and smi-4. On the other hand, for what concerns the massive-SMIs group, we selected the one with the lowest unused resources, (i.e. smi-7), since it is more efficient.

As shown in Figs. 13, 14, 16 and 18, number of subscribers, travel distances, CO_2 emissions and resources usage are almost the same between Tangramob and ToolTRain. For the mobility costs parameter, Fig. 17 shows that both smi-1 and smi-4 are very similar; whereas for smi-7 the difference is less than one euro, which is acceptable. On the other hand, travel times (Fig. 15) are different, but at least they follow the same upward trend. Nevertheless, even though the TRebeca model still lacks a realistic representation of traffic, we can conclude that H1 is verified, with some precautions concerning the travel times output.

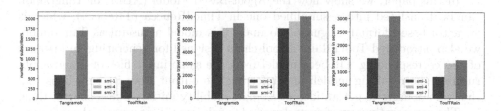

Fig. 13. Subscriptions   **Fig. 14.** Travel distances   **Fig. 15.** Travel times

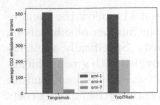 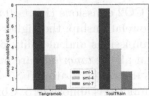 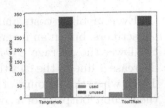

Fig. 16. CO2 emissions   **Fig. 17.** Mobility costs   **Fig. 18.** Mobility fleet usage

Table 3. Computational times

	SMI-1	SMI-4	SMI-7	Iterations
Tangramob	693413 ms	841782 ms	947465 ms	110
ToolTRain	45641 ms	57882 ms	69242 ms	-

6.3 Computational Performance Statistics

In order to compare Tangramob and ToolTRain in terms of computational time, Table 3 reports the CPU time of each selected SMI for both a Tangramob simulation and a ToolTRain run. More in detail, the experiments are performed on a Manjaro Linux desktop with an i7-4790S CPU @ 3.20 GHz and 16 GB RAM. Each Tangramob simulation is configured for 110 iterations.

7 Conclusions and Future Work

Assessing the effects of smart mobility initiatives is a complex and risk-bearing task in urban planning. A Decision Support System (DSS) like Tangramob can support urban planners and transport companies in such a duty, even though the computational requirements might be considerable in case of large scenarios.

In this paper, we show how the Agent-Based Model (ABM) of Tangramob can be translated into a simplified one in TimedRebeca (TRebeca), which is an actor-based formal language. To make this model as useful as Tangramob, we also introduced ToolTRain, a tool-chain designed for generating an instance of the corresponding TRebeca model from the same input files of Tangramob; running the resulting model; and inferring the output from its run. This tool thus allows users to get an idea of a smart mobility initiative in a shorter time.

The comparative experiment designed to validate this approach, shows a positive correlation between the output variables of both Tangramob and ToolTRain. Also, the computational time comparison reported in Table 3 confirms the validity of the proposed approach, since a ToolTRain run requires less than 10% of time needed for its corresponding Tangramob simulation. Considering such promising results, we would like to emphasize that the conceptual organization and architecture of ToolTRain can be reused in other AB contexts. This would even allow to exploit the power and the expressiveness of actor-based formal languages like Rebeca in order to reproduce the behavior of a certain phenomenon with an acceptable fidelity and few implementation efforts.

As future work, we are planning to improve the TRebeca model in order to introduce new mobility services as well as finding a better way to emulate traffic, due to its implication on travel times. Moreover, we will extend a fully automated tool to provide the modeling and analysis of self-adaptive urban planning systems at runtime. The resulting system would allow *tangrhubs* to adapt their mobility services at runtime, in response to service disruptions, commuters' traveling experience and changes in the environment (e.g. car accidents, strikes).

References

1. ToolTRain project. https://rebeca-lang.github.io/allprojects/Tangramob
2. Benevolo, C., Dameri, R.P., D'Auria, B.: Smart mobility in smart city. In: Torre, T., Braccini, A.M., Spinelli, R. (eds.) Empowering Organizations. LNISO, vol. 11, pp. 13–28. Springer, Cham (2016). https://doi.org/10.1007/978-3-319-23784-8_2
3. Bosch, P.M., Ciari, F.: Macrosim - a macroscopic mobsim for MATSim. Procedia Comput. Sci. **109** (2017). https://doi.org/10.1016/j.procs.2017.05.406
4. Castagnari, C., De Angelis, F., de Berardinis, J., Forcina, G., Polini, A.: Tangramob: an agent-based simulation framework for validating smart mobility solutions. https://www.tangramob.com/docs/SmartHub_Thesis.pdf
5. Charypar, D., Axhausen, K., Nagel, K.: Event-driven queue-based traffic flow microsimulation. Transp. Res. Record: J. Transp. Res. Board **2003**, 35–40 (2007)
6. Fehrenbacher, K.: Another failed attempt to make ride sharing work in the U.S., ridejoy to shut down. https://goo.gl/3ITYce
7. Horni, A., Nagel, K., Axhausen, K.W.: The Multi-Agent Transport Simulation MATSim. Ubiquity-Press, London (2016)
8. Khamespanah, E., Sirjani, M., Kaviani, Z.S., Khosravi, R., Izadi, M.J.: Timed rebeca schedulability and deadlock freedom analysis using bounded floating time transition system. Sci. Comput. Program. **98**, 184–204 (2015)
9. Mamiit, A.: Why the ride-sharing company failed to conquer China and what it means for everyone else (2016). https://goo.gl/cHuC9n
10. Reynisson, A.H., Sirjani, M., Aceto, L., Cimini, M., Jafari, A., Ingolfsdottir, A., Sigurdarson, S.H.: Modelling and simulation of asynchronous real-time systems using timed rebeca. Sci. Comput. Program. **89**, 41–68 (2014)
11. Sirjani, M.: Rebeca: theory, applications, and tools. In: de Boer, F.S., Bonsangue, M.M., Graf, S., de Roever, W.-P. (eds.) FMCO 2006. LNCS, vol. 4709, pp. 102–126. Springer, Heidelberg (2007). https://doi.org/10.1007/978-3-540-74792-5_5
12. Sirjani, M., Khamespanah, E.: On time actors. In: Ábrahám, E., Bonsangue, M., Johnsen, E.B. (eds.) Theory and Practice of Formal Methods. LNCS, vol. 9660, pp. 373–392. Springer, Cham (2016). https://doi.org/10.1007/978-3-319-30734-3_25
13. Strippgen, D., Nagel, K.: Multi-agent traffic simulation with cuda. In: High Performance Computing and Simulation, HPCS 2009. IEEE (2009)
14. United Nations: The World's Cities in 2016. United Nations, New York (2016)

Using Coq for Formal Modeling and Verification of Timed Connectors

Weijiang Hong, M. Saqib Nawaz, Xiyue Zhang, Yi Li, and Meng Sun(✉)

Department of Informatics and LMAM, School of Mathematical Sciences,
Peking University, Beijing, China
{wj.hong,msaqibnawaz,zhangxiyue,liyi_math,sunm}@pku.edu.cn

Abstract. Formal modeling and verification of connectors in component-based software systems are getting more interest with recent advancements and evolution in modern software systems. In this paper, we use the proof assistant Coq for modeling and verification of timed connectors. We first present the definition of timed channels and the composition operators for constructing timed connectors in Coq. Basic timed channels are interpreted as axioms and inference rules are used for the specification of composition operators. Furthermore, timed connectors being built by composing basic timed/untimed channels, are defined as logical predicates which describe the relations between inputs and outputs. Within this framework, timed connector properties can be naturally formalized and proved in Coq.

Keywords: Reo · Timed connector · Coq · Modeling · Verification

1 Introduction

Most modern software systems today are distributed over large networks of computing devices. However, software components that comprise the whole system usually do not fit together exactly and leave significant interfacing gaps among them. Such interfacing gaps are generally filled with additional code known as "glue code". Compositional coordination languages offer such a "glue code" for components and facilitate the mutual interactions between components in a distributed processing environment. Reo [1] and Linda [11] are two popular examples of such compositional coordination languages, which have played an important role in the success of component-based systems in the past decades.

Reo is a channel-based exogenous coordination language where complex component connectors are orchestrated from channels via certain composition operators. Connectors provide the protocols that control and organize the communication, synchronization and cooperation among the components that they interconnect. Despite its simplicity, Reo has been used successfully in various application domains, such as service-oriented computing [10,20], business processes [23] or biological systems [7].

The reliability of component-based systems highly depend on the correctness of connectors. Formal analysis and verification of connectors is gaining more

© Springer International Publishing AG 2018
A. Cerone and M. Roveri (Eds.): SEFM 2017 Workshops, LNCS 10729, pp. 558–573, 2018.
https://doi.org/10.1007/978-3-319-74781-1_37

interest in recent years with the evolution of software systems and advancements in Cloud and Grid computing technologies. Furthermore, the increasing growth in size and complexity of computing infrastructure has made the modeling and verification of connectors properties a more difficult and challenging task. From modeling and analysis context, the formal semantics for Reo allow us to specify and analyze the behavior of connectors precisely. In literature, different formal semantics have been proposed for Reo [13], such as the coalgebraic semantics in terms of relations on infinite timed data streams [3], operational semantics using constraint automata [5], the coloring semantics by coloring a connector with possible data flows [8] in order to resolve synchronization and exclusion constraints, and the UTP (Unified Theories of Programming) semantics [21].

Our aim in this paper is to provide an approach for formal modeling and reasoning about timed Reo connectors under the UTP semantic framework [19] in the proof assistant Coq [12]. Our mechanized verification of connectors in Coq is certainly not the first one. Much work has been carried out in the past for formal verification of connectors. Baier et al. [4] developed a symbolic model checker Vereofy for checking CTL-like properties of systems with exogenous coordination. Another approach is to take advantage of existing verification tools by translating Reo model to other formal models such as Alloy [14], mCRL2 [15], etc. However, since infinite behavior is usually taken into consideration for connectors during the modeling and verification process of their properties, the analysis and verification can be achieved efficiently in theorem provers. In [16], we provided a method for formal modeling and verification of Reo connectors in Coq. Reo connectors were represented in a constructive way and verification was based on the simulation of the behavior and output of Reo connectors. Later in [22] a different approach was proposed, where primitive channels and connectors in Reo were modeled and analyzed in Coq, based on the UTP semantics.

Both [16,22] only took untimed connectors into consideration. A family of timed channels and connectors has been provided in [2,19], which can be used to measure the time elapsed between two events at input/output nodes and specify timed behavior happening in coordination. In this paper, the modeling and verification framework for connectors in [22] is extended to cover timed connectors as well. We first provide the definition for a family of timed channels in Coq, then we present our approach on how to model and reason about timed connectors. The basic idea is to model the observable behavior of a (timed) connector as a relation on the timed data streams as its input and output. In Coq, this can be naturally achieved by representing a connector as a logical predicate that describes the relation among the timed data streams on its input and output nodes. The details of the implementation in Coq can be found at [9].

The rest of this paper is organized as follows: Reo and Coq are briefly discussed in Sect. 2. Specifications for timed data streams, some pre-defined auxiliary functions and predicates in Coq are presented in Sect. 3, followed by the formal modeling of basic timed channels and compositional operators in Sect. 4. Section 5 provides the approach for reasoning about connector properties in our framework. Finally, Sect. 6 concludes the paper and discusses some future research directions.

2   Preliminaries

A brief introduction to the coordination language Reo and the proof assistant Coq is provided in this section.

2.1   Reo

Reo is a channel-based exogenous coordination language where complex *component connectors* are compositionally constructed out of simpler ones. Further details on Reo can be found in [1,3,5]. Connectors provide the protocol to control and organize the communication, synchronization and cooperation between concurrent components. The simplest connectors are channels with well-defined behavior. Each channel has two channel ends and there are two types of channel ends in Reo: *source* ends and *sink* ends. A source channel end accepts data into the channel and a sink channel end dispenses data out of the channel. A few examples of basic channel types in Reo are shown in Fig. 1.

| Sync | LossySync | FIFO1 | SyncDrain | t-Timer |
| Channel | Channel | Channel | Channel | Channel |

Fig. 1. Some basic channels in Reo

A *synchronous (Sync) channel* has one source and one sink end. I/O operations can succeed only if the writing operation at source end is synchronized with the read operation at its sink end. A *lossy synchronous (LossySync) channel* is a variant of synchronous channel that accepts all data through its source end. The written data is lost immediately if no corresponding read operation is available at its sink end. A *FIFO1 channel* is an asynchronous channel with one buffer cell, one source end and one sink end. The channel accepts a data item whenever the buffer is empty. The data item is kept in the buffer and dispensed to the sink end in the FIFO order. A *Synchronous Drain (SyncDrain) channel* has two source ends and no sink end, which means that no data can be obtained from such channels. The write operation on both sourced ends should happen simultaneously and the data items written to this channel are irrelevant. A *t-timer* channel accepts any data item at its source end and produces a *timeout* signal after a delay of t time units on its sink end.

In Reo, complex connectors are constructed by composition of different channels with *join* and *hide* operations on the channel ends. The result can be represented visually as a graph where a node represents a set of channel ends that are combined together through the join operation, while the edges in the graph represent the channels between the corresponding nodes. Nodes are categorized into source, sink or mixed nodes, depending on whether the node contain only source channel ends, sink channel ends, or both source and sink channel ends.

The internal topology of any component connector can be hidden with hiding operations. The hidden nodes can not be accessed or observed from outside. The behavior of a Reo connector can be formalized by data-flow at its source and sink nodes. Source nodes are analogous to input ports, sink nodes to output ports and mixed nodes are internal details of a connector that are hidden.

2.2 Coq Proof Assistant

Coq is a widely used proof assistant that is based on higher order logic and λ-calculus. It offers a formal specification language called *Gallina* and a mechanical (semi-interactive) theorem proving environment. *Gallina* can be used for writing specifications, mathematical definitions, propositions and functions, executable algorithms and theorems, for example:

```
(* Variables declaration *)
Variables a b: nat.
(* Factorial Function *)
Fixpoint fact(n: nat): nat=
 match n with
  | 0 => 1
  | S n' => n * fact n'
 end
(* Theorem Declaration *)
Theorem fact_gre n m: n <= m -> fact n <= fact m
Proof.
(* interactive theorem proving *)
auto.
Qed.
```

This example describes a recursive function for computing factorial of a natural type number. Theorem can be proved interactively with tactics that Coq offers. Coq is also equipped with a rich set of standard libraries. Some of the libraries that we used in this work include *Reals*, *Stream*, *Arith* and *Logic*. Proofs can be reconstructed in other proof assistants such as Isabelle [17] and PVS [18]. Further details on Coq can be found in [6,12].

3 Basic Definitions in Coq

The notion of timed data (TD) streams and some pre-defined auxiliary functions and predicates in Coq are briefly introduced in this section. These functions and predicates are used in the following sections for modeling timed channels and compositional operators.

In our previous work [22], behavior of connectors is formalized by means of data flows at its sink and source nodes. In Coq, such behavior over infinite data-flows is modeled by defining *TD streams* as follows:

```
Definition Time := R.
Definition Data := nat.
(*Inductive Data : Set :=
  |Natdata : nat-> Data
  |Empty : Data.*)
Definition TD := Time * Data.
```

Time is represented by real numbers ($\mathbb{R}$) and data by natural numbers ($\mathbb{N}$). The continuous time model captured by $\mathbb{R}$ is suitable as it is very expressive and close to the nature of time in the real world. Therefore, the time sequence consists of increasing and diverging time moments. Representation of data with natural numbers enables us to expand the model for different application domains by *Inductive*. Cartesian product of time and data items defines a TD object. The stream module in Coq is used to produce streams of TD objects.

To capture the timed behavior of connectors, we extend our model in [22] from primitive channels to timed channels. One of the important differences between primitive channels and timed channels is the time requirement of input TD streams. For primitive channels, we only require that time of input TD streams is a simulation of real time which means that time stream is increasing as time passes by. Thus, we have the following representative definition about time stream where the terms *PrL* and *PrR* take a pair of values (a, b) as an argument and return the first or second value of the pair, respectively.

```
Axiom Inc_T : forall (T: Stream TD) (n:nat),
PrL(Str_nth n T) < PrL(Str_nth n (tl T)).
```

However, for basic timed channels, we require that another input data is not accepted when there is no timeout signal for the last data. This constraint is reflected in the construct of basic timed channels as follows (the variable t is defined in the respective timed channel):

```
forall n:nat,PrL(Str_nth n Input) + t < PrL(Str_nth n (tl Input))
```

We use the basic predicate formulas of judgment about time and data in [22] and introduce some new judgment definitions for timed channels. As defined in [22], predicate *Teq* means that the time components of two streams are equal. *Tlt* means that each time dimension of the first stream is strictly less than the other stream while *Tgt* means that every time dimension of the first stream is greater than the other stream. The judgment about equality of data which is defined as *Deq* is analogous to the judgment of time. The following three definitions that serve to facilitate the modeling of timed channels are plain and easy to understand with one of the time streams is added by a t time delay. An extra t is appended to the names of these new predicates about judgment of time to distinguish them from the original ones.

```
Definition Teqt(s1 s2:Stream TD)(t:Time): Prop :=
  forall n:nat, PrL(Str_nth n s1) + t = PrL(Str_nth n s2)
Definition Tltt(s1 s2:Stream TD)(t:Time): Prop :=
```

```
    forall n:nat, PrL(Str_nth n s1) + t < PrL(Str_nth n s2)
Definition Tgtt(s1 s2:Stream TD)(t:Time): Prop :=
    forall n:nat, PrL(Str_nth n s1) + t > PrL(Str_nth n s2)
```

Teqt means that time of the second stream is equal to time of the first stream with an addition of t time units. *Tltt* represents that time of the first stream with an addition of t is less than the second stream and *Tgtt* has the opposite meaning to *Tltt*.

4 Basic Timed Channels and Operators

In this section, we describe the modeling of a few timed channels in Reo that can be used to measure the time between two events and produce timeout signals. We also show the definition of composition operators to construct timed connectors.

4.1 Basic Timed Channels

Predicates are used to describe the constraints on time and data for timed channels in Coq, and such predicates can be combined (with intersection) together to provide the complete specification of timed channels. This approach also offers convenience for the analysis and proof of timed connector properties. In the following, we present the formal definition of some basic timed channels in Coq.

t-**Timer:** The basic t-*timer channel* $A \overset{t}{\longrightarrow} B$ accepts any input value through its source end A and returns a *timeout* signal on its sink end B exactly after a delay of t time units. The following definition specifies the design model for the t-*timer* channel in Coq.

```
Parameter timeout: Data
Definition Timert (Input Output: Stream TD)(t: Time): Prop:=
    (forall n:nat,
    PrL(Str_nth n Input) + t < PrL(Str_nth n (tl Input)))
    /\ Teqt Input Output t
    /\ forall n:nat, PrR (Str_nth n Output) = timeout
```

In this specification, the first conjunction requires that an input data item cannot be accepted by the channel when there is no timeout signal for the previous data item it receives. This means that there should be no other input actions during the delay of t time units. The second requirement describes the relation on the time dimension of the input and output streams. The last one presents that after a delay of t time units for every data item it received at the source end, a timeout signal will be generated at the sink end.

OFF-t-Timer: A t-*timer* with the *off*-option $A \overset{}{\multimap} \overset{t}{\textcircled{t}} \longrightarrow B$ which allows the timer to be stopped before the expiration of its delay t is designed in case users require the timer to stop working as soon as possible. Under this circumstance, a special *off* value whose type is also assumed to be *Data* can be consumed through the source end. We define the t-*timer* with the *off*-option inductively as follows:

```
Parameter off: Data.
Parameter OFFTimert: Stream TD -> Stream TD -> Time -> Prop.
Axiom OFFTimert_coind:
 forall (Input Output: Stream TD)(t:Time),
 OFFTimert Input Output t ->
 (forall n:nat, PrR(Str_nth n Input) = off  \/
  PrL(Str_nth n Input) + t  <  PrL(Str_nth n (tl Input)))
 /\ ( (PrR (hd (tl Input)) = off) ->
      (OFFTimert (tl (tl Input)) Output t)  )
 /\ ( (~PrR (hd (tl Input)) = off) ->
      (PrL (hd Output) = PrL (hd Input) + t)
        /\ (PrR (hd Output) = timeout)
        /\ OFFTimert (tl Input) (tl Output) t  ).
```

The first predicate in the specification specifies the behavior of input, whereas the next two predicates specify the output behavior. There are some requirements on the inter-arrival time of the inputs that depends on the value of incoming data. So the inputs need to meet such requirements which are specified in the first predicate. For the output, different actions are taken to deal with the data element to be accepted, which is PrR (hd (tl $Input$)). There are two cases which are captured by the two predicates respectively:

- Case I: If the data element to be accepted is *off*, the timer is stopped and we remove the data *off* and the current data without any output. Then resume a new input stream, i.e. *OFFTimert (tl (tl Input)) Output t*.
- Case II: If the data element to be accepted is not *off*, a *timeout* signal is produced as output after a delay of t time units. Then resume a new input stream, i.e. *OFFTimert (tl Input) (tl Output) t*.

RST-t-Timer: Similarly, a *reset*-option is needed when the users require the timer to be reset to 0 at once as the values in the stream remain unchanged. A t-*timer* channel with the *reset*-option $A \xrightarrow{r}{t} \rightarrow B$ is activated as soon as a special *reset* value is consumed through its source end.

EXP-t-Timer: When an early expiration is needed for a t-timer channel, like the above two cases, an *expire* value is needed for input. For the t-timer channel with *expire*-option $A \xrightarrow{e}{t} \rightarrow B$, once the *expire* value is consumed through the source end, a *timeout* signal is produced through the sink end instantaneously.

The modeling of the RST-t-Timer and the EXP-t-Timer in Coq are similar to the OFF-t-Timer. The details can be found at [9].

In Coq, specifying timed channels by intersection of predicates makes the model intuitive and concise as each predicate describes a simple order relation on time or data. Moreover, we can easily split these predicates to make the process of proving connector properties simpler.

4.2   Modeling Operators in Coq

We now describe how composition operators for construction of complex connectors from basic channels can be modeled in Coq. We have three types of composition operators which are graphically represented in Fig. 2:

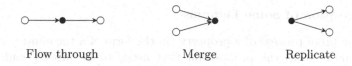

Flow through   Merge   Replicate

Fig. 2. Channel composition operators

The *flow-through* operator which acts on mixed nodes simply allows data items to flow through the junction node, from one channel to the other. Thus, we need not to give the *flow-through* operator a specific definition since it can be achieved implicitly. For example, while we specify two channels $Sync(A, B)$ and $FIFO1(B, C)$, the *flow-through* operator that acts on node B for these two channels has been achieved.

Similar to the *flow-through* operator, the *replicate* operator can also be achieved implicitly by means of renaming. For example, for channels $Sync(A, B)$ and $FIFO1(C, D)$, we can illustrate $Sync(A, B)$ and $FIFO1(A, D)$ instead of defining a function like $rep(Sync(A, B), FIFO1(C, D))$ and the *replicate* operator is achieved directly by renaming C with A for the FIFO1 channel.

The modeling of the *merge* operator in Coq is more complicated. When the *merge* operator acts on two channels AB and CD, it leads to a choice of data items being taken from AB or CD. Similar to the definition of timed channels, we define *merge* as the intersection of two predicates and use the recursive definition:

```
Parameter merge:Stream TD -> Stream TD -> Stream TD -> Prop.
Axiom merge_coind:
    forall s1 s2 s3:Stream TD,
    merge s1 s2 s3->(~(PrL(hd s1) = PrL(hd s2))
 /\ (((PrL(hd s1) < PrL(hd s2))  ->
 ((hd s3 = hd s1)   /\ merge (tl s1) s2 (tl s3)))
 /\ ((PrL(hd s1) > PrL(hd s2))   ->
 ((hd s3 = hd s2)   /\ merge s1 (tl s2) (tl s3)))))).
```

The three timed data streams *s1*, *s2*, *s3* are located in two source ports and one sink port, respectively. If time corresponding to the first data of *s1* is less than time corresponding to the first data of *s2*, then the first data and time elements of stream *s3* are equal to the elements of stream *s1*. Meanwhile, *Merge* is called again for the next data and time elements, but the arguments need to be changed to *tl s1*, *s2* and *tl s3*. For the circumstance that time corresponding to the first data of *s1* is greater than time corresponding to the first data of *s2*, the constraints are similar to the first case.

5   Reasoning About Connectors

With time channels, we can analyze and prove some interesting and important properties of timed connectors in Coq. In this section, we give some examples to elucidate how to reason about timed connector properties.

5.1   Derivation of Some Lemmas

In Coq, the proof process of a property (in the form of a theorem) is as follows: First the user states the proposition that needs to be proved, called a *goal*. Then user applies commands called *tactics* to decompose this goal into simpler subgoals or solve it directly. This decomposition process ends when all subgoals are completely solved. Before proving properties, we first introduce some lemmas that are used to facilitate the proofs.

```
[1]Lemma Eq_Tltt : forall(A B:Stream TD)(t:Time)(n:nat),
      Tltt A B t  ->  PrL(Str_nth n A) + t < PrL(Str_nth n B).

[2]Lemma Eq_Teqt : forall(A B:Stream TD)(t:Time)(n:nat),
      Teqt A B t  ->  PrL(Str_nth n A) + t = PrL(Str_nth n B).

[3]Lemma transfer_eqt_lt : forall(s1 s2 s3:Stream TD)(t:Time),
      (Teqt s1 s2 t) /\ (Tlt s2 s3)  ->  Tltt(s1 s3 t).

[4]Lemma transfer_gt_tl : forall s1 s2:Stream TD,
      Tgt s1 s2  ->  Tgt (tl s1) (tl s2).

[5]Lemma transfer_gt_gt : forall s1 s2 s3:Stream TD,
      (Tgt (tl s2) s1) /\ (Tgt (tl s3) s2) -> (Tgt (tl(tl s3)) s1).

[6]Lemma transfer_lt_lt : forall s1 s2 s3:Stream TD,
      (Tlt s1 s2 ) /\ (Tlt s2 s3) -> (Tlt s1 s3 ).

[7]Lemma transfer_eqt : forall(s1 s2 s3:Stream TD)(t:Time),
      (Teq s1 s2) /\ (Teqt s2 s3 t)  ->  (Teqt s1 s3 t).

[8]Lemma transfer_merge : forall (s11 s12 s13 s21 s22 s23:
      Stream TD)(t:Time),(merge s11 s12 s13)/\(Teqt s11 s21 t)
      /\(merge s21 s22 s23)/\(Teqt s12 s22 t)
      ->  (Teqt s13 s23 t).
```

Lemma 1 means that $PrL(Str\_nth\, n\, A) + t < PrL(Str\_nth\, n\, B)$ can be derived from $Tltt(A, B, t)$. Similarly, Lemma 2 means that $PrL(Str\_nth\, n\, A) + t = PrL(Str\_nth\, n\, B)$ can be derived from $Teqt(A, B, t)$. Lemmas 3–7 describe the transitivity on the time dimension. Take lemma *transfer_eqt_lt* as an example: If we have one function $Teqt$ with time streams $s1$ and $s2$, such that

$s1 + t = s2$, and another function Tlt with time streams $s2$ and $s3$, such that $s2 < s3$, then we can deduce $Tltt(s1, s3, t)$, such that $s1 + t < s3$. Lemma 8 means that the transitivity for time also holds for the *merge* operator. We obtain $s13$ and $s23$ by merging $s11$, $s12$ and $s21$, $s22$ respectively. Then if we have $s11 + t = s21$ and $s12 + t = s22$, we can easily deduce $s13 + t = s23$.

5.2   Verification of Connector Properties

Example 1. We consider the timed connector shown in Fig. 3. The node A in the connector is a source node, whereas C, D and E are mixed nodes and B is a sink node. This connector consists of five channels AC, AD, CE, DE and DB with channel type *t-timer*, $FIFO1$, $FIFO1$, $SyncDrain$ and $Sync$ respectively. This connector ensures the lower bound "$> t$" for a take operation on node B. Every data item being received at A will be kept in the buffer of channel AD for more than t time units before it can be taken out at node B.

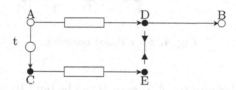

Fig. 3. Lower bounded FIFO1 channel

The relations between source node A and sink node B on both time and data dimensions for this connector are specified in Theorem 1. If we use α, β to represent the data streams that flow through the nodes A and B, and use a, b to denote the time stream corresponding to α and β respectively, i.e., the i-th element $a(i)$ in a denotes exactly the time moment of the occurrence of $\alpha(i)$, then Theorem 1 states the property that $\alpha = \beta$ and $a + t < b$ for the connector in Fig. 3.

The connector is built from axioms $Sync$, $SyncDrain$, $FIFO1$ and $Timert$ for its basic channels, which are used as hypothesis for the proof of Theorem 1.

Theorem 1 (LB FIFO1 Channel). $\forall A, B, C, D, E \in Stream\ TD, t \in Time$

$$Timert(A, C, t) \wedge FIFO1(A, D) \wedge SyncDrain(D, E) \wedge FIFO1(C, E) \wedge Sync(D, B)$$
$$\rightarrow Deq(A, B) \wedge Tltt(A, B, t)$$

Proof. First we consider the case for data. In this connector, we have predicate $Deq(A, D)$ which can be obtained from $FIFO1(A, D)$ and predicate $Deq(D, B)$ which is specified by $Sync(D, B)$. The combination of both predicates with *flow_through* operator results in $Deq(A, B)$.

For the case of time, we have four predicates, $Teqt(A, C, t)$, $Tlt(C, E)$, $Teq(E, D)$ and $Teq(D, B)$ respectively, such that the constraints $A + t = C$, $C < E$, $E = D$, $D = B$ hold for time. The combination of these four predicates results in $Tltt(A, B, t)$, such that $A + t < B$ holds on time. The proof of Theorem 1 has been implemented in Coq with the help of *tactics*.

Note that we have a constraint on the input for timed channel *t-timer*, which requires the inter-arrival time of the inputs is at least t. This condition may bring inconvenience if we hope to produce a timeout after a delay t for every input even if sometimes the inter-arrival time of the inputs is less than t. We show how to weaken this restriction in the following example.

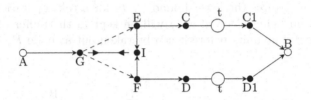

Fig. 4. $2 \times t$ timed connector

Example 2. A timed connector $A \xrightarrow{n \times t} B$ can be built by using n t-timer channels and an exclusive router (with n sink nodes), whose behavior is to produce a *timeout* after a delay t for every input (i). What we deserve to notice is that the arrival time between $input_i$ and $input_{i+j}$ ($j < n$) can be less than t whereas the arrival time between $input_i$ and $input_{i+n}$ should be at least t. The connector in Fig. 4 shows the topology structure of $A \xrightarrow{2 \times t} B$ where A is a source node, B is a sink node and all other nodes are mixed nodes.

Let a and b represent the time streams that correspond to the data flowing into A and out of B, respectively. Theorem 2 states the property that $a + t = b$ for the $2 \times t$ timed connector which can be derived from axioms *Sync*, *LossySync*, *SyncDrain* and *Timert*.

Theorem 2 ($2 \times t$ Timed Channel). $\forall A, B, C, D, E, F, G, I \in Stream\ TD$, $t \in Time$

$$Sync(A, G) \land LossySync(G, E) \land LossySync(G, F) \land Sync(E, I) \land$$
$$Sync(F, I) \land SyncDrain(G, I) \land merge(E, F, I) \land Sync(E, C) \land$$
$$Sync(F, D) \land Timert(C, C1, t) \land Timert(D, D1, t) \land merge(C1, D1, B)$$
$$\rightarrow Teqt(A, B, t)$$

```
Section example2.
Theorem nt_Timed : forall (A B C D E F G I C1 D1 :Stream TD)(t:Time),
  (Sync A G)  /\ (LossySync G E) /\ (LossySync G F) /\ (Sync E I)      /\
  (Sync F I)  /\ (SyncDrain G I)  /\ (merge E F I)     /\ (Sync E C)     /\
  (Sync F D) /\ (Timert C C1 t)   /\ (Timert D D1 t)  /\ (merge C1 D1 B)
  -> (Teqt A B t).
Proof.
intros.
destruct H;destruct H0;destruct H1.
destruct H2;destruct H3;destruct H4.

(*Prepare for Lemma transfer_eqt*)
assert((Teq A I)/\(Teqt I B t)).
split.
(*Proof for Teq A I*)
rewrite H.
apply H4.
(*Proof for Teqt I B t*)
        (*Prepare for Lemma transfer_merge*)
        assert ((merge C D I) /\ (Teqt C C1 t) /\ (Teqt D D1 t) /\ (merge C1 D1 B)).
        repeat split.
        (*Proof for merge C D I*)
        destruct H5.
        destruct H6.
        rewrite <- H6.
        destruct H7.
        rewrite <- H7.
        assumption.
        (*Proof for Teqt C C1 t*)
        destruct H5.
        destruct H6.
        destruct H7.
        destruct H8.
        destruct H8.
        destruct H10.
        assumption.
        (*Proof for Teqt D D1 t*)
        destruct H5.
        destruct H6.
        destruct H7.
        destruct H8.
        destruct H9.
        destruct H9.
        destruct H11.
        assumption.
        (*Proof for merge C1 D1 B*)
        destruct H5.
        destruct H6.
        destruct H7.
        destruct H8.
        destruct H9.
        assumption.

        generalize H6.
        apply transfer_merge.

generalize H6.
apply transfer_eqt.
Qed.
End example2.
```

Fig. 5. Proof steps for Example 2 in Coq

Proof. The main *goal* $Teqt(A, B, t)$ is first split in two *subgoals* $Teq(A, I)$ and $Teqt(I, B, t)$ with Lemma 7. For the first subgoal $Teq(A, I)$, we have $Teq(A, G)$ ($A = G$ on the time dimension) which is derived from $Sync(A, G)$ and $Teq(G, I)$ ($G = I$ on the time dimension) which is derived from $SyncDrain(G, I)$. So we can easily deduce that $Teq(A, I)$. For the second subgoal $Teqt(I, B, t)$, the proof is supported by Lemma 8. Consequently, we only need to prove the premise condition of the Lemma. Note that $merge(C, D, I)$ which can be deduced by $merge(E, F, I), Sync(E, C), Sync(F, D)$ and $merge(C1, D1, B)$ is given by Hypothesis. Further, $Teqt(C, C1, t)$ and $Teqt(D, D1, t)$ can be easily obtained from the definition of channels $Timert(C, C1, t)$ and $Timert(D, D1, t)$ respectively. So for the time dimension, we have $merge(C, D, I)$, $merge(C1, D1, B)$, $Teqt(C, C1, t)$ and $Teqt(D, D1, t)$ such that $C \wedge D = I, C1 \wedge D1 = B, C + t = C1$, and $D + t = D1$. Then we can draw the conclusion that $I + t = B$, i.e. $Teqt(I, B, t)$. A sample of concrete proof steps in Coq is provided in Fig. 5.

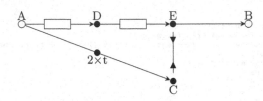

Fig. 6. Timer FIFO2 channel

Example 3. Another useful connector that can be used to model a real-time network is a timed *FIFOn* that delays every input for t time units, even if the inter-arrival time of the inputs is less than t (for up to n such inputs). Such a connector can not be obtained by just composing n timed FIFO1 channels. However, it is still easy to construct such connectors by using $\xrightarrow{n \times t} \bullet \rightarrow$. Figure 6 shows an example of such a timed FIFO2 connector. We can parameterize this connector to have as many buffers as we want simply by inserting more (or fewer) FIFO1 channels between nodes A and E and using a corresponding $\xrightarrow{n \times t} \bullet \rightarrow$ where n is the number of *FIFO1* channels.

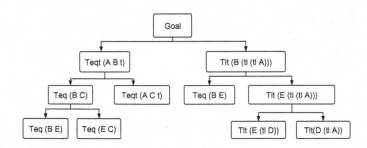

Fig. 7. Proof steps of Theorem 3

Theorem 3 (Timed FIFO2 Channel). $\forall A, B, C, D, E \in Stream\ TD, t \in Time$

$$FIFO1(A, D) \wedge FIFO1(D, E) \wedge Sync(E, B) \wedge SyncDrain(C, E) \wedge Teqt(A, C, t)$$
$$\rightarrow Teqt(A, B, t) \wedge Tlt(B, tl(tlA))$$

Proof. The proof process is based on divide and conquer technique. There are two goals in this theorem: $Teqt(A, B, t)$ and $Tlt(B, tl(tlA))$. The first goal $Teqt(A, B, t)$ is split into two subgoals $Teq(B, C)$ and $Teqt(A, C, t)$. Furthermore, the *subgoal* $Teq(B, C)$ can be split into $Teq(B, E)$ and $Teq(E, C)$. The second goal $Tlt(B, tl(tlA))$ is split into two subgoals $Teq(B, E)$ and $Tlt(E, (tl(tlA)))$ and $Tlt(E, (tl(tlA)))$ into $Tlt(E, (tlD))$ and $Tlt(D, (tlA))$. All of these six subgoals as shown in Fig. 7 are easy to solve.

Example 4. In this example, we show a more interesting generalized property of connector *FIFOn(A, B)* for arbitrary n, in terms of predicates $Tlt(A, B)$ and $Deq(A, B)$. Similar to *FIFO2 connector*, that is constructed by 2 *FIFO1 channels*, *FIFOn+1 connector* can be composed by a *FIFOn connector* and a *FIFO1 channel*, as shown in Fig. 8.

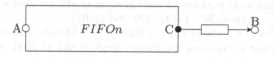

Fig. 8. FIFOn+1

Theorem 4 (Generalized Property). $\forall n \in Nat, A\ B \in Stream\ TD$

$$FIFO(n, A, B) \rightarrow Tlt(A, B) \wedge Deq(A, B)$$

Proof. We make use of mathematical induction to tackle this issue. First of all, the channel $FIFO1(A, B)$ have this property obviously. Then if the statement is assumed to be true for any natural number, then it must be true for the next natural number as well. The detailed proof of this inductive step can be found at [9].

6 Conclusion

As an extension of the work in [22], this paper presents a method for formal modeling of timed channels and reasoning about timed connector properties in Coq. The model preserves the original structure of timed channels and composition operators, which makes their description reasonably readable. Connector properties are defined with predicates which offer an appropriate description of the relations between different TD streams on the nodes of a connector. The proofs of connector properties are completed with the help of pre-defined techniques and tactics that Coq offers. Comparing with other verification techniques (like model checking), using theorem provers like Coq makes it possible to prove more generic properties that are harder or infeasible with model checkers, like the generalized property for *FIFOn* connector which has been proved in Theorem 4. Such properties for arbitrary n cannot be verified explicitly with model checkers.

Analysis and proof process of complex connectors in Coq is hard and time-consuming as it depends on more tactics and decision procedures. The proof process can become easier by adding frequently-used proof patterns as new tactics. Furthermore, automation methods may also help us to avoid tons of hand-written proofs and Coq offers several auto tactics to solve proof goals. With proper configuration, perhaps such tactics will work well in our framework. Another possible future work is to prove more generic and complex properties, like generalizations of Theorems 2 and 3 for any size n, that we believe to be more interesting.

Acknowledgement. The work was partially supported by the National Natural Science Foundation of China under grant no. 61772038, 61532019, 61202069 and 61272160.

References

1. Arbab, F.: Reo: a channel-based coordination model for component composition. Math. Struct. Comput. Sci. **14**(3), 329–366 (2004)
2. Arbab, F., Baier, C., de Boer, F., Rutten, J.: Models and temporal logics for timed component connectors. In: Proceedings of SEFM 2004, pp. 198–207. IEEE Computer Society (2004)
3. Arbab, F., Rutten, J.: A coinductive calculus of component connectors. Technical report, SEN-R0216, CWI, Amsterdam (2002)
4. Baier, C., Blechmann, T., Klein, J., Klüppelholz, S., Leister, W.: Design and verification of systems with exogenous coordination using vereofy. In: Margaria, T., Steffen, B. (eds.) ISoLA 2010. LNCS, vol. 6416, pp. 97–111. Springer, Heidelberg (2010). https://doi.org/10.1007/978-3-642-16561-0_15
5. Baier, C., Sirjani, M., Arbab, F., Rutten, J.: Modeling component connectors in Reo by constraint automata. Sci. Comput. Program. **61**, 75–113 (2006)
6. Bertot, Y., Casteran, P.: Interactive Theorem Proving and Program Development. Coq'Art: The Calculus of Inductive Construction. Texts in Theoretical Computer Science. An EATCS Series. Springer, Heidelberg (2003). https://doi.org/10.1007/978-3-662-07964-5
7. Clarke, D., Costa, D., Arbab, F.: Modelling coordination in biological systems. In: Margaria, T., Steffen, B. (eds.) ISoLA 2004. LNCS, vol. 4313, pp. 9–25. Springer, Heidelberg (2006). https://doi.org/10.1007/11925040_2
8. Clarke, D., Costa, D., Arbab, F.: Connector coloring I: synchronization and context dependency. Sci. Comput. Program. **66**(3), 205–225 (2007)
9. Coq Implementation of Connectors. https://github.com/WJ-Hong/Timed-Reo
10. Diakov, N., Arbab, F.: Compositional construction of web services using Reo. In: Proceedings of International Workshop on Web Services: Modeling, Architecture and Infrastructure (ICEIS 2004), pp. 13–14. INSTIC Press (2004)
11. Gelernter, D., Carriero, N.: Coordination languages and their significance. Coomun. ACM **35**(2), 96 (1992)
12. Huet, G., Kahn, G., Paulin-Mohring, C.: The Coq proof assistant a tutorial. Rapport Technique, 178 (1997)
13. Jongmans, S.T.Q., Arbab, F.: Overview of thirty semantic formalisms for Reo. Sci. Ann. Comp. Sci. **22**(1), 201–251 (2012)
14. Khosravi, R., Sirjani, M., Asoudeh, N., Sahebi, S., Iravanchi, H.: Modeling and analysis of Reo connectors using alloy. In: Lea, D., Zavattaro, G. (eds.) COORDINATION 2008. LNCS, vol. 5052, pp. 169–183. Springer, Heidelberg (2008). https://doi.org/10.1007/978-3-540-68265-3_11

15. Kokash, N., Krause, C., de Vink, E.: Reo+mCRL2: a framework for model-checking dataflow in service compositions. Formal Aspects Comput. **24**, 187–216 (2012)
16. Li, Y., Sun, M.: Modeling and verification of component connectors in Coq. Sci. Comput. Program. **113**(3), 285–301 (2015)
17. Nipkow, T., Wenzel, M., Paulson, L.C. (eds.): Isabelle/HOL: A Proof Assistant for Higher-Order Logic. LNCS, vol. 2283. Springer, Heidelberg (2002). https://doi.org/10.1007/3-540-45949-9
18. Owre, S., Rushby, J.M., Shankar, N.: PVS: a prototype verification system. In: Kapur, D. (ed.) CADE 1992. LNCS, vol. 607, pp. 748–752. Springer, Heidelberg (1992). https://doi.org/10.1007/3-540-55602-8_217
19. Sun, M.: Connectors as designs: the time dimension. In: Proceedings of TASE 2012, pp. 201–208. IEEE Computer Society (2012)
20. Sun, M., Arbab, F.: Web services choreography and orchestration in Reo and constraint automata. In: Proceedings of SAC 2007, pp. 346–353. ACM (2007)
21. Sun, M., Arbab, F., Aichernig, B.K., Astefanoaei, L., de Boer, F.S., Rutten, J.: Connectors as designs: modeling, refinement and test case generation. Sci. Comput. Program. **77**(7–8), 799–822 (2012)
22. Zhang, X., Hong, W., Li, Y., Sun, M.: Reasoning about connectors in Coq. In: Kouchnarenko, O., Khosravi, R. (eds.) FACS 2016. LNCS, vol. 10231, pp. 172–190. Springer, Cham (2017). https://doi.org/10.1007/978-3-319-57666-4_11
23. Zlatev, Z., Diakov, N., Porkaev, S.: Construction of negotiation protocols for e-commerce applications. ACM SIGecom Exch. **5**(2), 12–22 (2004)

An Initial User Study Comparing the Readability of a Graphical Coordination Model with Event-B Notation

Eva Kühn[✉] and Sophie Therese Radschek[✉]

Institute of Computer Languages, TU Wien, Vienna, Austria
{eva.kuehn,sophie.radschek}@tuwien.ac.at
http://www.complang.tuwien.ac.at/eva

Abstract. Given the advance of IoT applications, coordination of concurrent and distributed systems will become ever more important. However, the concepts are sometimes hard to grasp and comprehensive modelling tools with a high level of abstraction from cumbersome messaging code must be found. Readability and compact representation is often a selling point for graphical notations. But how does one substantiate that claim? How can textual and graphical notations be compared? We have conducted a small readability study comparing the basic Event-B to the graphical notation of the Peer Model - a compact and powerful coordination model. We discuss the results and lessons learned from this initial study.

Keywords: Coordination model · Peer Model · Event-B
Readability of designs

1 Introduction

Coordination of distributed and concurrent collaboration is a challenging task in modern computing. The understandable specification of coordination aspects is therefore of particular importance. Coordination models are specifically tailored to provide the developer with special elements to express coordination logic. Some of them even feature graphical notations. On the other hand, formal notations can also be used for specifying coordination problems. They are unambiguous and often accompanied by some proof method. Börger [1] identifies the lack of a ground model and stepwise refinement to be a disadvantage of workflow systems compared to popular formal specification methods like Abstract State Machines [2] or Event-B [3].

We think that the combination of formal foundation and a graphical representation is required and that a formal model alone will not provide enough efficiency for developers. This paper therefore evaluates the readability of graphical coordination models compared to pure formal models, using a well founded graphical coordination model which provides translations to different verification tools (e.g. Event-B). It can therefore serve as a "facade" to these formal

© Springer International Publishing AG 2018
A. Cerone and M. Roveri (Eds.): SEFM 2017 Workshops, LNCS 10729, pp. 574–590, 2018.
https://doi.org/10.1007/978-3-319-74781-1_38

methods. This paper helps to argue that said facade approach is useful and – as an enhancement of existing formal methods – can serve to bring formal methods closer to average developers not trained in mathematical methods. Usability testing and user studies are well established as a method to identify usability problems or to establish confidence in the usability of products and tools. However, there is little to be found on usability testing of specification and modelling languages, especially regarding comparisons between textual and graphical notations.

We explore how textual formal notations can be compared to graphical coordination notations. Our main concern is intuitiveness of notation and readability of existing specifications without or with little prior knowledge, because specifications are not only used by experts but have to be understood by anyone connected to the development cycle.

A small initial user study was conducted comparing the graphical notation of the Peer Model to basic Event-B. The Peer Model was chosen as a well-founded programming model for coordination (see [4] for a comparison to other coordination models) that has a graphical notation, a ground model and good abstraction from coordination communication via space containers. Currently, it is being extended by invariant assertions and a translation to Event-B to allow verification. Event-B was chosen as a representative of a textual formal specification language [3] with a close relationship to the Peer Model (see above) that is easy to learn (it is closely related to the B Method [5] which is claimed to be usable by engineers without special knowledge of formal methods [6]). The setup, results of and lessons learned from the experiment are discussed.

An initial study was carried out and its results contribute to establishing more comprehensive evaluation methods of the usability of concepts. The study was successful insofar as it showed that the test setup provided comparable results, helped identify usability issues with invariant assertions and showed a tendency toward the higher efficiency in understanding the Peer Model over Event-B which we are confident to substantiate in a larger, more elaborate study.

The paper is structured as follows: Sect. 2 relates our work to the state of art in usability testing. Section 3 outlines the foundations of Event-B and the Peer Model. Section 4 explains the setup and results of the initial study. Section 5 evaluates the relevance of this particular study for our main study to be conducted. Section 6 draws a conclusion from the results as to the usefulness of the study and lays out a plan for future studies.

2   Related Work

Our target audience is restricted to software developers and other professionals involved in the software development process. We therefore consider our related work to be methods of evaluation of tools or concepts for developers and experts rather than usability evaluation in general.

Barišić et al. propose usability testing for the evaluation of usability of domain-specific languages [7]. They propose an incorporation of usability evaluation in the development process of domain specific languages in order to increase usability and give substance to the claim of productivity improvements over general purpose languages. Contrary to our approach, they give no recommendation for a test setting and do not consider comparative usability tests.

Birkmeier et al. compare BPMN and UML Activity Diagrams [8] by means of usability tests. They compare the performance of users solving a real world problem with BPMN and UML Activity Diagrams. They consider users of all levels (from untrained to experts) to compare two graphical notations. Unlike them, we compare a graphical notation with a textual formal notation. In addition, our main concern is readability by untrained users.

Ottensooser et al. compare BPMN notation with *written use cases* [9]. Their approach is somewhat similar to ours as they compare a graphical notation with a textual one using usability testing, but they focus on the intelligibility of business processes by business students.

Green and Petre introduce the *Cognitive Dimensions Framework* [10]. They give a catalogue of dimensions to evaluate visual programming environments. These dimensions are interesting when analysing the results of a usability test and identifying changes to be made, but do little to help create an empirical study.

In Scheller and Kühn we introduce the *API Concepts Framework* for automatic usability evaluation of APIs [11]. Usability tests were used to tune and verify the framework. These tests foresee programming tasks to be performed by developers familiar with the language for which the API shall be used.

Piccioni et al. also conduct an empirical study on API usability [12].

What differentiates our approach from the above mentioned, is that we compare a graphical coordination model with a formal specification of the same system where the software developers have no prior knowledge about these notations. The comparison is non-trivial because software developers are much more accustomed to textual notations, as they use them daily. It is therefore interesting to investigate whether the advantages of graphical coordination models lead to a better performance than the familiarity of textual notations. Our approach is aimed at comparing the readability of the notations.

3   Background

In this section, we give background information on the concepts our work is based on. We introduce the concepts of the Peer Model, Event-B and usability tests.

3.1   Peer Model

The Peer Model [4,13,14] is a programming model for coordination on top of tuple-space-based communication. It aims at being a usable model which raises the specification of coordination to a high level of abstraction. It is an extensible model providing domain specific modelling constructs.

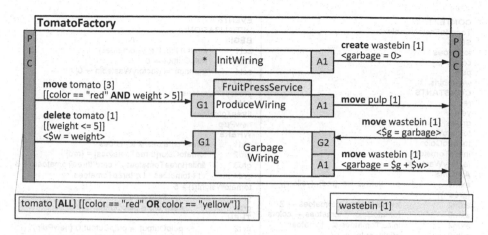

Fig. 1. Peer Model specification of the tomato factory use case as presented to the participants.

It relies on known foundations like shared spaces [15, 16], Actor Model [17], and Petri Nets [18]. So far, we have presented modelling constructs for remoting, flow correlation, basic time constraints, exceptions, and flexible distributed transactions [4].

The main artefacts of the Peer Model are: *Peer, Container, Entry, Wiring, Link, Query* and *Service*. All of them possess application as well as system *Properties*; application properties being user defined coordination properties and system properties being predefined properties with special semantics (e.g.: ttl – "time to live" – specifies the lifespan of an element while user defined properties have to be given their semantics explicitly). There is ongoing work to extend the Peer Model with invariant assertions on containers based on the query language.

The *graphical notation* of the Peer Model is demonstrated in Fig. 1. It shows a peer representing a tomato factory (named TomatoFactory) with 3 wirings (InitWiring, ProduceWiring and GarbageWiring) and 2 invariant assertions. Init Wiring has one special guard *. This condition is true exactly once at peer start. When it is fulfilled, the wiring creates one wastebin entry with garbage property set to 0. The query on guard link G1 of ProduceWiring selects 3 red tomatoes with weight greater than 5 from the peer input container (PIC) and moves them to the wiring's internal container (WIC). The wiring then calls FruitPressService and moves the resulting pulp to the peer output container (POC). GarbageWiring demonstrates the use of variables. It deletes one tomato entry from the PIC, takes the wastebin, stores the weight of the tomato and the garbage of the wastebin in variables, and updates the wastebin's garbage property to be their sum when moving it back to the POC. One invariant asserts that all tomato entries in the PIC have color yellow or red. Another invariant asserts that there is always one wastebin in the POC.

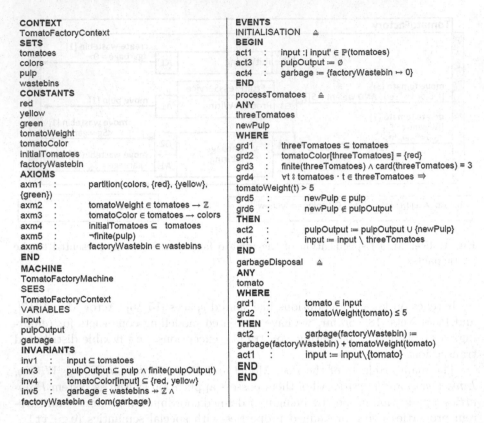

CONTEXT
TomatoFactoryContext
SETS
tomatoes
colors
pulp
wastebins
CONSTANTS
red
yellow
green
tomatoWeight
tomatoColor
initialTomatoes
factoryWastebin
AXIOMS
axm1   :   partition(colors, {red}, {yellow}, {green})
axm2   :   tomatoWeight ∈ tomatoes → ℤ
axm3   :   tomatoColor ∈ tomatoes → colors
axm4   :   initialTomatoes ⊆ tomatoes
axm5   :   ¬finite(pulp)
axm6   :   factoryWastebin ∈ wastebins
END
MACHINE
TomatoFactoryMachine
SEES
TomatoFactoryContext
VARIABLES
input
pulpOutput
garbage
INVARIANTS
inv1   :   input ⊆ tomatoes
inv3   :   pulpOutput ⊆ pulp ∧ finite(pulpOutput)
inv4   :   tomatoColor[input] ⊆ {red, yellow}
inv5   :   garbage ∈ wastebins ⇸ ℤ ∧ factoryWastebin ∈ dom(garbage)

EVENTS
INITIALISATION   ≙
BEGIN
act1   :   input :| input' ∈ ℙ(tomatoes)
act3   :   pulpOutput := ∅
act4   :   garbage := {factoryWastebin ↦ 0}
END
processTomatoes   ≙
ANY
threeTomatoes
newPulp
WHERE
grd1   :   threeTomatoes ⊆ tomatoes
grd2   :   tomatoColor[threeTomatoes] = {red}
grd3   :   finite(threeTomatoes) ∧ card(threeTomatoes) = 3
grd4   :   ∀t · tomatoes · t ∈ threeTomatoes ⇒ tomatoWeight(t) > 5
grd5   :   newPulp ∈ pulp
grd6   :   newPulp ∉ pulpOutput
THEN
act2   :   pulpOutput := pulpOutput ∪ {newPulp}
act1   :   input := input \ threeTomatoes
END
garbageDisposal   ≙
ANY
tomato
WHERE
grd1   :   tomato ∈ input
grd2   :   tomatoWeight(tomato) ≤ 5
THEN
act2   :   garbage(factoryWastebin) := garbage(factoryWastebin) + tomatoWeight(tomato)
act1   :   input := input\{tomato}
END
END

Fig. 2. Event-B specification of the tomato factory use case as presented to the participants.

A *peer* relates to an actor in the Actor Model [17]. It is an autonomous worker with a unique identifier and ingoing and outgoing mailboxes, termed input and output *containers* (PIC and POC).

Containers store entries. PIC and POC have transactional access and blocking behaviour. In addition, so-called wiring internal containers (WIC, see below) are supported.

Entries are stored in peer containers and passed between them via wirings (see below). A **type** property is mandatory for entries. It models the coordination type of the entry.

The coordination behaviour of the peer is explicitly modelled by *wirings* similar to Petri Net transitions [18]. Wirings have guard and action links and can call services where application logic is situated, which is out of scope for the Peer Model. Wiring instances have an internal container termed WIC without support of transactions and without blocking behaviour that serves as a local entry collection. Each wiring instance represents an atomic local space transaction, termed wiring transaction (WTX) [4]. If the wiring's `ttl` expires, this causes a rollback of the current WTX and starts a new wiring instance, if possible.

A *link* transports entries between a peer container and a wiring's WIC or in the other direction. Incoming links direct from a peer container to the WIC and are termed *guards*, whereas outgoing links are termed *actions*. The operational behaviour of a WTX is the sequential execution of all guard links, then service calls and finally action links. A link reads or takes entries from the source container (c1) and writes it to the target container (c2). In addition, entries can be dynamically created. Links can use variables (prefixed with a $ sign) whose scope is the current wiring instance and which they can set according to properties of the entries they transport.

The *Peer Model Query* consists of three parts: (1) `type` (entry type), (2) `cnt` (count specification), and (3) `sel` (a selector expression). It selects an appropriate amount of entries of the appropriate type that satisfy the selector expression [13]. Cnt states the number of entries that are to be selected. It can either be a number or keyword (e.g. **ALL**, see [19] for more detail). The selector expression specifies properties which the entries have to fulfil. It allows access to entry properties, link variables, the use of comparison operators ($==$, $>$, $<$, . . .), brackets and logical operators (**NOT, AND, OR**).

A *service* implements an application method that has access to all entries in the WIC; it may access the application specific value of the entry's `data` property.

There is ongoing work to extend the Peer Model with *invariant assertions* on containers. The assertions utilise the Peer Model Query and can be understood as a link that must always be executable. In the current version as used in the study, only simple queries that could also be used in links are allowed to be used.

3.2   Event-B

Event-B is the event-based variant of the B Method. Event-B specifications are meant for use in the design phase, before the implementation takes place. Event-B specifications consist of CONTEXTs[1] and MACHINEs.

CONTEXTs specify static aspects of models. They define types (SETS) and CONSTANTS and give information about them in AXIOMS. CONTEXTs can extend other CONTEXTs to use their information and augment them. Completely static models can be expressed using only CONTEXTs.

MACHINEs contain the dynamic aspects of models. They rely on static information from CONTEXTs and keep track of a state using VARIABLES. The state is changed by EVENTS. EVENTS have PARAMETERS, GUARDS (conditions that must hold for the event to be executed) and ACTIONS (activities to be executed with the event). INVARIANTS describe the state space and must be proven to hold after INITIALISATION, and after each EVENT execution – under the premise that they and the GUARDS were fulfilled before.

---

[1] For differentiation from Peer Model notation, we write Event-B keywords in capitals.

Event-B relies on REFINEMENT to concretise abstract models. More concrete specifications must provably fulfil the same invariants as the abstract model, but can hold more specific information.

The tool suite enabling Event-B development is called Rodin [20]. It is an open platform with automatic generation of proof obligations and support for automatic and semi-automatic proofs.

Figure 2 shows the aforementioned example of an Event-B ground model (without refinement).

3.3   Usability Tests

ISO 9241, treating human computer interaction, defines usability as the extent to which a product can be used by specified users to achieve specified goals with effectiveness, efficiency and satisfaction in a specified context of use [21].

Effectiveness signifies the quality and correctness of the solutions users find for the problems presented to them. In our case where we measure understanding, effectiveness is the degree to which the user understands the notation.

Efficiency is measured in the amount of resources the users need to complete the tasks (consumed time is usually a big part of this aspect).

Satisfaction connotes the users' perception of the tool and their own performance using it.

One way to evaluate the usability of tools is to carry out usability tests. Test participants use the tool to complete tasks while being observed [21]. Usability tests can, for instance, uncover usability problems or show the difference in usability of two or more products. When comparing two products, quantitative measurements for effectiveness, efficiency and satisfaction must be introduced. Section 4.2 elaborates the metrics used in our test.

Our initial study can be described as a usability test as potential users participated and that they were asked to perform a task with the tools in question. It is different from a classical usability test insofar as (1) the observer assisted the users when prompted and (2) an important part of the task was to understand the notation.

4   The User Study

The goal of our study is to establish methods of comparing usability aspects (and in particular readability) of specifications, especially between formal notations and coordination models. These methods shall then be applied to different specification and modelling approaches, resulting in a comprehensive comparison of different approaches. A first step in this direction has been taken by carrying out a small user study comparing the intuitiveness of the graphical Peer Model notation with basic Event-B. The following sections present the study and its results. The study's impact on our work of comparing the usability of coordination modelling will be discussed in Sect. 5.

4.1   Test Setting

The participants were software developers and other professionals in the area of software engineering. They were confronted with a task description, a use case, one example specification of the use case in the graphical Peer Model notation (see Fig. 1) and one in basic Event-B notation (see Fig. 2). They were neither given an introduction nor an explanation. They were only instructed to study the specifications and answer a few questions about them. A coordinator answered questions they asked about the elements of the notations. The technique was used to understand which parts of the notations were understood on their own and which needed explaining. The participants were encouraged to ask as many questions as they deemed necessary to understand the notations, but to always try and find a solution on their own first. Task and use case description were provided in the beginning and were available to the participants throughout the test. The two example solutions were provided one after the other. Both specifications are equivalent solutions, but use different notations. They treated the same aspects of the system at a similar level of abstraction. To minimise the bias, half of the participants received the Peer Model example first, half of them the Event-B example. After having completed the task for both notations, the users were asked to fill out a questionnaire to indicate their own perception of their performance and their preference. All tests were voice recorded to allow later evaluation of the participants' performance.

Tomato factory use case: The participants were asked to consider the coordination flow of a fully automatized tomato factory. They were provided with the following description:

> The modeled flow of the tomato factory is the production of tomato puree: Suppliers deliver red and yellow tomatoes. One unit of puree is made out of three tomatoes that must be red and weigh more than 5 dag[2]. Too small tomatoes are thrown away. A waste bin is provided for their disposal.

Task: Participants had to carefully inspect the notations in order to answer the following questions:

- How is the tomato factory modelled?
- How are tomatoes modelled?
- How are workflows in the tomato factory modelled?
- How is the manufacturing of tomatoes into tomato puree modelled?
- How is the disposal of waste modelled?
- How is the waste bin modelled?
- How does the specification assert that only red and yellow tomatoes end up in the factory?
- How are assertions modelled in general?

---

[2] Dag is a metric weight unit, 5 dag $\hat{=}$ 1.76 oz.

The participants were allowed to investigate the models and ask questions until they were convinced they understood them. Then, the above questions were discussed. Questions that the participants had already answered by thinking aloud [21] were omitted from this discussion.

After the discussion, the participants were asked to extend the model by adding the invariant assertion that the weight of the waste in the waste bin may not be negative. The intention for the Peer Model example was to add the constraint [[garbage ≥ 0]] to the existing POC invariant and for Event-B example it was to add an invariant garbage (factoryWastebin) ≥ 0.

Example specifications: The participants were provided with the Peer Model specification of the use case as shown in Fig. 1 and the Event-B specification as shown in Fig. 2.

Questionnaire: At the end of the interview, participants were asked to fill out a questionnaire about their perception of the two example specifications and their performance on completing the task. They had to assess their performance and preference with respect to the following criteria:

- How well they understood the respective specifications in general (not at all, with difficulty, well enough or very well).
- How well they could answer the questions posed in the task for each model (not at all, with help or immediately).
- Whether they knew what and where to insert to extend the notations by the assertion (does not apply, applies little, applies some, applies).
- What they liked or did not like about the notations.
- Which notation they preferred.

4.2   Metrics

The interviews were evaluated in two categories: user performance and satisfaction. User satisfaction was determined using the questionnaire at the end of the interview while performance was determined using the audio recording of the interview. Both aspects were formalised in metrics and the different notations' scores were compared.

Satisfaction: Satisfaction was measured in two metrics: (1) preference of notation and (2) confidence of the participants in their own performance.

(1) was interrogated at the end of the questionnaire. The preceding questions about (dis-)advantages of the respective notations were meant to help the participants to identify such a preference. The participants were not required to answer them.

(2) was established by assigning scores to the participants' answers. The most confident answer was awarded a score of 1, the least confident a score of zero and the answers in between were weighed in equal intervals. E.g.: The answer "with help" to the question "I understood how the waste bin is modelled in the Peer Model" was awarded a score of 0.5, and the answer "well enough" to the question "I understood the Event-B specification" was awarded a score of 0.67.

These scores were added up per notation and the results were compared to each other.

Performance: The participants' performance was measured by (1) the needed time for the notation specific parts of the test (2) by the number of (a) notation and use case specific, (b) confirmation and (c) overall questions asked per notation and (3) by the percentage of use case specific elements understood.

(1) and (2c) are efficiency related metrics. (2a) and (3) are effectiveness related metrics. (2b) had no influence on effectiveness.

(1) was measured using the voice recording of the interview (intervals of 10 s).

(2) was counted off the voice recordings.

(3) was measured by asking the test participants to explain the elements and to add an assertion to the specification. Their performance was awarded scores 0, 0.5 or 1, 0 indicating the participant not being able to explain the element correctly, 0.5 that they could explain it partly right but made mistakes or overlooked something and 1 that they completely explained it the way it was intended. These scores were summed up per notation and compared to each other.

4.3   Results

We tested 13 users working and studying in fields of computer science. 5 were female and 8 male. 6 were 30 years or younger, 4 between 30 and 40 and 3 over 40. 6 were software developers, 5 students and 2 had other occupations in the area of computer science. 5 indicated a low prior knowledge of formal notations, 6 a medium prior knowledge and 2 a high prior knowledge. None of the participants had ever worked with the Peer Model or Event-B, though one had knowledge of the Z Method [22] which is closely related to Event-B.

Satisfaction: 8 participants preferred the Peer Model notation over the Event-B notation, 4 preferred the Event-B notation and 1 did not indicate a preference to either. Not all participants gave answers to the questions what aspects of the notations they liked or disliked. Most commonly, the compactness and graphical notation of the Peer Model representation and the clear structure of the Event-B representation were mentioned as advantages while the numerous symbols and length of the Event-B representation were mentioned as disadvantages. When asked to evaluate their performance, participants scored comparably on both notations. 12 out of 13 participants awarded comparable scores to their performance in the different notations (40–60% of overall score for each notation). Only one felt significantly more confident with the Peer Model than with the

Event-B notation (83% of overall score awarded to Peer Model performance). See Table 1 for a detailed overview. In summary, participants were comparably satisfied with their performance in both notations.

Table 1. Overview of satisfaction measurements.

% of awarded points awarded to					% of possible points awarded to			
	Min	Max	Mean	Median	>90% within	Min	Max	Mean	Median
Peer Model	40	83	52	53	40–55	53	95	76	78
Event-B	17	60	48	47	45–60	18	100	73	77

Efficiency: 11 out of 13 participants were faster with the Peer Model notation than with the Event-B notation, 10 even significantly faster (at least 20% faster). On average, the time spent on the Peer Model notation was 67% the time spent on the Event-B notation (mean 67%, median: 66%). On average, a participant asked 8 questions about the Peer model and 10 about the Event-B notation and 42% (median 43%) of their total questions about the Peer Model (and 58% - resp. 57% about Event-B). Table 2 shows an overview of interesting comparisons. The efficiency evaluation shows that without prior knowledge about the notations, the Peer Model can be used with slightly higher efficiency than the Event-B notation.

Effectiveness: The number of use case and notation related questions that were asked was roughly balanced between the notations. On average, about 43% (median 44%) of such questions asked by participants related to the Peer Model and 57% (resp. 56%) to the Event-B notation. Questions about Event-B notation most commonly included questions about guards, parameters and function or relation symbols. Questions about the Peer Model notation most commonly included questions about execution sequences, the significance of the cardinalities in queries and the meaning of "PIC" and "POC". Understanding of the use case and ability to place the invariant were similarly balanced. On average, the participants scored roughly the same on both notations – on average roughly 50% of the overall performance score was awarded to either notation. This suggests a comparable understanding of both notations. See Table 3 for the detailed numbers.

Identified Problems: Participants had comprehension problems with invariant assertions. Many (9 out of 13) at least partially misunderstood the concept and as a result had difficulties placing an invariant assertion in both models. The Peer Model notation for invariants was understood from the query point of view, but, due to the missing know-how as to what invariants are or due to misinterpretations of the graphical representation, they were not identified as invariants. Participants took them to be descriptions of input and output in a sense of a flow rather than a sense of static truth value.

Table 2. Overview of efficiency measurements.

	Min	Max	Mean	Median
Absolute time in minutes				
Peer Model	5:00	19:00	9:52	9:30
Event-B	8:20	25:30	15:13	15:00
Overall	18:00	50:00	32:43	29:00
Percentage of overall time spent on				
Peer Model	18%	38%	30%	32%
Event-B	34%	54%	47%	48%
Percentage of notation time spent on				
Peer Model	27%	52%	39%	40%
Event-B	48%	73%	61%	60%
Ratio of notation length to each other				
Peer Model/Event-B	66%	110%	67%	66%
Event-B/Peer Model	91%	270%	165%	152%
Total number of questions asked				
Peer Model	104			
Event-B	129			
Number of questions asked				
Peer Model	1	24	8	5
Event-B	2	21	10	8
Percentage of question asked for one notation				
Peer Model	17%	60%	42%	43%
Event-B	4%	83%	58%	57%

Some participants (2 out of 13) criticised the usage of the same arrowheads for different operations on links.

Most (12 out of 13) participants found the numerous symbols for functions and relations in Event-B to be confusing. They asked questions about them and sometimes confused symbols.

4.4 Threats to Validity

As the study setting is quite small and unconventional, there are some threats to the validity of its results to be discussed. We address the impact that sample size, score system, choice of notation and choice of example could have on the results of comparability.

While the number of 13 participants is small, we argue that it is big enough to argue the method's fairness. Participants were chosen particularly to include as many different levels of experience and previous knowledge as possible. 11 out of

Table 3. Effectiveness.

Total number of use case and notation questions asked			
Peer Model	81		
Event-B	111		

Number of use case and notation questions asked per participant			
	Min	Max	Mean	Median
Peer Model	1	16	6.23	5
Event-B	1	15	8.54	8

Percentage of use case and notation question asked for one notation per participant			
	Min	Max	Mean	Median
Peer Model	43%	52%	48%	46%
Event-B	48%	57%	52%	54%

Absolute percentage of score per participant			
	Min	Max	Mean	Median
Peer Model	44%	94%	72%	75%
Event-B	31%	100%	71%	69%

Percentage of participant's score for each notation			
	Min	Max	Mean	Median
Peer Model	41%	65%	51%	50%
Event-B	35%	59%	49%	50%

the 13 participants had no less than 40 and no more than 60% of their altogether score of understanding awarded to either one of the notations, which makes us confident that the sample size was big enough and a larger group of participants would not have changed the result of comparability of the two notations.

The score system used for the measurement of understanding of the notations appears rough. A grade system was originally intended, but as most scores were either perfect or fail, a cruder score system was introduced.

The example and its representations in Peer Model and Event-B notation were specifically chosen to be a compact coordination problem and to use a comparable subset of concepts of the two notations, i.e. they use components you would teach a student in the first session. Refinement, variants, the use of multiple peers, exception handling and other more advanced features of the two notations were deliberately left out. We are aware that this limits the results to initial readability understandability, but since this is exactly what we want to research, the bias this might create is not relevant here.

The notations chosen for this study are easily comparable as they both allow the parts of one coherent task to be kept together visually (e.g. one task can be treated as an event in Event-B or as a wiring in the Peer Model). Also, both use the notion of invariants to restrict the allowed state space of the system. However, these similarities are not excessive and the differences far outweigh them. The similarities in name and differences in purpose of some elements might even make a comparison harder than necessary.

5   Discussion

In the following, we discuss the results of our study with regard to usefulness of the method used.

Comparability of the Notations: One of the questions that prompted the initial study was whether graphical coordination models could be compared to textual formal specification notations. One concern was therefore to create a method that does not favour the understanding of one notation over the other. All measurements were in comparable ranges and even fairly distributed for effectiveness and confidence, which confirmed our assumption that the two notations can be compared in this study setting without giving an advantage to one of the notations. This aspect of the study will therefore stay the same: no initial tutorials and questions instead.

Measurability of Effectiveness: The fact that a major part of the task that participants had to perform was understanding the model, made evaluation of effectiveness hard. The small number of elements to be explained and only one active task leads to only an approximate measurement of effectiveness. This was acceptable for the initial study, where effectiveness was only used as a control measurement to make sure the test does not favour one notation. In the planned main study we will include more questions and tasks to allow for a more precise measurement.

Questionnaire: Giving the users the questionnaire at the very end of the test had the advantage that participants compared the notations before answering and the disadvantage that the first notation was less well remembered by some participants. We suggest splitting the questionnaire into assessment and likability parts. Assessment of one's own performance should be done immediately after the task was completed, while the comparison of which notation was preferred should be done at the very end of the test.

Choice of Use Case: The tomato factory use case is rather small (only two tasks have to be coordinated). In this setting, only few tasks and questions were possible. For a more elaborate measurement for effectiveness, more complex use cases have to be used. We also propose to use multiple use cases to minimise bias.

Sample Size: We were able to identify a slightly better acceptance of the Peer Model and a sightly higher efficiency (in time) even in this small sample size. However, for all other metrics, we are not confident concerning the statistical relevance of the results. The sample sizes in the main study will therefore be bigger.

Efficiency of the Method: The method of answering questions that were asked by the participants, had the disadvantage that all interviews had to be conducted by the same person. We propose to compile a set of standardised answers, in order to allow parallel testing using multiple observers.

6   Conclusion and Future Work

A small initial comparative readability study has been conducted to bootstrap a bigger study that compares graphical coordination models to formal specification notations. Its results are discussed and evaluated to improve it for the main study. The conclusions drawn from the study are:

Lessons learned: Our study was successful as such that it helped identify a setting for the main study we are working on. We learned that a setting for comparing textual and graphical notations without tutorial introductions can be used without unfair bias to one of the notations. The study helped identify usability problems with the Peer Model and Event-B notation.

Improved study setting: Based on the results of this study, the proposed improved study setting is as follows:

Two notations are compared with help of multiple use cases. Participants from the software development area without special prior knowledge should be chosen. They are given information about a use case beforehand, but no information about the notation. They are presented with two example solutions in different notations one after the other and asked to try and understand them on their own. The order of notations is assigned randomly. Then, they have to perform a catalogue of tasks covering the concepts of the notation. Participants are observed by means of voice recording and will be assisted by a searchable catalogue of answers to frequently asked questions. The observer will not assist. User satisfaction is measured in a questionnaire to be answered at the end of each part and a final questionnaire at the end of the entire test. Effectiveness is evaluated on the performance of tasks, which have to be constructed in a way that they require many concepts of the notation. Efficiency is evaluated on the amount of time spent on each notation. Number and kind of questions researched in the catalogue of answers are captured but used only for problem identification, as is the recording. The average test should last no longer than one hour to minimise fatigue phenomena (the average test took about 30 min in the study setting presented here).

Propositions to improve the notations: With the Peer Model, one major and one minor problem have been identified: (1) visualisation of assertions and (2) visualisation of links. To address these problems, we propose the following: ad (1) remove the invariant boxes from the containers and to introduce one single box of invariant assertions for all containers using the name of the container to identify invariant location; and ad (2) to introduce different shapes for the links to distinguish between create, move, etc. and intend to find the best notation by means of another usability test.

With Event-B, the main issue was the multitude of symbols for functions and relations (12 out of 13 users asked questions about symbols and/or confused them). While the symbols are mainly standard mathematical notation, they appear not to be intuitive for many developers.

References

1. Börger, E.: Approaches to modeling business processes: a critical analysis of BPMN, workflow patterns and YAWL. Softw. Syst. Model. **11**(3), 305–318 (2012)
2. Börger, E., Huggins, J.K.: Abstract State Machines 1988–1998: Commented ASM Bibliography. CoRR cs.SE/9811014 (1998)
3. Abrial, J.R.: Modeling in Event-B: System and Software Engineering. Cambridge University Press, Cambridge (2010)
4. Kühn, E.: Flexible transactional coordination in the peer model. In: Dastani, M., Sirjani, M. (eds.) FSEN 2017. LNCS, vol. 10522, pp. 116–131. Springer, Cham (2017). https://doi.org/10.1007/978-3-319-68972-2_8
5. Abrial, J.R.: The B-book - Assigning Programs to Meanings. Cambridge University Press, Cambridge (2005)
6. Behm, P., Benoit, P., Faivre, A., Meynadier, J.-M.: Météor: a successful application of B in a large project. In: Wing, J.M., Woodcock, J., Davies, J. (eds.) FM 1999. LNCS, vol. 1708, pp. 369–387. Springer, Heidelberg (1999). https://doi.org/10.1007/3-540-48119-2_22
7. Barišić, A., Amaral, V., Goulao, M., Barroca, B.: Quality in use of domain-specific languages: a case study. In: Proceedings of 3rd ACM SIGPLAN Workshop on Evaluation and Usability of Programming Languages and Tools, pp. 65–72. ACM (2011)
8. Birkmeier, D., Kloeckner, S., Overhage, S.: An empirical comparison of the usability of BPMN and UML activity diagrams for business users. In: ECIS, vol. 2010, p. 2 (2010)
9. Ottensooser, A., Fekete, A., Reijers, H.A., Mendling, J., Menictas, C.: Making sense of business process descriptions: an experimental comparison of graphical and textual notations. J. Syst. Softw. **85**(3), 596–606 (2012). Novel approaches in the design and implementation of systems/software architecture
10. Green, T.R.G., Petre, M.: Usability analysis of visual programming environments: a 'cognitive dimensions' framework. J. Vis. Lang. Comput. **7**(2), 131–174 (1996)
11. Scheller, T., Kühn, E.: Automated measurement of API usability: the API concepts framework. Inf. Softw. Technol. **61**, 145–162 (2015)
12. Piccioni, M., Furia, C.A., Meyer, B.: An empirical study of API usability. In: 2013 ACM / IEEE International Symposium on Empirical Software Engineering and Measurement, pp. 5–14, October 2013
13. Kühn, E.: Reusable coordination components: reliable development of cooperative information systems. Int. J. Coop. Inf. Syst. **25**(4), 1740001 (2016). World Scientific Publishing Company
14. Kühn, E., Craß, S., Joskowicz, G., Marek, A., Scheller, T.: Peer-based programming model for coordination patterns. In: De Nicola, R., Julien, C. (eds.) COORDINATION 2013. LNCS, vol. 7890, pp. 121–135. Springer, Heidelberg (2013). https://doi.org/10.1007/978-3-642-38493-6_9

15. Gelernter, D.: Generative communication in Linda. ACM Trans. Program. Lang. Syst. (TOPLAS) **7**(1), 80–112 (1985)
16. Kühn, E., Mordinyi, R., Keszthelyi, L., Schreiber, C.: Introducing the concept of customizable structured spaces for agent coordination in the production automation domain. In: 8th International Conference on Autonomous Agents and Multiagent Systems (AAMAS), IFAAMAS, pp. 625–632 (2009)
17. Agha, G.A.: ACTORS: A Model Of Concurrent Computation in Distributed Systems. MIT Press, Cambridge (1990)
18. Petri, C.A.: Kommunikation mit Automaten. Ph.D. thesis, Technische Hochschule, Darmstadt (1962)
19. Craß, S., Kühn, E., Salzer, G.: Algebraic foundation of a data model for an extensible space-based collaboration protocol. In: International Database Engineering and Applications Symposium (IDEAS), pp. 301–306. ACM (2009)
20. Abrial, J., Butler, M.J., Hallerstede, S., Hoang, T.S., Mehta, F., Voisin, L.: Rodin: an open toolset for modelling and reasoning in Event-B. STTT **12**(6), 447–466 (2010)
21. Lewis, J.R.: Usability testing. In: Handbook of Human Factors and Ergonomics, vol. 12, p. e30 (2006)
22. Spivey, J.M.: The Z Notation: A Reference Manual. Prentice-Hall Inc., Upper Saddle River (1989)

Author Index

Printed in the United States
By Bookmasters